Call ~of the~ Wild

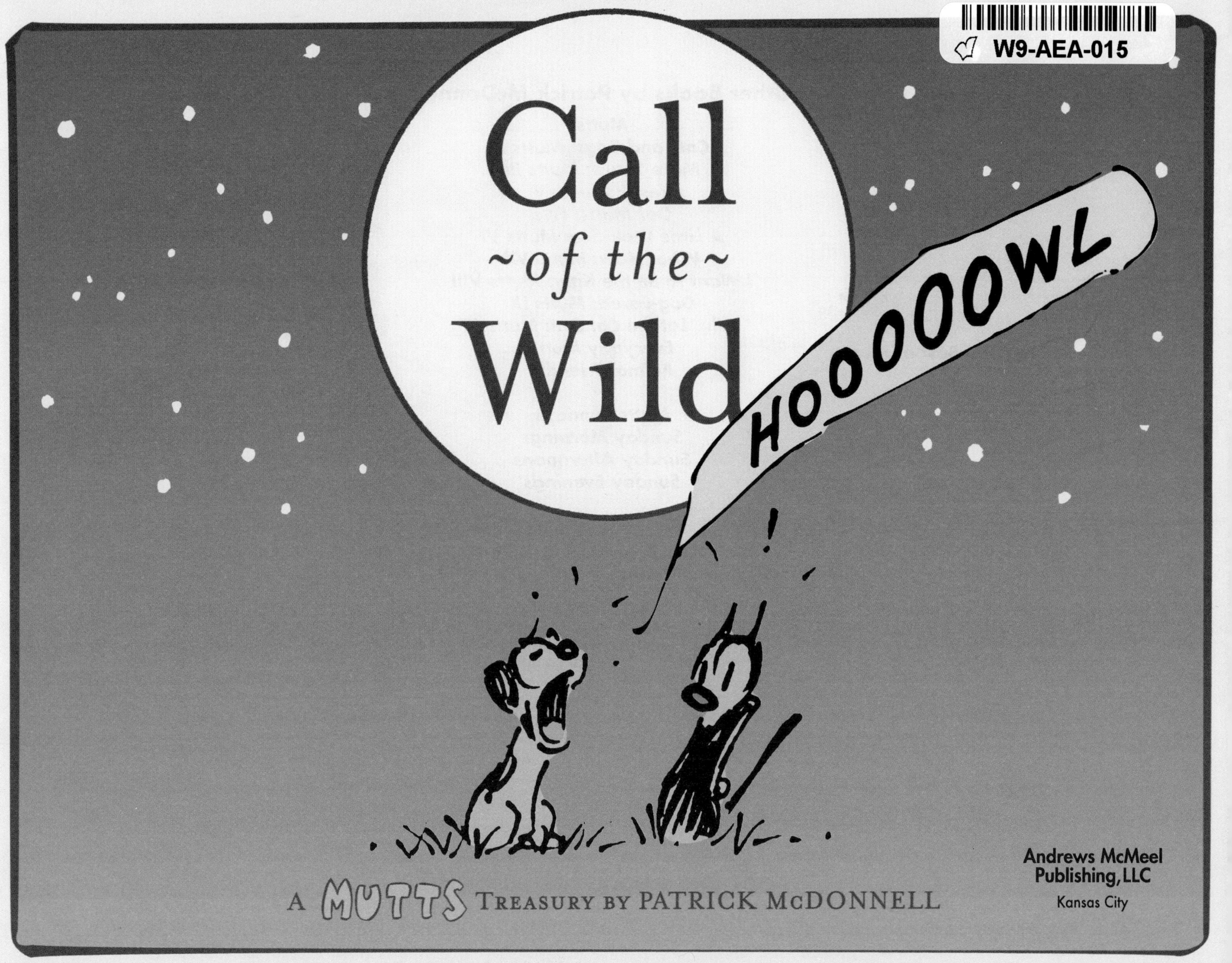
HOOOOOWL

A MUTTS TREASURY BY PATRICK McDONNELL

Andrews McMeel Publishing, LLC
Kansas City

Other Books by Patrick McDonnell

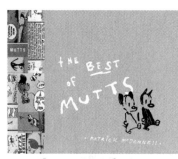

Mutts
Cats and Dogs: Mutts II
More Shtuff: Mutts III
Yesh!: Mutts IV
Our Mutts: Five
A Little Look-See: Mutts VI
What Now: Mutts VII
I Want to Be the Kitty: Mutts VIII
Dog-Eared: Mutts IX
Who Let the Cat Out: Mutts X
Everyday Mutts
Animal Friendly

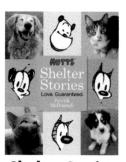

Mutts Sundays
Sunday Mornings
Sunday Afternoons
Sunday Evenings

THE BEST OF MUTTS
PATRICK McDONNELL
The Best of Mutts

MUTTS
Shelter Stories
Love. Guaranteed.
Patrick McDonnell
Shelter Stories

Mutts is distributed internationally by King Features Syndicate, Inc. For information write King Features Syndicate, Inc., 300 West Fifty-Seventh Street, New York, New York 10019.

08 09 10 11 12 BAM 10 9 8 7 6 5 4 3 2 1

ISBN-13: 978-0-7407-7099-9
ISBN-10: 0-7407-7099-3

Library of Congress Control Number: 2008922538

Call of the Wild is printed on recycled paper.

Mutts can now be found on the Internet at www.muttscomics.com.

Cover design by Jeff Schulz, Command-Z Design.

ATTENTION: SCHOOLS AND BUSINESSES
Andrews McMeel books are available at quantity discounts with bulk purchase for educational, business, or sales promotional use.
For information, please write to: Special Sales Department, Andrews McMeel Publishing, LLC, 1130 Walnut Street, Kansas City, Missouri 64106.

THIS WHOLE WORLD IS WILD AT HEART...
—DAVID LYNCH

IN THIS AGE OF VIRTUAL REALITY WE LIVE IN A CONSTANT DRONE OF
ELECTRONIC-DIGITAL STIMULATION INCESSANTLY DROWNING OUT THE REAL WORLD.

BE STILL, BE SILENT. LISTEN TO NATURE.

TREES WHISPERING IN THE AUTUMN BREEZE.
BIRDS SINGING THEIR SPRING SONGS.
OCEAN WAVES LAPPING THE SEASHORE.
THE CAT PURRING PEACEFULLY ON YOUR LAP.
YOUR OWN SWEET HEART EFFORTLESSLY BEATING...BEATING.

AND THAT LITTLE WHITE DOG IN THE DISTANCE HOWLING, URGING YOU
TO "COME BACK...COME BACK."

THE CALL OF THE WILD.

Patrick McDonnell

YEEPA
YEEPA
YEEG HA!

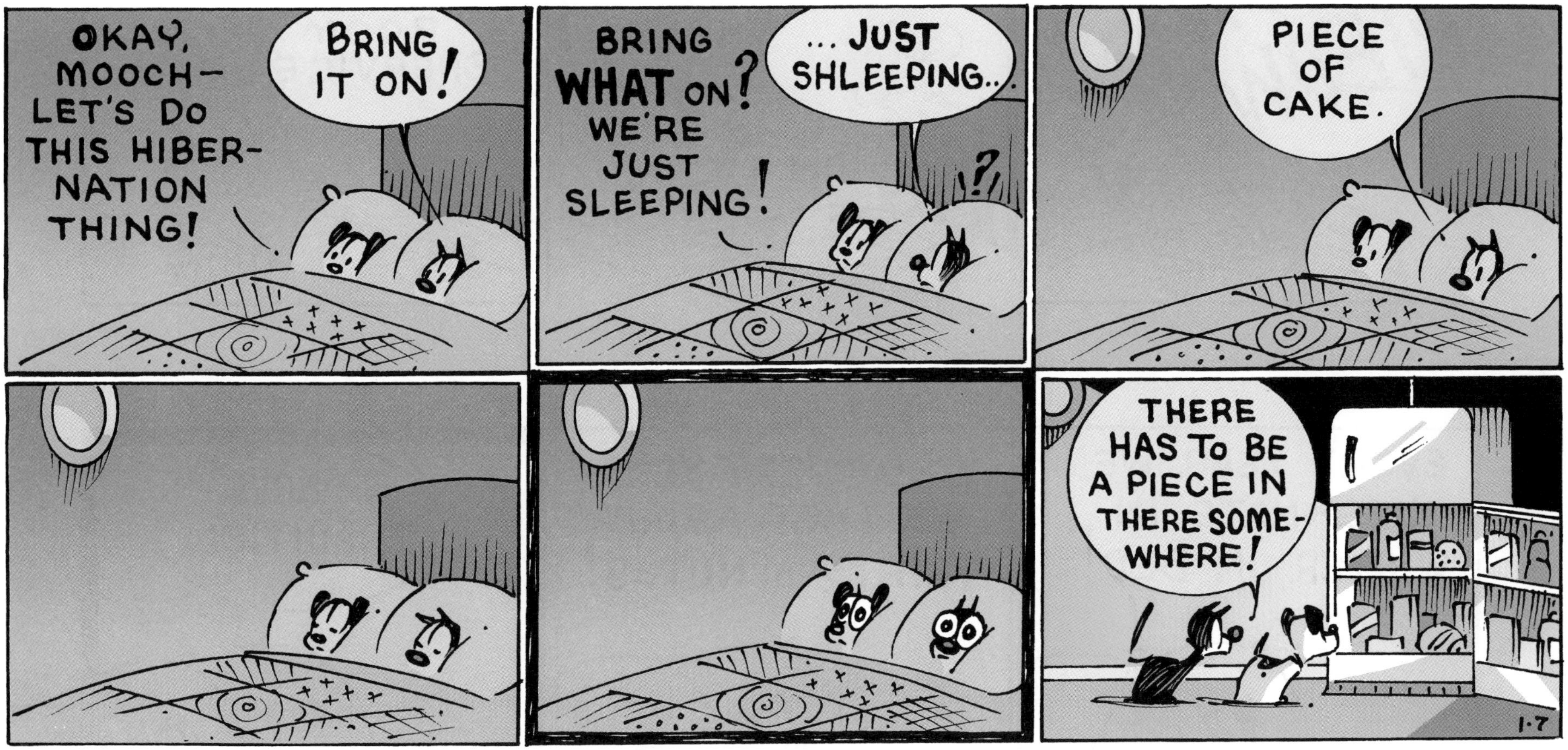
OKAY, MOOCH— LET'S DO THIS HIBER-NATION THING!
BRING IT ON!
BRING WHAT ON? WE'RE JUST SLEEPING!
... JUST SHLEEPING...
?!
PIECE OF CAKE.
THERE HAS TO BE A PIECE IN THERE SOME-WHERE!
1·7

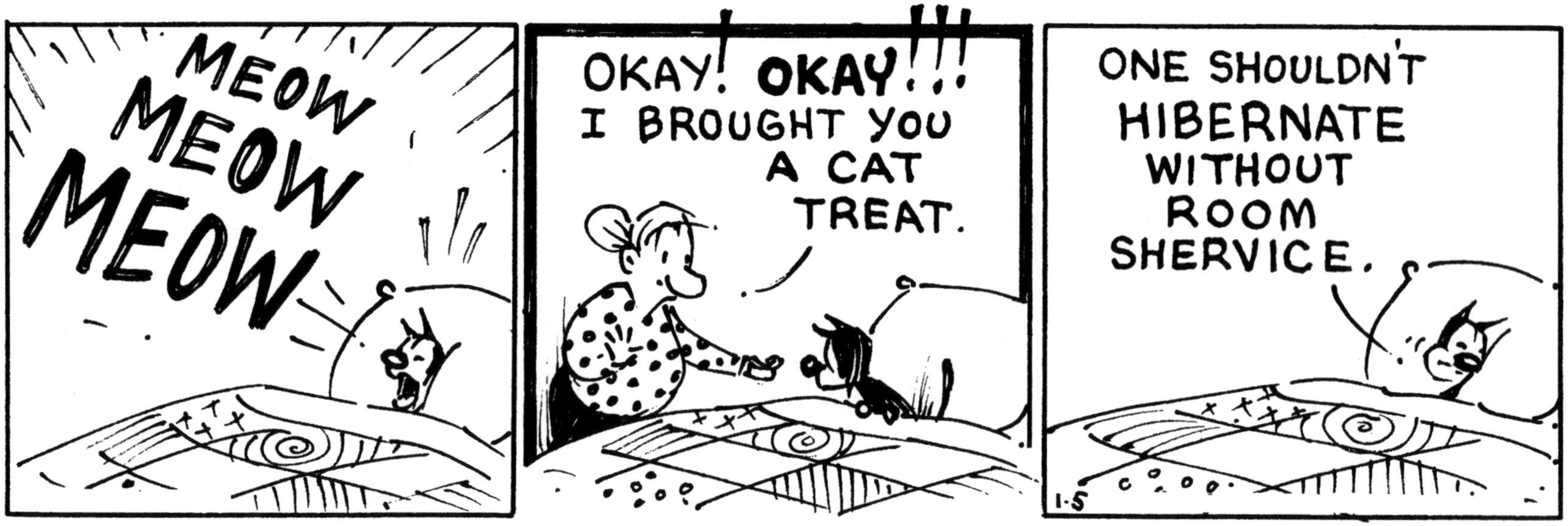
MEOW MEOW MEOW
OKAY! OKAY!!! I BROUGHT YOU A CAT TREAT.
ONE SHOULDN'T HIBERNATE WITHOUT ROOM SHERVICE.

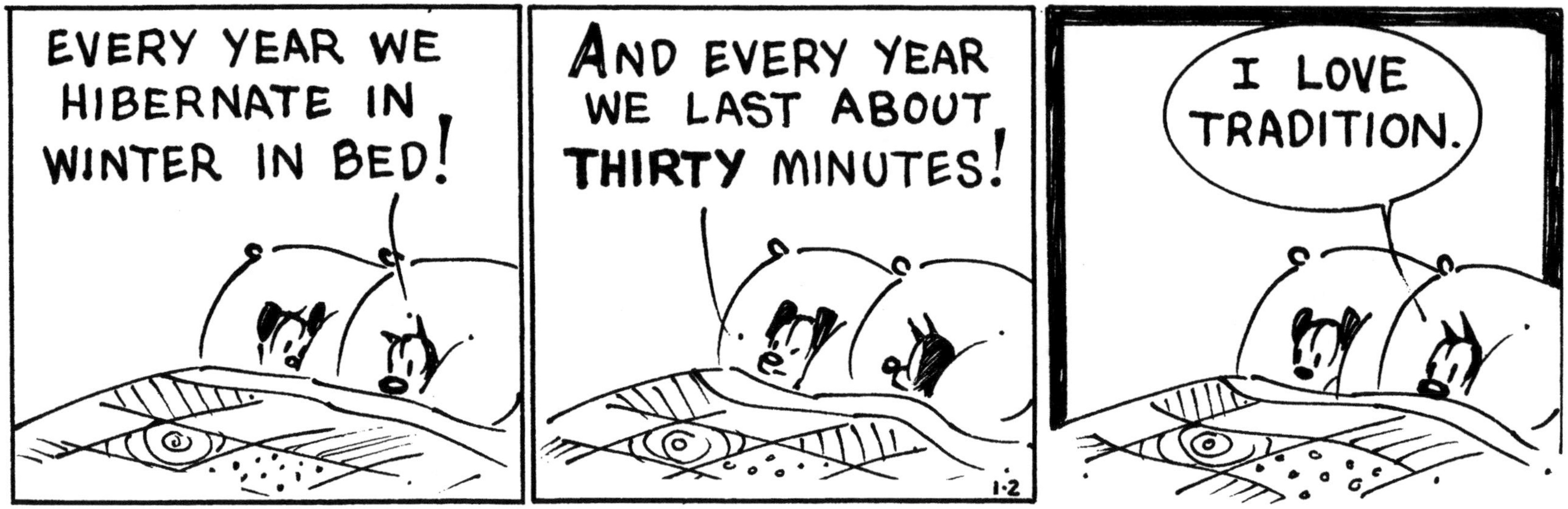
EVERY YEAR WE HIBERNATE IN WINTER IN BED!
AND EVERY YEAR WE LAST ABOUT THIRTY MINUTES!
I LOVE TRADITION.

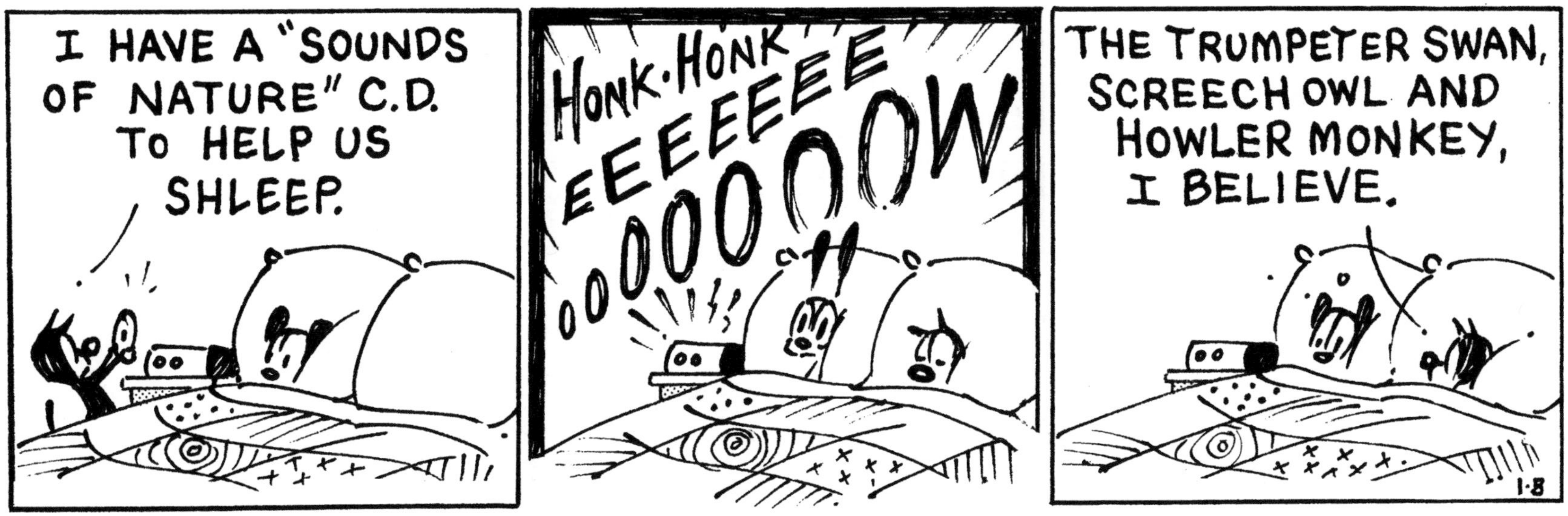
I HAVE A "SOUNDS OF NATURE" C.D. TO HELP US SHLEEP.
HONK·HONK
EEEEEEEE
OOOOOOOOOW
THE TRUMPETER SWAN, SCREECH OWL AND HOWLER MONKEY, I BELIEVE.
1·8

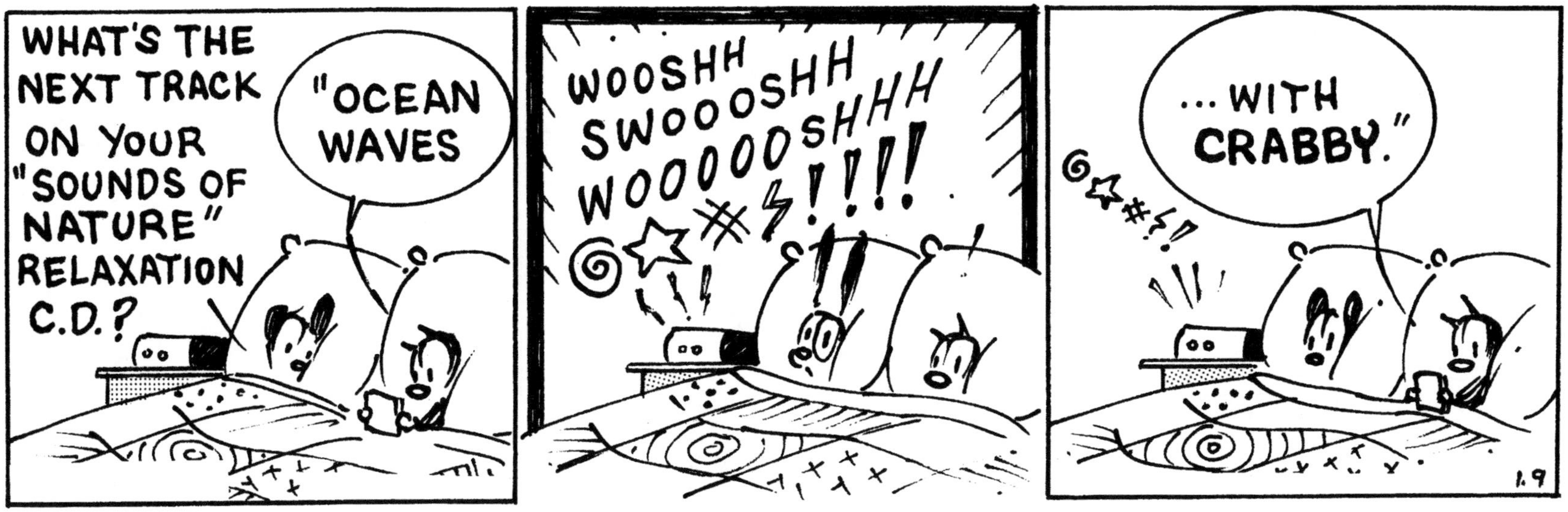
WHAT'S THE NEXT TRACK ON YOUR "SOUNDS OF NATURE" RELAXATION C.D.?
"OCEAN WAVES
WOOSHH
SWOOOSHHH
WOOOOOSHH!!!!
...WITH **CRABBY**."
1·9

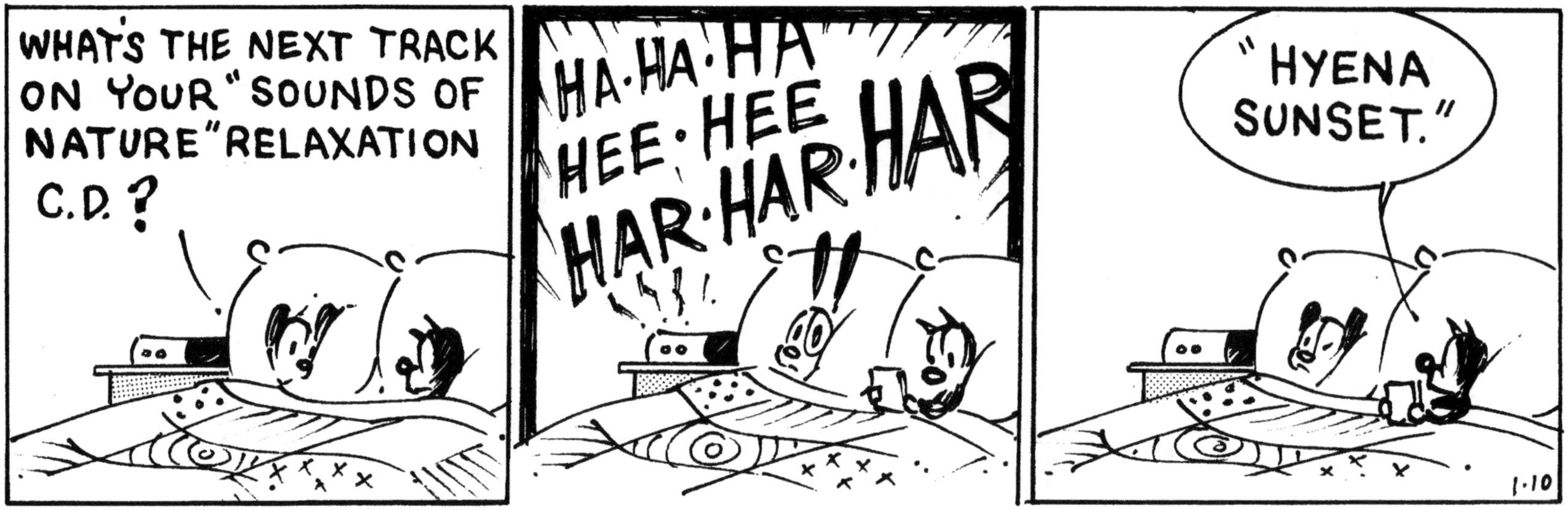
WHAT'S THE NEXT TRACK ON YOUR "SOUNDS OF NATURE" RELAXATION C.D.?
HA·HA·HA HEE·HEE HAR·HAR·HAR
"HYENA SUNSET."
1·10

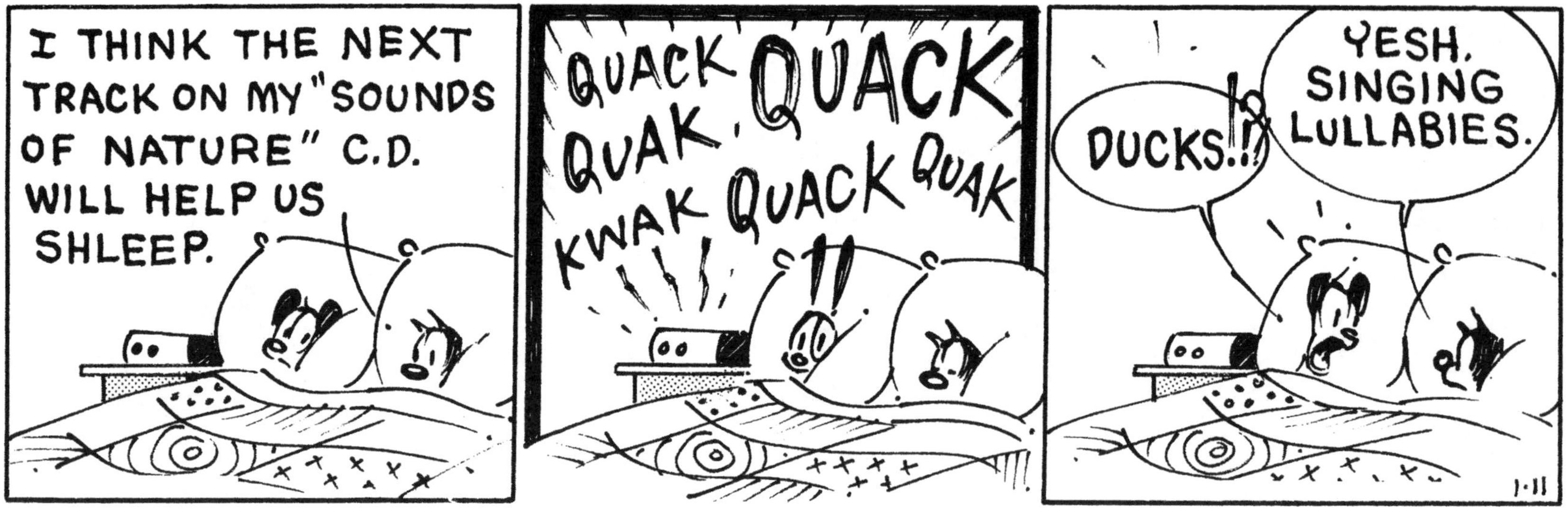
I THINK THE NEXT TRACK ON MY "SOUNDS OF NATURE" C.D. WILL HELP US SHLEEP.
QUACK QUACK QUAK KWAK QUACK QUAK
DUCKS!!?
YESH. SINGING LULLABIES.
1·11

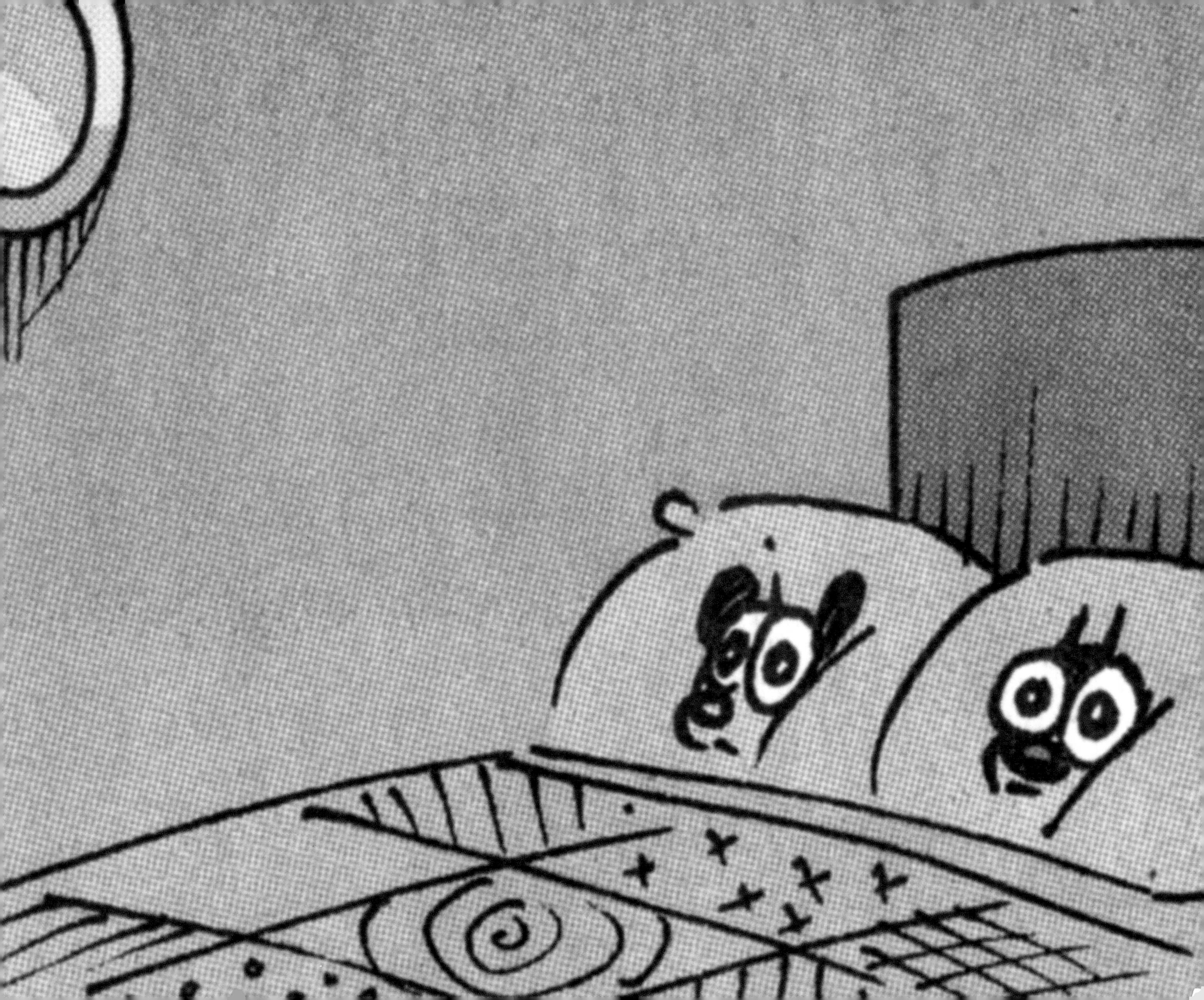

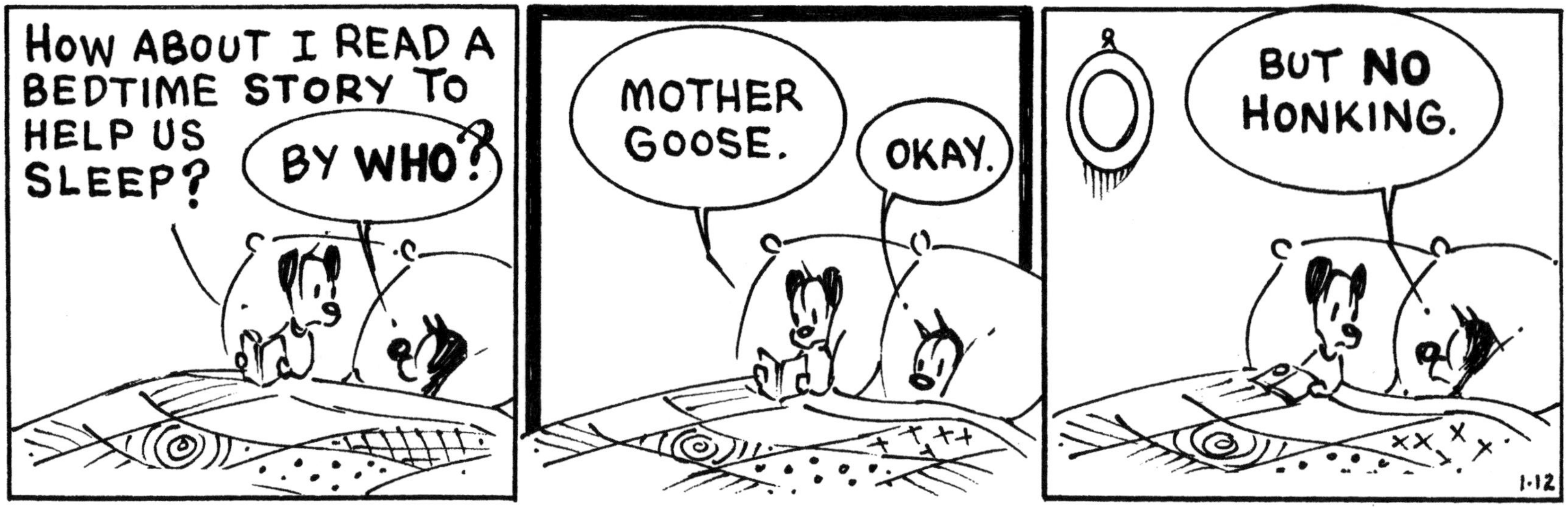
HOW ABOUT I READ A BEDTIME STORY TO HELP US SLEEP?
BY WHO?
MOTHER GOOSE.
OKAY.
BUT NO HONKING.
1·12

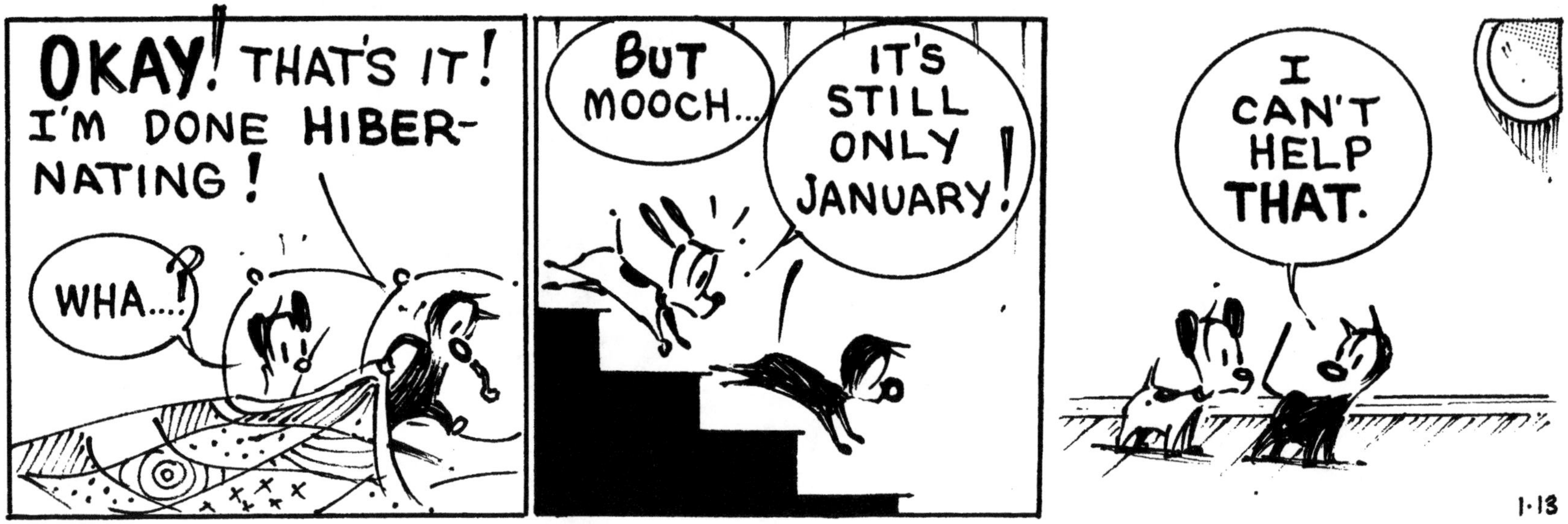
OKAY! THAT'S IT! I'M DONE HIBER-NATING!
WHA...?
BUT MOOCH...
IT'S STILL ONLY JANUARY!
I CAN'T HELP THAT.
1·13

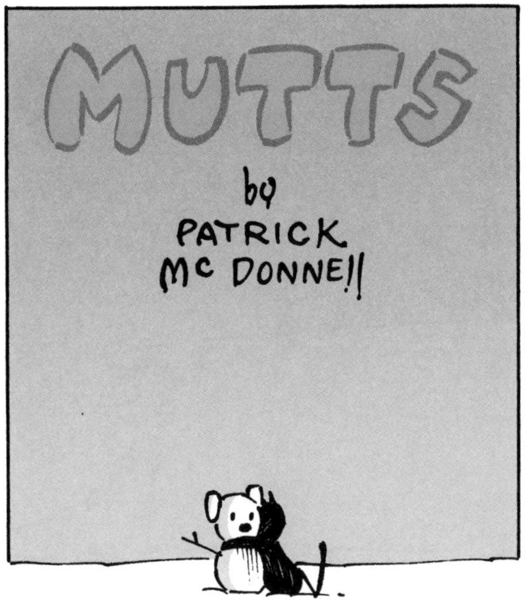
MUTTS
by
PATRICK
MC DONNELL

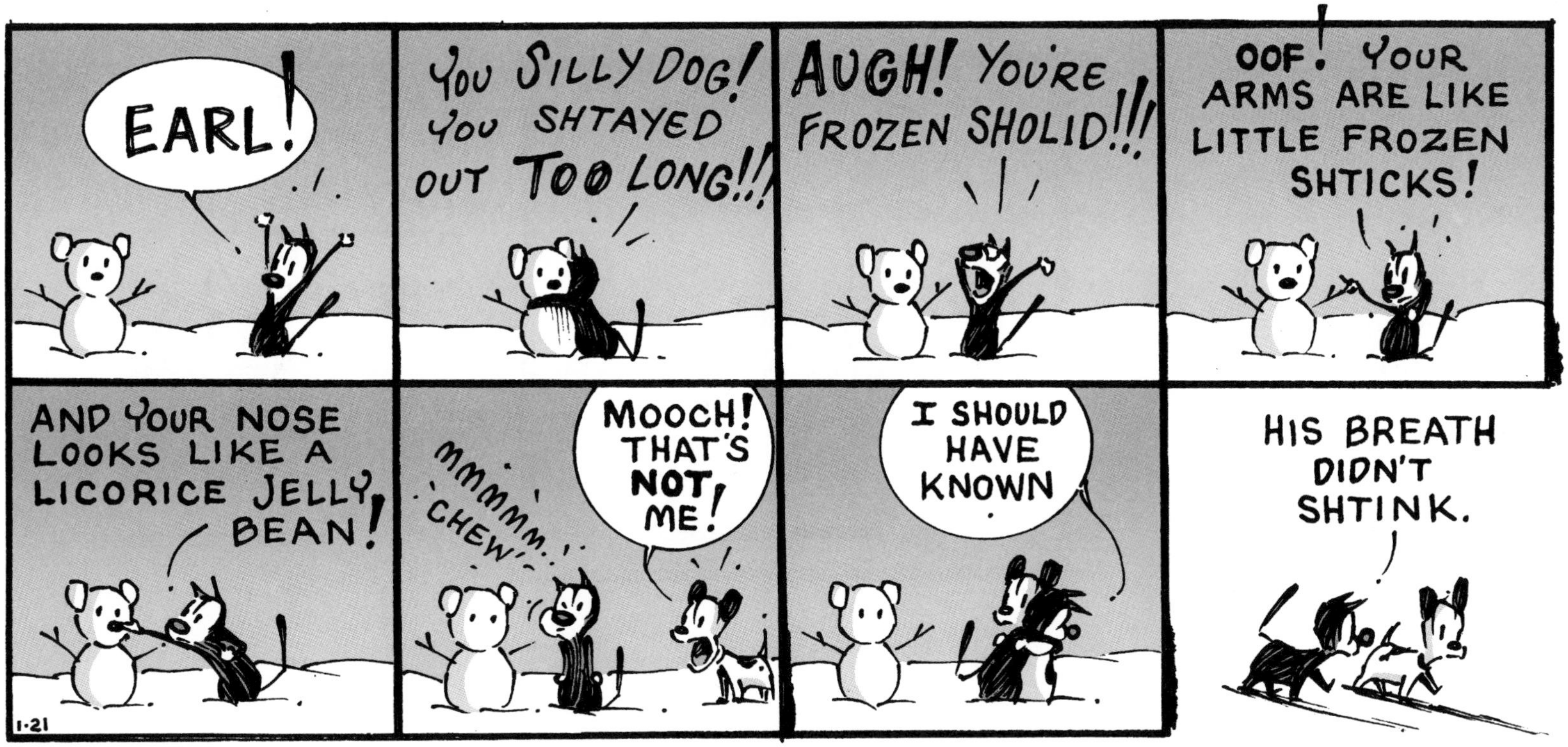
EARL!
YOU SILLY DOG! YOU SHTAYED OUT TOO LONG!!
AUGH! YOU'RE FROZEN SHOLID!!!
OOF! YOUR ARMS ARE LIKE LITTLE FROZEN SHTICKS!
AND YOUR NOSE LOOKS LIKE A LICORICE JELLY BEAN!
1-21
MMMMM... CHEW
MOOCH! THAT'S NOT ME!
I SHOULD HAVE KNOWN
HIS BREATH DIDN'T SHTINK.

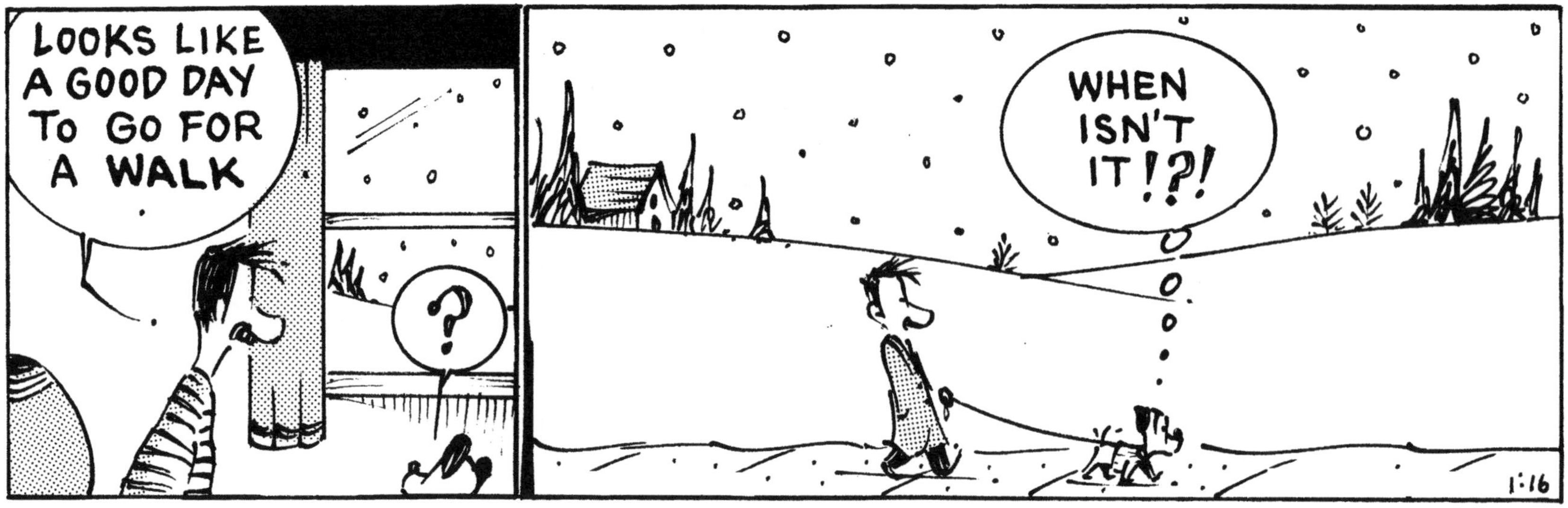
LOOKS LIKE A GOOD DAY TO GO FOR A WALK
?
WHEN ISN'T IT!?!
1·16

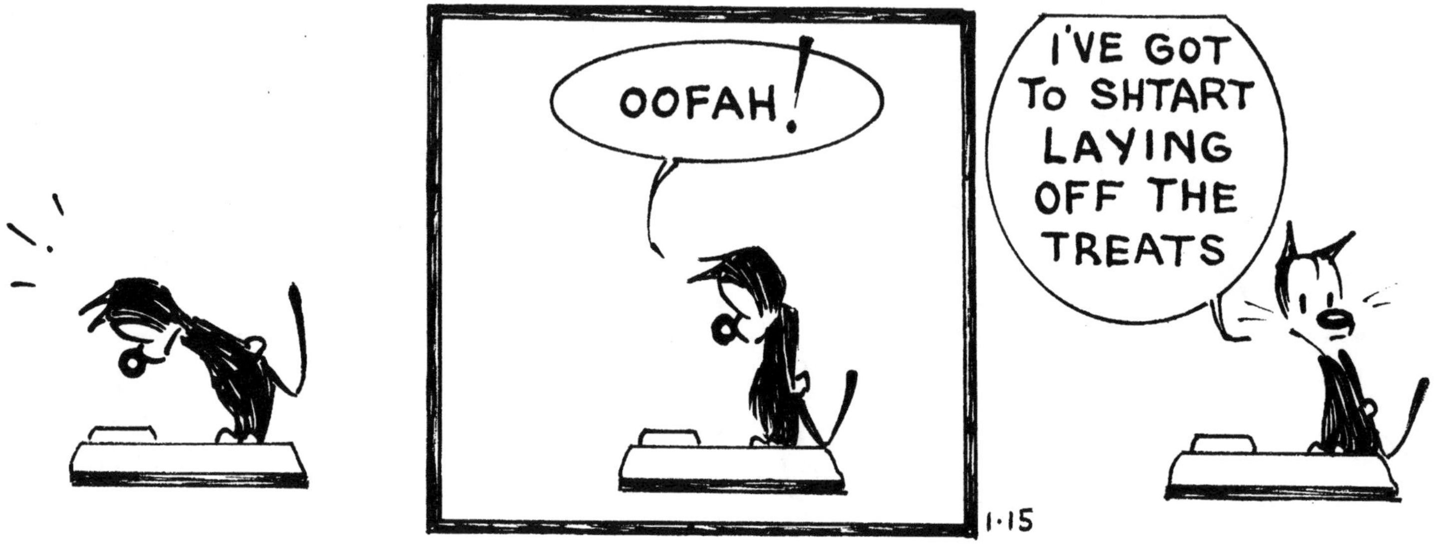
OOFAH!
I'VE GOT TO SHTART LAYING OFF THE TREATS
1·15

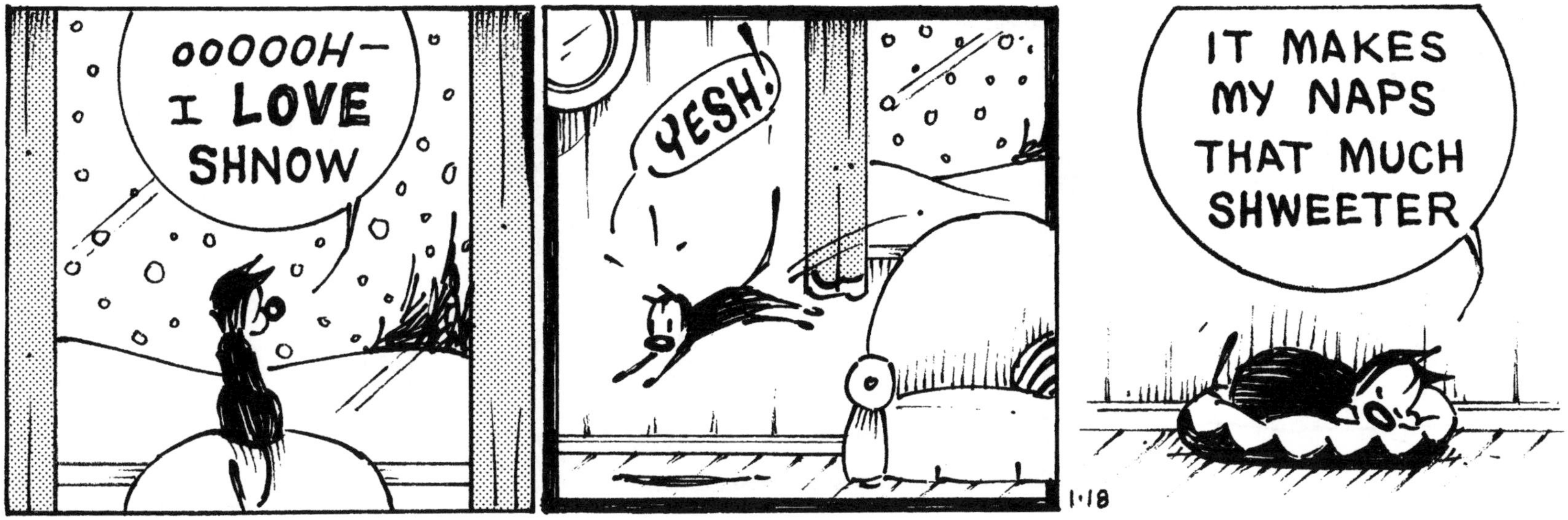
OOOOOH—
I LOVE
SHNOW
YESH!
IT MAKES
MY NAPS
THAT MUCH
SHWEETER
1·18

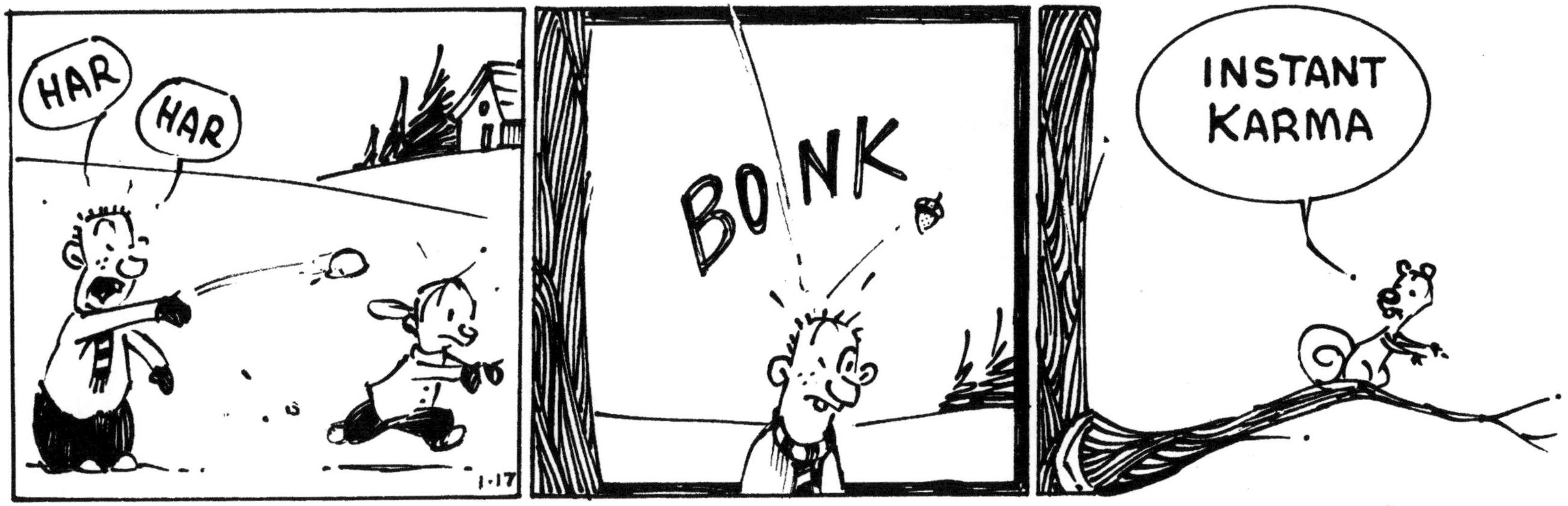
HAR
HAR
1·17
BONK
INSTANT
KARMA

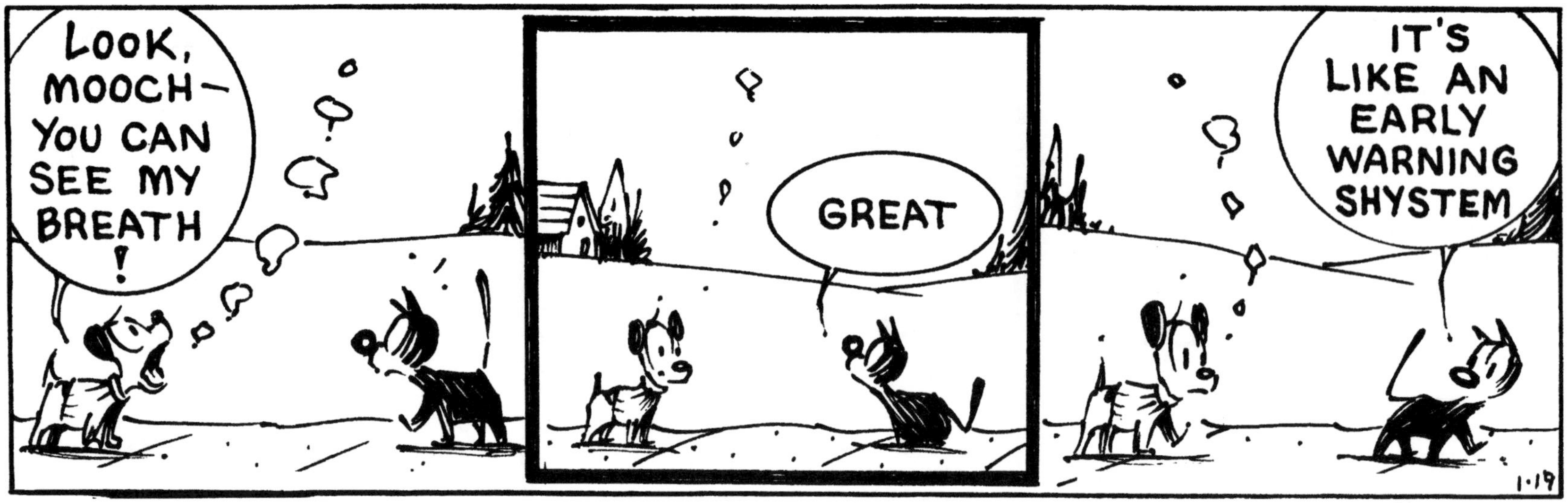
LOOK, MOOCH– YOU CAN SEE MY BREATH!
GREAT
IT'S LIKE AN EARLY WARNING SHYSTEM
1·19

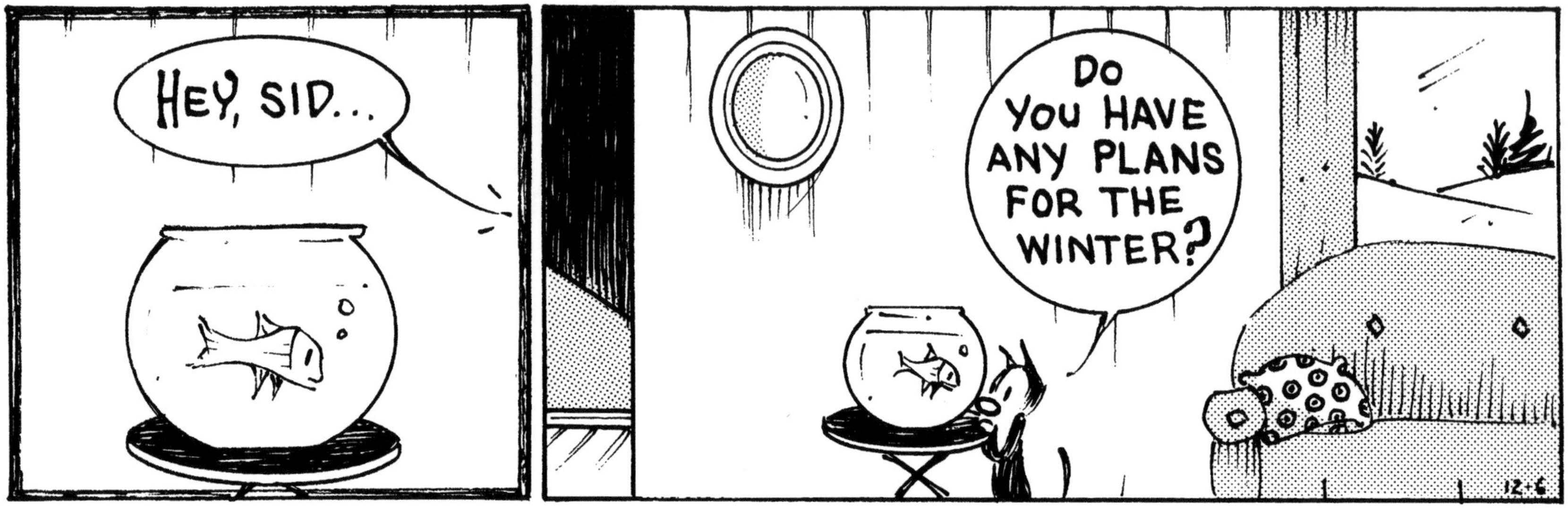
HEY, SID...
DO YOU HAVE ANY PLANS FOR THE WINTER?
12·6

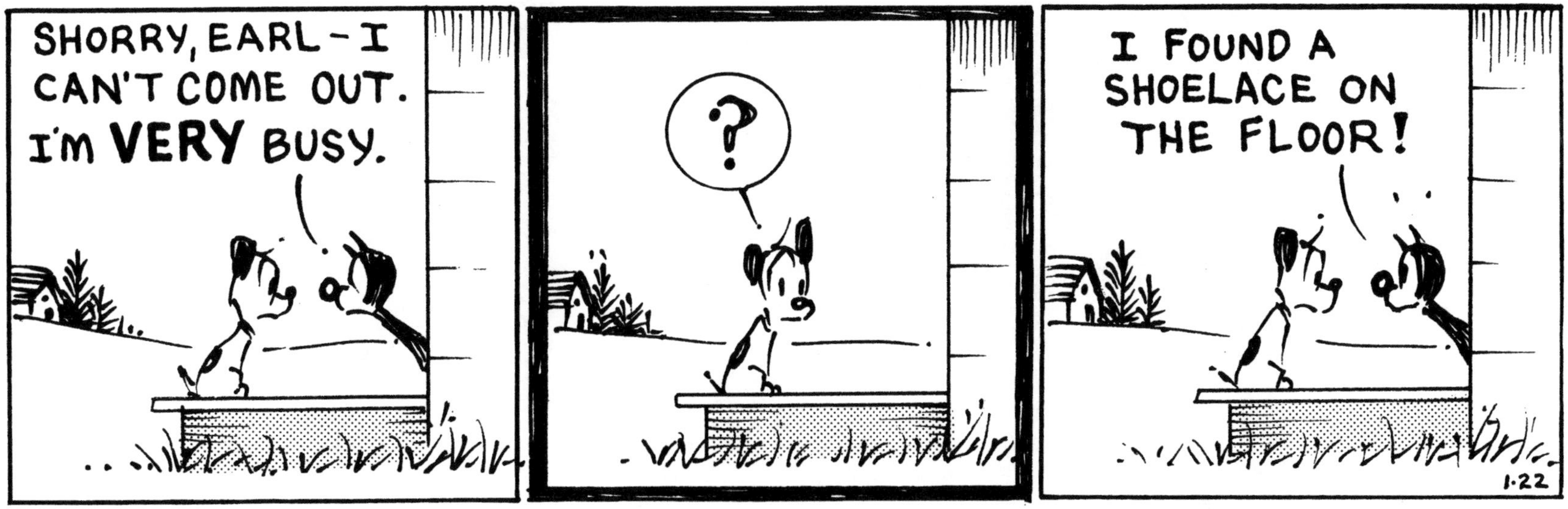
SHORRY, EARL - I CAN'T COME OUT. I'M VERY BUSY.
?
I FOUND A SHOELACE ON THE FLOOR!
1·22

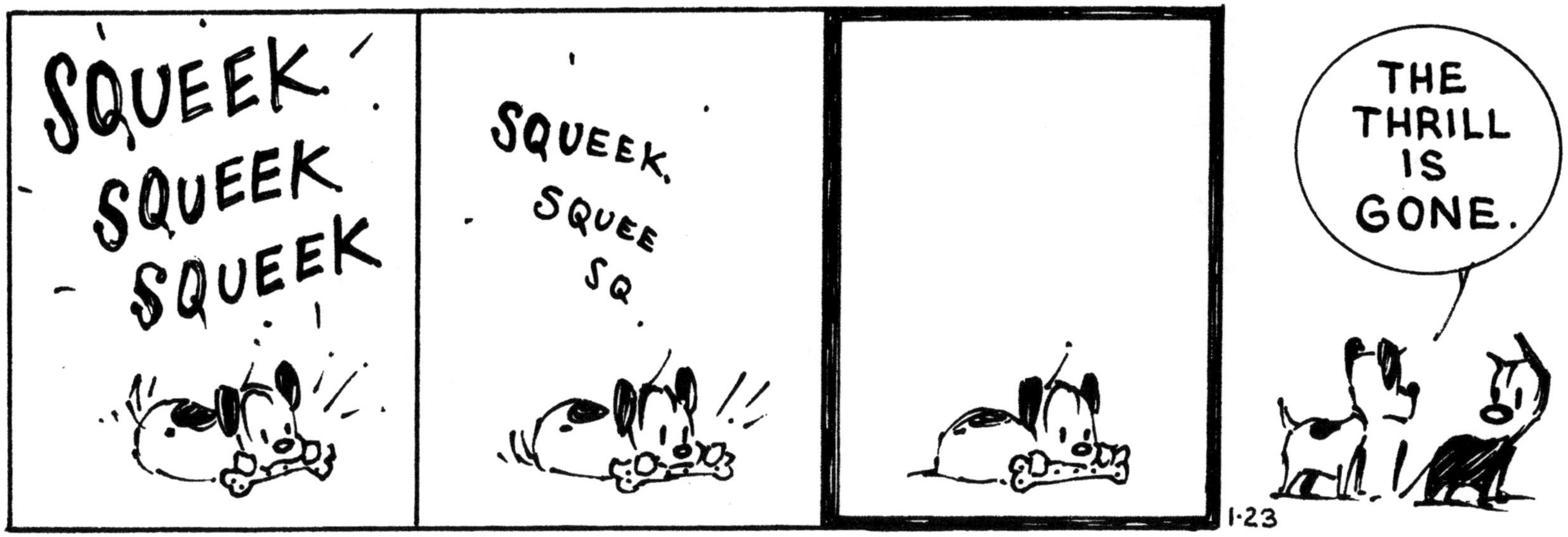
SQUEEK SQUEEK SQUEEK SQUEEK
SQUEEK. SQUEE SQ.
THE THRILL IS GONE.
1·23

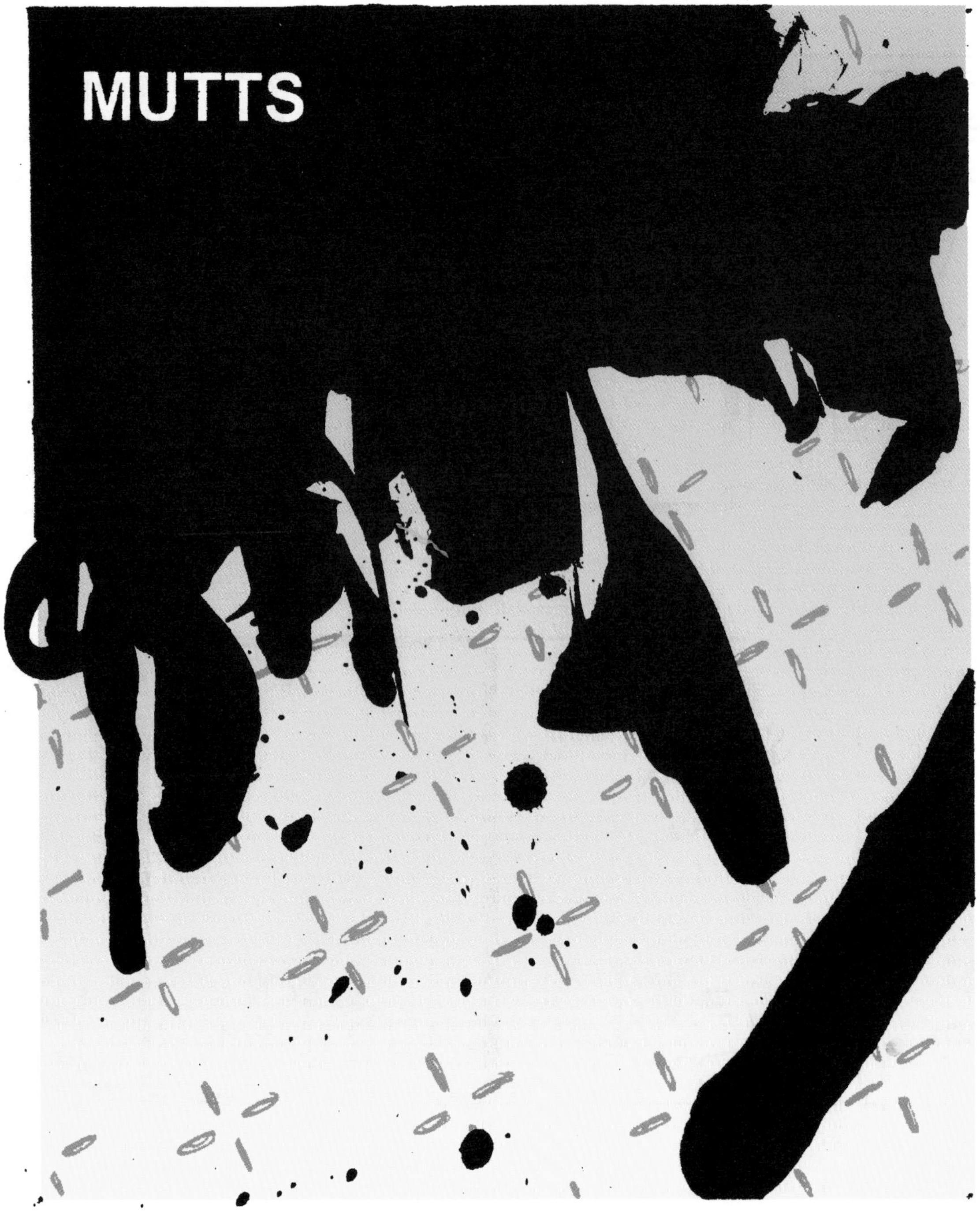
MUTTS

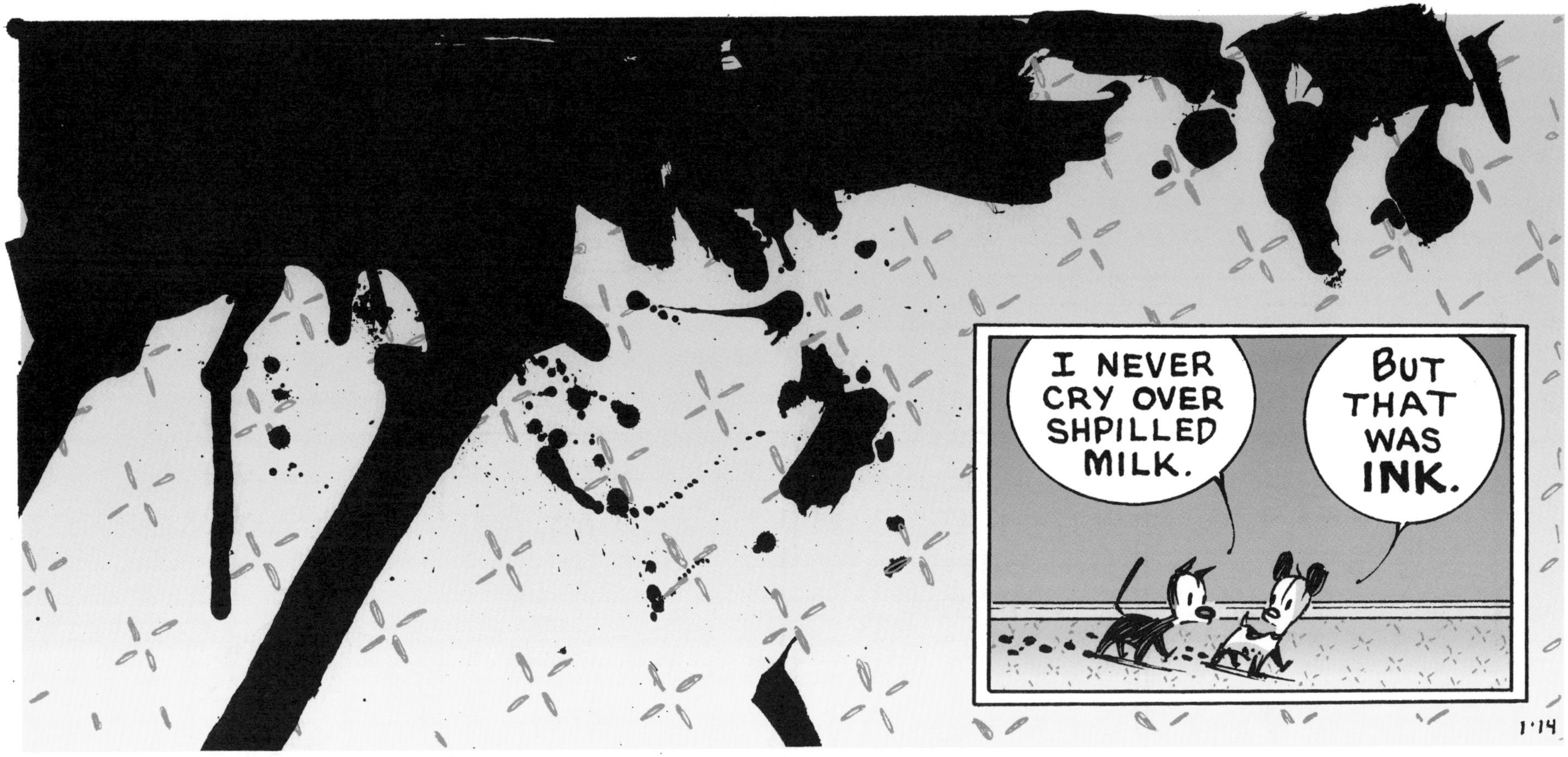
I NEVER CRY OVER SHPILLED MILK.
BUT THAT WAS INK.
1·14

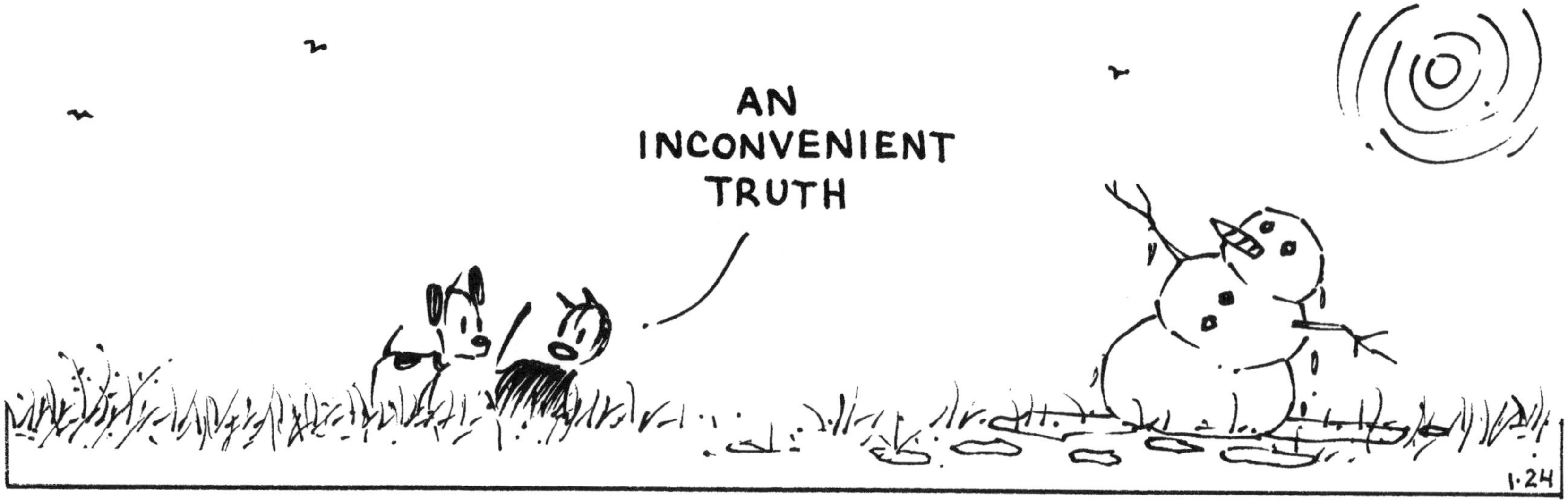
AN INCONVENIENT TRUTH
1·24

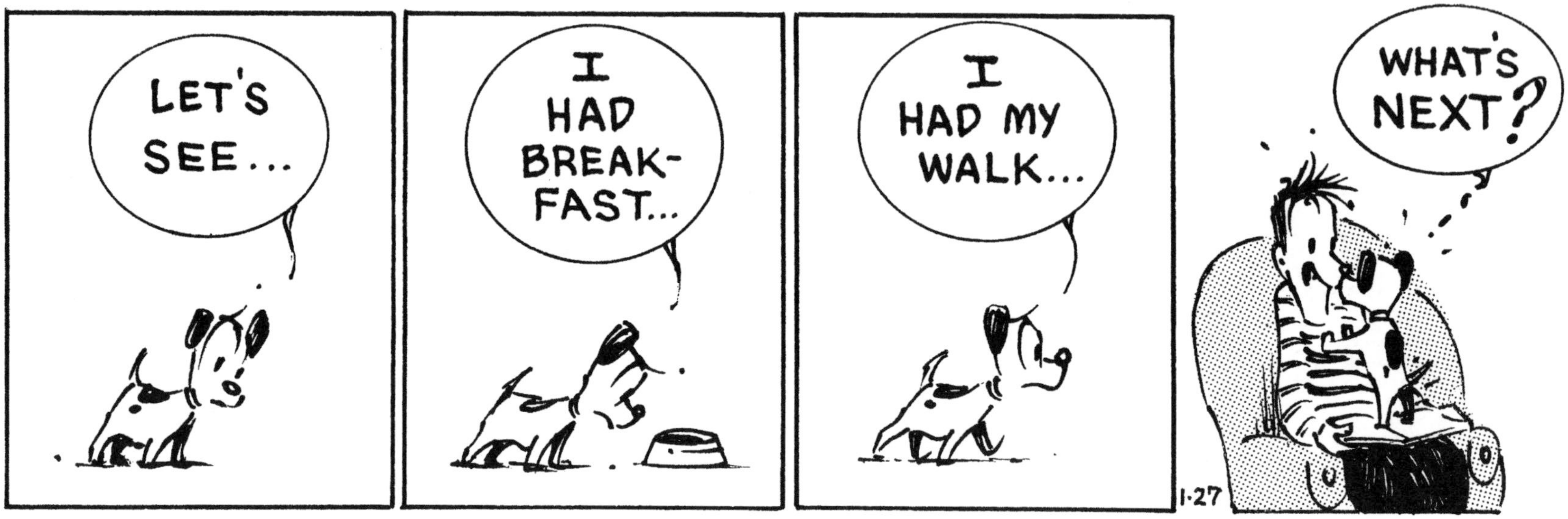
LET'S SEE...
I HAD BREAK-FAST...
I HAD MY WALK...
1·27
WHAT'S NEXT?

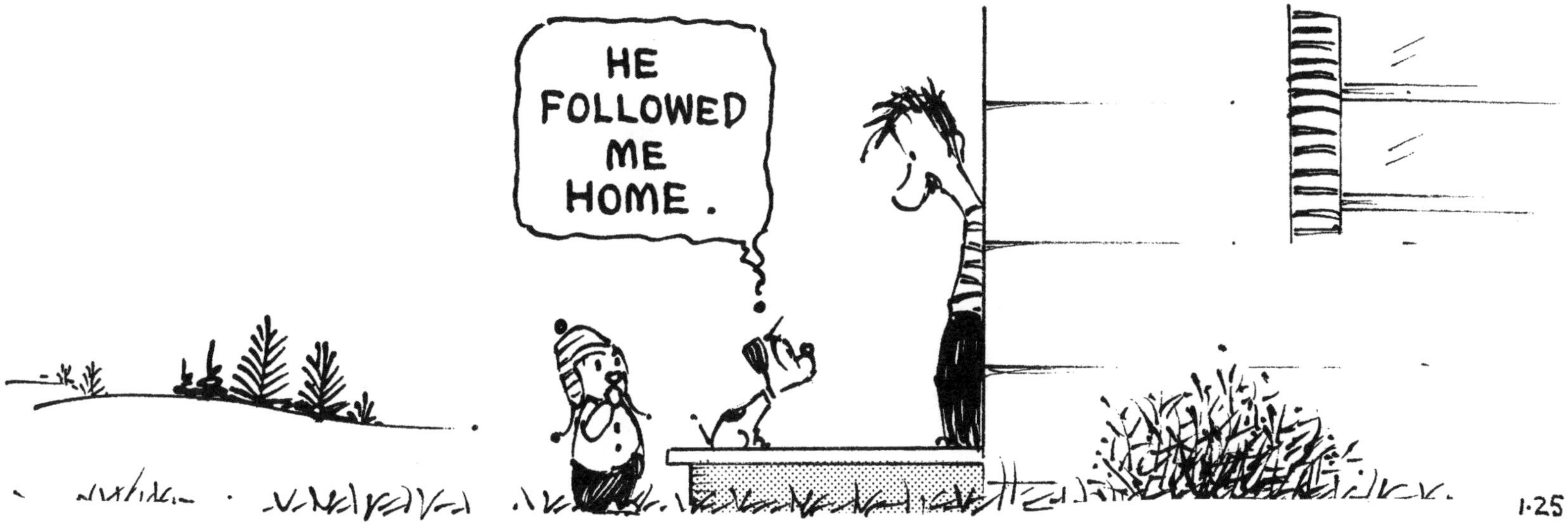
HE FOLLOWED ME HOME.
1·25

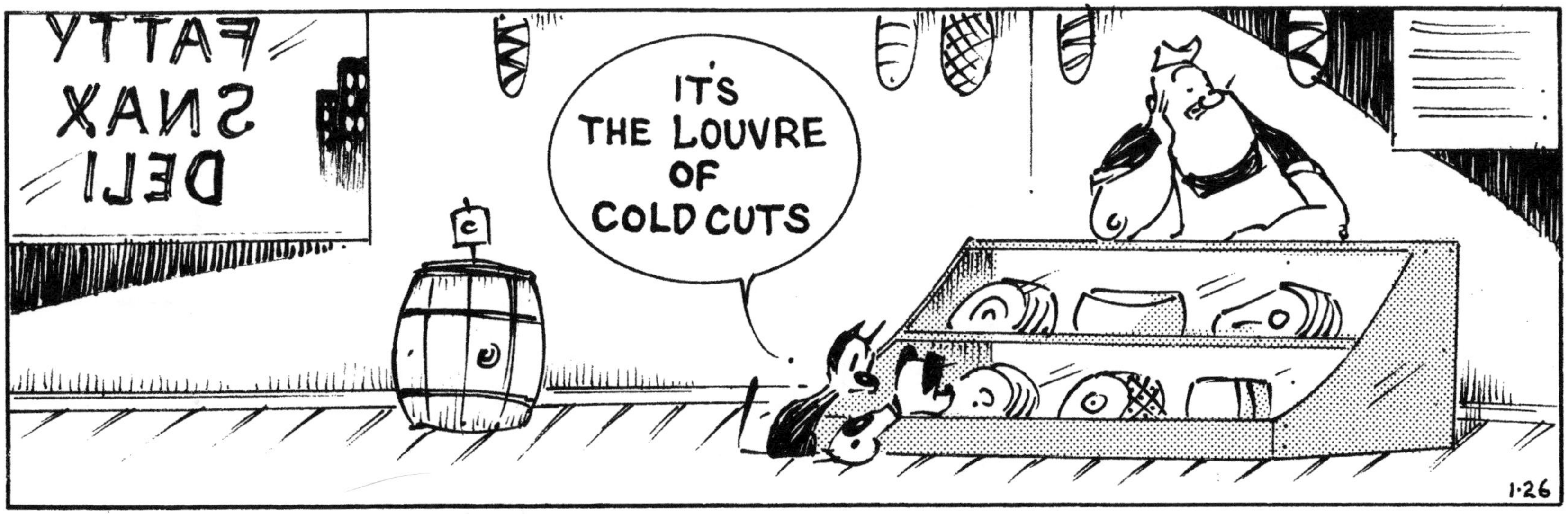
FATTY SNAX DELI
IT'S THE LOUVRE OF COLD CUTS
1·26

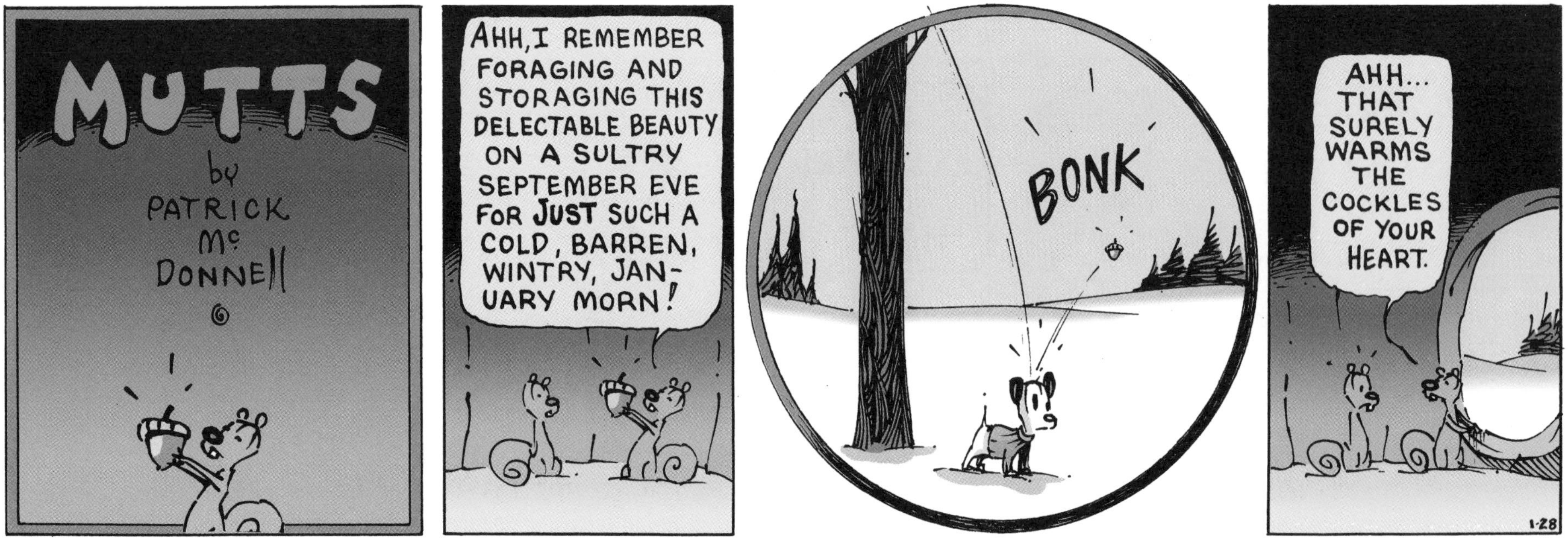
MUTTS
by PATRICK McDONNELL
AHH, I REMEMBER FORAGING AND STORAGING THIS DELECTABLE BEAUTY ON A SULTRY SEPTEMBER EVE FOR JUST SUCH A COLD, BARREN, WINTRY, JANUARY MORN!
BONK
AHH... THAT SURELY WARMS THE COCKLES OF YOUR HEART.
1·28

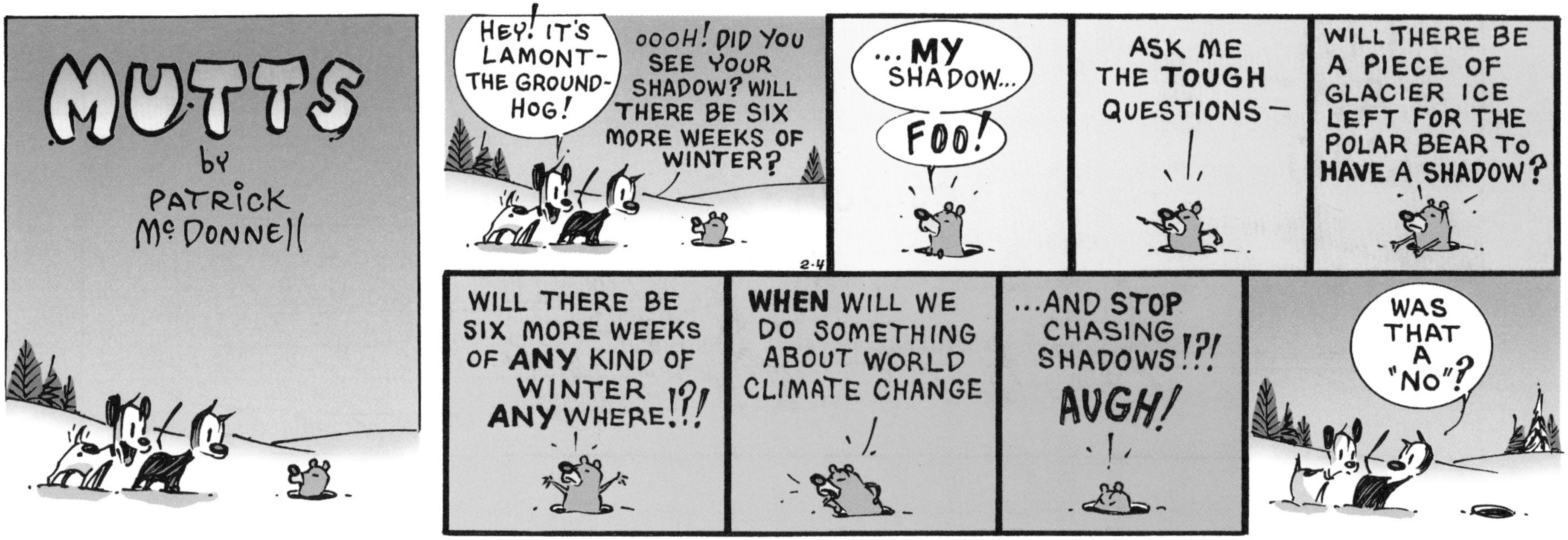
MUTTS
by PATRICK McDONNELL
HEY! IT'S LAMONT-THE GROUND-HOG!
OOOH! DID YOU SEE YOUR SHADOW? WILL THERE BE SIX MORE WEEKS OF WINTER?
2·4
...MY SHADOW...
FOO!
ASK ME THE TOUGH QUESTIONS—
WILL THERE BE A PIECE OF GLACIER ICE LEFT FOR THE POLAR BEAR TO HAVE A SHADOW?
WILL THERE BE SIX MORE WEEKS OF ANY KIND OF WINTER ANY WHERE!?!
WHEN WILL WE DO SOMETHING ABOUT WORLD CLIMATE CHANGE
...AND STOP CHASING SHADOWS!?!
AUGH!
WAS THAT A "NO"?

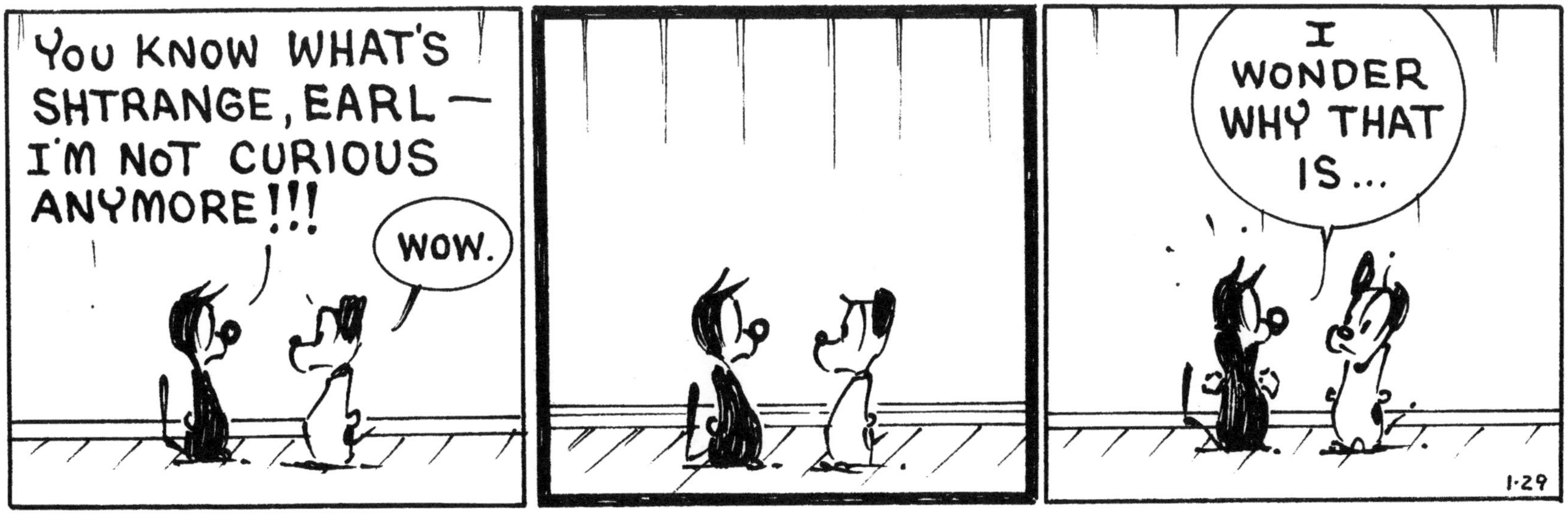
YOU KNOW WHAT'S SHTRANGE, EARL— I'M NOT CURIOUS ANYMORE!!!
WOW.
I WONDER WHY THAT IS...
1·29

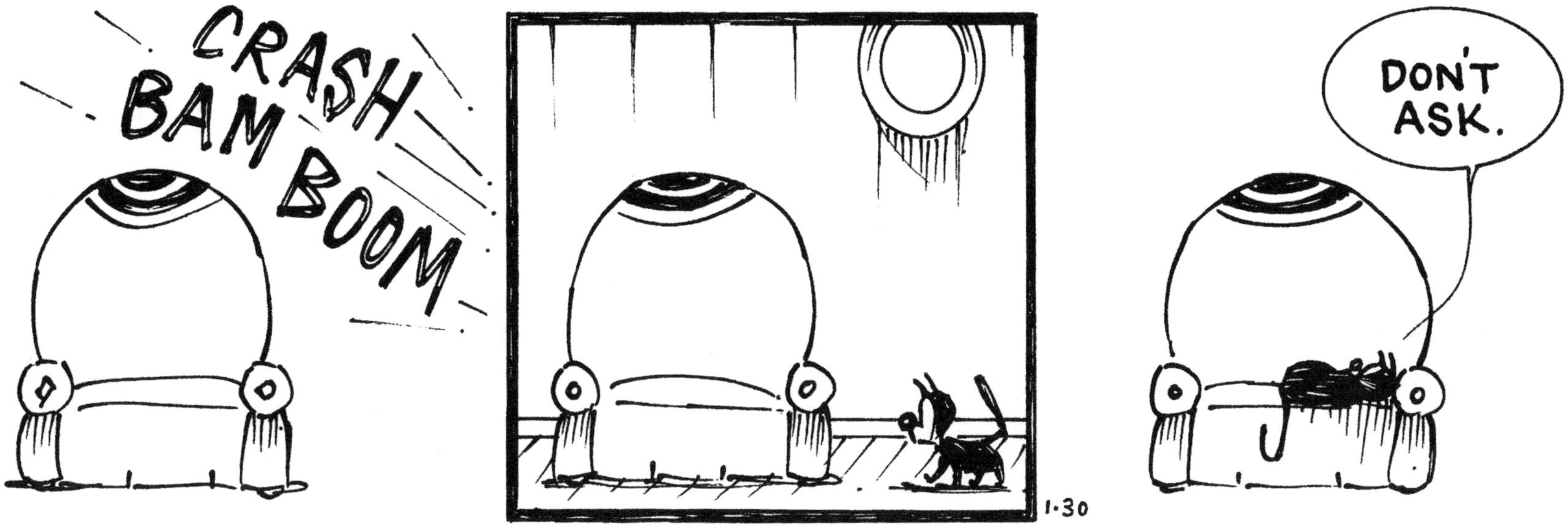
CRASH BAM BOOM
1·30
DON'T ASK.

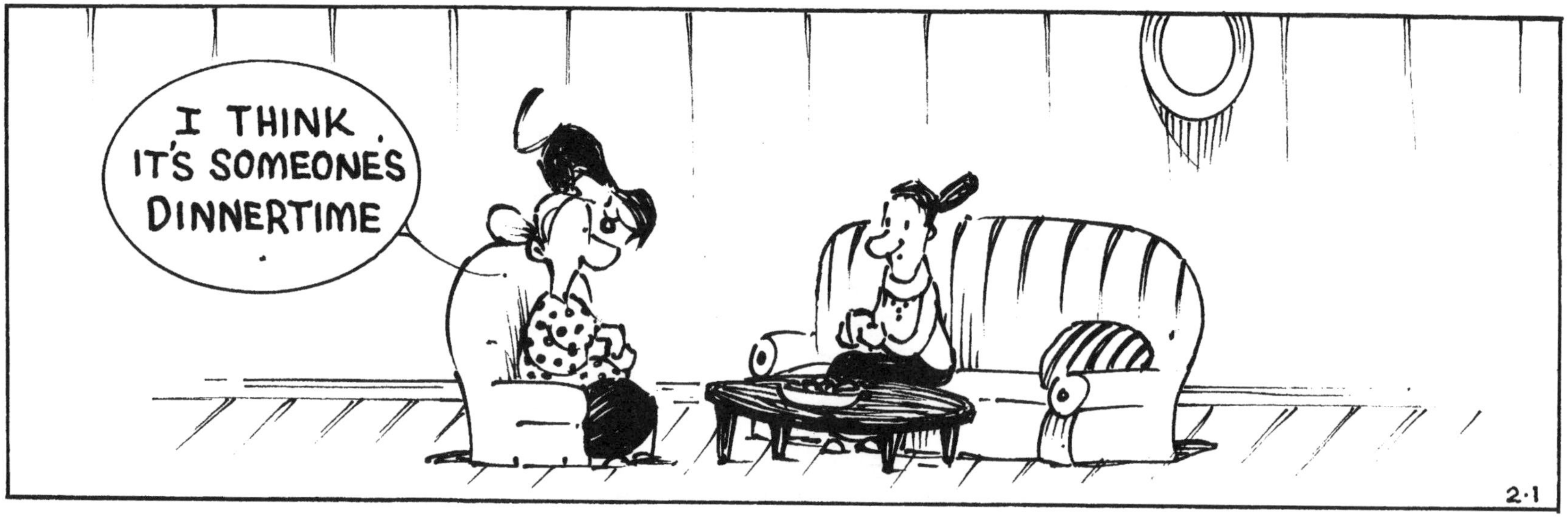
I THINK IT'S SOMEONE'S DINNERTIME.
2·1

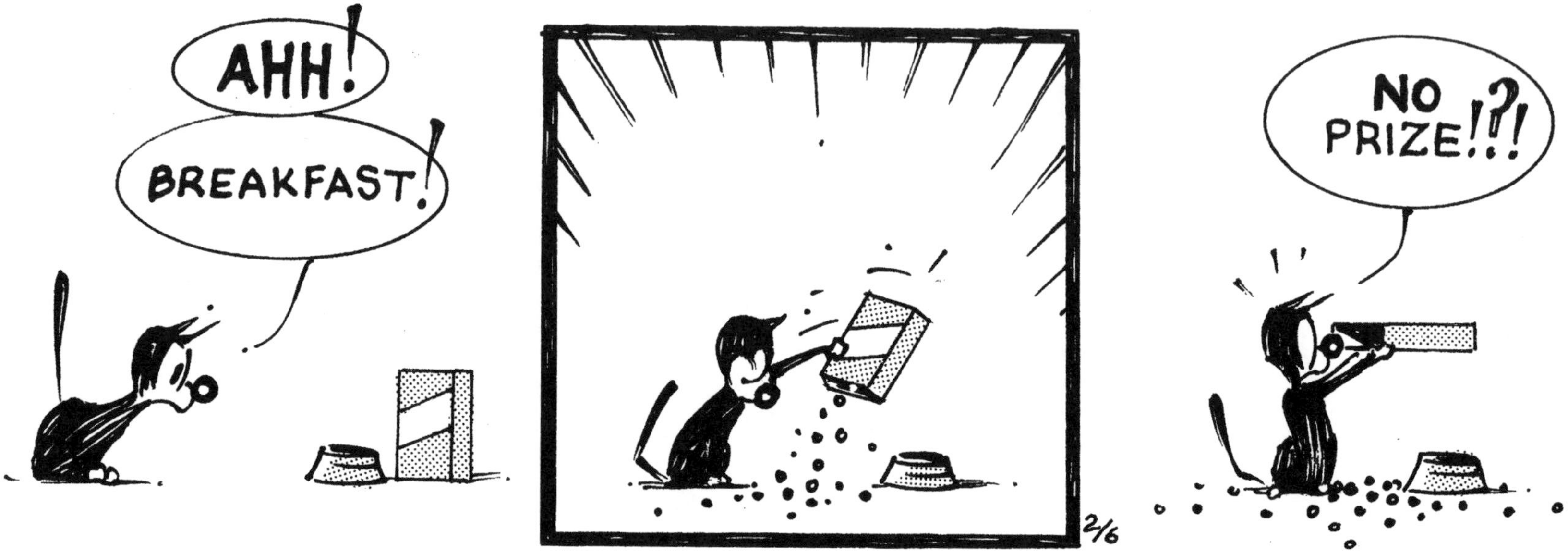
AHH!
BREAKFAST!
2/6
NO PRIZE!?!

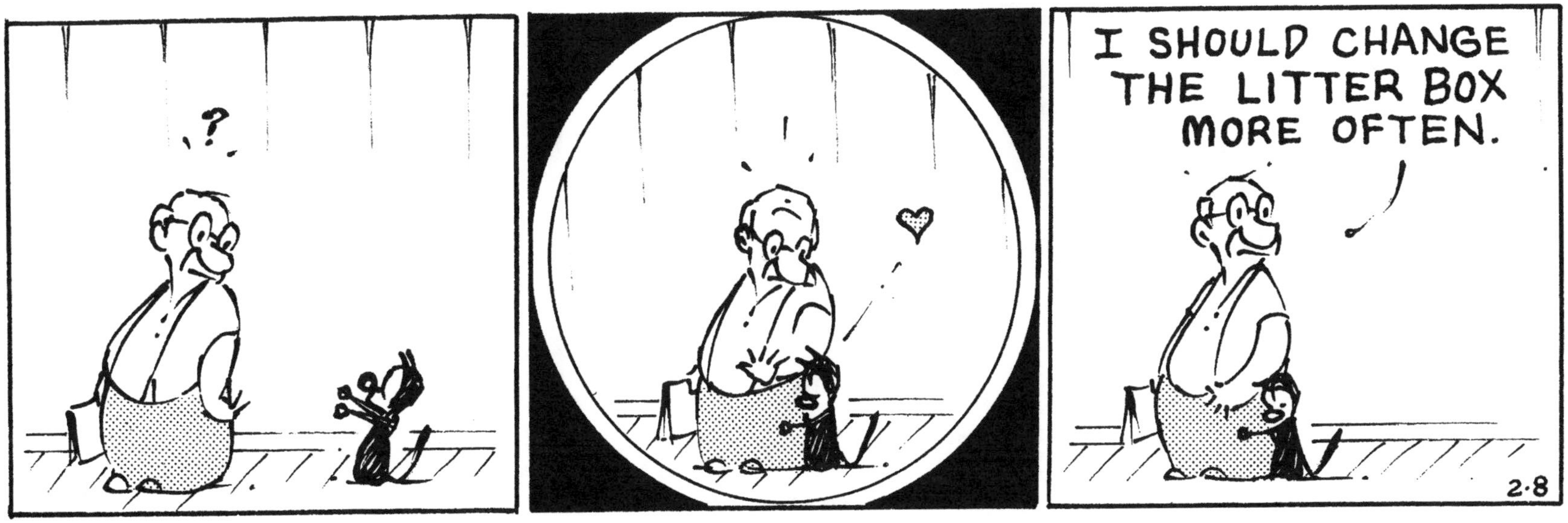
?
I SHOULD CHANGE THE LITTER BOX MORE OFTEN.
2·8

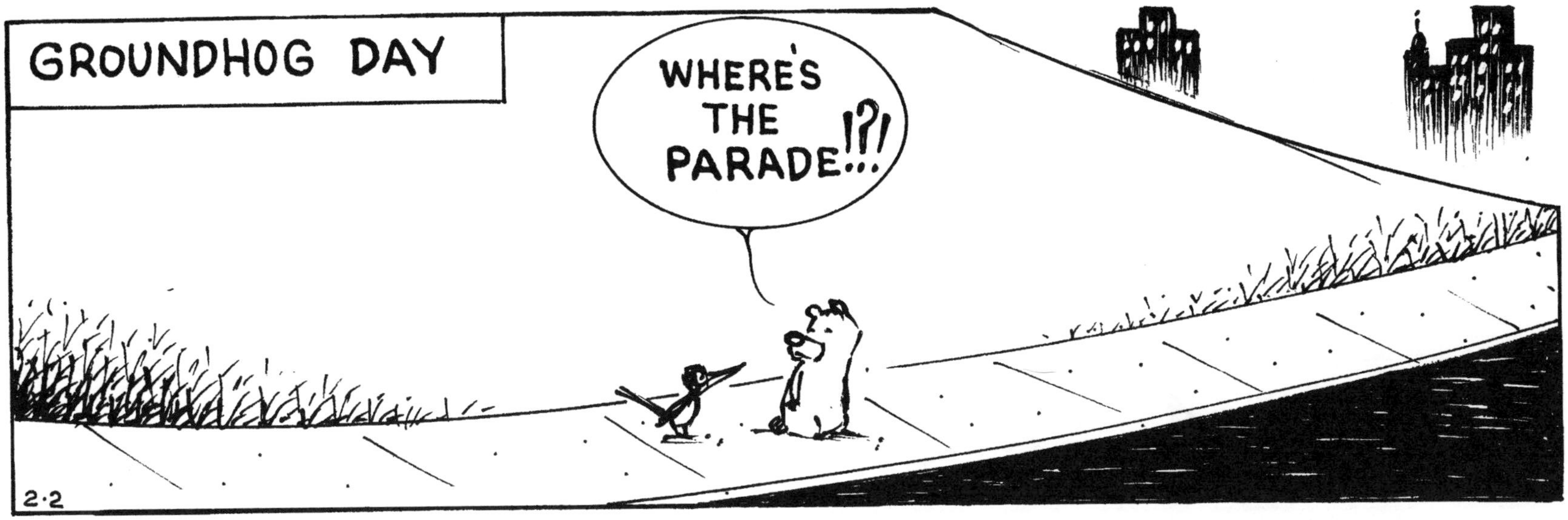
GROUNDHOG DAY
WHERE'S THE PARADE!?!
2·2

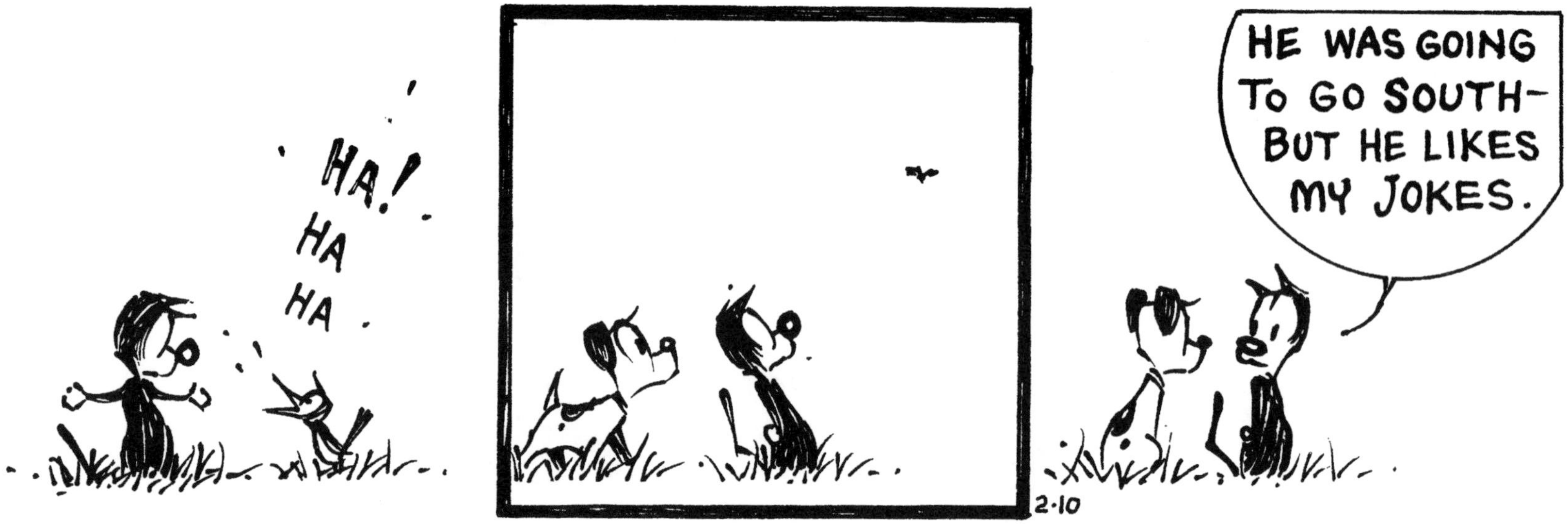
HA! HA HA HA
HE WAS GOING TO GO SOUTH— BUT HE LIKES MY JOKES.
2-10

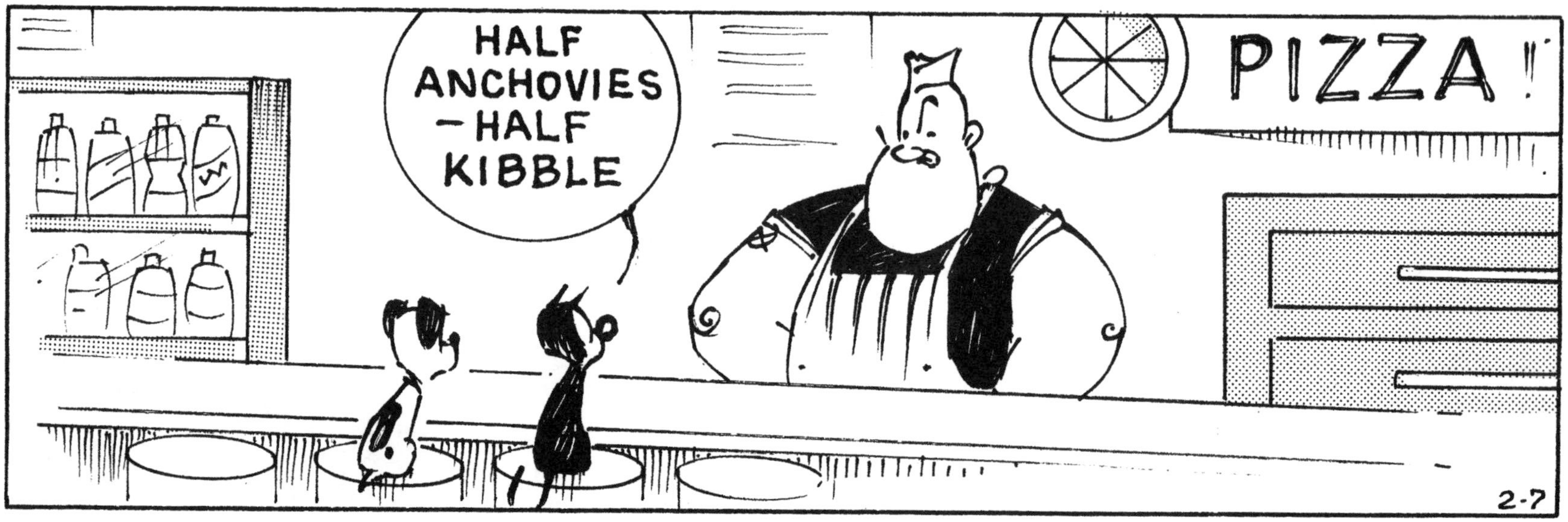
HALF ANCHOVIES —HALF KIBBLE
PIZZA!
2-7

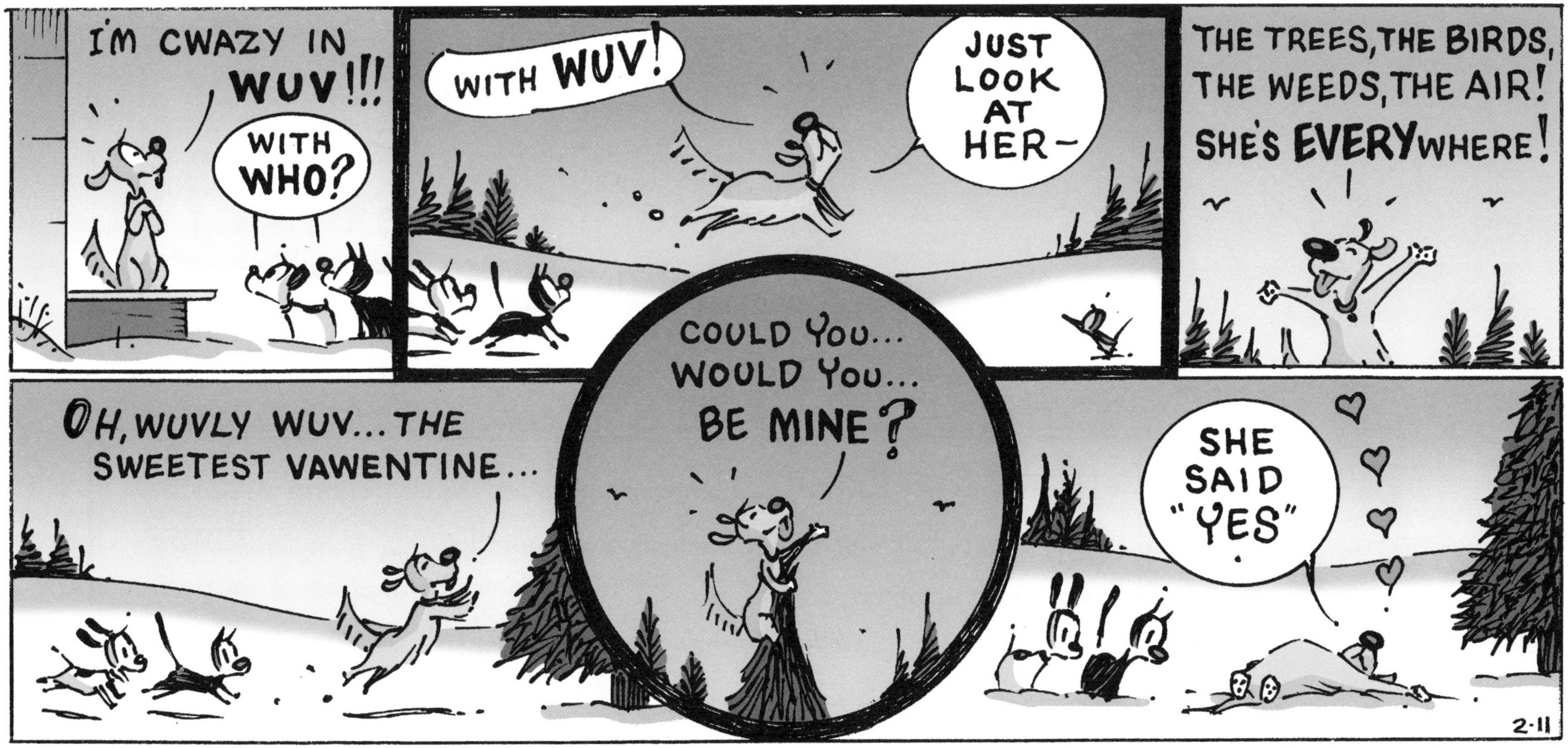
I'M CWAZY IN WUV!!!
WITH WHO?
WITH WUV!
JUST LOOK AT HER—
THE TREES, THE BIRDS, THE WEEDS, THE AIR! SHE'S EVERYWHERE!
OH, WUVLY WUV... THE SWEETEST VAWENTINE...
COULD YOU... WOULD YOU... BE MINE?
SHE SAID "YES"
2-11

All animals except man know that the principal business of life is to enjoy it.
   - Samuel Butler

2·12

Happiness is a butterfly, which when pursued is just beyond your grasp, but which, if you will sit down quietly, may alight upon you.
   - Nathaniel Hawthorne

2·13

In love, there is always one who kisses and one who offers the cheek.

— *French Proverb*

2·14

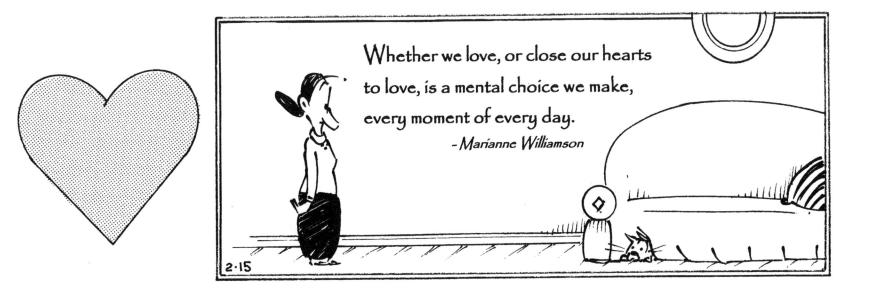

Whether we love, or close our hearts to love, is a mental choice we make, every moment of every day.

— *Marianne Williamson*

2·15

27

You cannot always *have* happiness,
but you can always *give* happiness.
— *Anonymous*

We find rest in those we love,
and we provide a resting place
for those who love us.
— *Saint Bernard of Clairvaux*

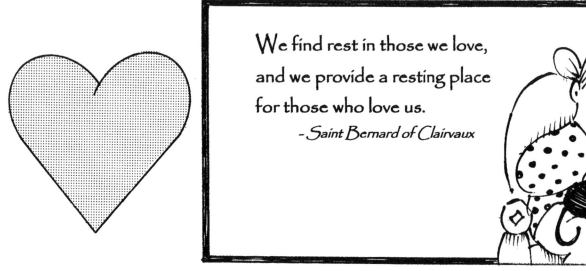

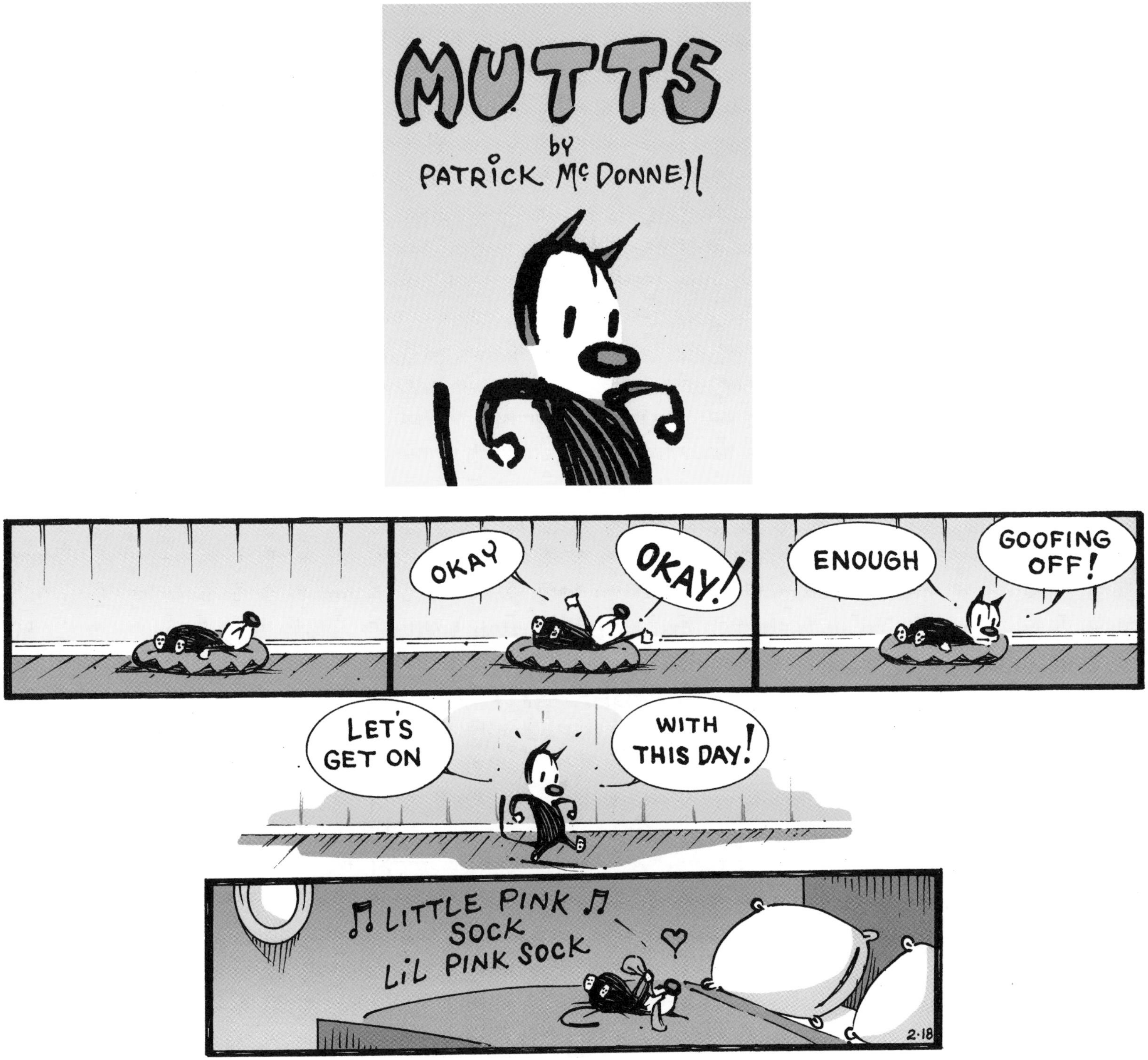
MUTTS
by
PATRICK McDONNELL
OKAY
OKAY!
ENOUGH
GOOFING OFF!
LET'S GET ON
WITH THIS DAY!
♫ LITTLE PINK ♫
SOCK
LIL PINK SOCK
2·18

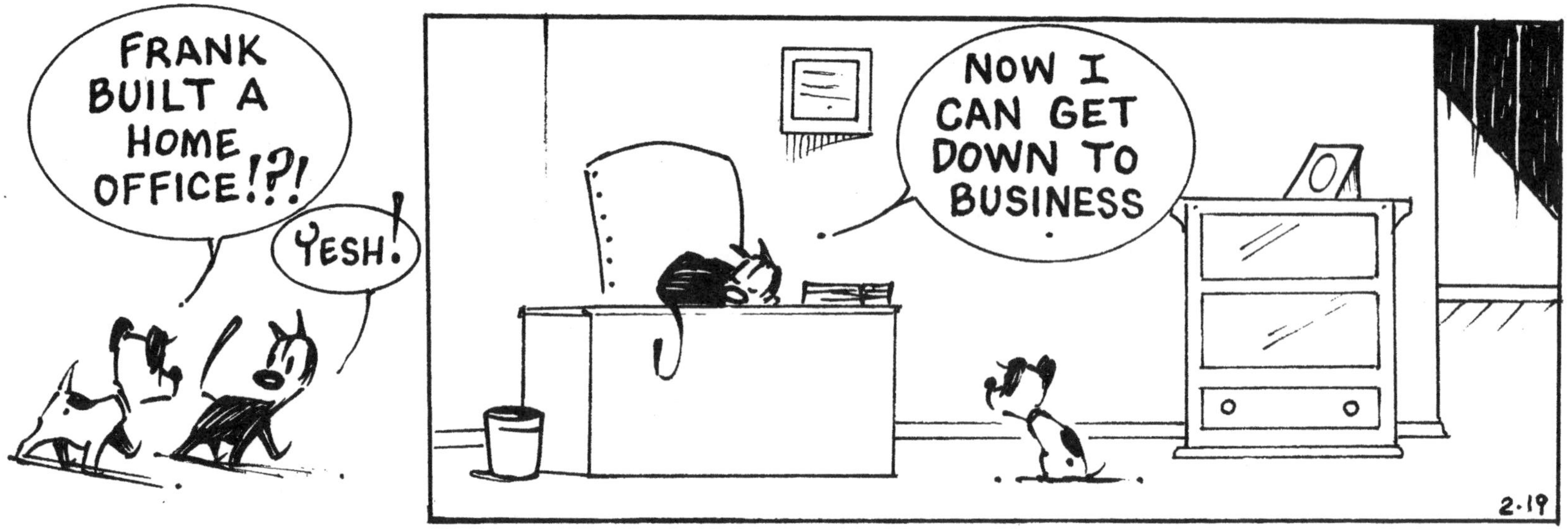
FRANK BUILT A HOME OFFICE!?!
YESH!
NOW I CAN GET DOWN TO BUSINESS.
2·19

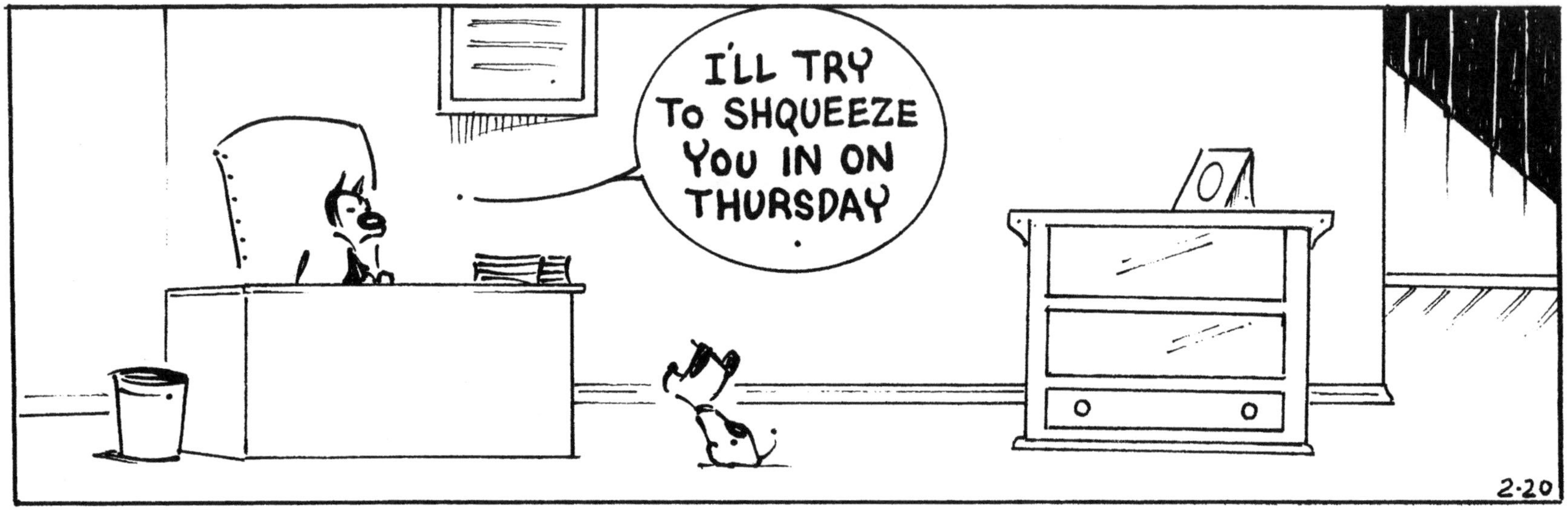
I'LL TRY TO SHQUEEZE YOU IN ON THURSDAY.
2·20

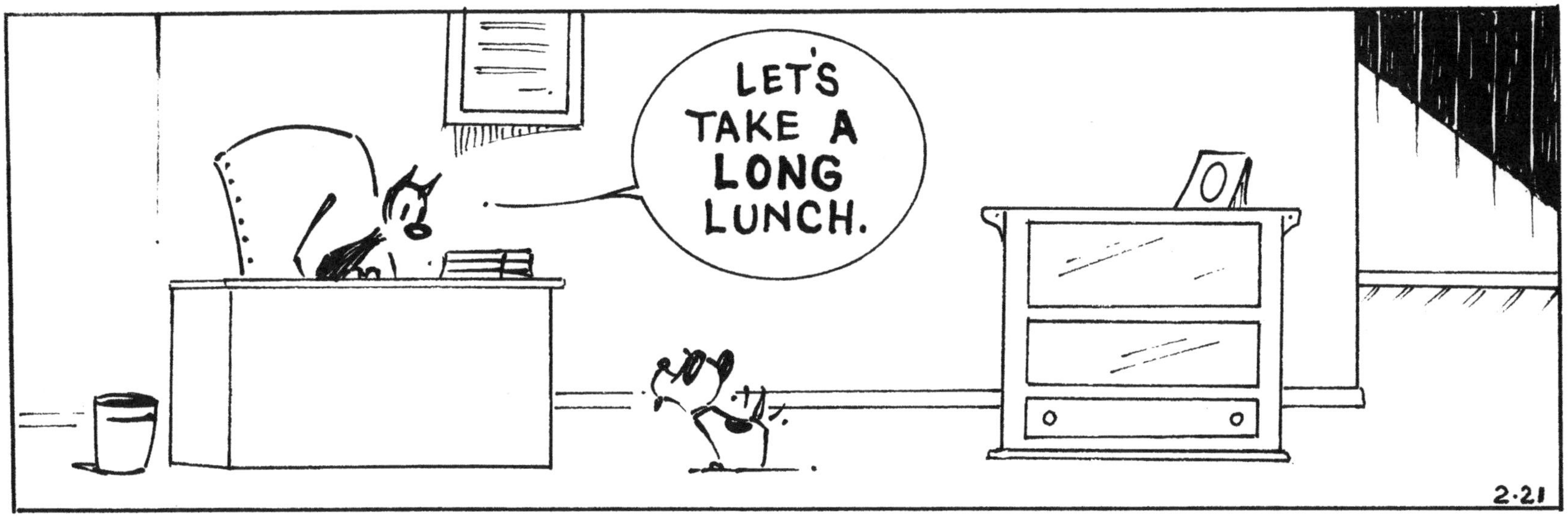
LET'S TAKE A LONG LUNCH.
2·21

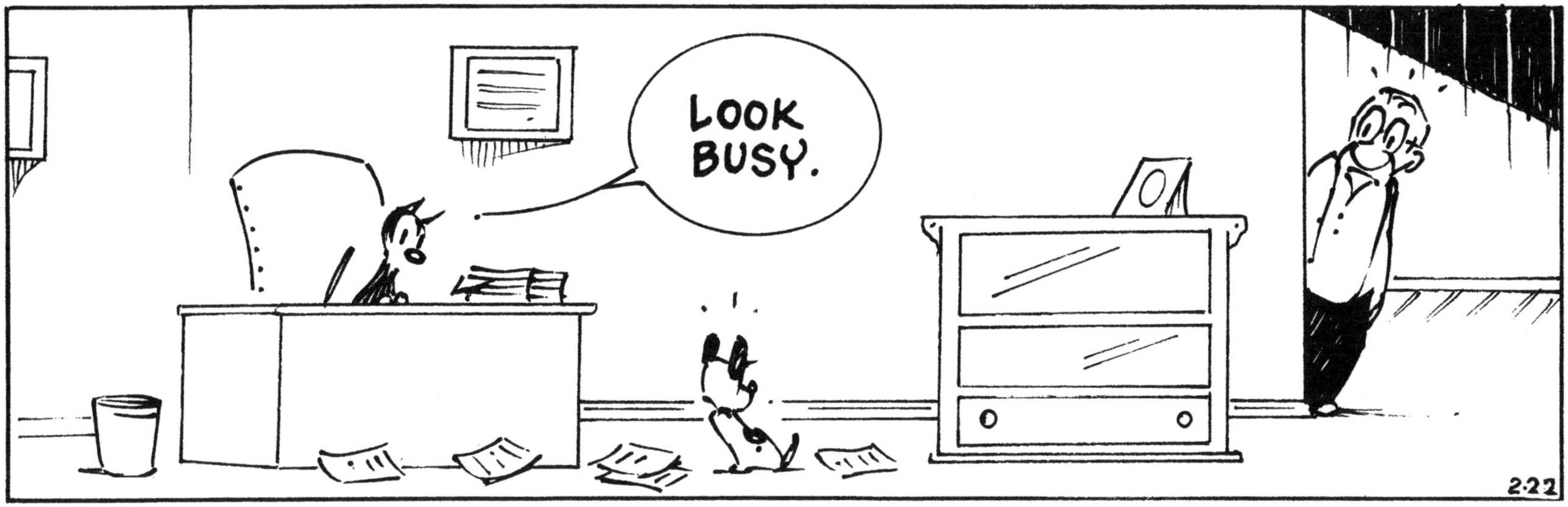
LOOK BUSY.
2·22

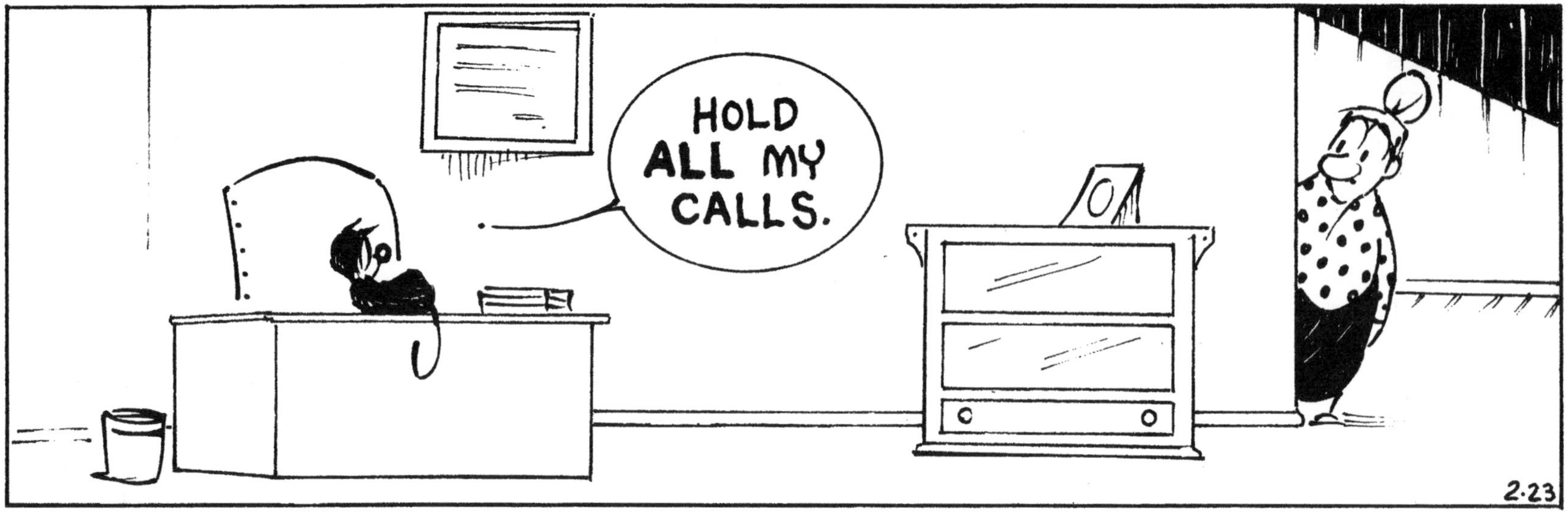
HOLD **ALL** MY CALLS.
2·23

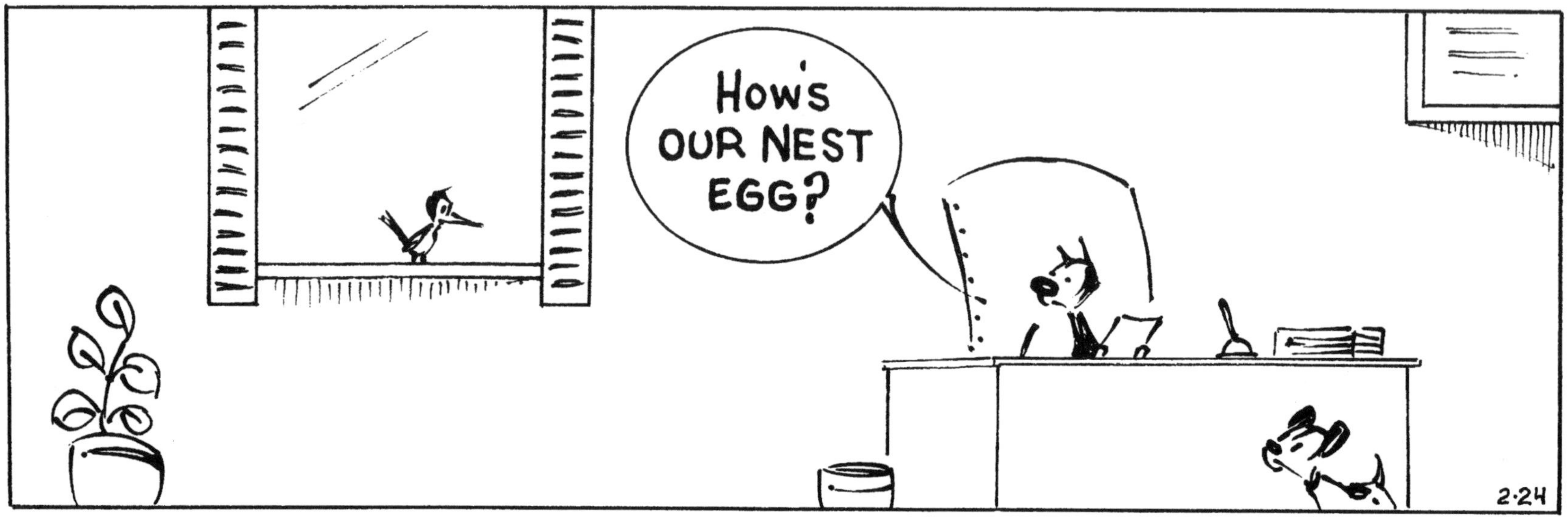
HOW'S OUR NEST EGG?
2·24

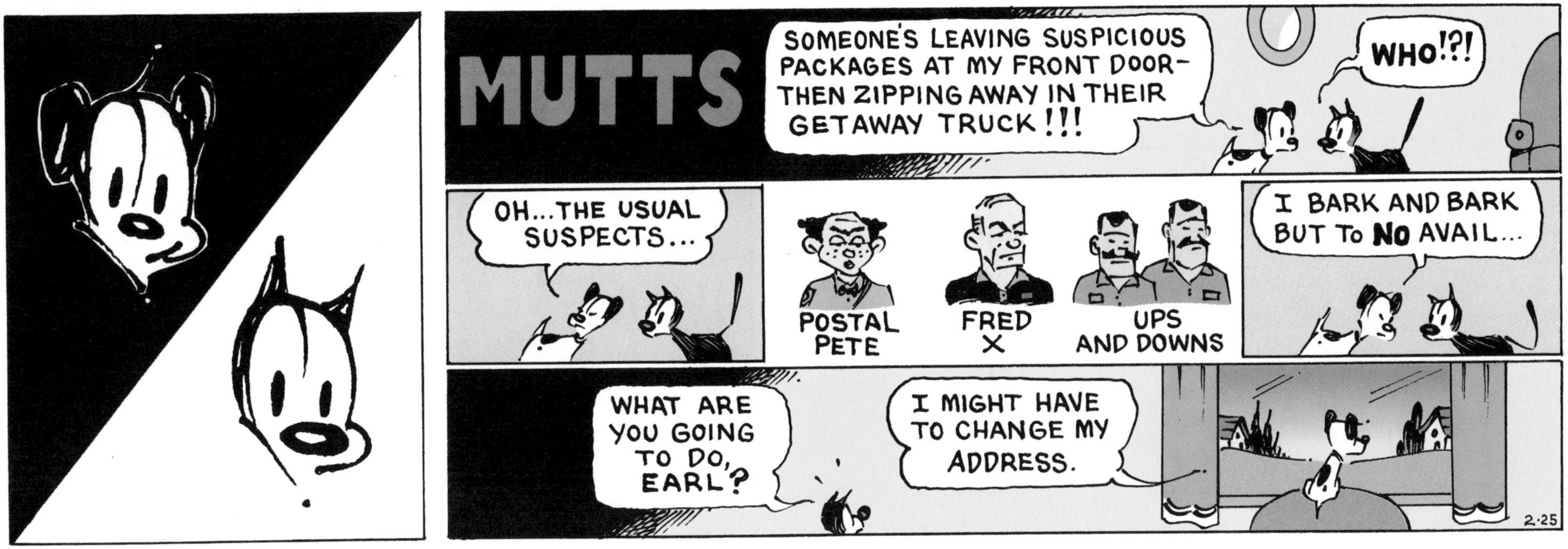
MUTTS
SOMEONE'S LEAVING SUSPICIOUS PACKAGES AT MY FRONT DOOR– THEN ZIPPING AWAY IN THEIR GETAWAY TRUCK!!!
WHO!?!
OH... THE USUAL SUSPECTS...
POSTAL PETE
FRED X
UPS AND DOWNS
I BARK AND BARK BUT TO NO AVAIL...
WHAT ARE YOU GOING TO DO, EARL?
I MIGHT HAVE TO CHANGE MY ADDRESS.
2·25

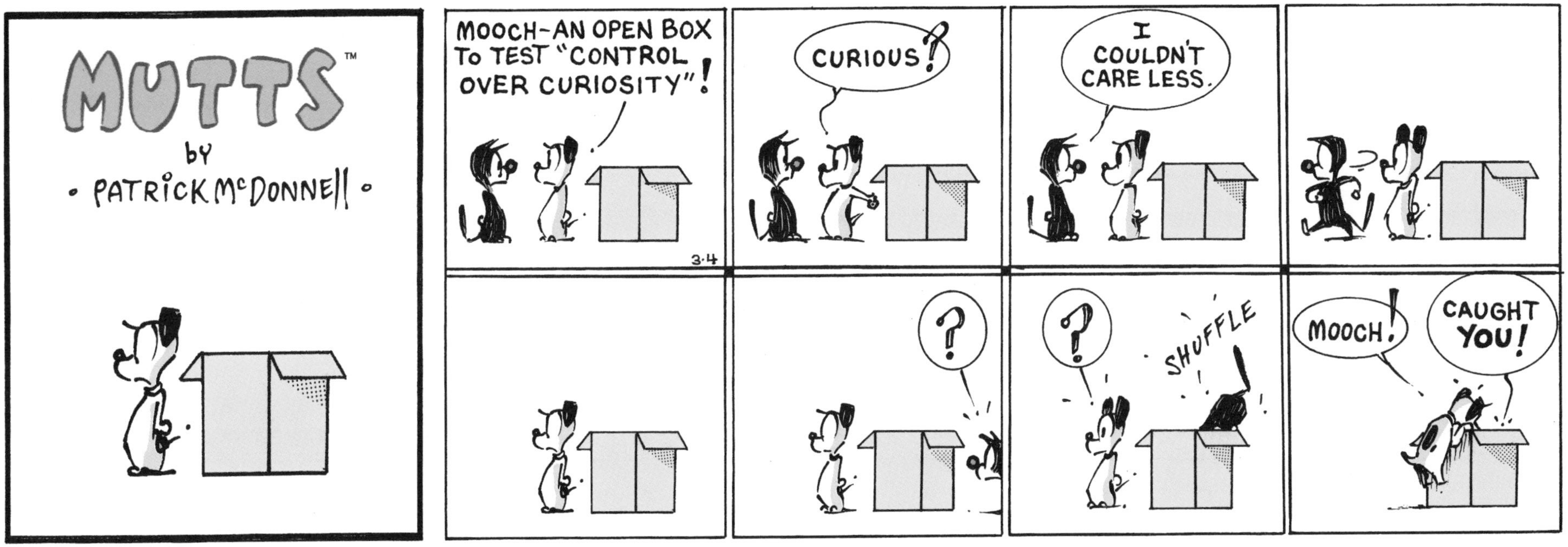
MUTTS™
by
PATRICK McDONNELL
MOOCH–AN OPEN BOX TO TEST "CONTROL OVER CURIOSITY"!
3·4
CURIOUS?
I COULDN'T CARE LESS.
?
?
SHUFFLE
MOOCH!
CAUGHT YOU!

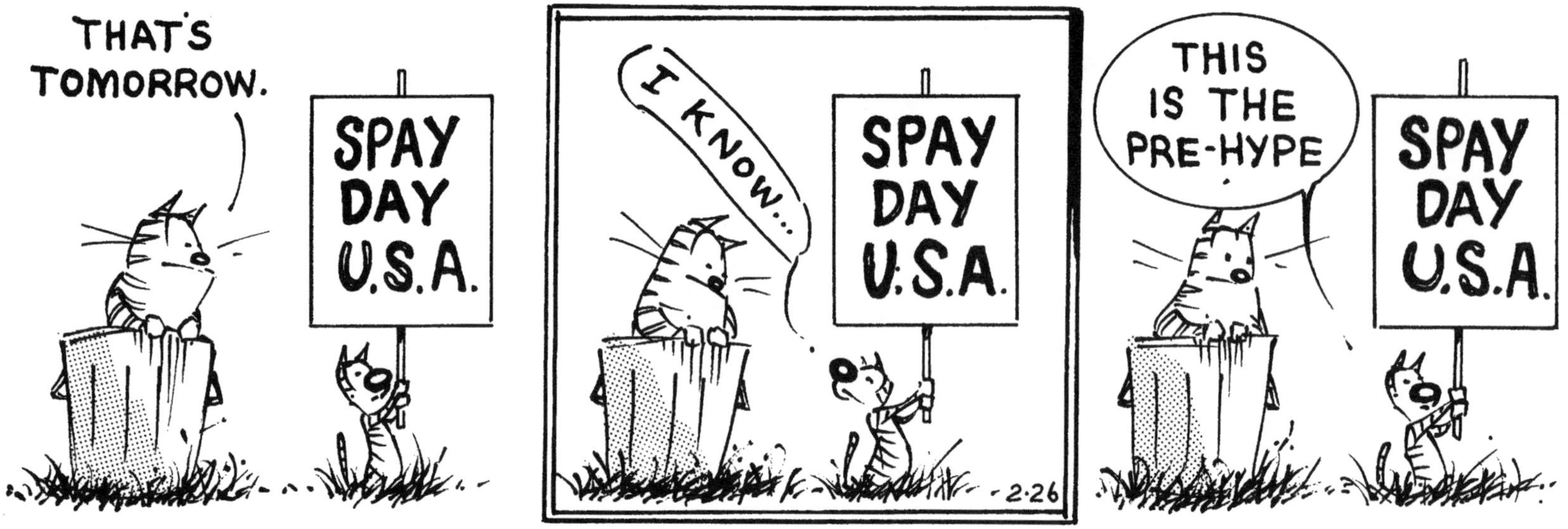
THAT'S TOMORROW.
SPAY DAY U.S.A.
I KNOW...
SPAY DAY U.S.A.
2·26
THIS IS THE PRE-HYPE
SPAY DAY U.S.A.

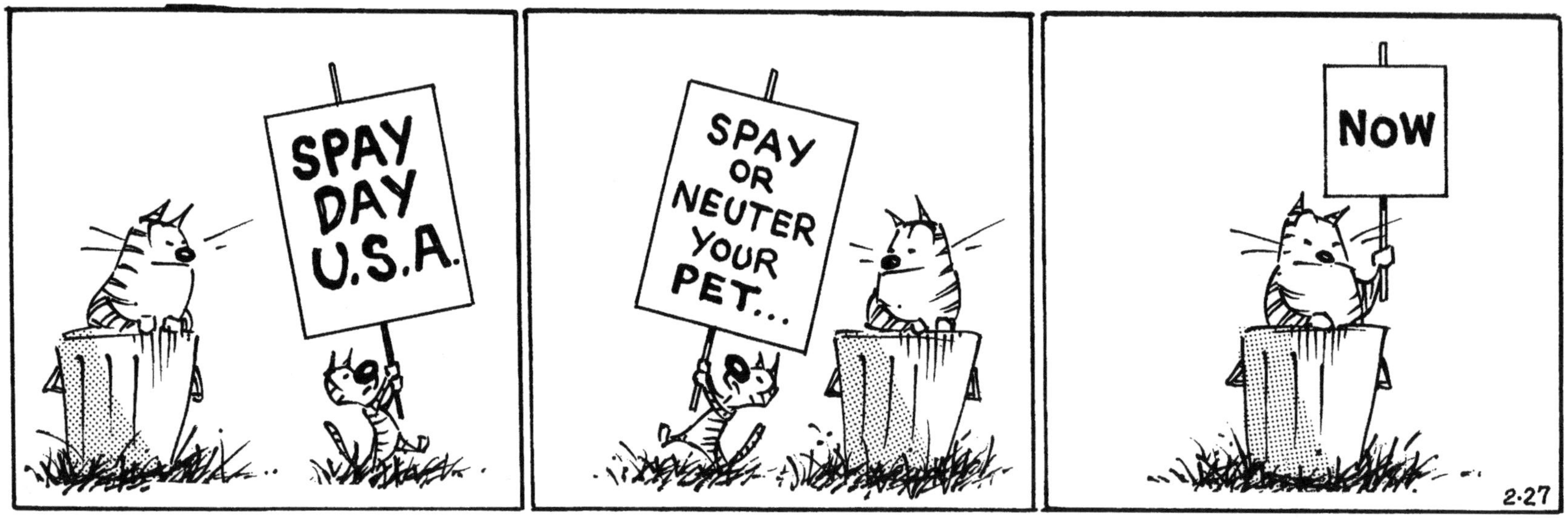
SPAY DAY U.S.A.
SPAY OR NEUTER YOUR PET...
NOW
2·27

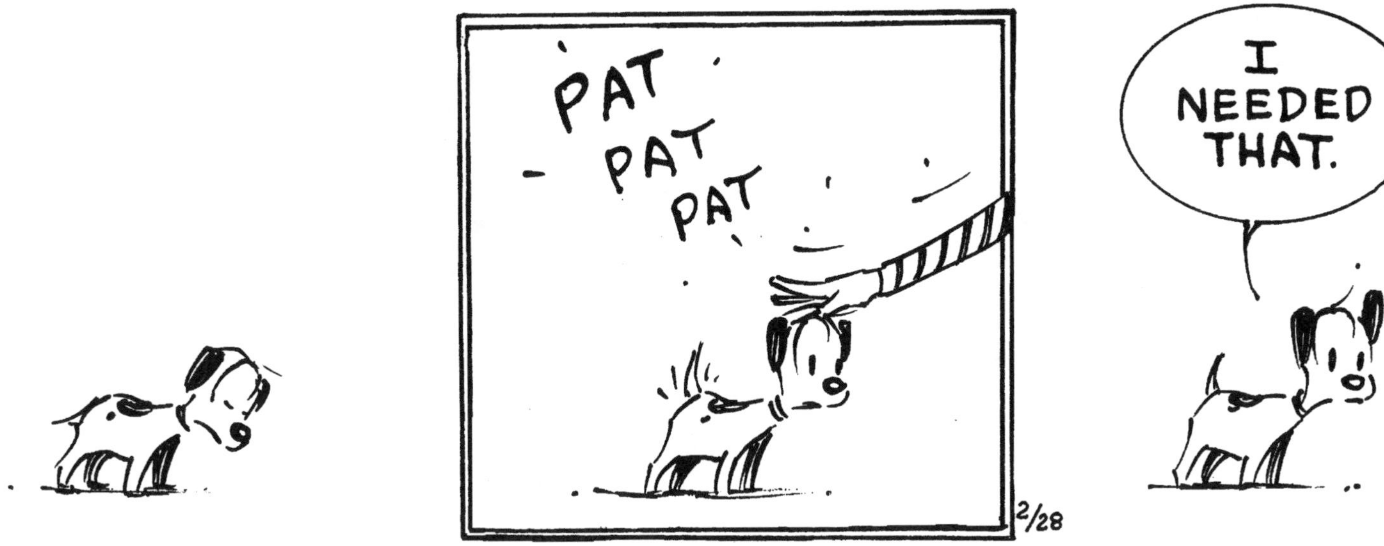
PAT PAT PAT
I NEEDED THAT.
2/28

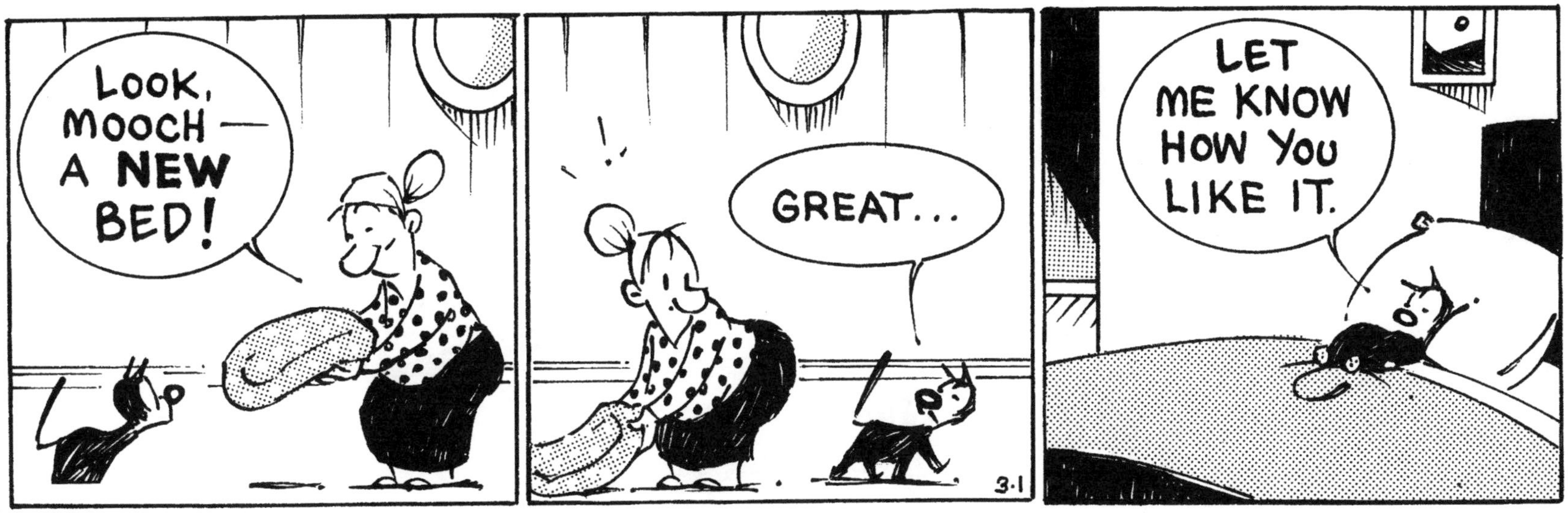
LOOK, MOOCH — A **NEW** BED!
!
GREAT...
3·1
LET ME KNOW HOW YOU LIKE IT.

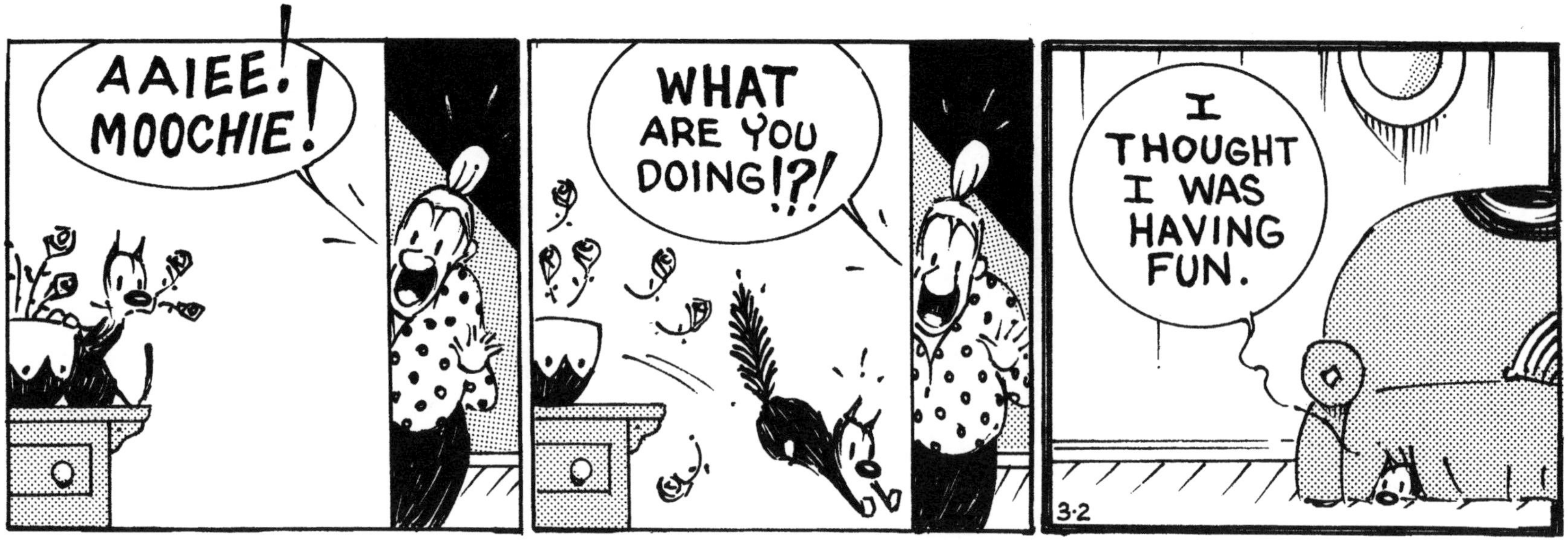
AAIEE! MOOCHIE!
WHAT ARE YOU DOING!?!
I THOUGHT I WAS HAVING FUN.
3·2

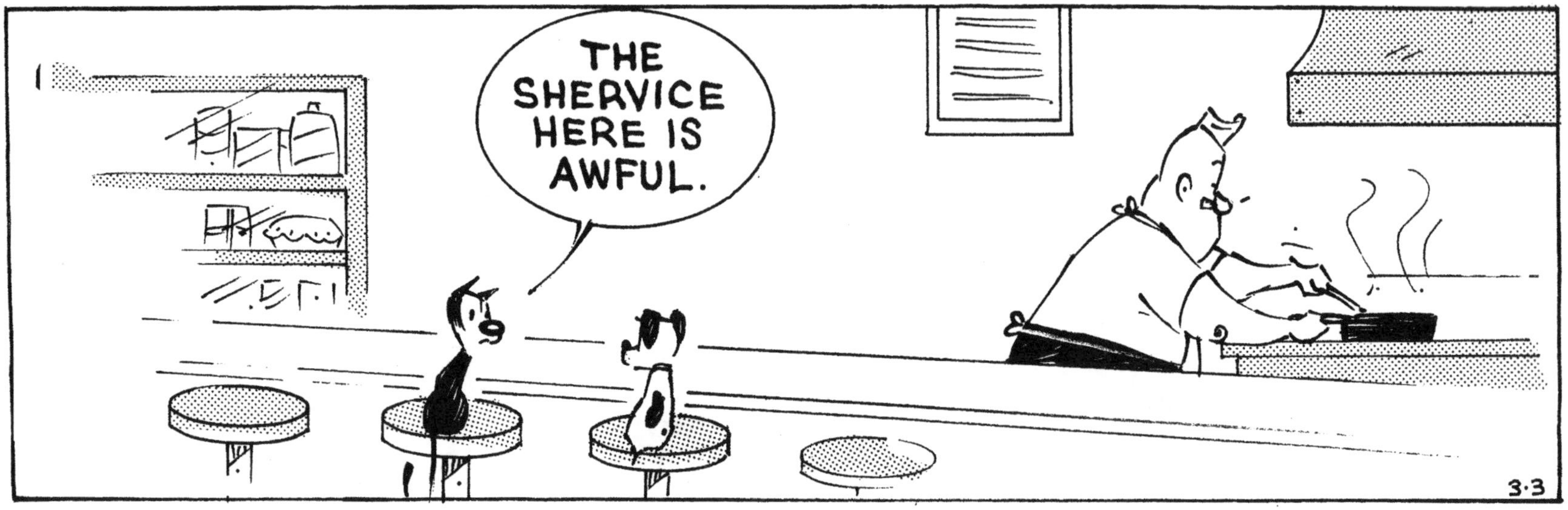
THE SHERVICE HERE IS AWFUL.
3·3

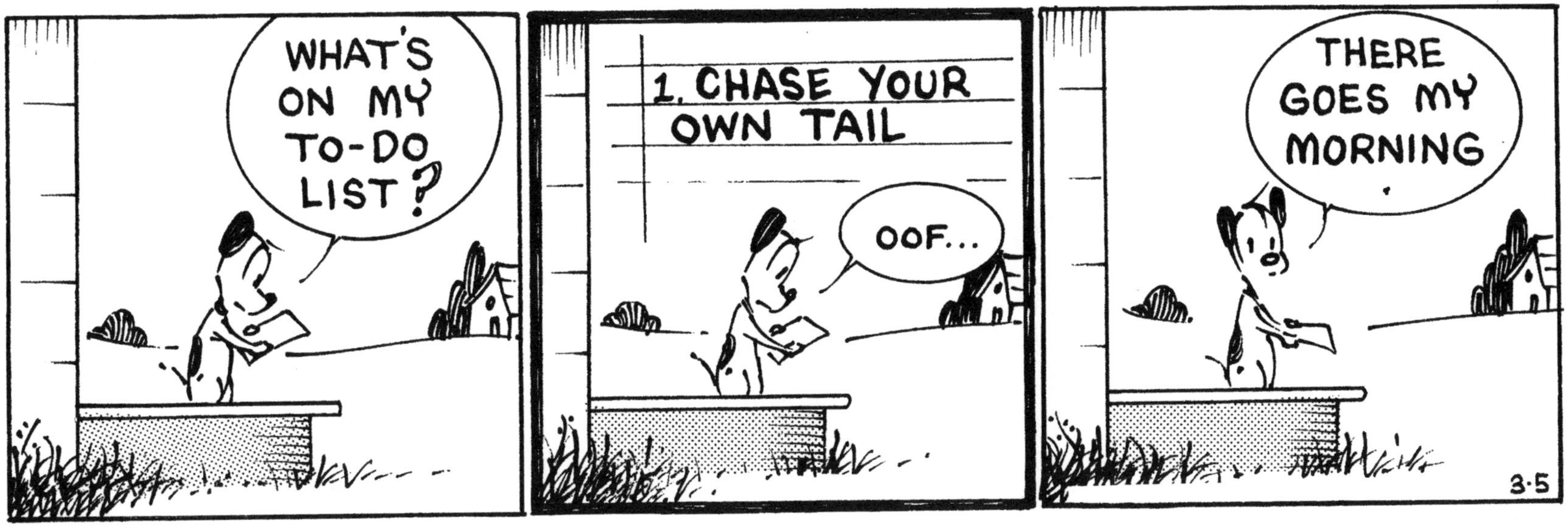
WHAT'S ON MY TO-DO LIST?
1. CHASE YOUR OWN TAIL
OOF...
THERE GOES MY MORNING
3·5

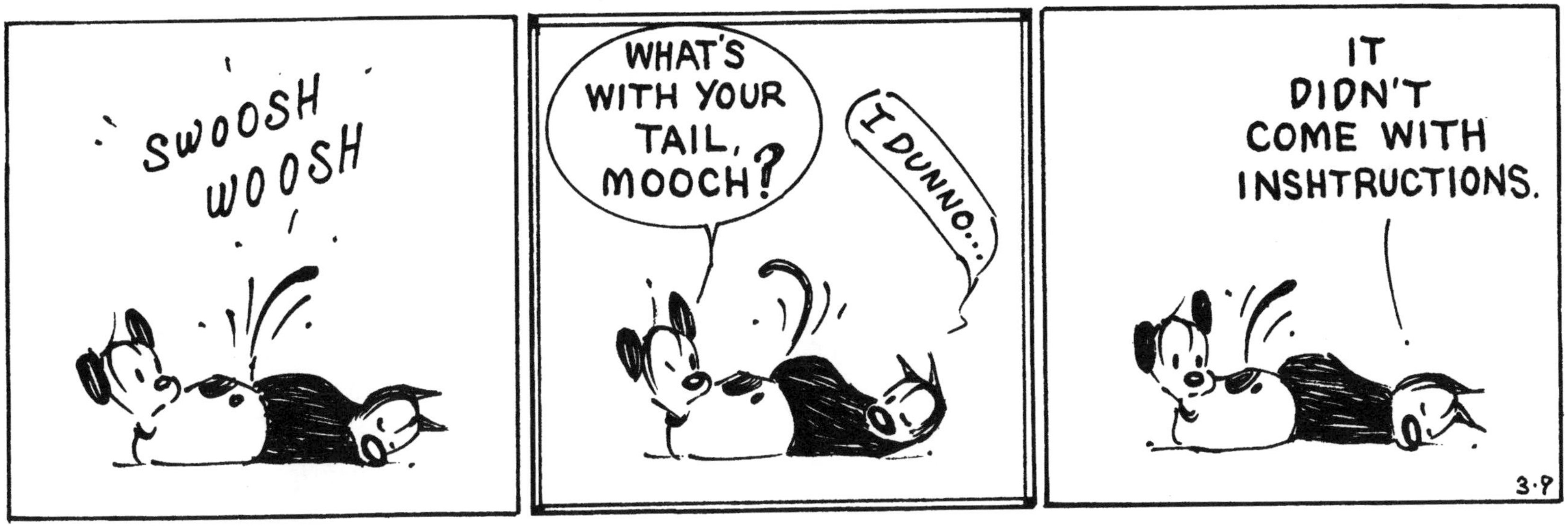
SWOOSH WOOSH
WHAT'S WITH YOUR TAIL, MOOCH?
I DUNNO...
IT DIDN'T COME WITH INSHTRUCTIONS.
3·9

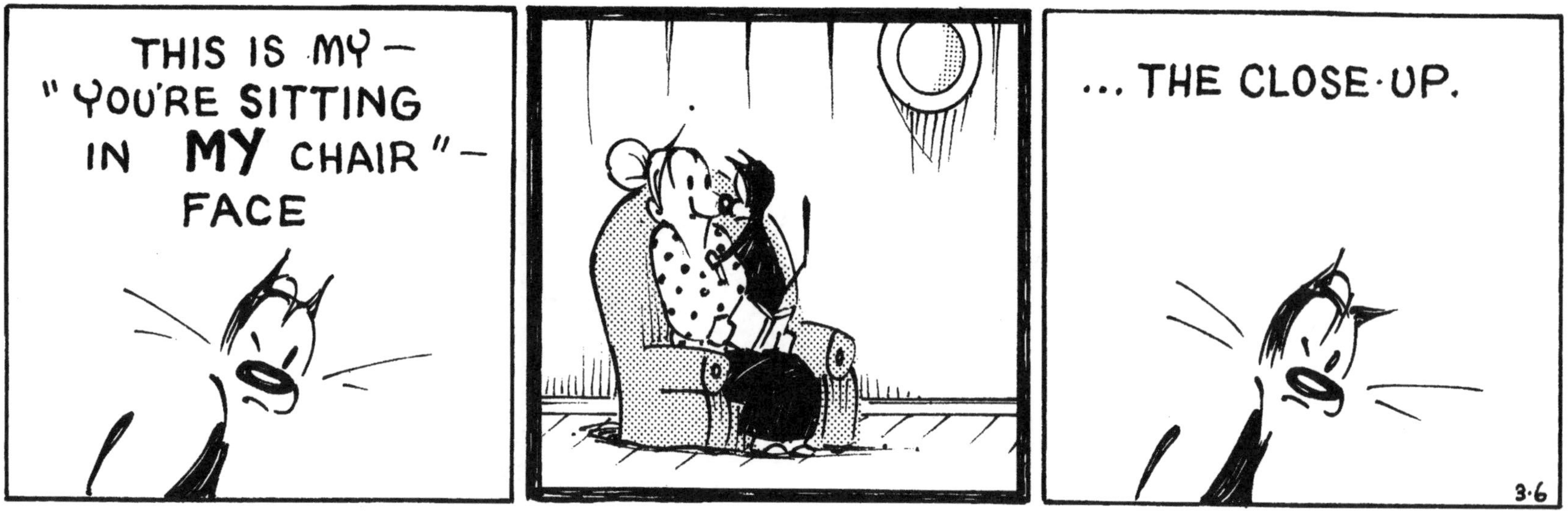
THIS IS MY— "YOU'RE SITTING IN MY CHAIR"— FACE
... THE CLOSE-UP.
3·6

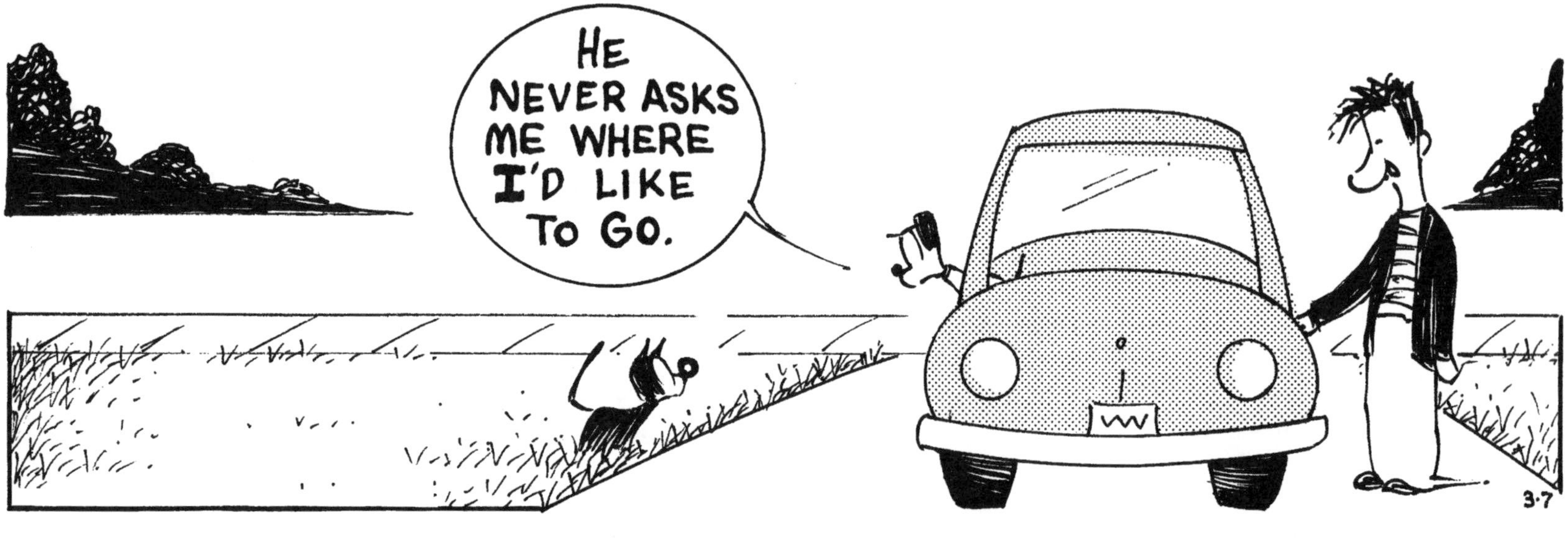
HE NEVER ASKS ME WHERE I'D LIKE TO GO.
3·7

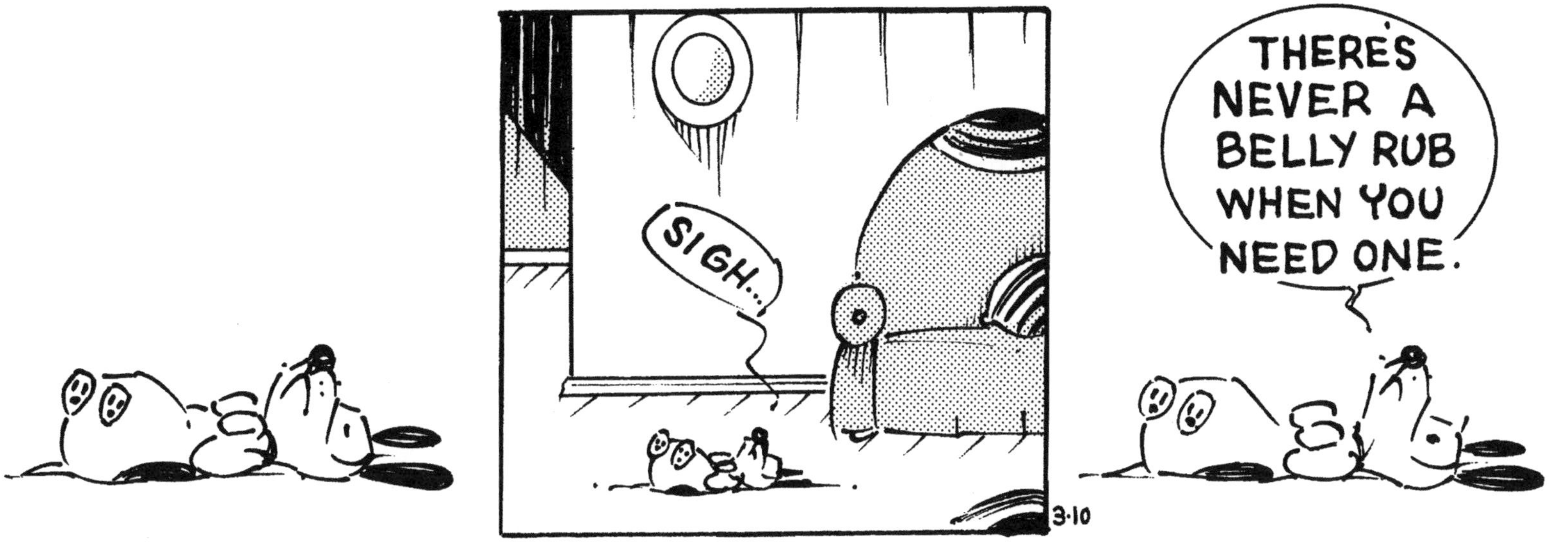
SIGH...
THERE'S NEVER A BELLY RUB WHEN YOU NEED ONE.
3·10

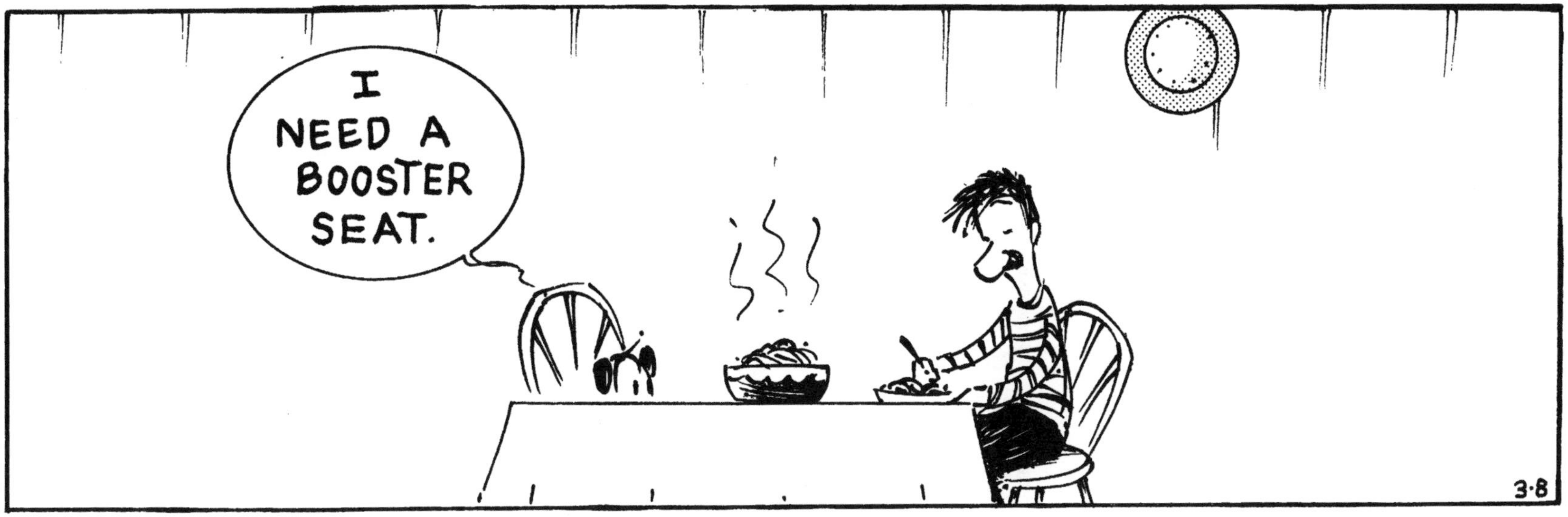
I NEED A BOOSTER SEAT.
3·8

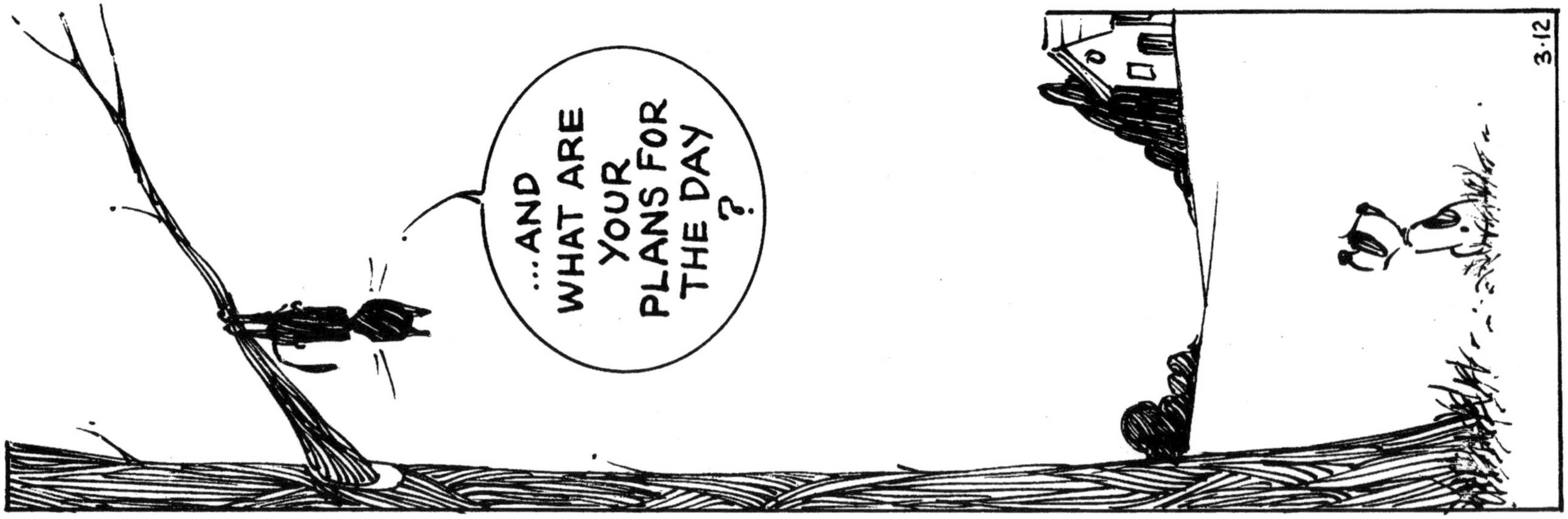
...AND WHAT ARE YOUR PLANS FOR THE DAY ?
3·12

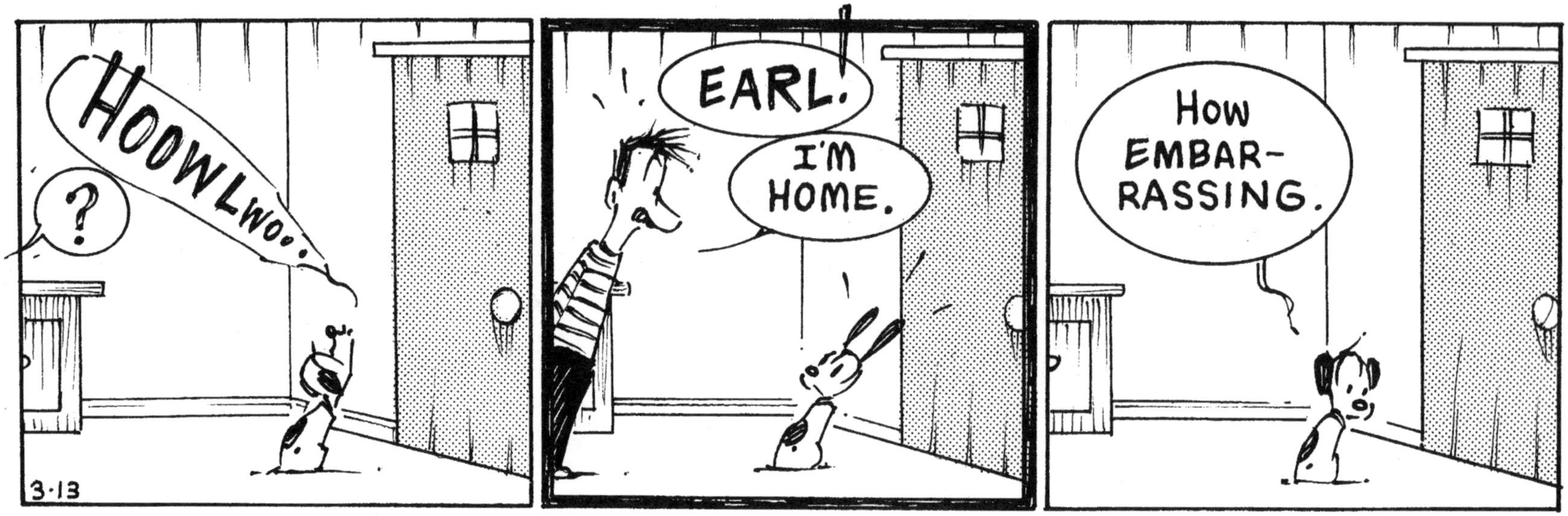
HOOWLwo..
?
3·13
EARL!
I'M HOME.
How EMBAR-RASSING.

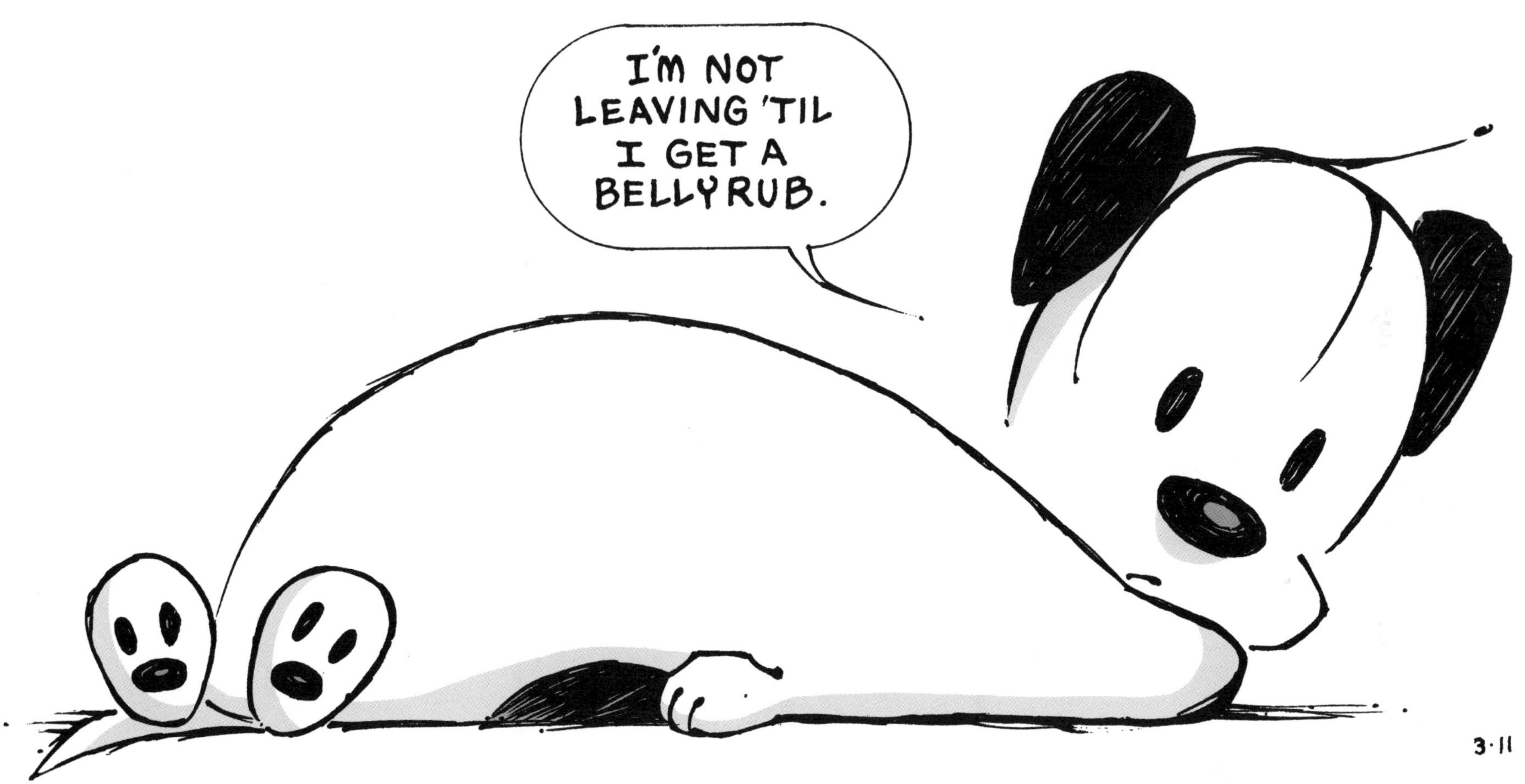
I'M NOT LEAVING 'TIL I GET A BELLYRUB.
3·11

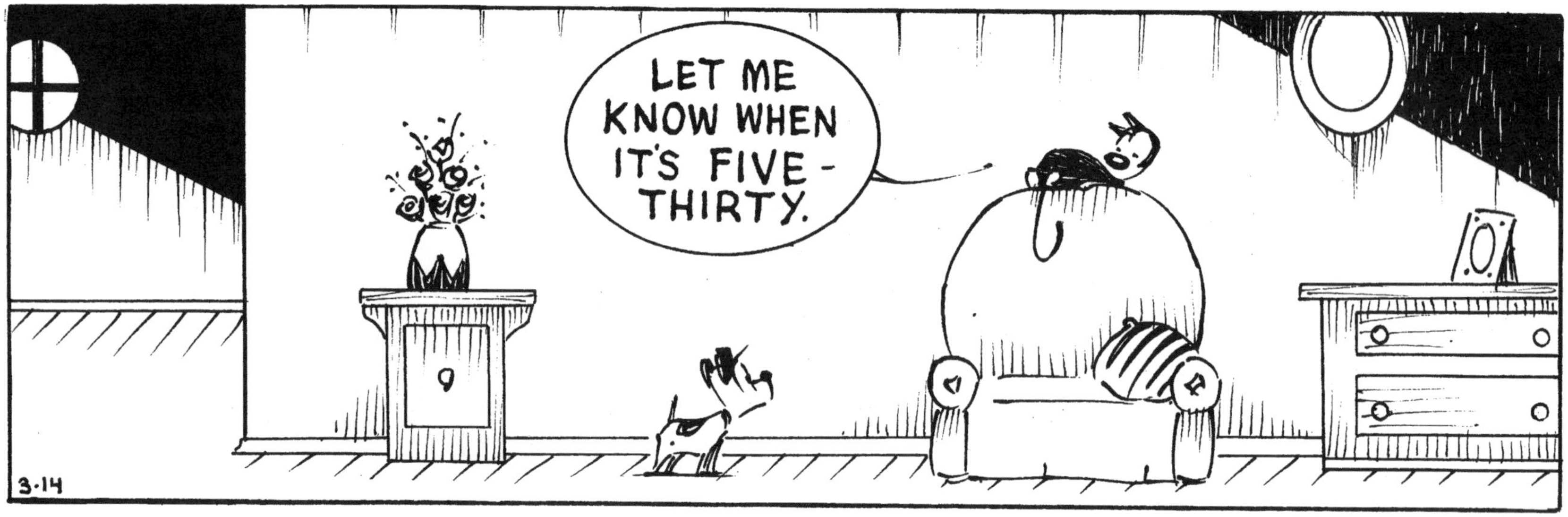
LET ME KNOW WHEN IT'S FIVE-THIRTY.
3·14

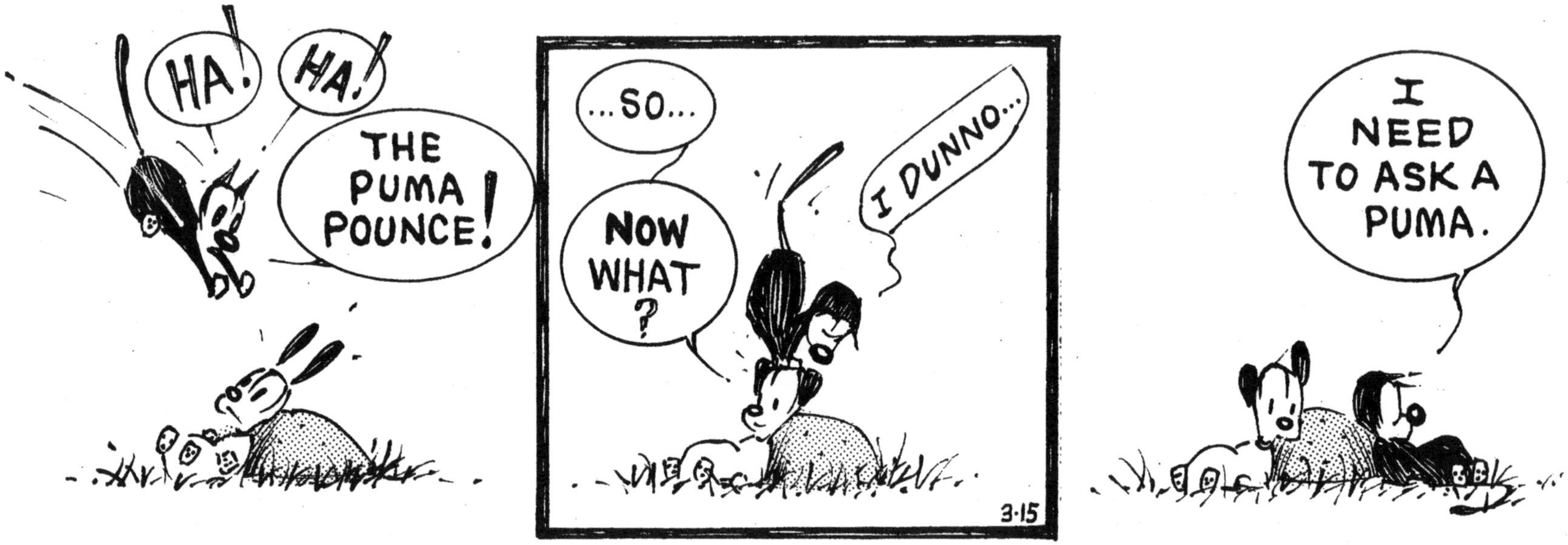
HA!
HA!
THE PUMA POUNCE!
...SO...
NOW WHAT?
I DUNNO...
3·15
I NEED TO ASK A PUMA.

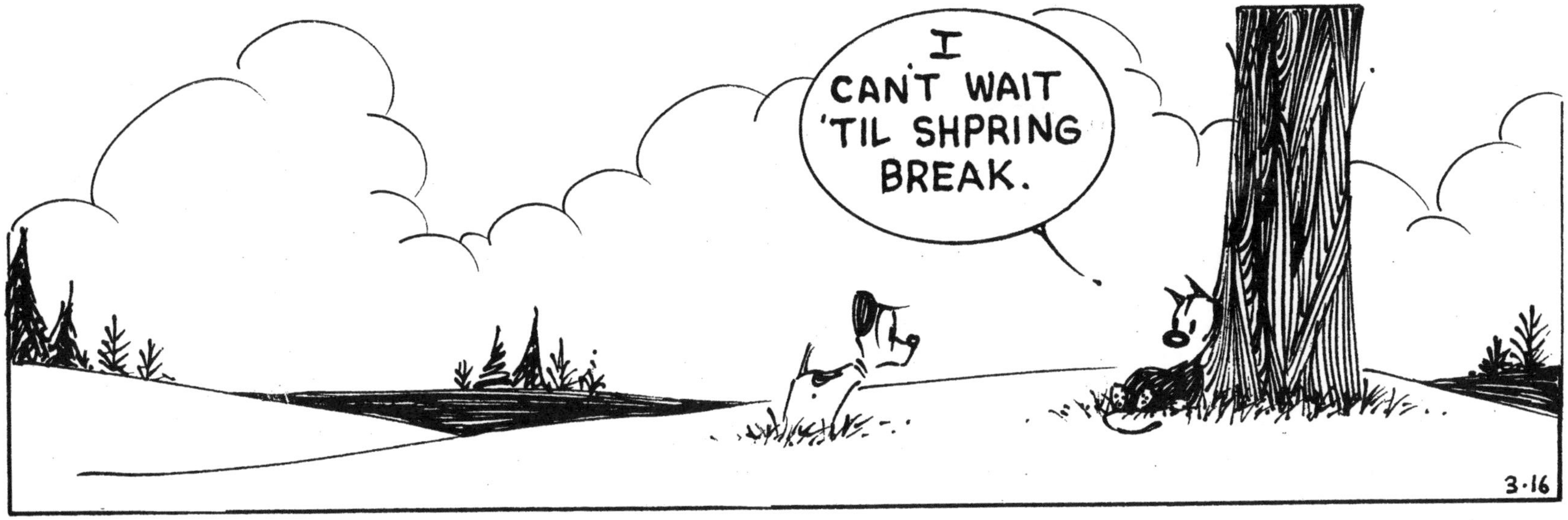
I CAN'T WAIT 'TIL SHPRING BREAK.
3·16

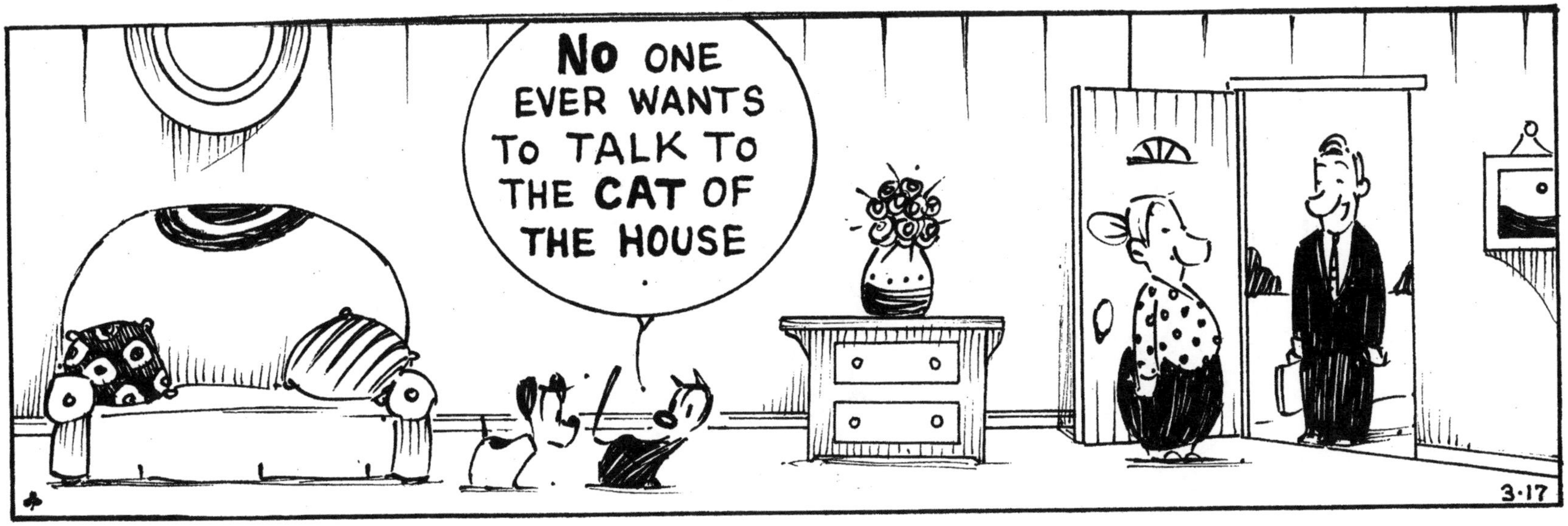
NO ONE EVER WANTS TO TALK TO THE CAT OF THE HOUSE.
3·17

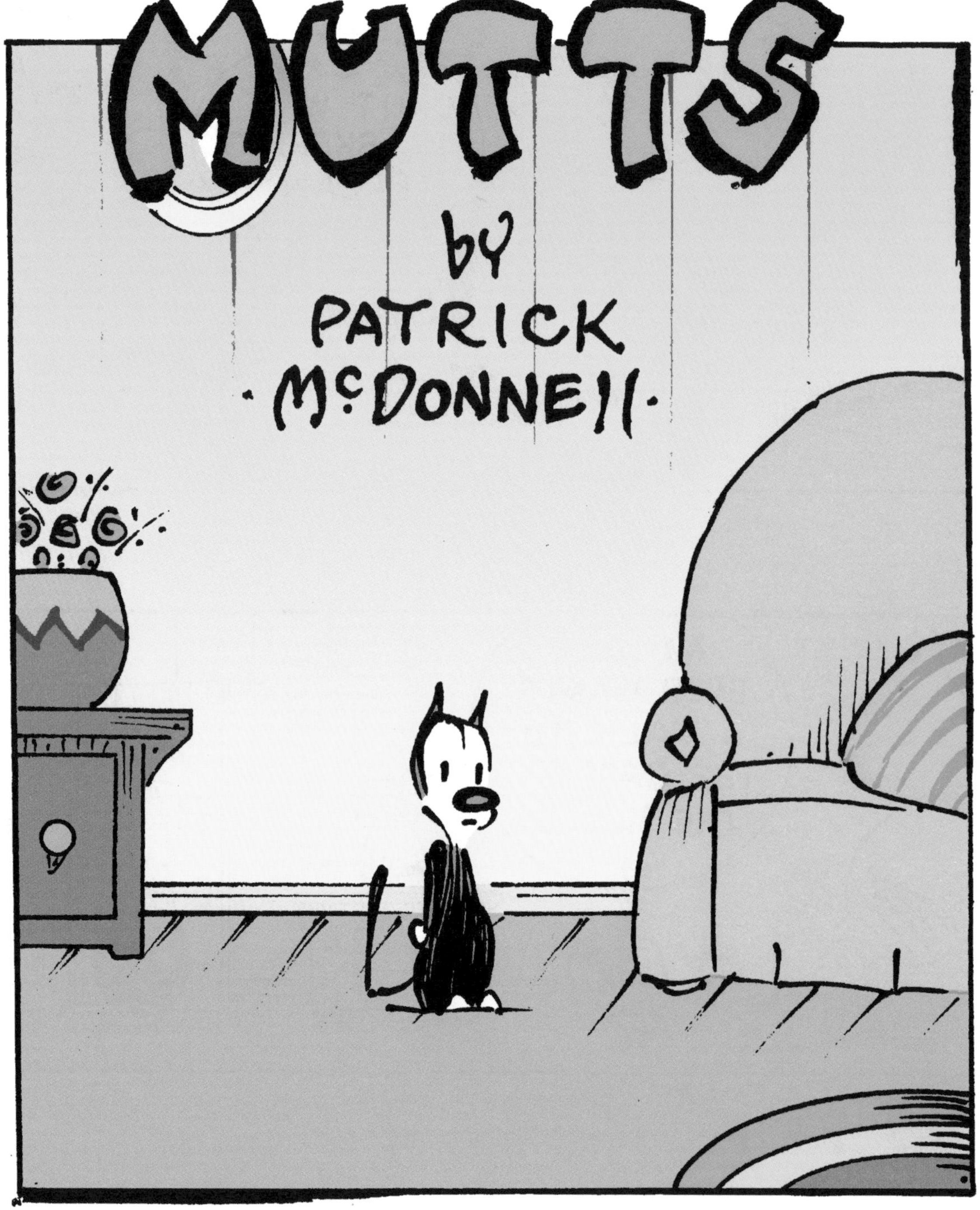
MUTTS
by
PATRICK
·McDONNELL·

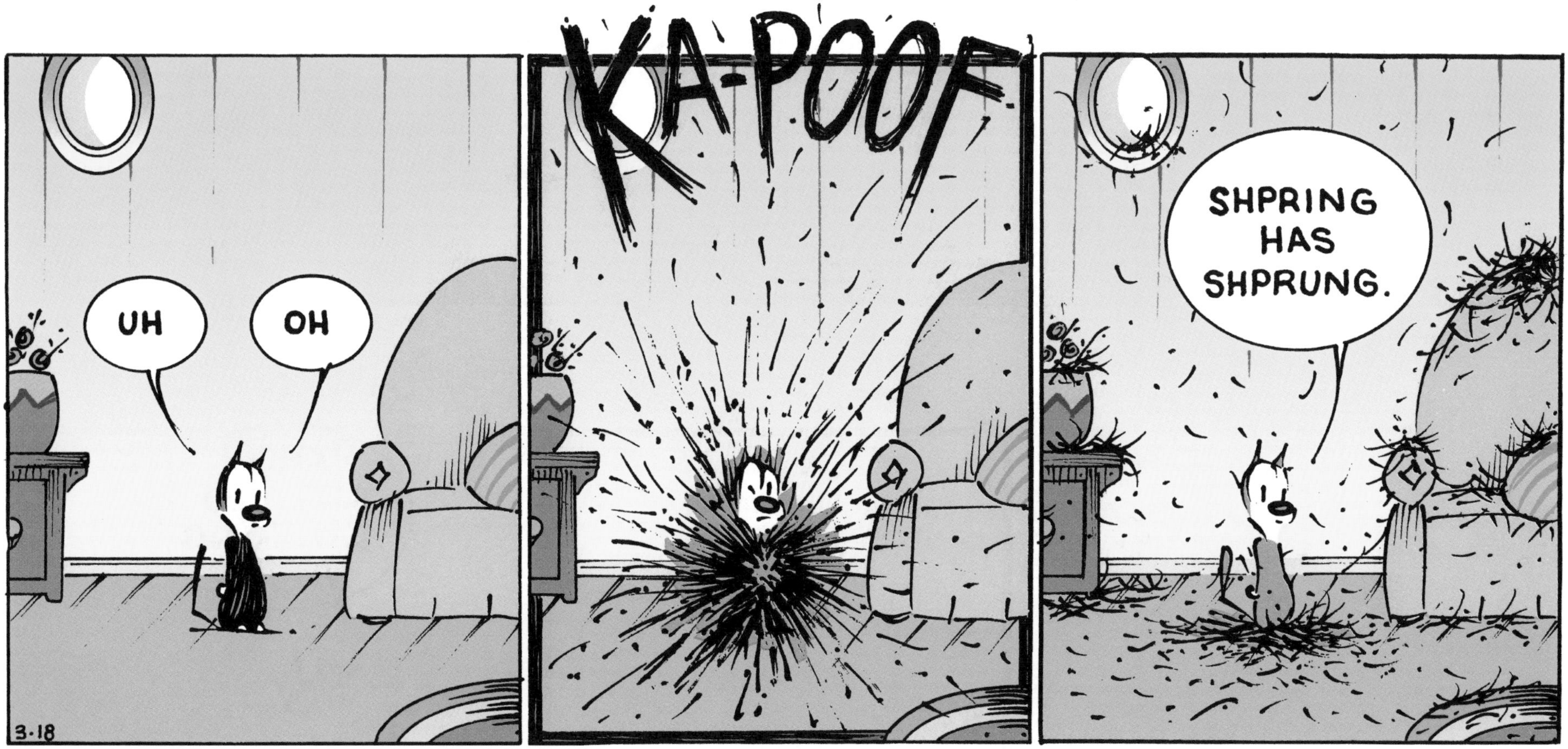
3-18
UH
OH
KA-POOF
SHPRING HAS SHPRUNG.

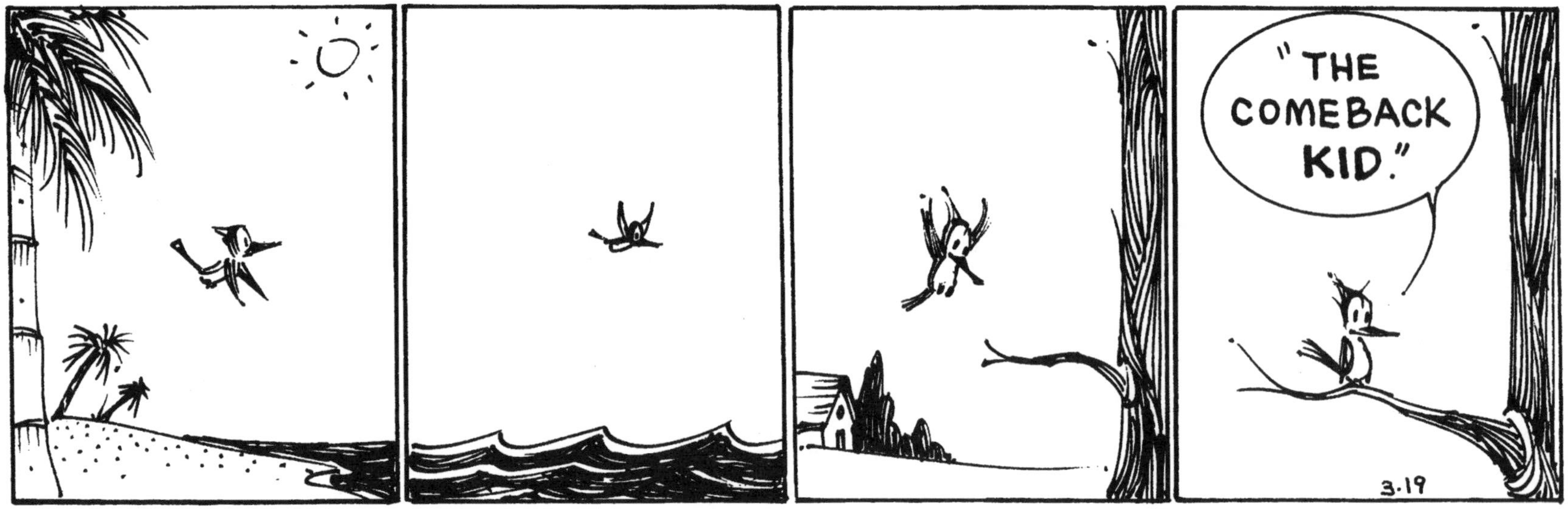
"THE COMEBACK KID."
3.19

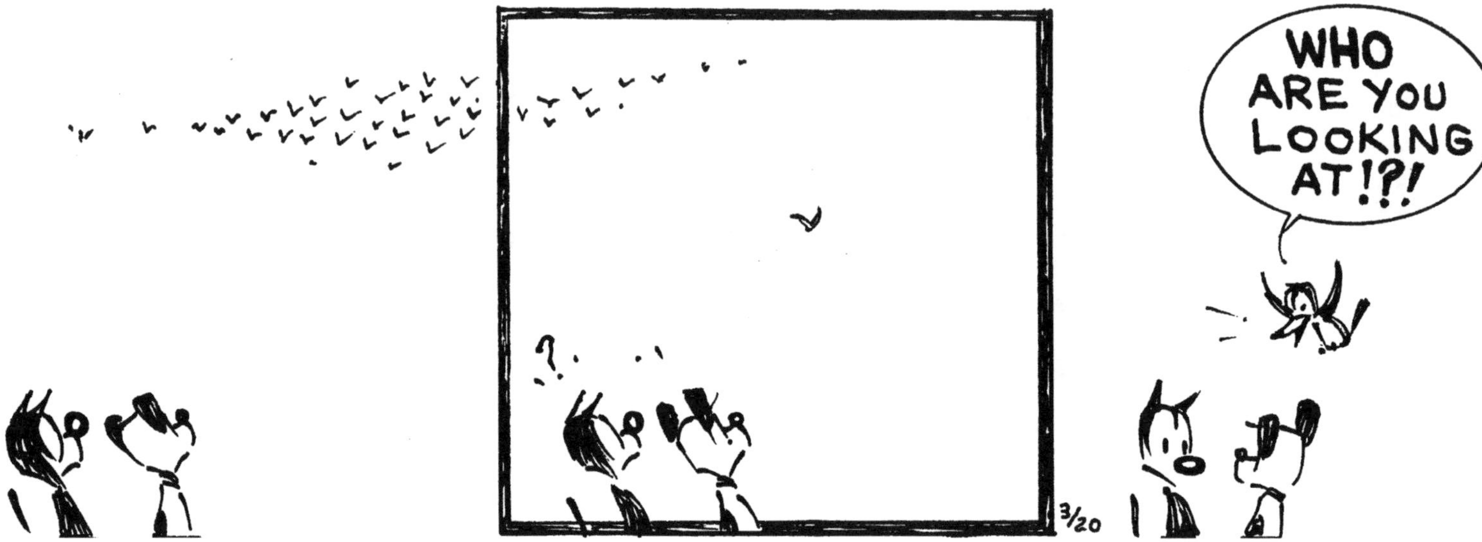
?
3/20
WHO ARE YOU LOOKING AT!?!

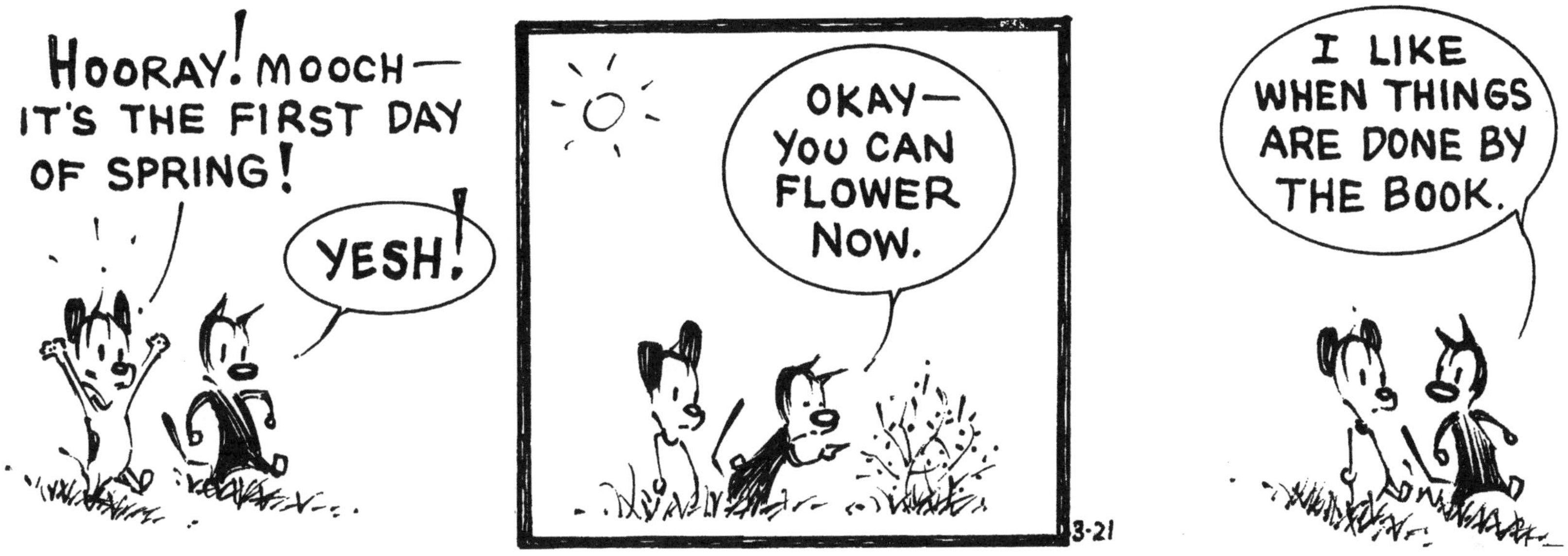
HOORAY! MOOCH— IT'S THE FIRST DAY OF SPRING!
YESH!
OKAY— YOU CAN FLOWER NOW.
3-21
I LIKE WHEN THINGS ARE DONE BY THE BOOK.

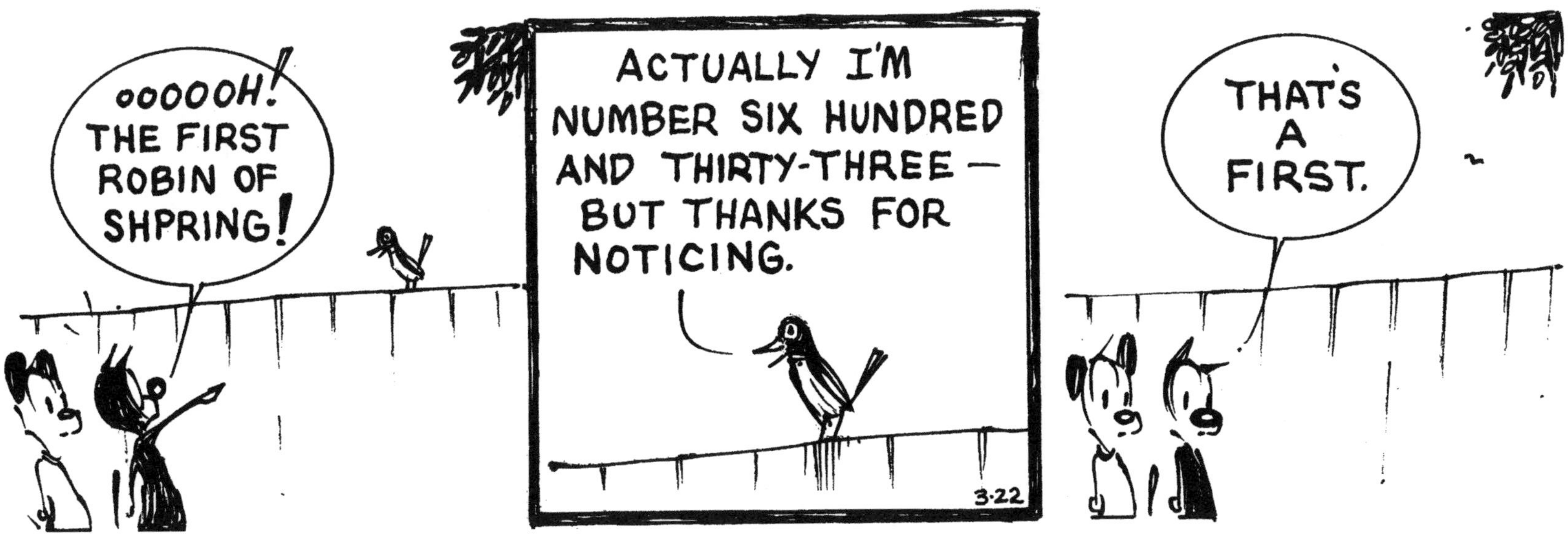
OOOOOH! THE FIRST ROBIN OF SHPRING!
ACTUALLY I'M NUMBER SIX HUNDRED AND THIRTY-THREE— BUT THANKS FOR NOTICING.
3-22
THAT'S A FIRST.

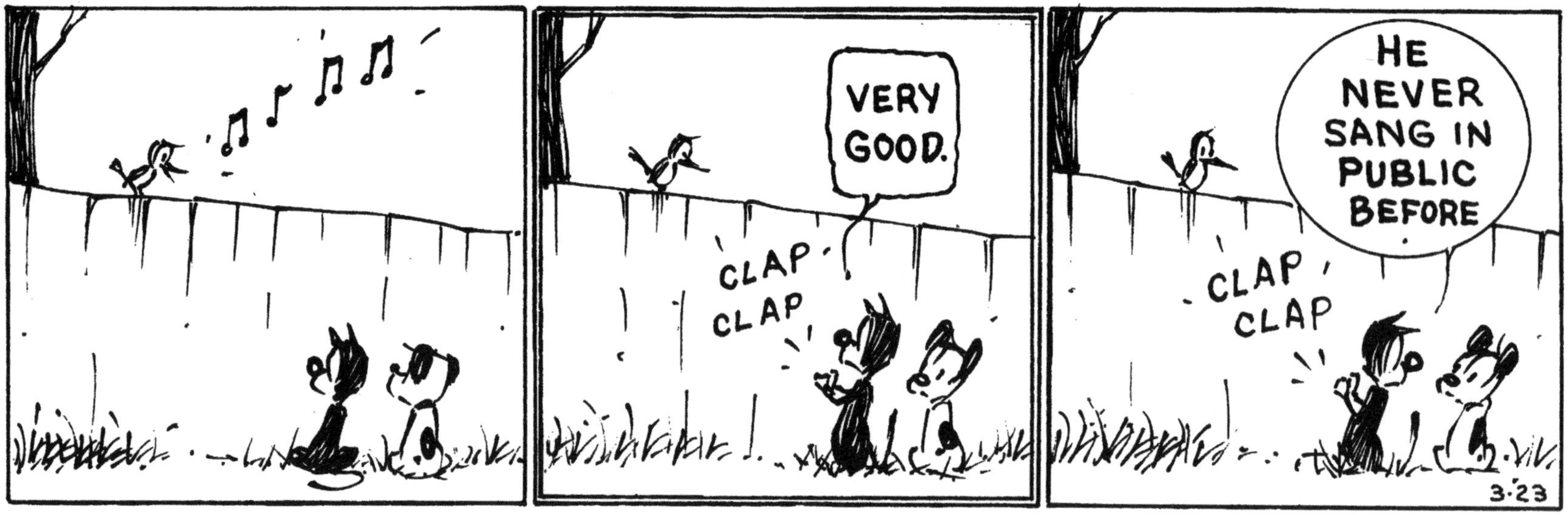
VERY GOOD.
CLAP CLAP
HE NEVER SANG IN PUBLIC BEFORE.
CLAP CLAP
3·23

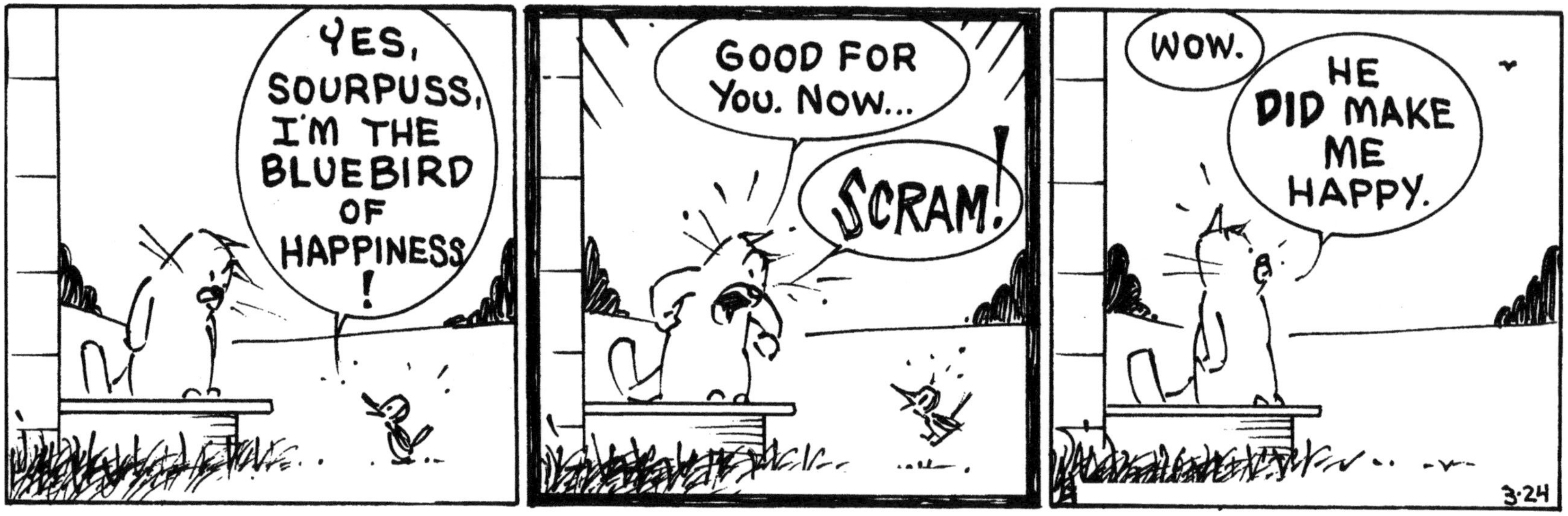
YES, SOURPUSS, I'M THE BLUEBIRD OF HAPPINESS!
GOOD FOR YOU. NOW...
SCRAM!
WOW.
HE DID MAKE ME HAPPY.
3·24

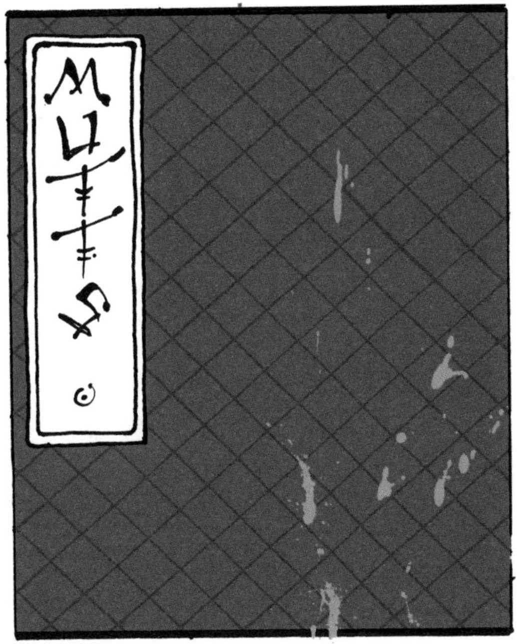
MUTTS ©

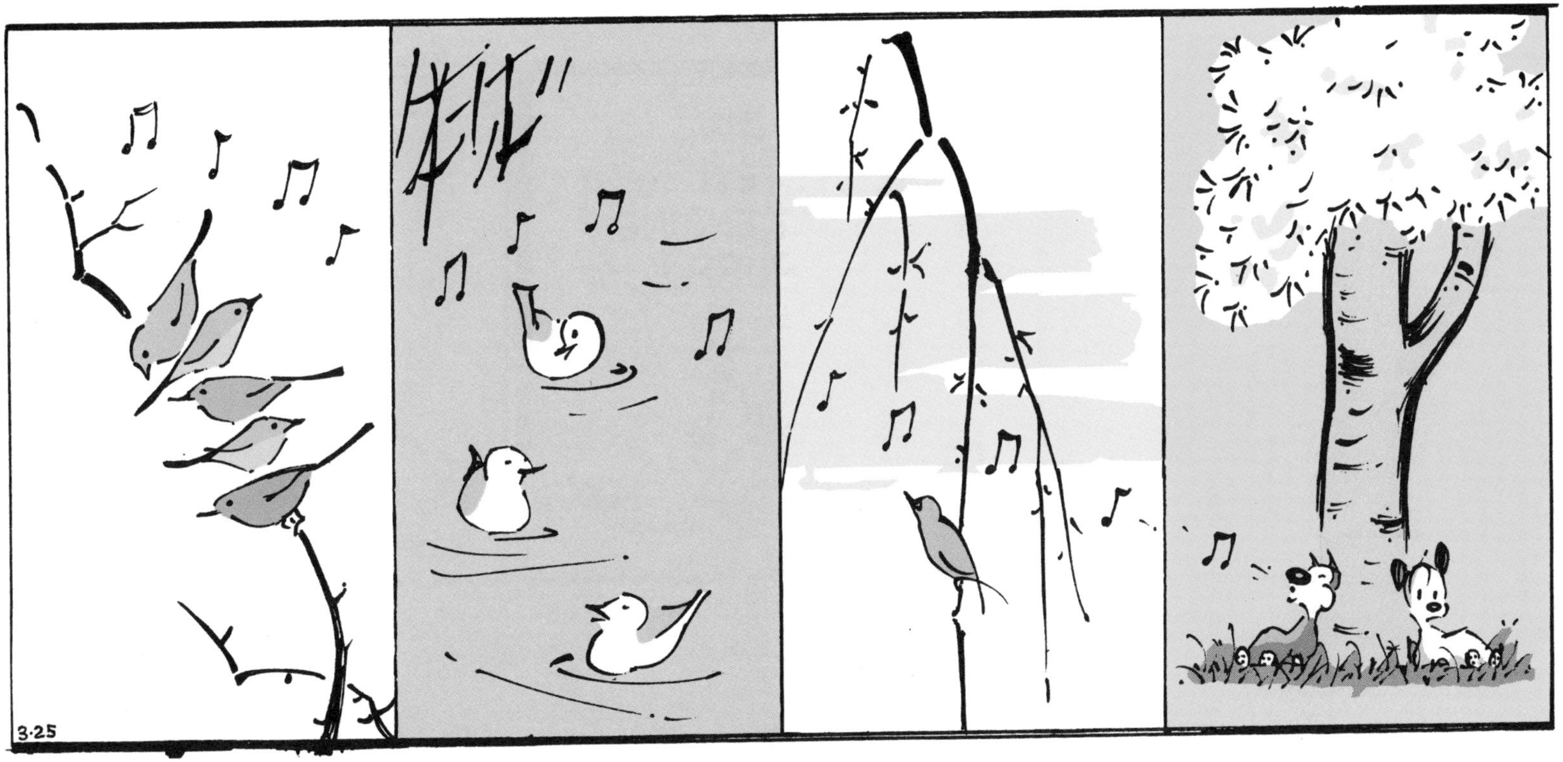
3·25

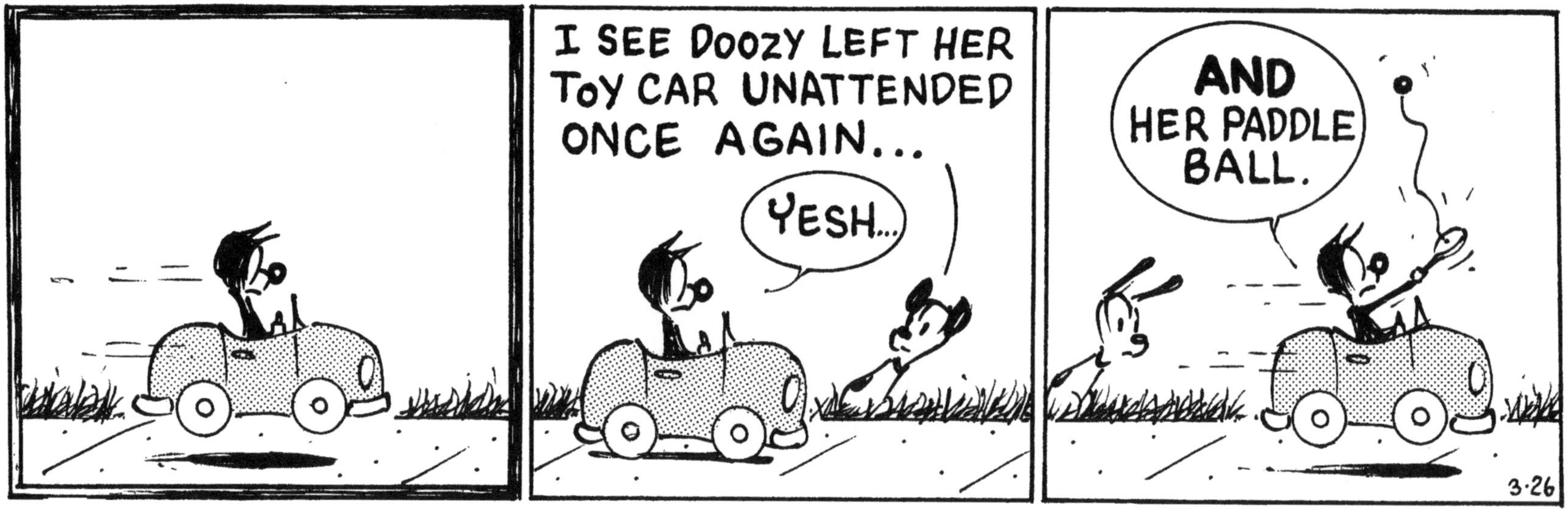
I SEE DOOZY LEFT HER TOY CAR UNATTENDED ONCE AGAIN...
YESH...
AND HER PADDLE BALL.
3·26

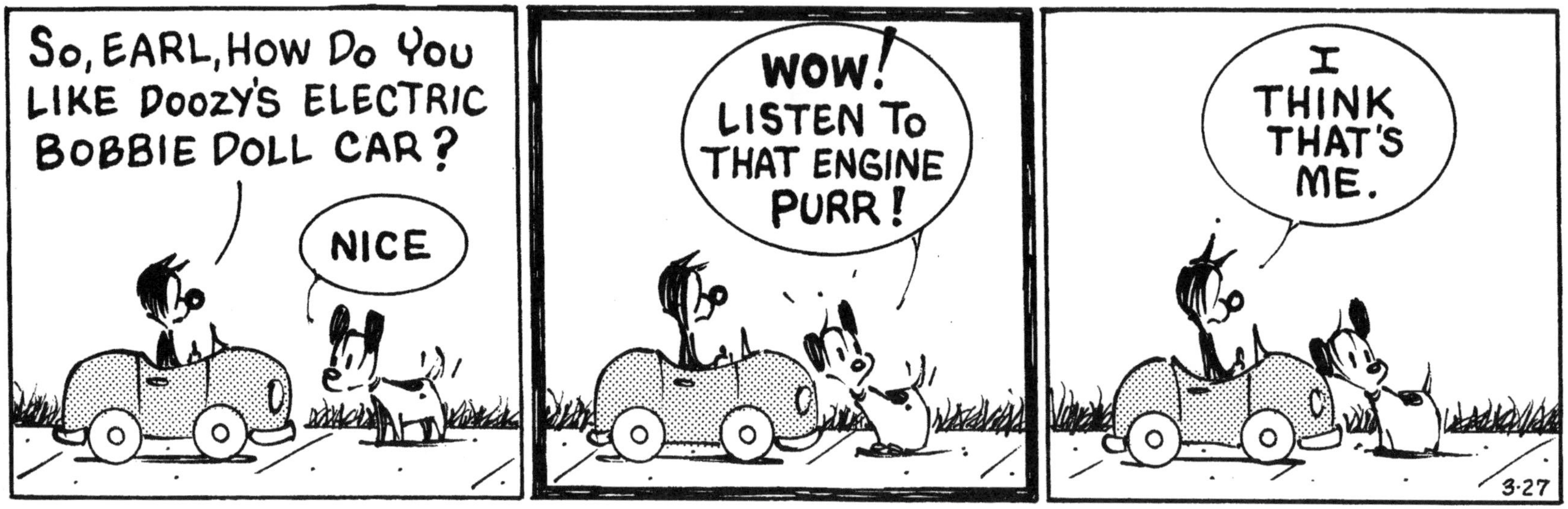
SO, EARL, HOW DO YOU LIKE DOOZY'S ELECTRIC BOBBIE DOLL CAR?
NICE
WOW! LISTEN TO THAT ENGINE PURR!
I THINK THAT'S ME.
3·27

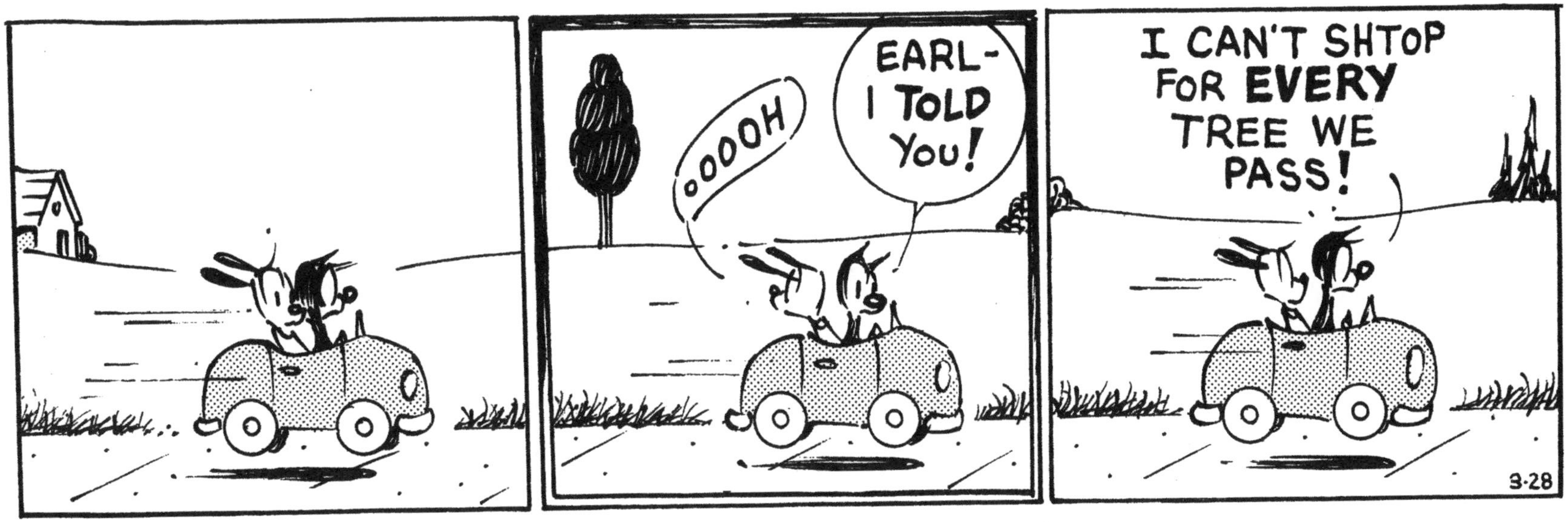
oOOOH
EARL- I TOLD YOU!
I CAN'T SHTOP FOR EVERY TREE WE PASS!
3-28

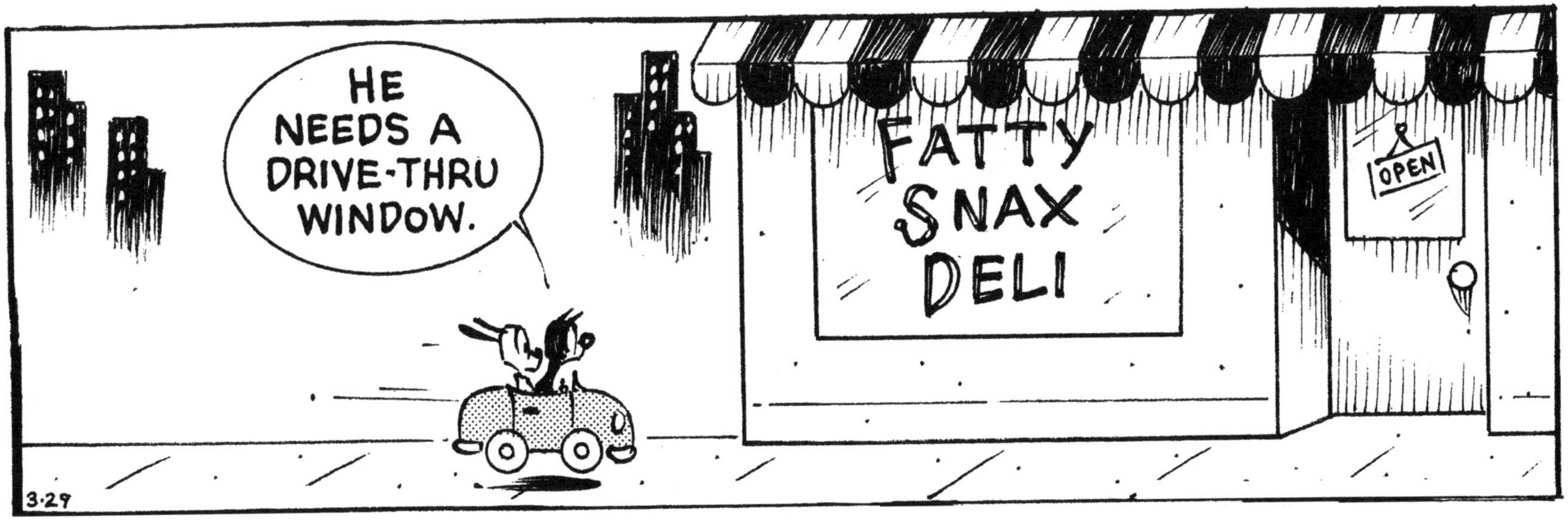
HE NEEDS A DRIVE-THRU WINDOW.
FATTY SNAX DELI
OPEN
3-29

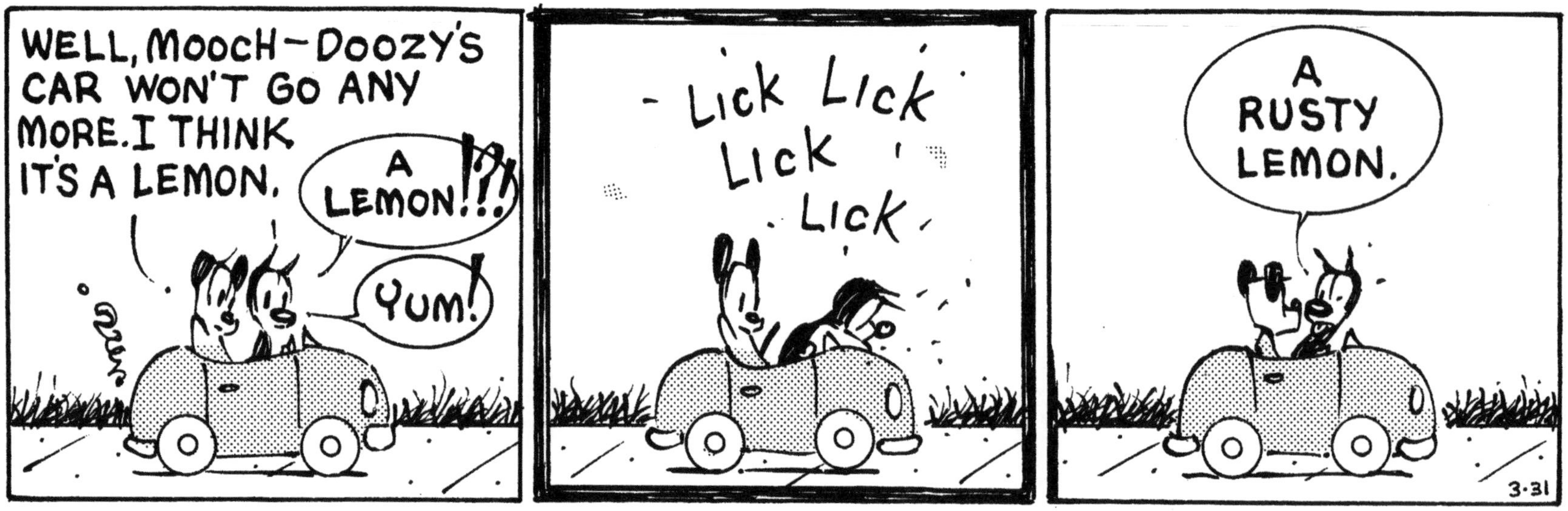

WELL, MOOCH—DOOZY'S CAR WON'T GO ANY MORE. I THINK IT'S A LEMON.
A LEMON!?!
YUM!
Lick Lick Lick Lick
A RUSTY LEMON.
3·31

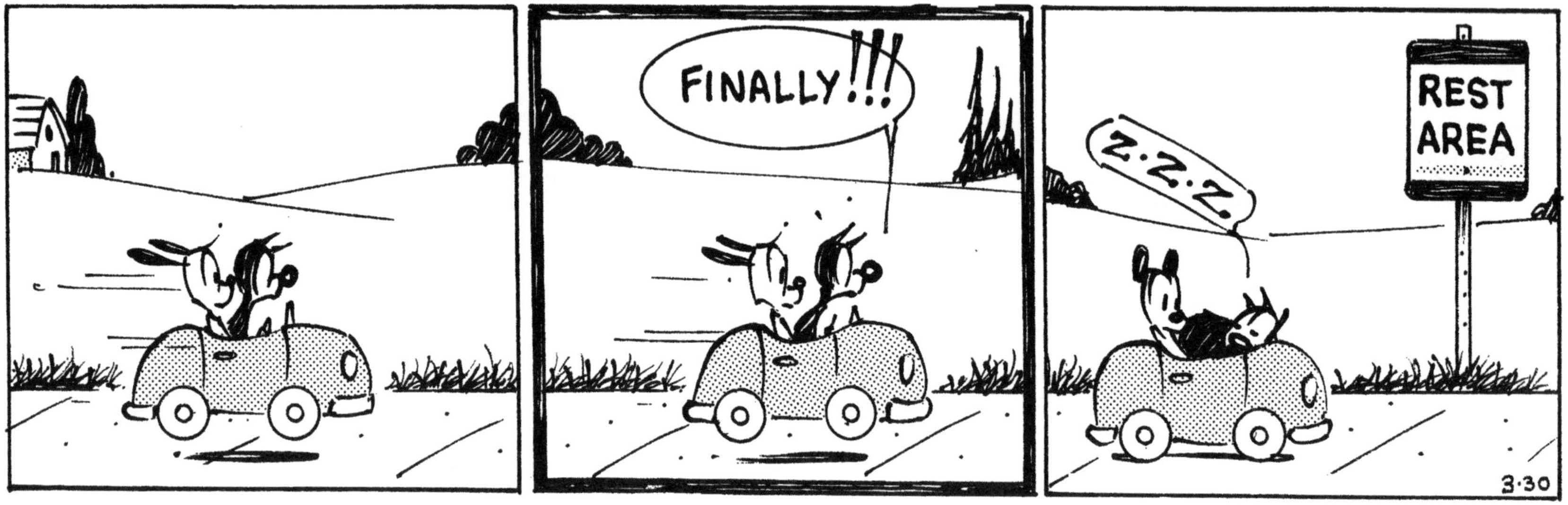

FINALLY!!!
Z·Z·Z
REST AREA
3·30

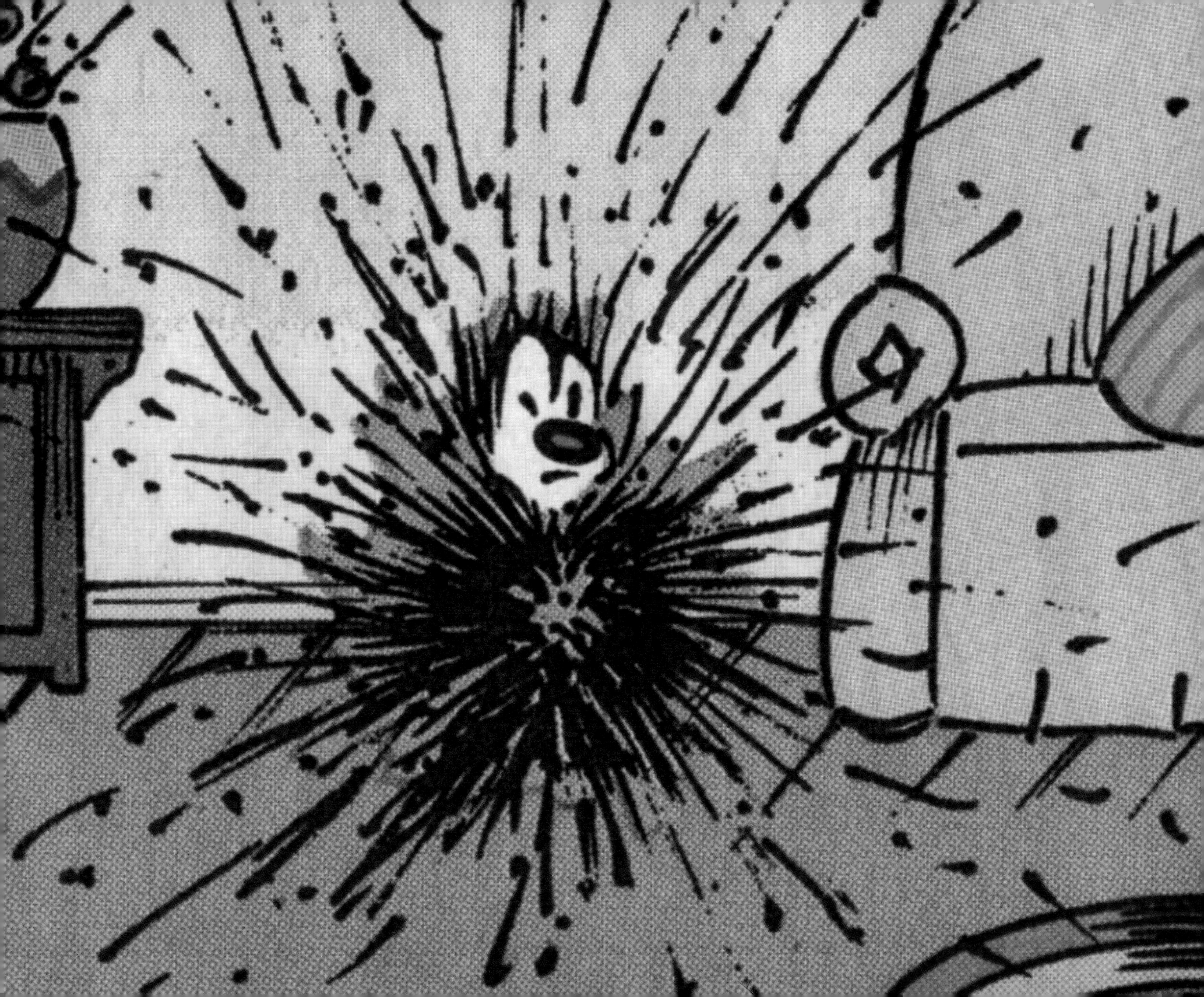

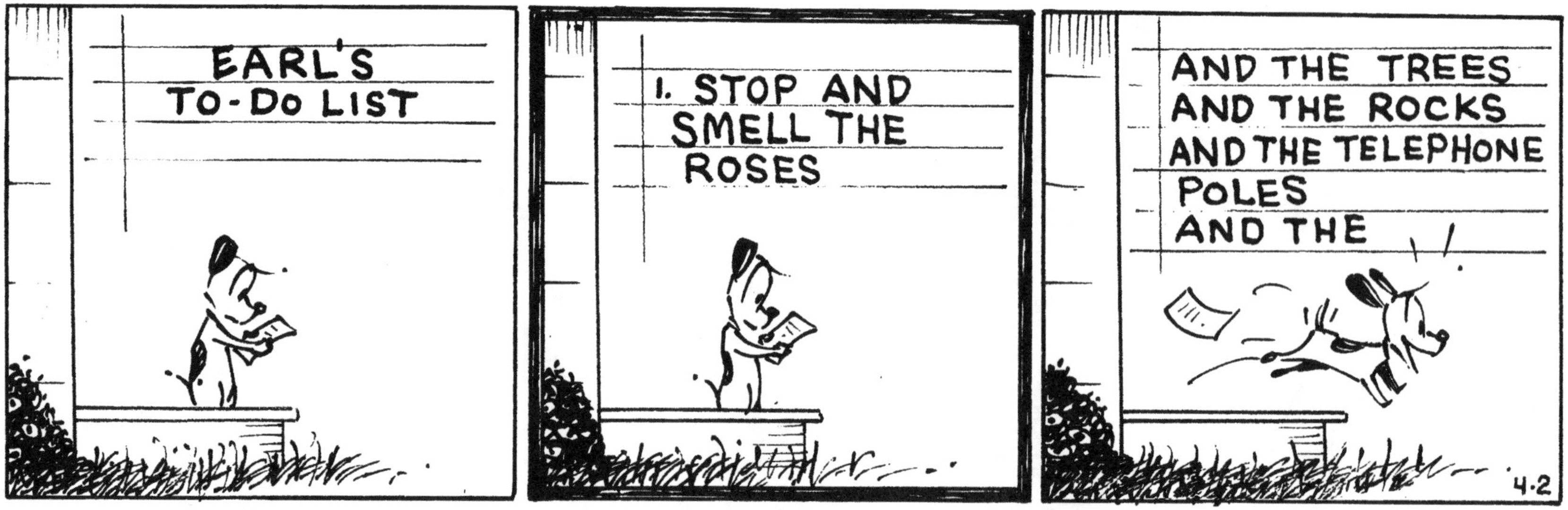
EARL'S TO-DO LIST
1. STOP AND SMELL THE ROSES
AND THE TREES AND THE ROCKS AND THE TELEPHONE POLES AND THE
4·2

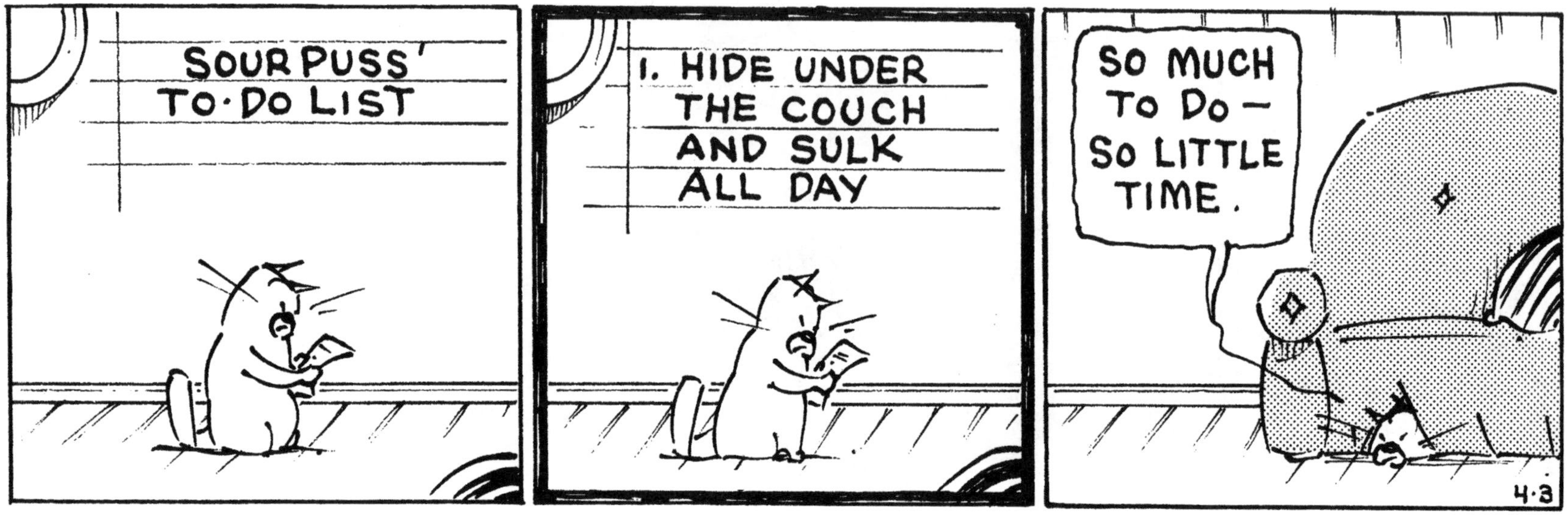
SOURPUSS' TO·DO LIST
1. HIDE UNDER THE COUCH AND SULK ALL DAY
SO MUCH TO DO — SO LITTLE TIME.
4·3

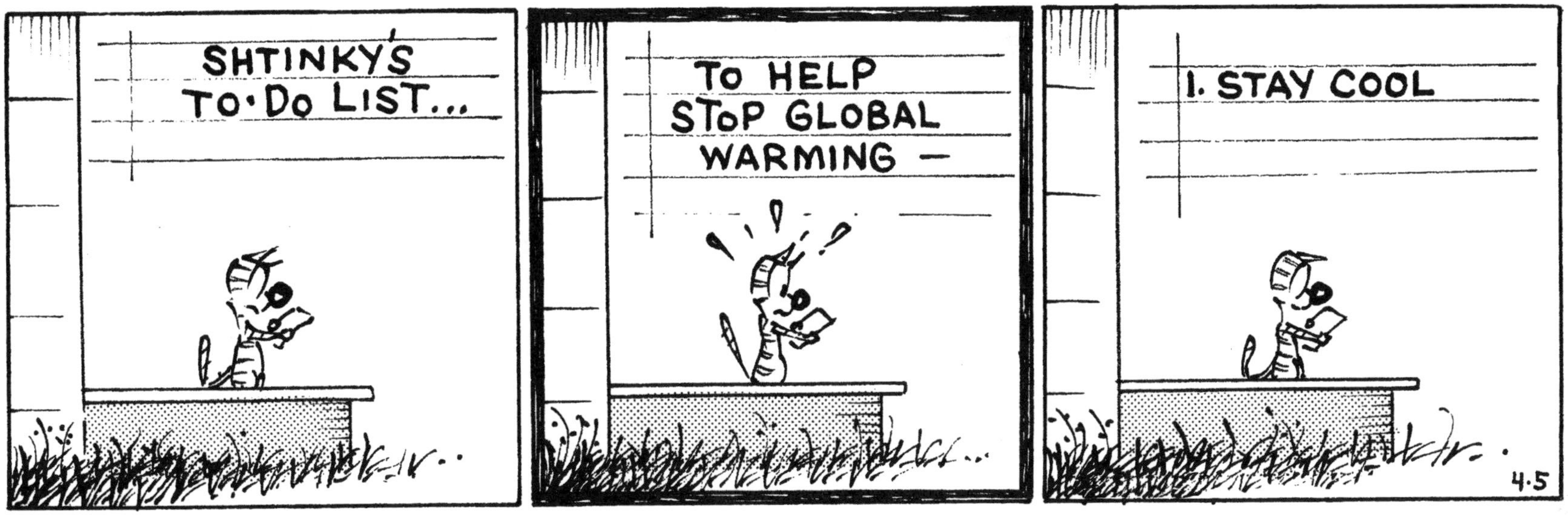
SHTINKY'S TO-DO LIST...
TO HELP STOP GLOBAL WARMING –
1. STAY COOL
4.5

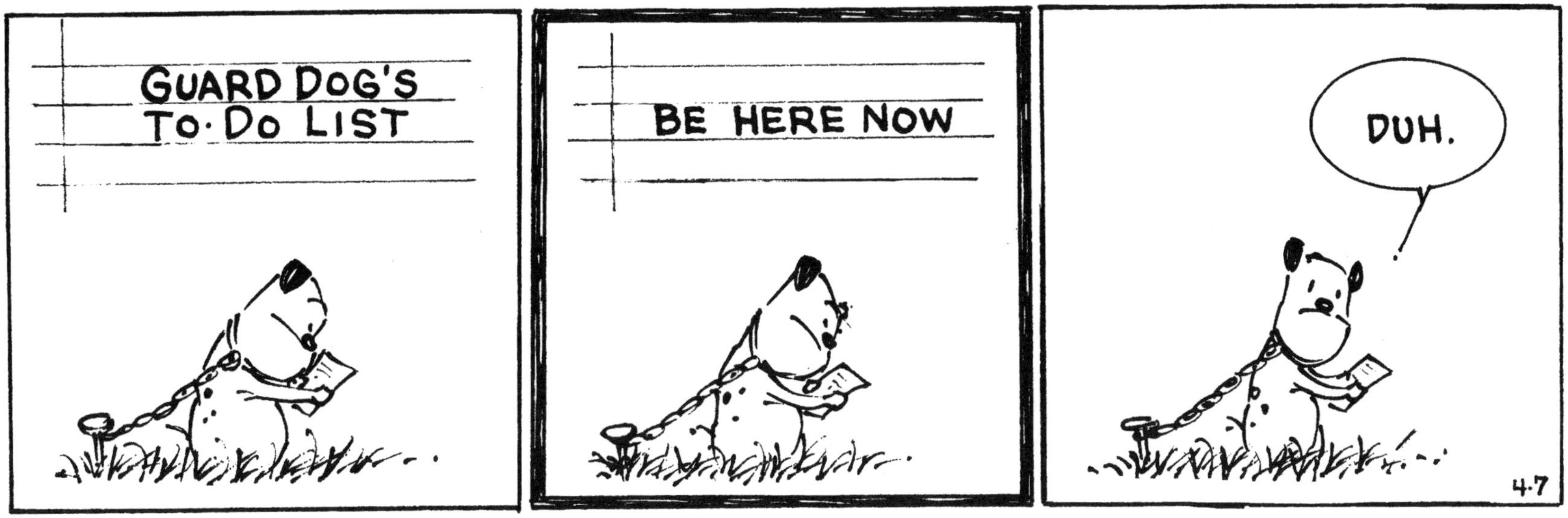
GUARD DOG'S TO-DO LIST
BE HERE NOW
DUH.
4.7

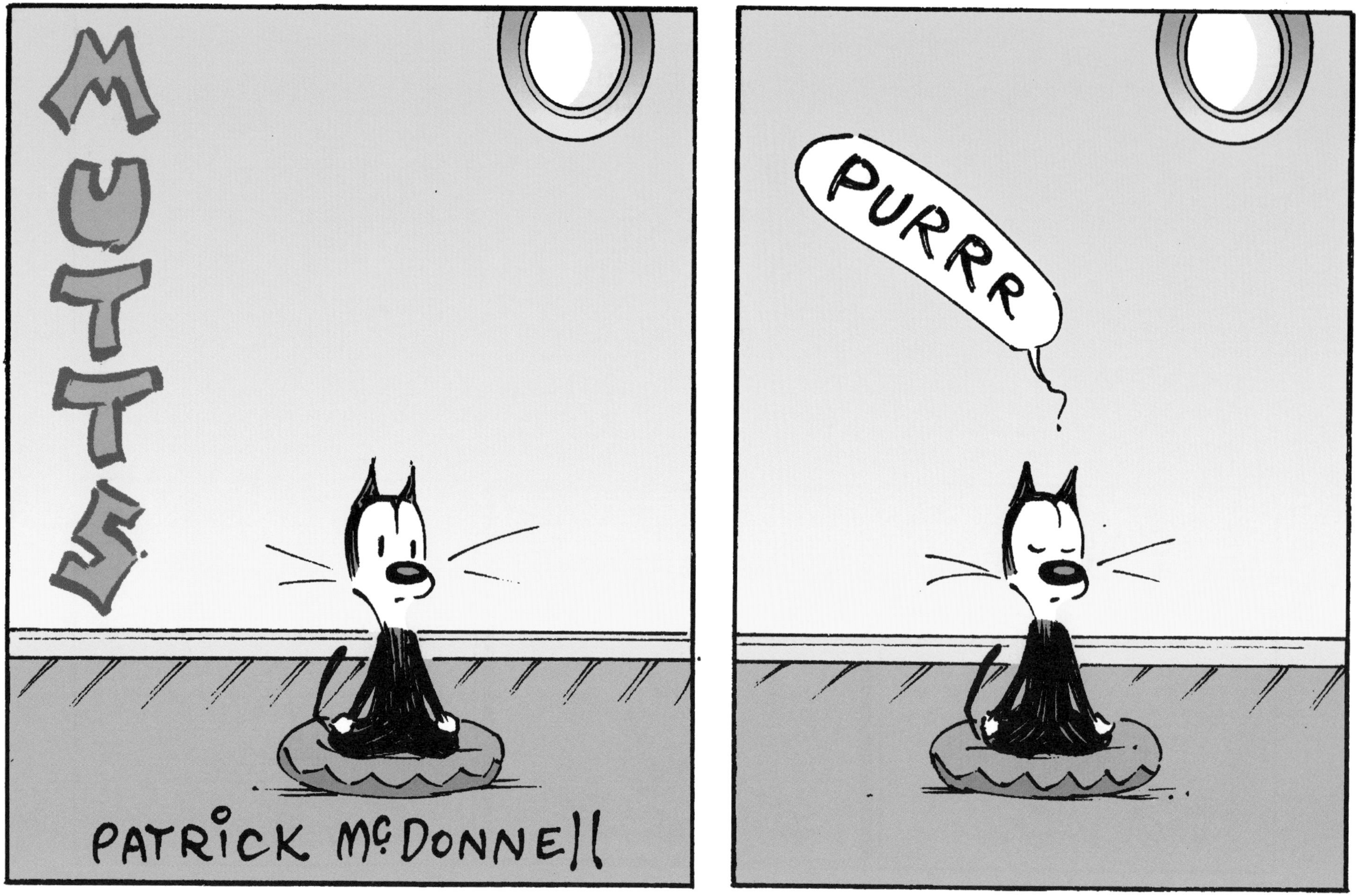
MUTTS
PATRICK McDONNELL
PURRR

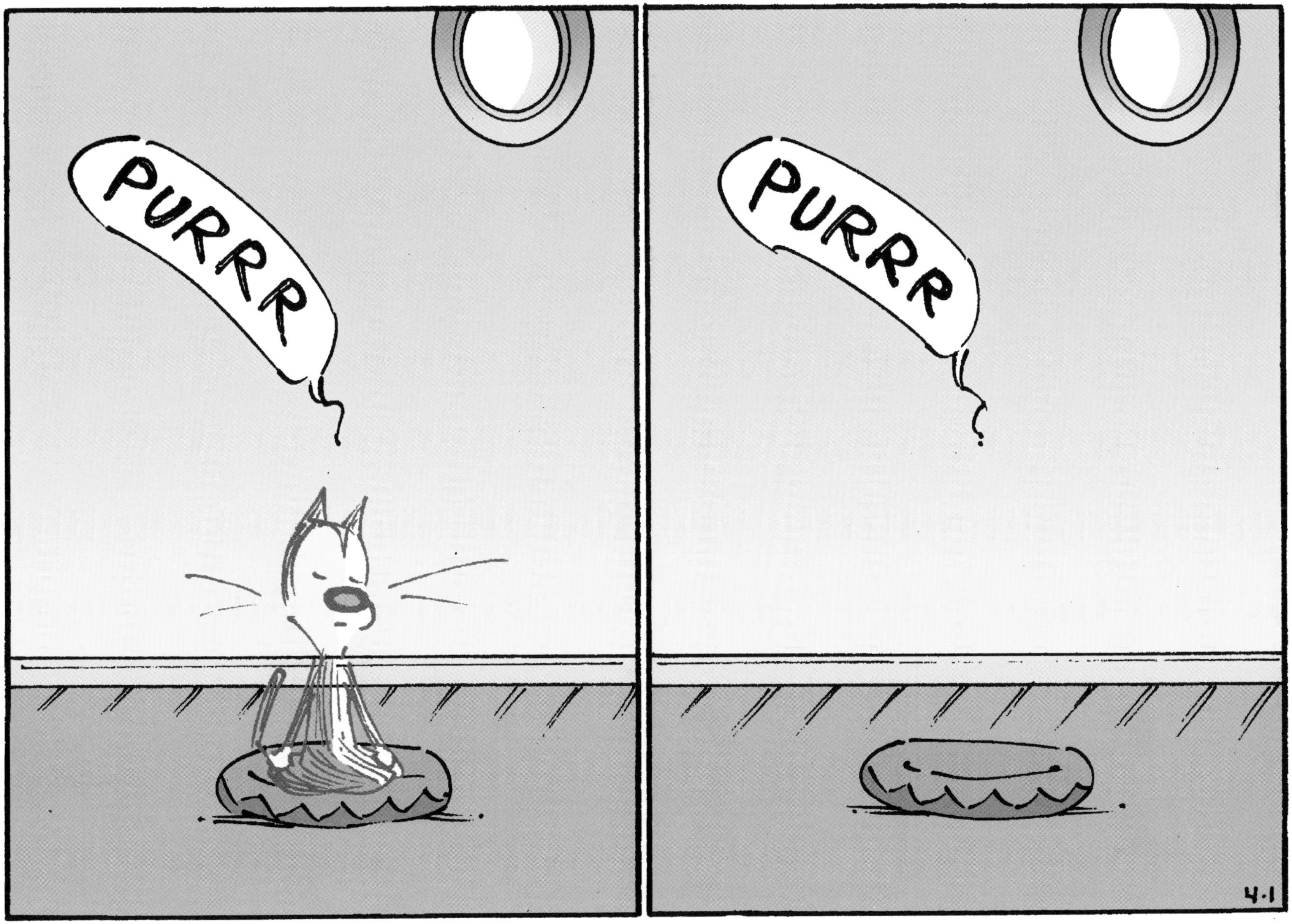
PURRR
PURRR
4-1

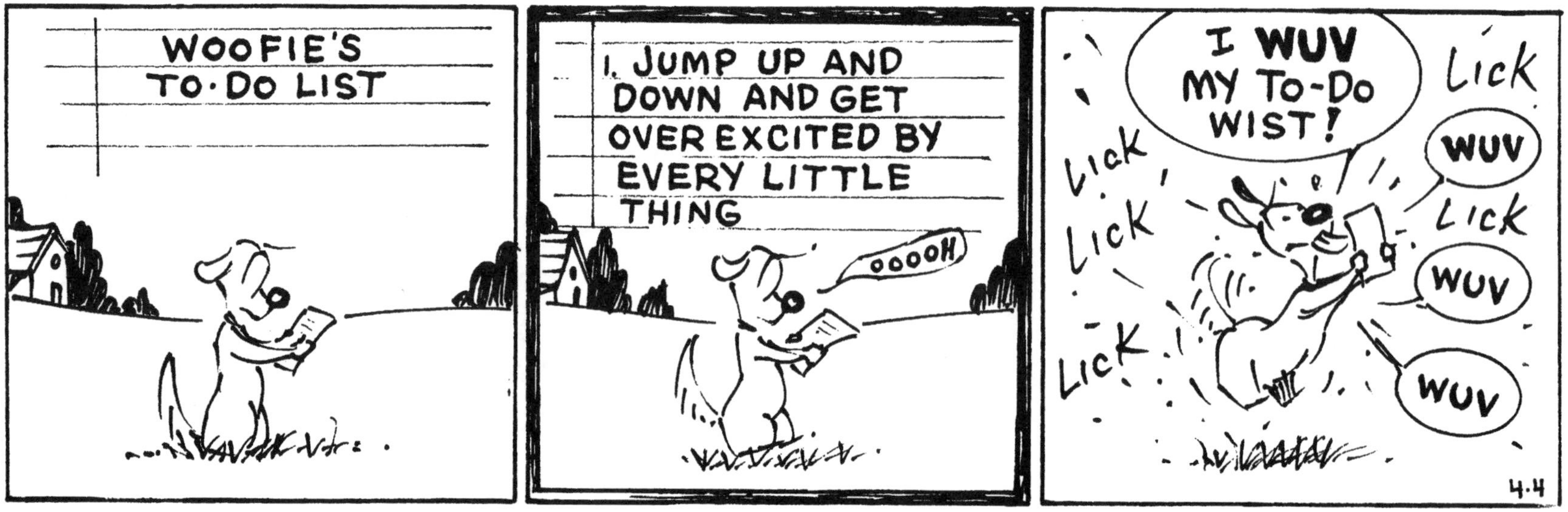
WOOFIE'S TO·DO LIST
1. JUMP UP AND DOWN AND GET OVER EXCITED BY EVERY LITTLE THING
OOOOH
I WUV MY TO-DO WIST!
LICK
WUV
LICK
WUV
LICK
LICK
WUV
LICK
4·4

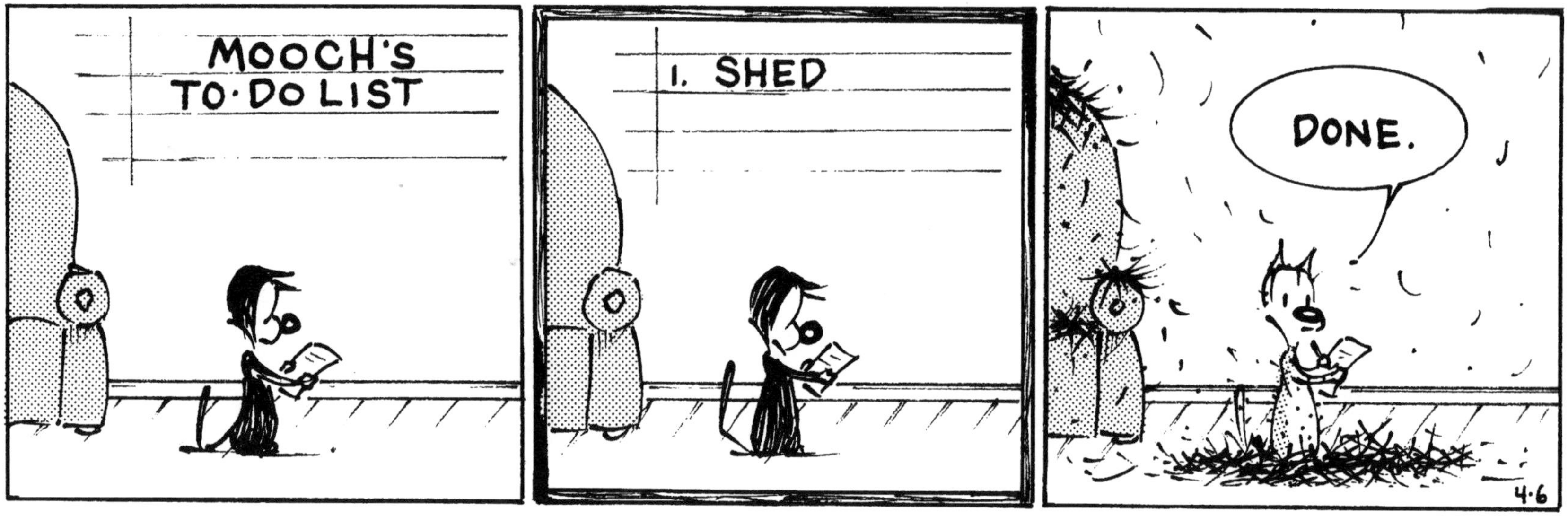
MOOCH'S TO·DO LIST
1. SHED
DONE.
4·6

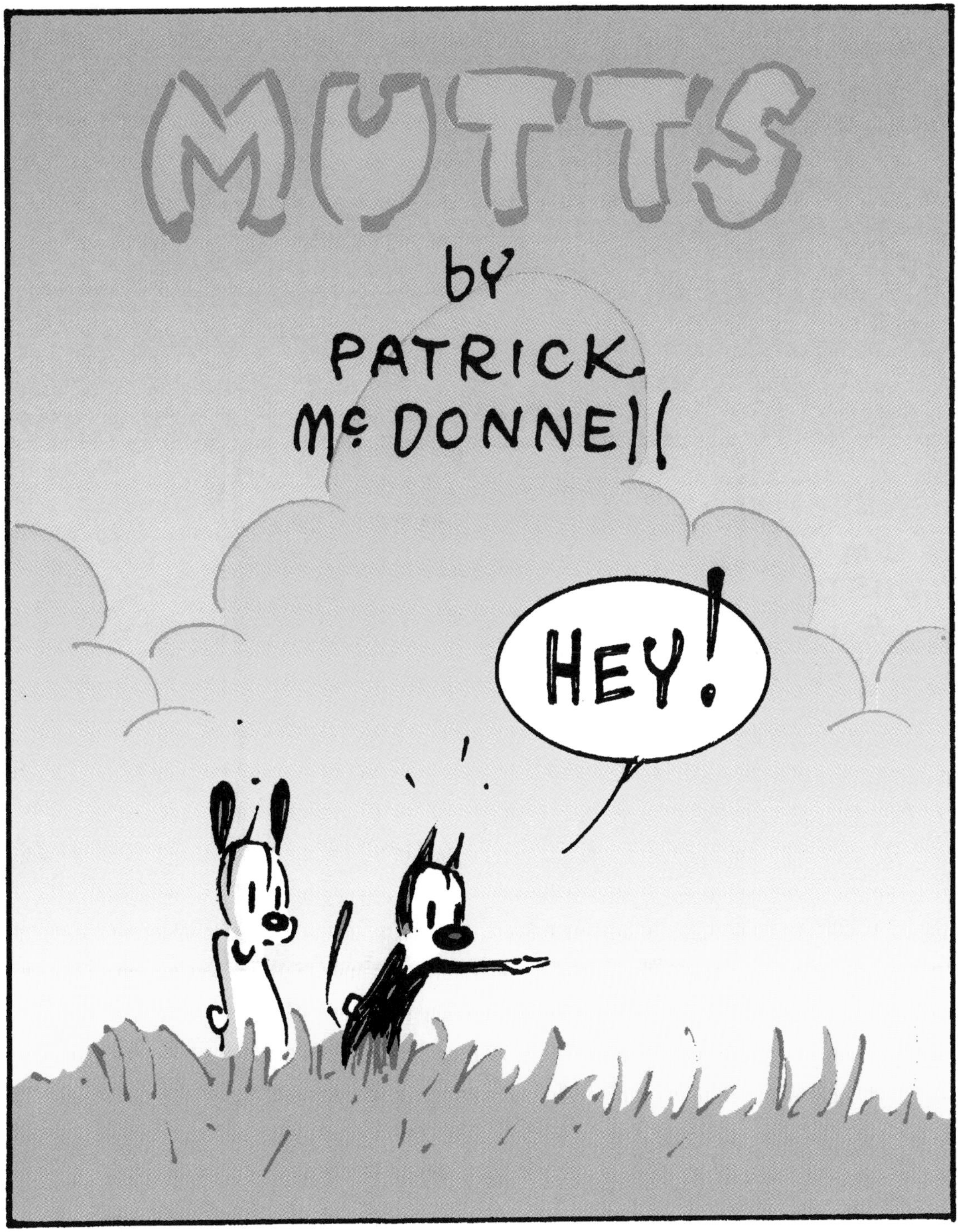
MUTTS
by PATRICK McDONNELL
HEY!

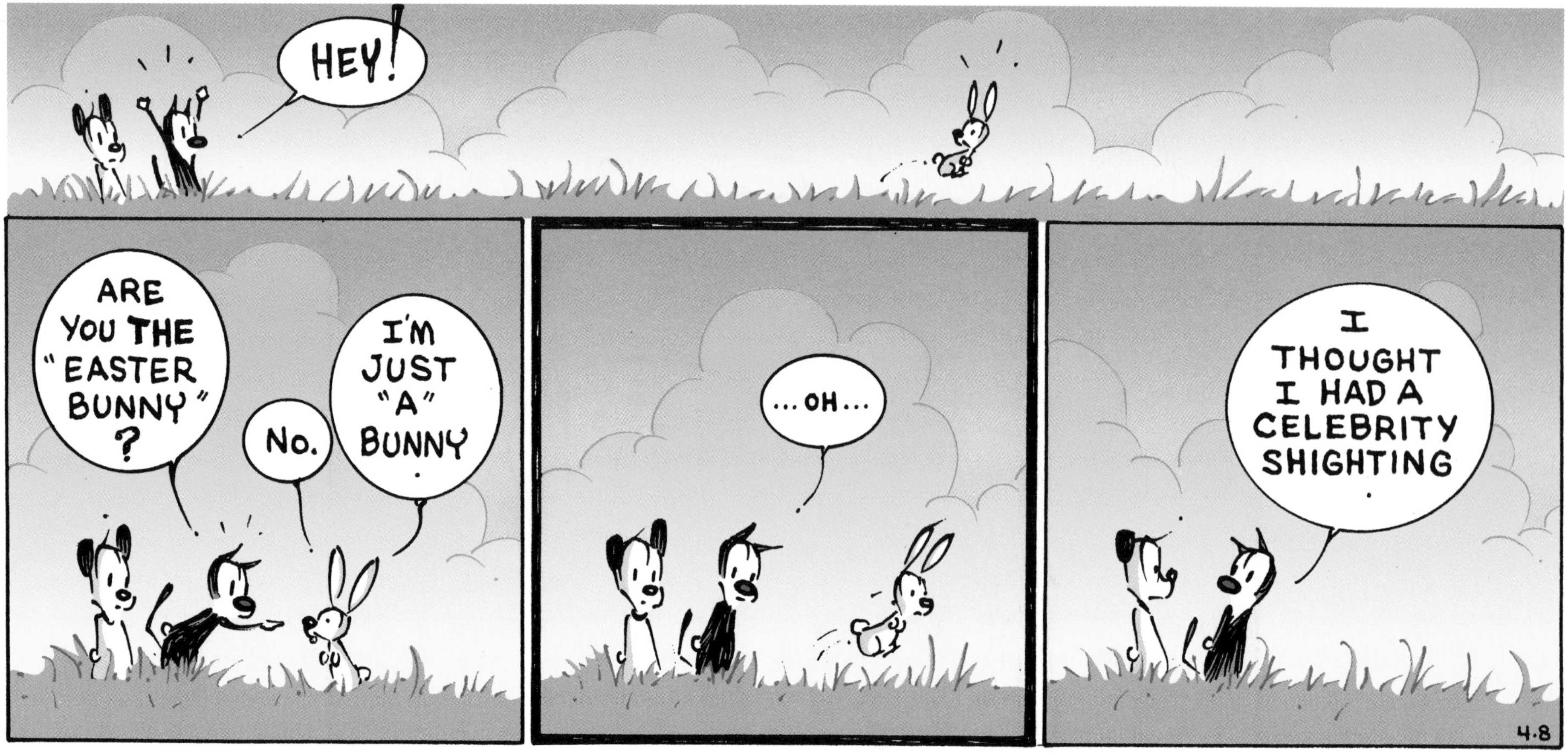
HEY!
ARE YOU THE "EASTER BUNNY" ?
No.
I'M JUST "A" BUNNY.
...OH...
I THOUGHT I HAD A CELEBRITY SHIGHTING.
4.8

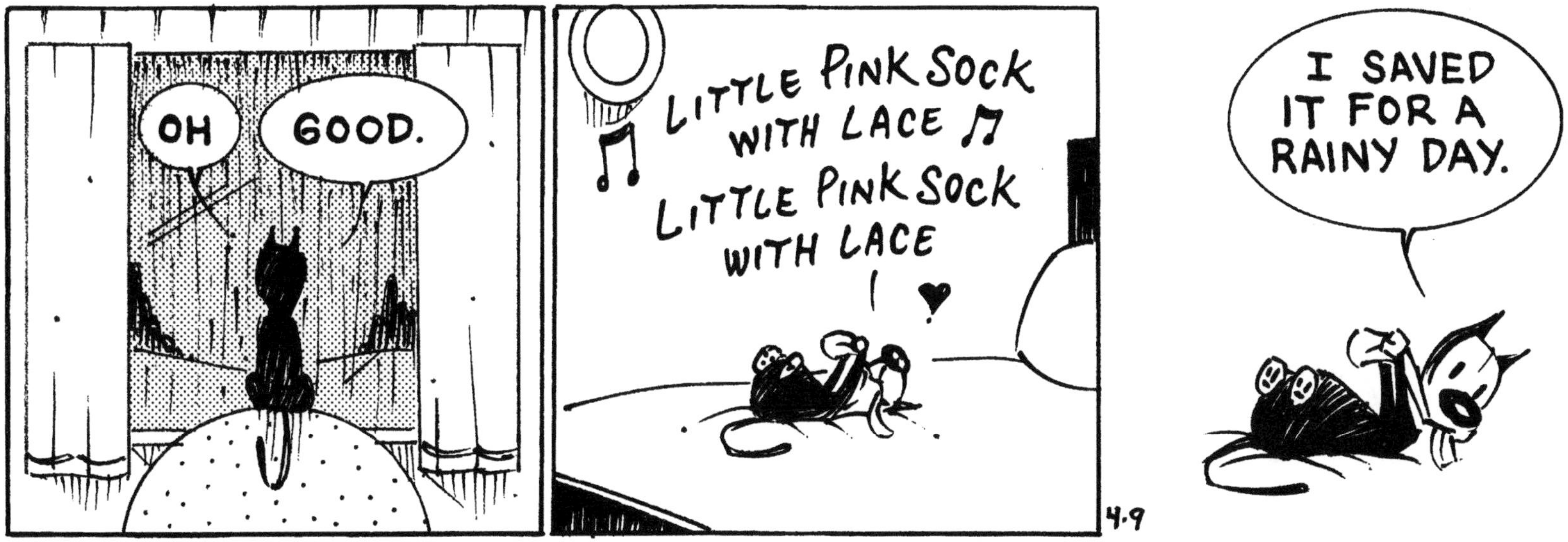
OH
GOOD.
LITTLE PINK SOCK WITH LACE
LITTLE PINK SOCK WITH LACE
I SAVED IT FOR A RAINY DAY.
4·9

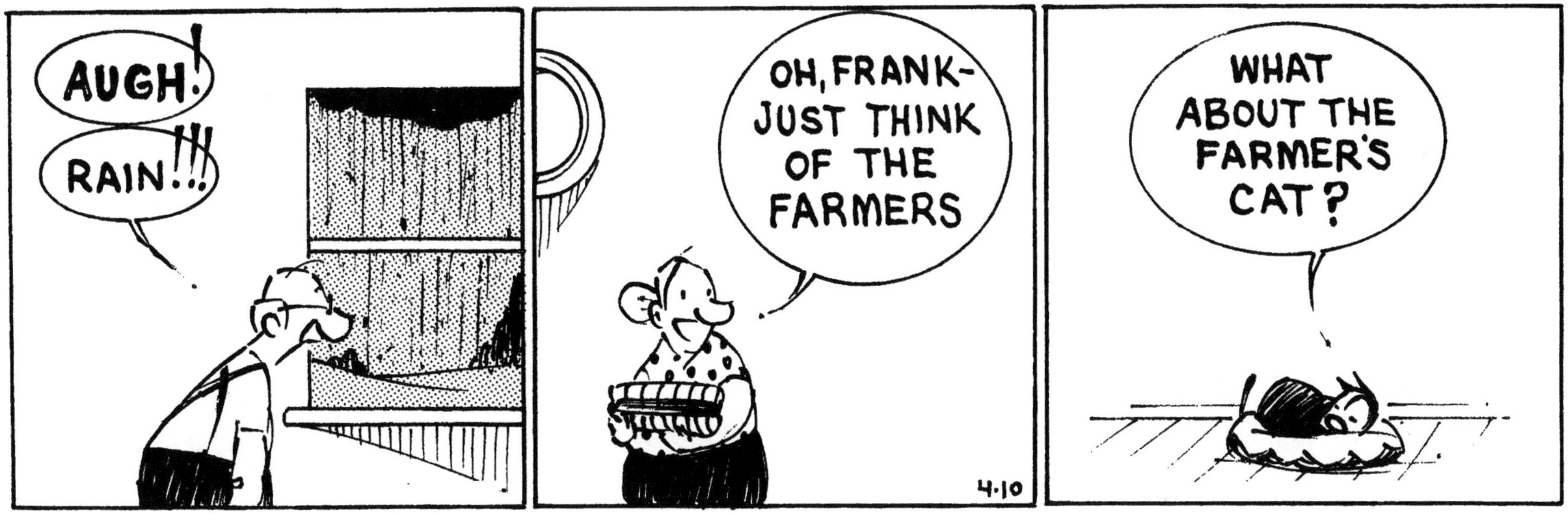
AUGH!
RAIN!!!
OH, FRANK- JUST THINK OF THE FARMERS
WHAT ABOUT THE FARMER'S CAT?
4·10

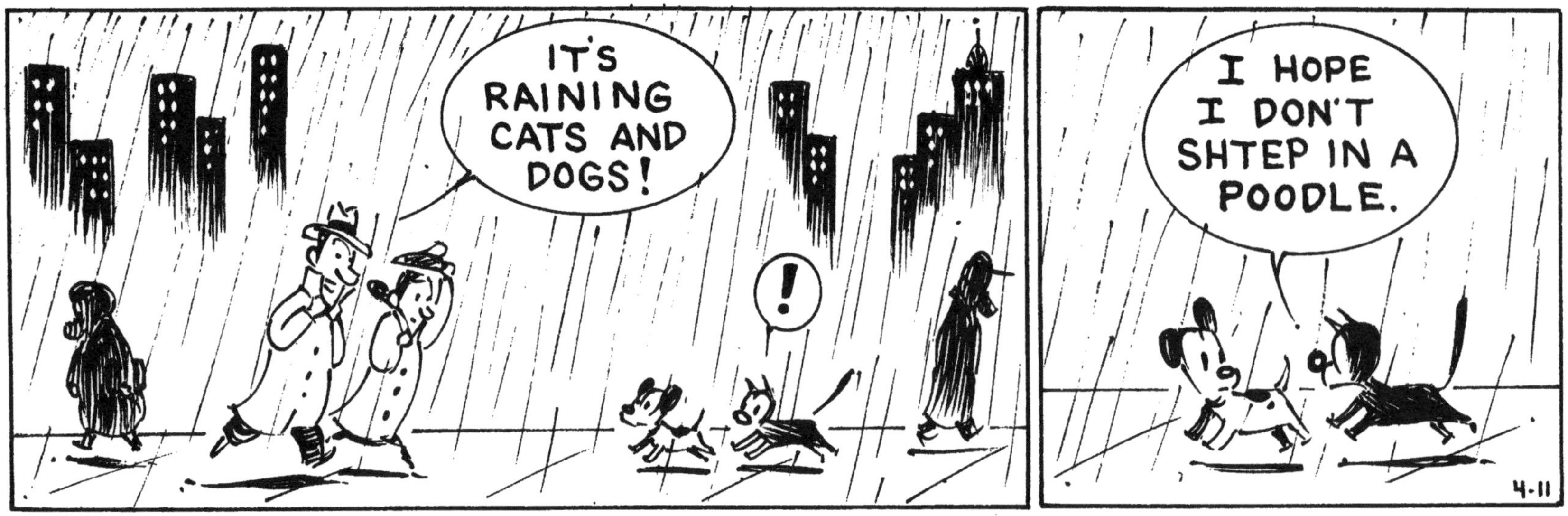
IT'S RAINING CATS AND DOGS!
!
I HOPE I DON'T SHTEP IN A POODLE.
4-11

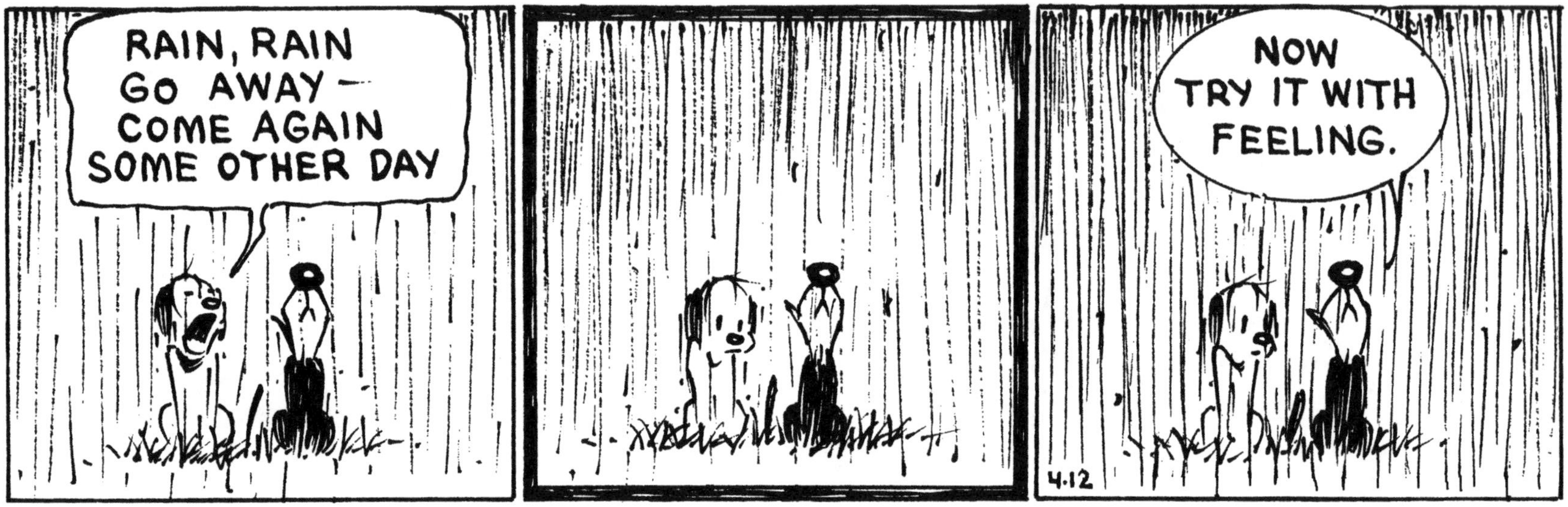
RAIN, RAIN GO AWAY— COME AGAIN SOME OTHER DAY
NOW TRY IT WITH FEELING.
4.12

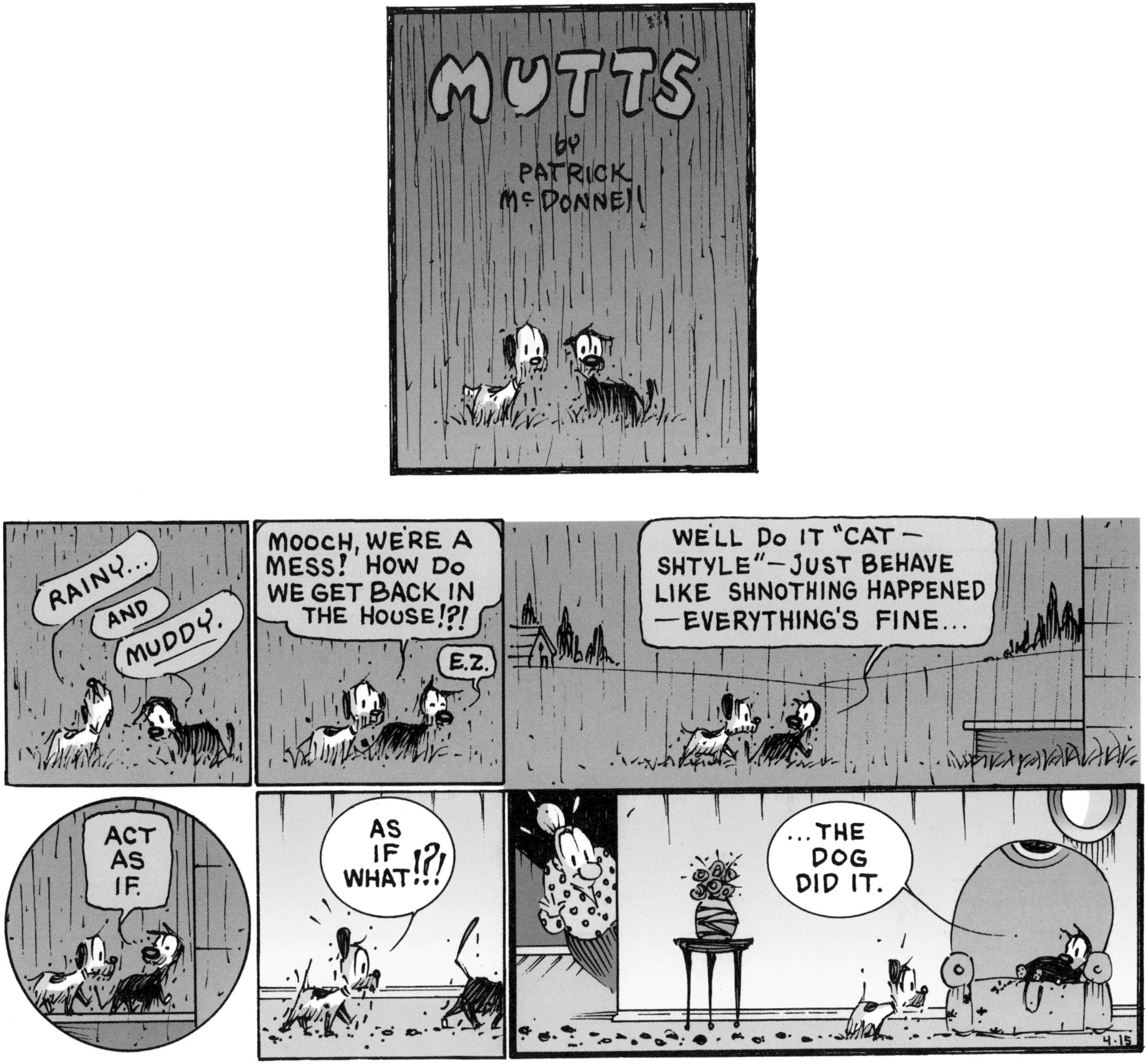
MUTTS
by
PATRICK
McDONNELL
RAINY...
AND
MUDDY.
MOOCH, WE'RE A MESS! HOW DO WE GET BACK IN THE HOUSE!?!
E.Z.
WE'LL DO IT "CAT-SHTYLE"—JUST BEHAVE LIKE SHNOTHING HAPPENED—EVERYTHING'S FINE...
ACT AS IF.
AS IF WHAT!?!
...THE DOG DID IT.
4·15

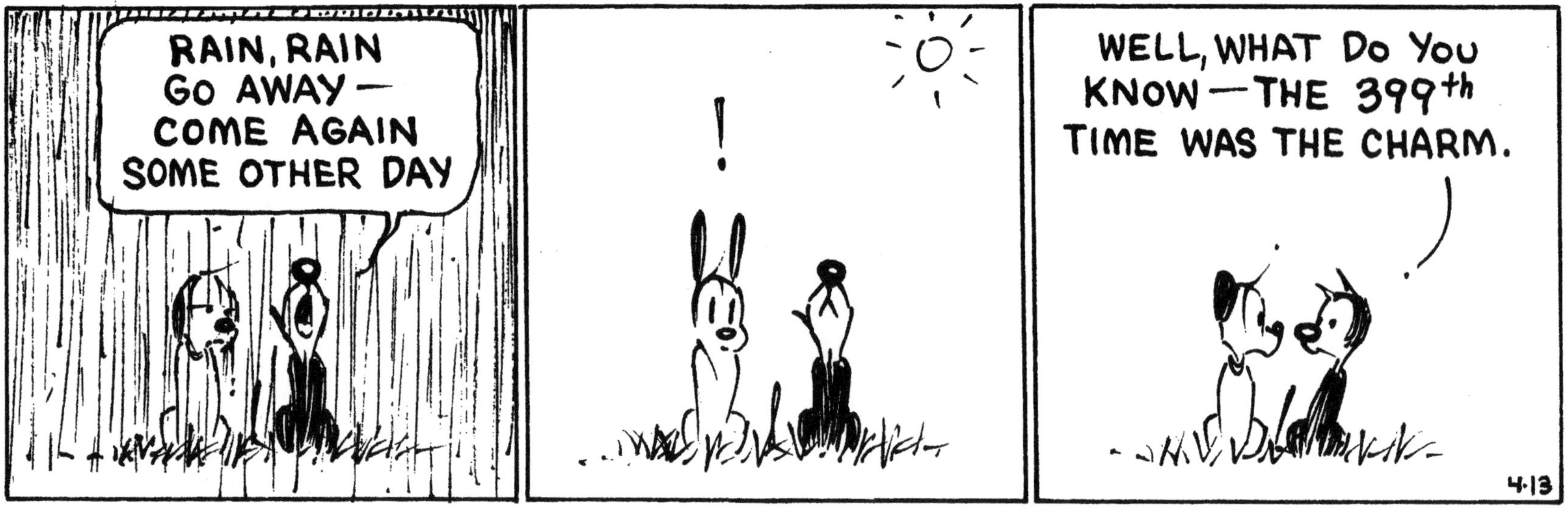
RAIN, RAIN GO AWAY— COME AGAIN SOME OTHER DAY
!
WELL, WHAT DO YOU KNOW—THE 399th TIME WAS THE CHARM.
4·13

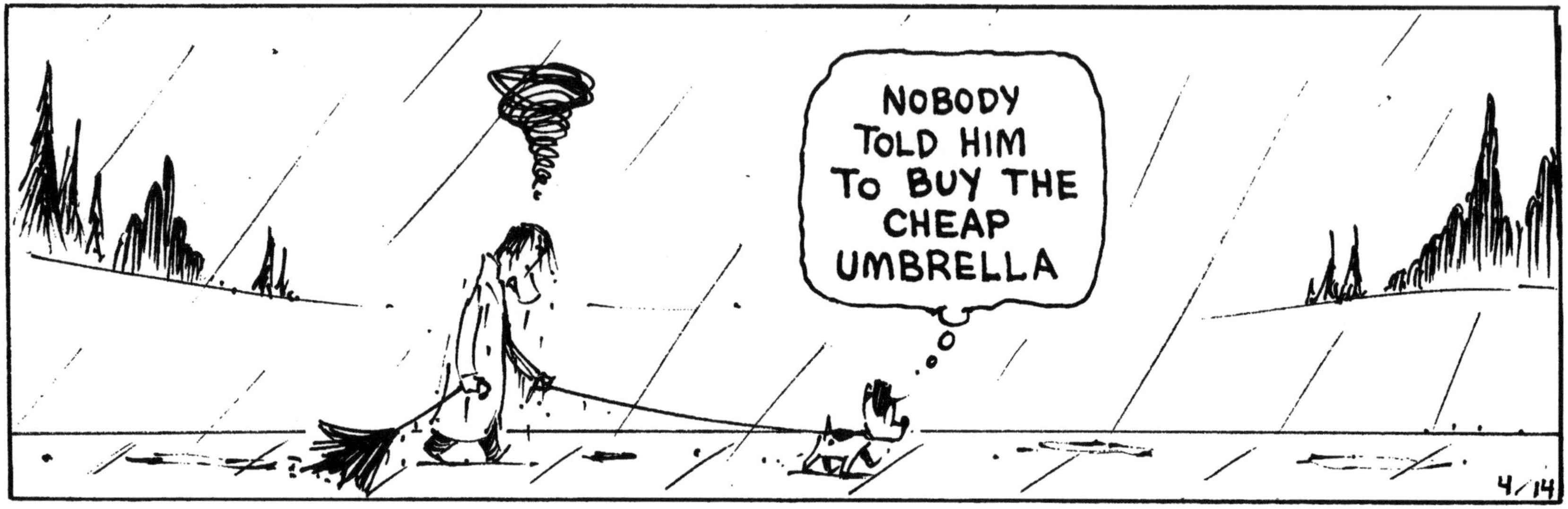
NOBODY TOLD HIM TO BUY THE CHEAP UMBRELLA
4/14

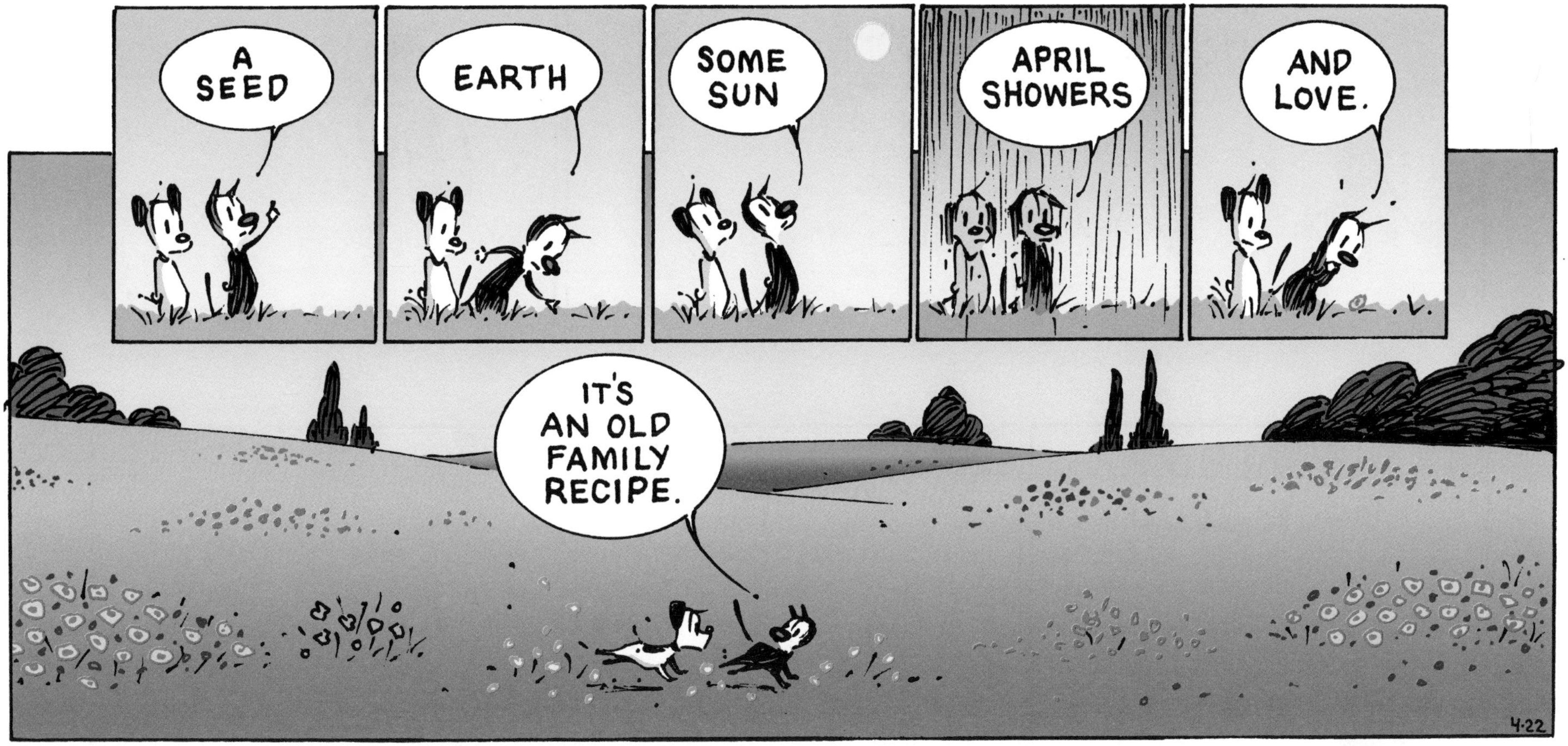
A SEED
EARTH
SOME SUN
APRIL SHOWERS
AND LOVE.
IT'S AN OLD FAMILY RECIPE.
4·22

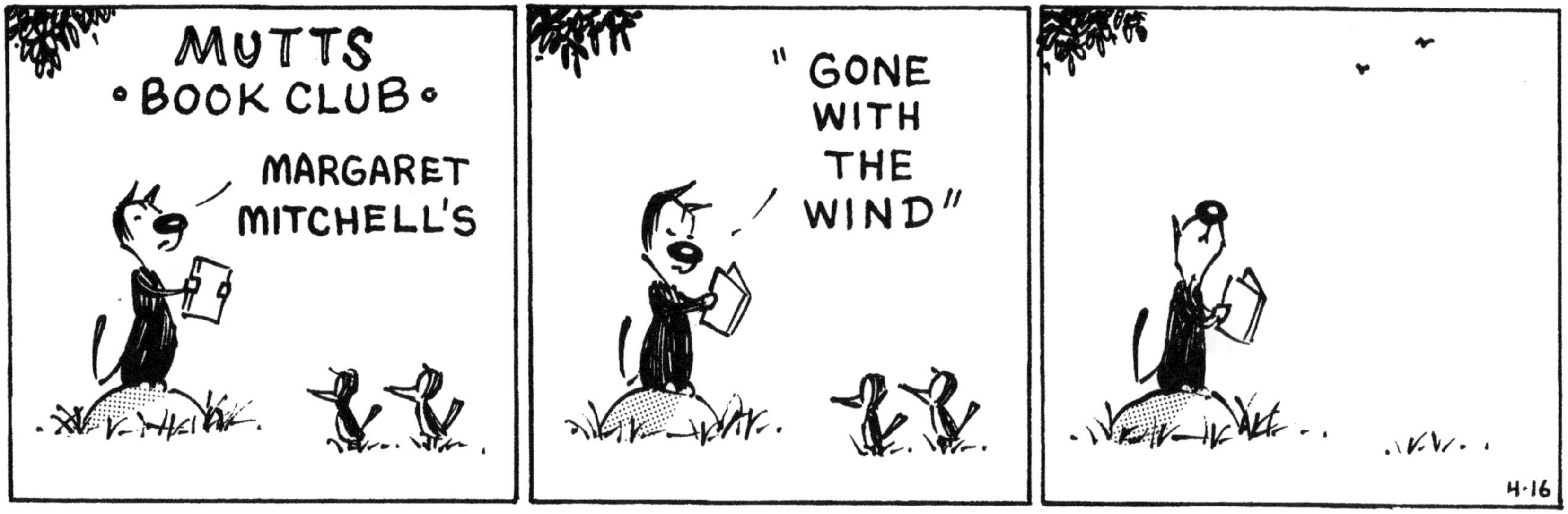
MUTTS
• BOOK CLUB •
MARGARET MITCHELL'S
"GONE WITH THE WIND"
4·16

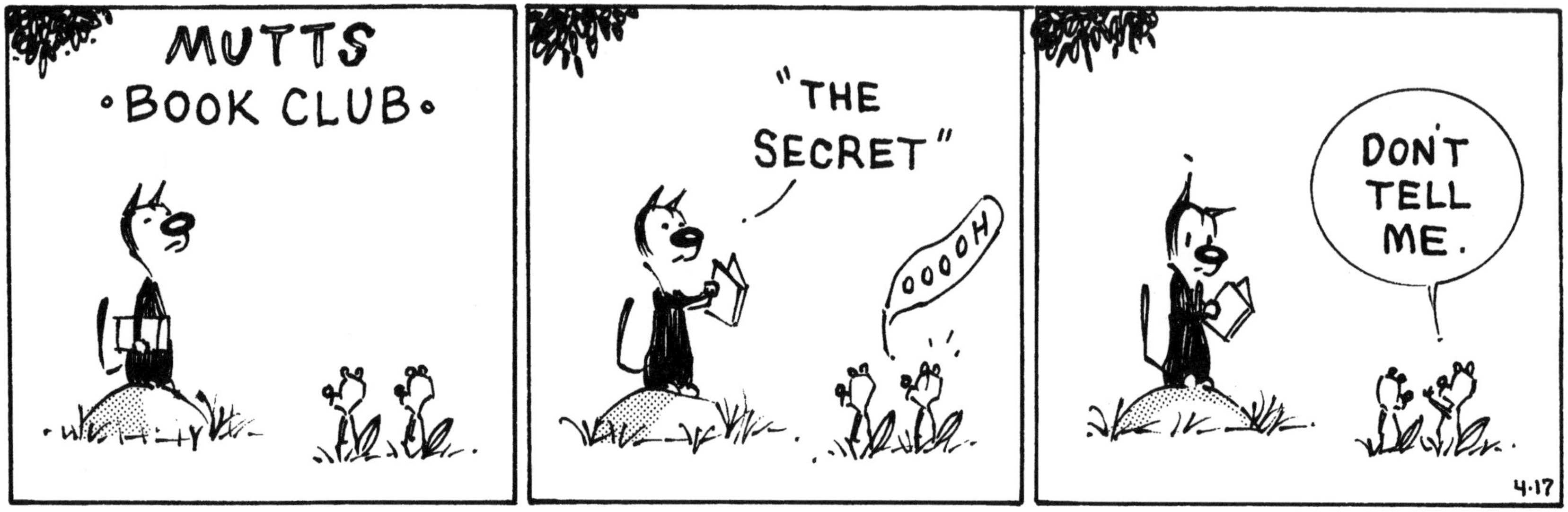
MUTTS
• BOOK CLUB •
"THE SECRET"
OOOOH
DON'T TELL ME.
4·17

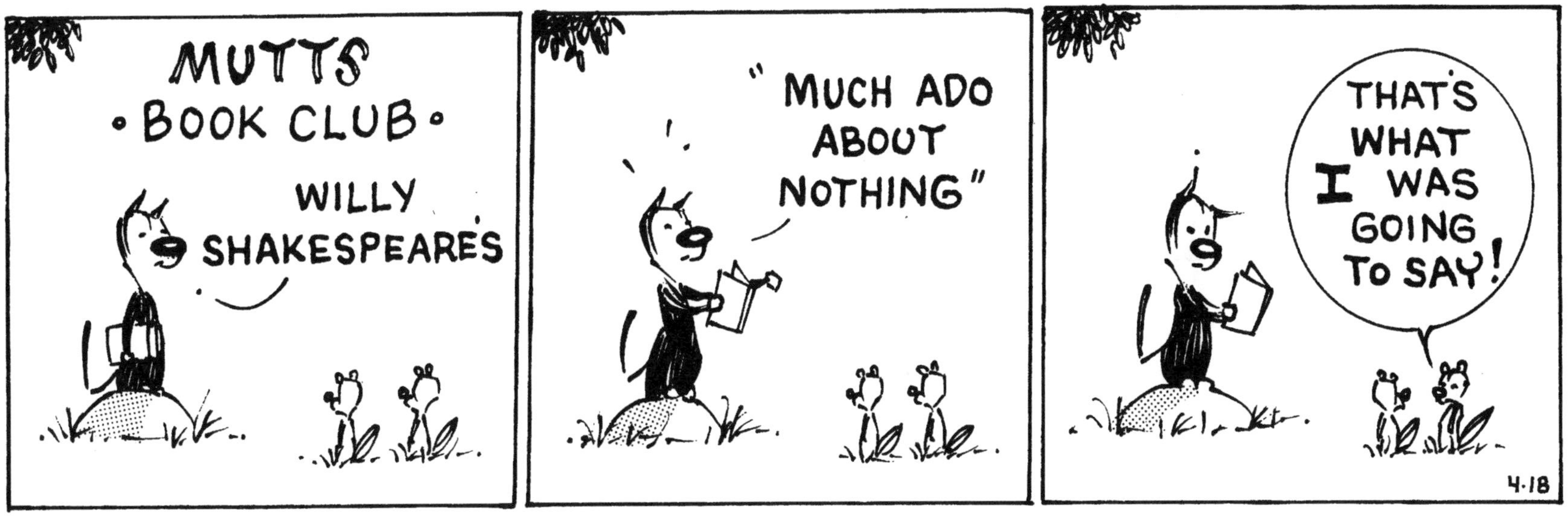
MUTTS
• BOOK CLUB •
WILLY SHAKESPEARE'S
" MUCH ADO ABOUT NOTHING "
THAT'S WHAT I WAS GOING TO SAY!
4·18

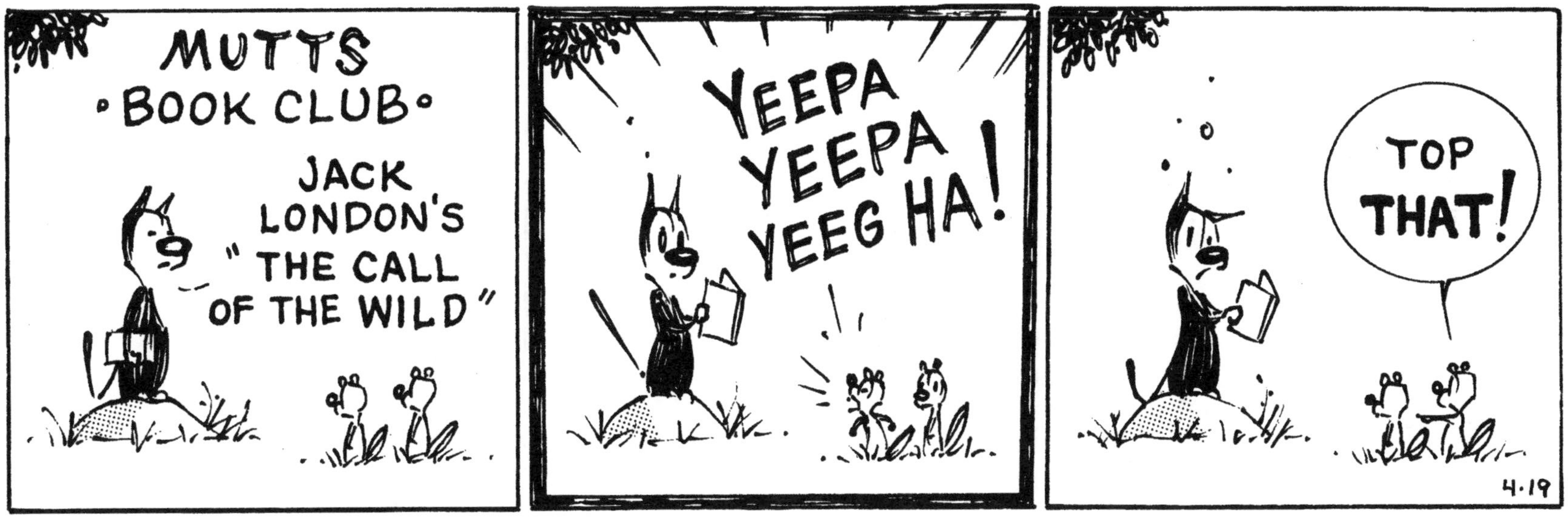
MUTTS
• BOOK CLUB •
JACK LONDON'S " THE CALL OF THE WILD "
YEEPA YEEPA YEEG HA!
TOP THAT!
4·19

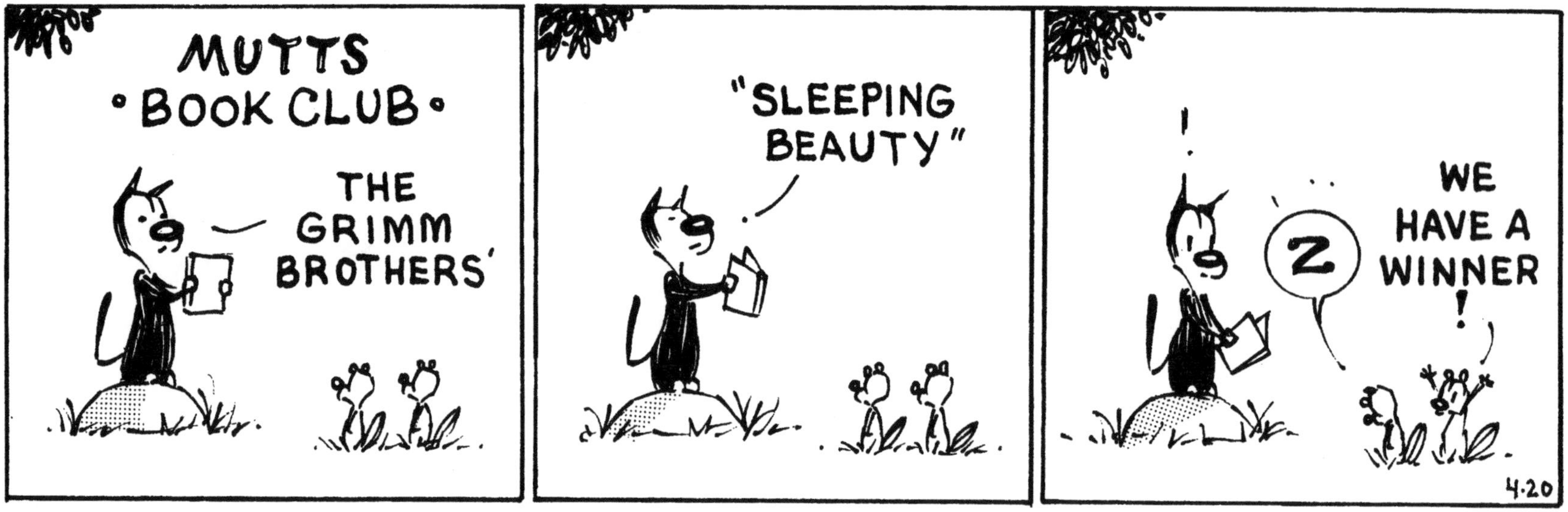
MUTTS
• BOOK CLUB •
THE GRIMM BROTHERS'
"SLEEPING BEAUTY"
Z
WE HAVE A WINNER!
4·20

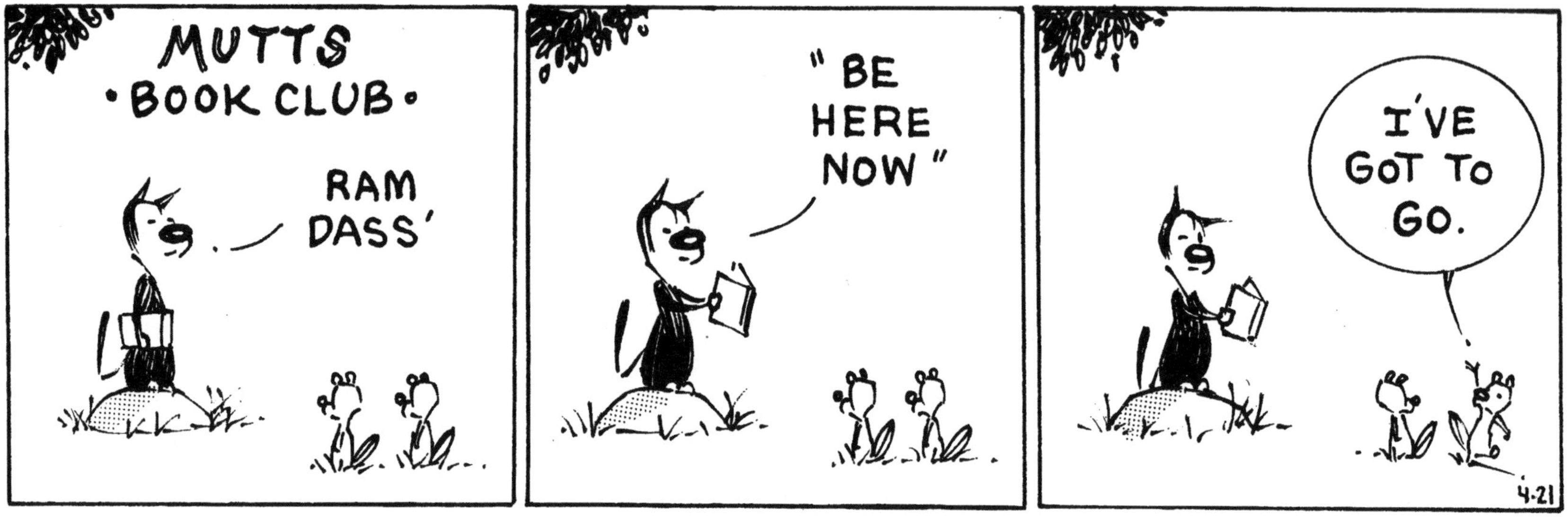
MUTTS
• BOOK CLUB •
RAM DASS'
"BE HERE NOW"
I'VE GOT TO GO.
4·21

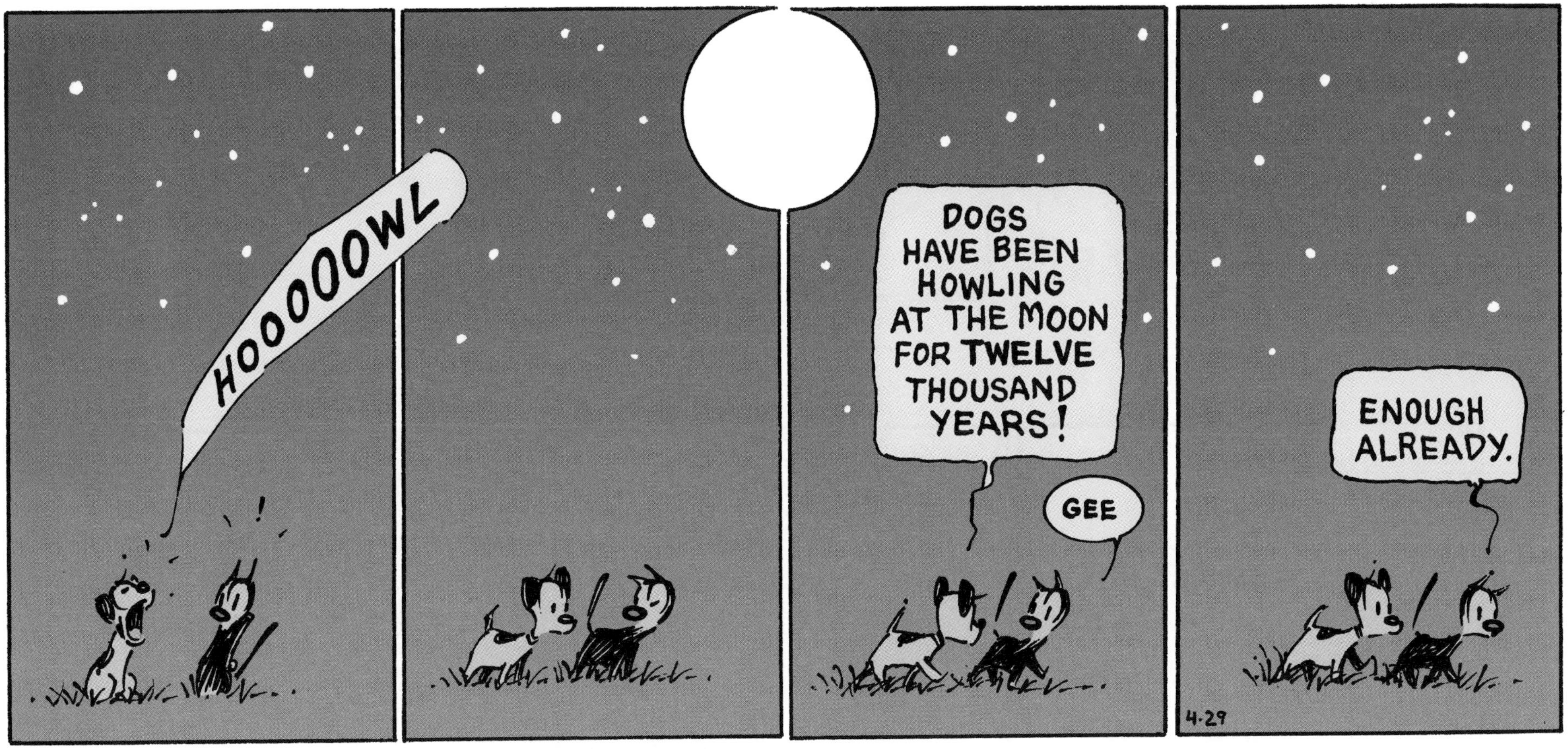
HOOOOOWL
DOGS HAVE BEEN HOWLING AT THE MOON FOR TWELVE THOUSAND YEARS!
GEE
ENOUGH ALREADY.
4.29

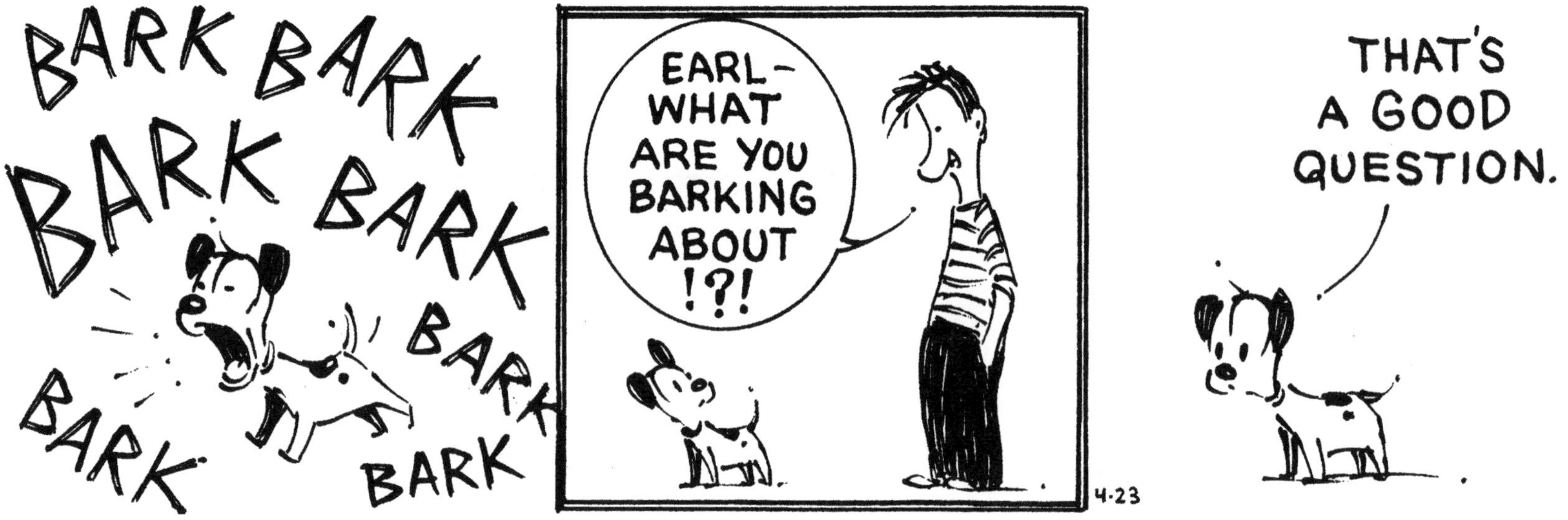
BARK BARK
BARK BARK
BARK
BARK
BARK
EARL- WHAT ARE YOU BARKING ABOUT !?!
4·23
THAT'S A GOOD QUESTION.

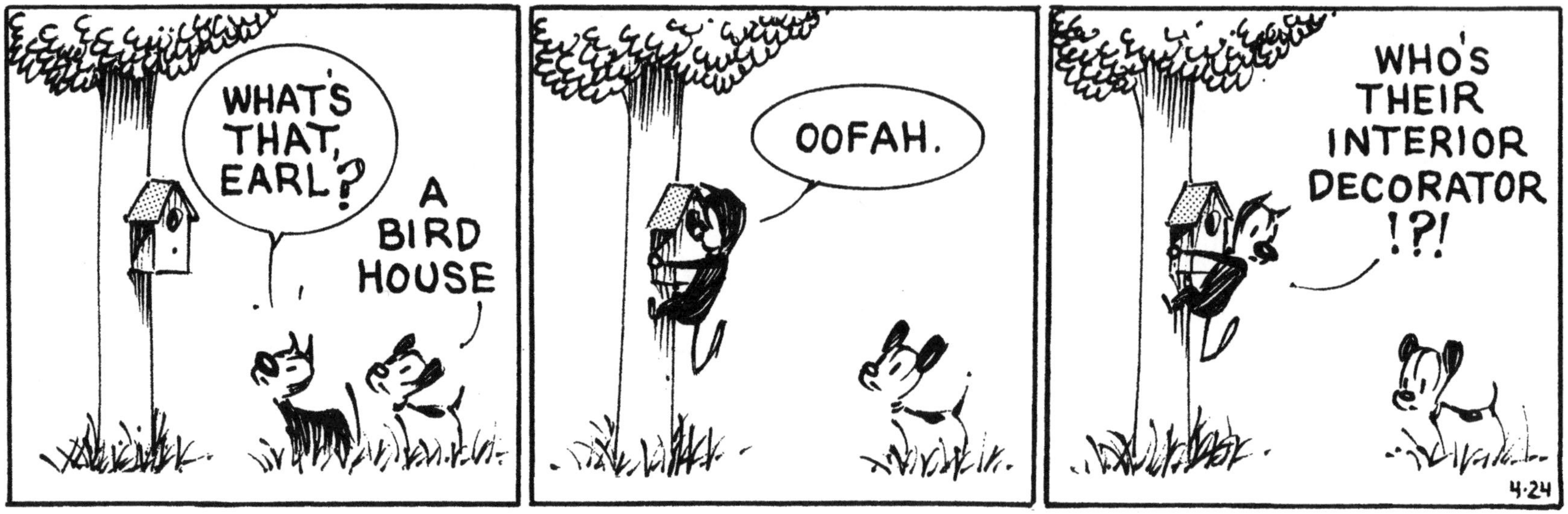
WHAT'S THAT, EARL?
A BIRD HOUSE
OOFAH.
WHO'S THEIR INTERIOR DECORATOR !?!
4·24

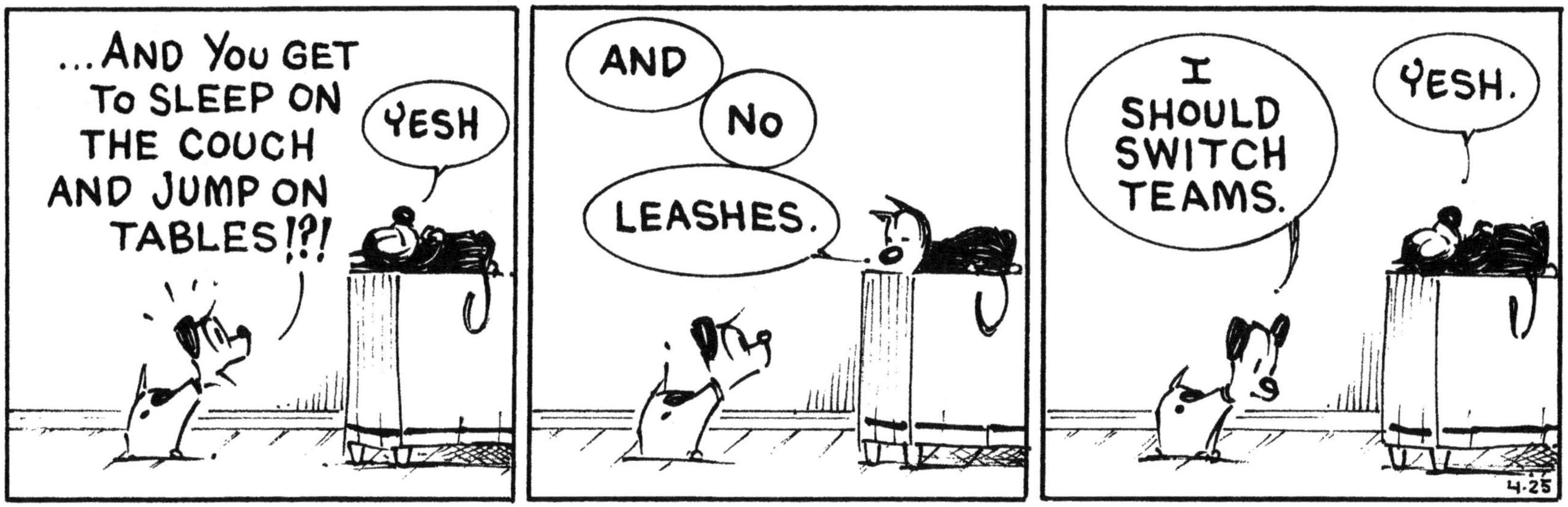
...AND YOU GET TO SLEEP ON THE COUCH AND JUMP ON TABLES!?!
YESH
AND
NO
LEASHES.
I SHOULD SWITCH TEAMS.
YESH.
4·25

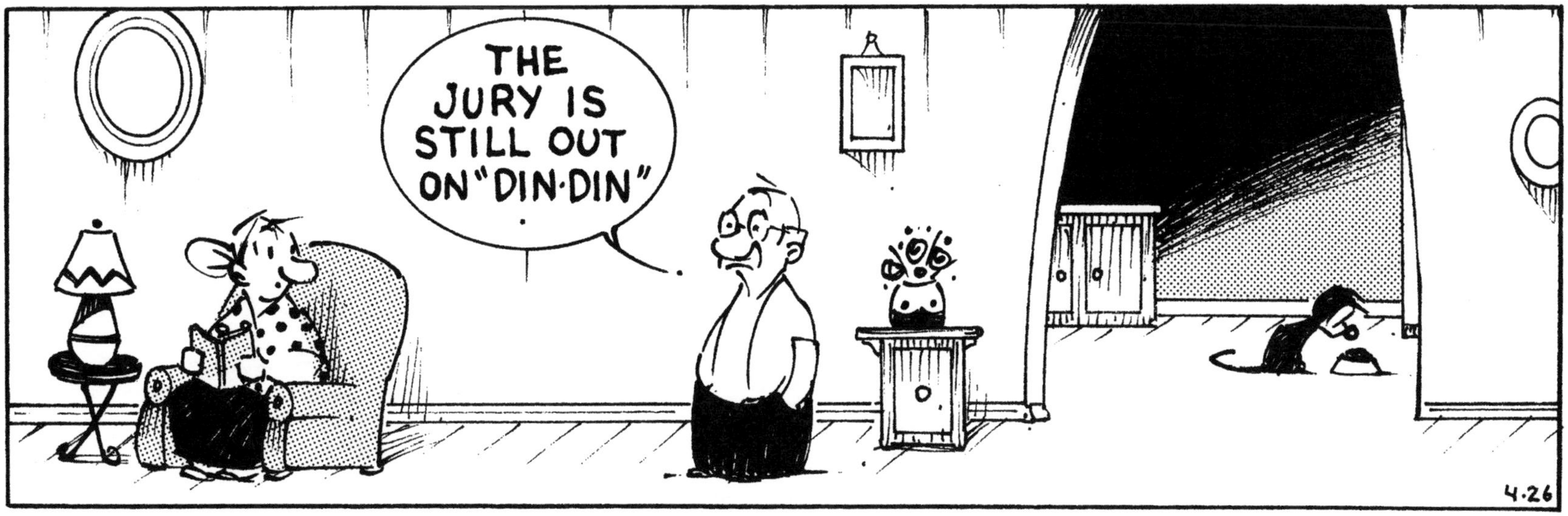
THE JURY IS STILL OUT ON "DIN·DIN".
4·26

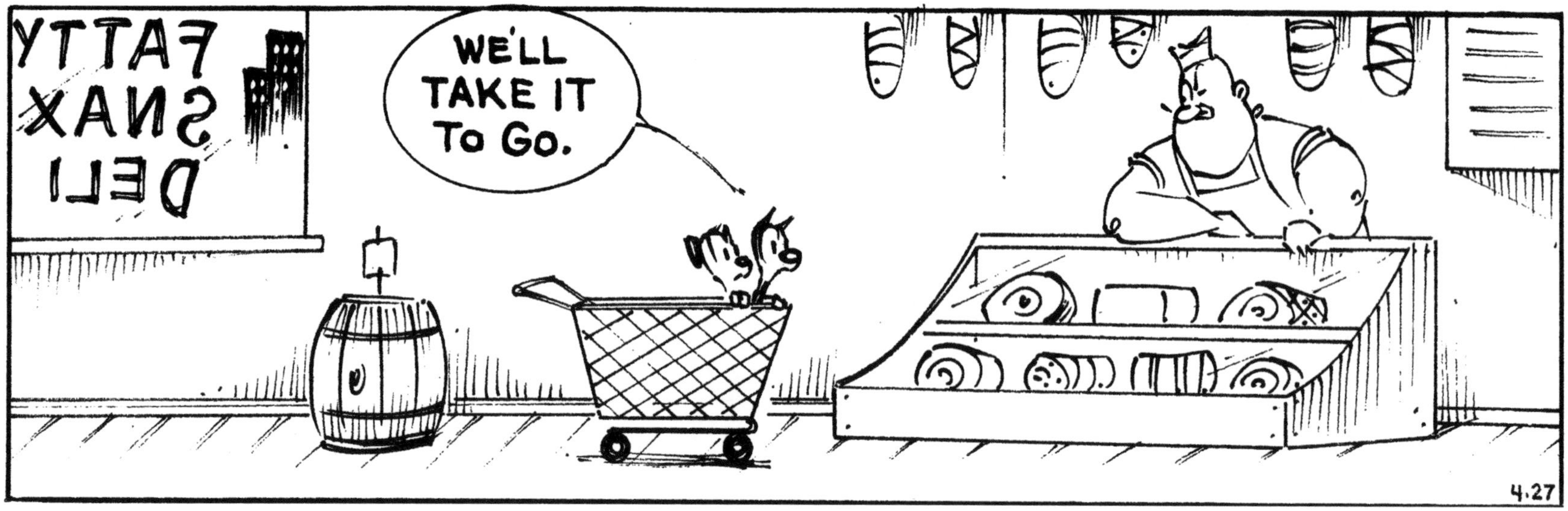
FATTY SNAX DELI
WE'LL TAKE IT To Go.
4.27

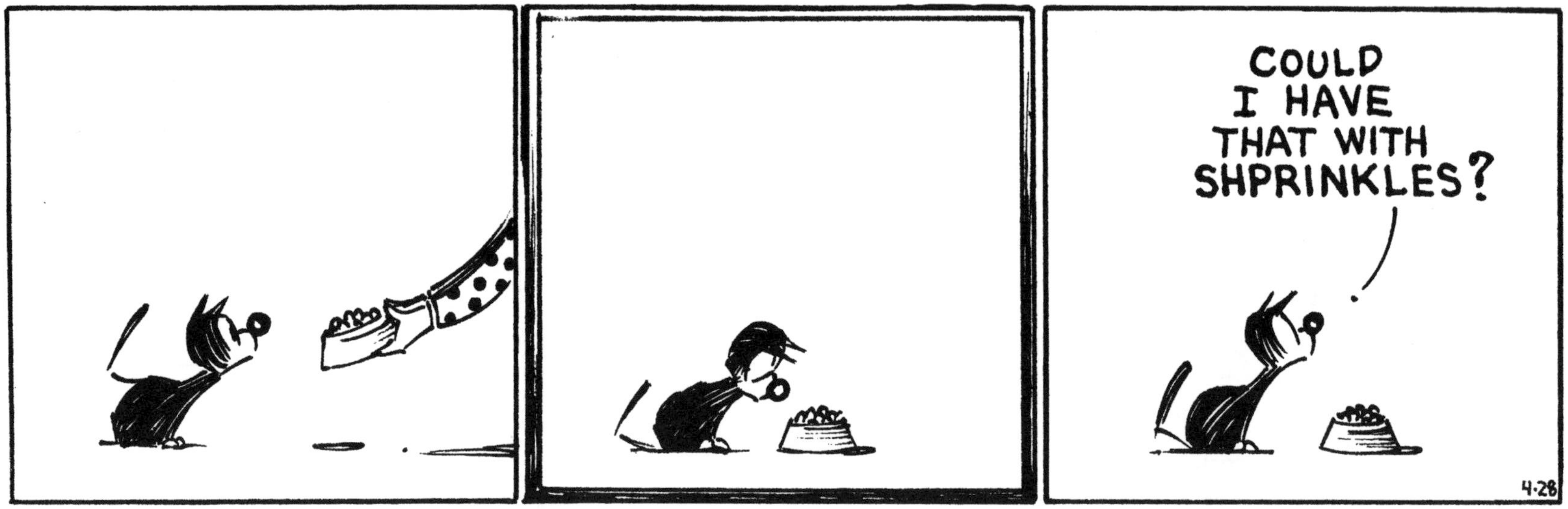
COULD I HAVE THAT WITH SHPRINKLES?
4.28

MUTTS
SHELTER STORIES

ANIMAL SHELTER
ADOPT A DOG TODAY
AND/OR A KITTY
PLEASE.
5/6

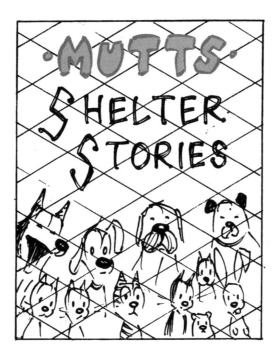

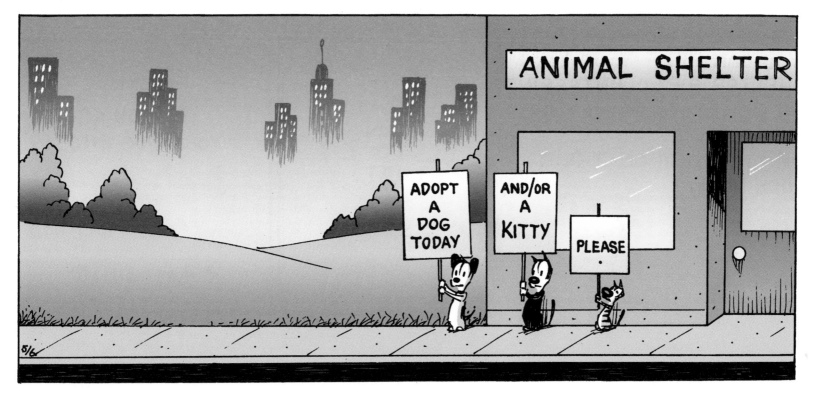

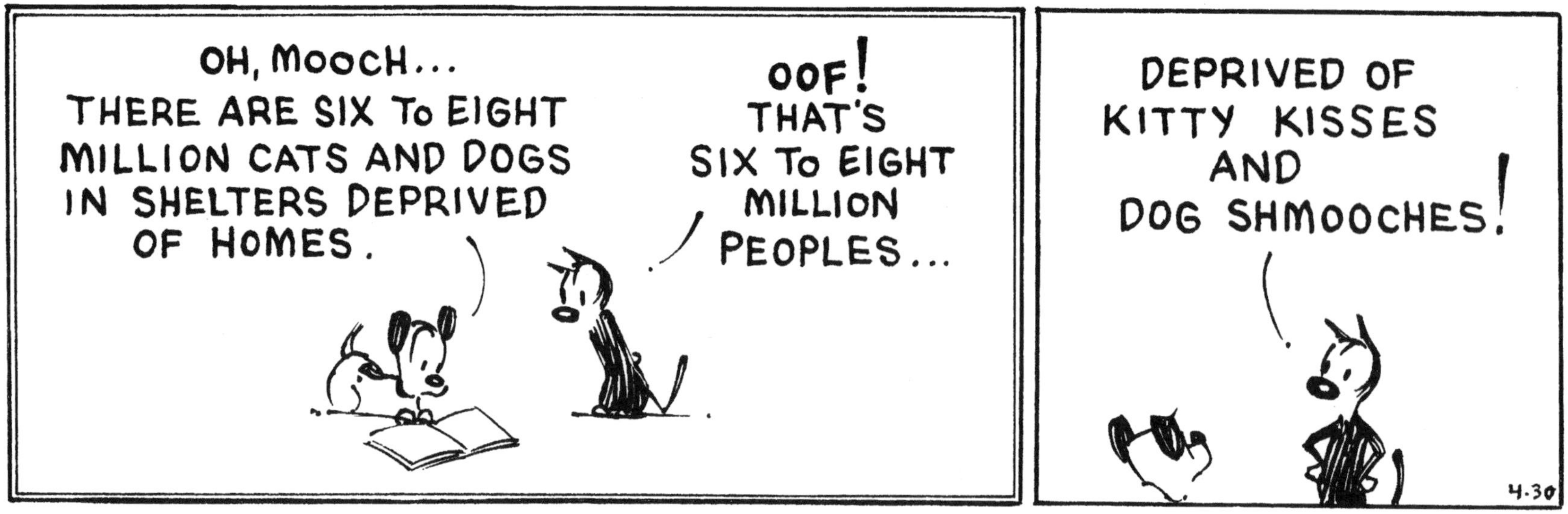
OH, MOOCH... THERE ARE SIX TO EIGHT MILLION CATS AND DOGS IN SHELTERS DEPRIVED OF HOMES.
OOF! THAT'S SIX TO EIGHT MILLION PEOPLES...
DEPRIVED OF KITTY KISSES AND DOG SHMOOCHES!
4-30

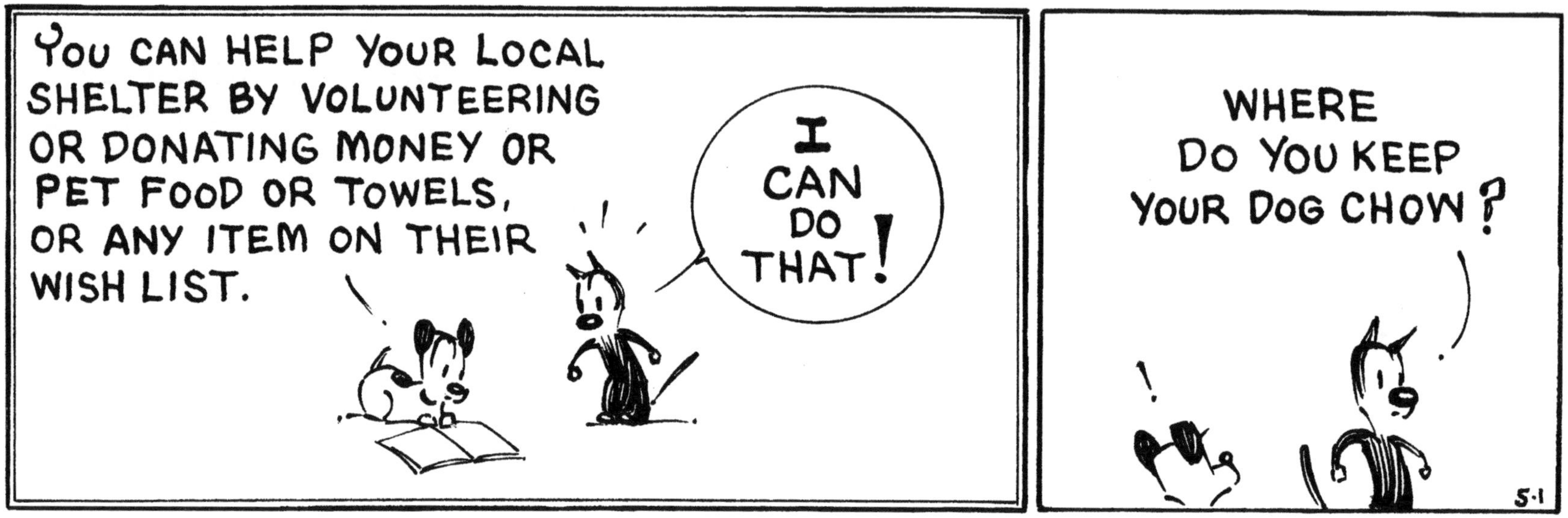
YOU CAN HELP YOUR LOCAL SHELTER BY VOLUNTEERING OR DONATING MONEY OR PET FOOD OR TOWELS, OR ANY ITEM ON THEIR WISH LIST.
I CAN DO THAT!
WHERE DO YOU KEEP YOUR DOG CHOW?
5-1

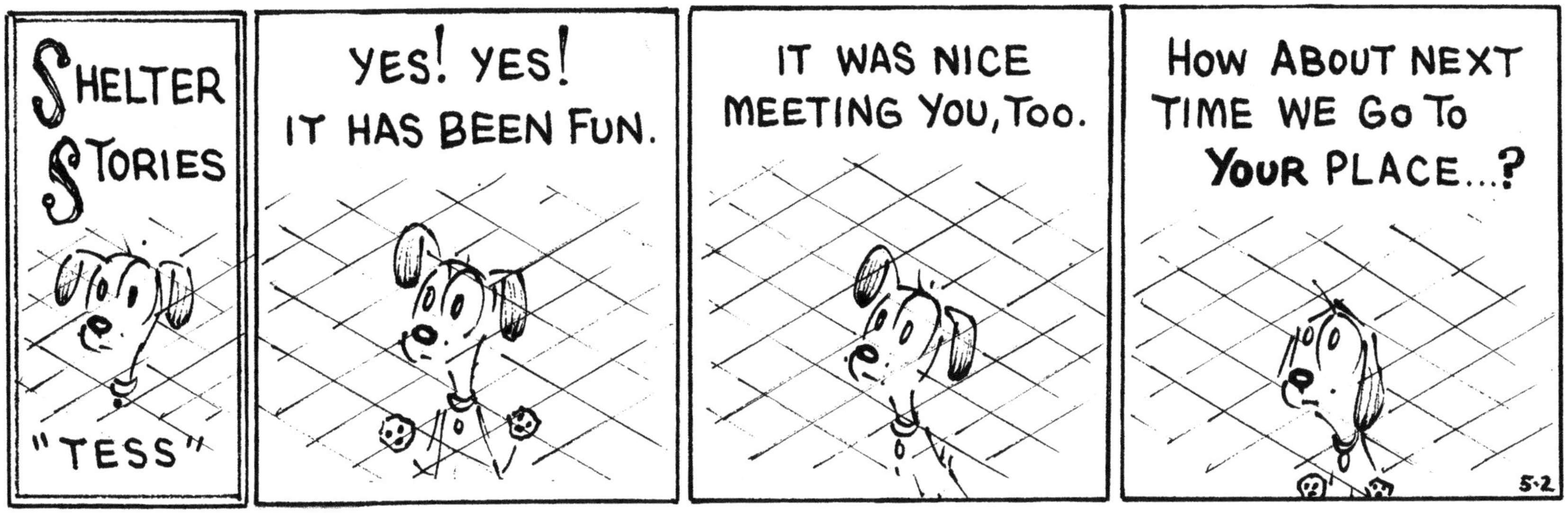
SHELTER STORIES
"TESS"
YES! YES! IT HAS BEEN FUN.
IT WAS NICE MEETING YOU, TOO.
HOW ABOUT NEXT TIME WE GO TO YOUR PLACE...?
5·2

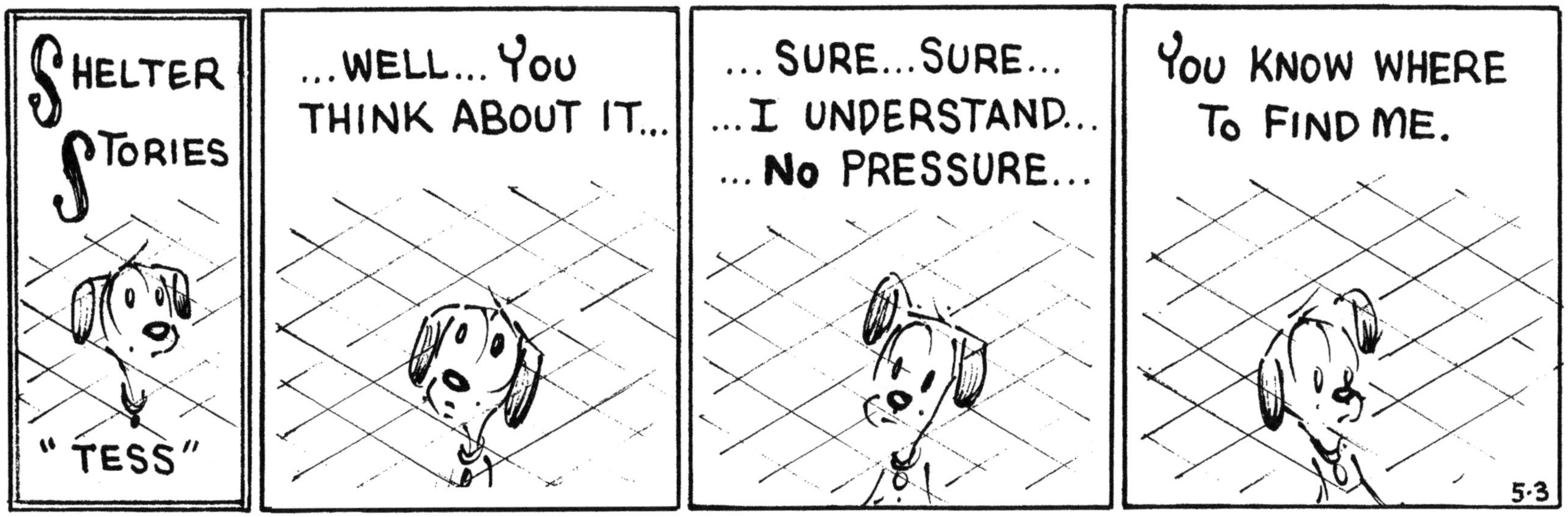
SHELTER STORIES
"TESS"
...WELL... YOU THINK ABOUT IT...
...SURE...SURE... ...I UNDERSTAND... ...NO PRESSURE...
YOU KNOW WHERE TO FIND ME.
5·3

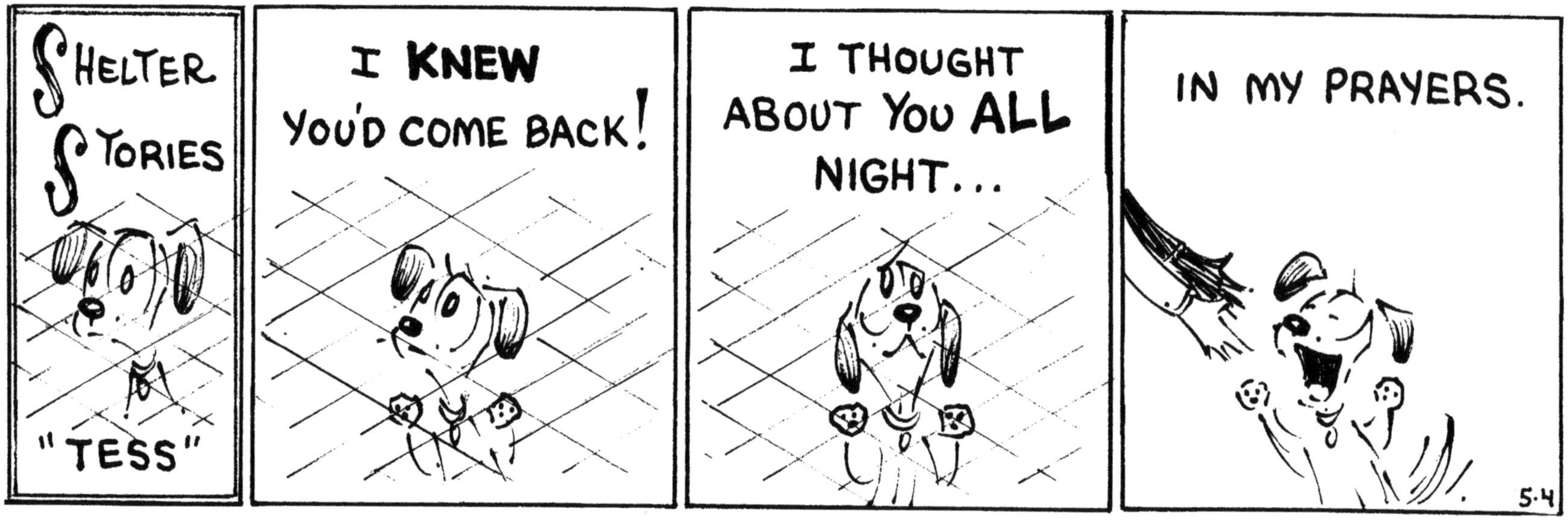
SHELTER STORIES
"TESS"
I KNEW YOU'D COME BACK!
I THOUGHT ABOUT YOU ALL NIGHT...
IN MY PRAYERS.
5·4

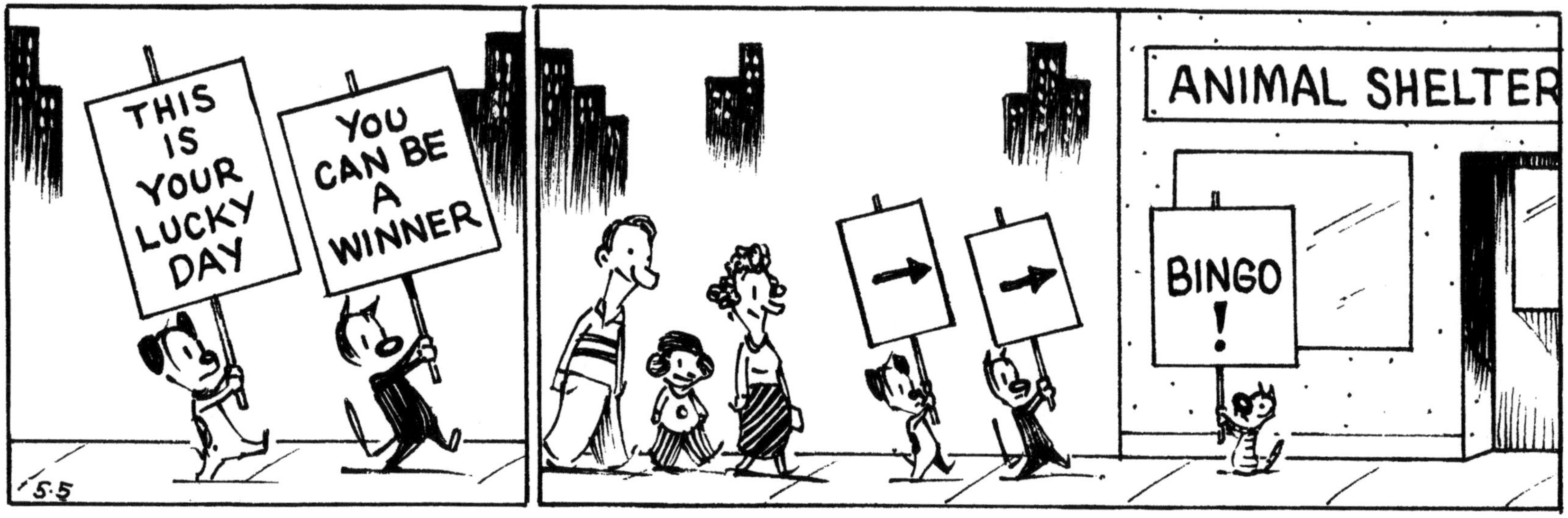
THIS IS YOUR LUCKY DAY
YOU CAN BE A WINNER
5·5
ANIMAL SHELTER
BINGO !

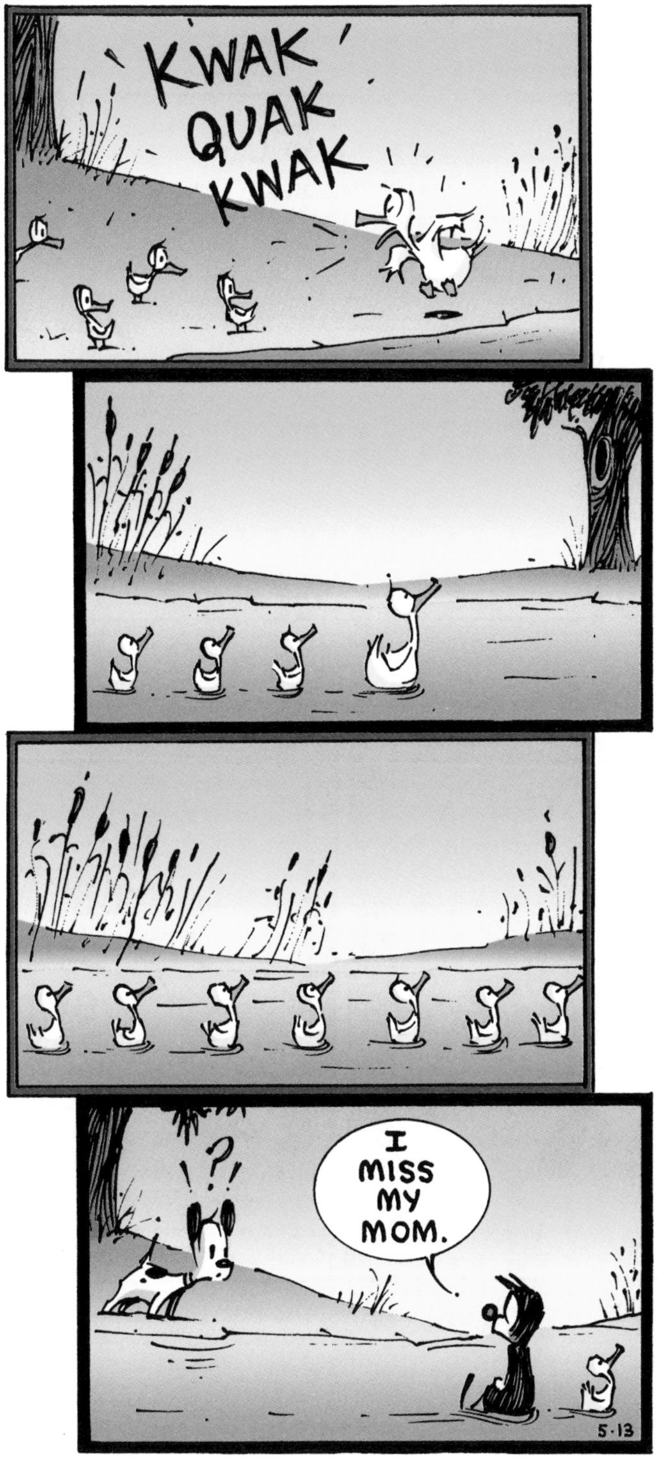
KWAK
QUAK
KWAK
!?!
I MISS MY MOM.
5·13

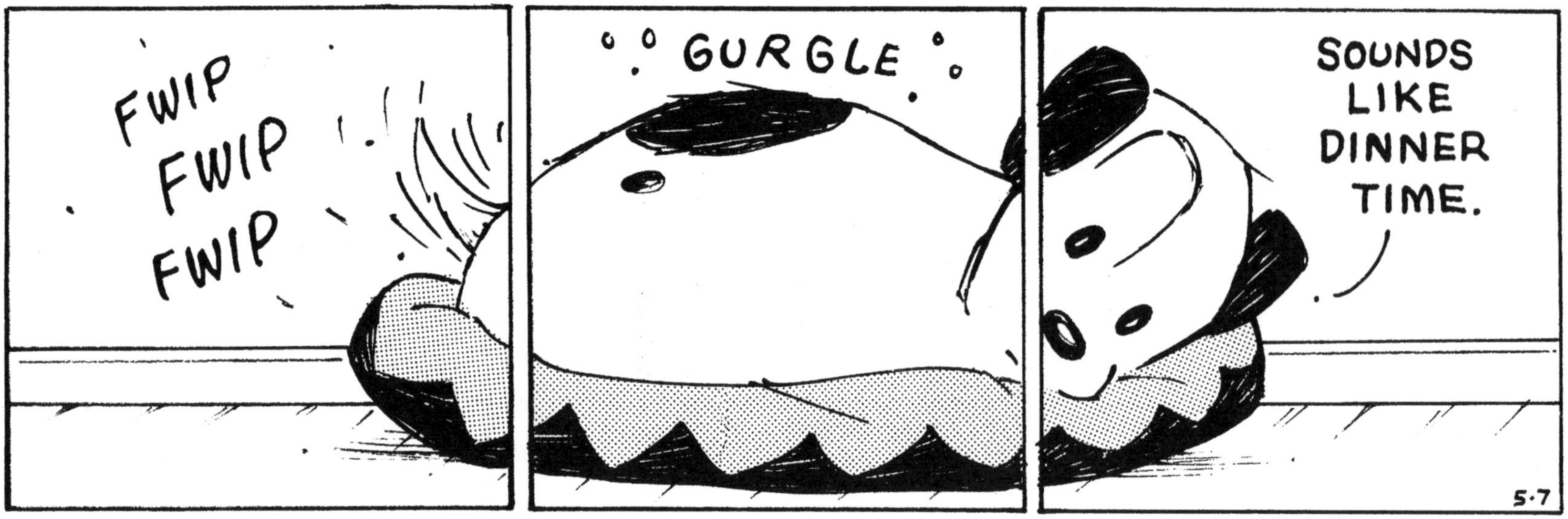
FWIP
FWIP
FWIP
GURGLE
SOUNDS LIKE DINNER TIME.
5·7

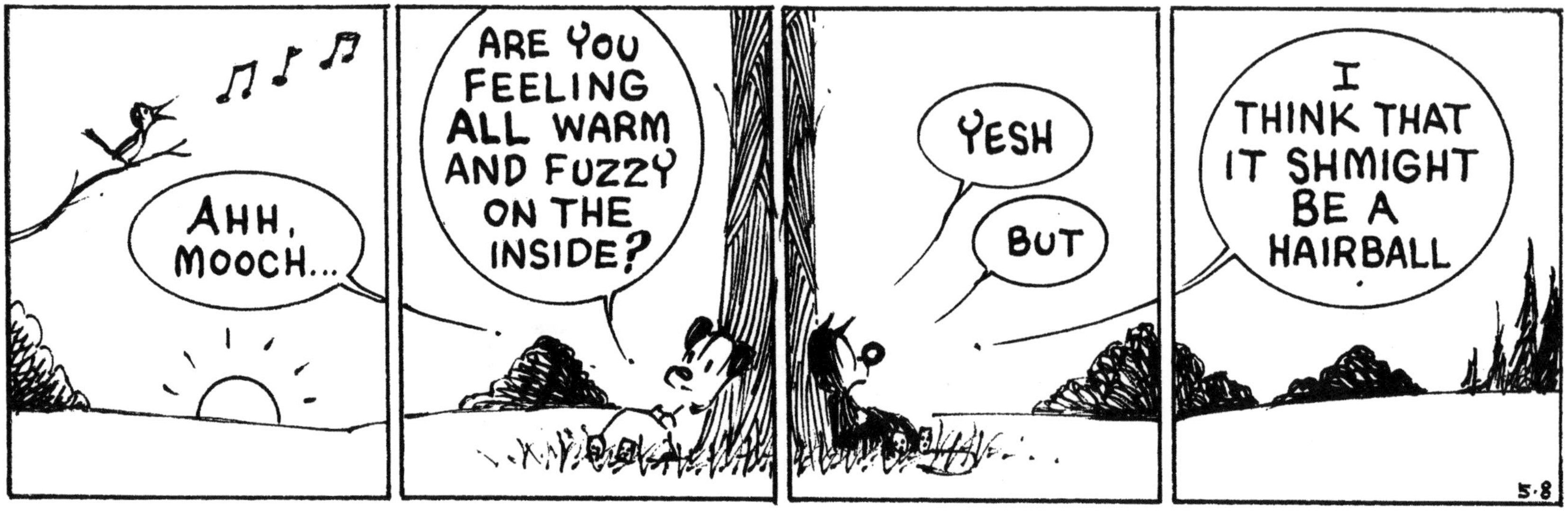
AHH, MOOCH...
ARE YOU FEELING ALL WARM AND FUZZY ON THE INSIDE?
YESH
BUT
I THINK THAT IT SHMIGHT BE A HAIRBALL
5·8

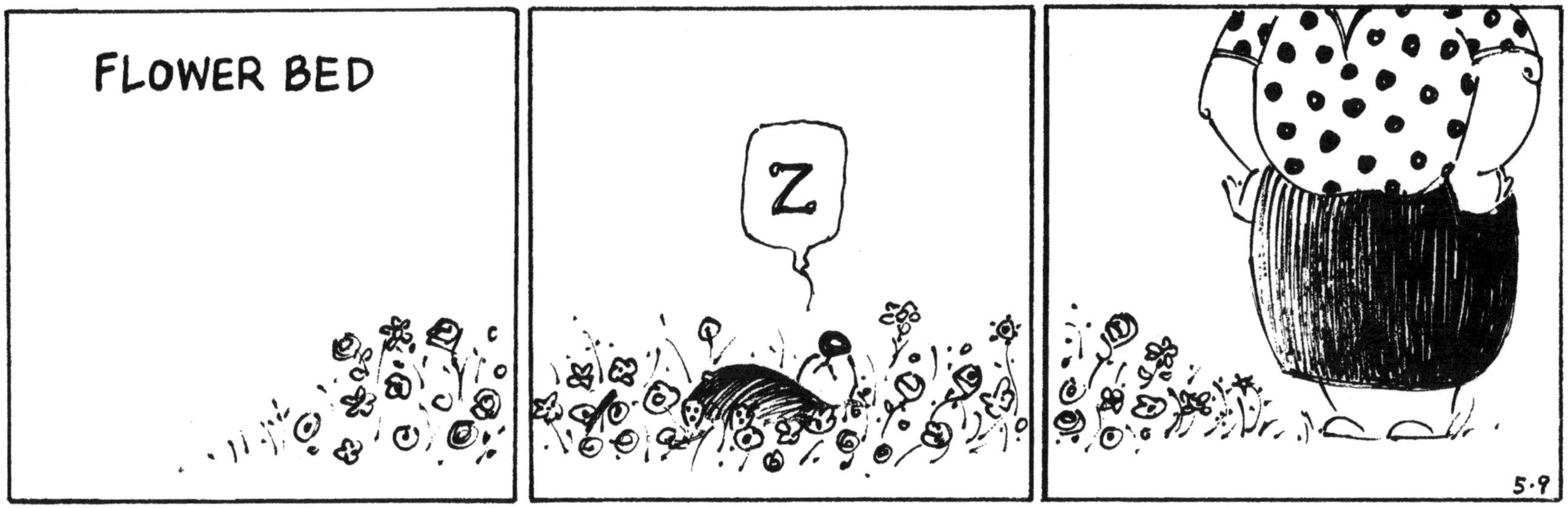
FLOWER BED
Z
5·9

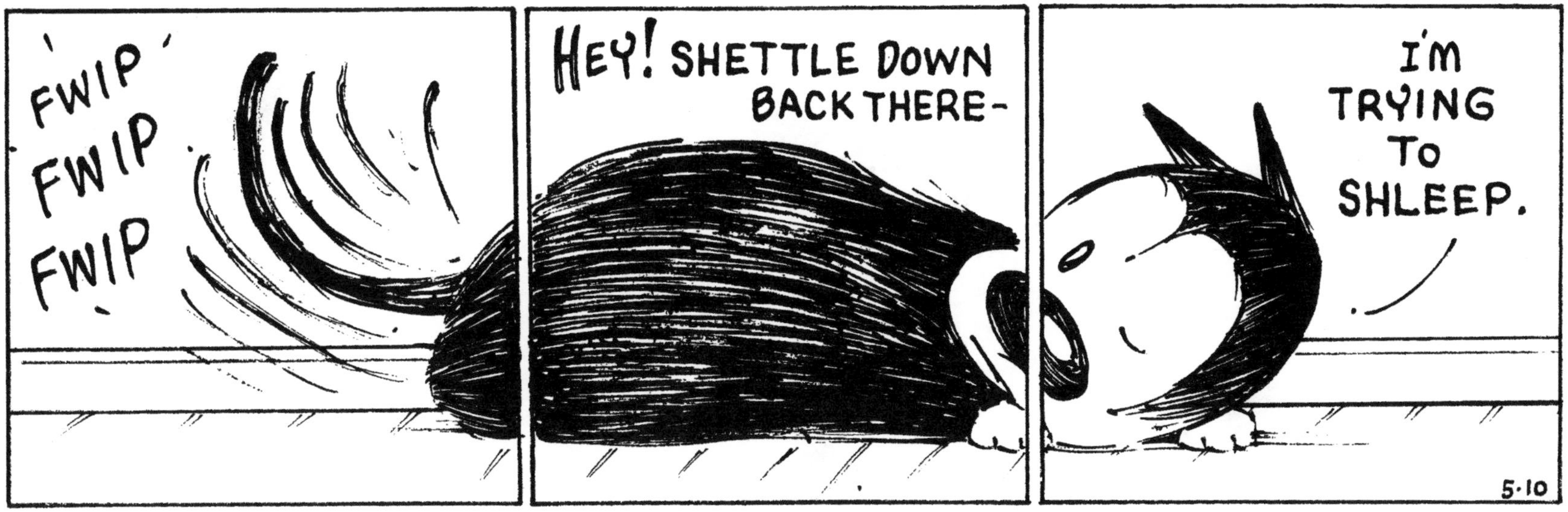
FWIP
FWIP
FWIP
HEY! SHETTLE DOWN BACK THERE-
I'M TRYING TO SHLEEP.
5·10

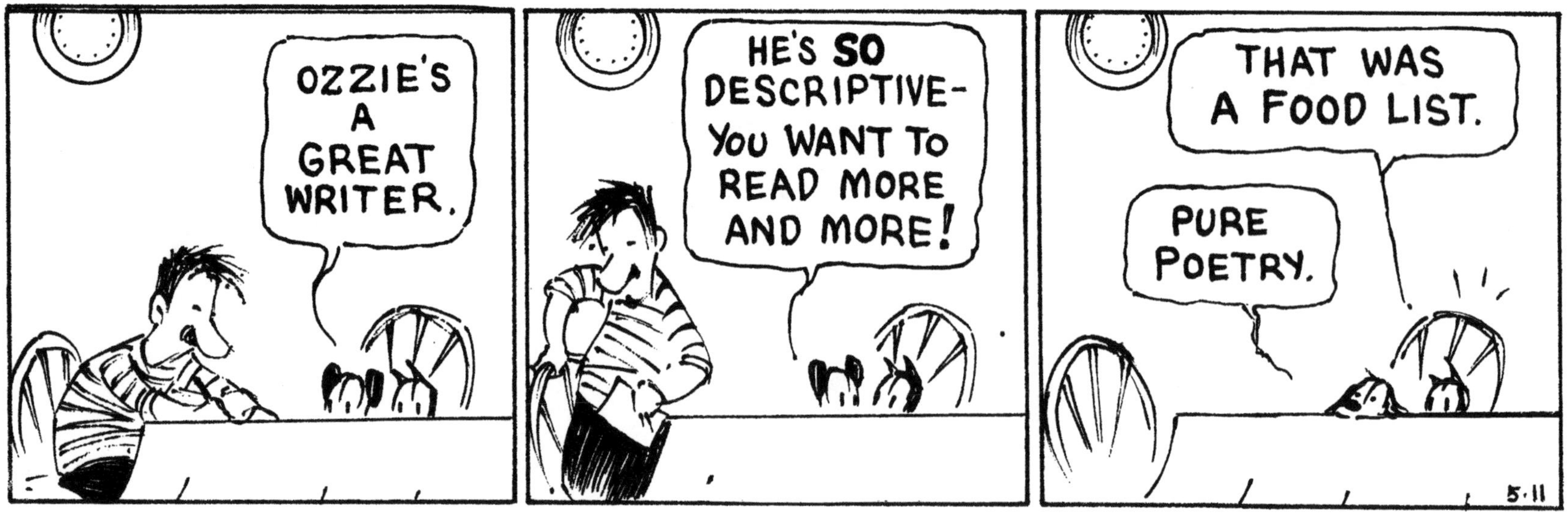
OZZIE'S A GREAT WRITER.
HE'S **SO** DESCRIPTIVE- YOU WANT TO READ MORE AND MORE!
THAT WAS A FOOD LIST.
PURE POETRY.
5·11

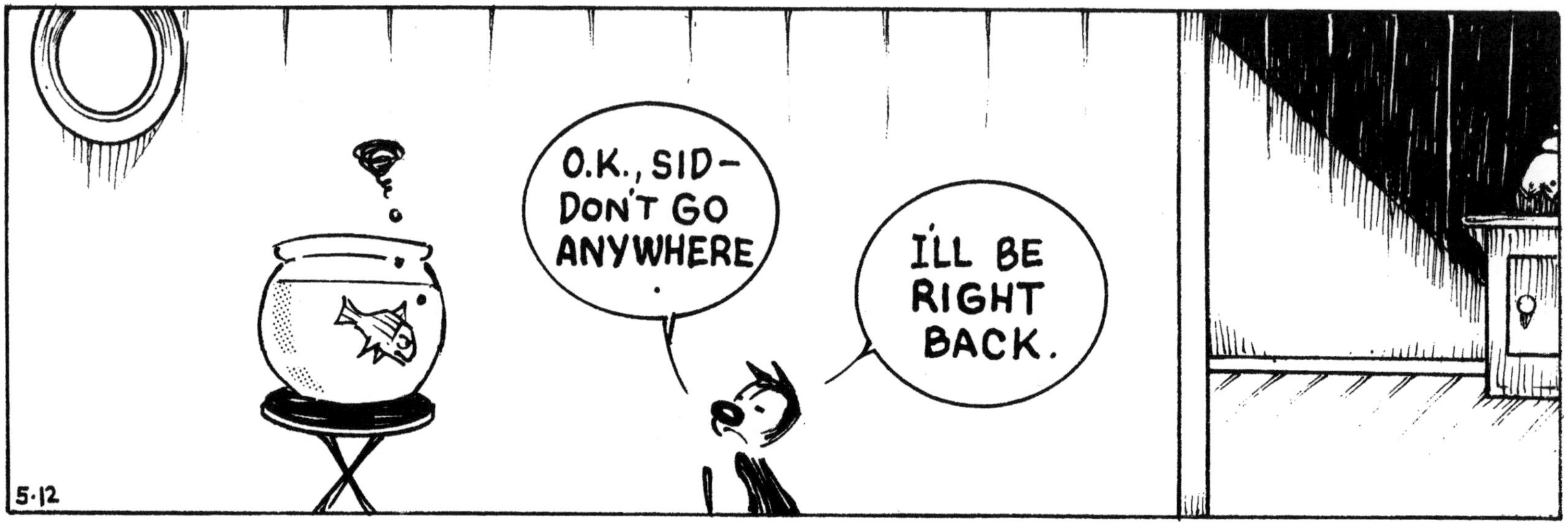
5·12
O.K., SID- DON'T GO ANYWHERE.
I'LL BE RIGHT BACK.

MUTTS
PATRICK McDONNELL

MOOCH!
YOU'RE GOING TO BE MY "SHOW AND TELL" TODAY!
ABCDEFGHIJKLMNOPQ
MEOW MEOW MEOW MEOW
MEOW MEOW
MEOW MEOW MEOW MEOW MEOW
MEOW MEOW MEOW
I TOLD THEM EVERYTHING.
5·27

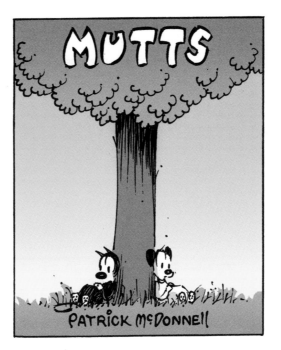

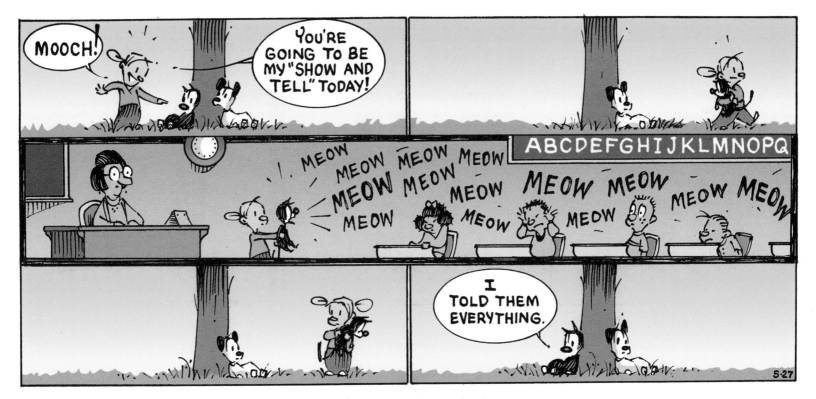

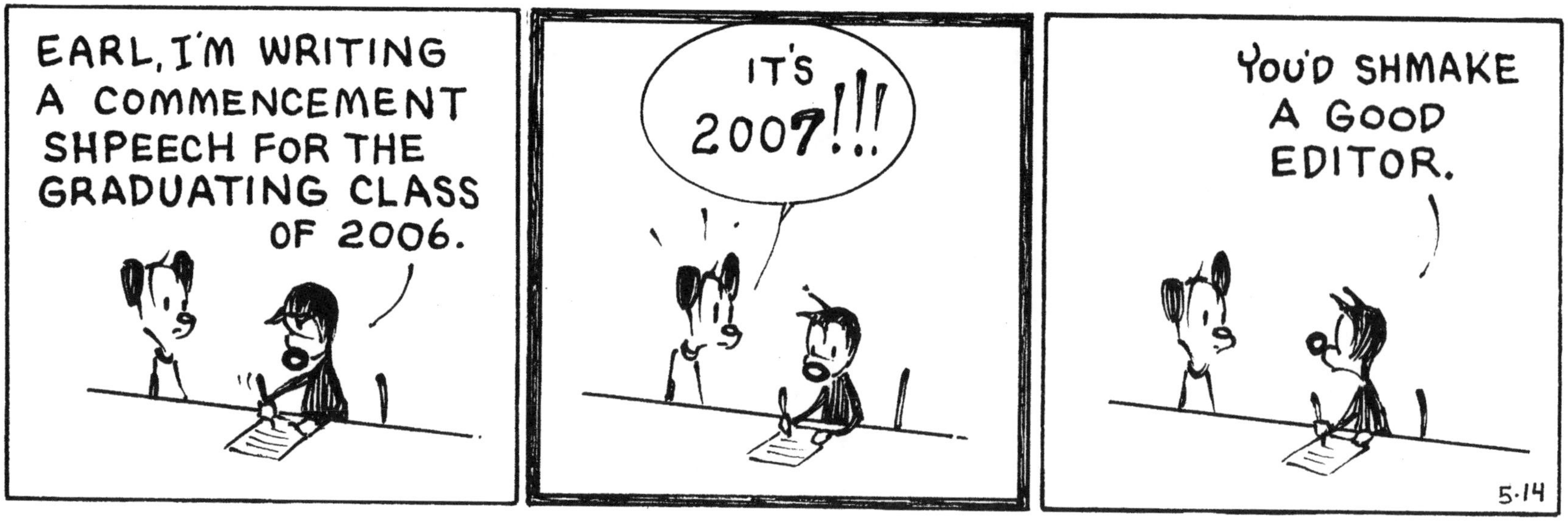

EARL, I'M WRITING A COMMENCEMENT SHPEECH FOR THE GRADUATING CLASS OF 2006.
IT'S 2007!!!
YOU'D SHMAKE A GOOD EDITOR.
5·14

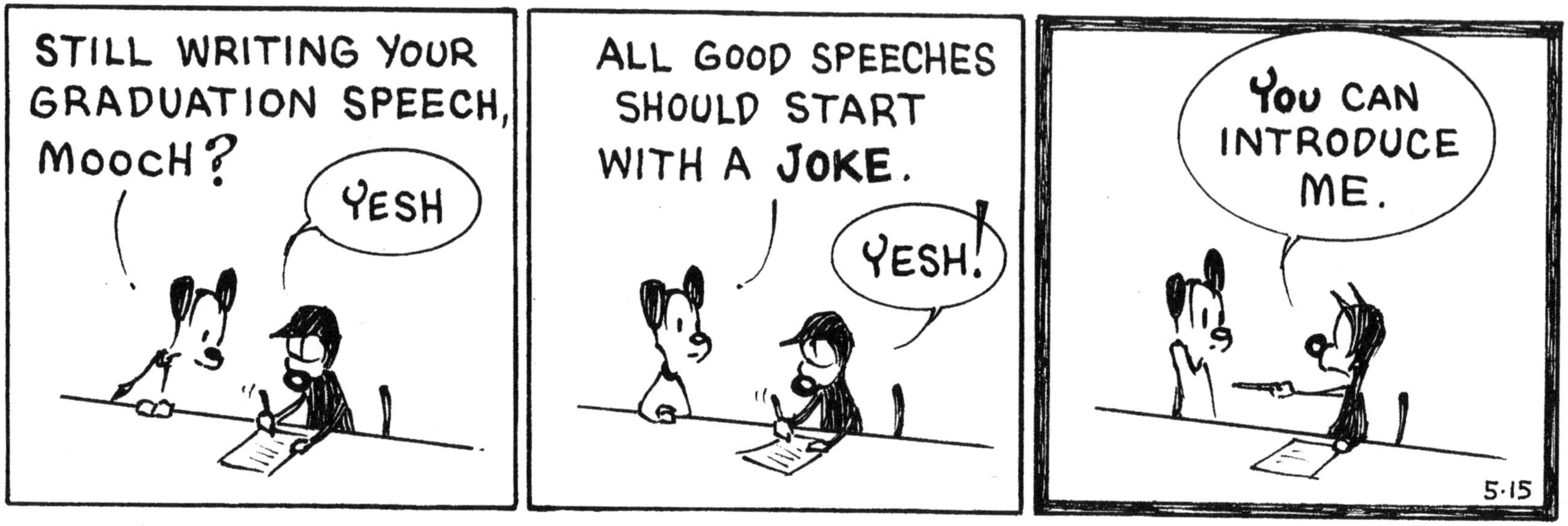

STILL WRITING YOUR GRADUATION SPEECH, MOOCH?
YESH
ALL GOOD SPEECHES SHOULD START WITH A JOKE.
YESH!
YOU CAN INTRODUCE ME.
5·15

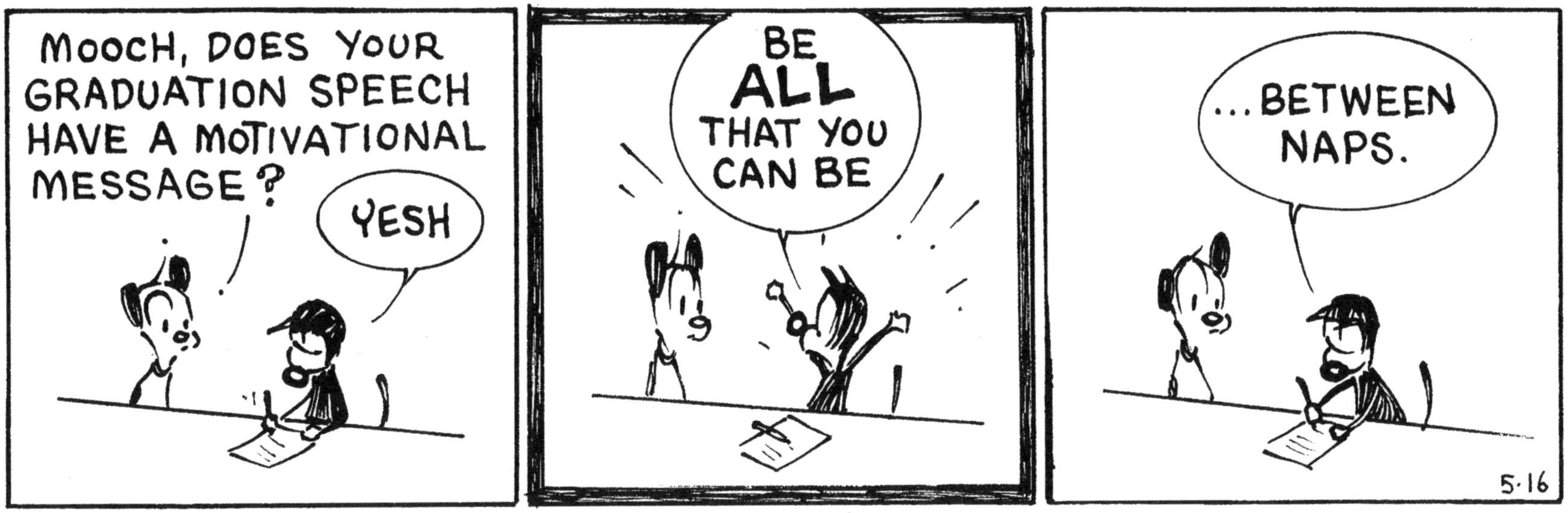
MOOCH, DOES YOUR GRADUATION SPEECH HAVE A MOTIVATIONAL MESSAGE?
YESH
BE ALL THAT YOU CAN BE
...BETWEEN NAPS.
5·16

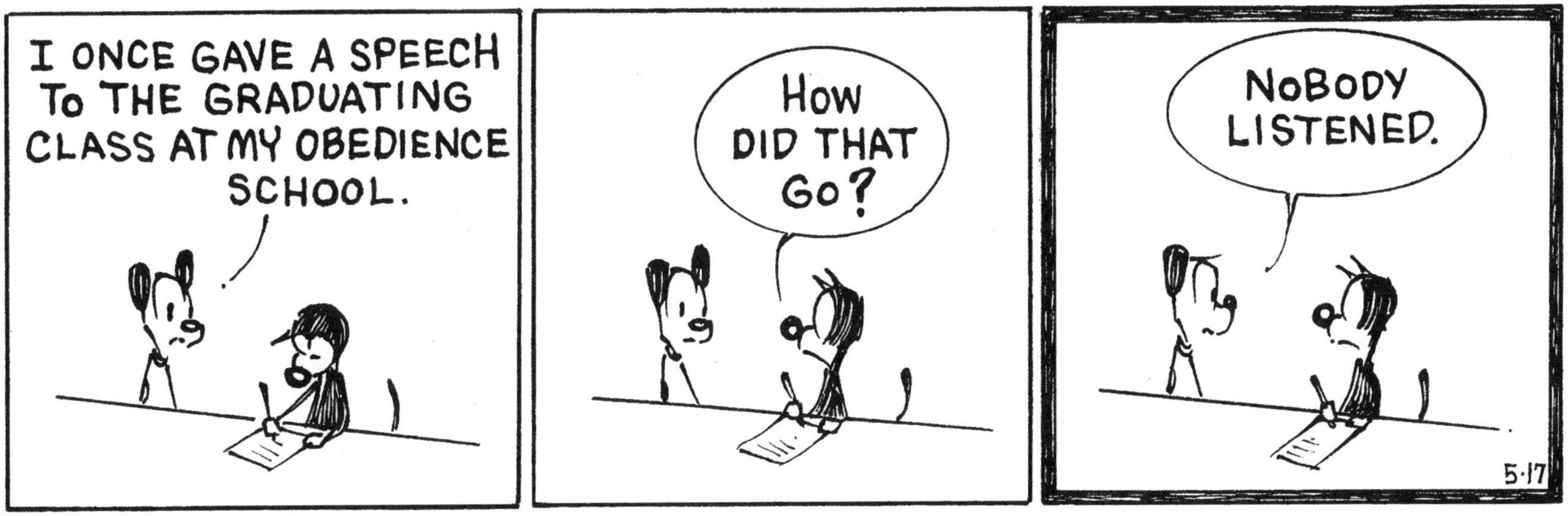
I ONCE GAVE A SPEECH TO THE GRADUATING CLASS AT MY OBEDIENCE SCHOOL.
HOW DID THAT GO?
NOBODY LISTENED.
5·17

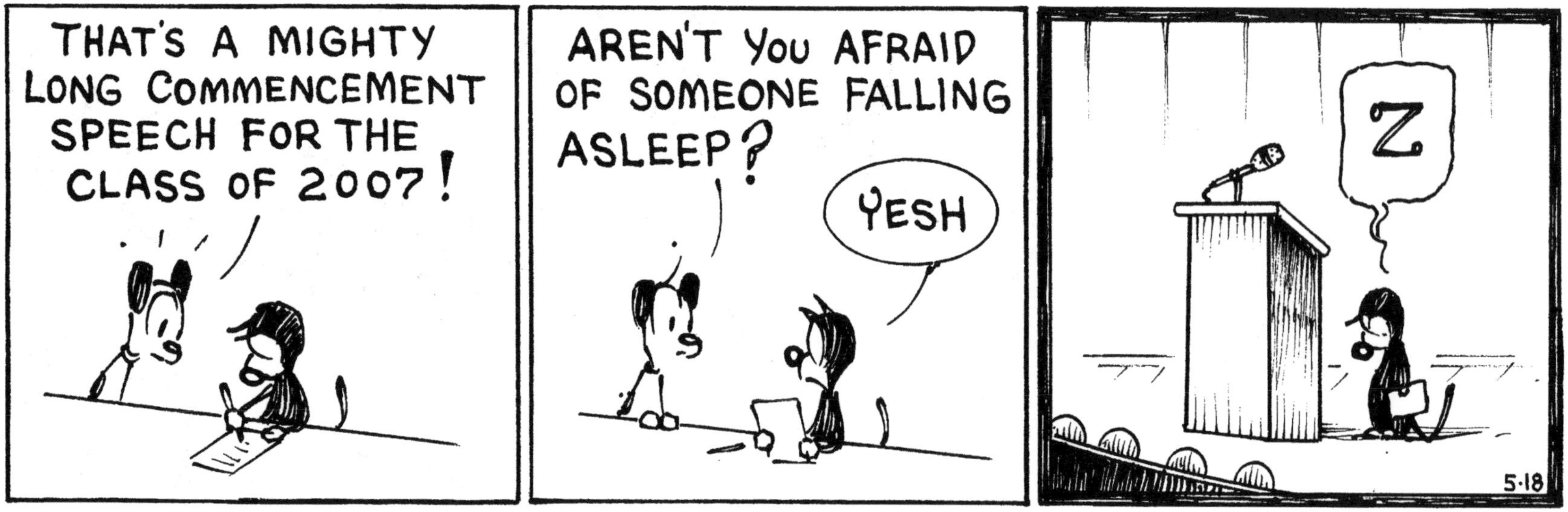
THAT'S A MIGHTY LONG COMMENCEMENT SPEECH FOR THE CLASS OF 2007!
AREN'T YOU AFRAID OF SOMEONE FALLING ASLEEP?
YESH
Z
5·18

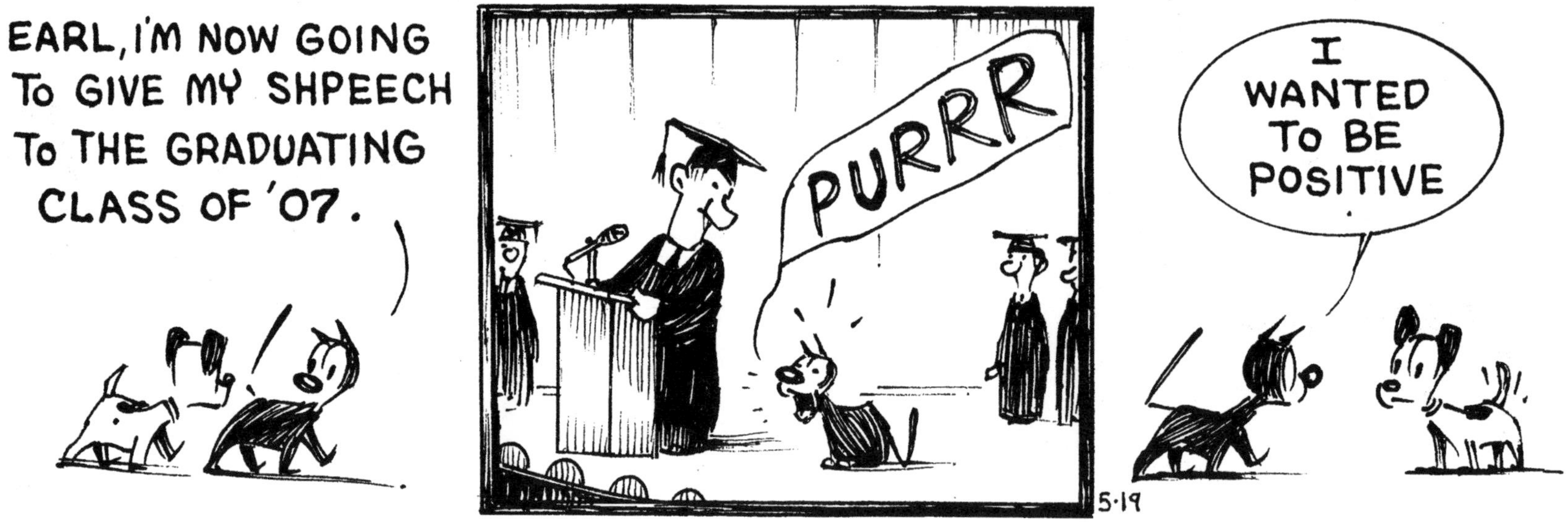
EARL, I'M NOW GOING TO GIVE MY SHPEECH TO THE GRADUATING CLASS OF '07.
PURRR
5·19
I WANTED TO BE POSITIVE

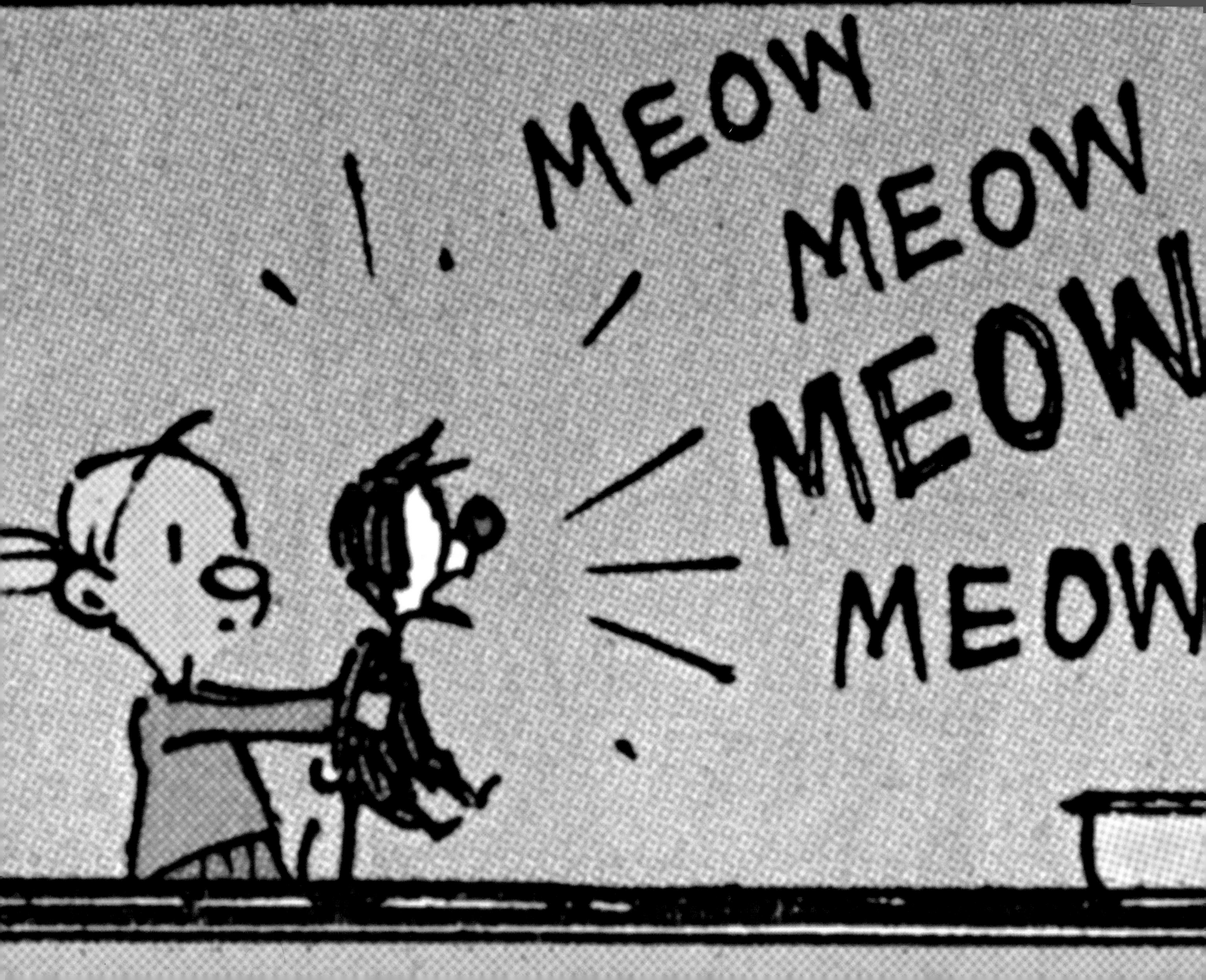
MEOW
MEOW
MEOW
MEOW

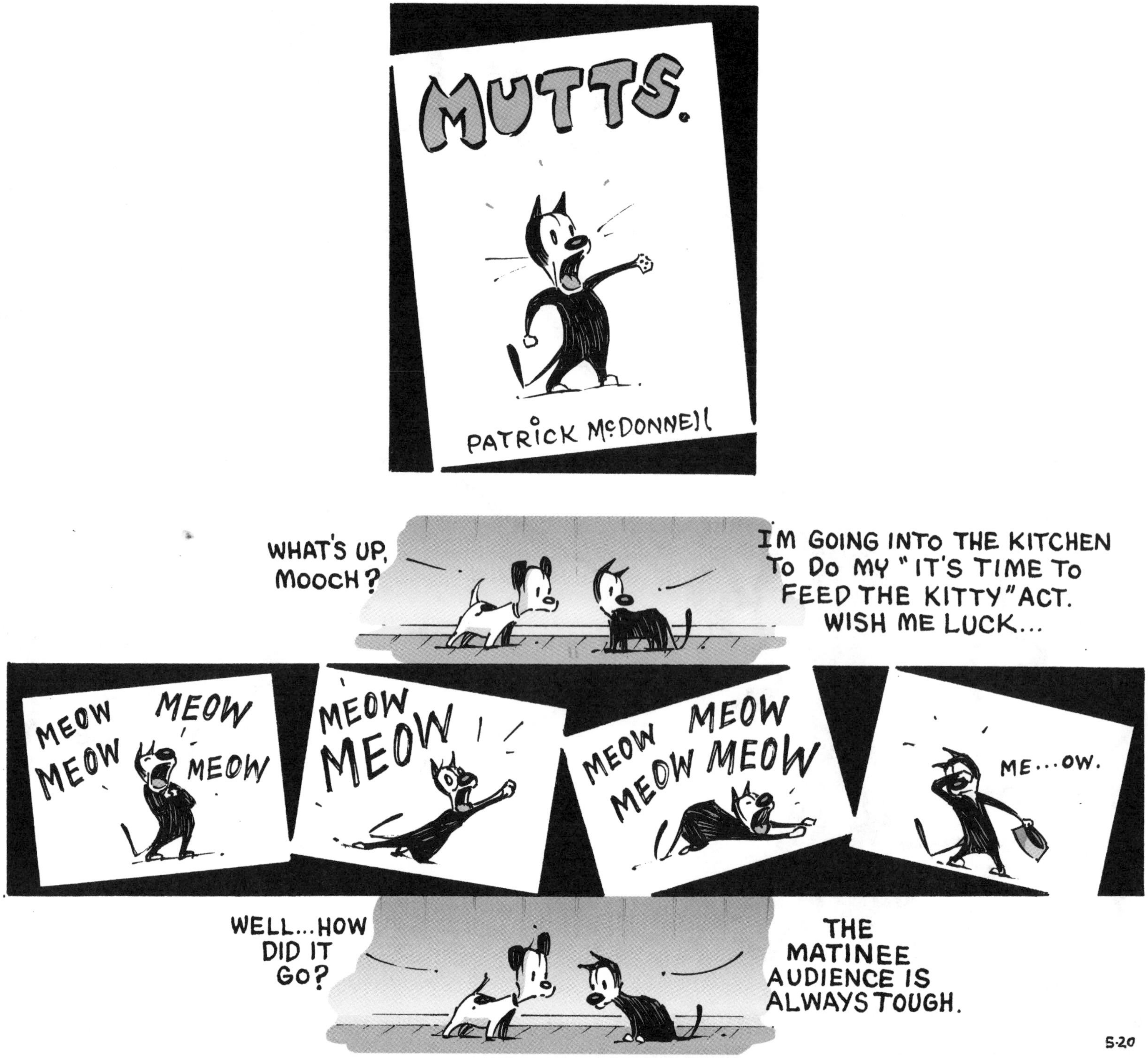
MUTTS.
PATRICK McDONNELL
WHAT'S UP, MOOCH?
I'M GOING INTO THE KITCHEN TO DO MY "IT'S TIME TO FEED THE KITTY" ACT. WISH ME LUCK...
MEOW MEOW MEOW MEOW
MEOW MEOW
MEOW MEOW MEOW MEOW
ME...OW.
WELL...HOW DID IT GO?
THE MATINEE AUDIENCE IS ALWAYS TOUGH.
5-20

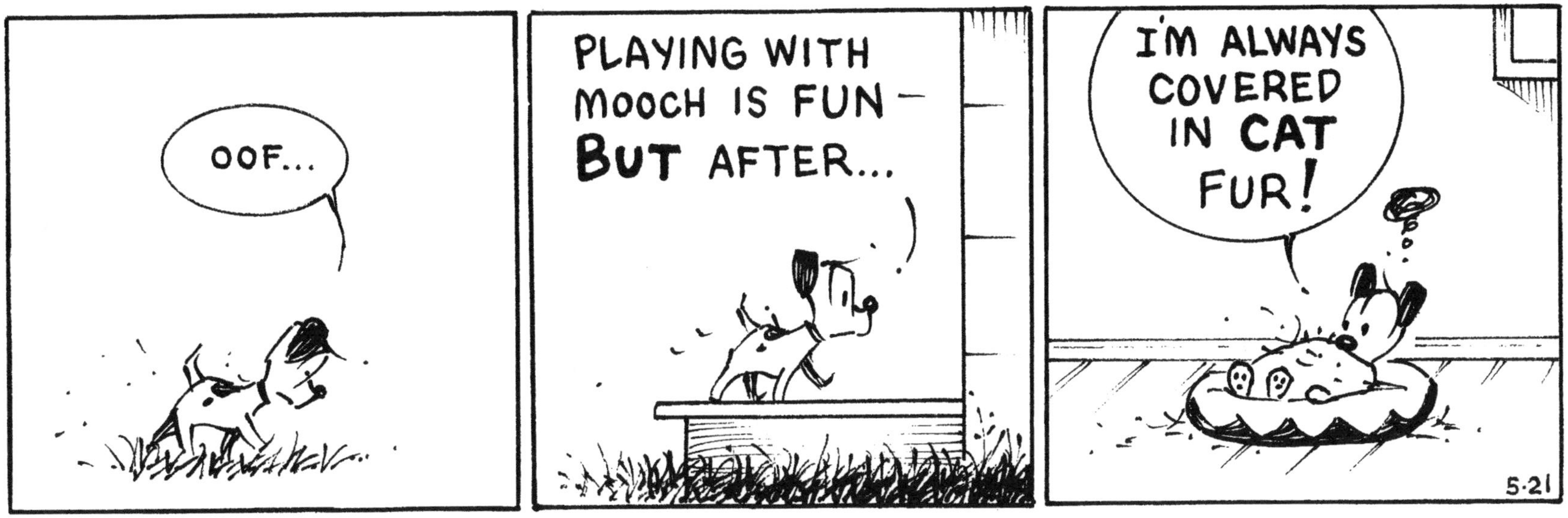
OOF...
PLAYING WITH MOOCH IS FUN – BUT AFTER...
I'M ALWAYS COVERED IN CAT FUR!
5·21

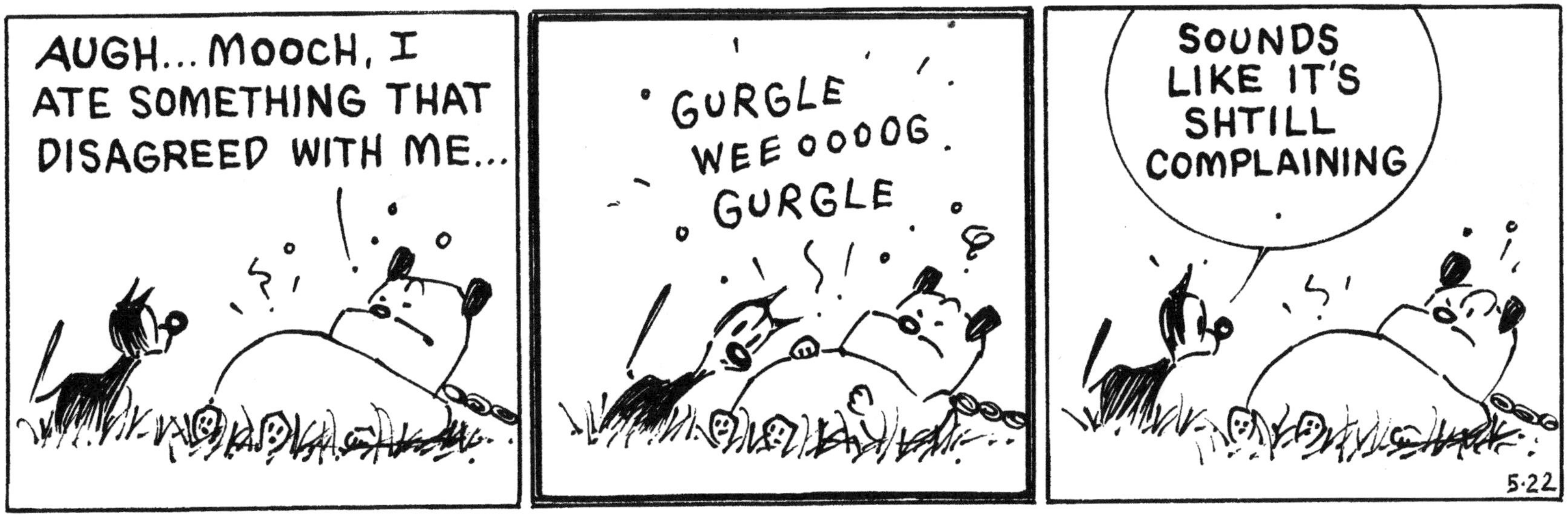
AUGH... MOOCH, I ATE SOMETHING THAT DISAGREED WITH ME...
GURGLE WEE OOOOG GURGLE
SOUNDS LIKE IT'S SHTILL COMPLAINING
5·22

I DON'T KNOW MY OWN STRENGTH.
5·25

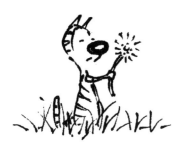

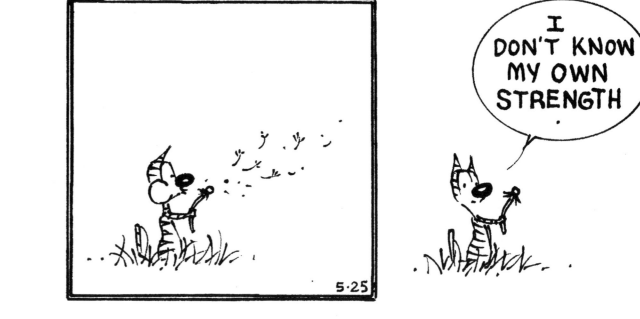

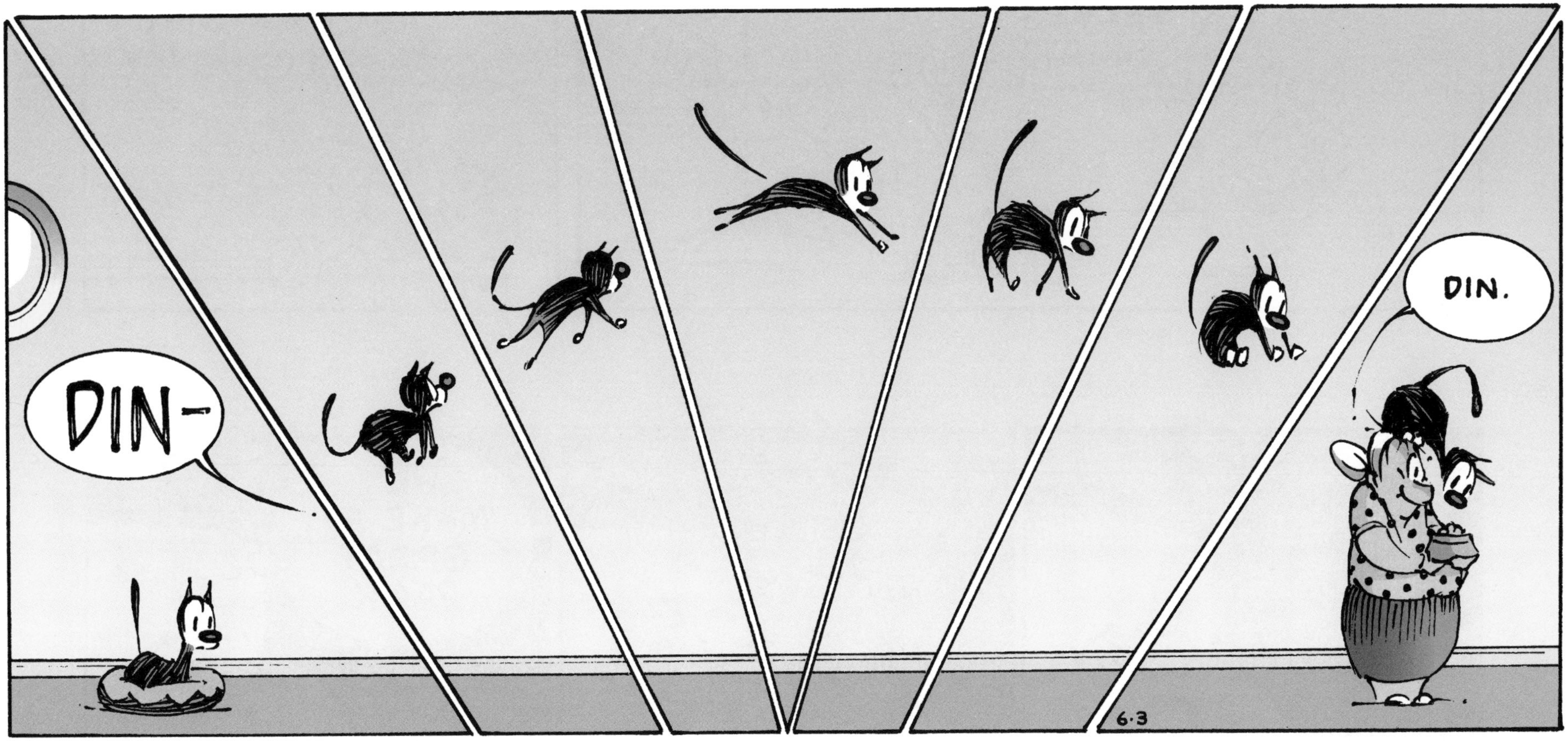
DIN-
DIN.
6·3

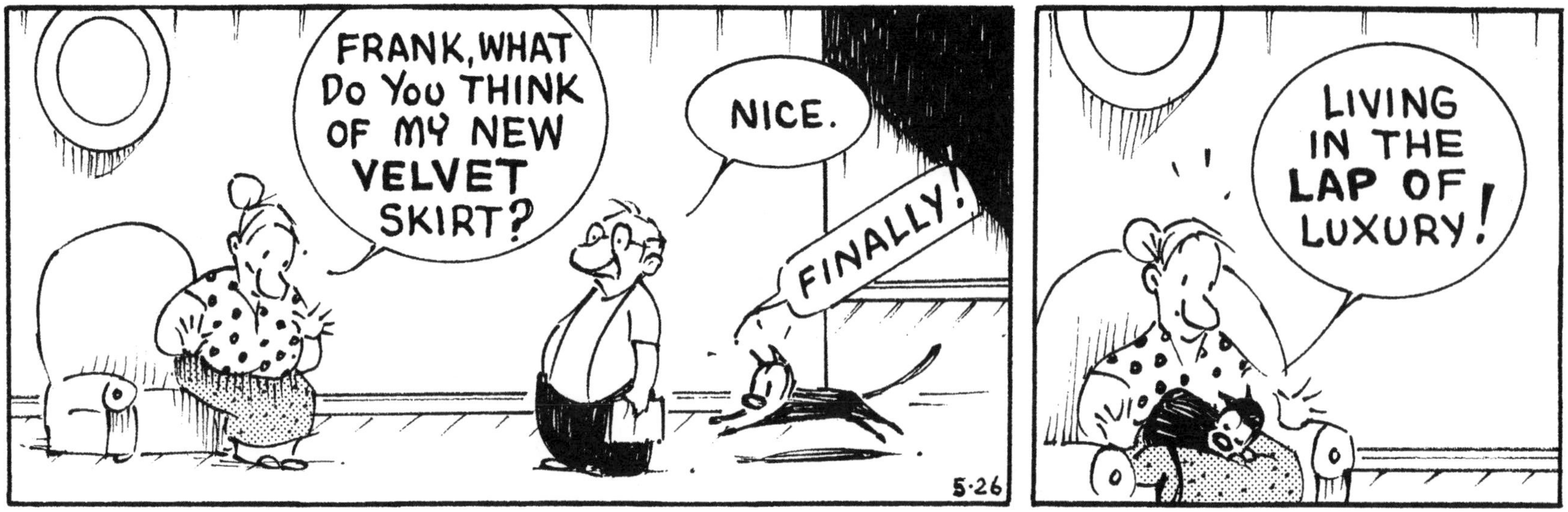
FRANK, WHAT DO YOU THINK OF MY NEW VELVET SKIRT?
NICE.
FINALLY!
LIVING IN THE LAP OF LUXURY!
5·26

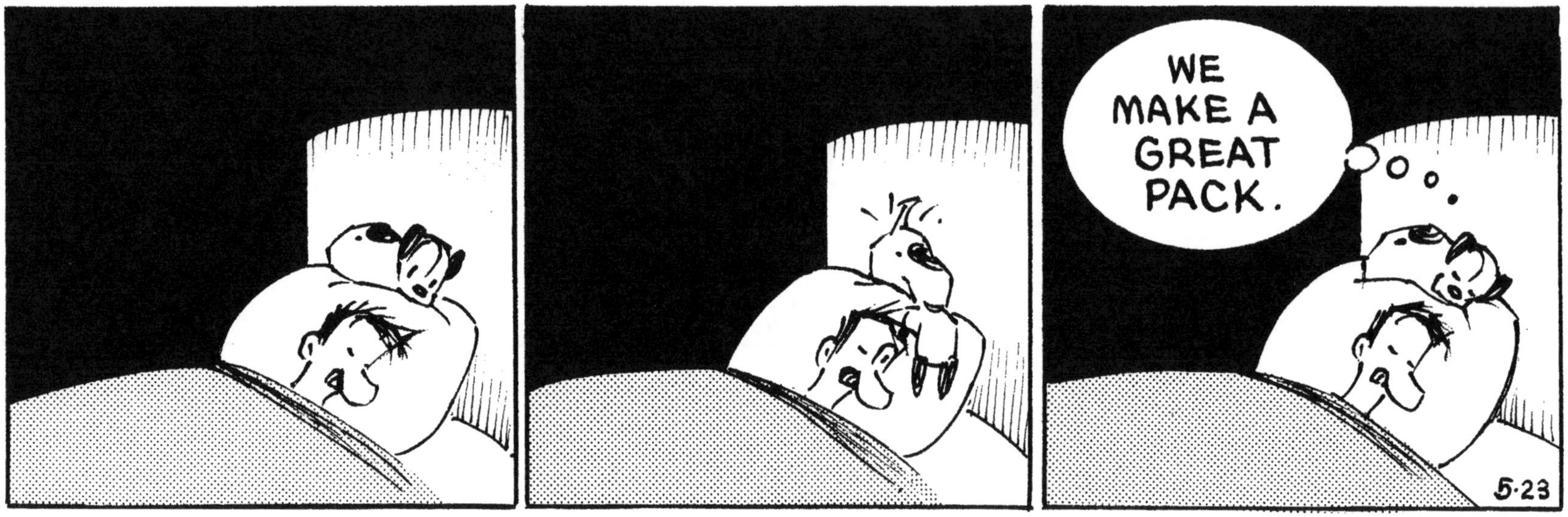
WE MAKE A GREAT PACK.
5·23

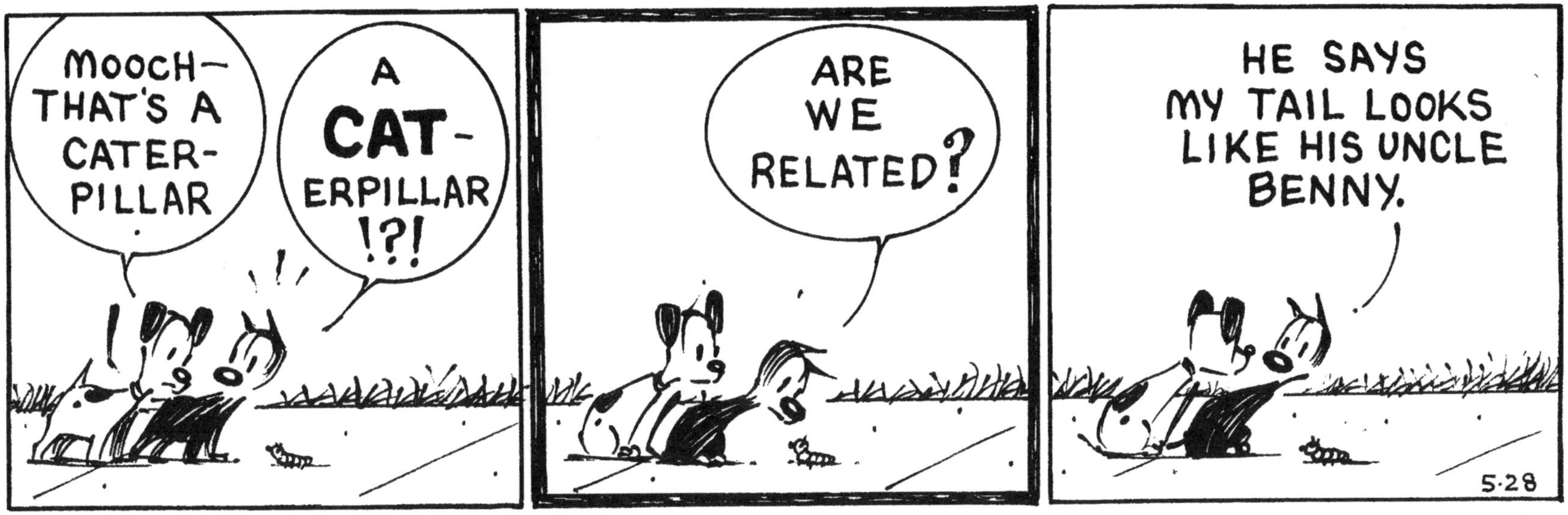
MOOCH— THAT'S A CATER-PILLAR
A CAT-ERPILLAR !?!
ARE WE RELATED?
HE SAYS MY TAIL LOOKS LIKE HIS UNCLE BENNY.
5·28

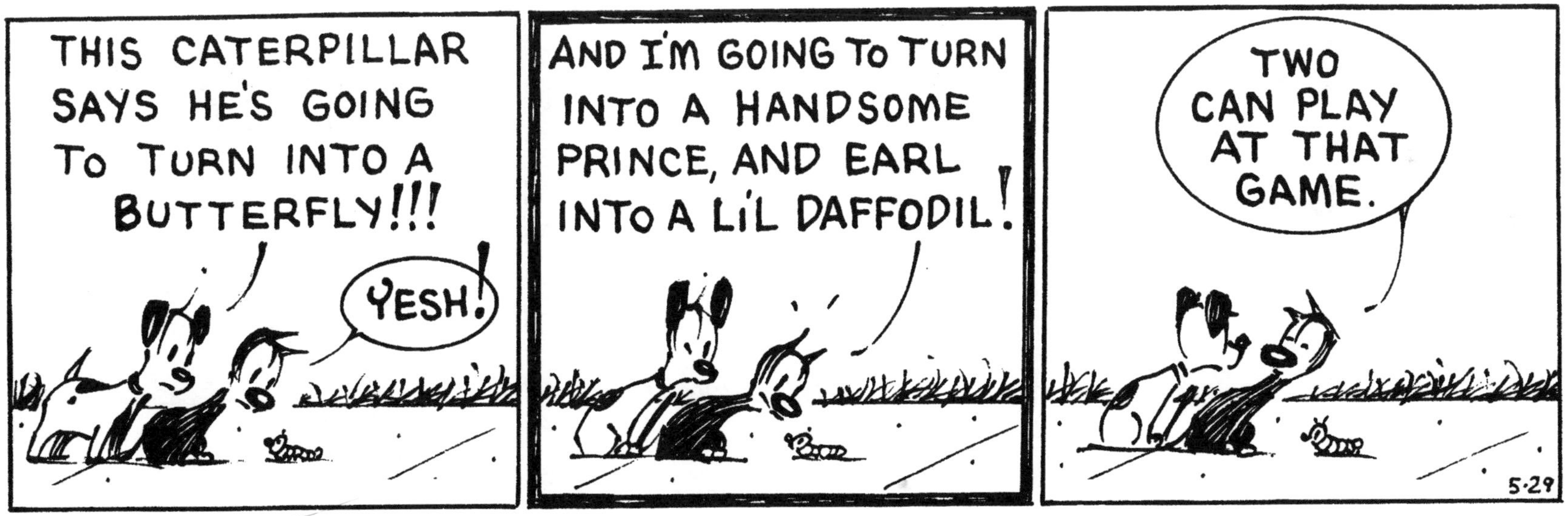
THIS CATERPILLAR SAYS HE'S GOING TO TURN INTO A BUTTERFLY!!!
YESH!
AND I'M GOING TO TURN INTO A HANDSOME PRINCE, AND EARL INTO A LI'L DAFFODIL!
TWO CAN PLAY AT THAT GAME.
5·29

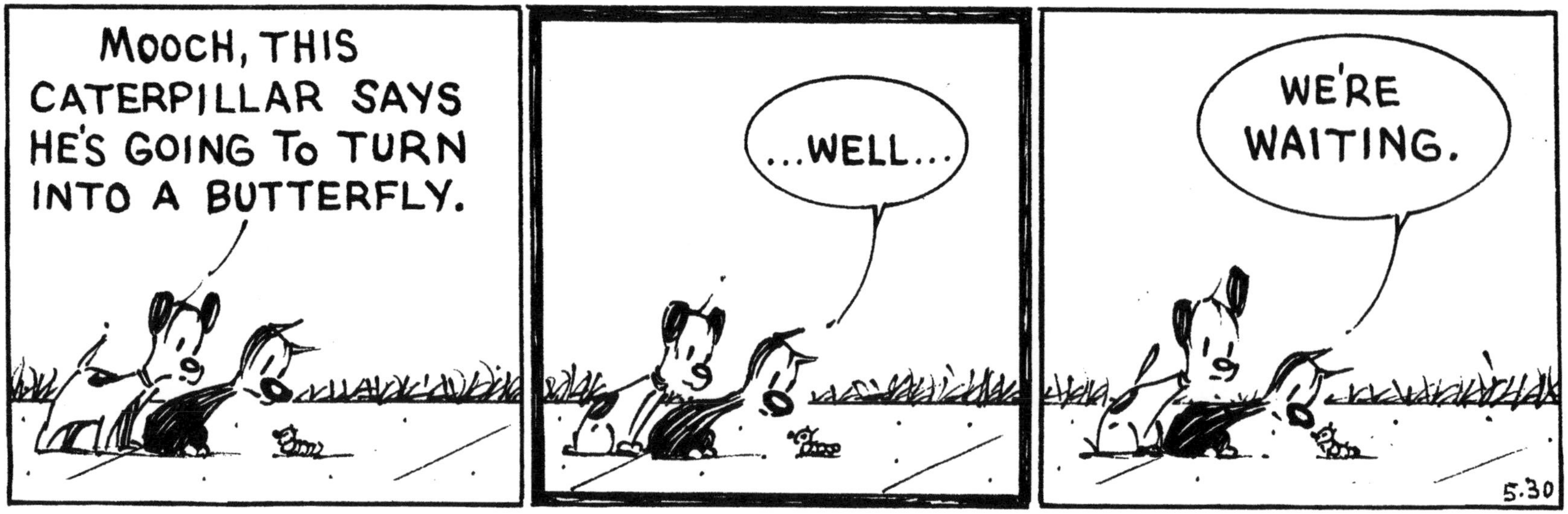
MOOCH, THIS CATERPILLAR SAYS HE'S GOING TO TURN INTO A BUTTERFLY.
...WELL...
WE'RE WAITING.
5.30

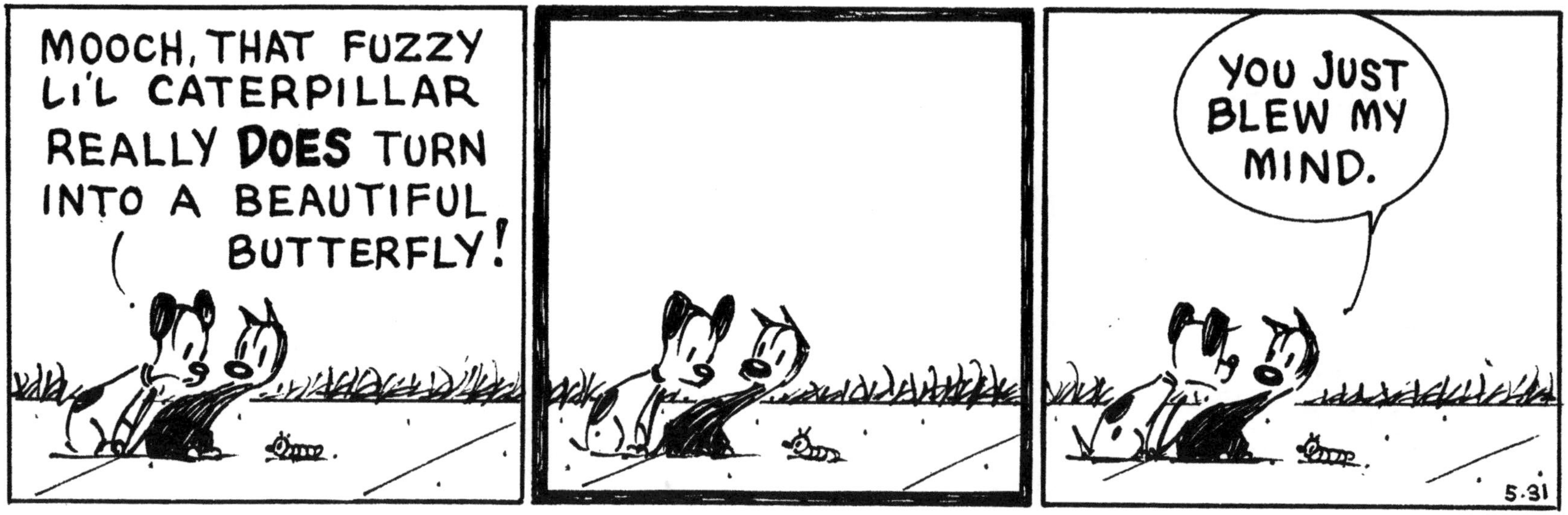
MOOCH, THAT FUZZY LI'L CATERPILLAR REALLY **DOES** TURN INTO A BEAUTIFUL BUTTERFLY!
YOU JUST BLEW MY MIND.
5.31

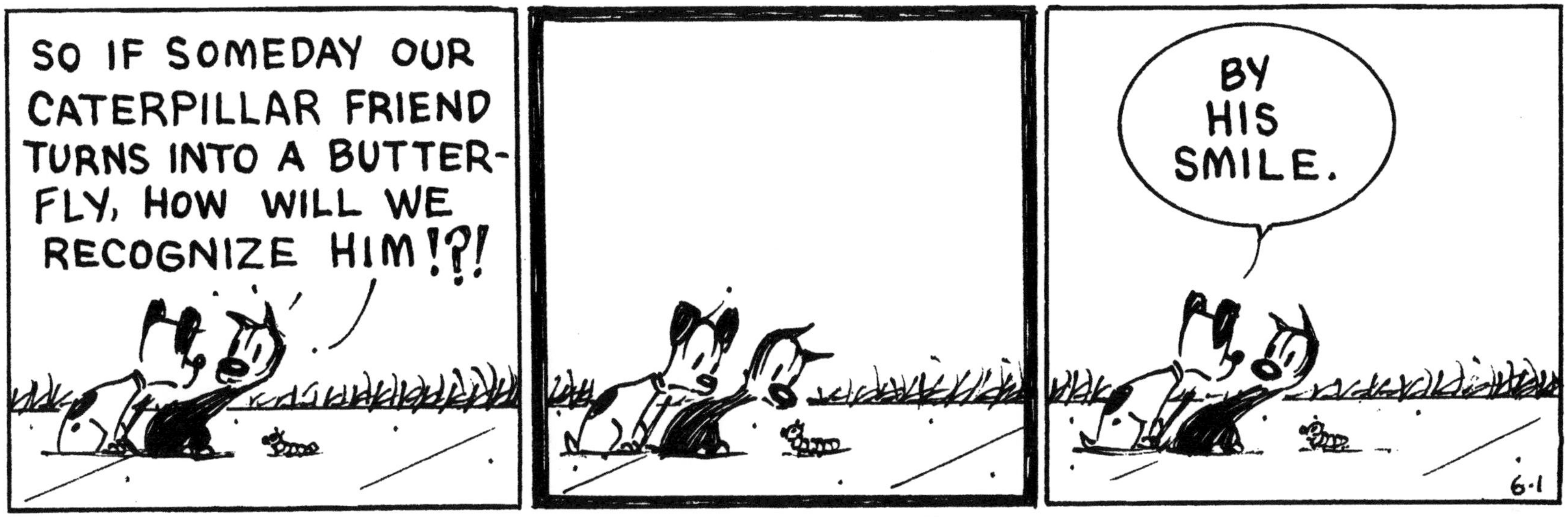
SO IF SOMEDAY OUR CATERPILLAR FRIEND TURNS INTO A BUTTER-FLY, HOW WILL WE RECOGNIZE HIM!?!
BY HIS SMILE.
6·1

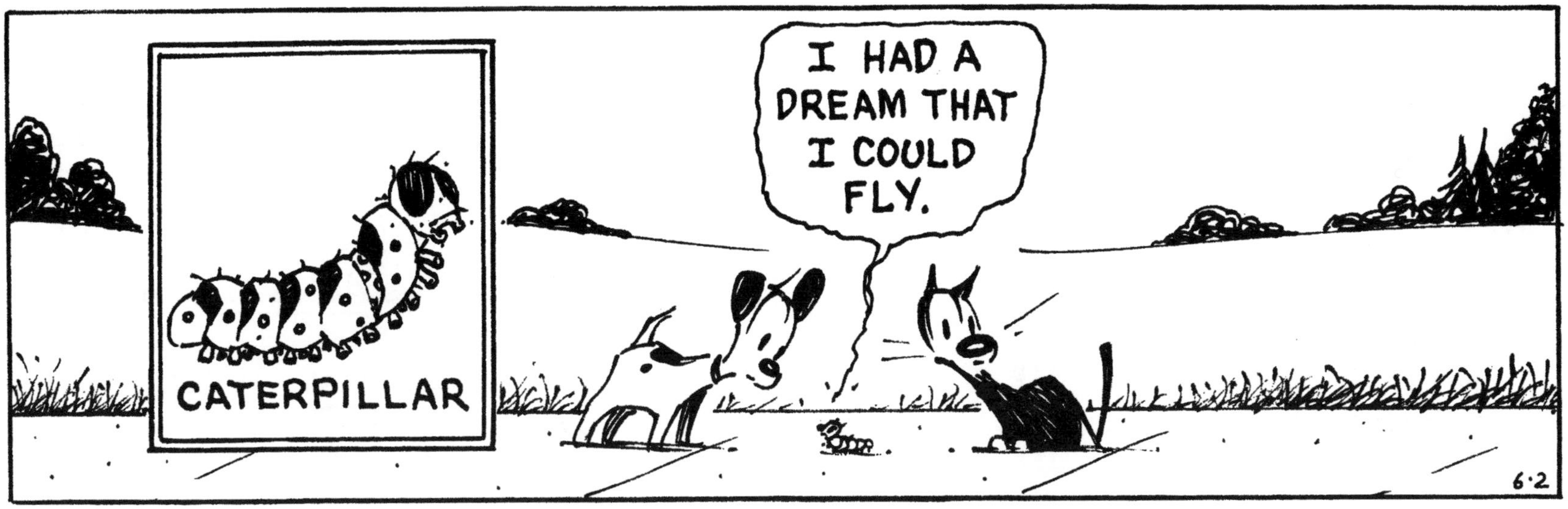
CATERPILLAR
I HAD A DREAM THAT I COULD FLY.
6·2

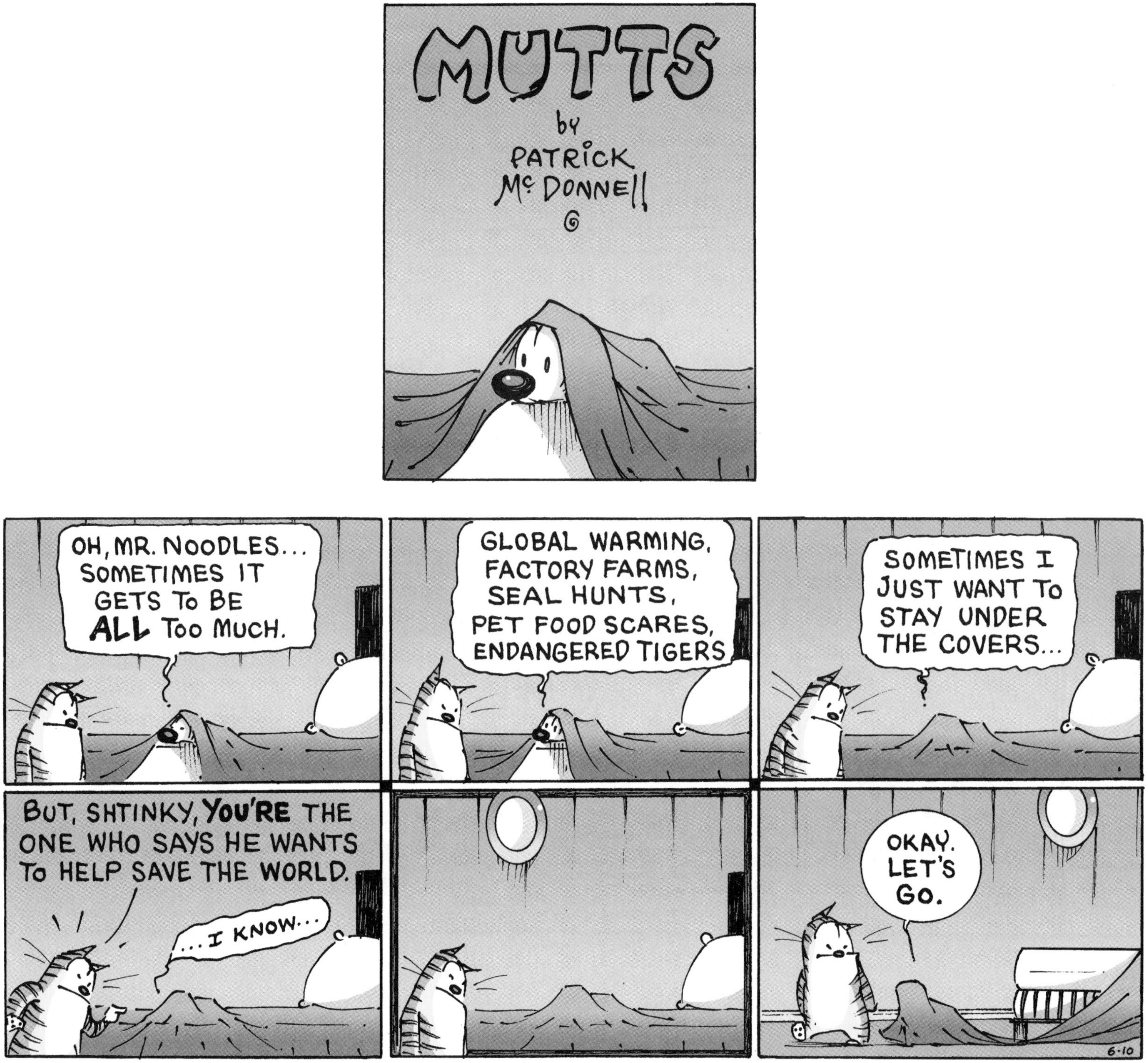
MUTTS
by
PATRICK
McDONNELL
OH, MR. NOODLES... SOMETIMES IT GETS TO BE ALL TOO MUCH.
GLOBAL WARMING, FACTORY FARMS, SEAL HUNTS, PET FOOD SCARES, ENDANGERED TIGERS
SOMETIMES I JUST WANT TO STAY UNDER THE COVERS...
BUT, SHTINKY, YOU'RE THE ONE WHO SAYS HE WANTS TO HELP SAVE THE WORLD.
...I KNOW...
OKAY. LET'S GO.
6-10

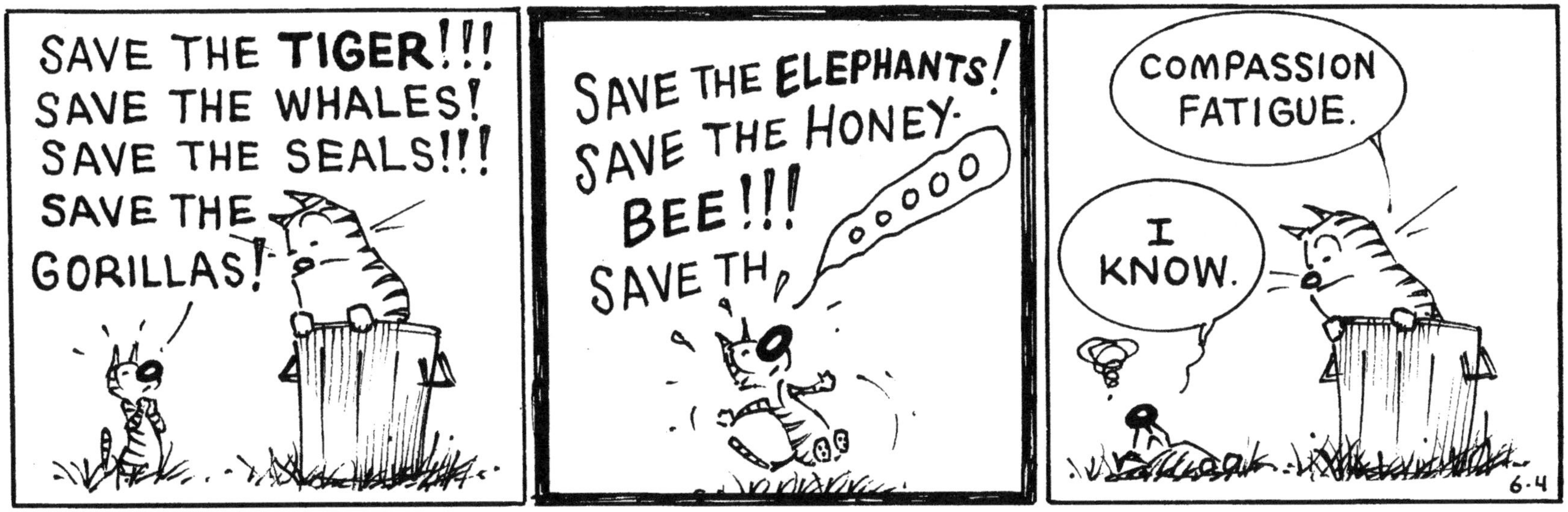
SAVE THE TIGER!!! SAVE THE WHALES! SAVE THE SEALS!!! SAVE THE GORILLAS!
SAVE THE ELEPHANTS! SAVE THE HONEY-BEE!!! SAVE TH
OOOOO
COMPASSION FATIGUE.
I KNOW.
6·4

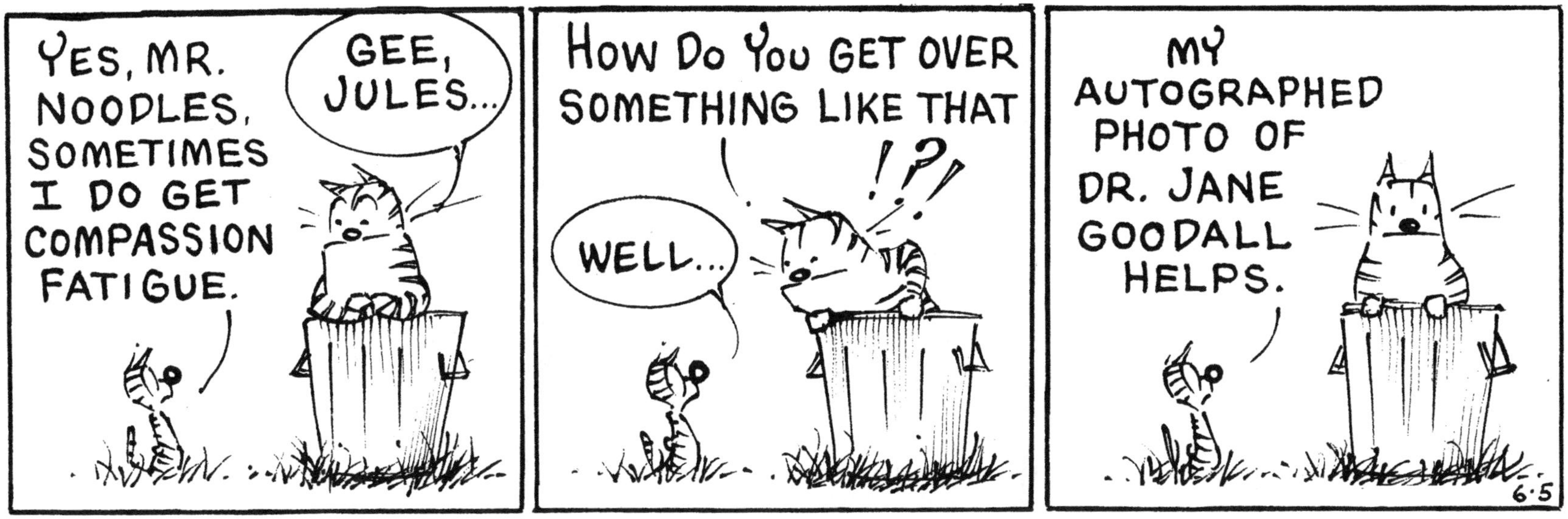
GEE, JULES...
YES, MR. NOODLES, SOMETIMES I DO GET COMPASSION FATIGUE.
HOW DO YOU GET OVER SOMETHING LIKE THAT
!?!
WELL...
MY AUTOGRAPHED PHOTO OF DR. JANE GOODALL HELPS.
6·5

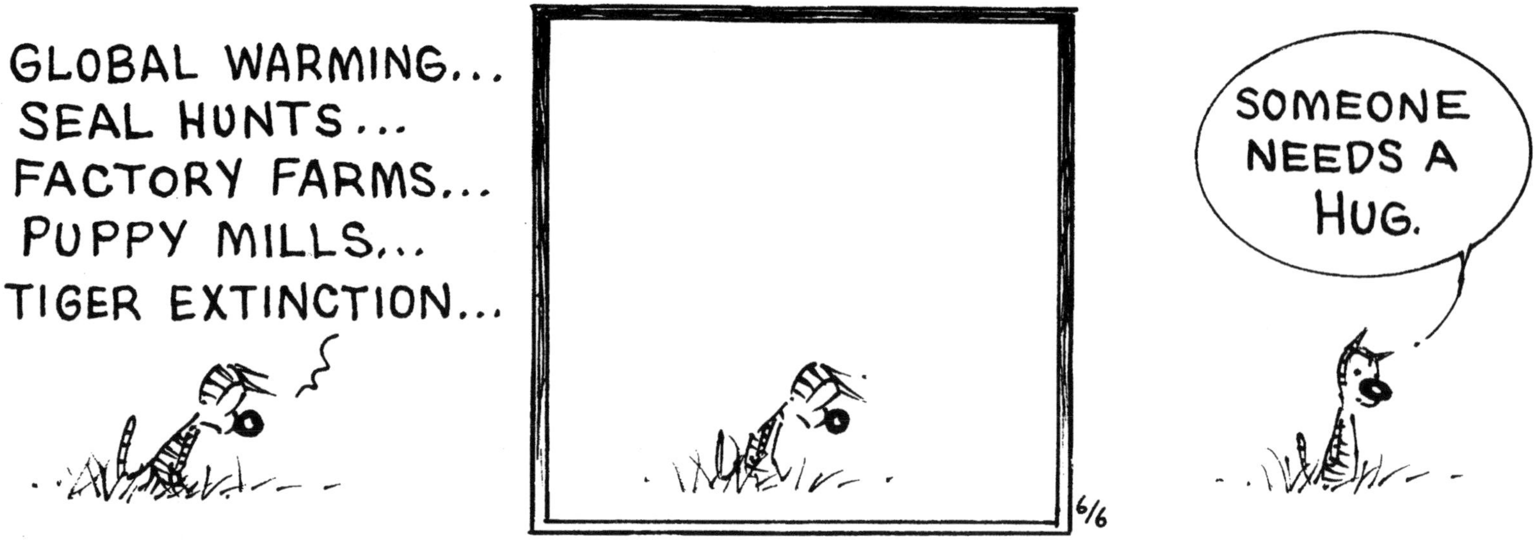
GLOBAL WARMING...
SEAL HUNTS...
FACTORY FARMS...
PUPPY MILLS...
TIGER EXTINCTION...
SOMEONE NEEDS A HUG.
6/6

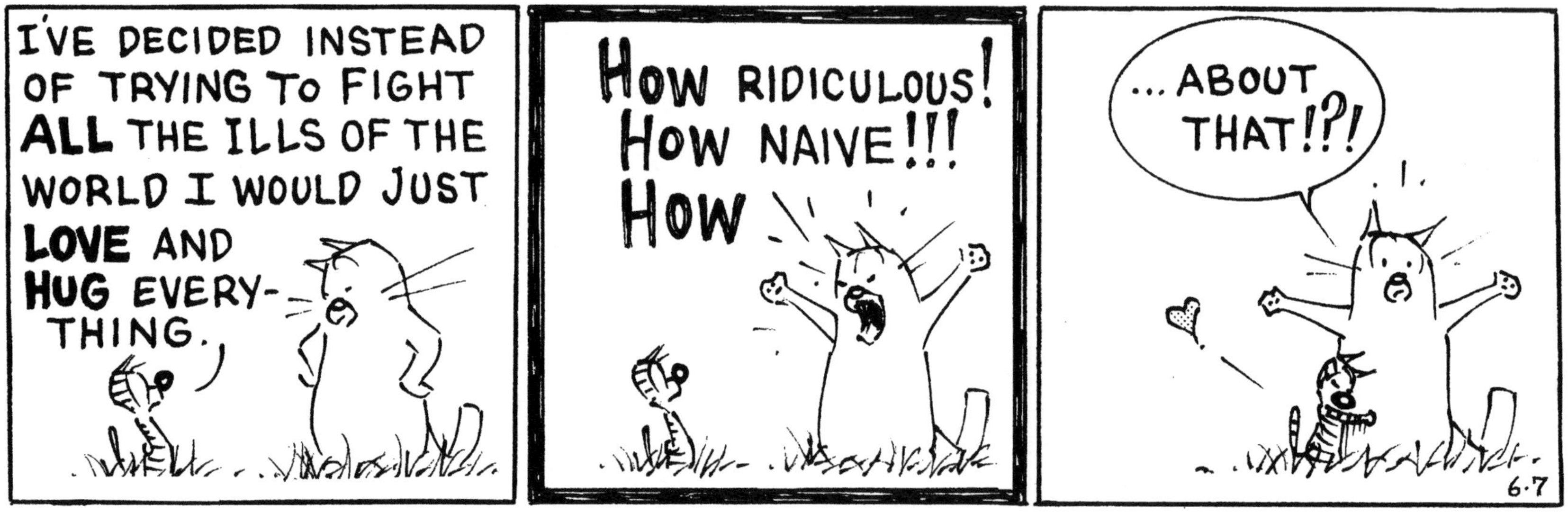
I'VE DECIDED INSTEAD OF TRYING TO FIGHT ALL THE ILLS OF THE WORLD I WOULD JUST LOVE AND HUG EVERY-THING.
HOW RIDICULOUS! HOW NAIVE!!! HOW
...ABOUT THAT!?!
6·7

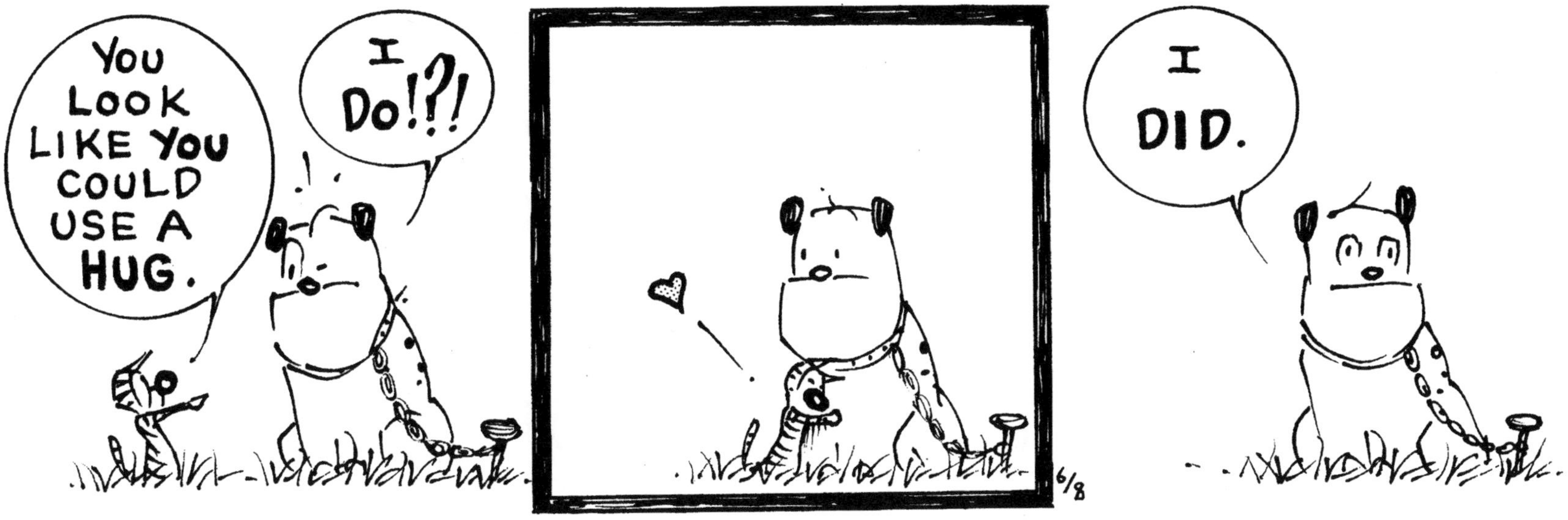
YOU LOOK LIKE YOU COULD USE A HUG.
I DO!?!
I DID.
6/8

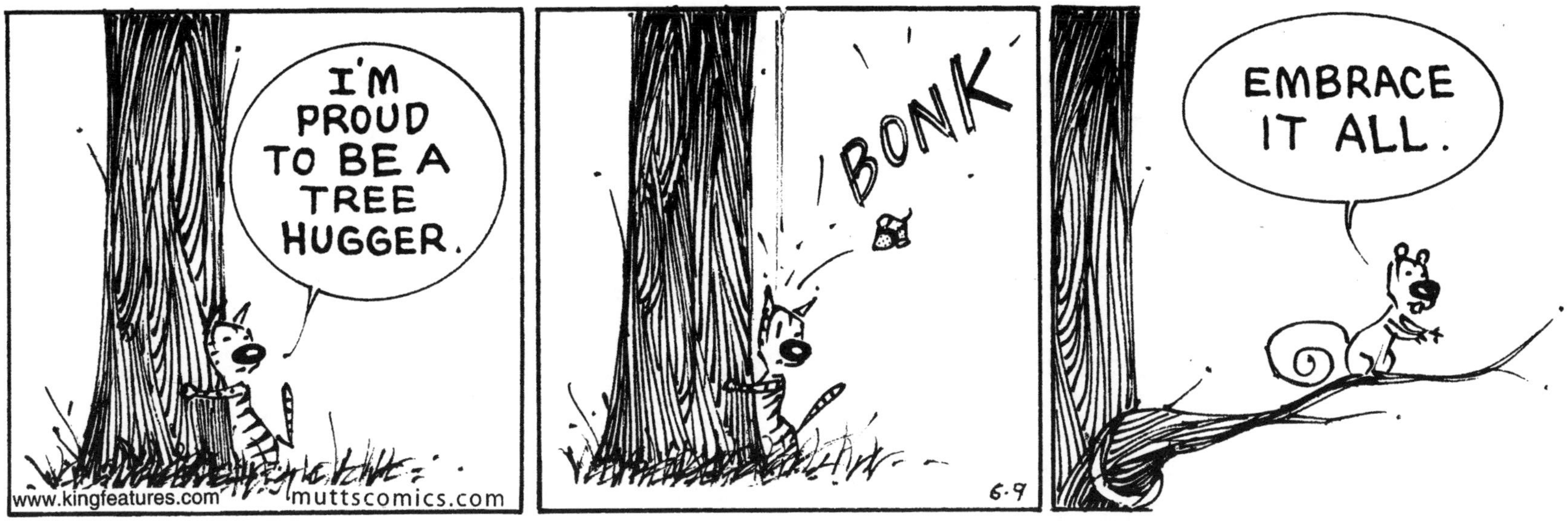
I'M PROUD TO BE A TREE HUGGER.
www.kingfeatures.com
muttscomics.com
BONK
6-9
EMBRACE IT ALL.

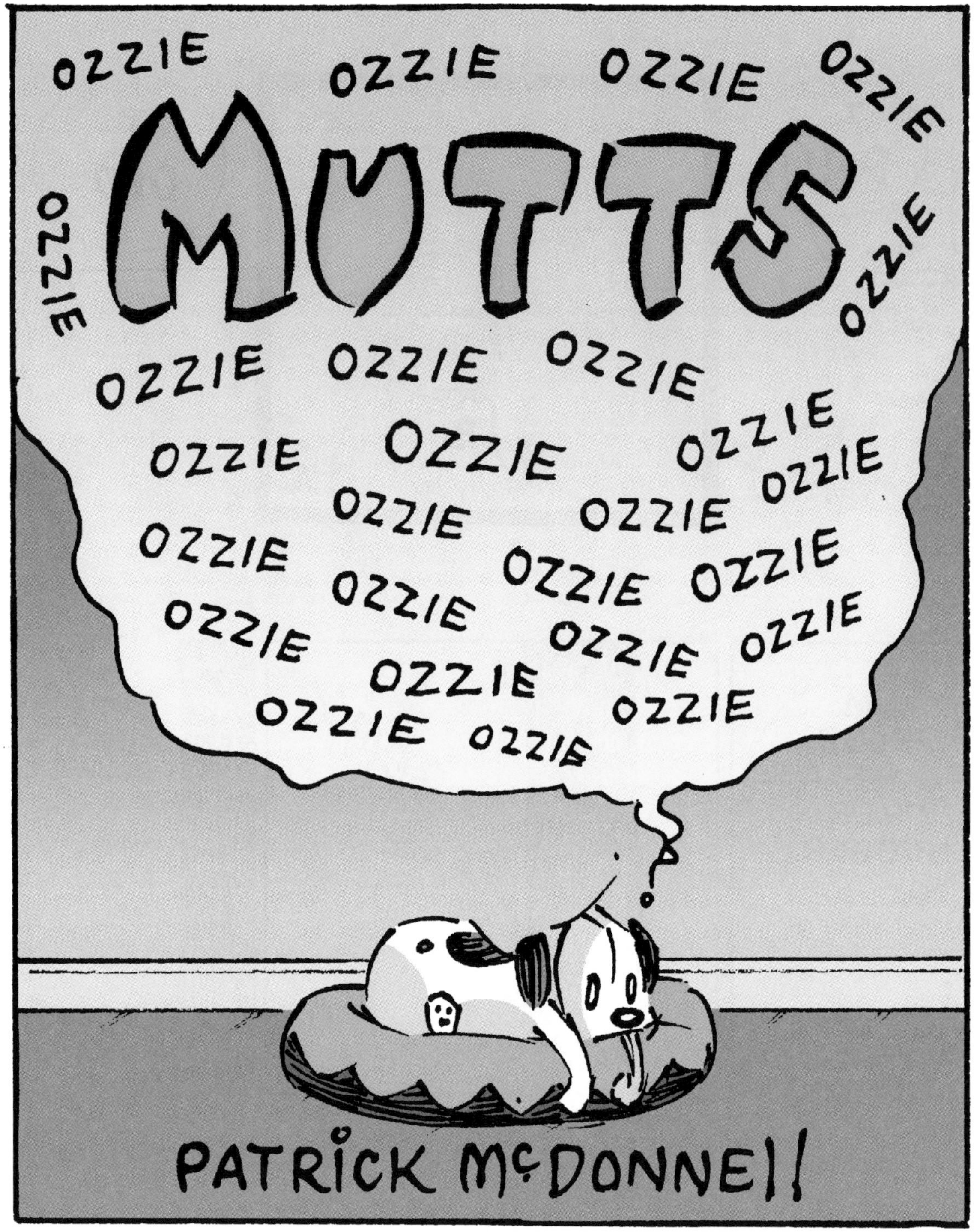
OZZIE OZZIE OZZIE OZZIE
MUTTS
OZZIE OZZIE
OZZIE OZZIE OZZIE
OZZIE OZZIE OZZIE
OZZIE OZZIE OZZIE
OZZIE OZZIE OZZIE
OZZIE OZZIE OZZIE OZZIE
OZZIE OZZIE
OZZIE OZZIE
PATRICK McDONNELL

99

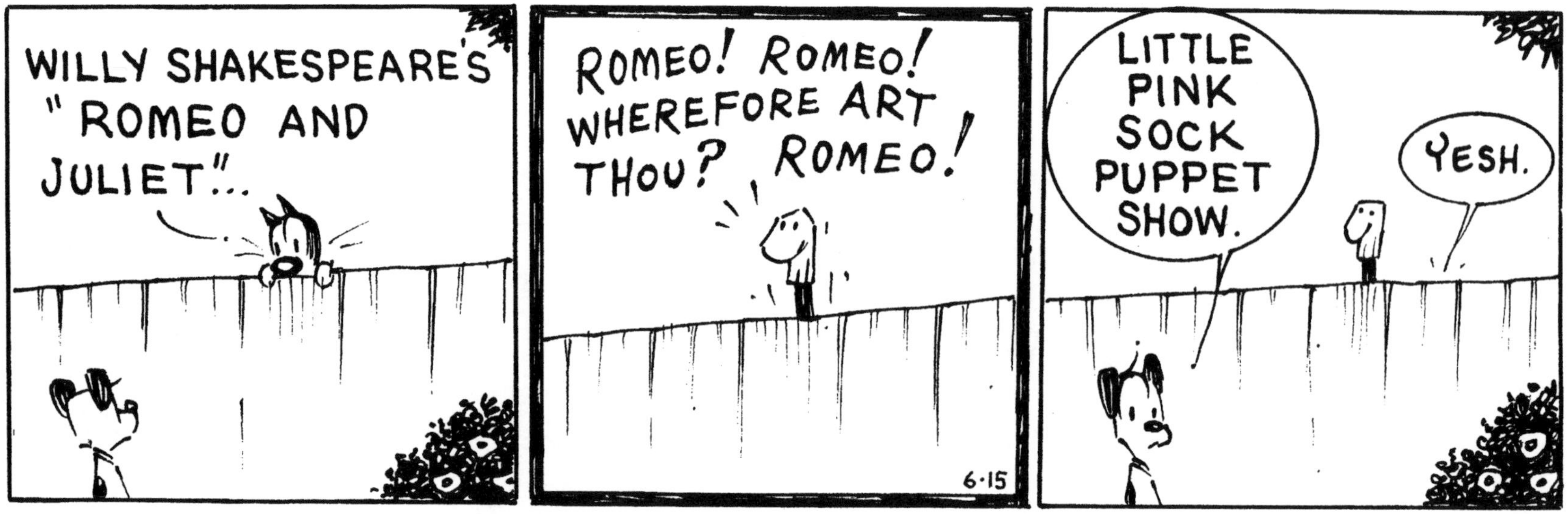
WILLY SHAKESPEARE'S "ROMEO AND JULIET"!...
ROMEO! ROMEO! WHEREFORE ART THOU? ROMEO!
6·15
LITTLE PINK SOCK PUPPET SHOW.
YESH.

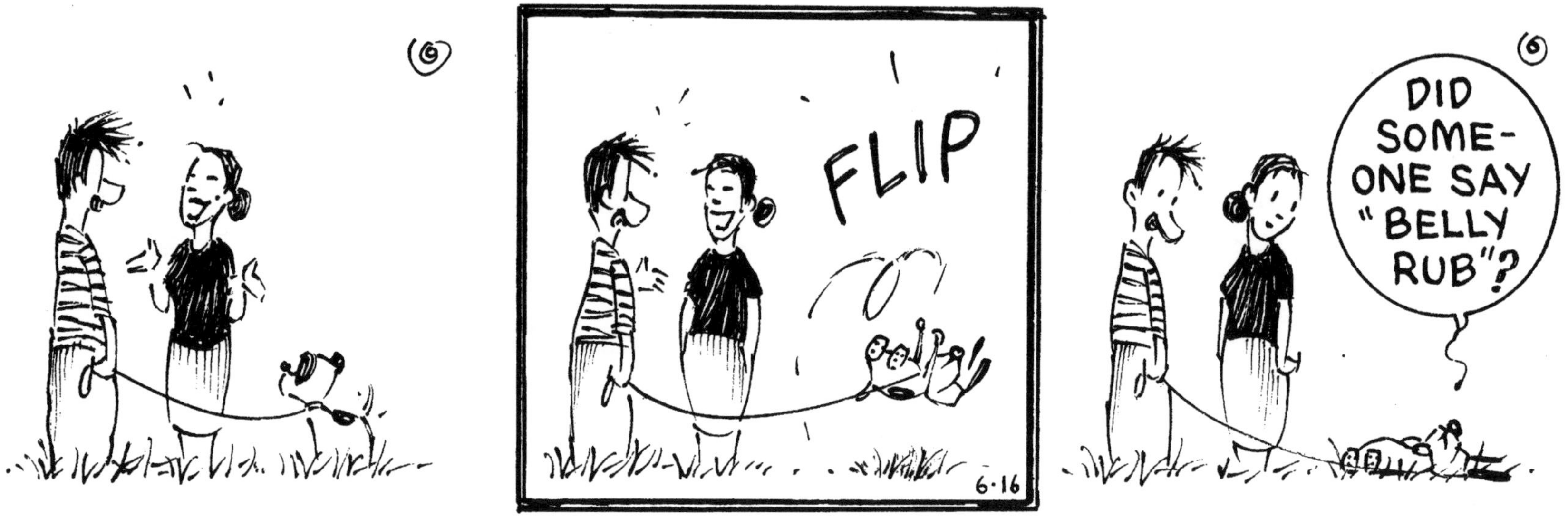
FLIP
6·16
DID SOME-ONE SAY "BELLY RUB"?

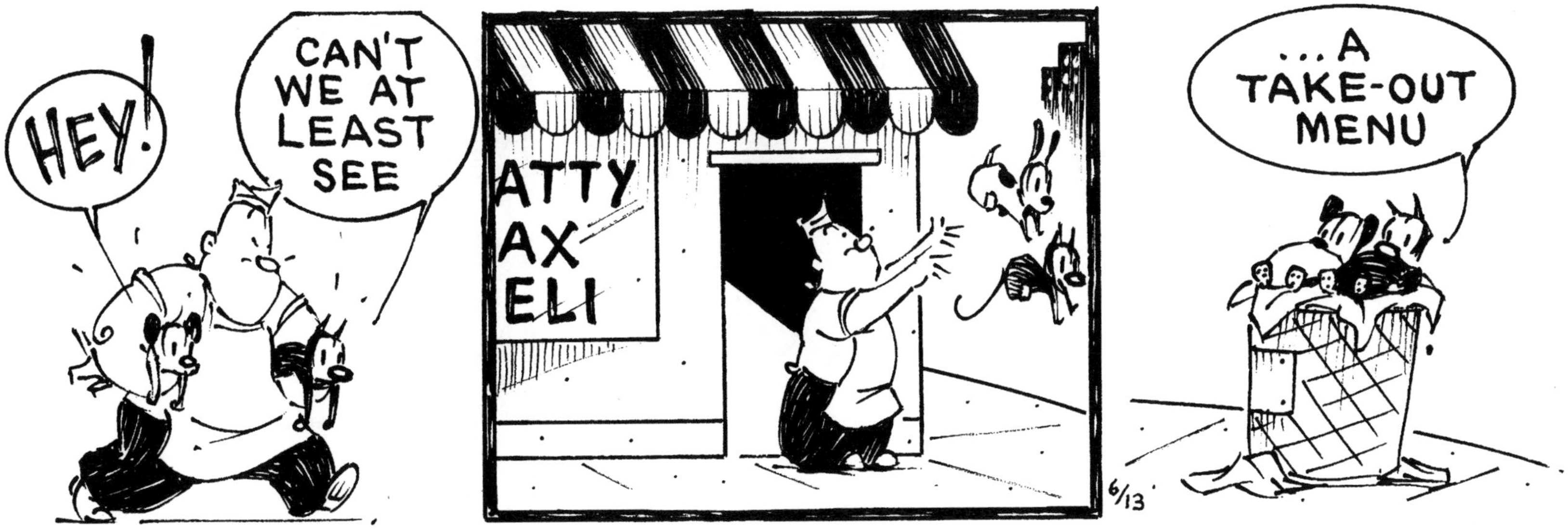
HEY!
CAN'T WE AT LEAST SEE
ATTY
AX
ELI
...A TAKE-OUT MENU
6/13

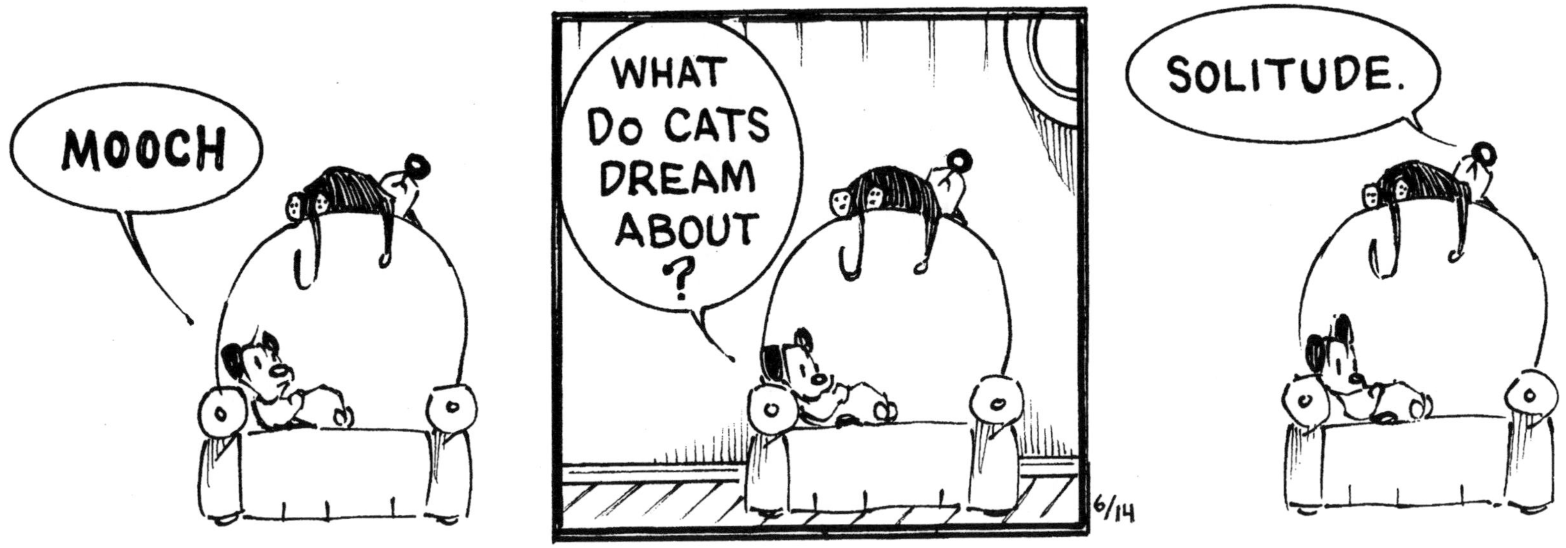
MOOCH
WHAT Do CATS DREAM ABOUT?
SOLITUDE.
6/14

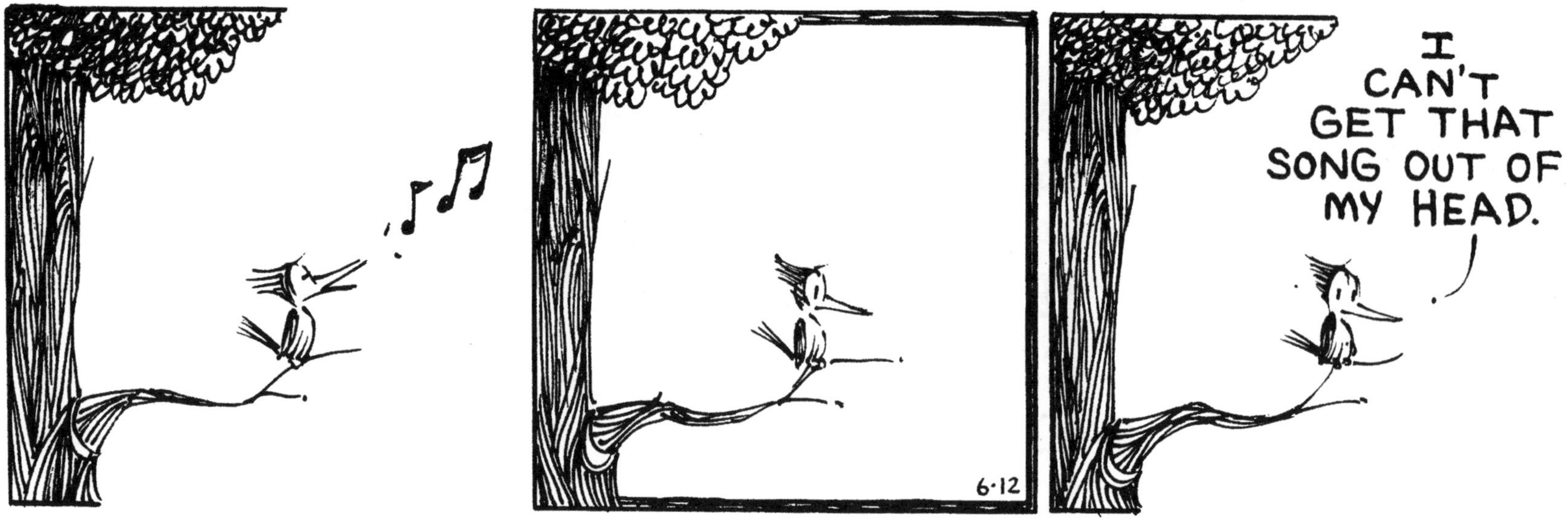
6·12
I CAN'T GET THAT SONG OUT OF MY HEAD.

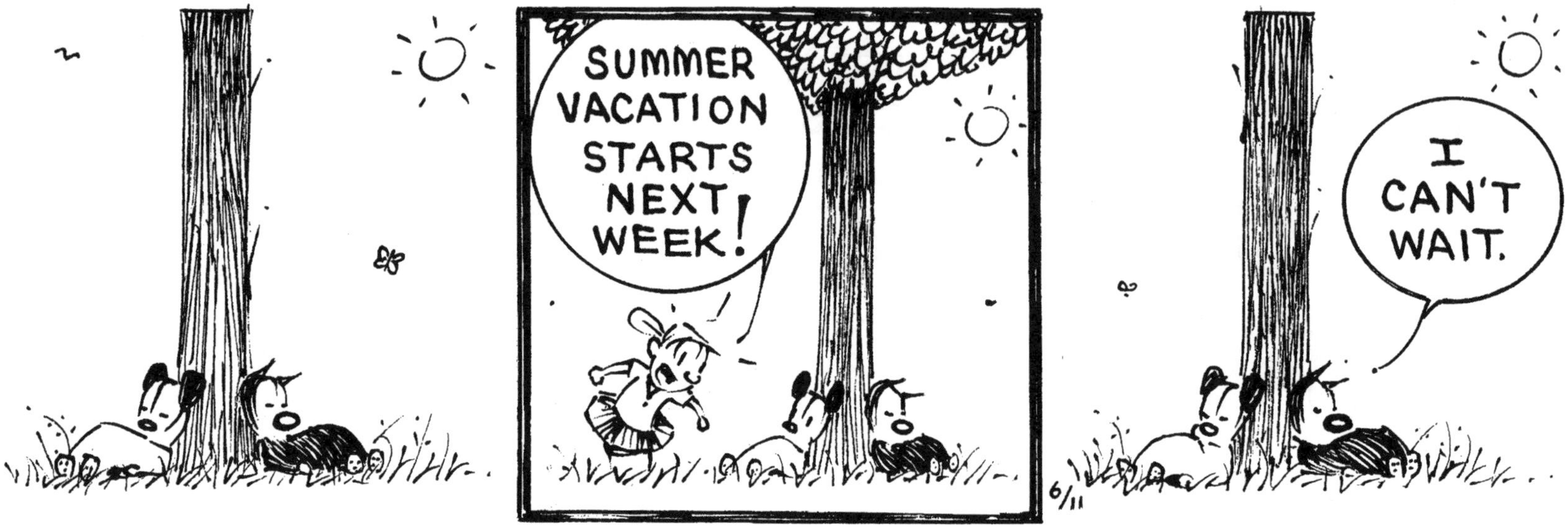
SUMMER VACATION STARTS NEXT WEEK!
6/11
I CAN'T WAIT.

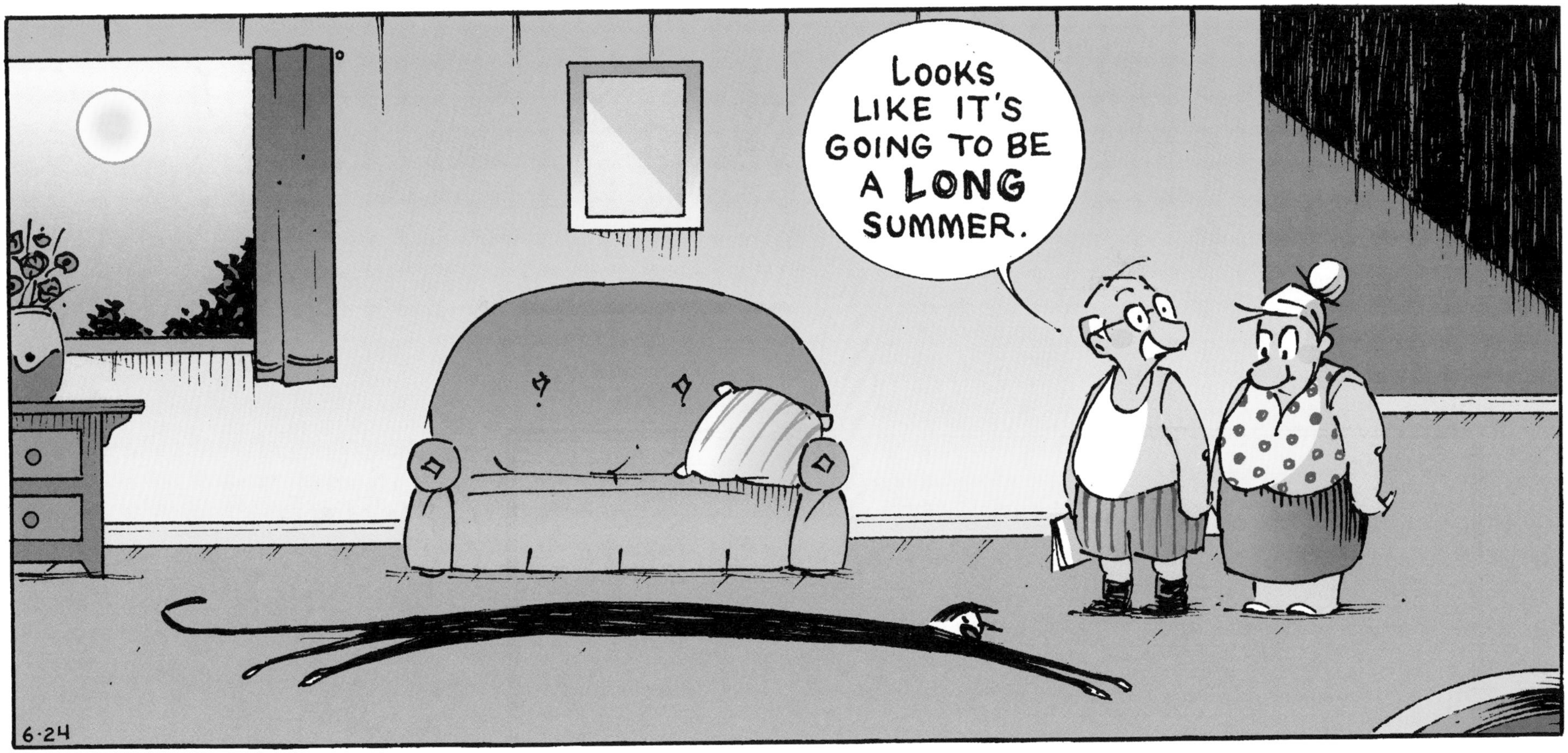
LOOKS LIKE IT'S GOING TO BE A **LONG** SUMMER.
6-24

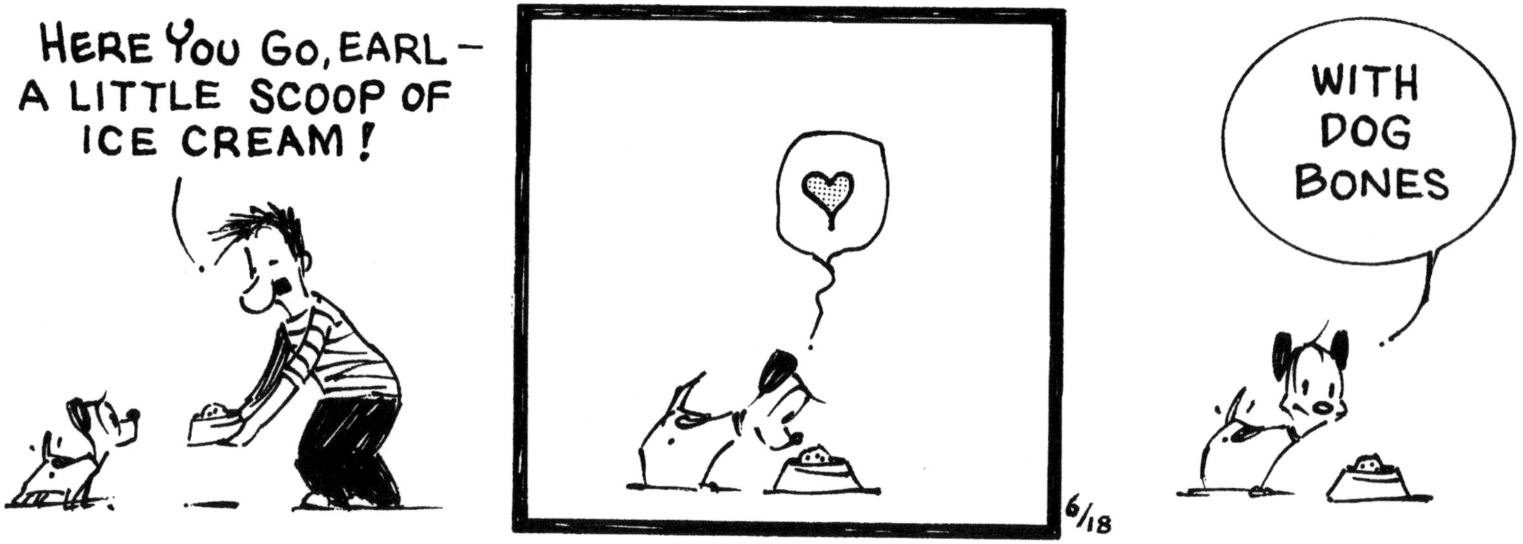
HERE YOU GO, EARL -
A LITTLE SCOOP OF
ICE CREAM!
WITH
DOG
BONES
6/18

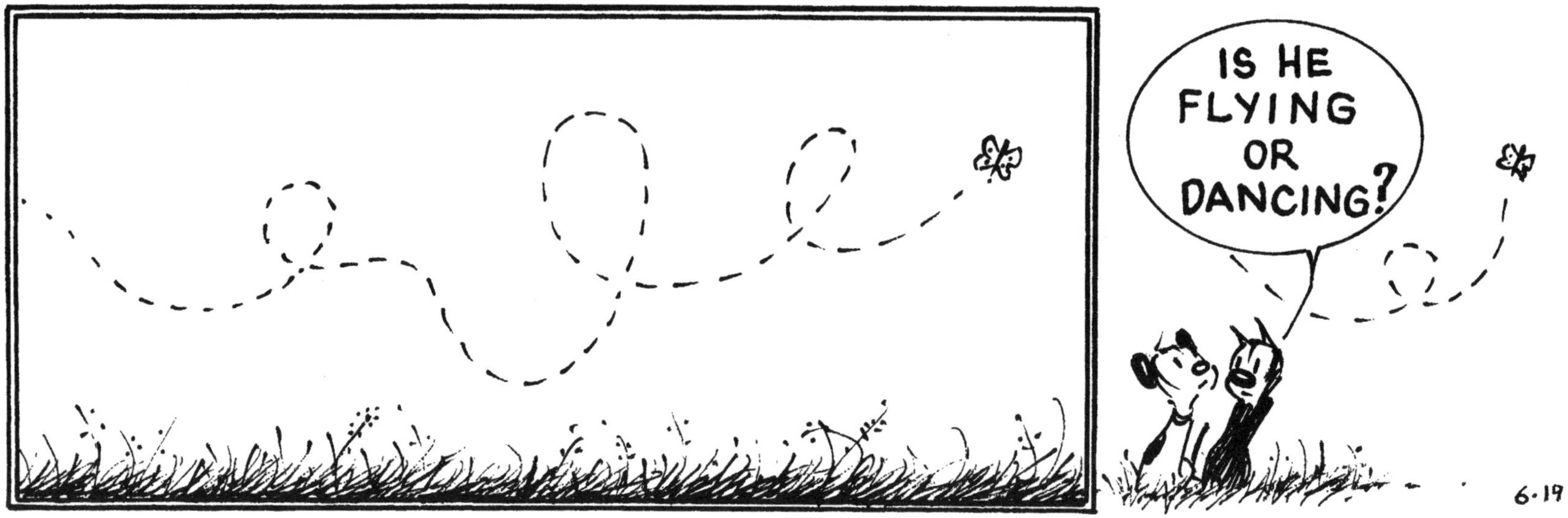
IS HE
FLYING
OR
DANCING?
6·19

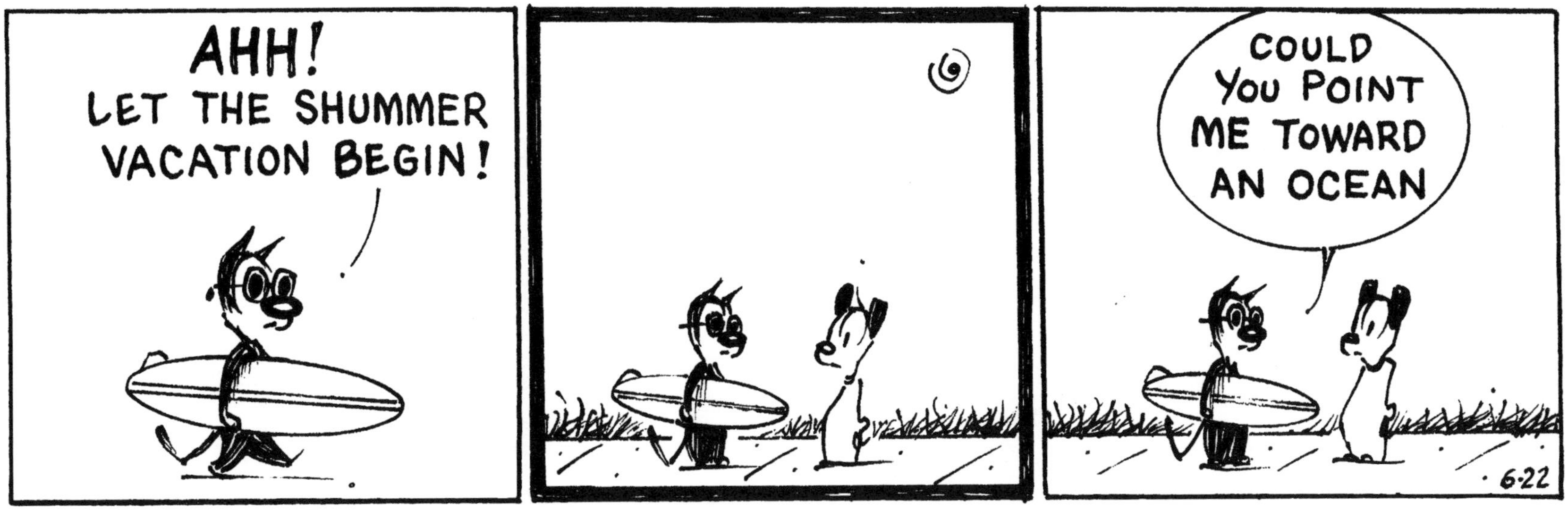
AHH! LET THE SHUMMER VACATION BEGIN!
COULD YOU POINT ME TOWARD AN OCEAN
6-22

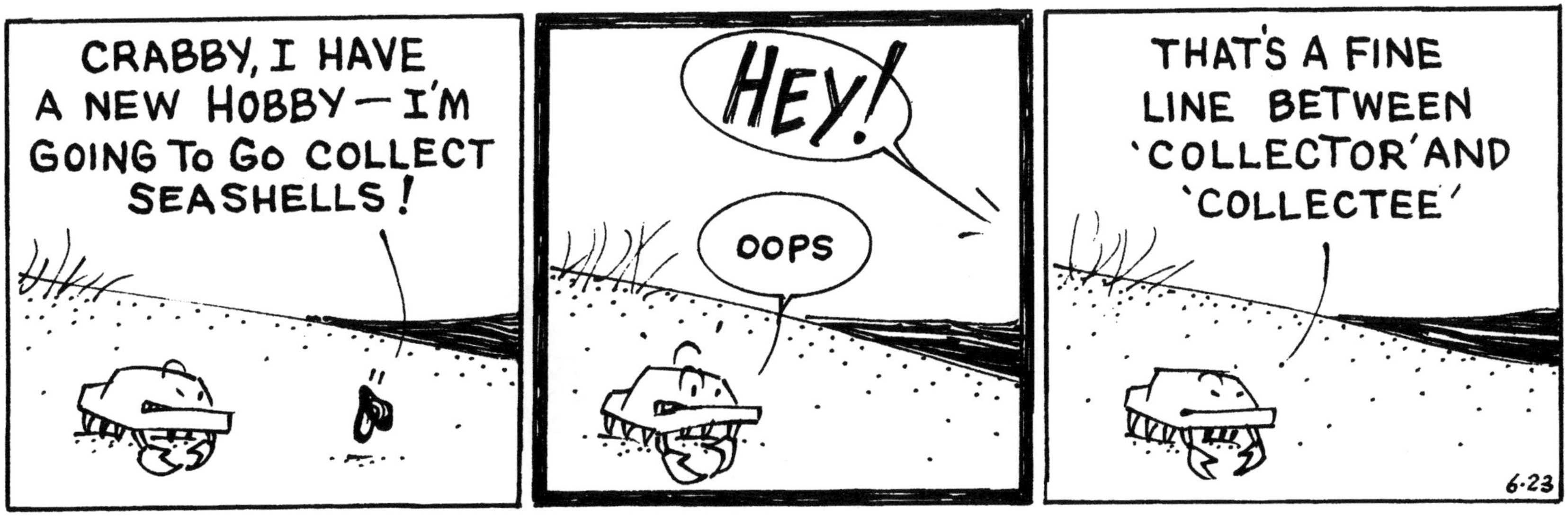
CRABBY, I HAVE A NEW HOBBY—I'M GOING TO GO COLLECT SEASHELLS!
HEY!
OOPS
THAT'S A FINE LINE BETWEEN 'COLLECTOR' AND 'COLLECTEE'
6-23

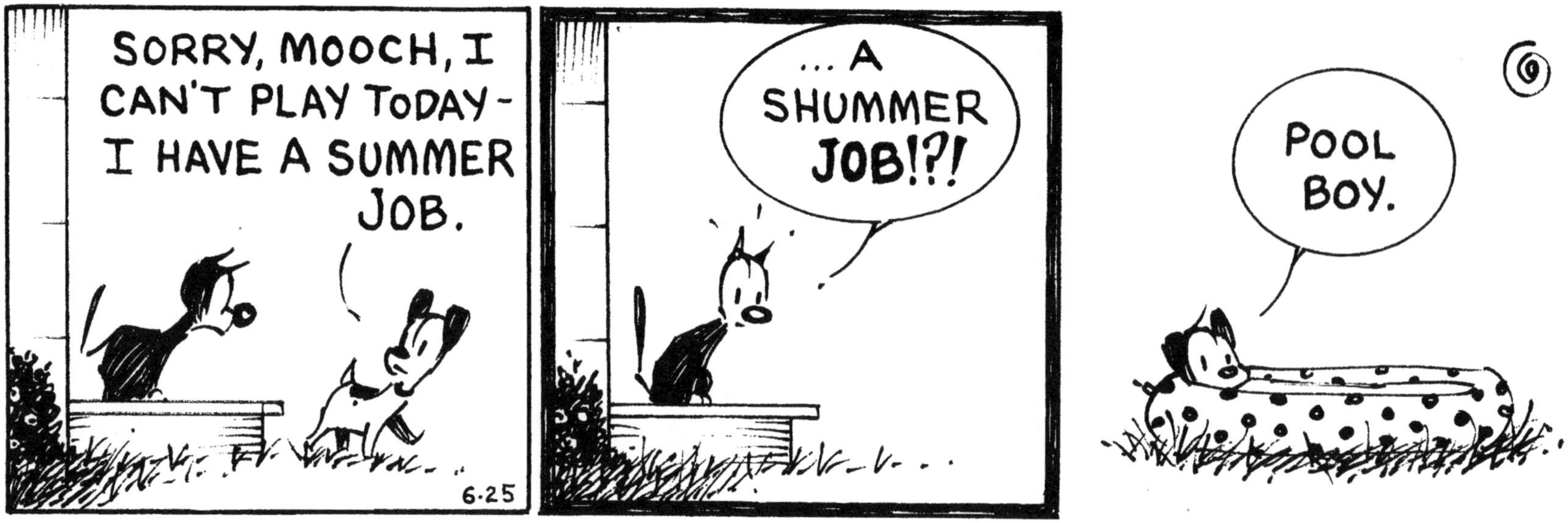
SORRY, MOOCH, I CAN'T PLAY TODAY - I HAVE A SUMMER JOB.
6·25
... A SHUMMER JOB!?!
POOL BOY.

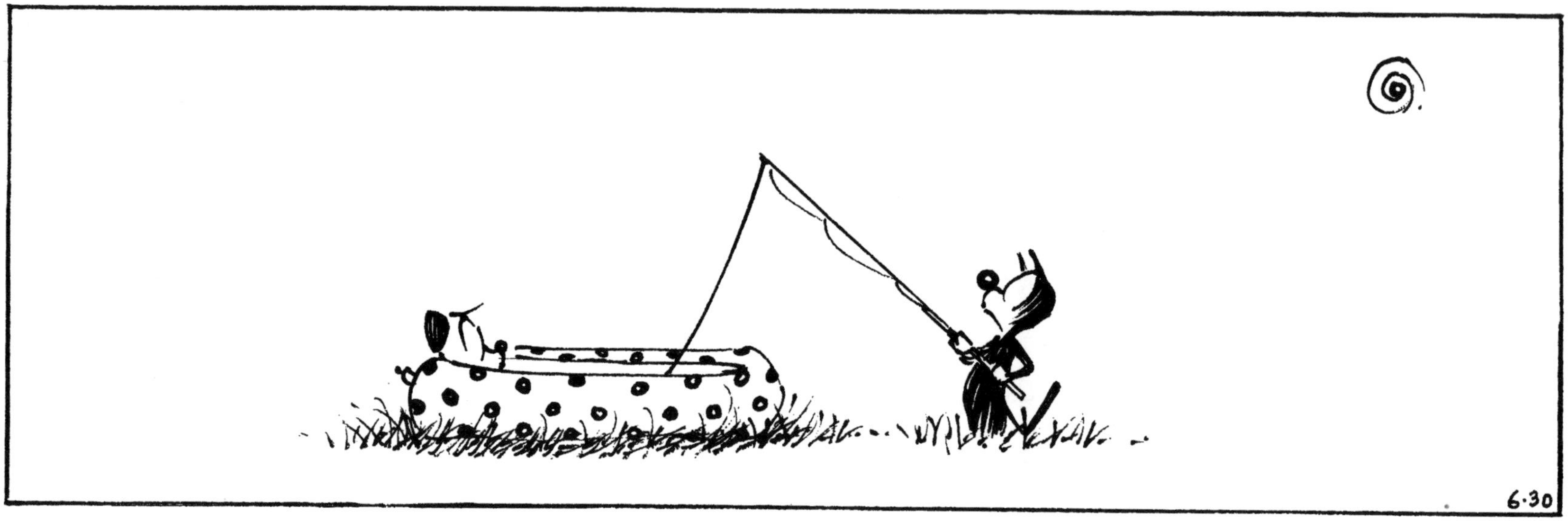
6·30

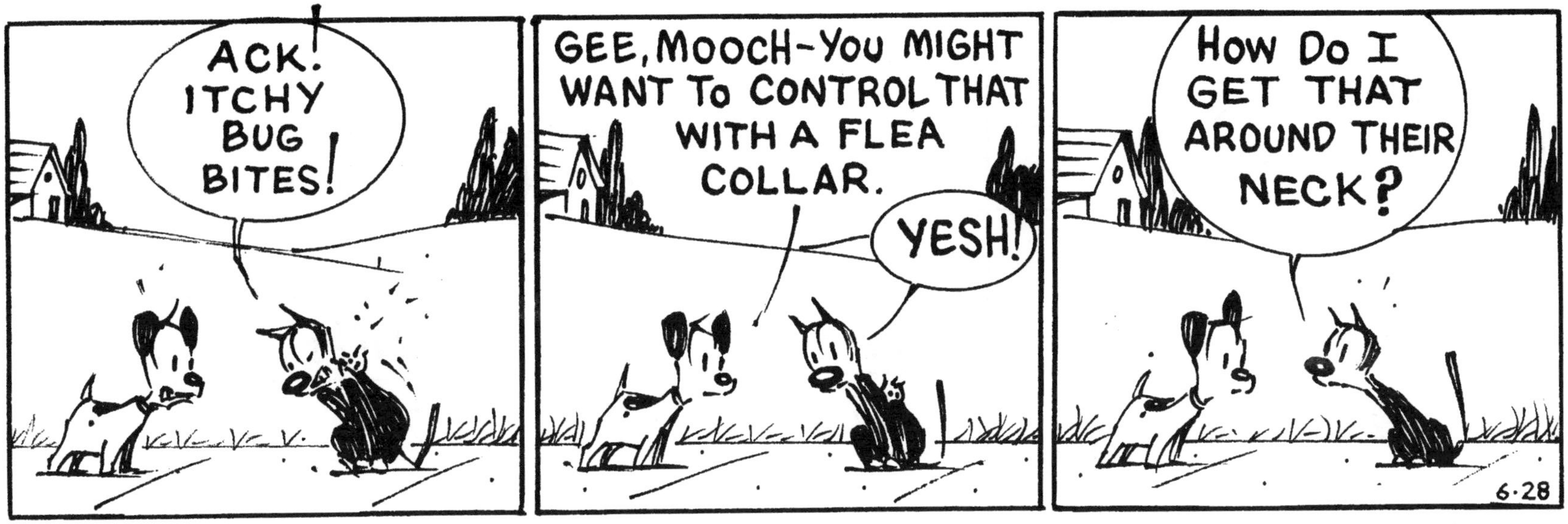
ACK! ITCHY BUG BITES!
GEE, MOOCH–YOU MIGHT WANT TO CONTROL THAT WITH A FLEA COLLAR.
YESH!
HOW DO I GET THAT AROUND THEIR NECK?
6·28

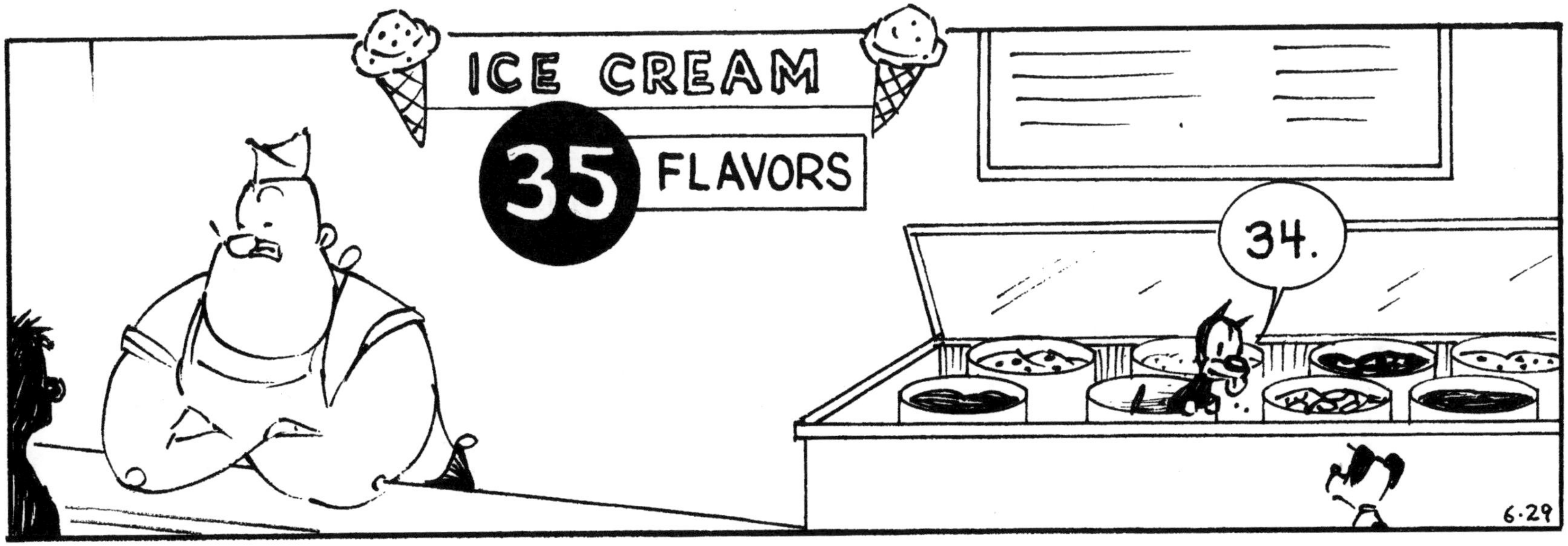
ICE CREAM
35 FLAVORS
34.
6·29

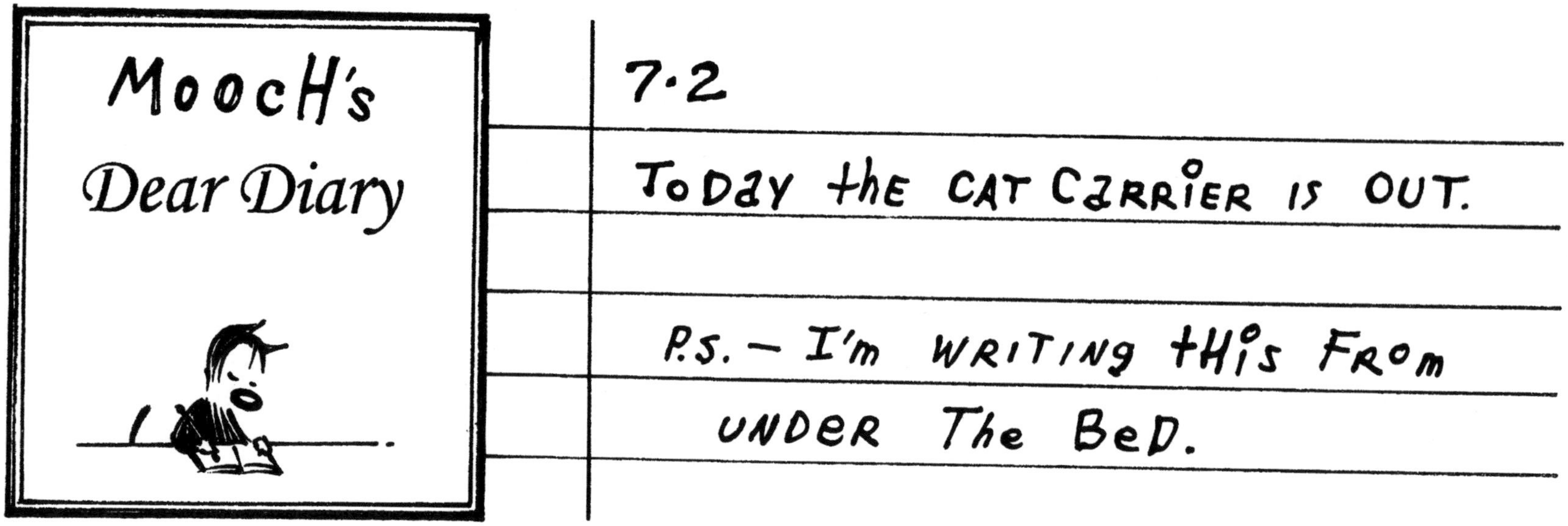
MoocH's
Dear Diary
7·2
Today the CAT Carrier is OUT.
P.S. – I'm WRITING this FROM
UNDER The BeD.

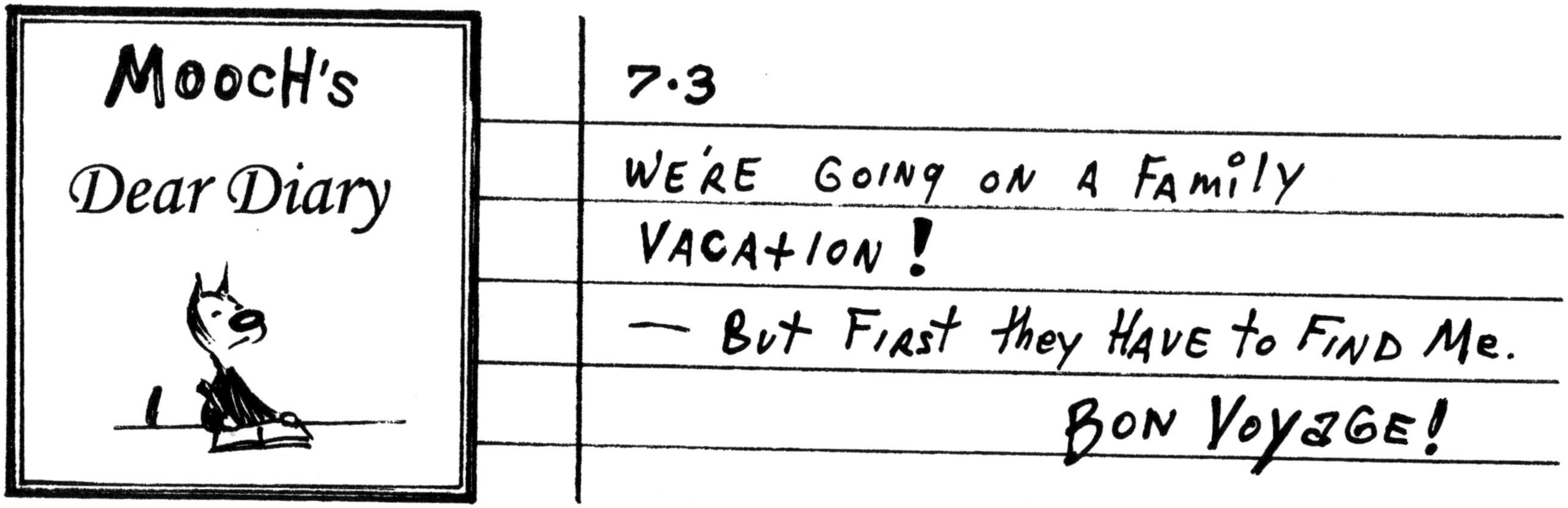
MoocH's
Dear Diary
7·3
WE'RE GOING ON A Family
VACAtION!
— But First they HAVE to FIND Me.
BON VoyaGE!

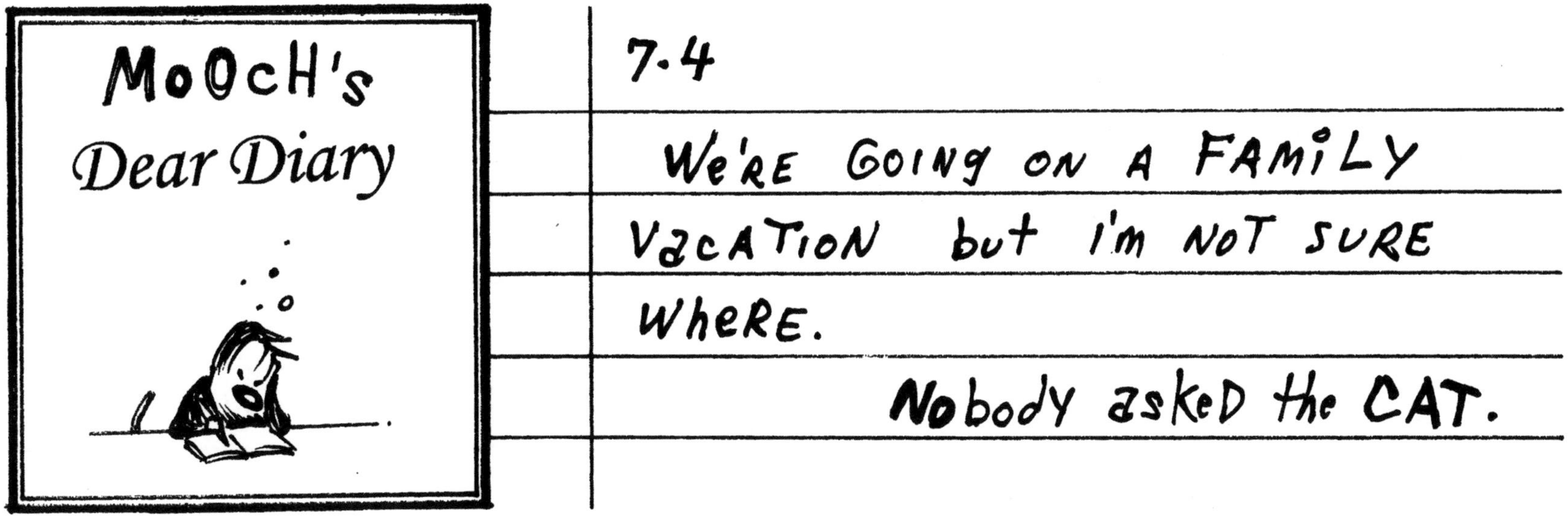
MOOCH'S
Dear Diary
7·4
WE'RE GOING ON A FAMILY VACATION but I'm NOT SURE WHERE.
Nobody asked the CAT.

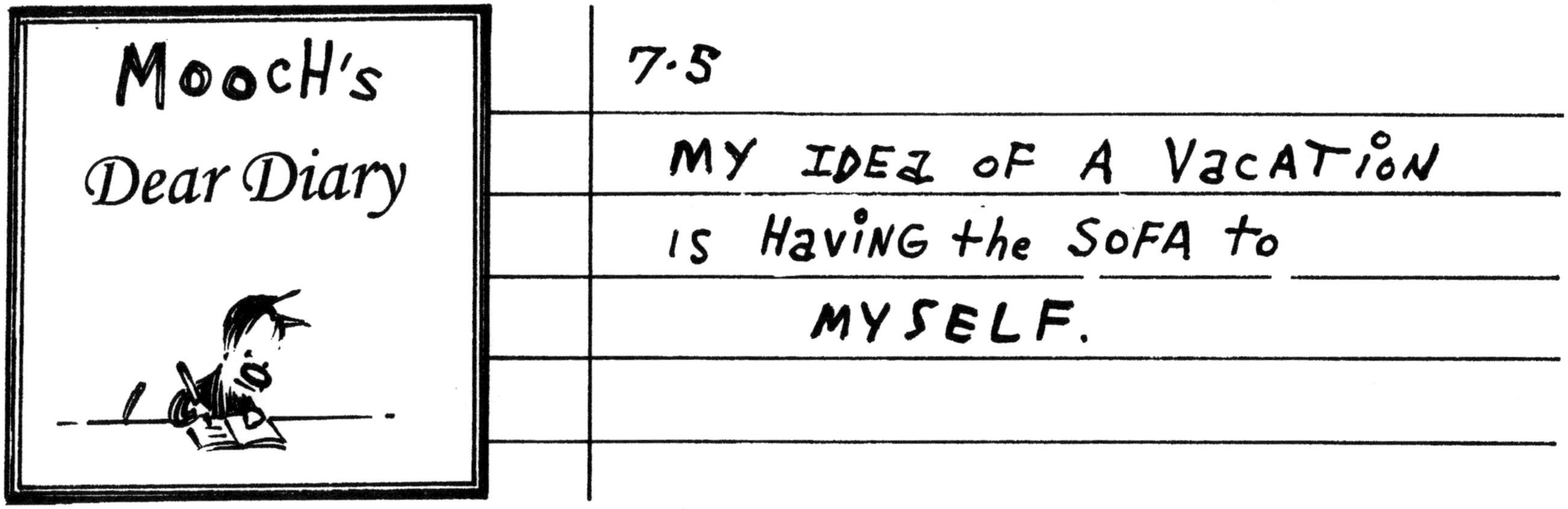
MOOCH'S
Dear Diary
7·5
MY IDEA OF A VACATION IS HAVING the SOFA to MYSELF.

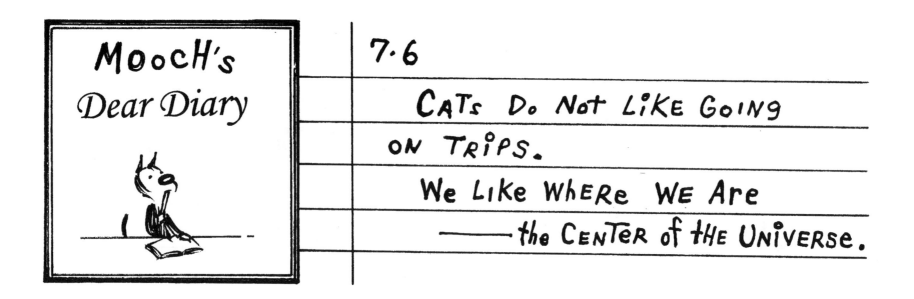

MOOCH's *Dear Diary*

7·6

CATS DO NOT LIKE GOING ON TRIPS.

We LIKE WHERE WE Are
—— the CENTER of tHE UNIVERSE.

MOOcH's *Dear Diary*

7·7

WE'RE GOING ON VACATION.
I HOPE WE GO ShomeWHeRE HoT AND EXOTIC!
— LIKE tHE Attic.

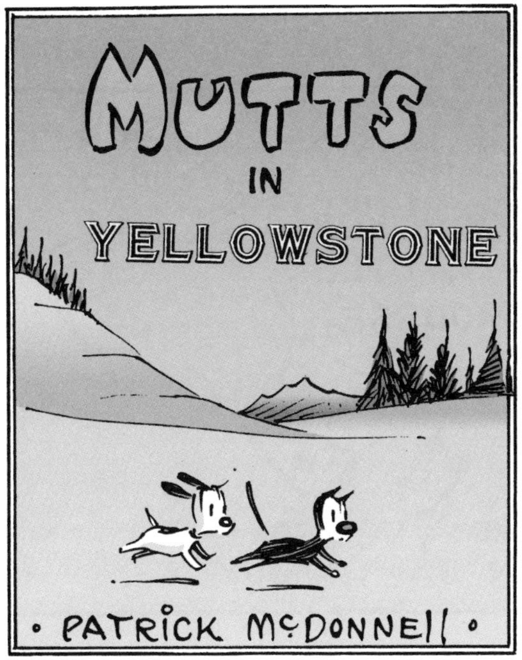
MUTTS
IN
YELLOWSTONE
• PATRICK McDONNELL •

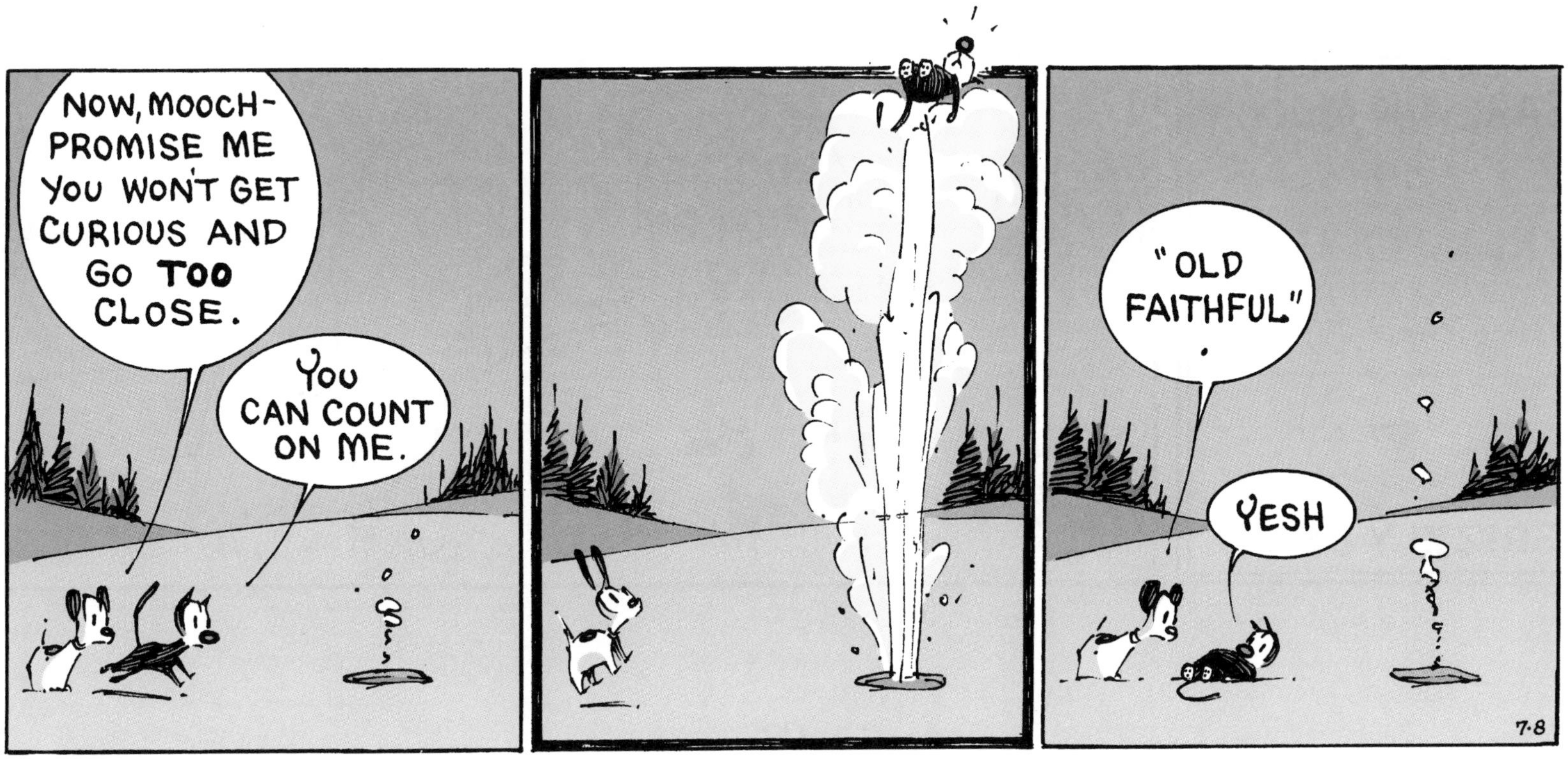
NOW, MOOCH- PROMISE ME YOU WON'T GET CURIOUS AND GO **TOO** CLOSE.
YOU CAN COUNT ON ME.
"OLD FAITHFUL".
YESH
7·8

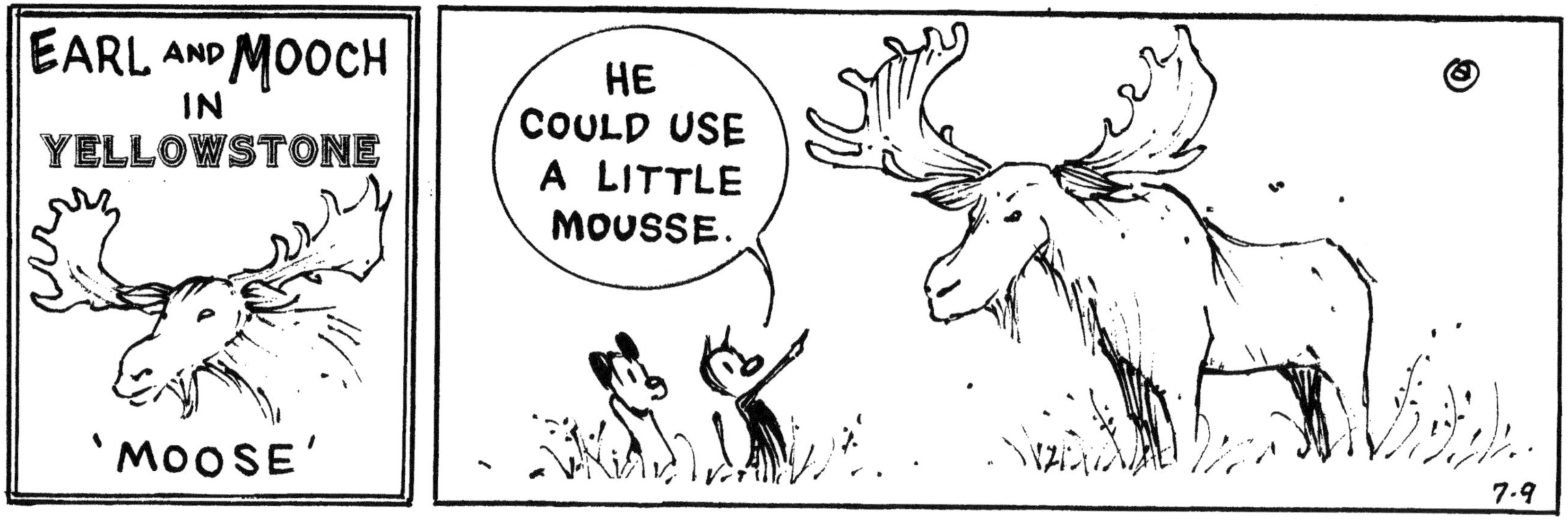
EARL AND MOOCH
IN
YELLOWSTONE
'MOOSE'
HE COULD USE A LITTLE MOUSSE.
7-9

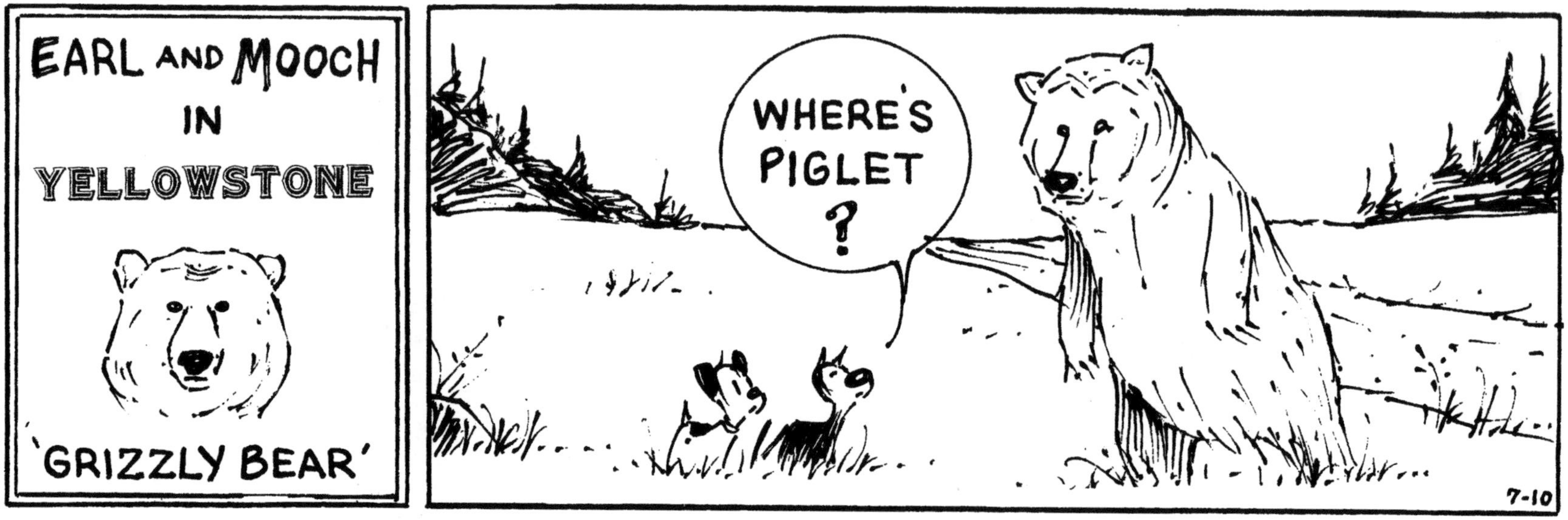
EARL AND MOOCH
IN
YELLOWSTONE
'GRIZZLY BEAR'
WHERE'S PIGLET ?
7-10

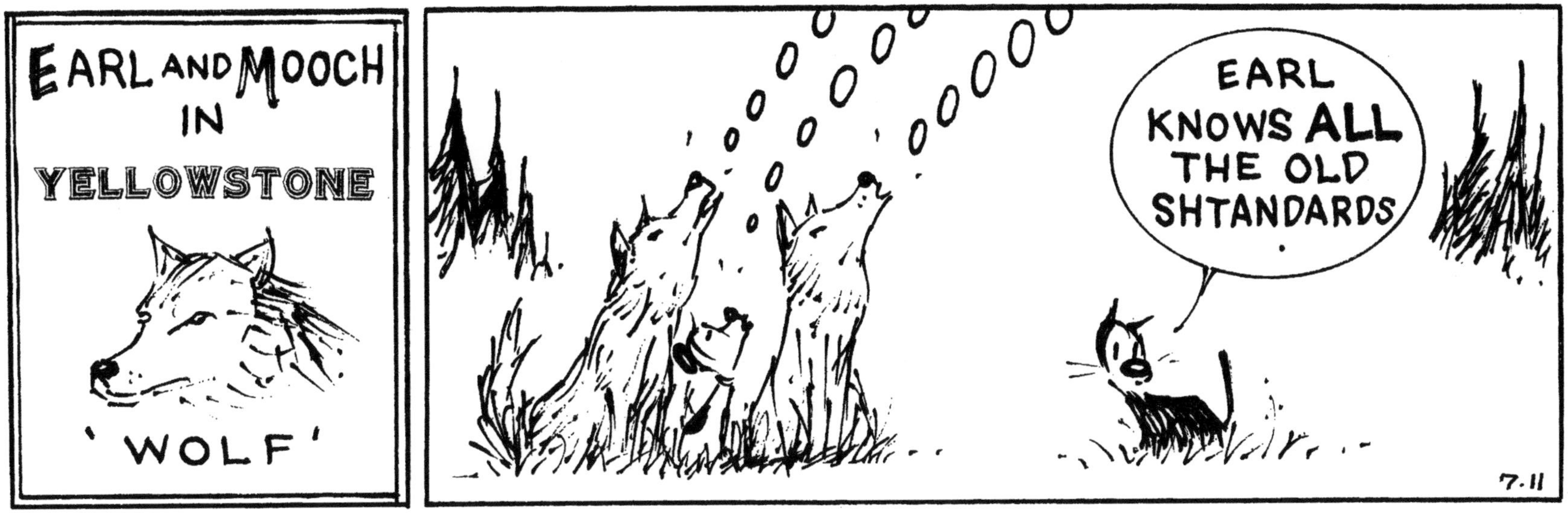
EARL AND MOOCH IN YELLOWSTONE
'WOLF'
EARL KNOWS ALL THE OLD SHTANDARDS.
7.11

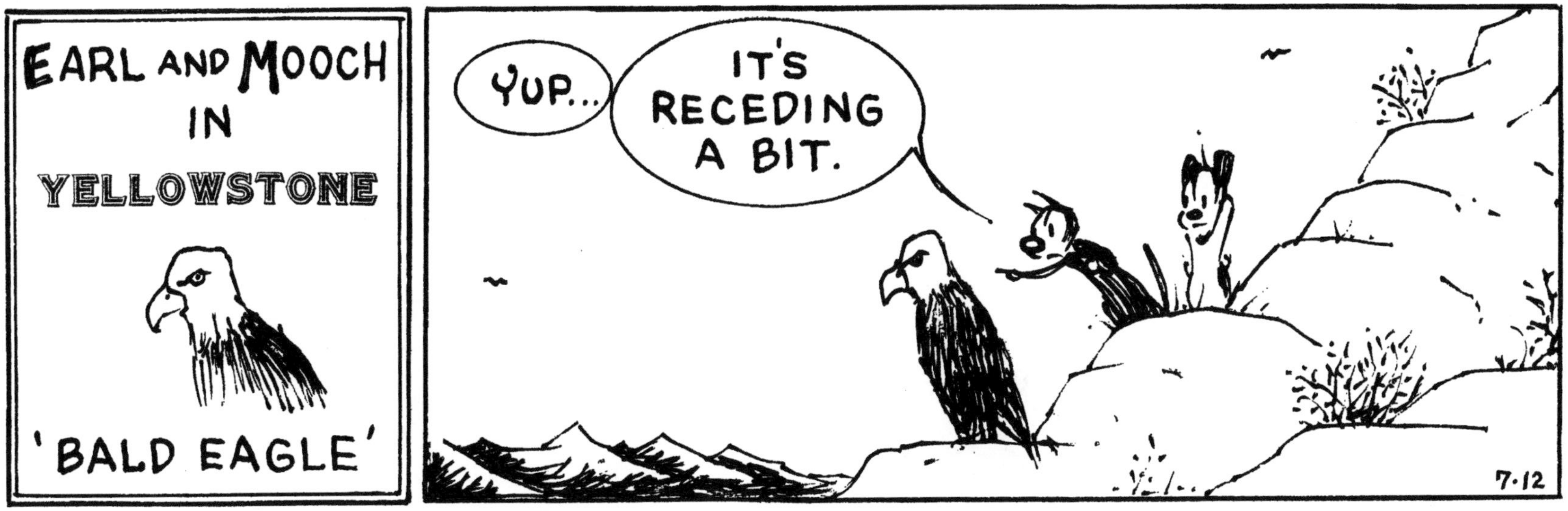
EARL AND MOOCH IN YELLOWSTONE
'BALD EAGLE'
YUP...
IT'S RECEDING A BIT.
7.12

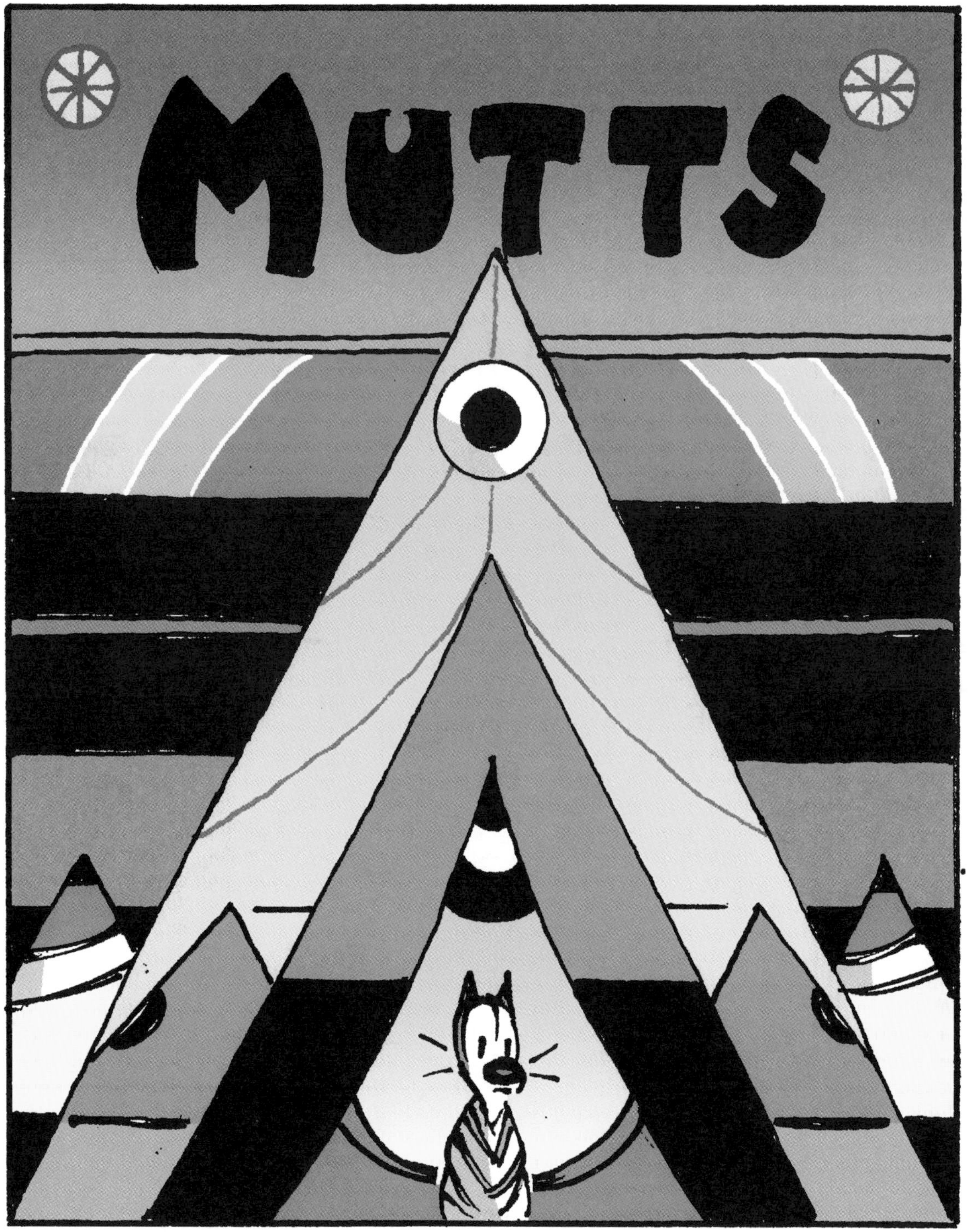
MUTTS

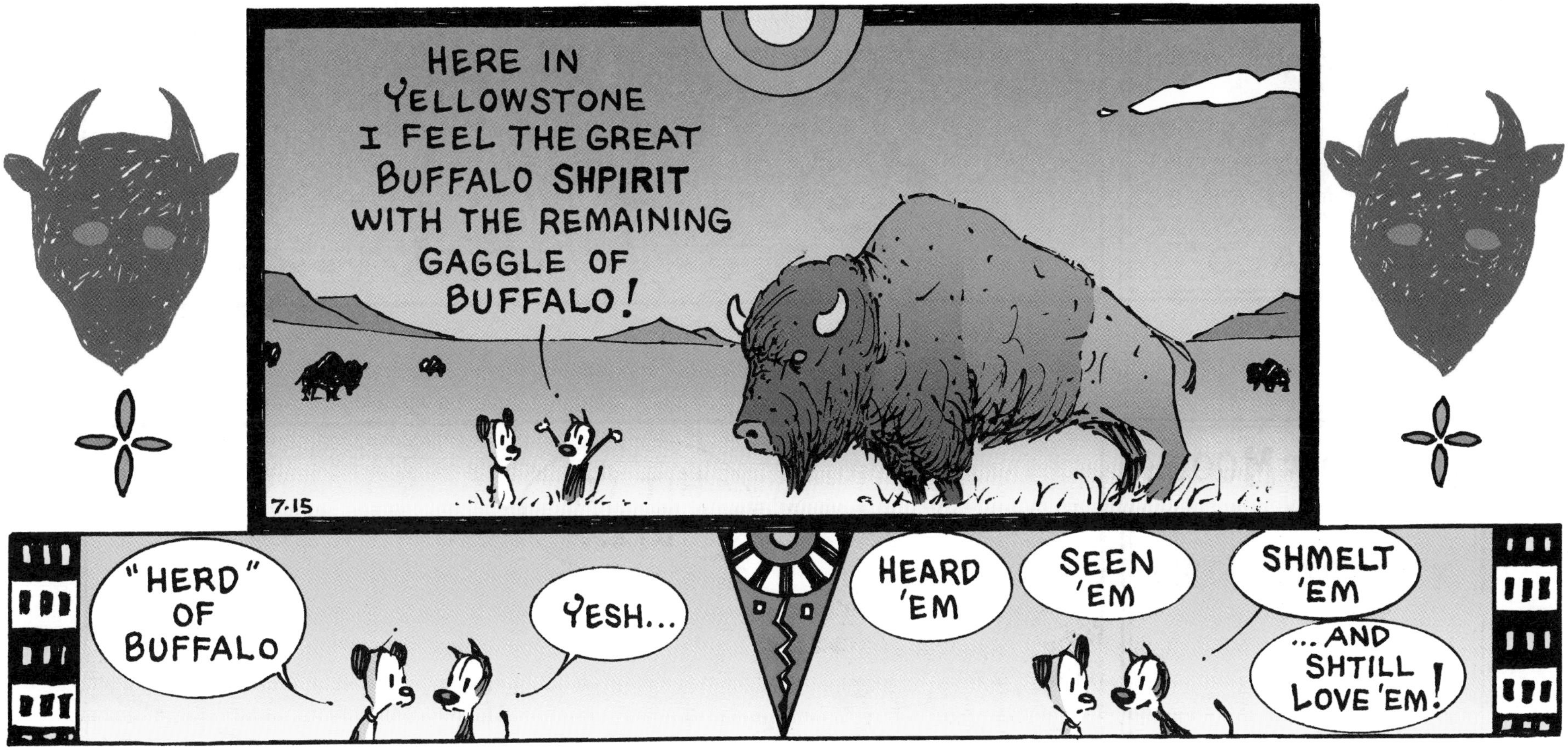
HERE IN YELLOWSTONE I FEEL THE GREAT BUFFALO SHPIRIT WITH THE REMAINING GAGGLE OF BUFFALO!
7.15
"HERD" OF BUFFALO
YESH...
HEARD 'EM
SEEN 'EM
SHMELT 'EM
...AND SHTILL LOVE 'EM!

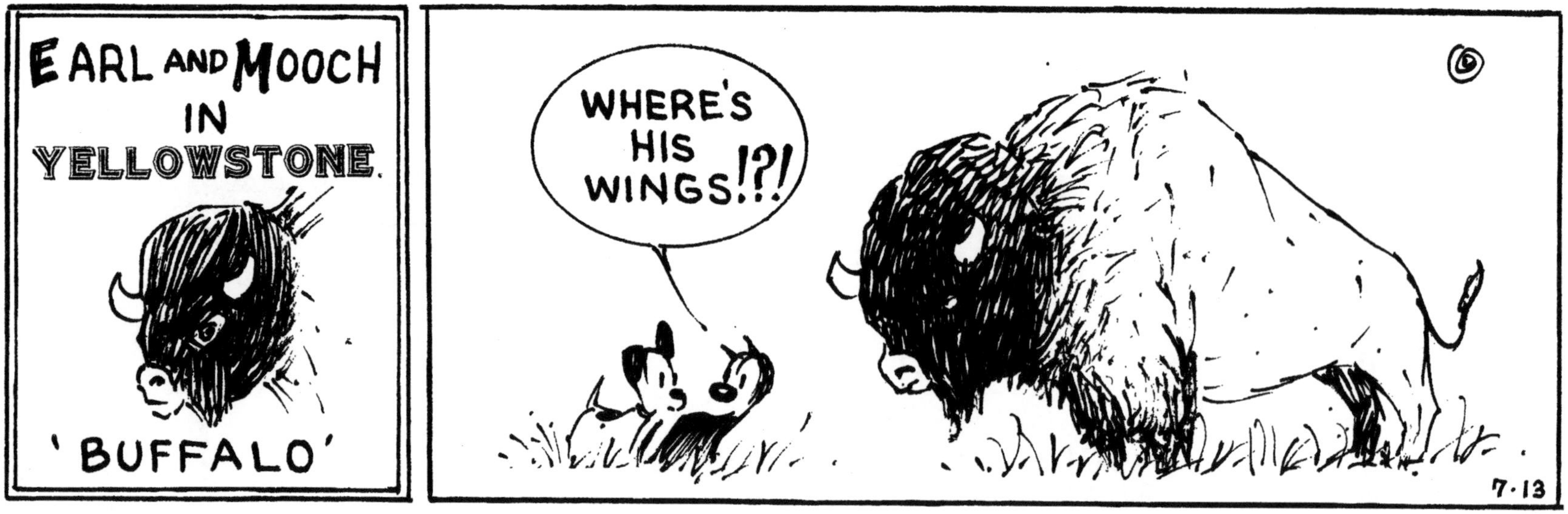
EARL AND MOOCH
IN
YELLOWSTONE.
'BUFFALO'
WHERE'S HIS WINGS!?!
©
7·13

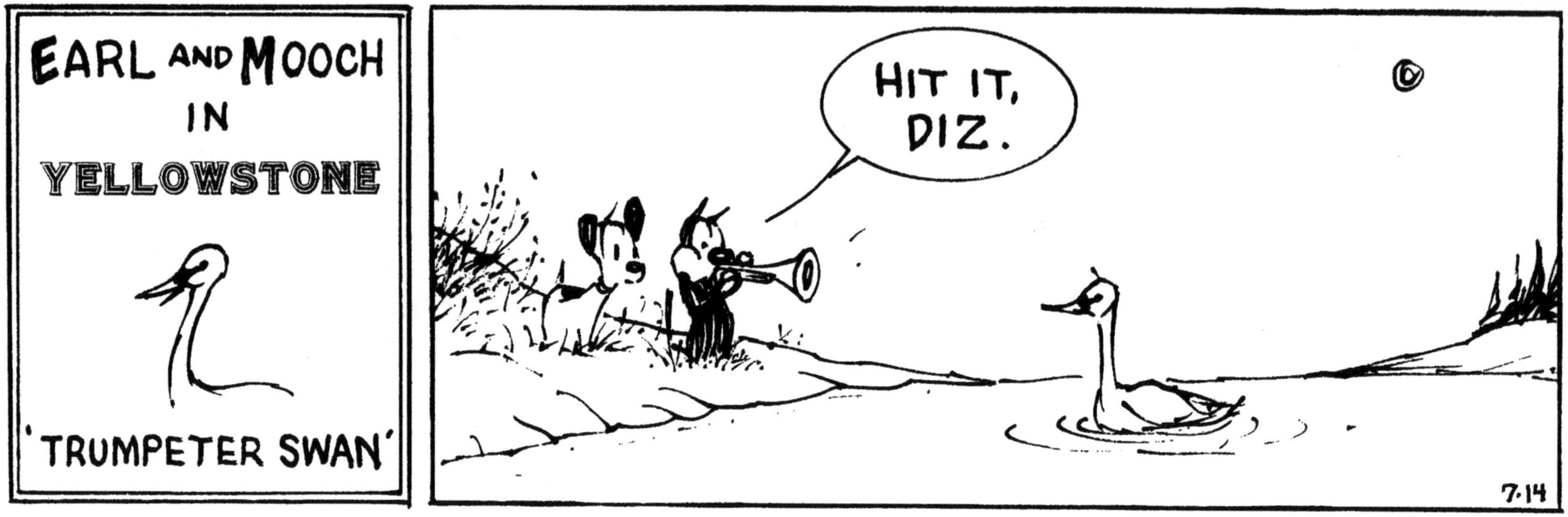
EARL AND MOOCH
IN
YELLOWSTONE
'TRUMPETER SWAN'
HIT IT, DIZ.
©
7·14

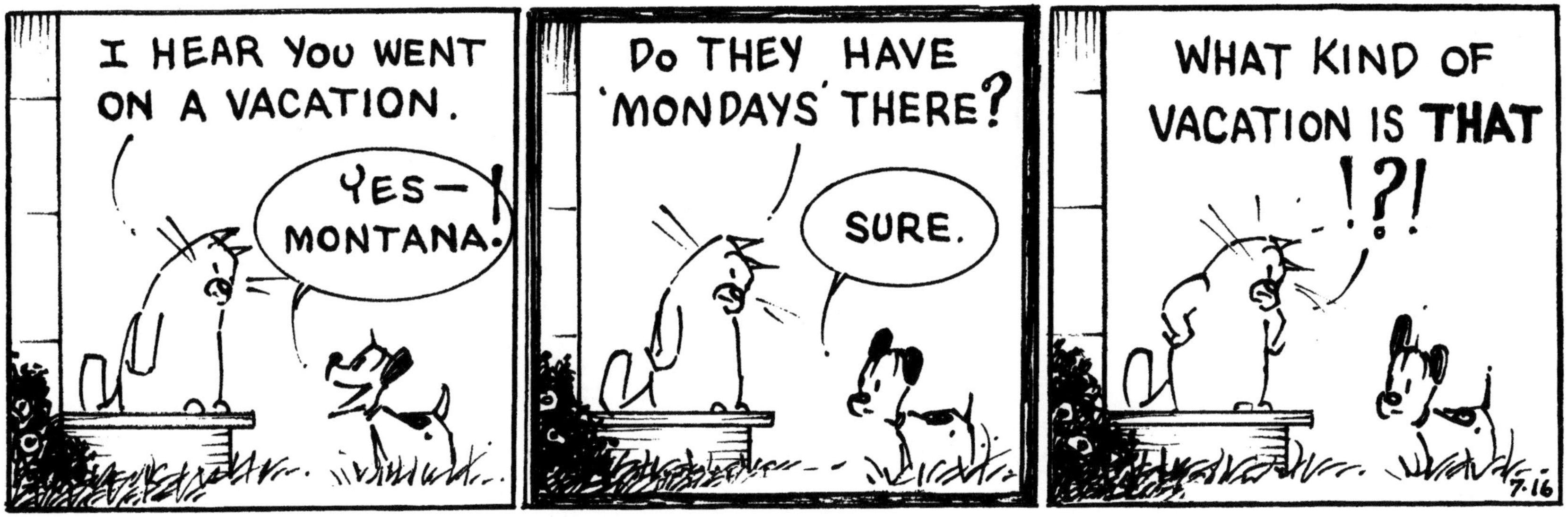
I HEAR YOU WENT ON A VACATION.
YES—MONTANA!
DO THEY HAVE 'MONDAYS' THERE?
SURE.
WHAT KIND OF VACATION IS THAT !?!
7.16

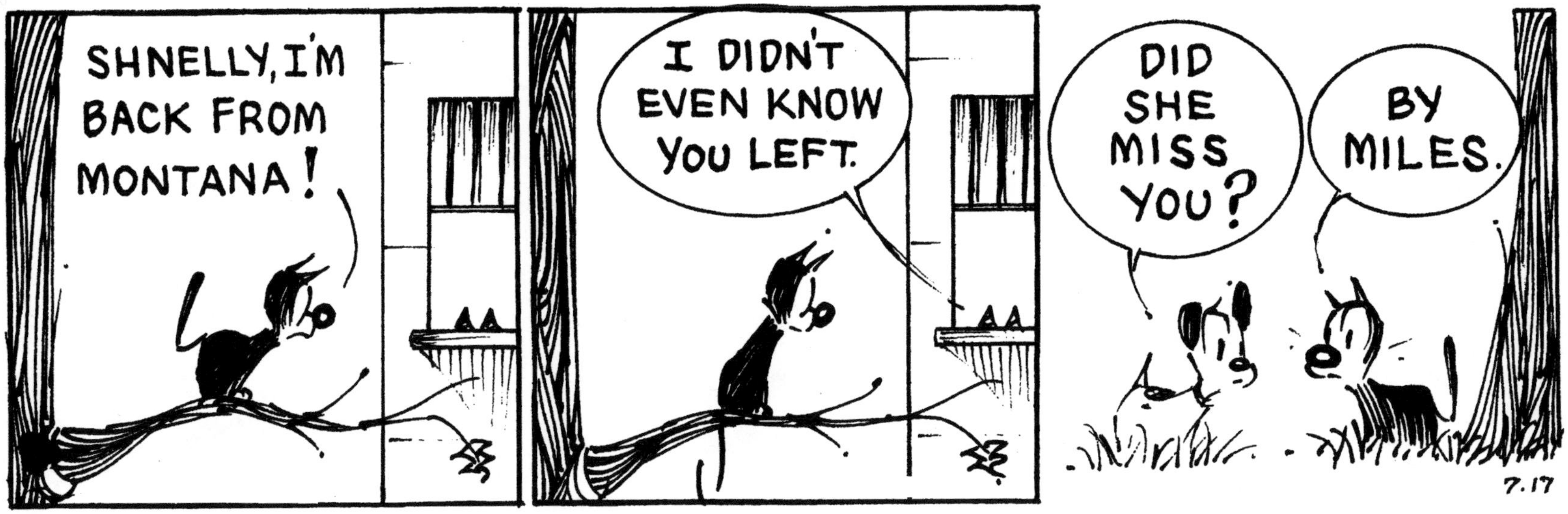
SHNELLY, I'M BACK FROM MONTANA!
I DIDN'T EVEN KNOW YOU LEFT.
DID SHE MISS YOU?
BY MILES.
7.17

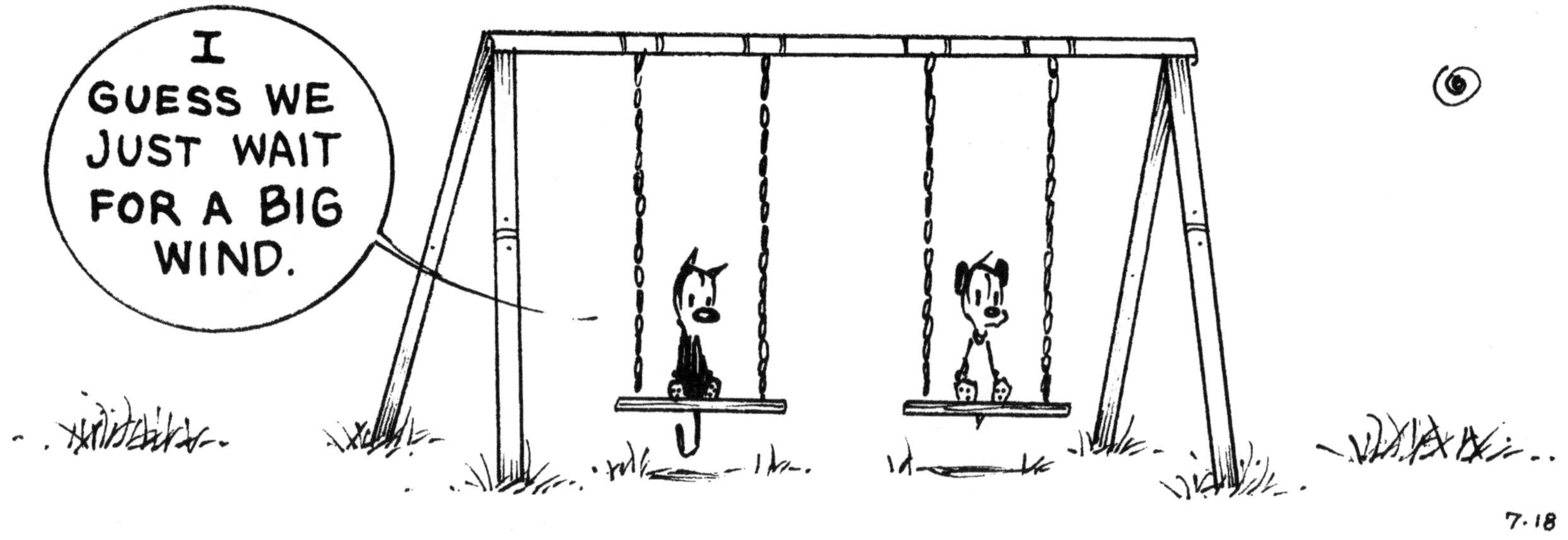
I GUESS WE JUST WAIT FOR A BIG WIND.
7.18

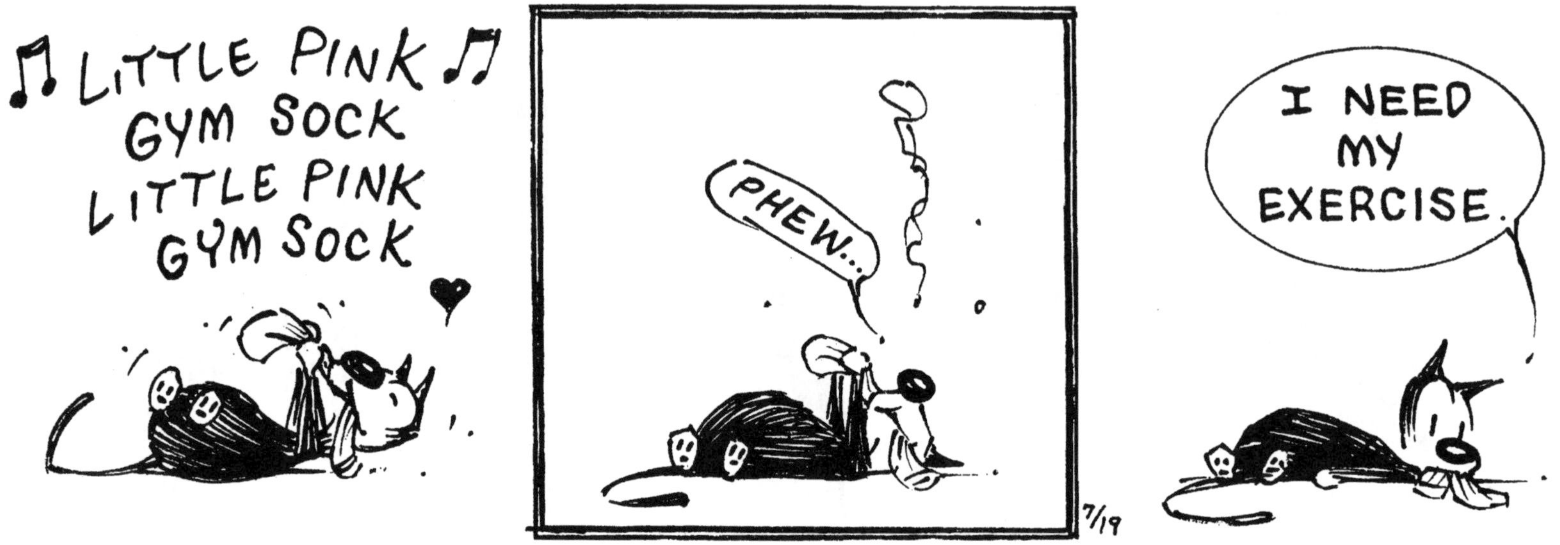
♫ LITTLE PINK ♫ GYM SOCK LITTLE PINK GYM SOCK
PHEW...
I NEED MY EXERCISE.
7/19

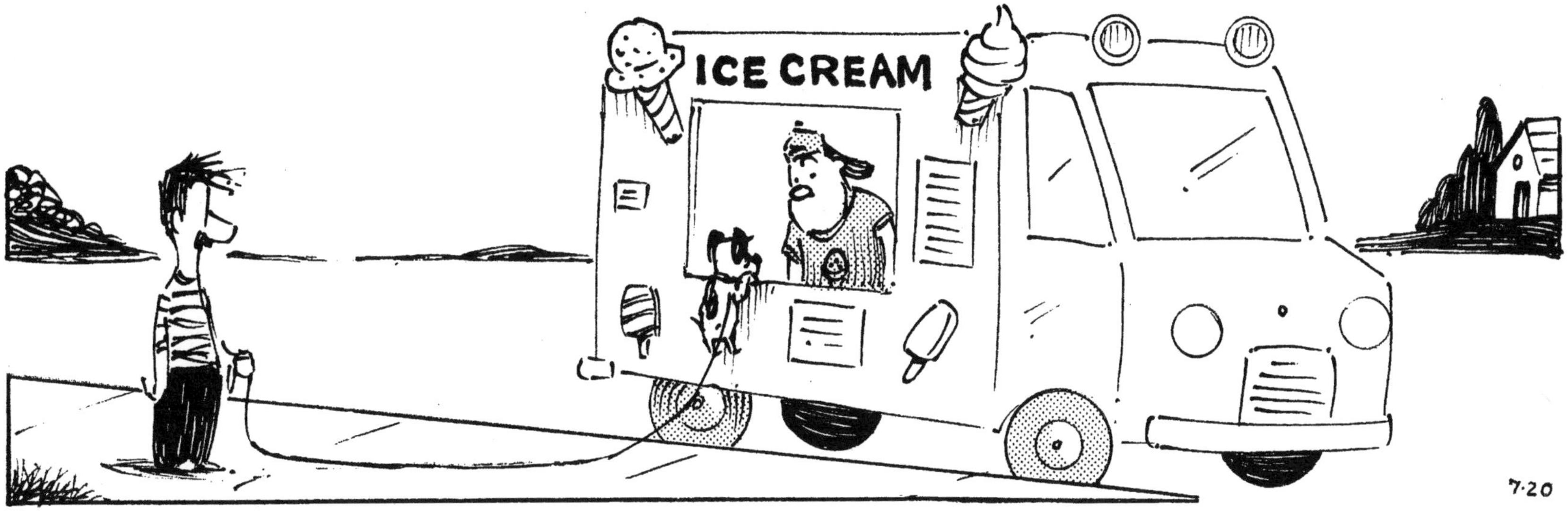
ICE CREAM
7·20

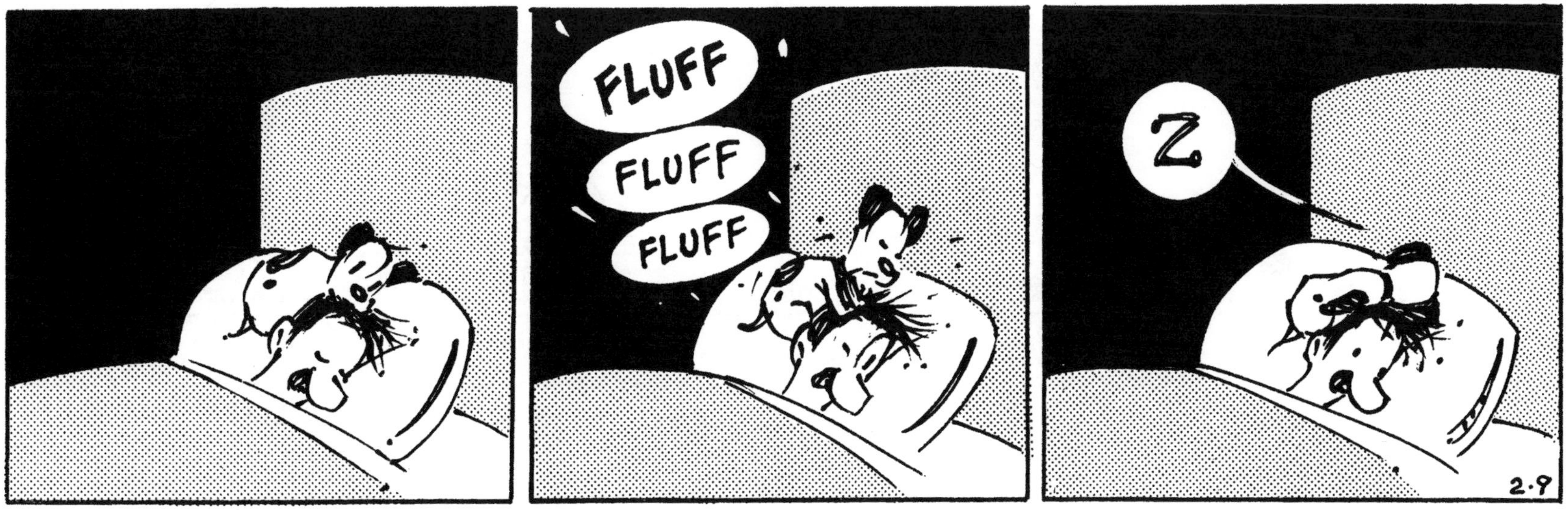
FLUFF
FLUFF
FLUFF
Z
2·9

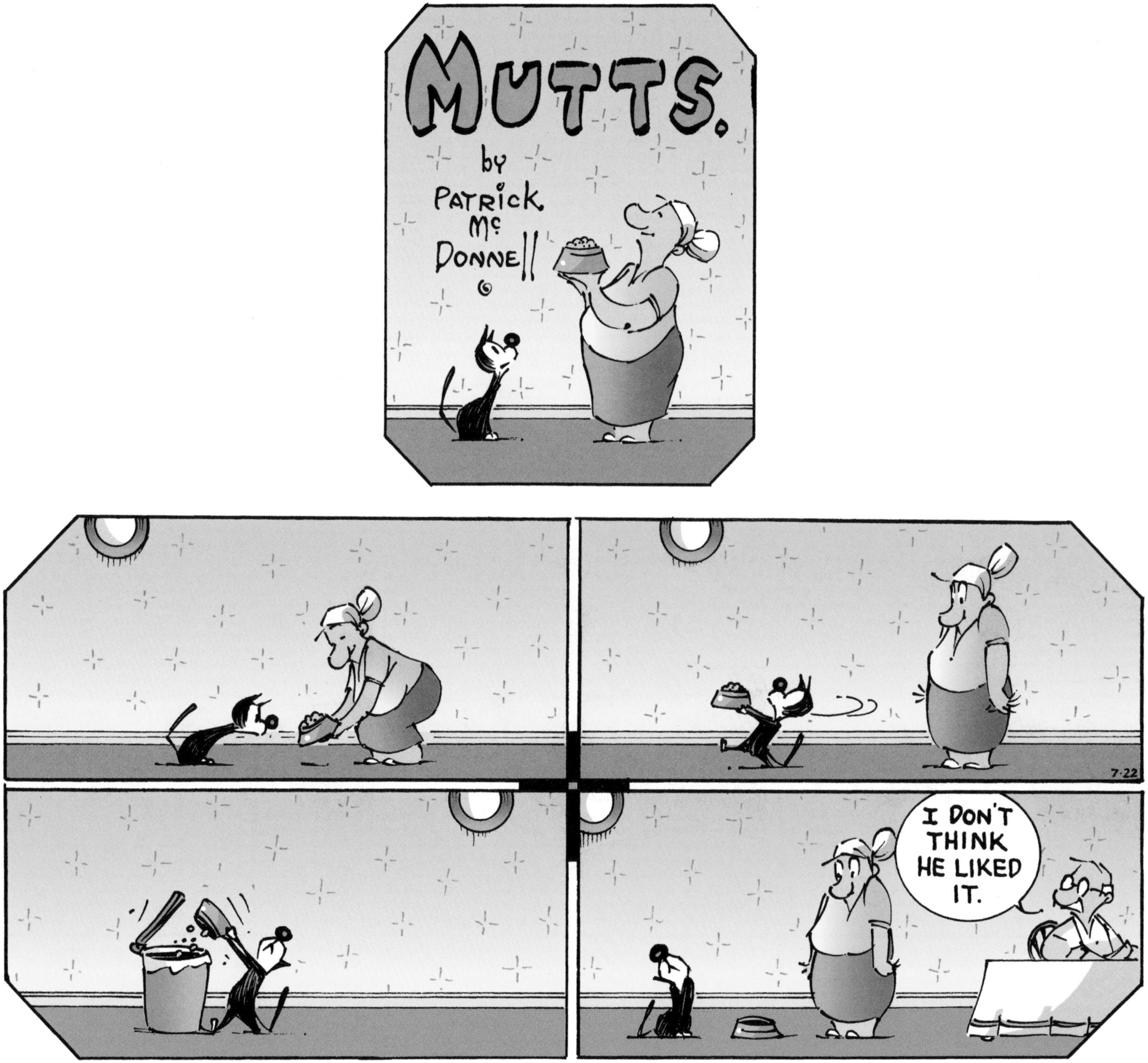
MUTTS.
by PATRICK McDONNELL ©
7-22
I DON'T THINK HE LIKED IT.

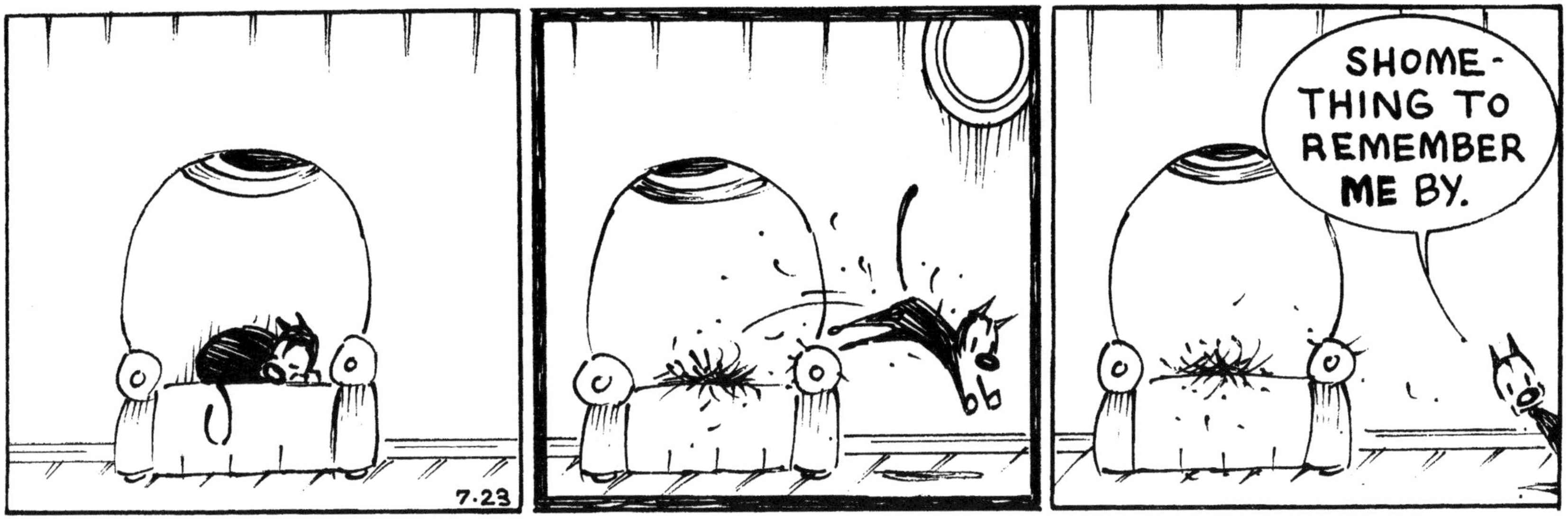
7·23
SHOME-THING TO REMEMBER ME BY.

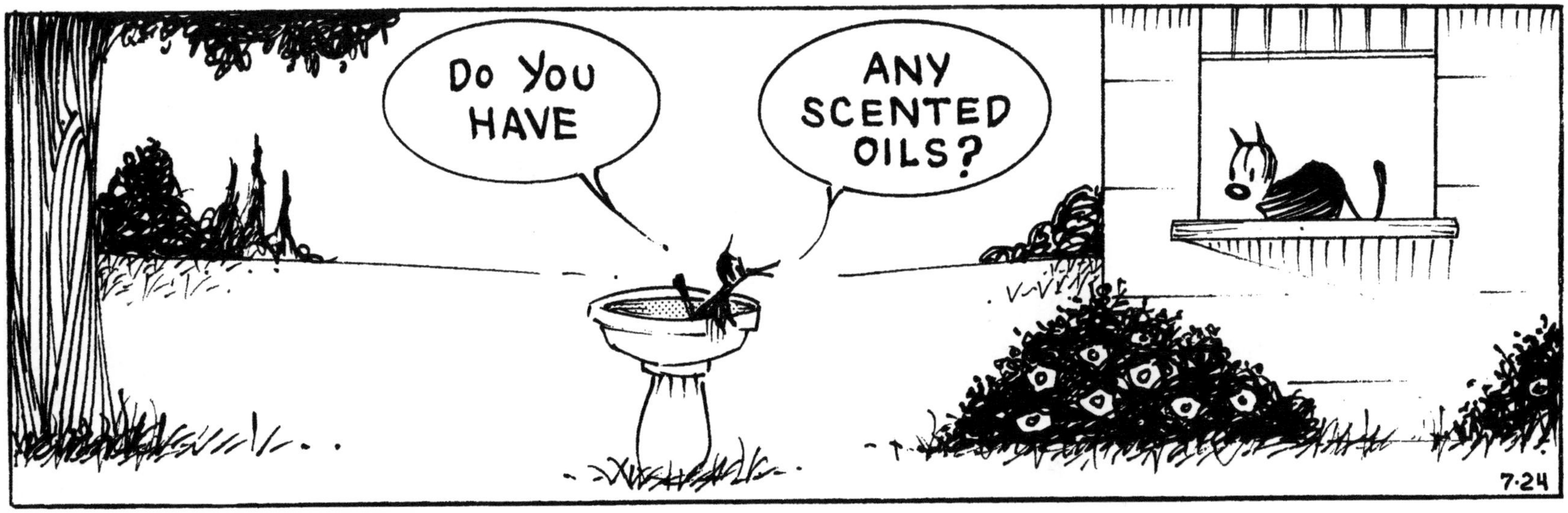
DO YOU HAVE
ANY SCENTED OILS?
7·24

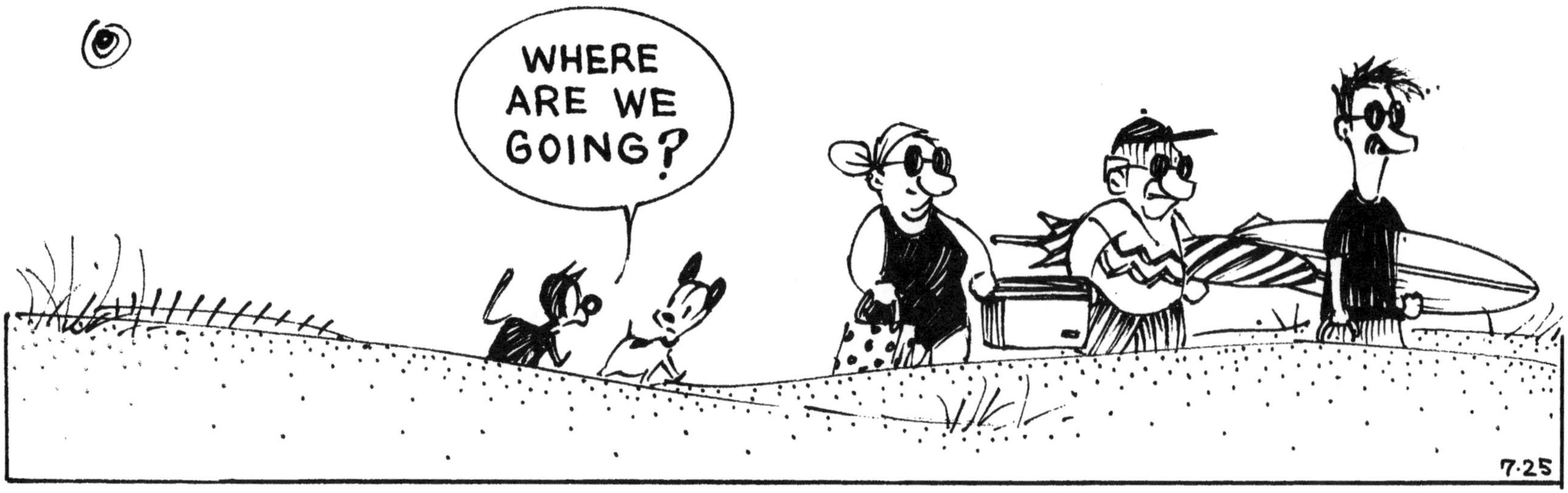
WHERE ARE WE GOING?
7·25

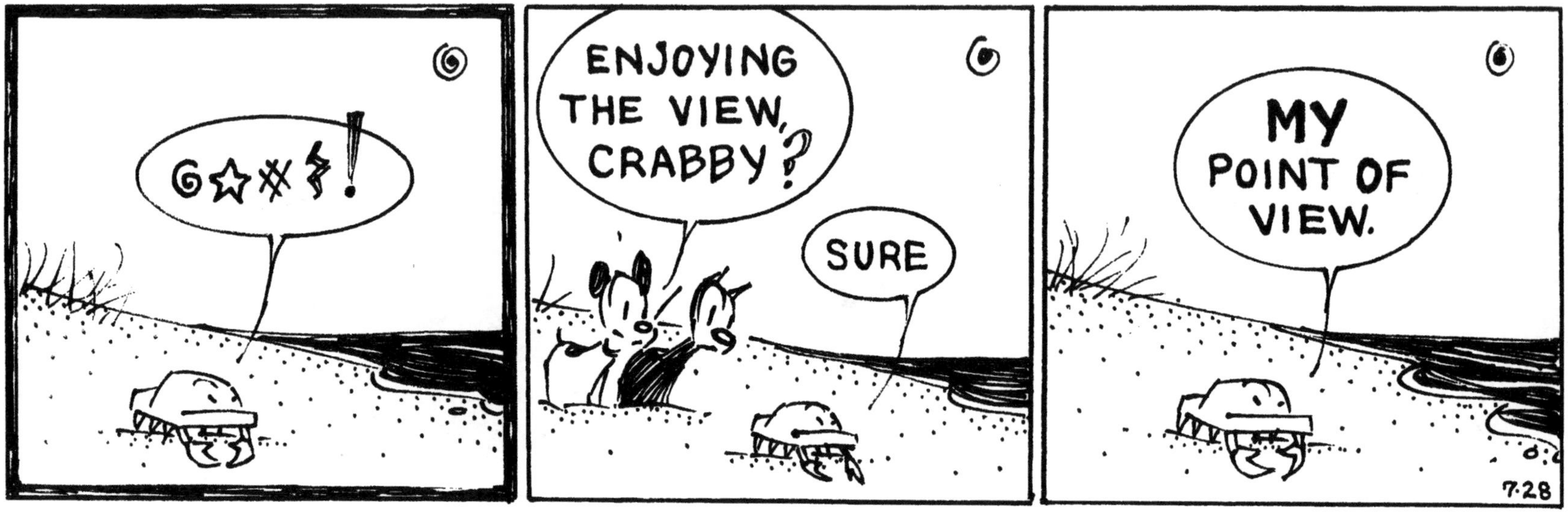
G☆#ϟ!
ENJOYING THE VIEW, CRABBY?
SURE
MY POINT OF VIEW.
7·28

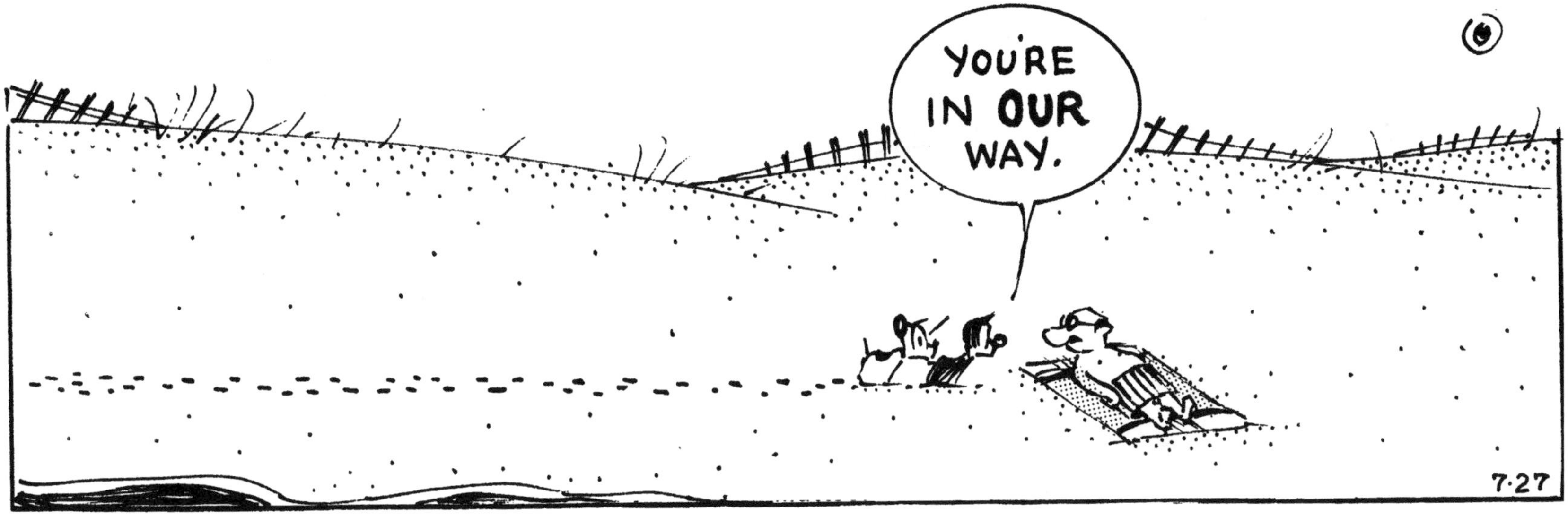
YOU'RE IN **OUR** WAY.
7·27

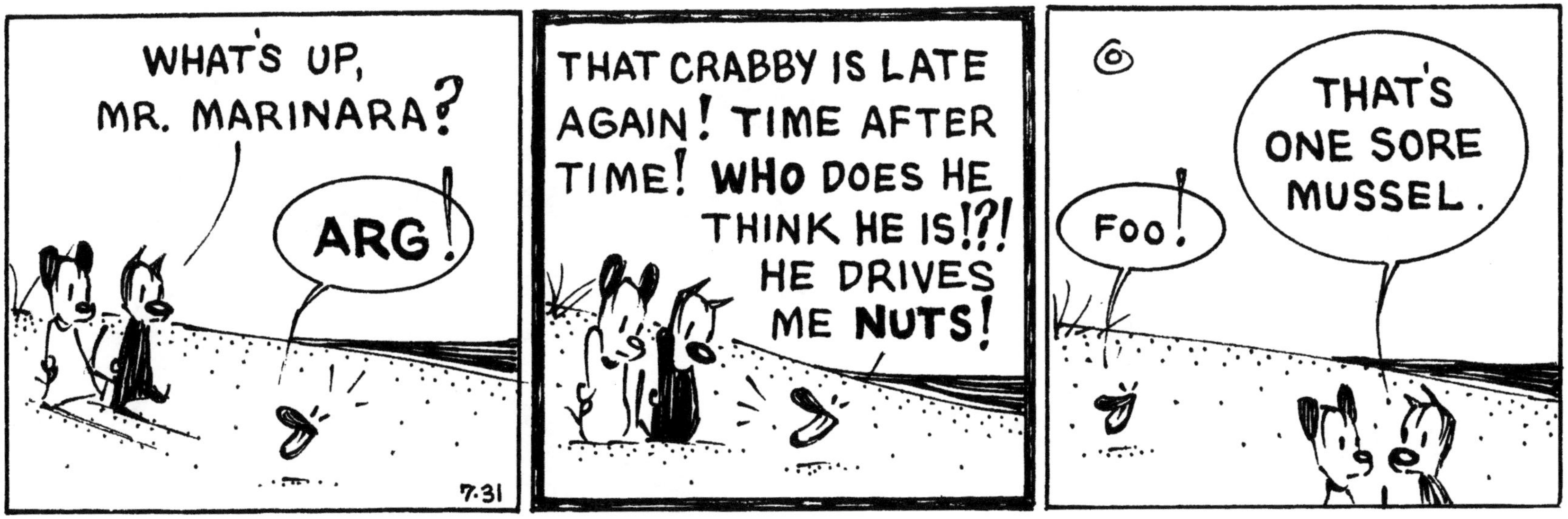
WHAT'S UP, MR. MARINARA?
ARG!
7·31
THAT CRABBY IS LATE AGAIN! TIME AFTER TIME! **WHO** DOES HE THINK HE IS!?! HE DRIVES ME **NUTS**!
FOO!
THAT'S ONE SORE MUSSEL.

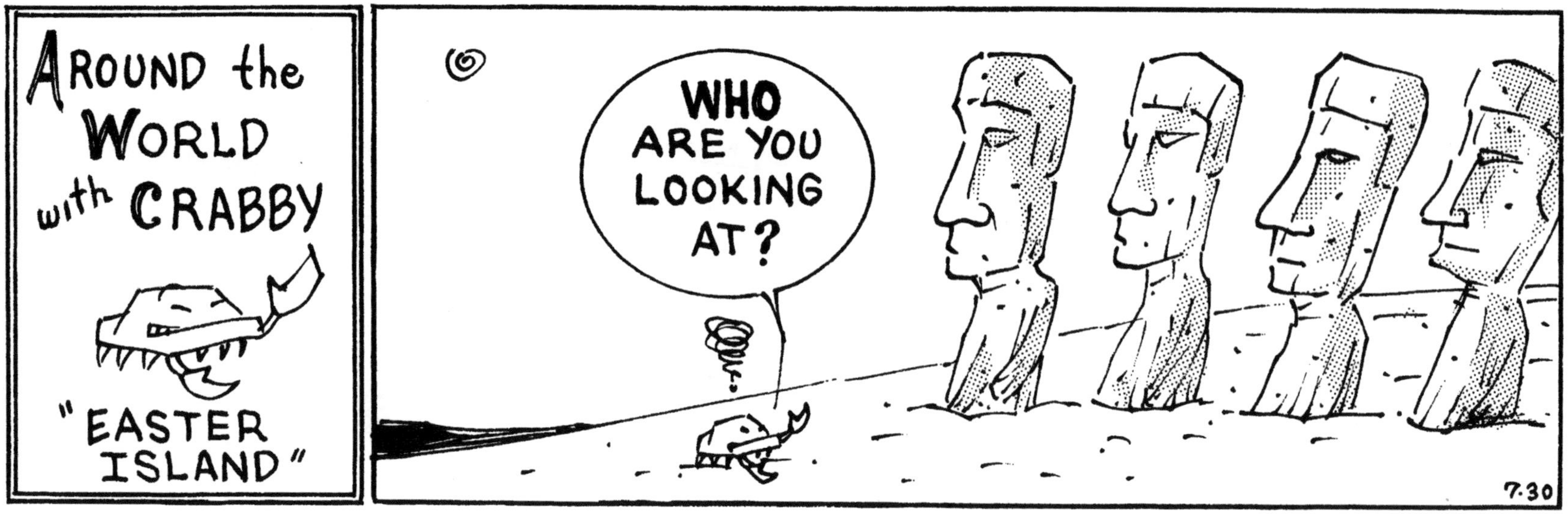
AROUND the WORLD with CRABBY
"EASTER ISLAND"
WHO ARE YOU LOOKING AT?
7.30

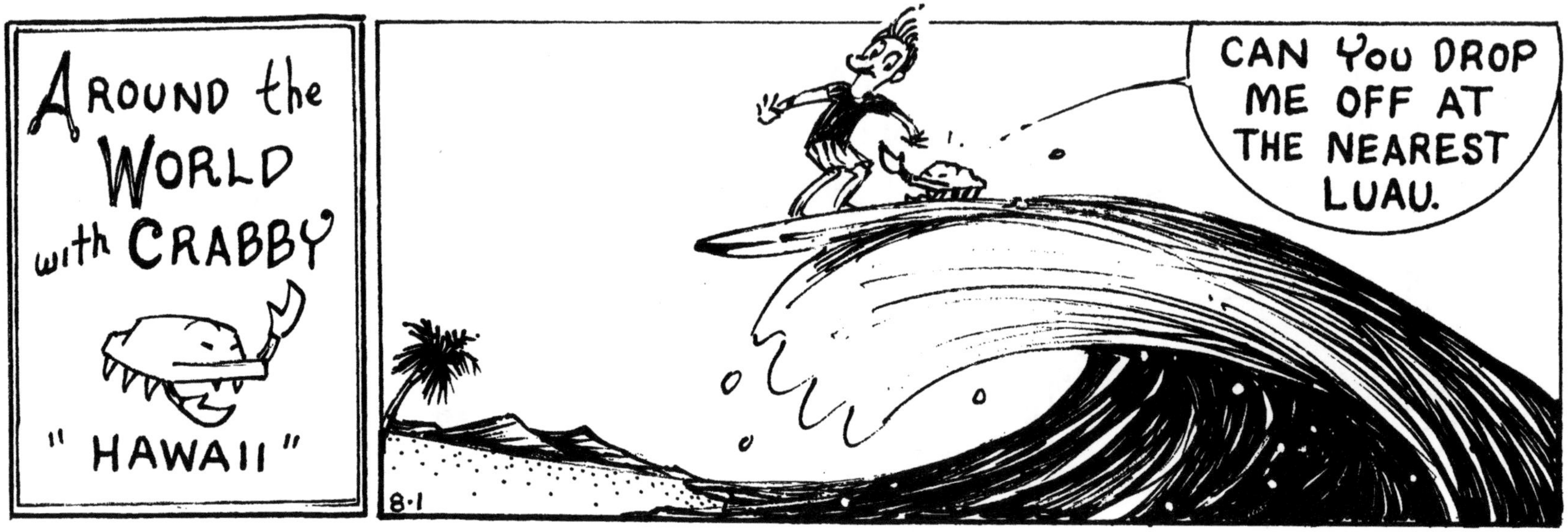
AROUND the WORLD with CRABBY
"HAWAII"
CAN YOU DROP ME OFF AT THE NEAREST LUAU.
8.1

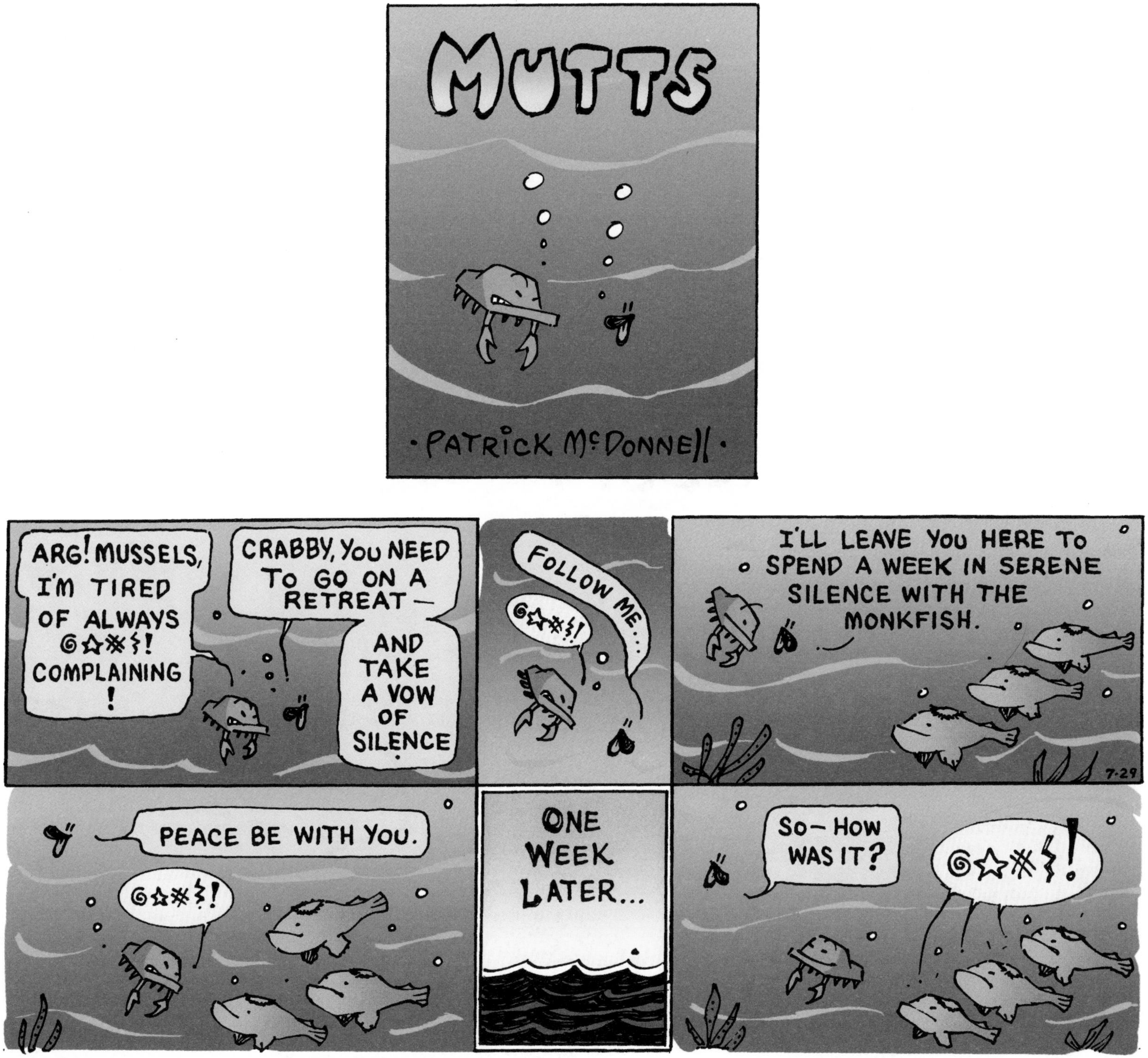
MUTTS
PATRICK McDONNELL
ARG! MUSSELS, I'M TIRED OF ALWAYS COMPLAINING!
CRABBY, YOU NEED TO GO ON A RETREAT—
AND TAKE A VOW OF SILENCE.
FOLLOW ME...
I'LL LEAVE YOU HERE TO SPEND A WEEK IN SERENE SILENCE WITH THE MONKFISH.
7-29
PEACE BE WITH YOU.
ONE WEEK LATER...
SO— HOW WAS IT?

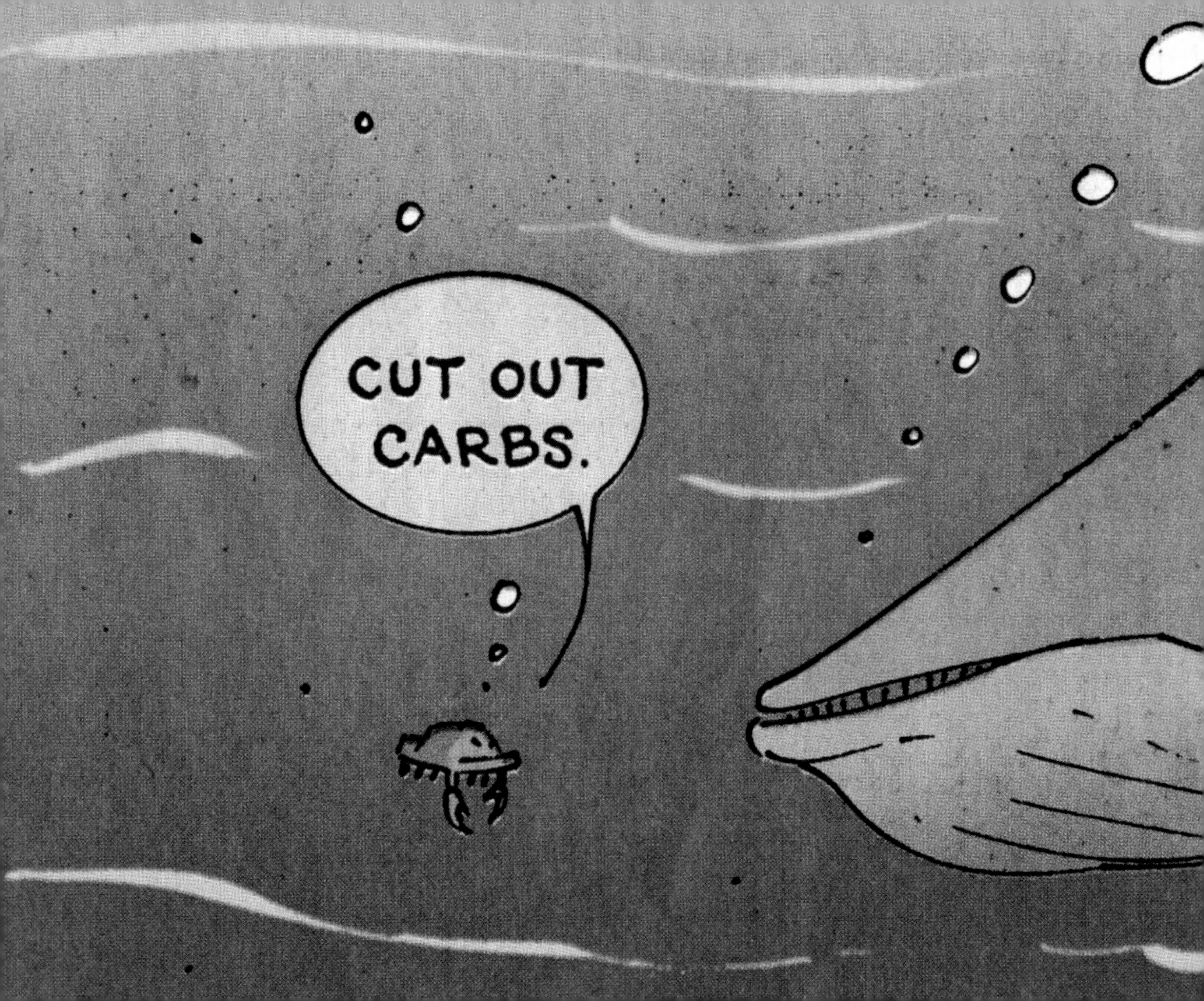
CUT OUT CARBS.

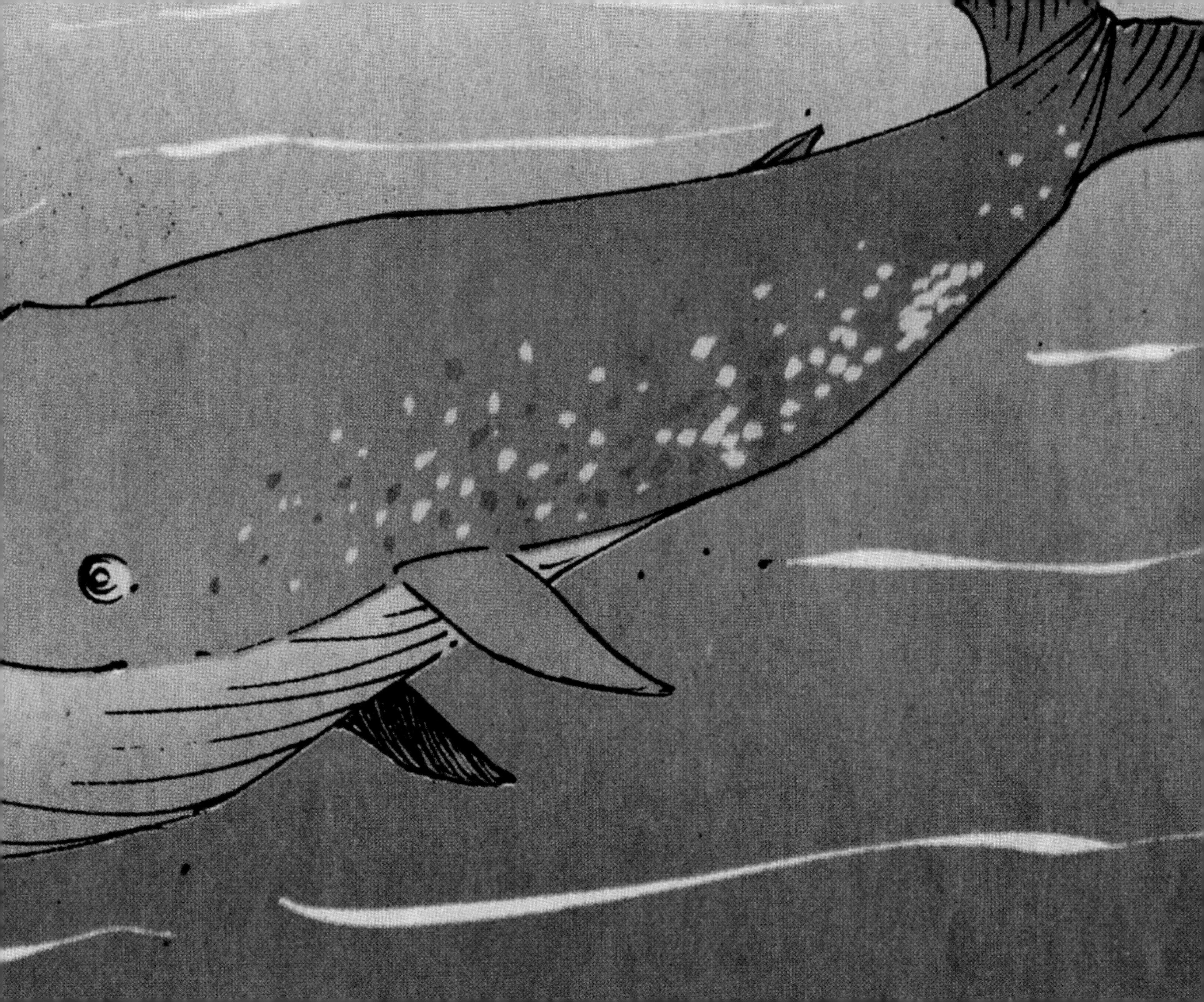

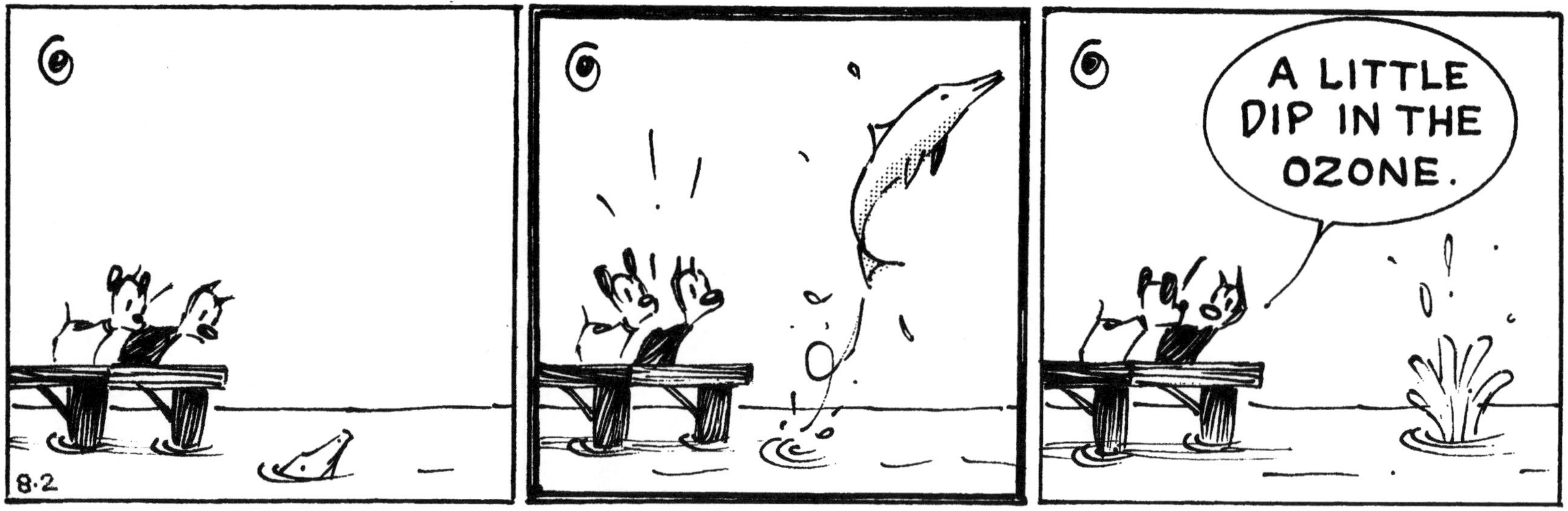
8·2
A LITTLE DIP IN THE OZONE.

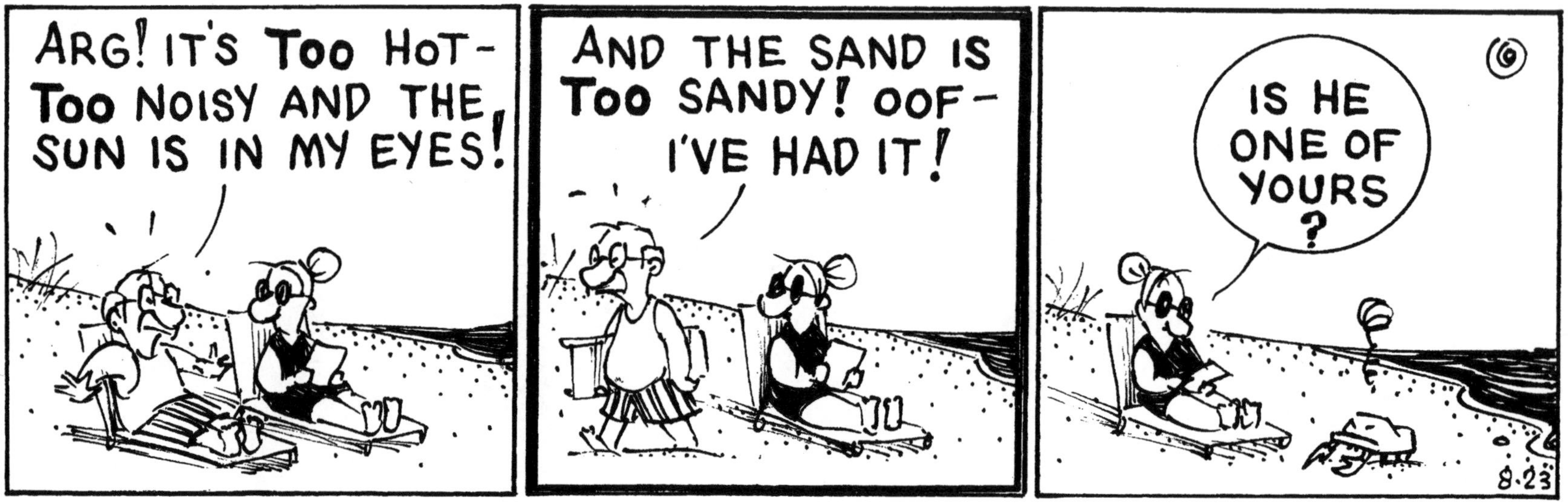
ARG! IT'S TOO HOT- TOO NOISY AND THE SUN IS IN MY EYES!
AND THE SAND IS TOO SANDY! OOF- I'VE HAD IT!
IS HE ONE OF YOURS?
8·23

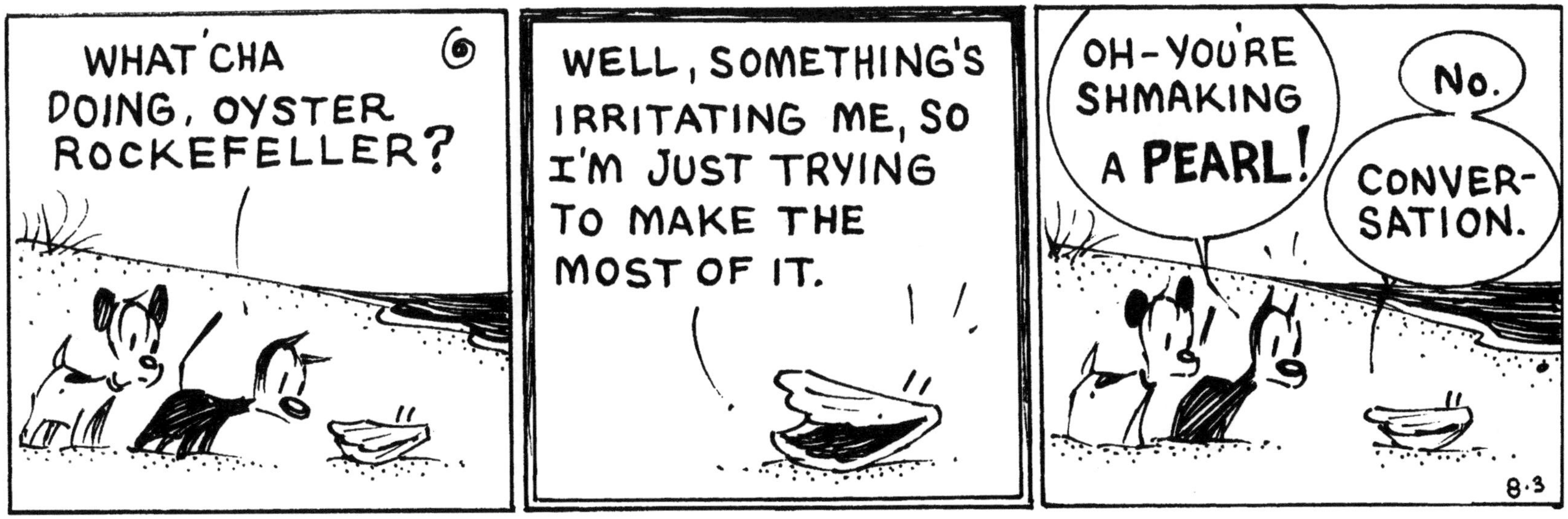
WHAT'CHA DOING, OYSTER ROCKEFELLER?
WELL, SOMETHING'S IRRITATING ME, SO I'M JUST TRYING TO MAKE THE MOST OF IT.
OH-YOU'RE SHMAKING A PEARL!
No.
CONVER-SATION.
8·3

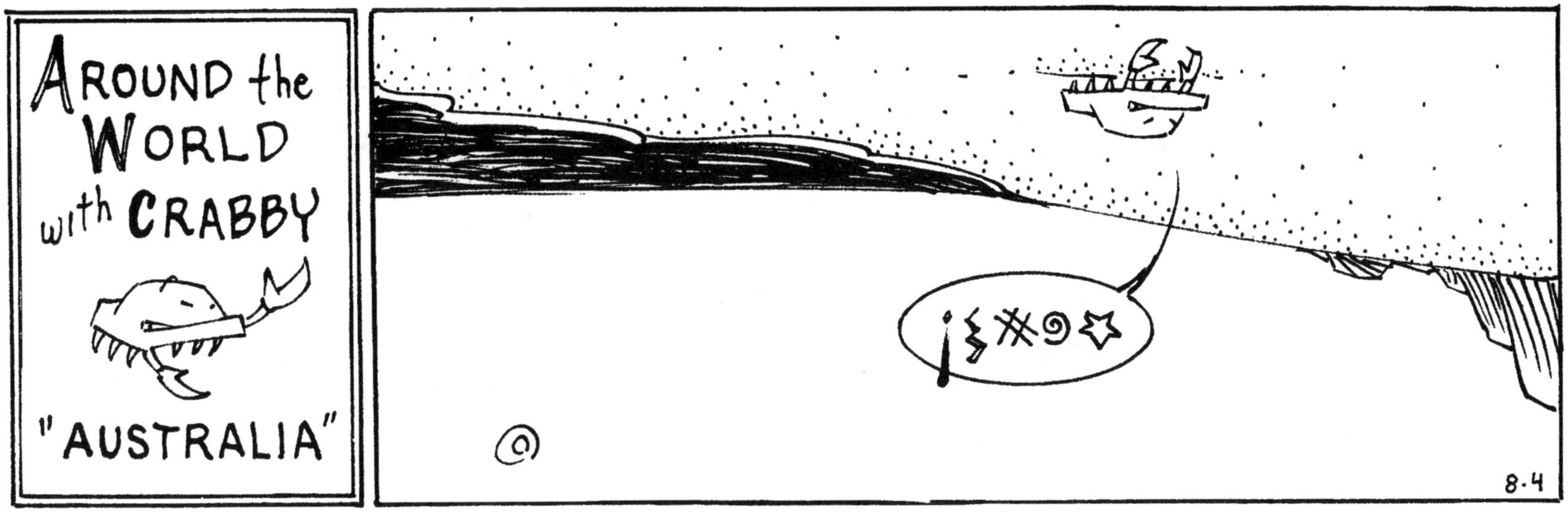
AROUND the WORLD with CRABBY
"AUSTRALIA"
8·4

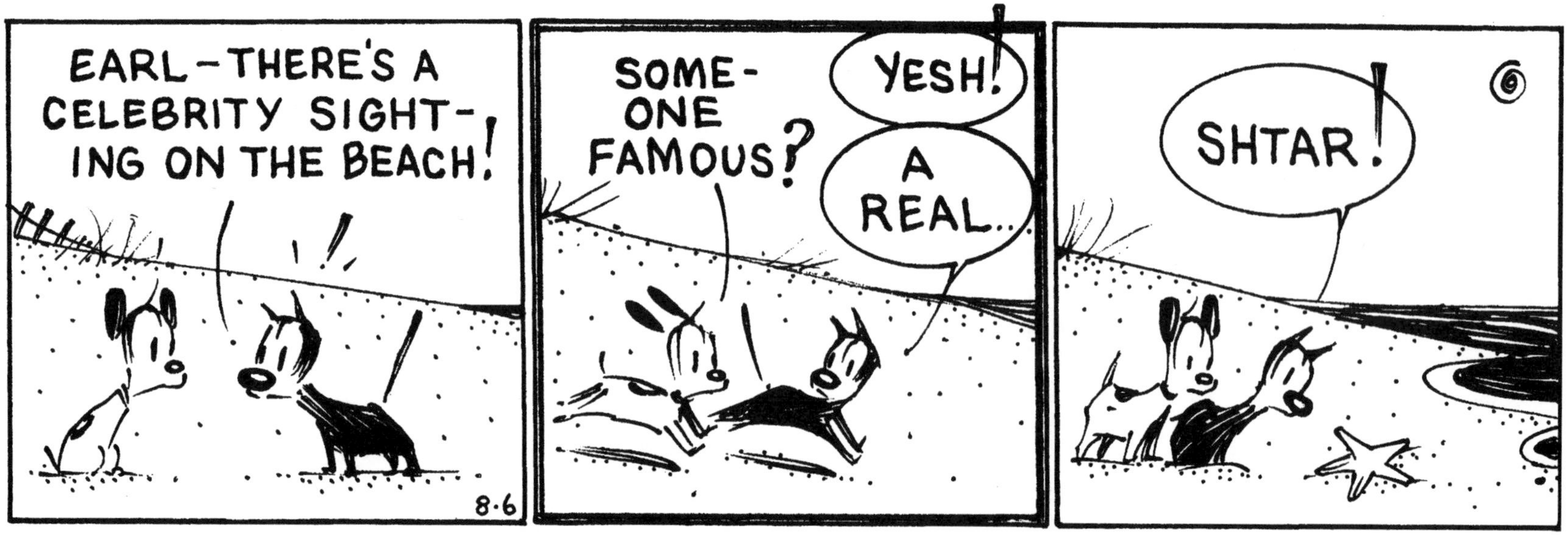
EARL—THERE'S A CELEBRITY SIGHTING ON THE BEACH!
8·6
SOME-ONE FAMOUS?
YESH!
A REAL...
SHTAR!

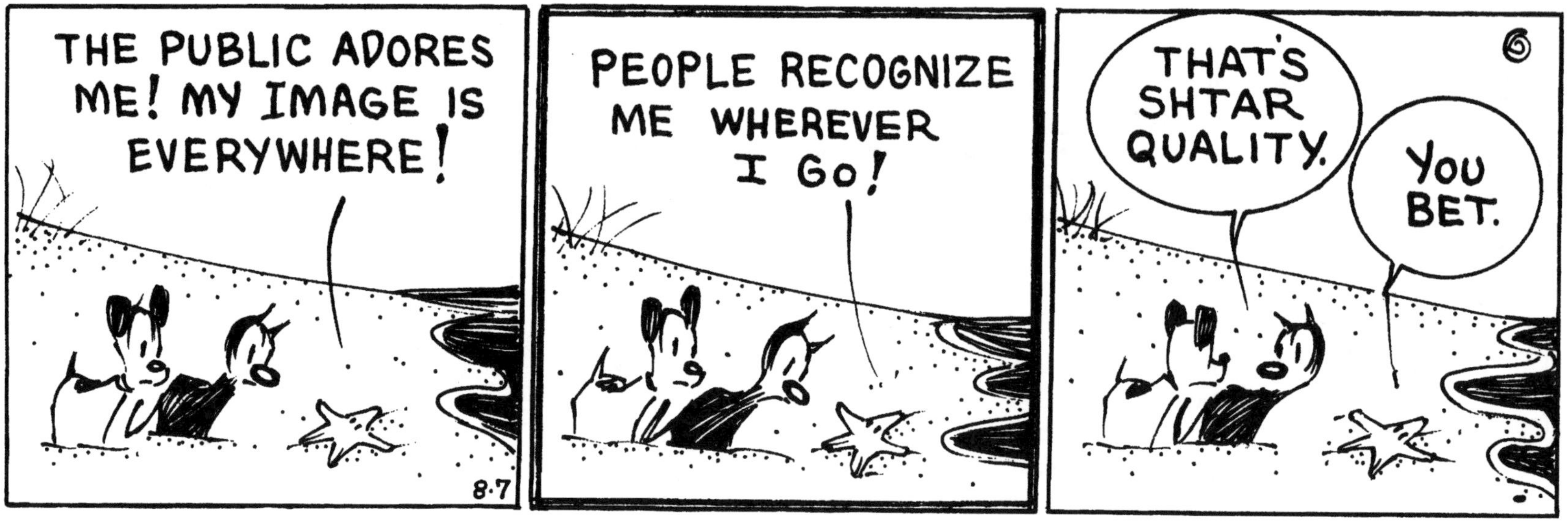
THE PUBLIC ADORES ME! MY IMAGE IS EVERYWHERE!
8·7
PEOPLE RECOGNIZE ME WHEREVER I GO!
THAT'S SHTAR QUALITY.
YOU BET.

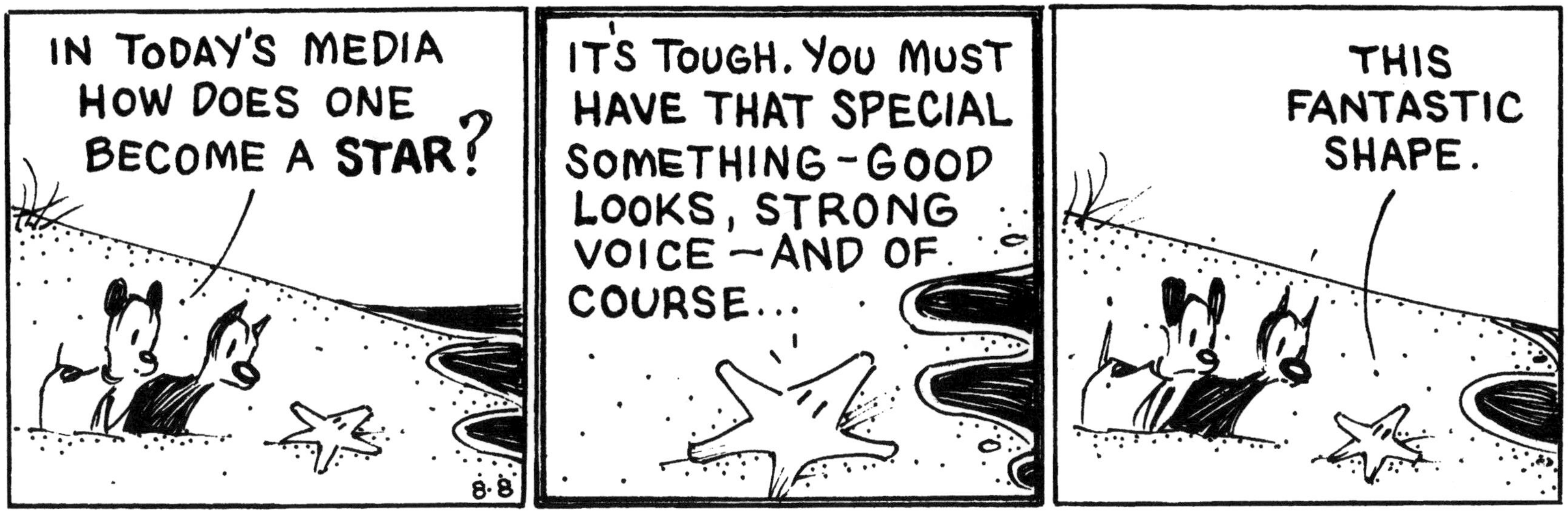
IN TODAY'S MEDIA HOW DOES ONE BECOME A **STAR**?
8·8
IT'S TOUGH. YOU MUST HAVE THAT SPECIAL SOMETHING—GOOD LOOKS, STRONG VOICE—AND OF COURSE...
THIS FANTASTIC SHAPE.

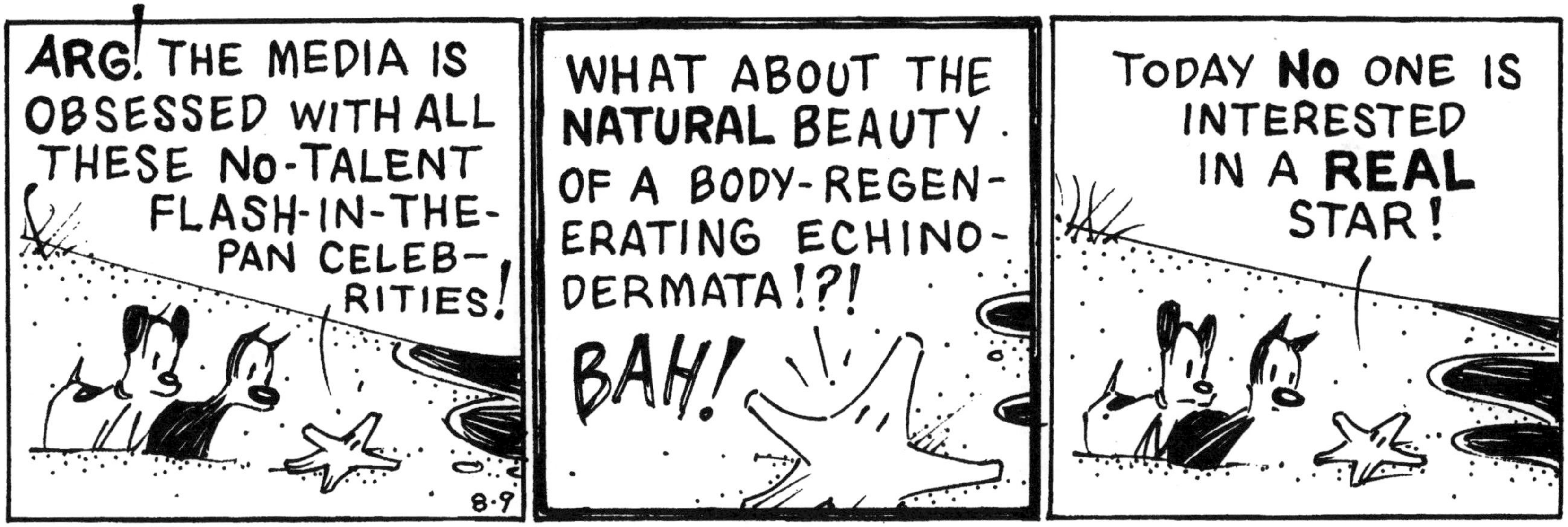
ARG! THE MEDIA IS OBSESSED WITH ALL THESE NO-TALENT FLASH-IN-THE-PAN CELEB-RITIES!
8·9
WHAT ABOUT THE **NATURAL** BEAUTY OF A BODY-REGEN-ERATING ECHINO-DERMATA!?!
BAH!
TODAY **NO** ONE IS INTERESTED IN A **REAL** STAR!

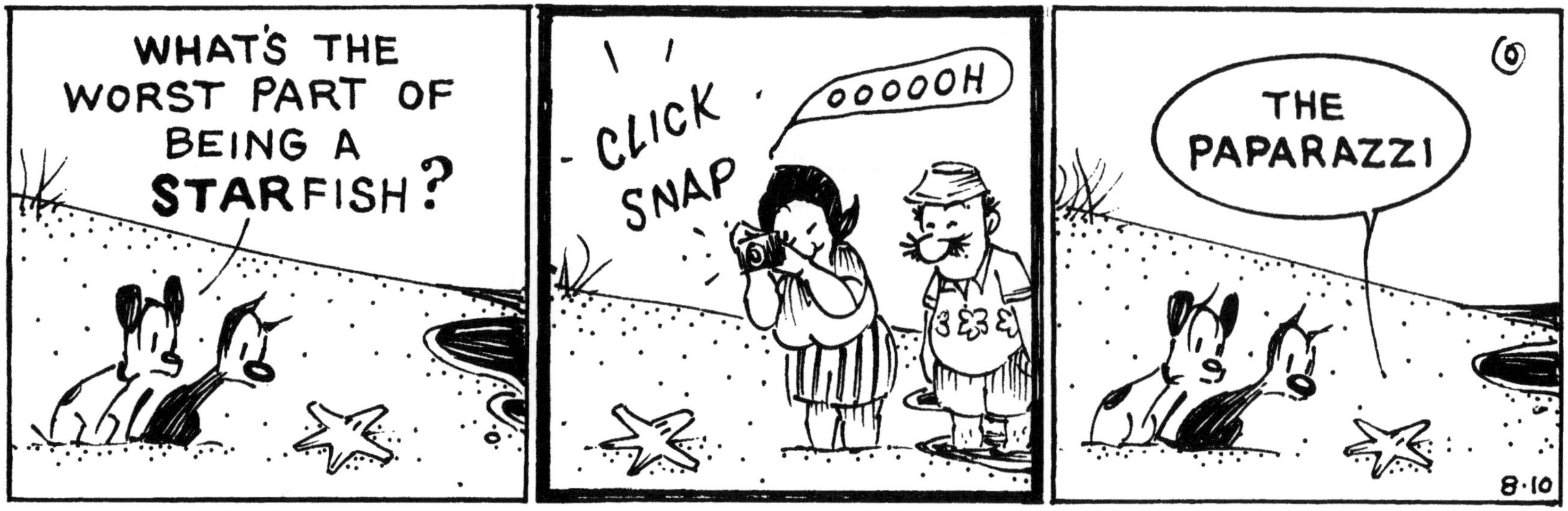
WHAT'S THE WORST PART OF BEING A STARFISH?
CLICK
SNAP
OOOOOH
THE PAPARAZZI
8·10

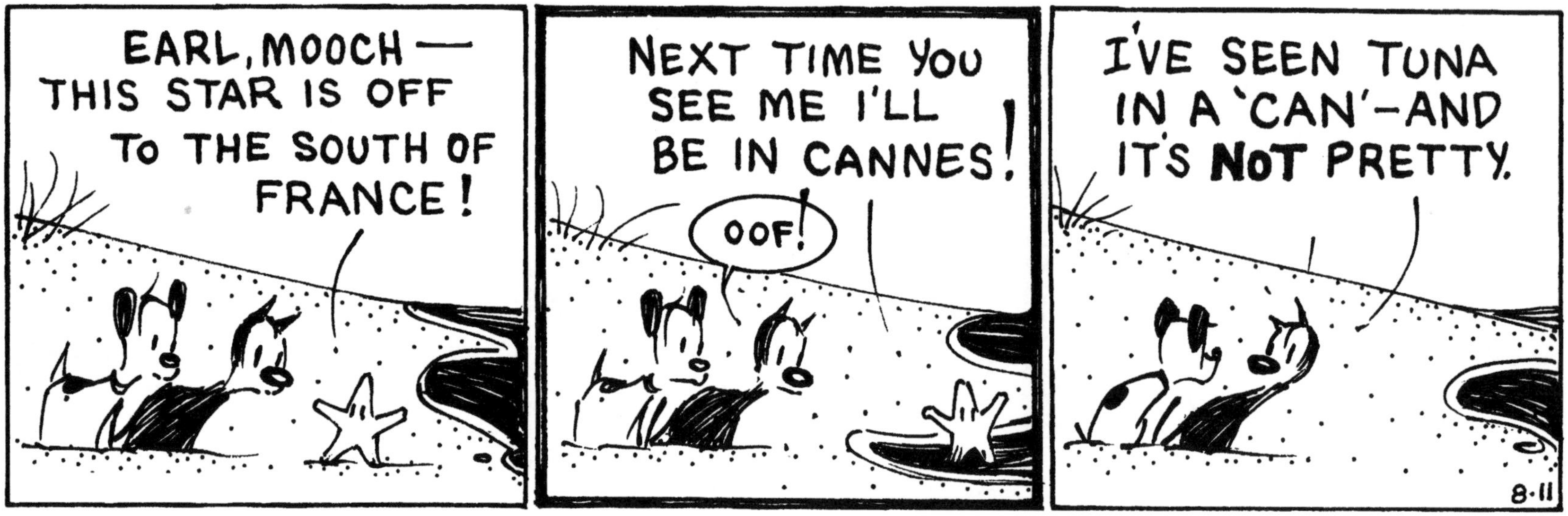
EARL, MOOCH — THIS STAR IS OFF TO THE SOUTH OF FRANCE!
NEXT TIME YOU SEE ME I'LL BE IN CANNES!
OOF!
I'VE SEEN TUNA IN A 'CAN'—AND IT'S NOT PRETTY.
8·11

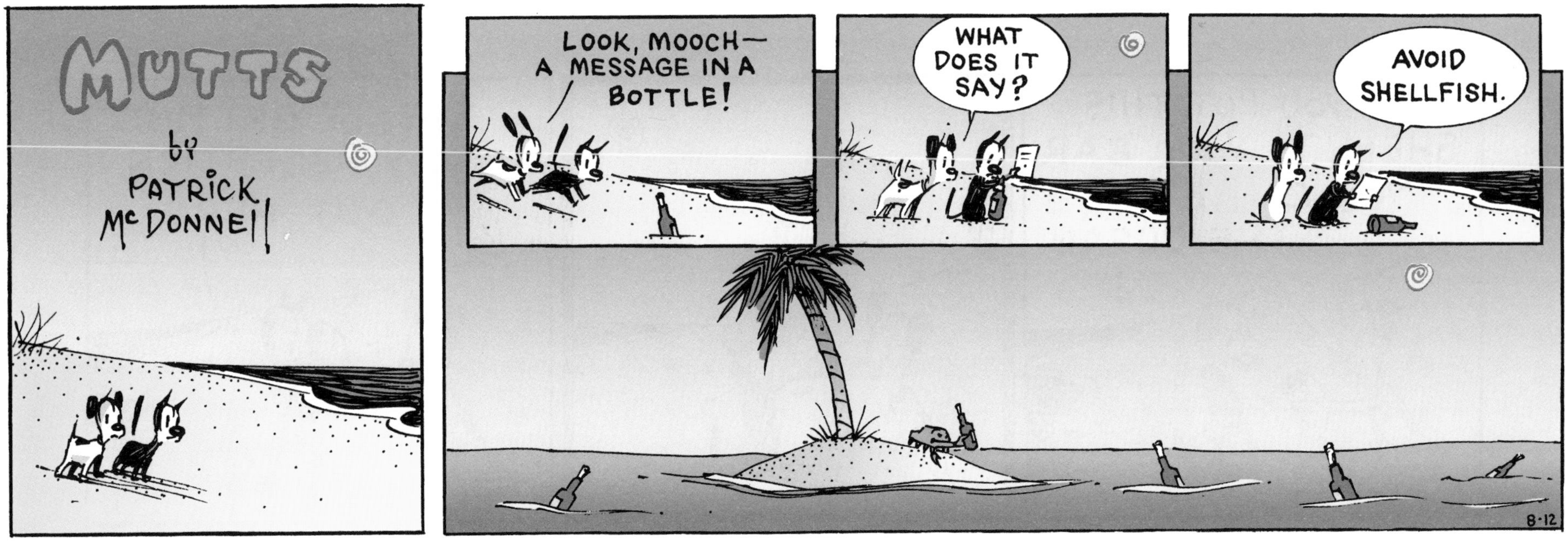
MUTTS
by PATRICK McDONNELL
LOOK, MOOCH— A MESSAGE IN A BOTTLE!
WHAT DOES IT SAY?
AVOID SHELLFISH.
8·12

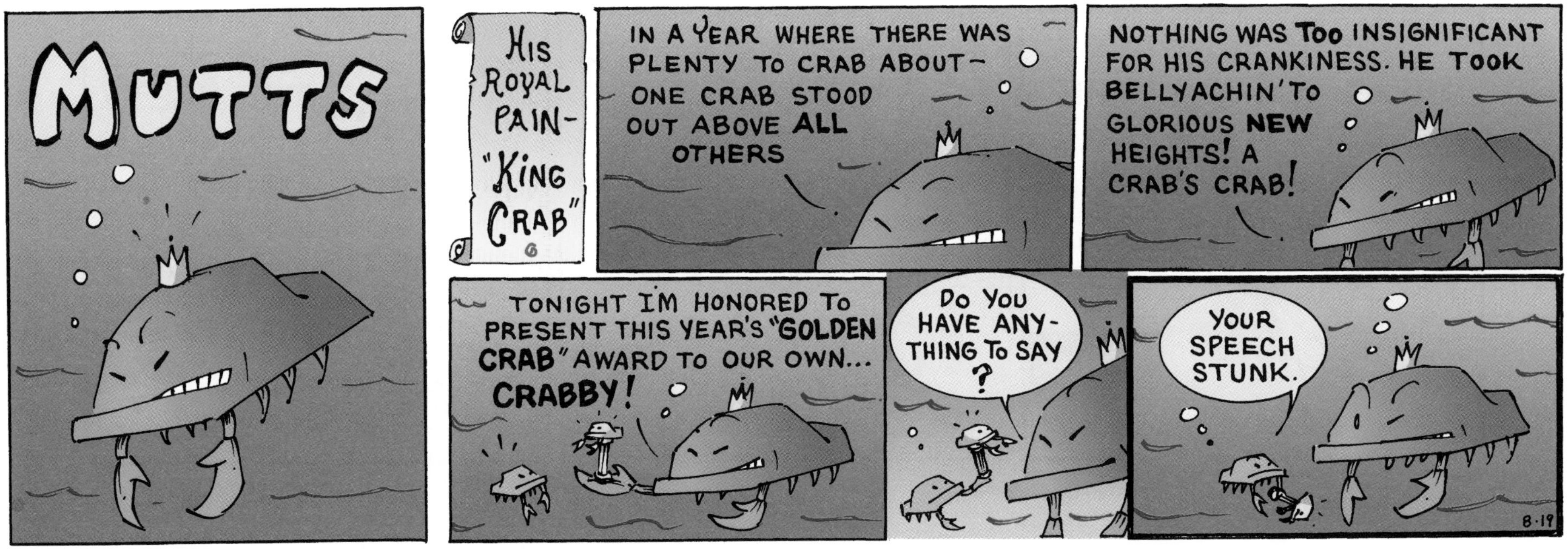
MUTTS
HIS ROYAL PAIN- "KING CRAB"
IN A YEAR WHERE THERE WAS PLENTY TO CRAB ABOUT— ONE CRAB STOOD OUT ABOVE ALL OTHERS
NOTHING WAS TOO INSIGNIFICANT FOR HIS CRANKINESS. HE TOOK BELLYACHIN' TO GLORIOUS NEW HEIGHTS! A CRAB'S CRAB!
TONIGHT I'M HONORED TO PRESENT THIS YEAR'S "GOLDEN CRAB" AWARD TO OUR OWN... CRABBY!
DO YOU HAVE ANYTHING TO SAY?
YOUR SPEECH STUNK.
8·19

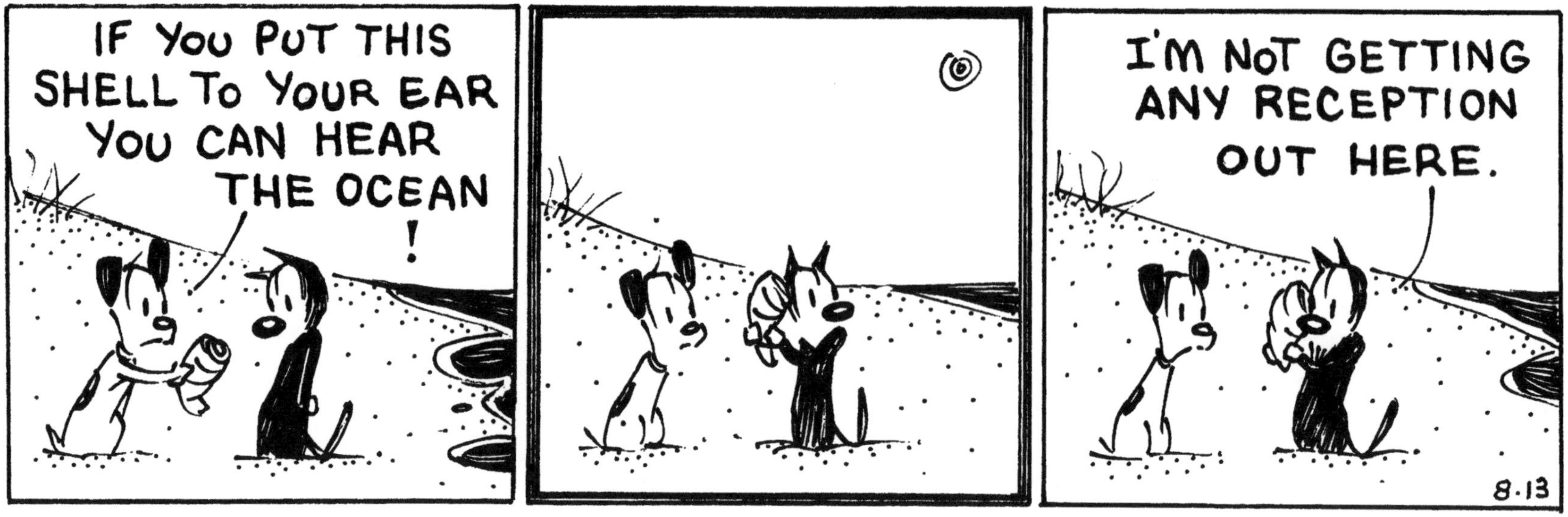
IF YOU PUT THIS SHELL TO YOUR EAR YOU CAN HEAR THE OCEAN !
I'M NOT GETTING ANY RECEPTION OUT HERE.
8·13

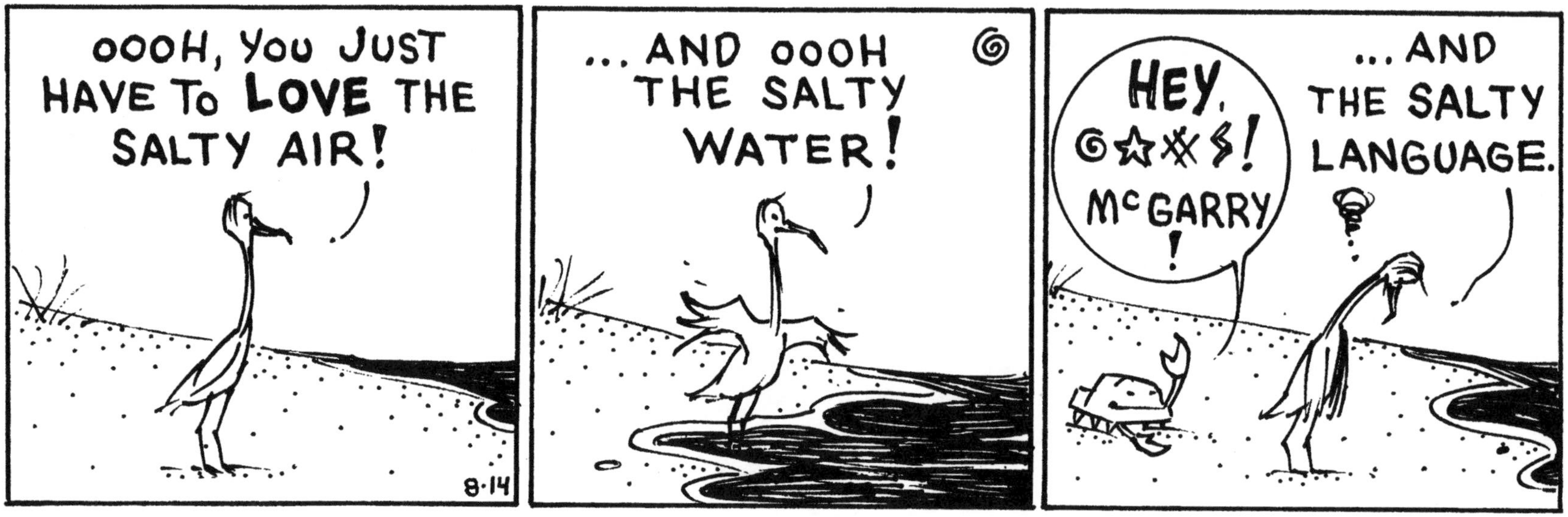
OOOH, YOU JUST HAVE TO **LOVE** THE SALTY AIR!
...AND OOOH THE SALTY WATER!
HEY, @☆※$! McGARRY!
...AND THE SALTY LANGUAGE.
8·14

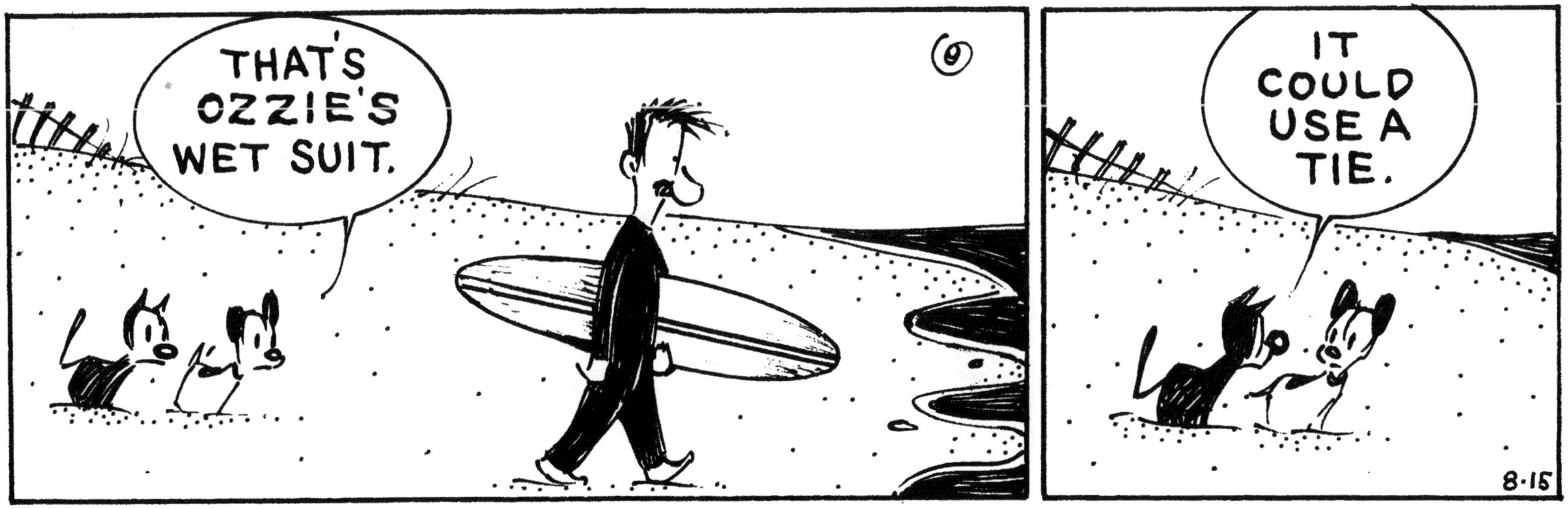
THAT'S OZZIE'S WET SUIT.
IT COULD USE A TIE.
8-15

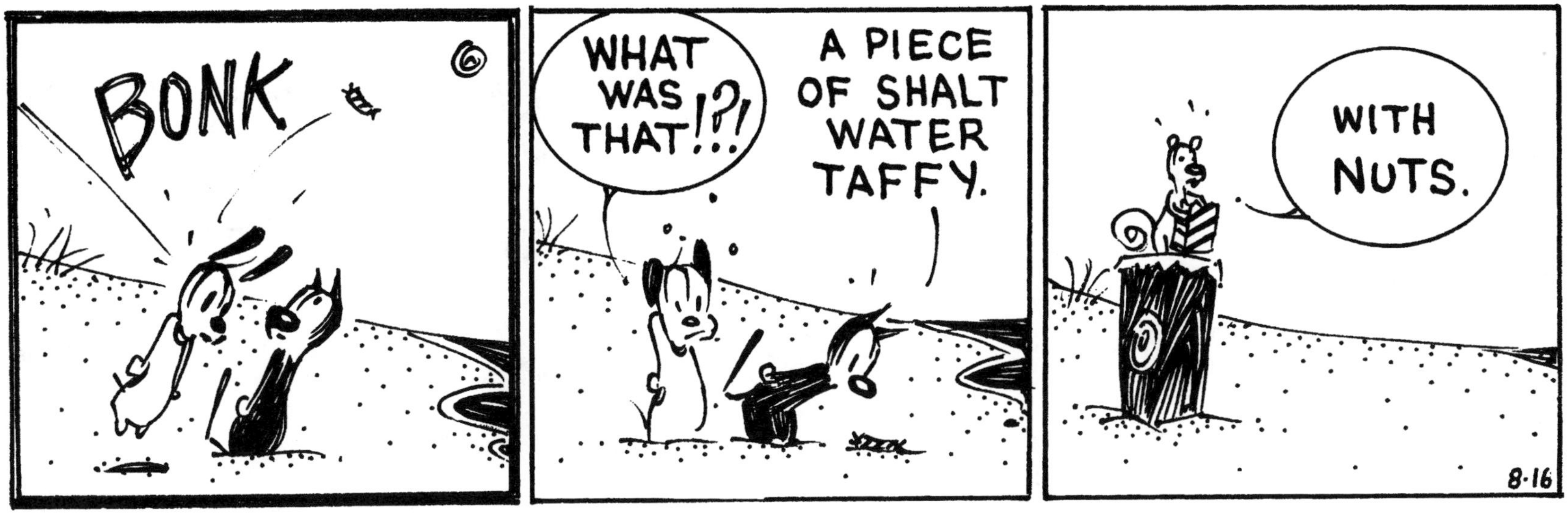
BONK
WHAT WAS THAT!?!
A PIECE OF SHALT WATER TAFFY.
WITH NUTS.
8-16

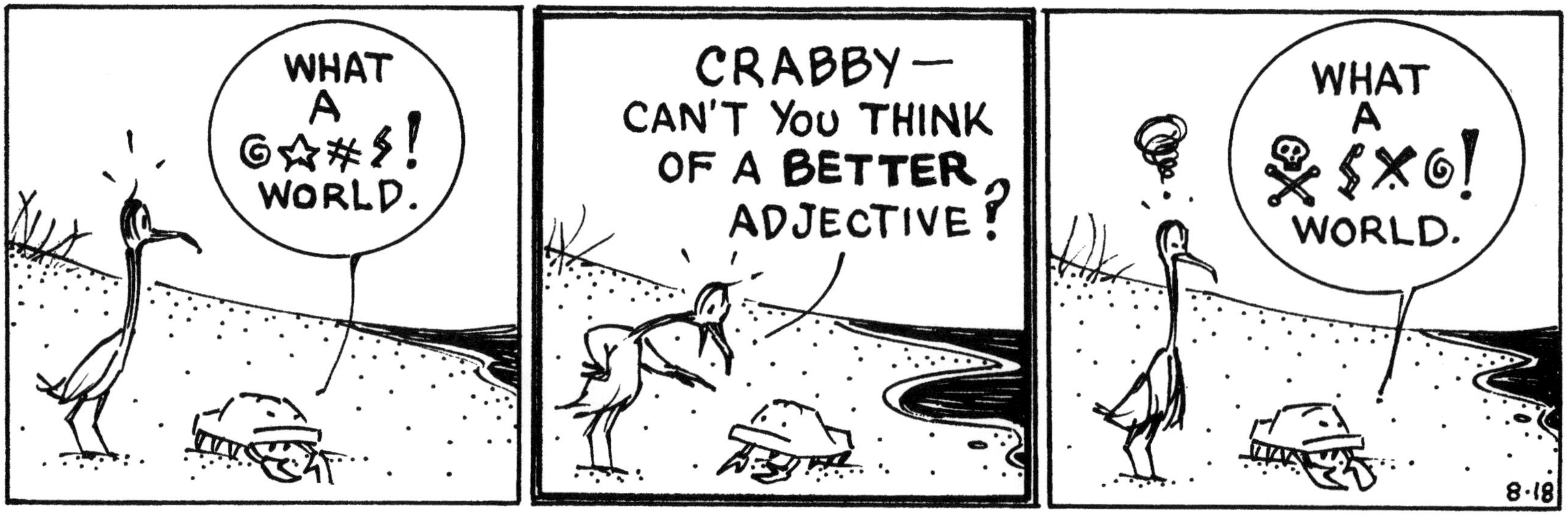
WHAT A
WORLD.
CRABBY— CAN'T YOU THINK OF A **BETTER** ADJECTIVE?
WHAT A
WORLD.
8·18

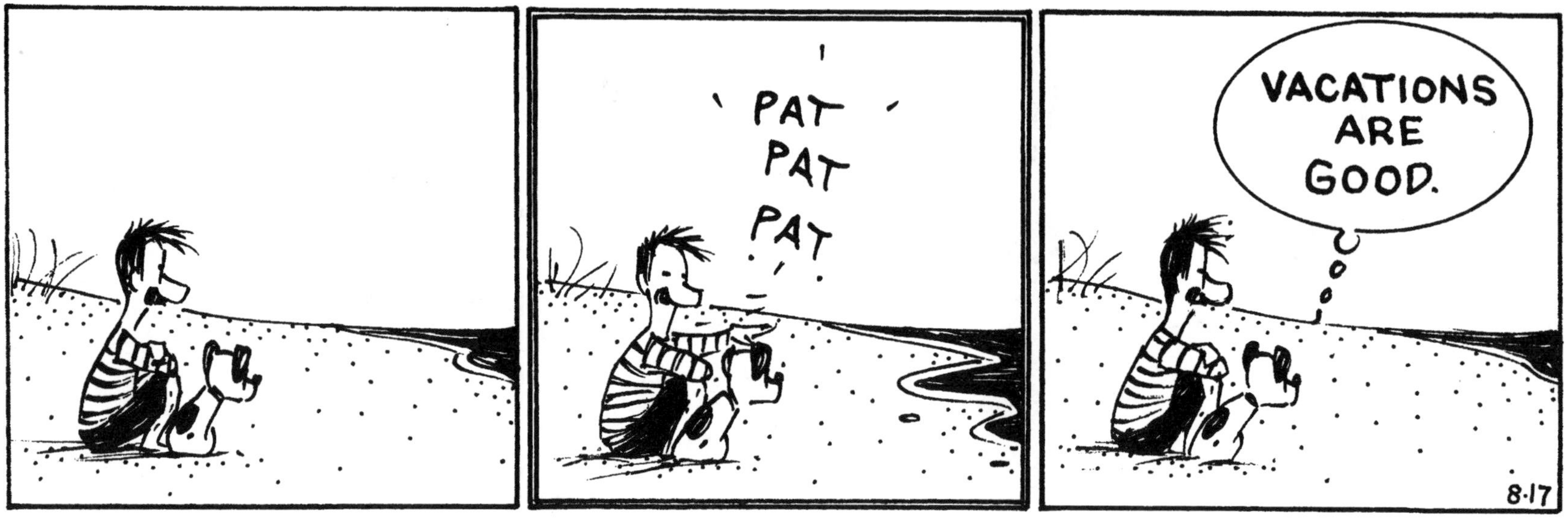
PAT PAT PAT
VACATIONS ARE GOOD.
8·17

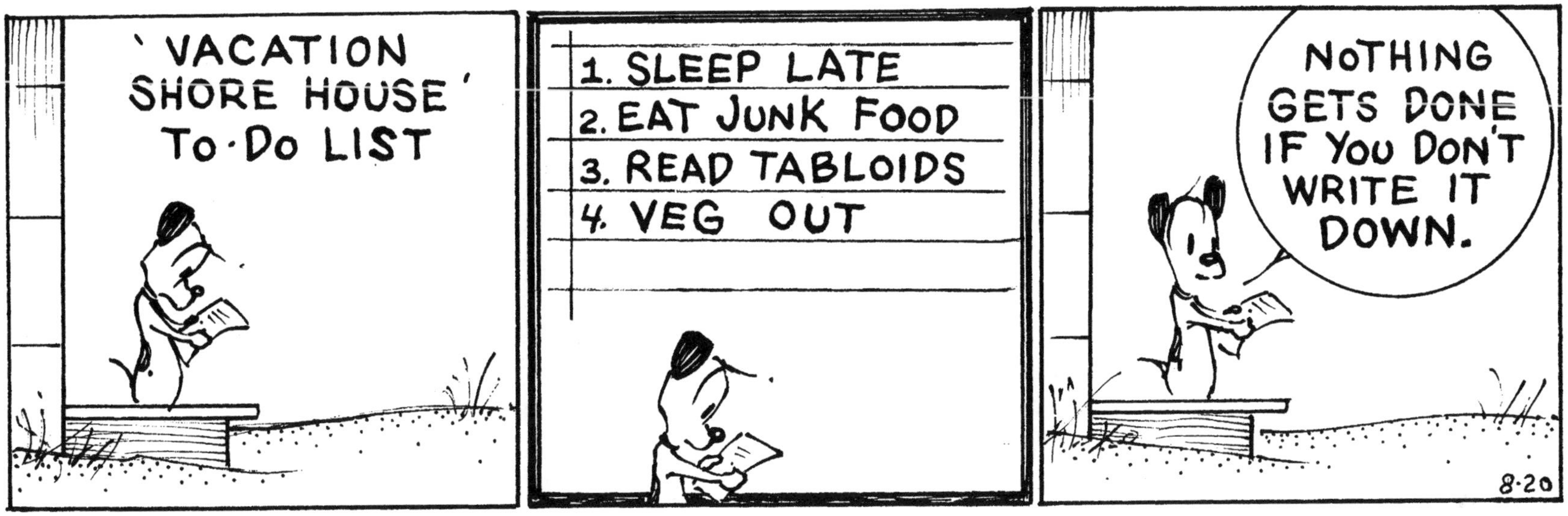
'VACATION SHORE HOUSE' TO-DO LIST
1. SLEEP LATE
2. EAT JUNK FOOD
3. READ TABLOIDS
4. VEG OUT
NOTHING GETS DONE IF YOU DON'T WRITE IT DOWN.
8·20

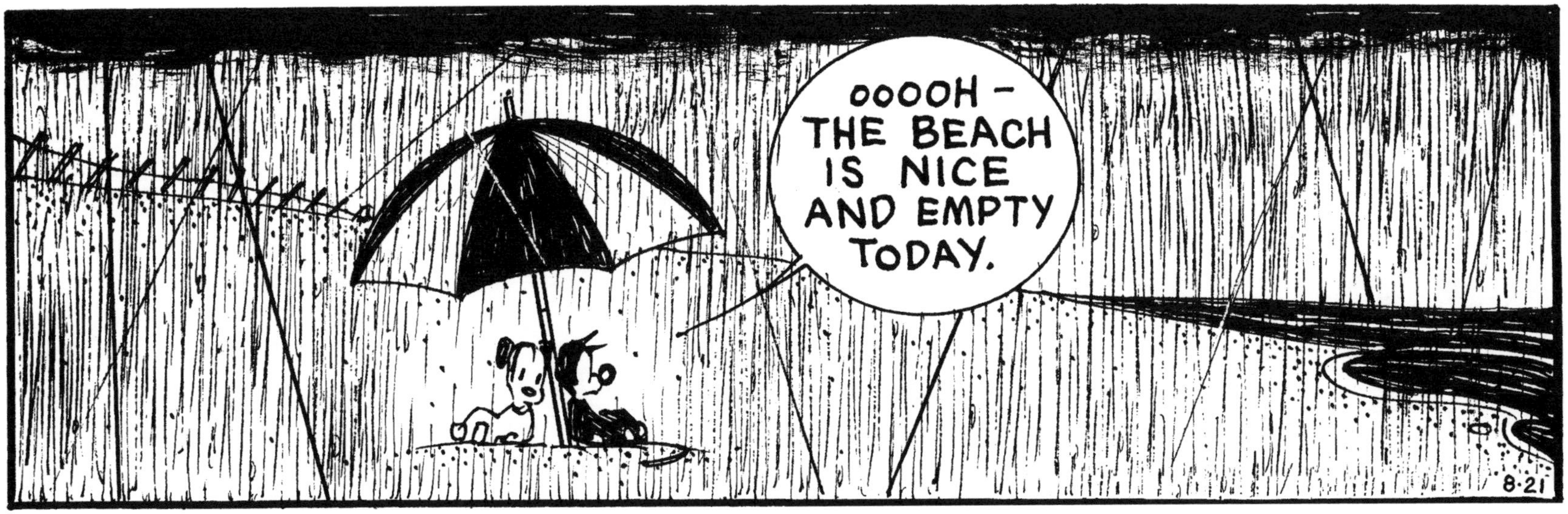
OOOOH - THE BEACH IS NICE AND EMPTY TODAY.
8·21

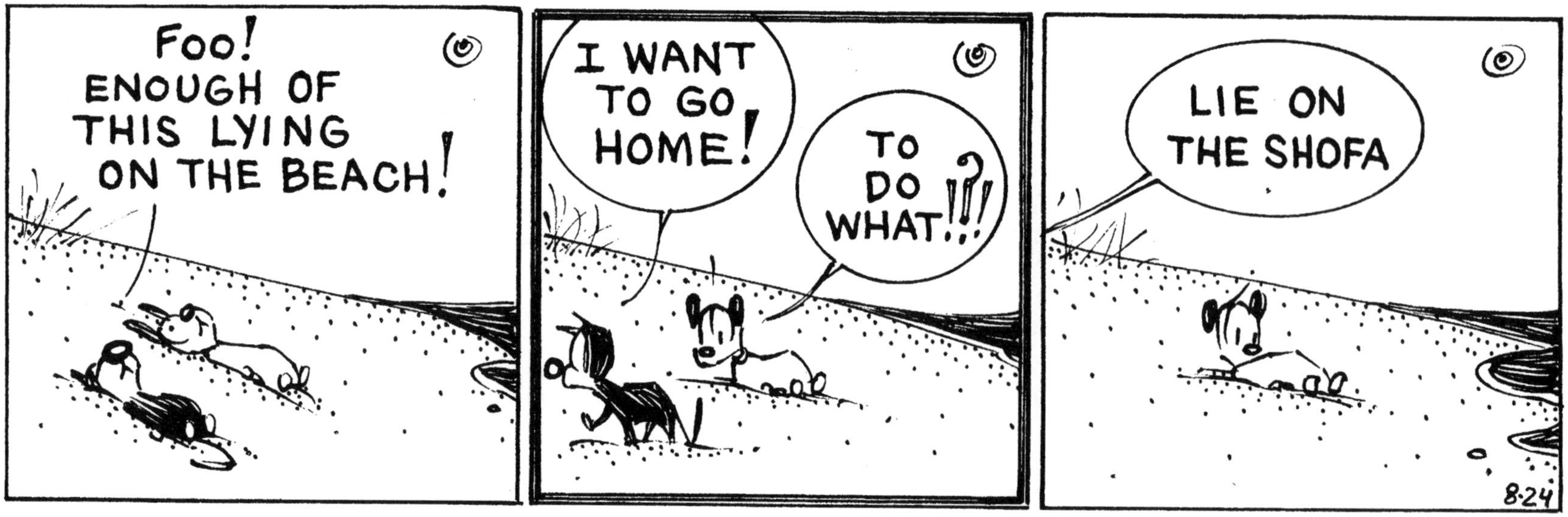
FOO! ENOUGH OF THIS LYING ON THE BEACH!
I WANT TO GO HOME!
TO DO WHAT!?!!
LIE ON THE SHOFA
8·24

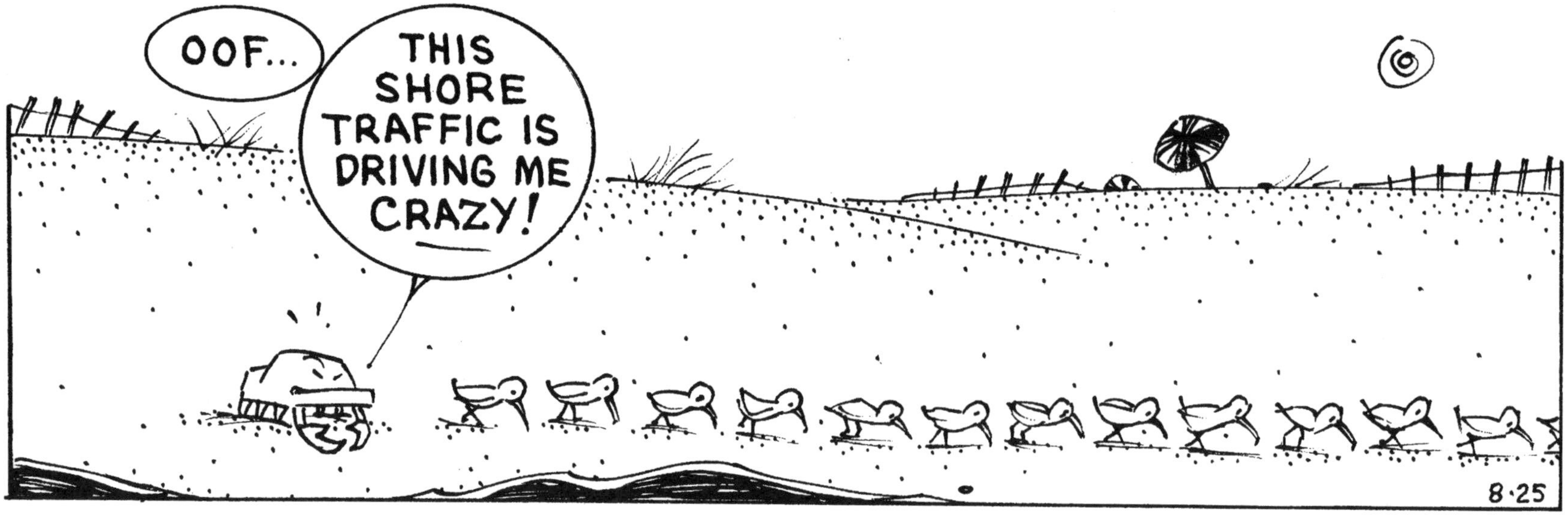
OOF...
THIS SHORE TRAFFIC IS DRIVING ME CRAZY!
8·25

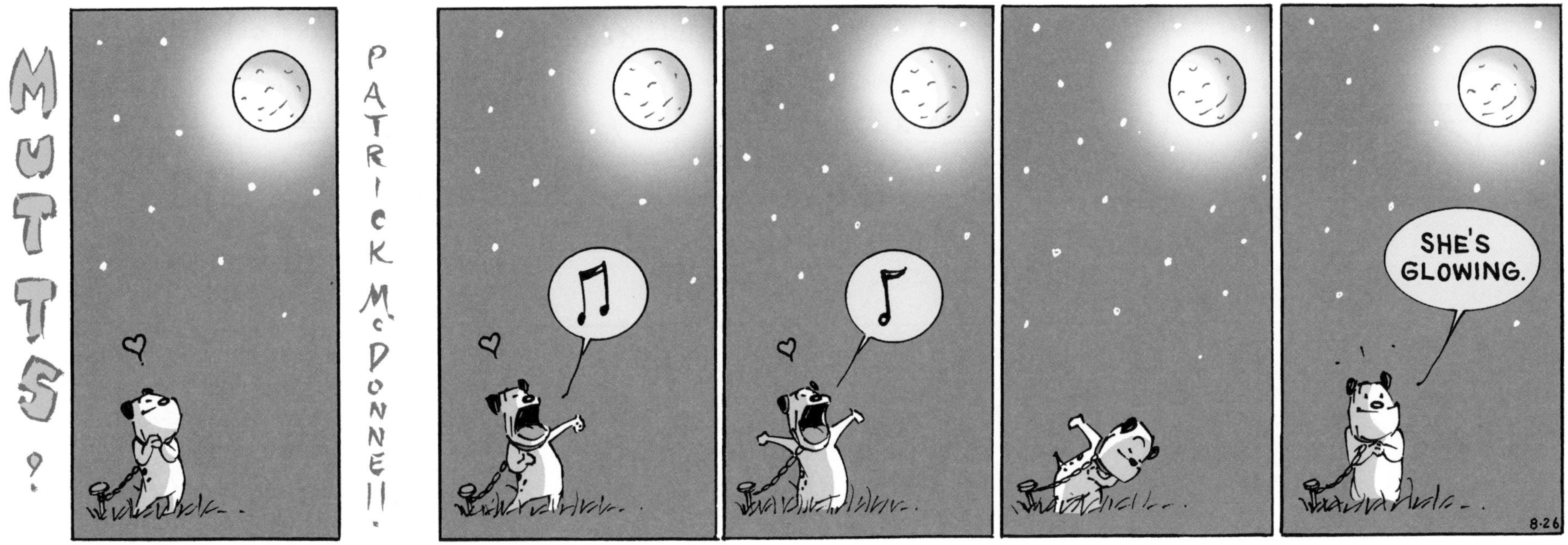
MUTTS
PATRICK McDONNELL
SHE'S GLOWING.
8-26

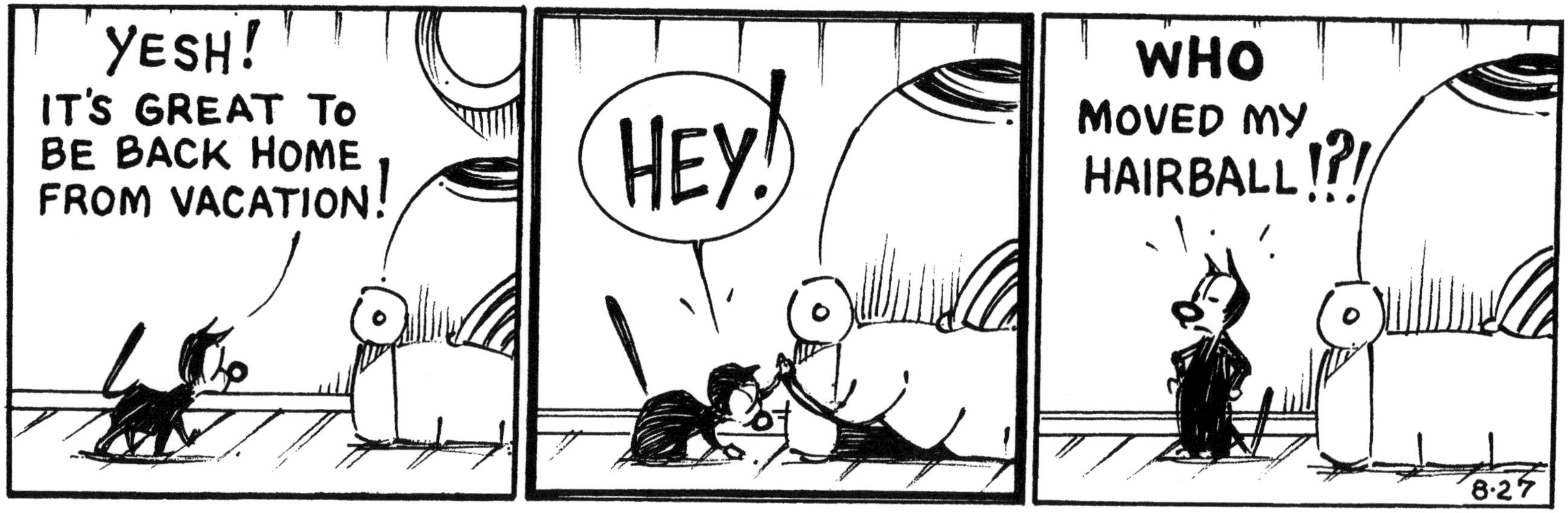
YESH! IT'S GREAT TO BE BACK HOME FROM VACATION!
HEY!
WHO MOVED MY HAIRBALL!?!
8·27

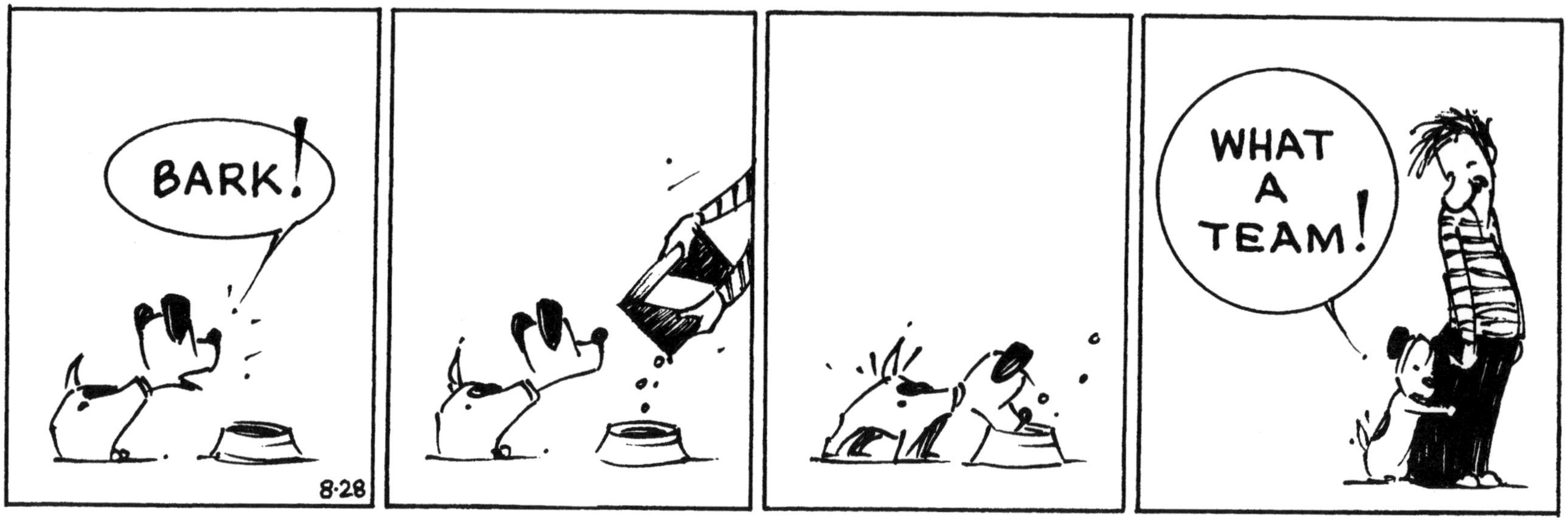
BARK!
8·28
WHAT A TEAM!

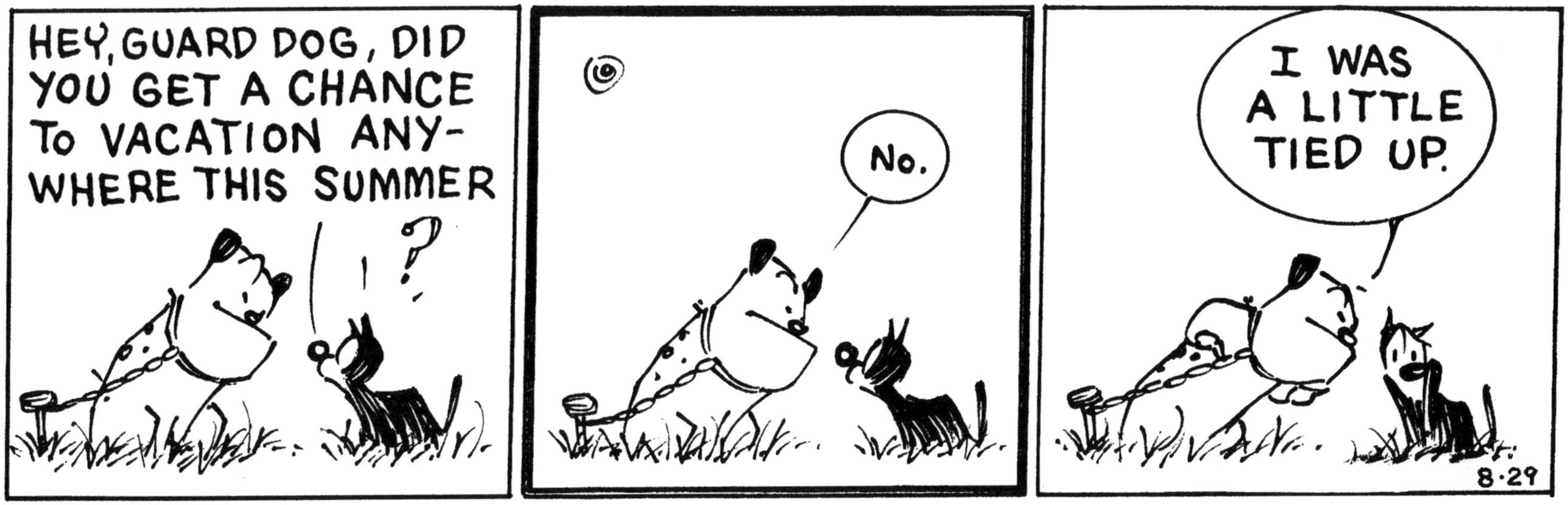
HEY, GUARD DOG, DID YOU GET A CHANCE TO VACATION ANY-WHERE THIS SUMMER
No.
I WAS A LITTLE TIED UP.
8·29

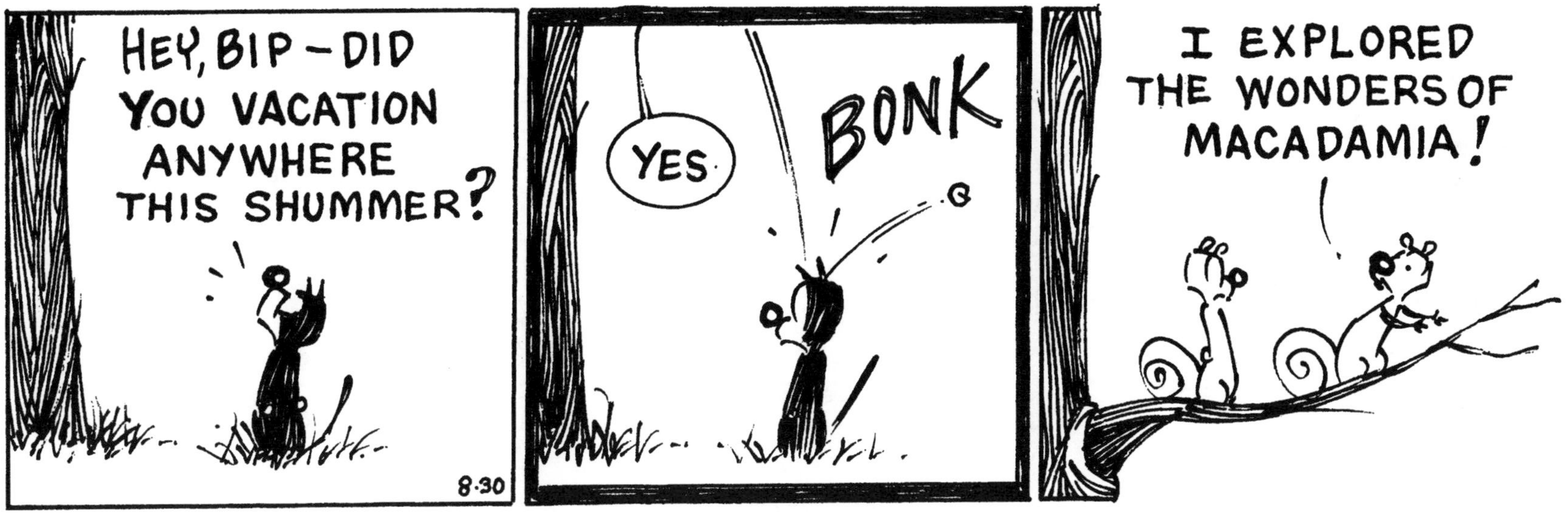
HEY, BIP - DID YOU VACATION ANYWHERE THIS SHUMMER?
8·30
YES.
BONK
I EXPLORED THE WONDERS OF MACADAMIA!

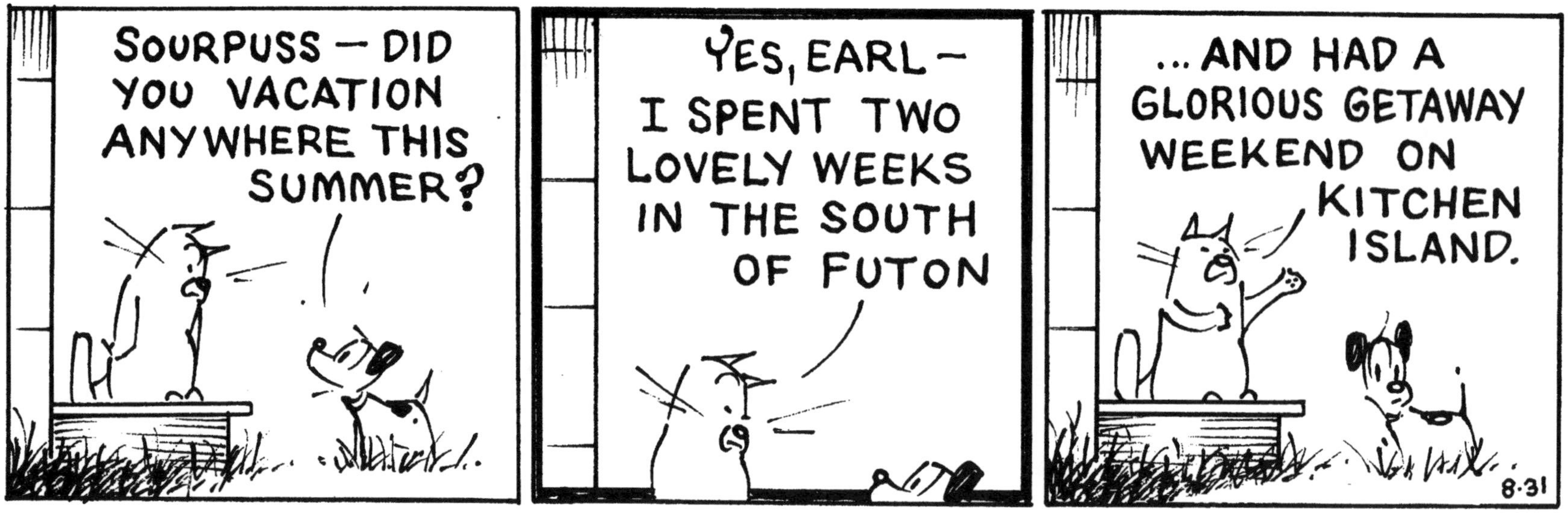
SOURPUSS — DID YOU VACATION ANYWHERE THIS SUMMER?
YES, EARL — I SPENT TWO LOVELY WEEKS IN THE SOUTH OF FUTON
... AND HAD A GLORIOUS GETAWAY WEEKEND ON KITCHEN ISLAND.
8·31

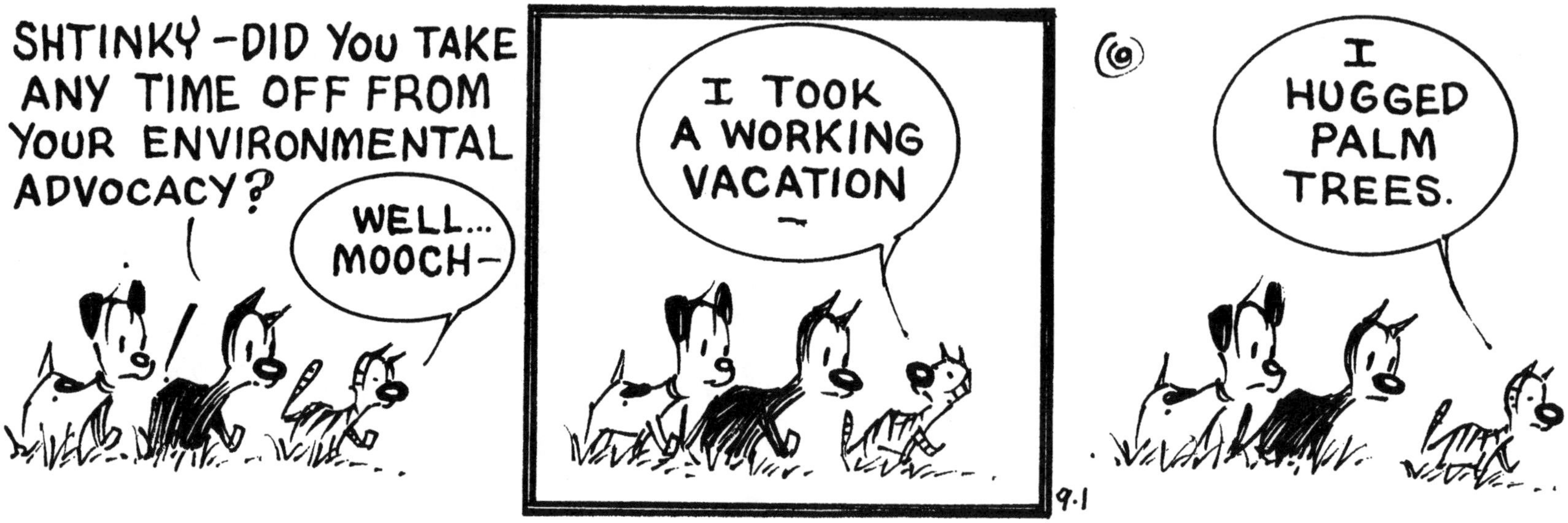
SHTINKY — DID YOU TAKE ANY TIME OFF FROM YOUR ENVIRONMENTAL ADVOCACY?
WELL... MOOCH —
I TOOK A WORKING VACATION —
I HUGGED PALM TREES.
9·1

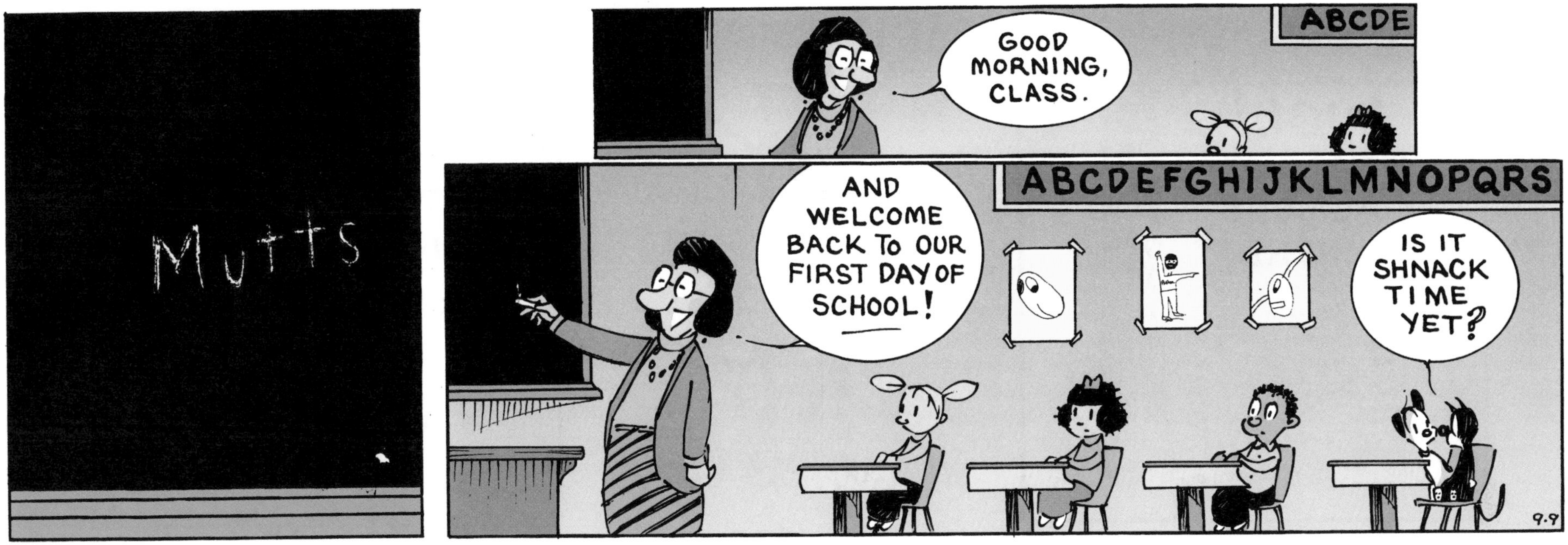
Mutts
ABCDE
GOOD MORNING, CLASS.
ABCDEFGHIJKLMNOPQRS
AND WELCOME BACK TO OUR FIRST DAY OF SCHOOL!
IS IT SHNACK TIME YET?
9.9

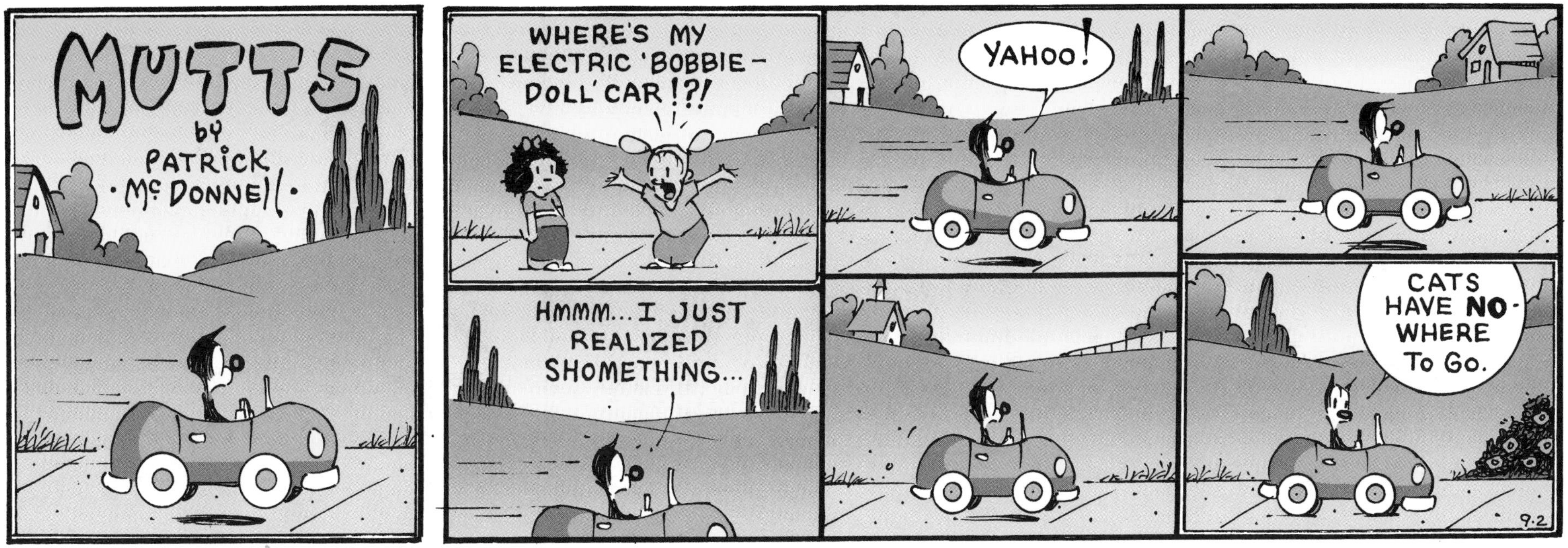
MUTTS
by PATRICK McDONNELL
WHERE'S MY ELECTRIC 'BOBBIE-DOLL' CAR!?!
YAHOO!
HMMM... I JUST REALIZED SHOMETHING...
CATS HAVE NO-WHERE TO GO.
9.2

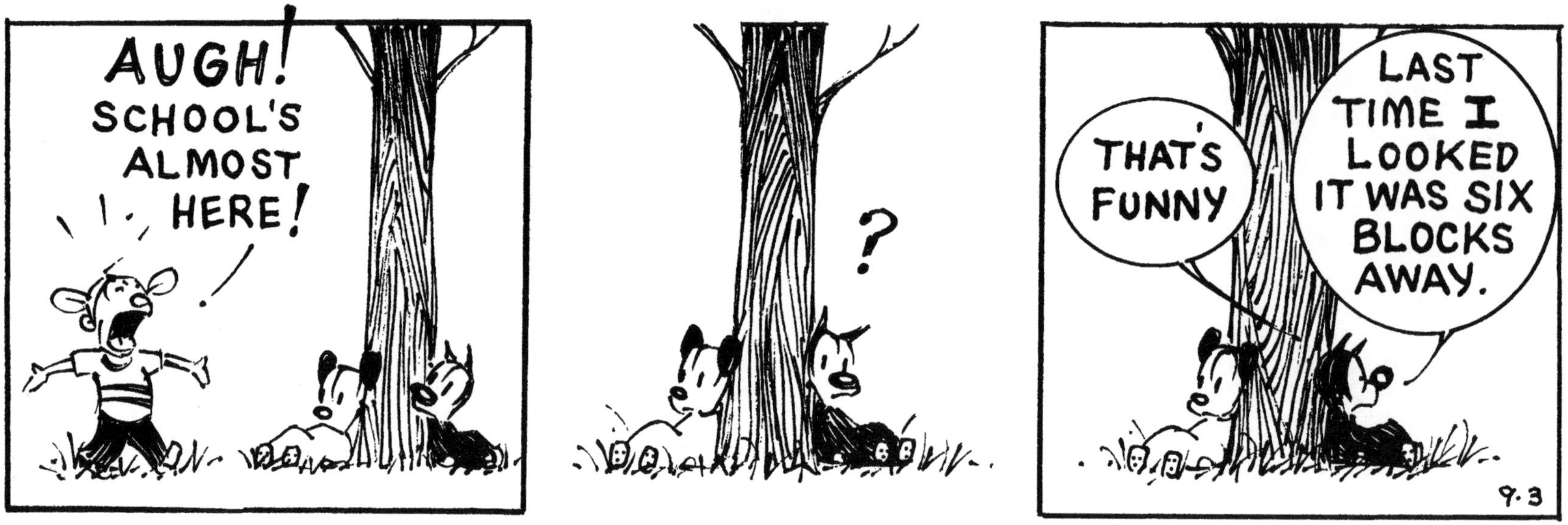
AUGH! SCHOOL'S ALMOST HERE!
?
THAT'S FUNNY
LAST TIME I LOOKED IT WAS SIX BLOCKS AWAY.
9.3

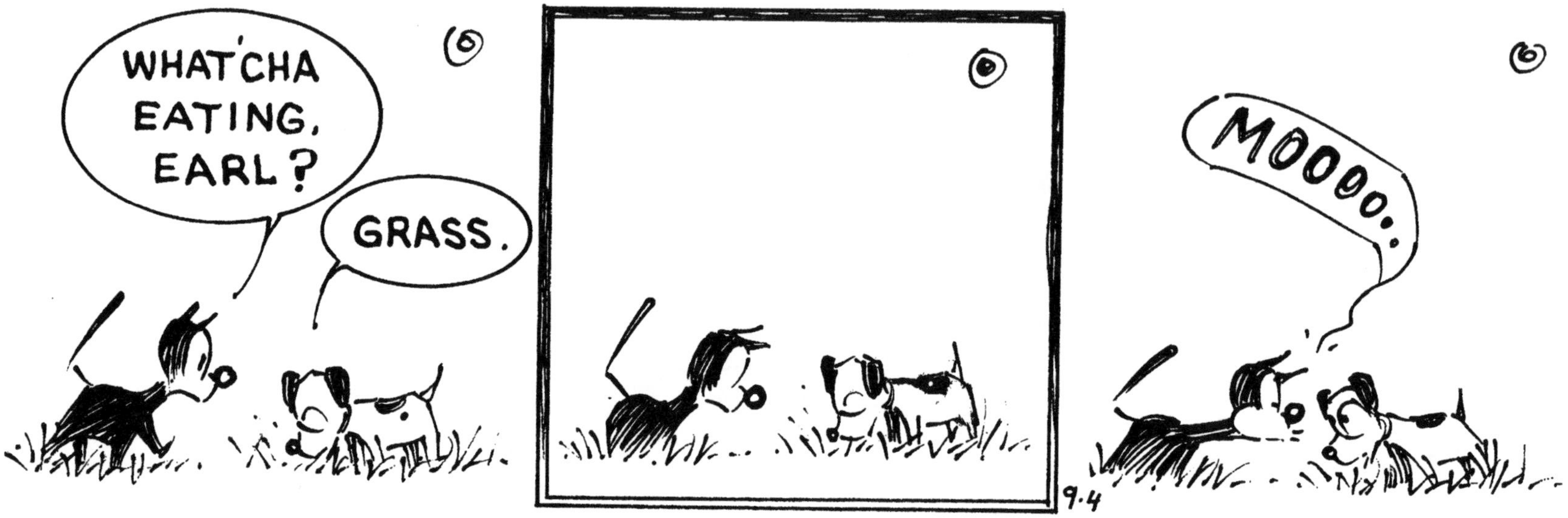
WHAT'CHA EATING, EARL?
GRASS.
MOOOO..
9.4

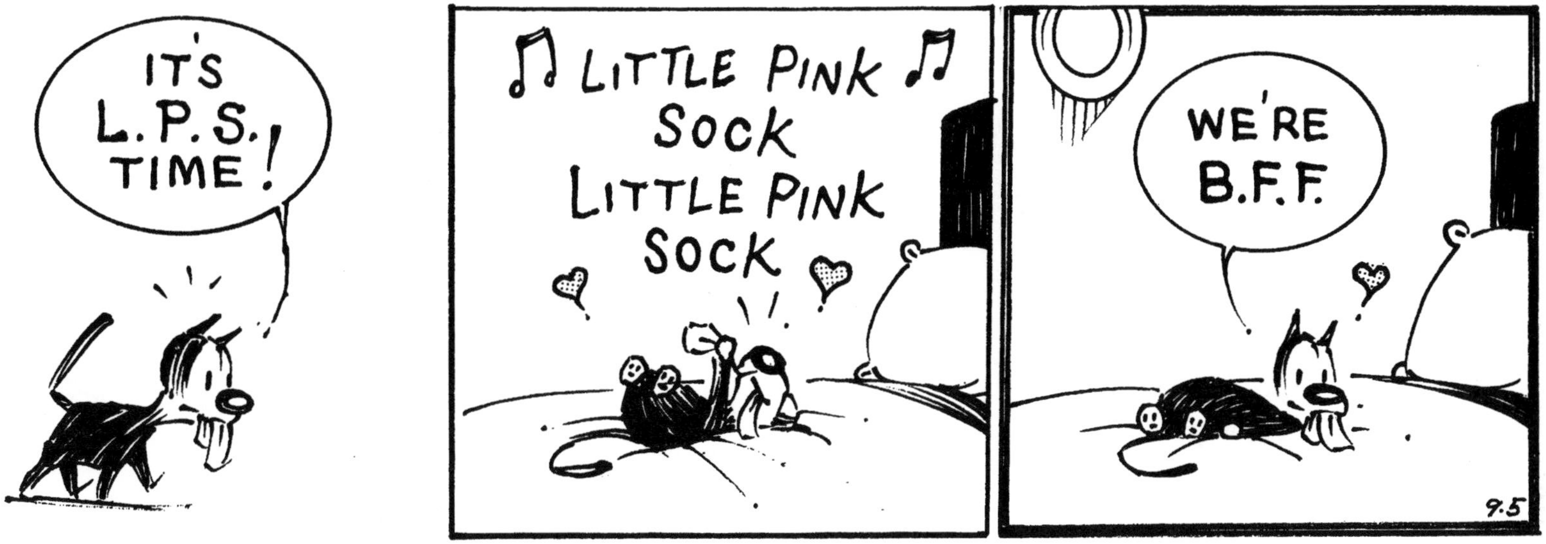
IT'S L.P.S. TIME!
♫ LITTLE PINK ♫ SOCK LITTLE PINK SOCK
WE'RE B.F.F.
9.5

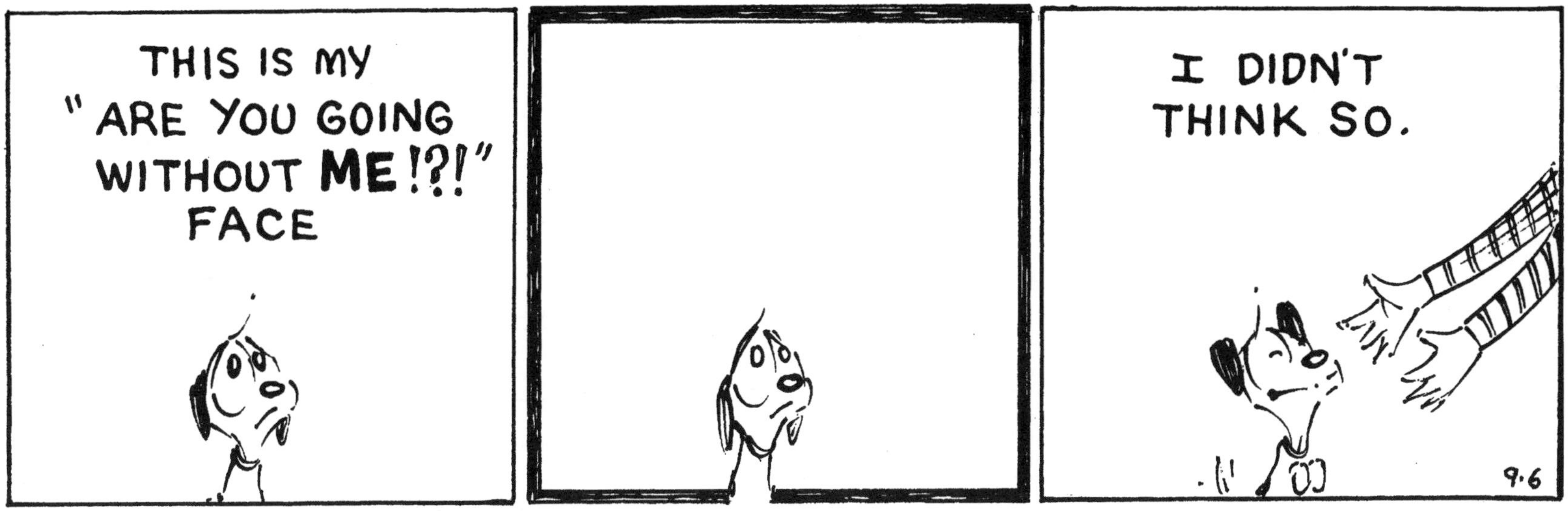
THIS IS MY "ARE YOU GOING WITHOUT **ME**!?!" FACE
I DIDN'T THINK SO.
9.6

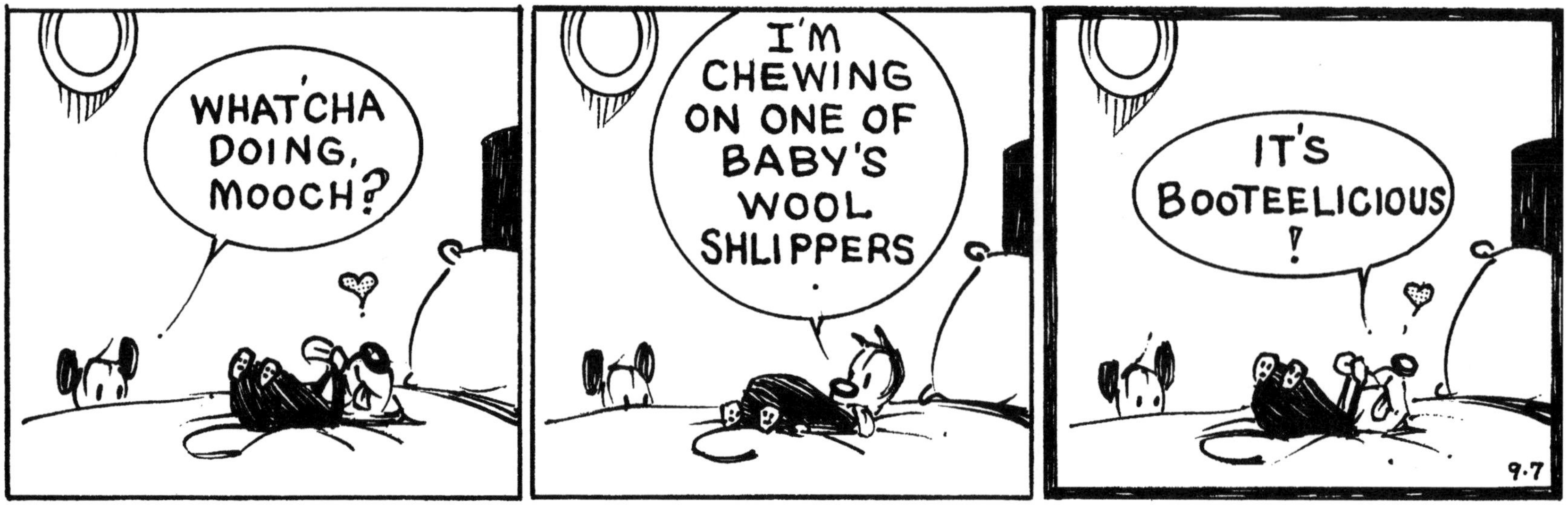
WHAT'CHA DOING, MOOCH?
I'M CHEWING ON ONE OF BABY'S WOOL SHLIPPERS
IT'S BOOTEELICIOUS!
9·7

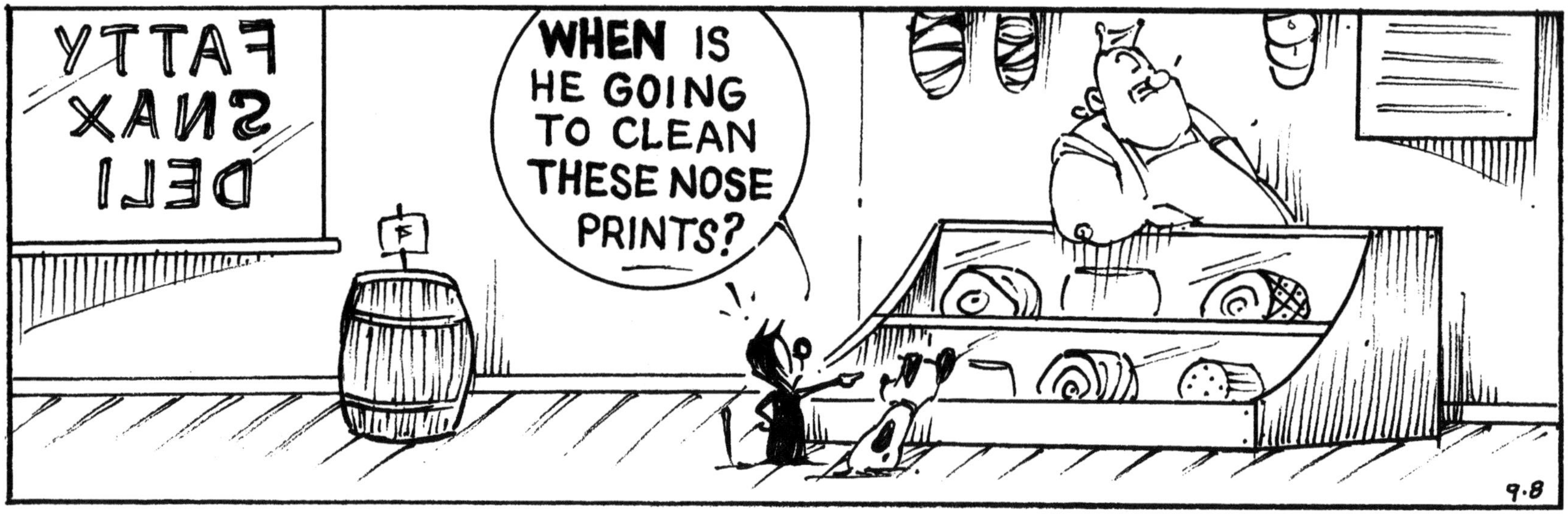
FATTY SNAX DELI
F
WHEN IS HE GOING TO CLEAN THESE NOSE PRINTS?
9·8

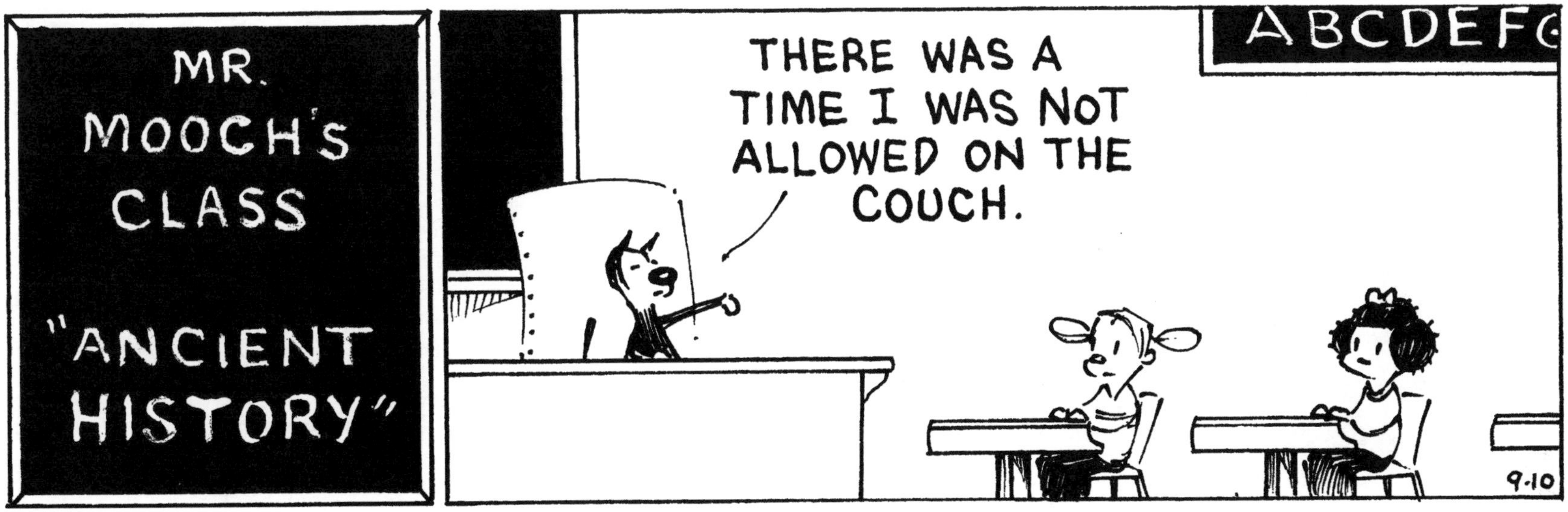
MR. MOOCH'S CLASS "ANCIENT HISTORY"
THERE WAS A TIME I WAS NOT ALLOWED ON THE COUCH.
ABCDEF
9·10

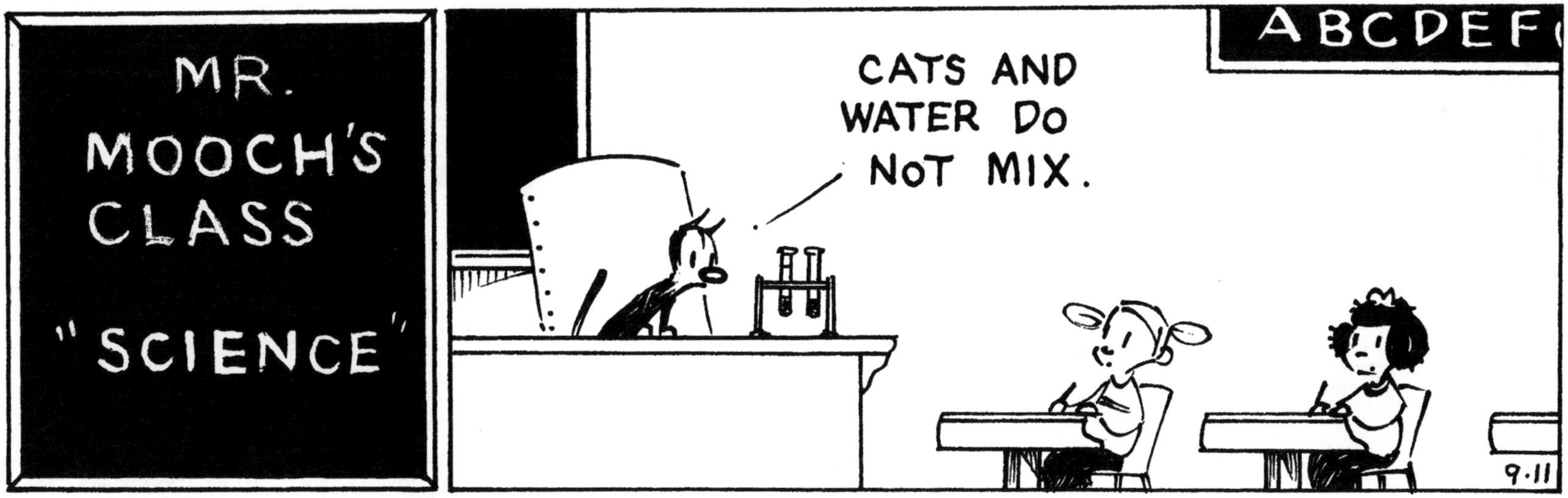
MR. MOOCH'S CLASS "SCIENCE"
CATS AND WATER DO NOT MIX.
ABCDEF
9·11

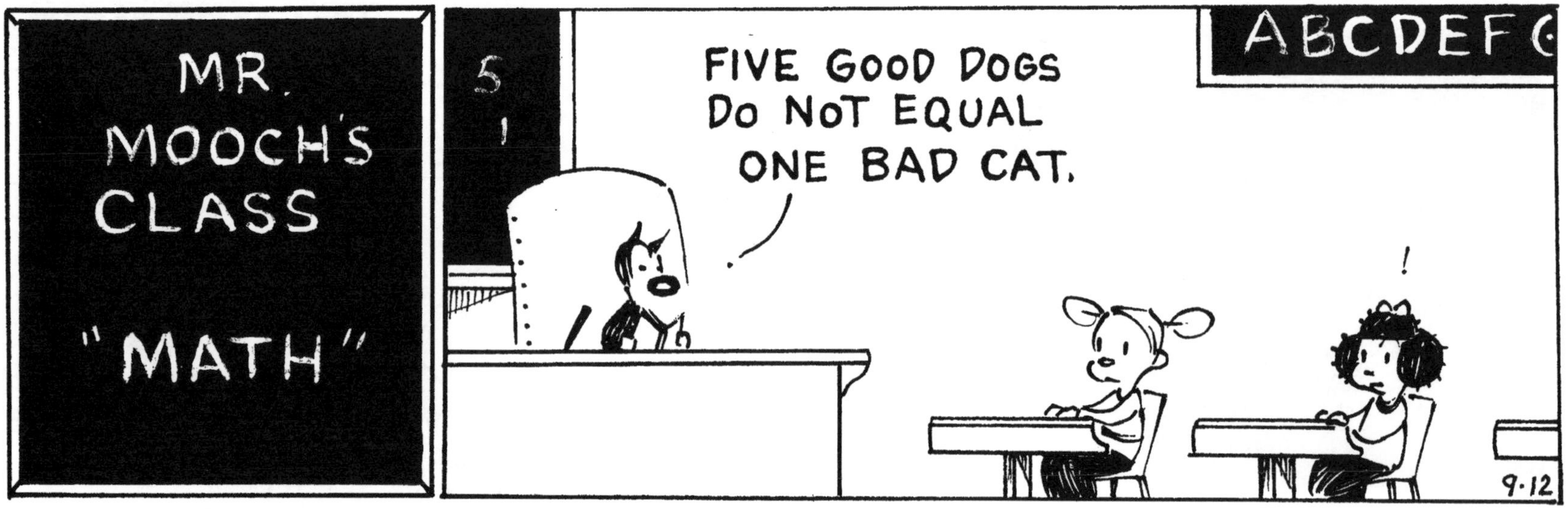
MR. MOOCH'S CLASS "MATH"
5
1
ABCDEFG
FIVE GOOD DOGS DO NOT EQUAL ONE BAD CAT.
!
9·12

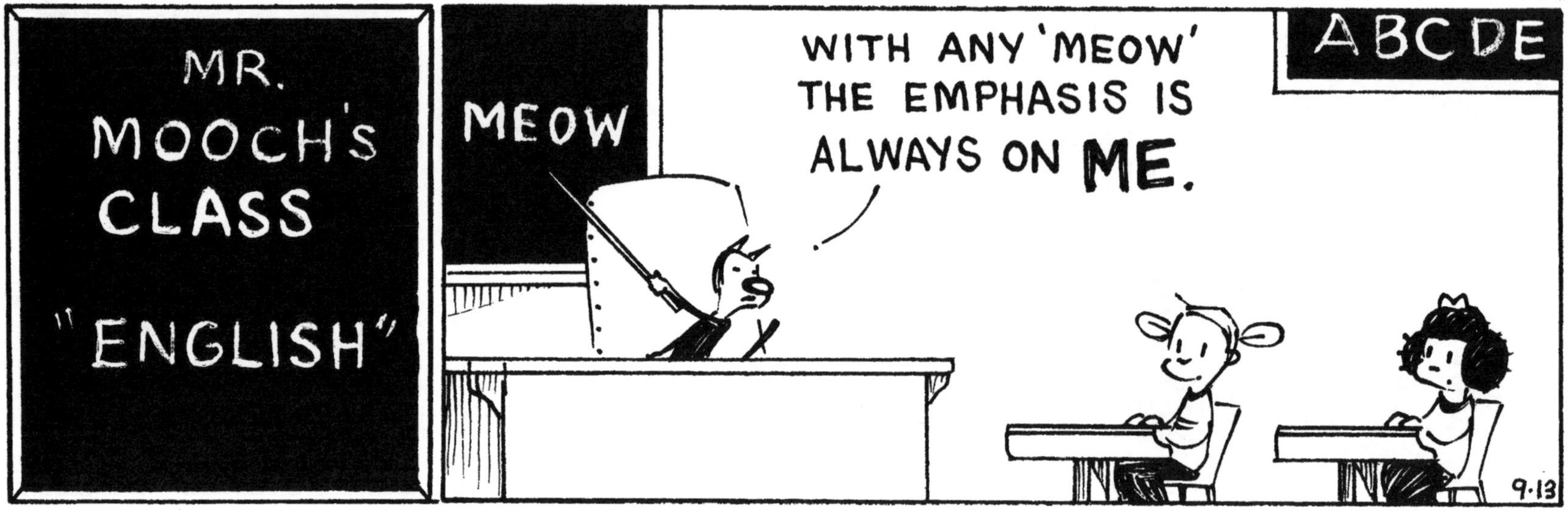
MR. MOOCH'S CLASS "ENGLISH"
MEOW
ABCDE
WITH ANY 'MEOW' THE EMPHASIS IS ALWAYS ON ME.
9·13

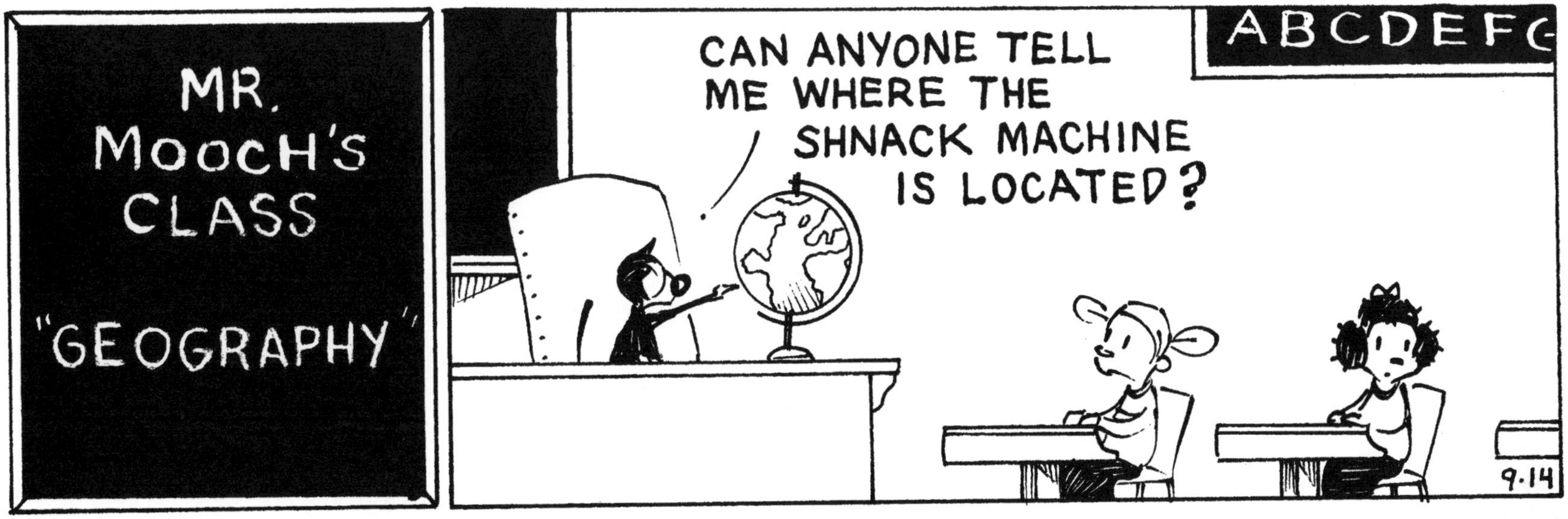
MR. MOOCH'S CLASS
"GEOGRAPHY"
ABCDEFG
CAN ANYONE TELL ME WHERE THE SHNACK MACHINE IS LOCATED?
9·14

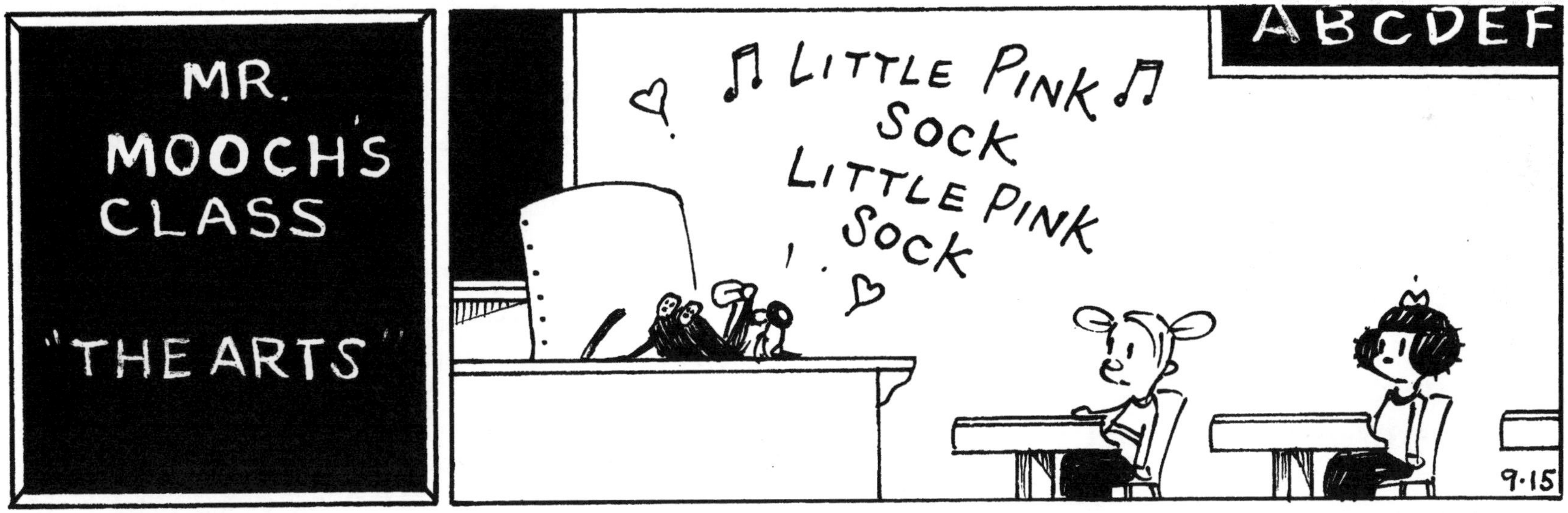
MR. MOOCH'S CLASS
"THE ARTS"
ABCDEF
LITTLE PINK SOCK
LITTLE PINK SOCK
9·15

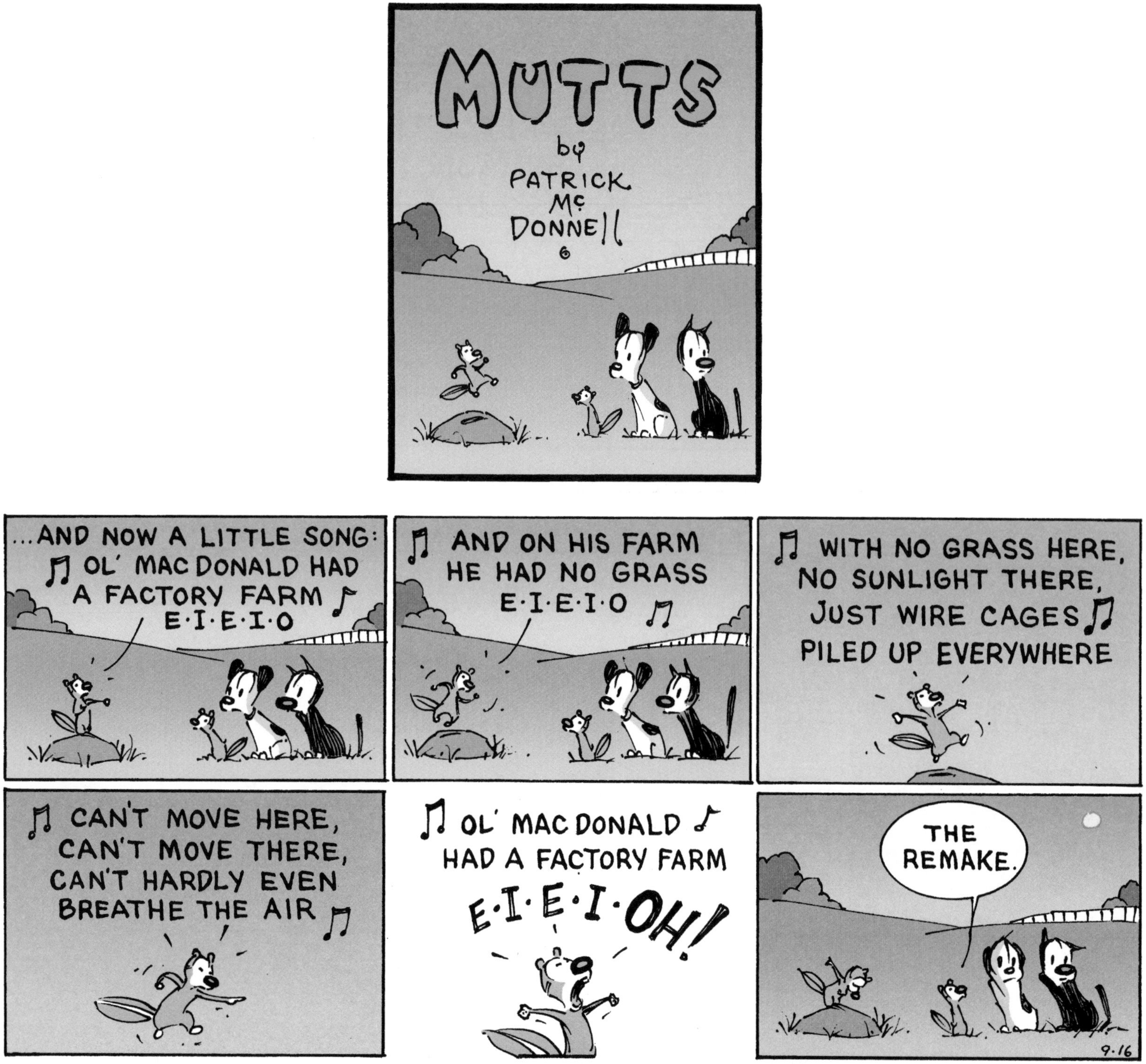
MUTTS
by PATRICK McDONNELL ©
...AND NOW A LITTLE SONG: OL' MAC DONALD HAD A FACTORY FARM E·I·E·I·O
AND ON HIS FARM HE HAD NO GRASS E·I·E·I·O
WITH NO GRASS HERE, NO SUNLIGHT THERE, JUST WIRE CAGES PILED UP EVERYWHERE
CAN'T MOVE HERE, CAN'T MOVE THERE, CAN'T HARDLY EVEN BREATHE THE AIR
OL' MAC DONALD HAD A FACTORY FARM
E·I·E·I·OH!
THE REMAKE.
9·16

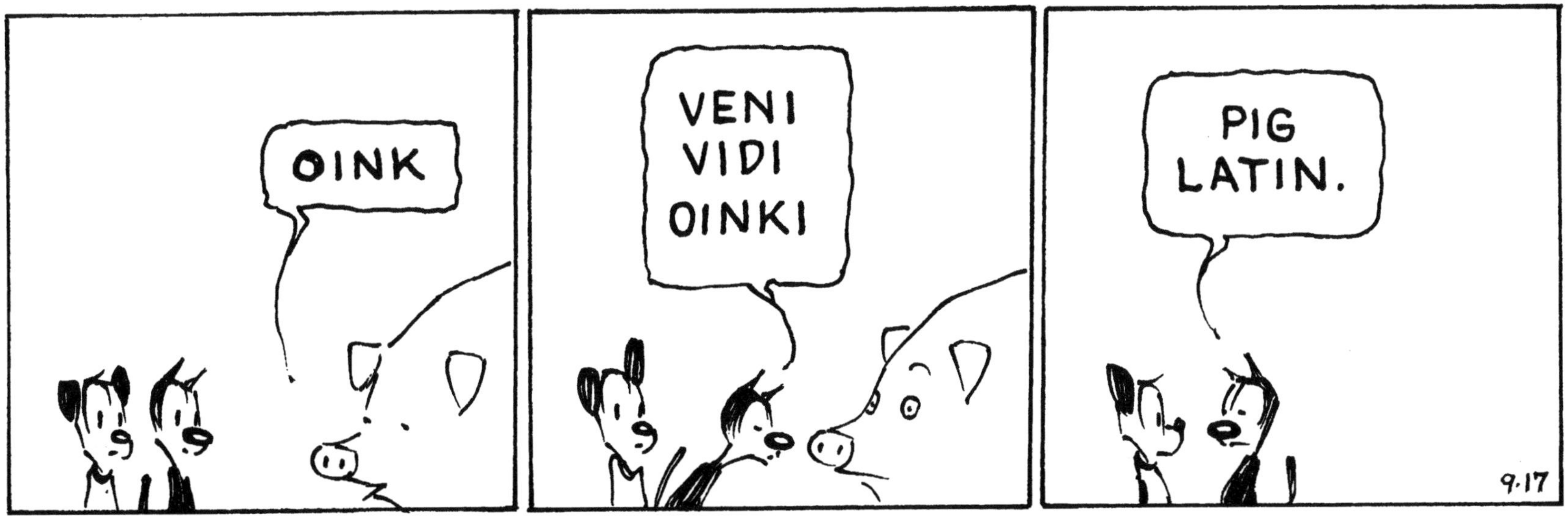
OINK
VENI VIDI OINKI
PIG LATIN.
9·17

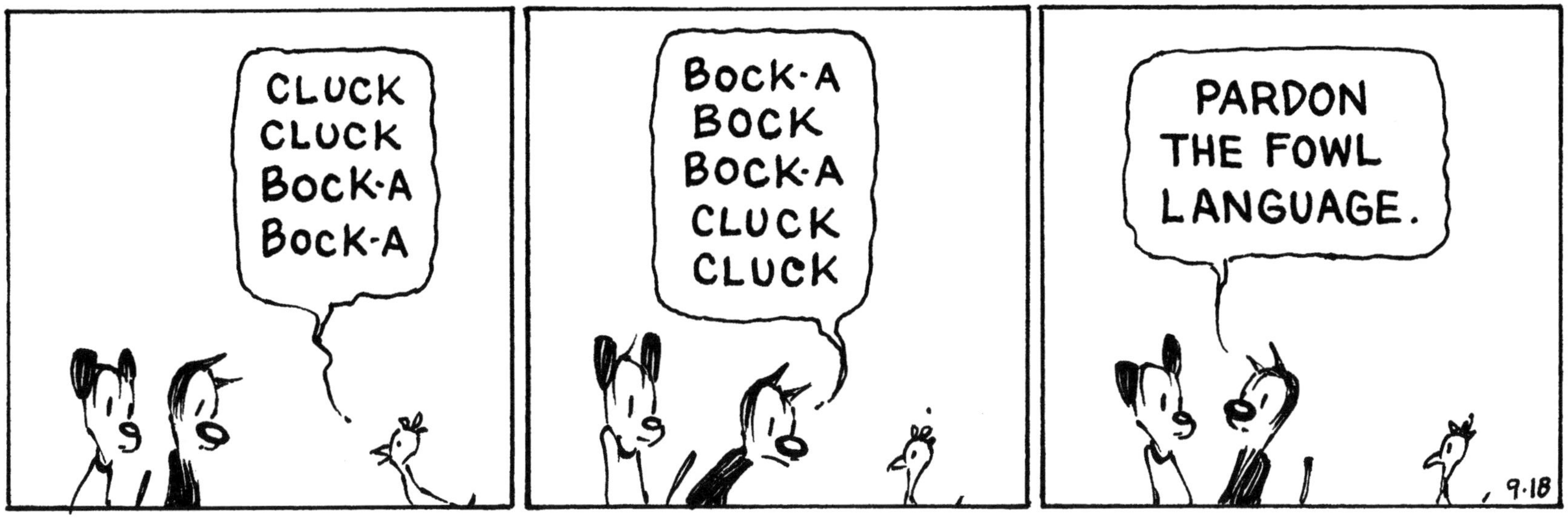
CLUCK CLUCK BOCK-A BOCK-A
BOCK-A BOCK BOCK-A CLUCK CLUCK
PARDON THE FOWL LANGUAGE.
9·18

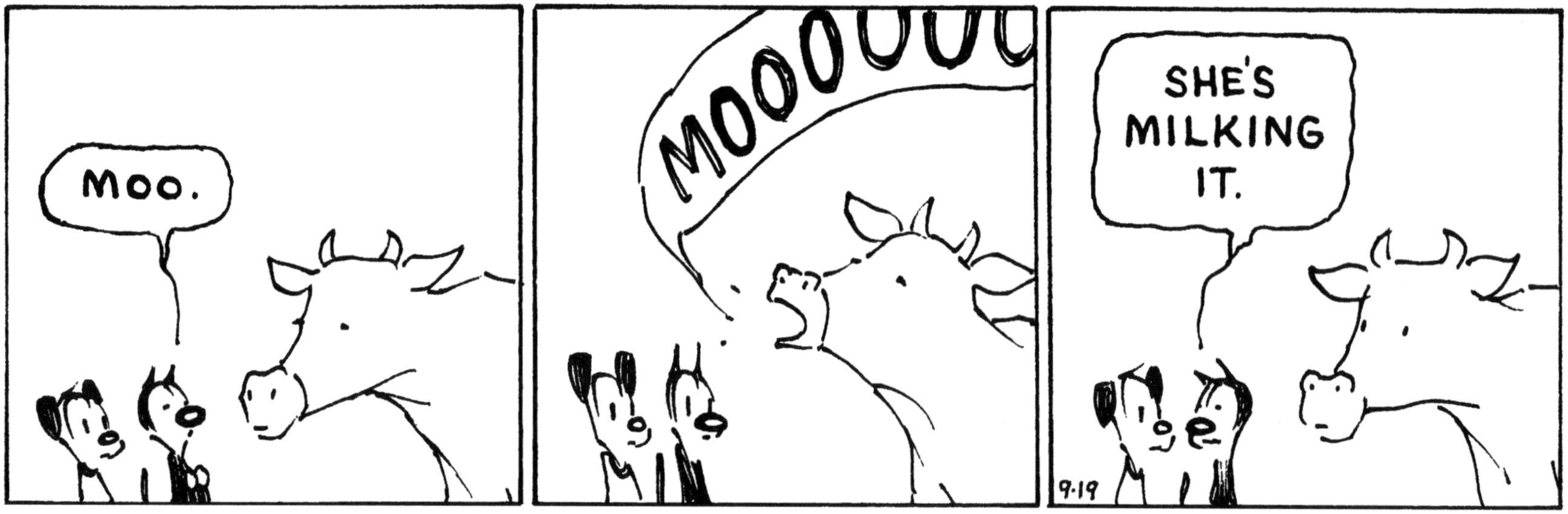
MOO.
MOOOUUU
SHE'S MILKING IT.
9·19

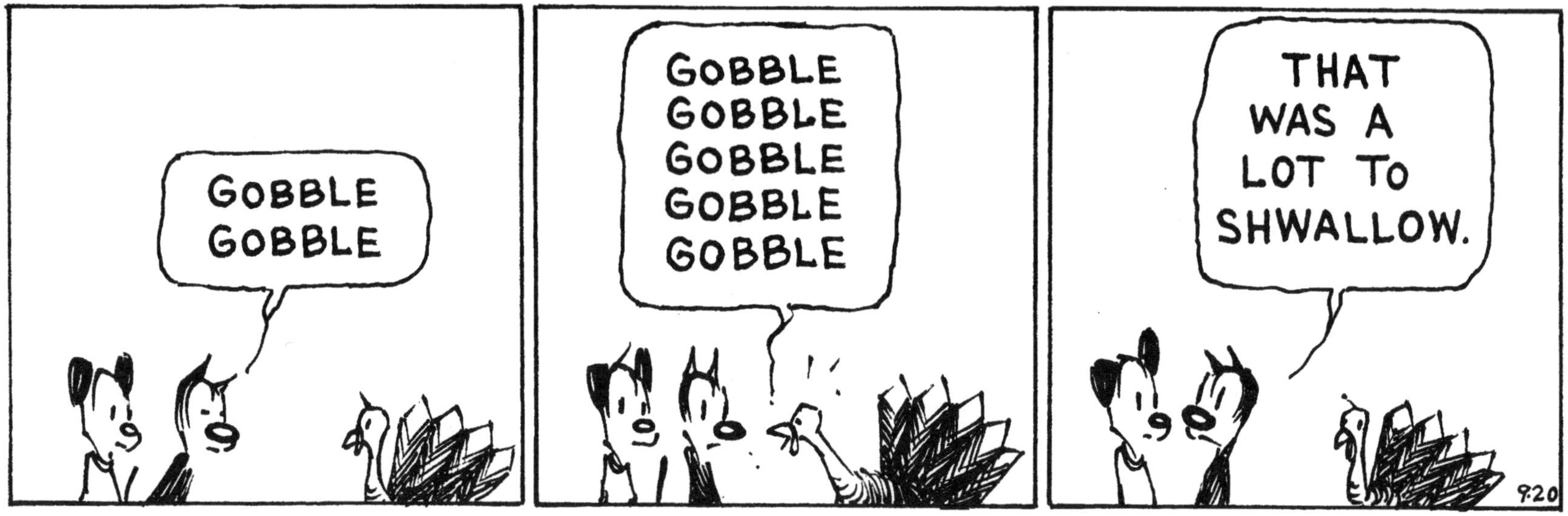
GOBBLE GOBBLE
GOBBLE GOBBLE GOBBLE GOBBLE GOBBLE
THAT WAS A LOT TO SHWALLOW.
9·20

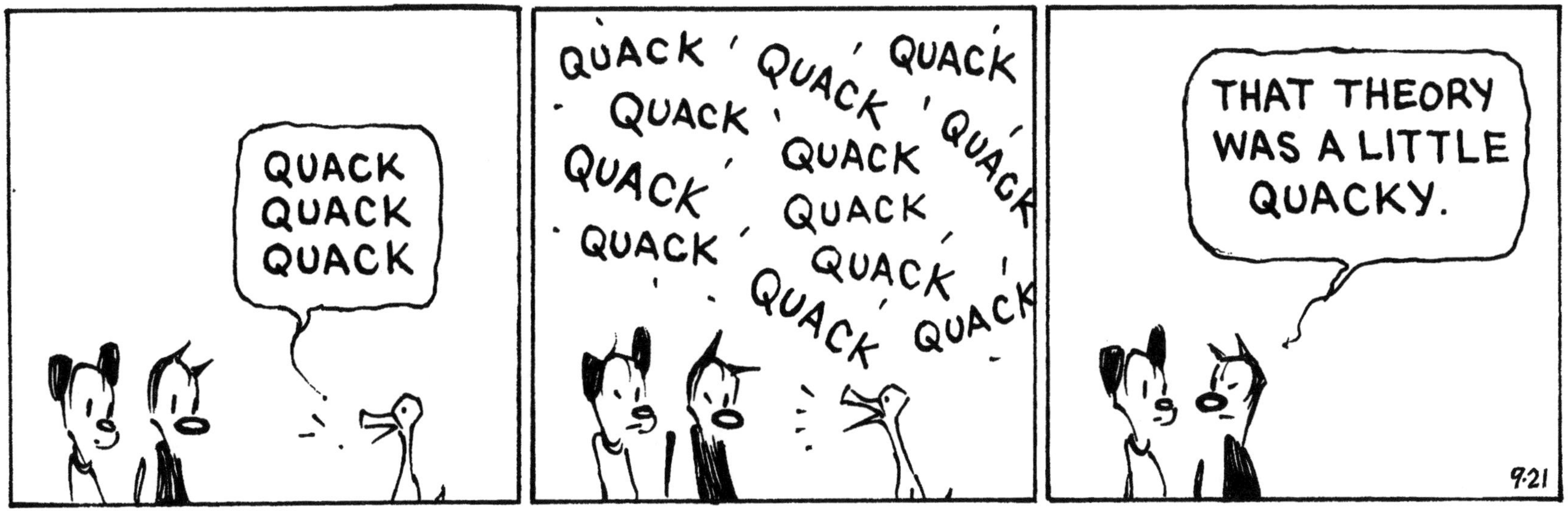
QUACK QUACK QUACK
QUACK QUACK QUACK QUACK QUACK QUACK QUACK QUACK QUACK QUACK QUACK QUACK
THAT THEORY WAS A LITTLE QUACKY.
9·21

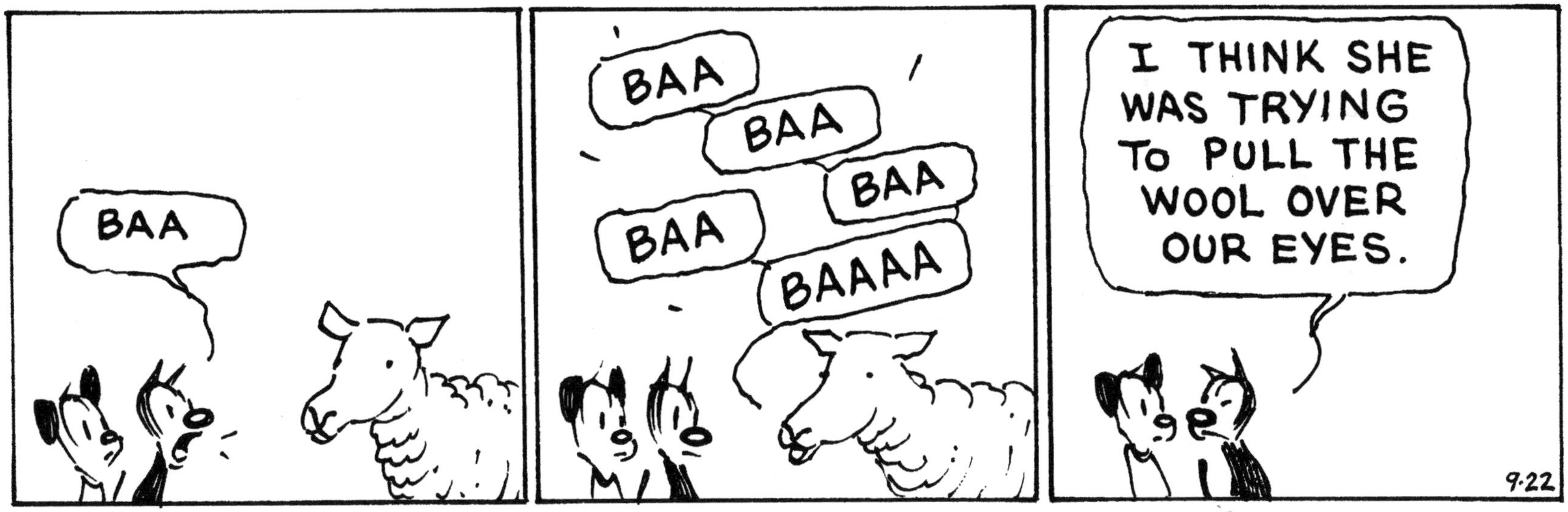
BAA
BAA
BAA
BAA
BAA
BAAAA
I THINK SHE WAS TRYING TO PULL THE WOOL OVER OUR EYES.
9·22

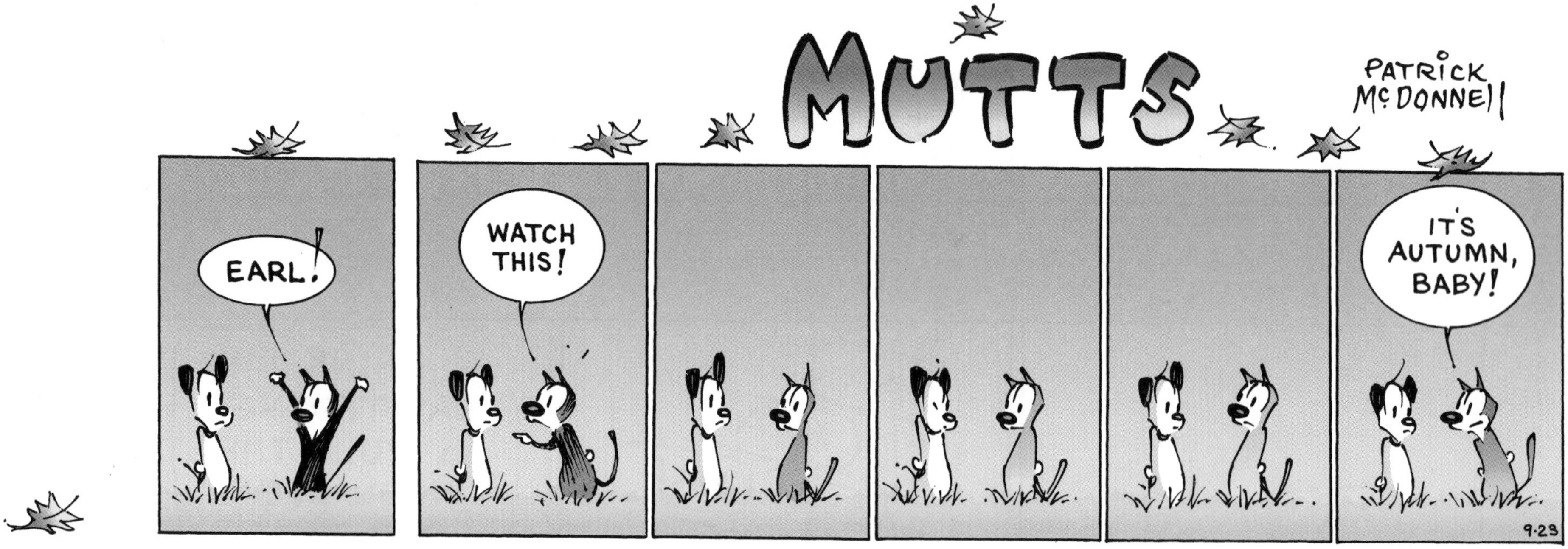
MUTTS
PATRICK McDONNELL
EARL!
WATCH THIS!
IT'S AUTUMN, BABY!
9·23

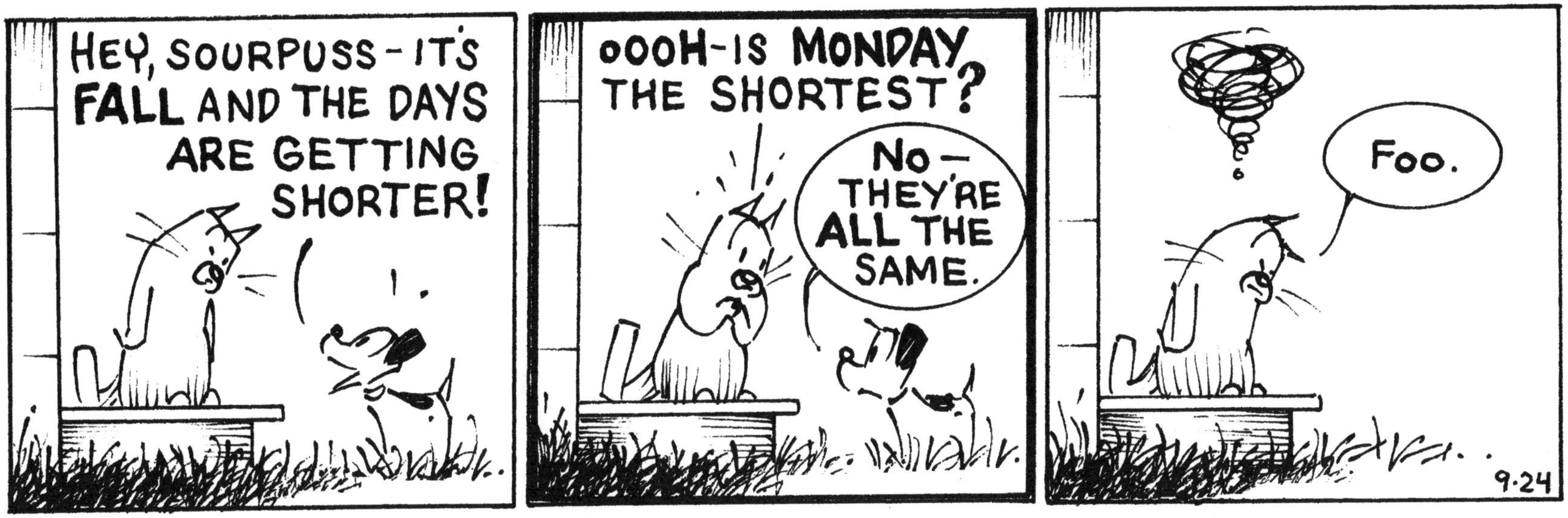
HEY, SOURPUSS - IT'S FALL AND THE DAYS ARE GETTING SHORTER!
OOOH - IS MONDAY THE SHORTEST?
NO - THEY'RE ALL THE SAME.
FOO.
9·24

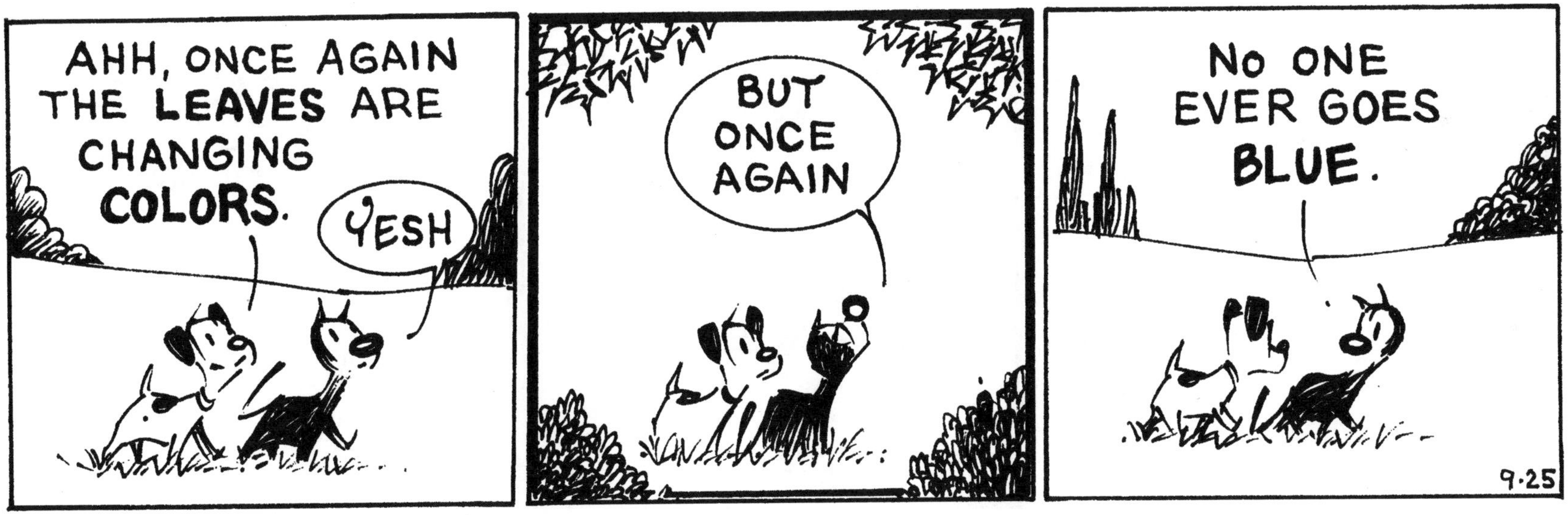
AHH, ONCE AGAIN THE LEAVES ARE CHANGING COLORS.
YESH
BUT ONCE AGAIN
NO ONE EVER GOES BLUE.
9·25

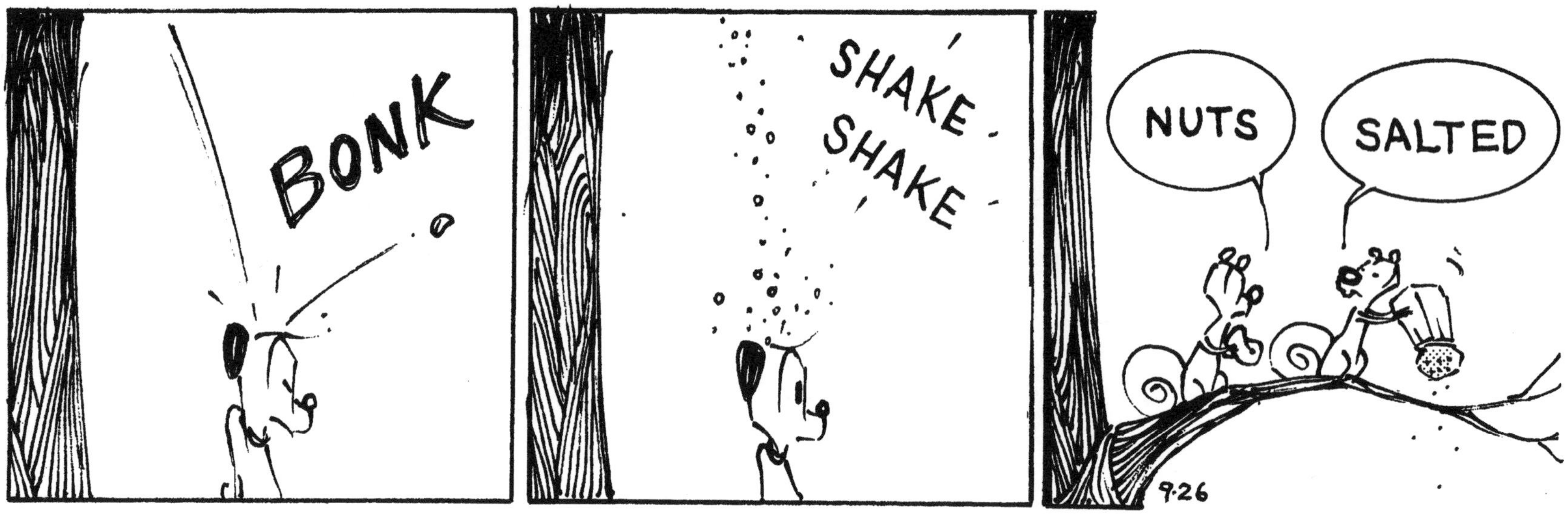
BONK
SHAKE SHAKE
NUTS
SALTED
9·26

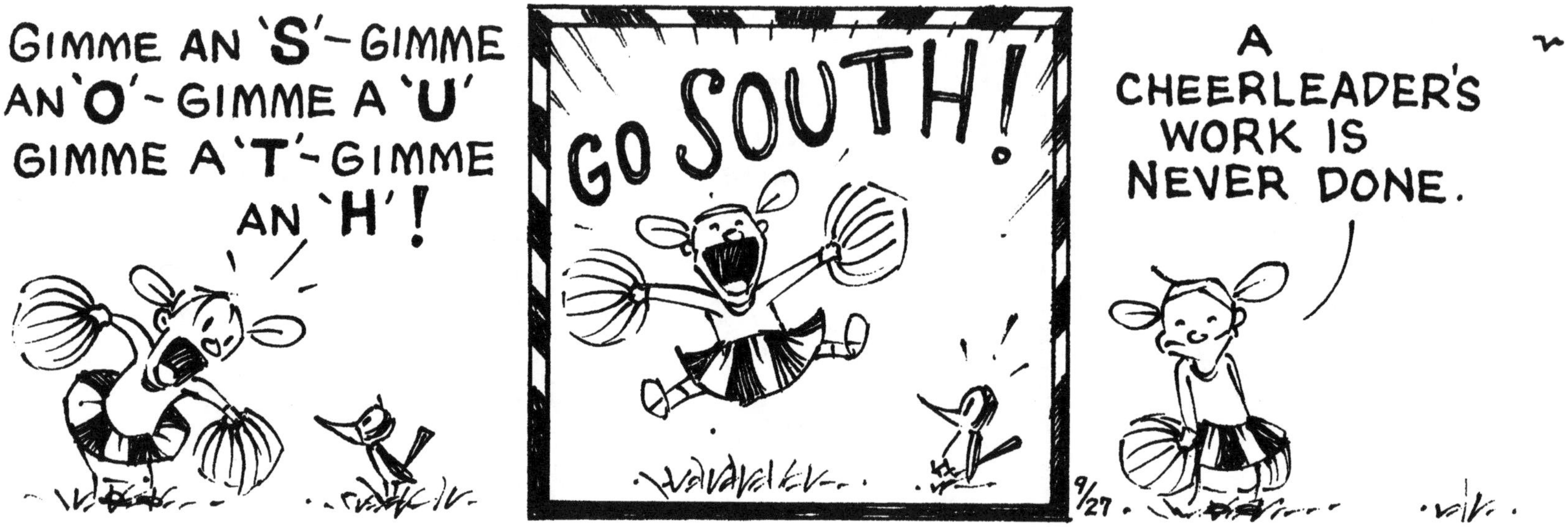
GIMME AN 'S'- GIMME AN 'O'- GIMME A 'U' GIMME A 'T'- GIMME AN 'H'!
GO SOUTH!
A CHEERLEADER'S WORK IS NEVER DONE.
9/27

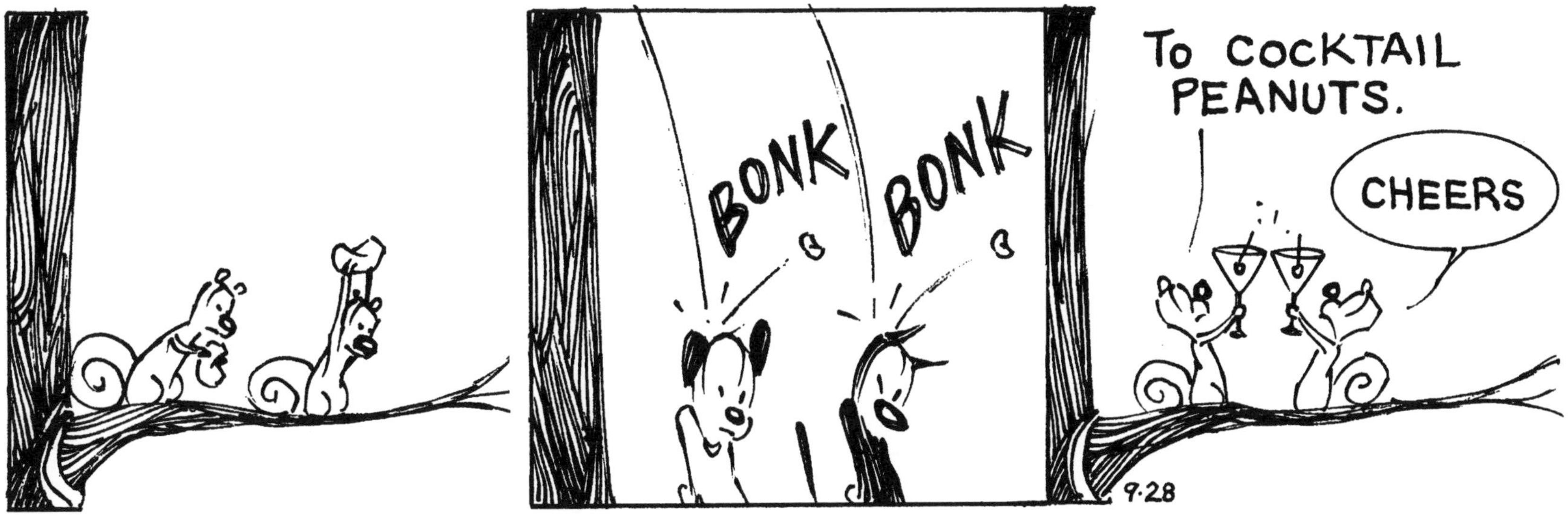
BONK
BONK
To COCKTAIL PEANUTS.
CHEERS
9·28

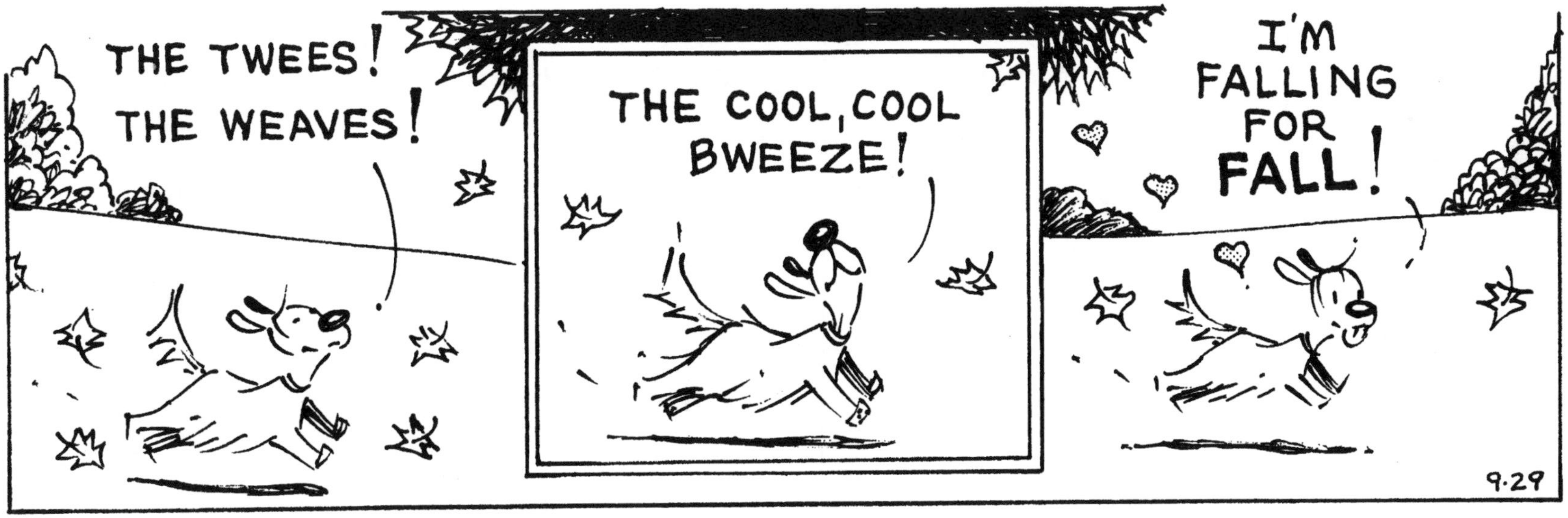
THE TWEES! THE WEAVES!
THE COOL, COOL BWEEZE!
I'M FALLING FOR FALL!
9·29

MUTTS
MY BOWL
MY CHEWY TOY
MY BED
MY OZZIE!
THERE'S NO PLACE LIKE HOME.
9·30

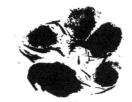

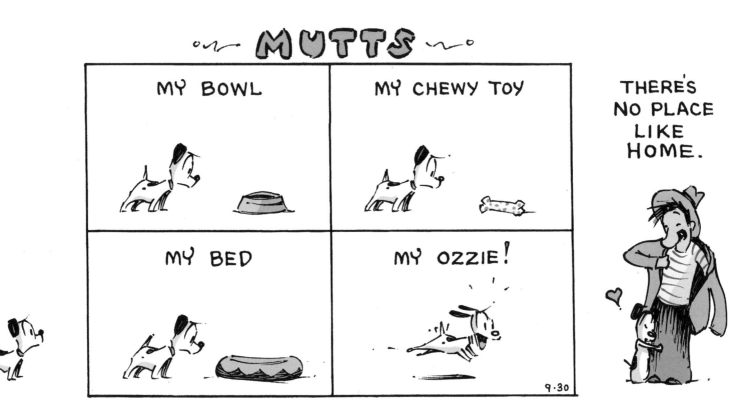

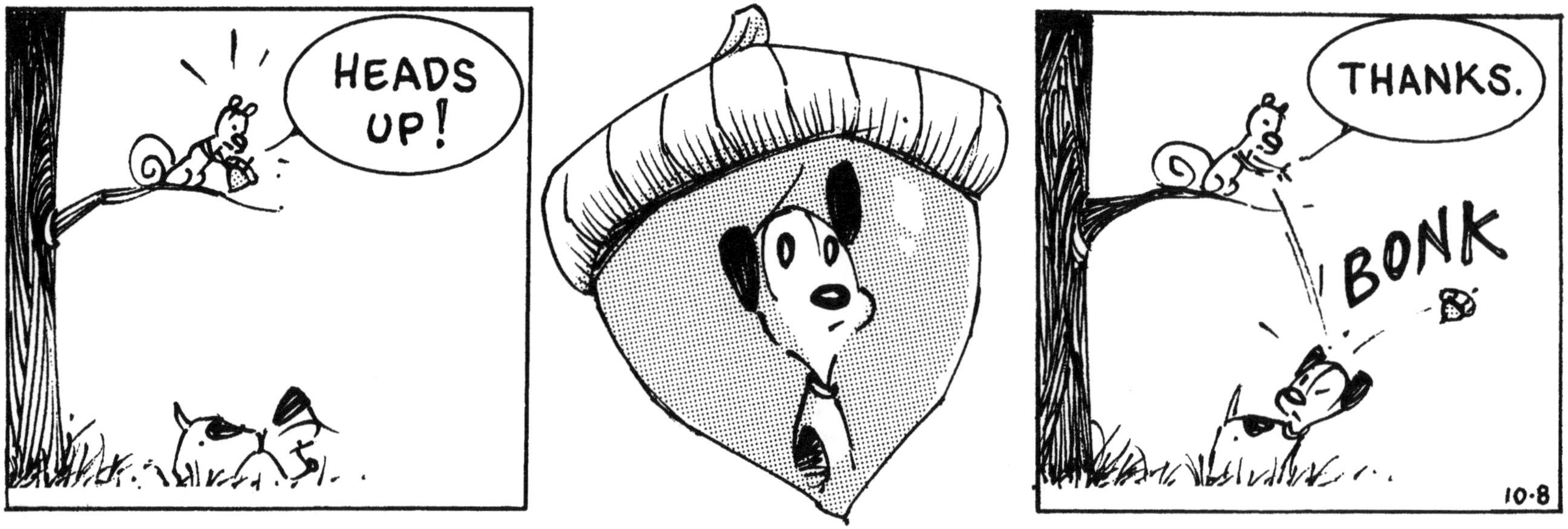
HEADS UP!
THANKS.
BONK
10·8

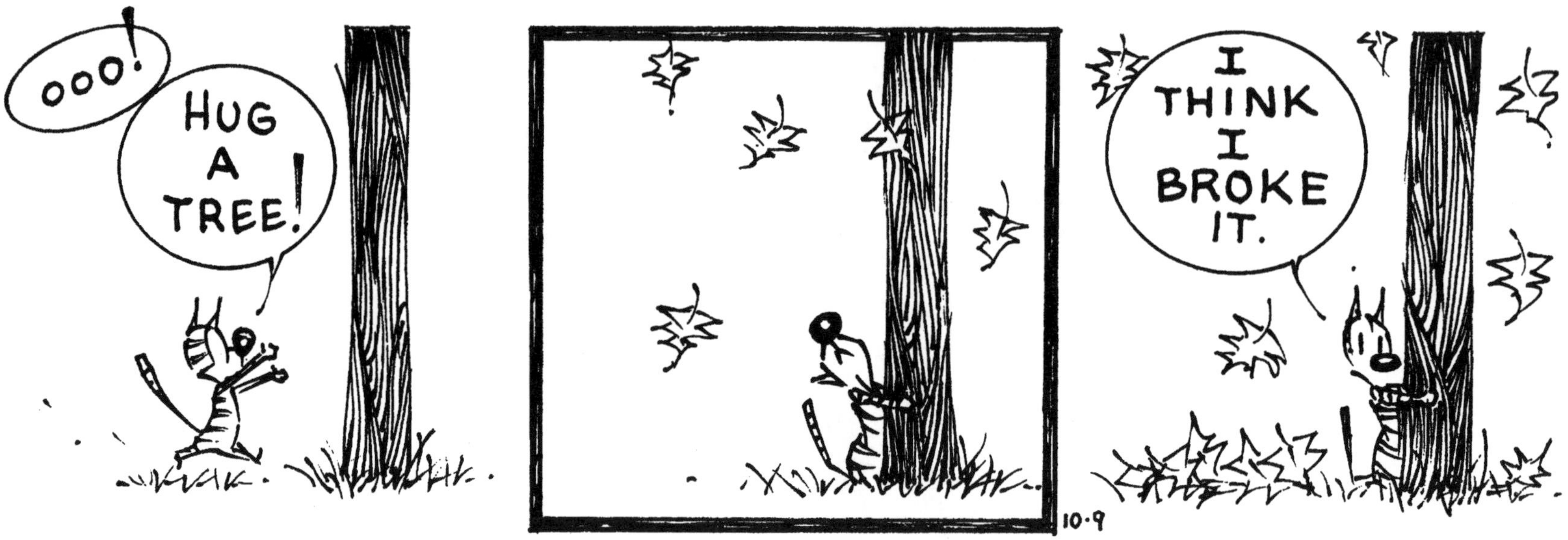
OOO!
HUG A TREE!
10·9
I THINK I BROKE IT.

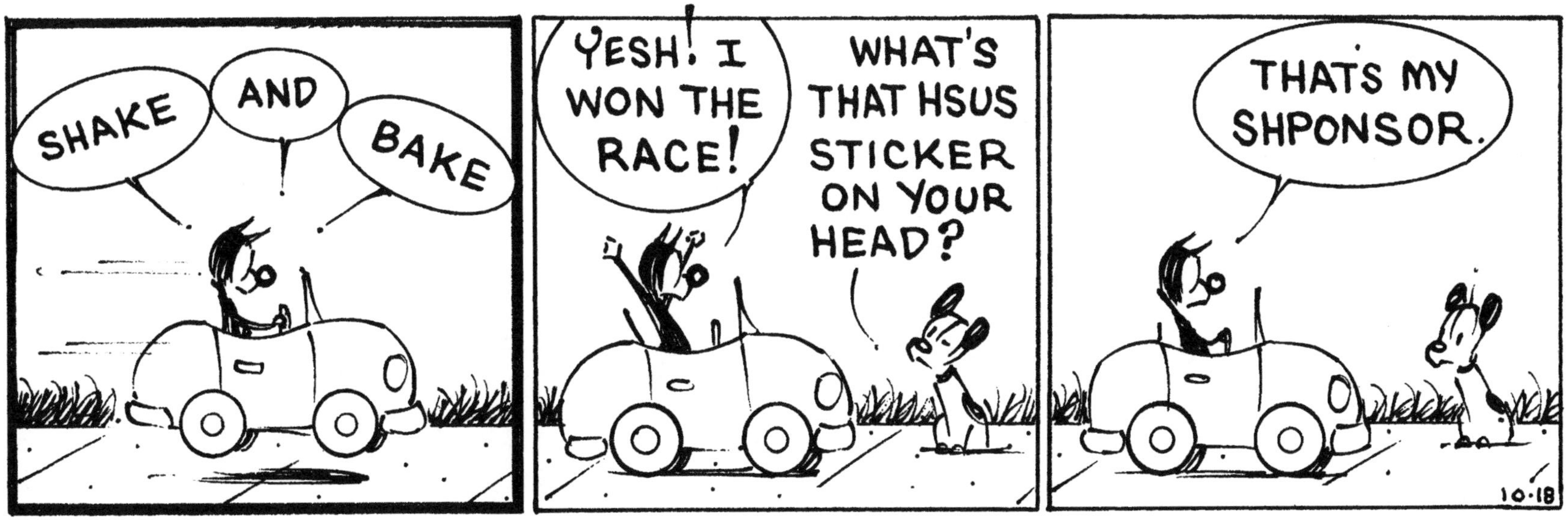
SHAKE
AND
BAKE
YESH! I WON THE RACE!
WHAT'S THAT HSUS STICKER ON YOUR HEAD?
THAT'S MY SHPONSOR.
10·18

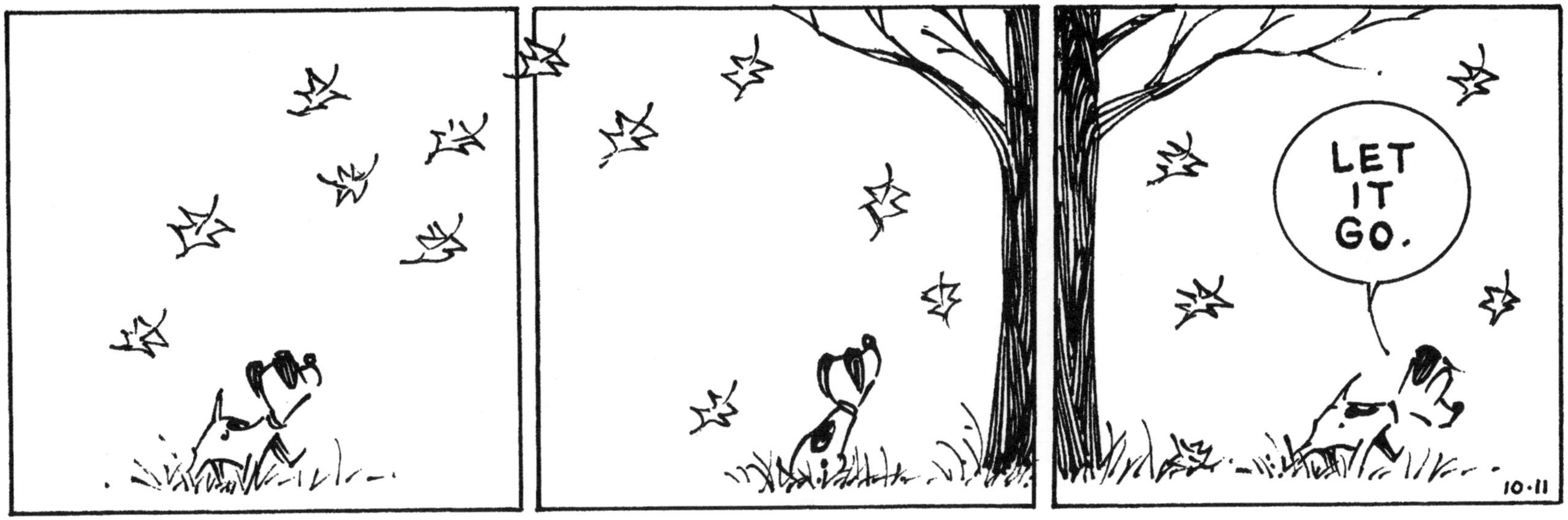
LET IT GO.
10·11

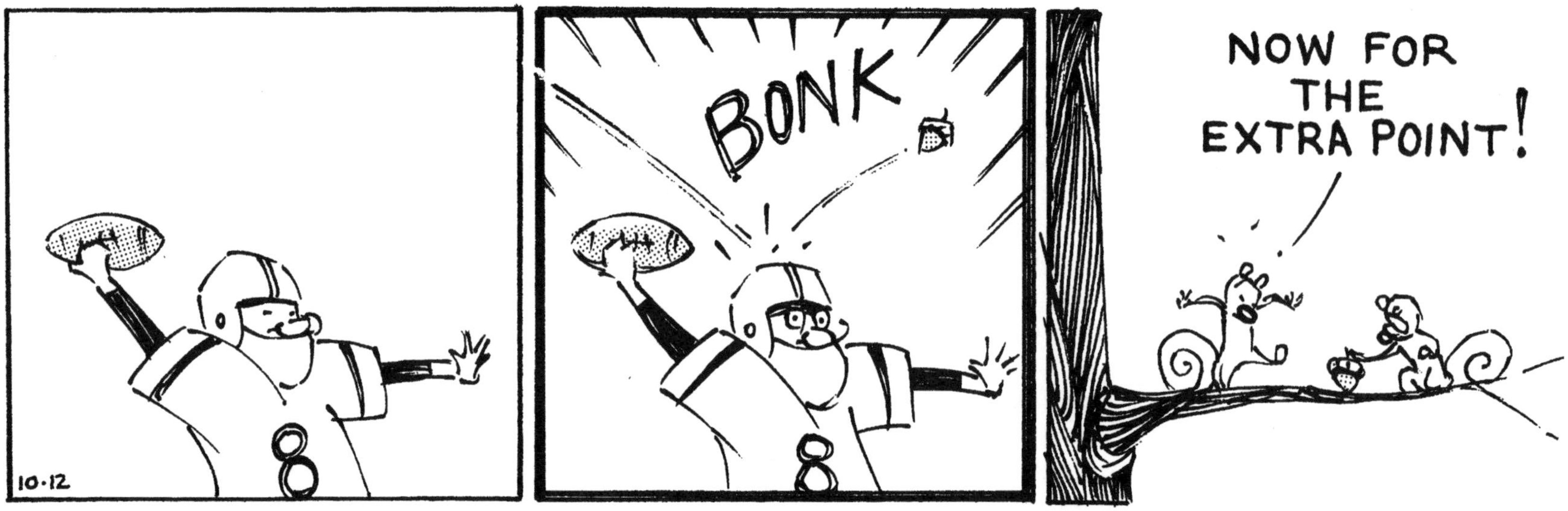
10·12
BONK
NOW FOR THE EXTRA POINT!

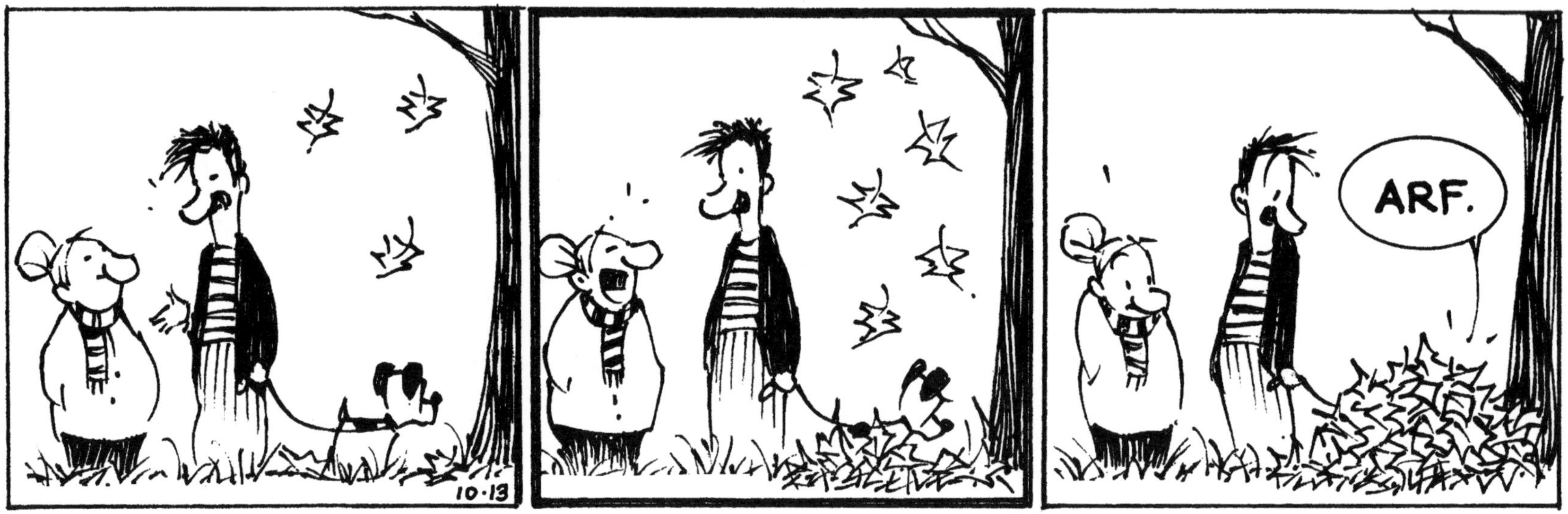
10·13
ARF.

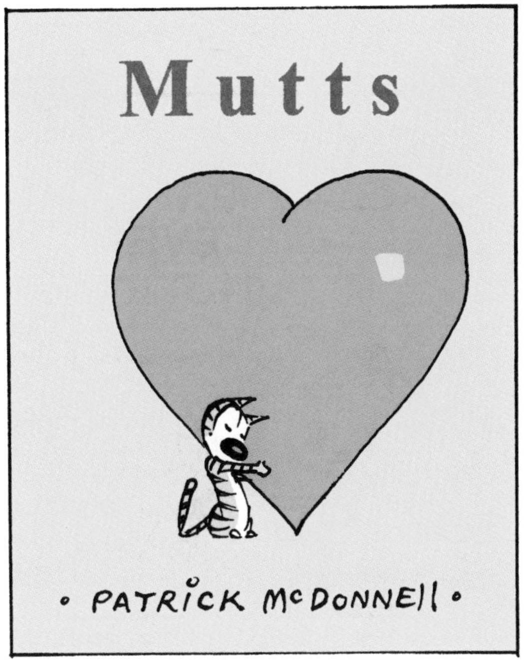
Mutts
• PATRICK McDONNELL •

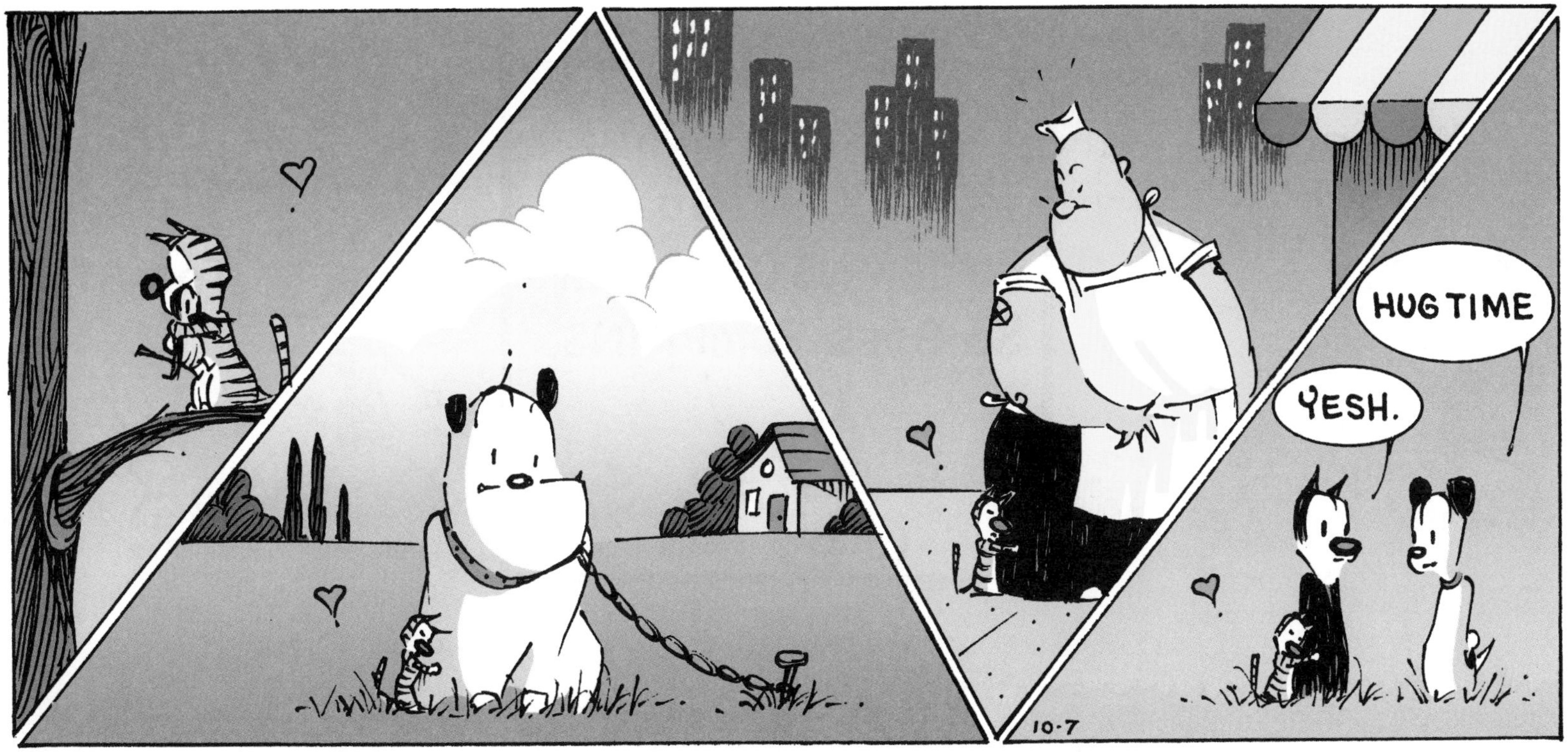
HUG TIME
YESH.
10-7

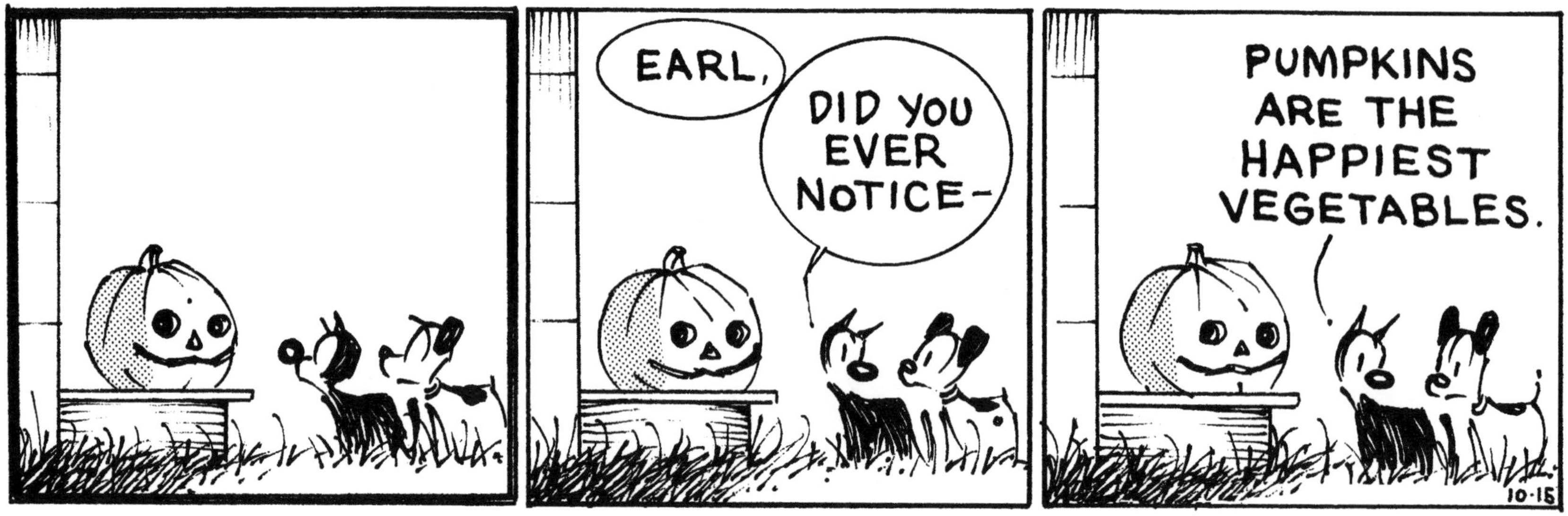
EARL,
DID YOU EVER NOTICE-
PUMPKINS ARE THE HAPPIEST VEGETABLES.
10-15

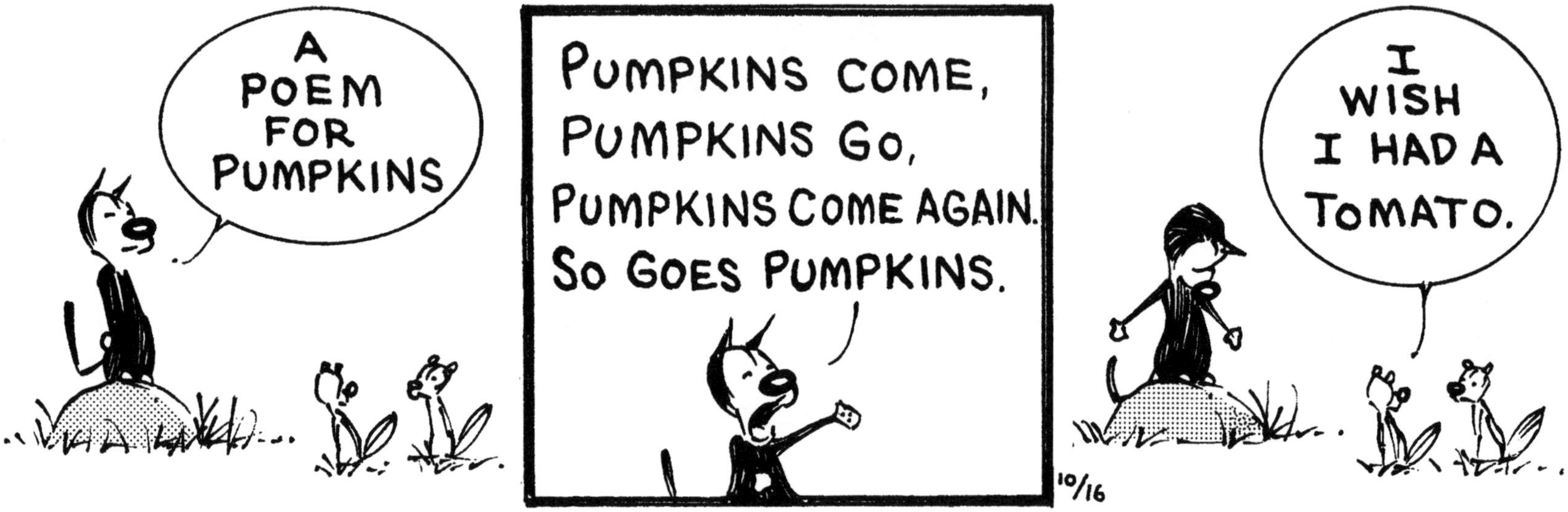
A POEM FOR PUMPKINS
PUMPKINS COME,
PUMPKINS GO,
PUMPKINS COME AGAIN.
SO GOES PUMPKINS.
I WISH I HAD A TOMATO.
10/16

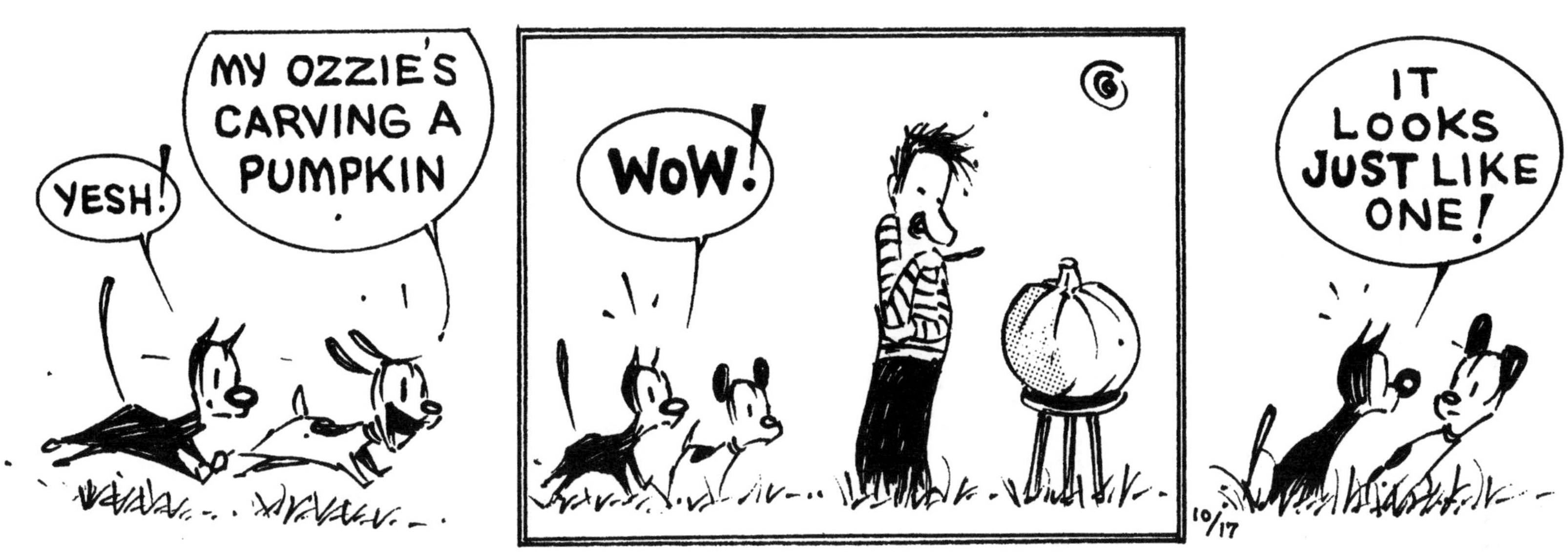
MY OZZIE'S CARVING A PUMPKIN
YESH!
WOW!
IT LOOKS JUST LIKE ONE!
10/17

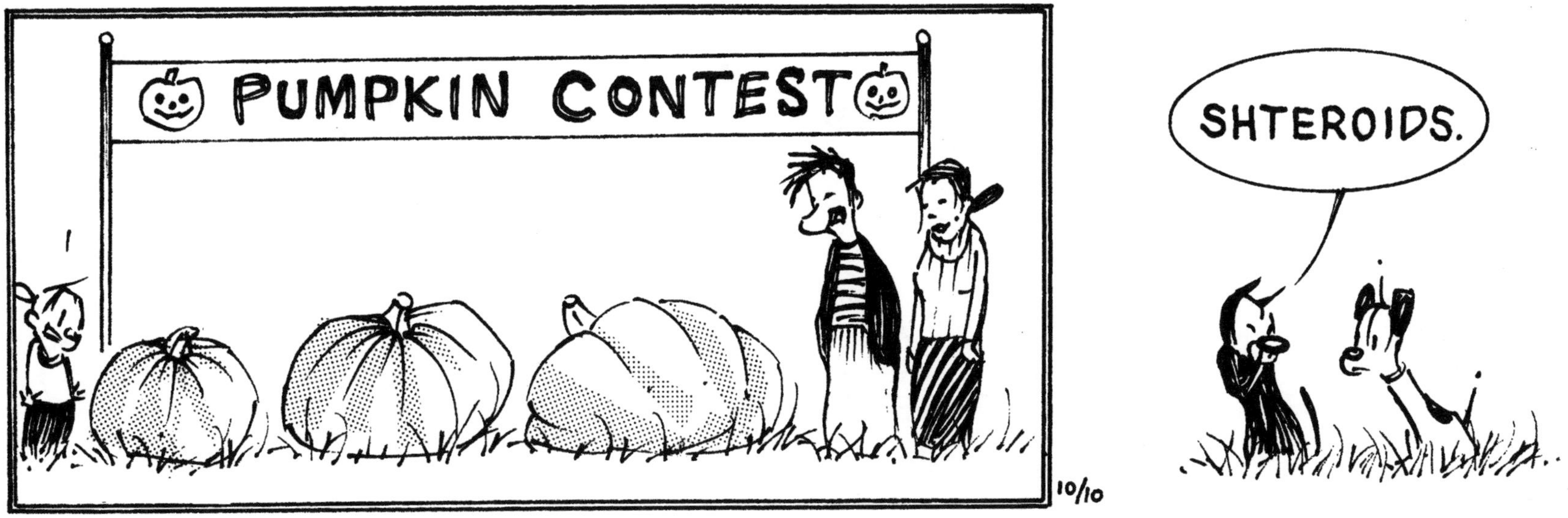
PUMPKIN CONTEST
10/10
SHTEROIDS.

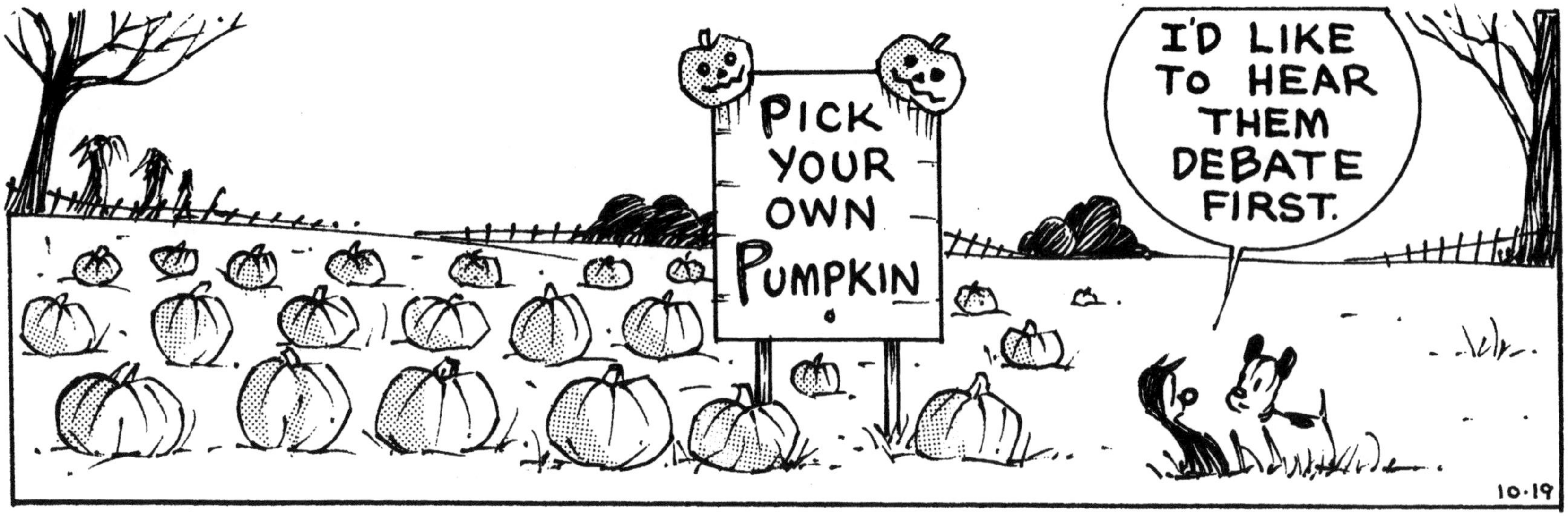
PICK YOUR OWN PUMPKIN
I'D LIKE TO HEAR THEM DEBATE FIRST.
10·19

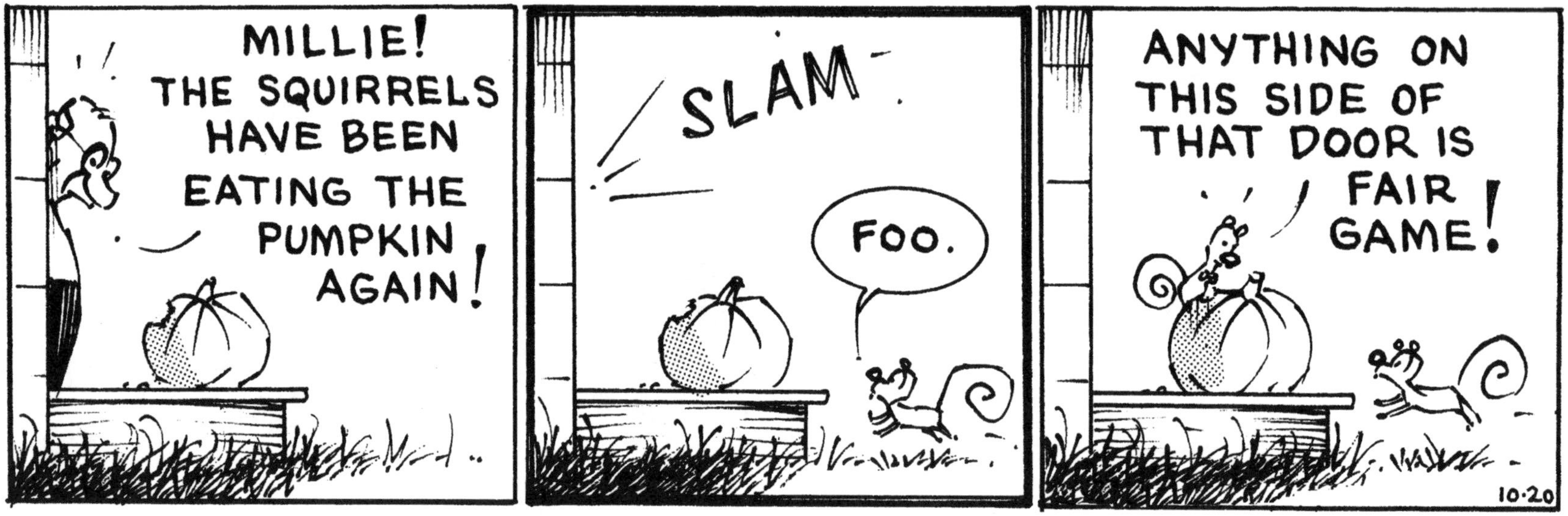
MILLIE! THE SQUIRRELS HAVE BEEN EATING THE PUMPKIN AGAIN!
SLAM
FOO.
ANYTHING ON THIS SIDE OF THAT DOOR IS FAIR GAME!
10·20

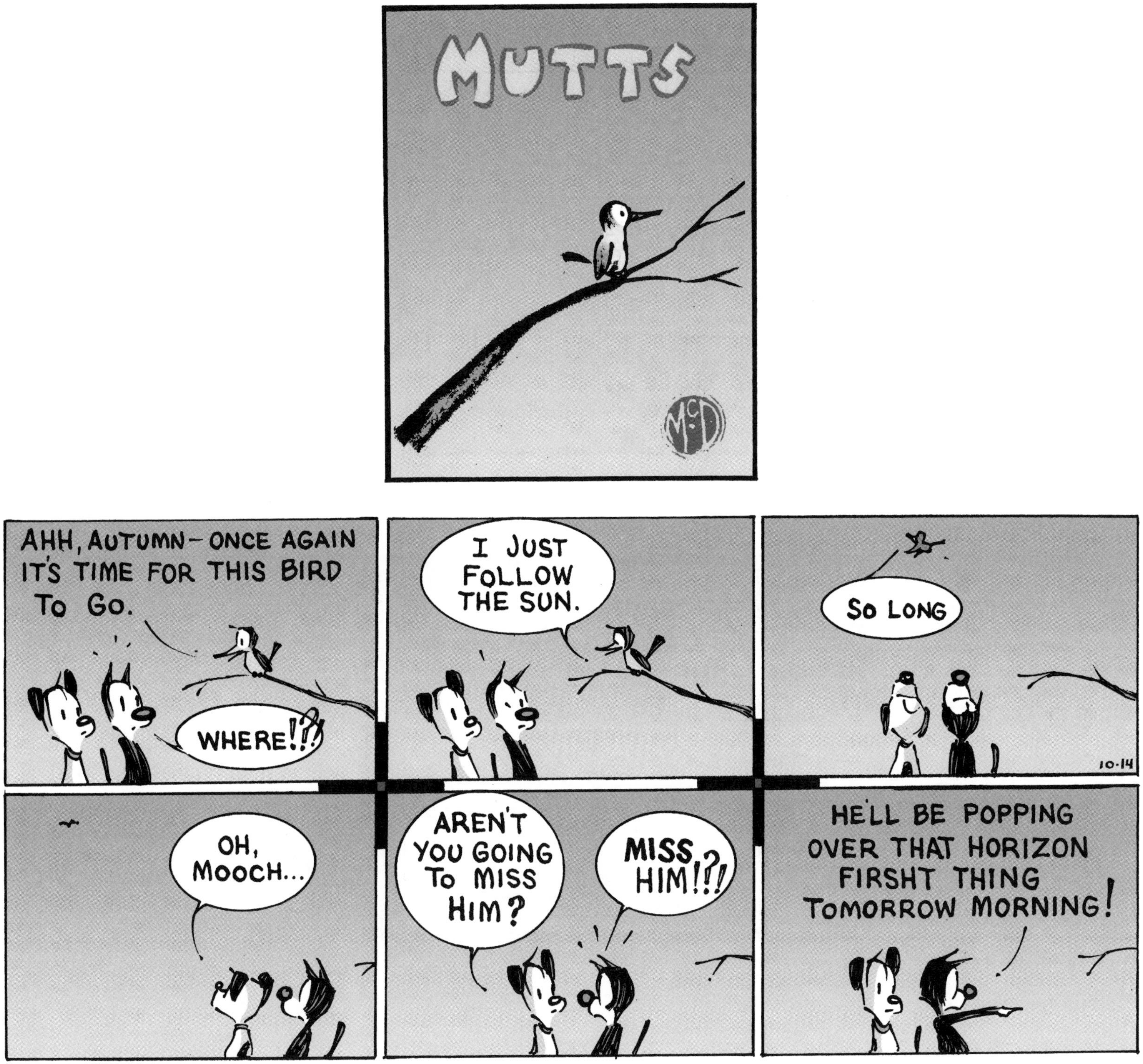
MUTTS
AHH, AUTUMN– ONCE AGAIN IT'S TIME FOR THIS BIRD TO GO.
WHERE!?!
I JUST FOLLOW THE SUN.
SO LONG
10-14
OH, MOOCH...
AREN'T YOU GOING TO MISS HIM?
MISS HIM!?!
HE'LL BE POPPING OVER THAT HORIZON FIRSHT THING TOMORROW MORNING!

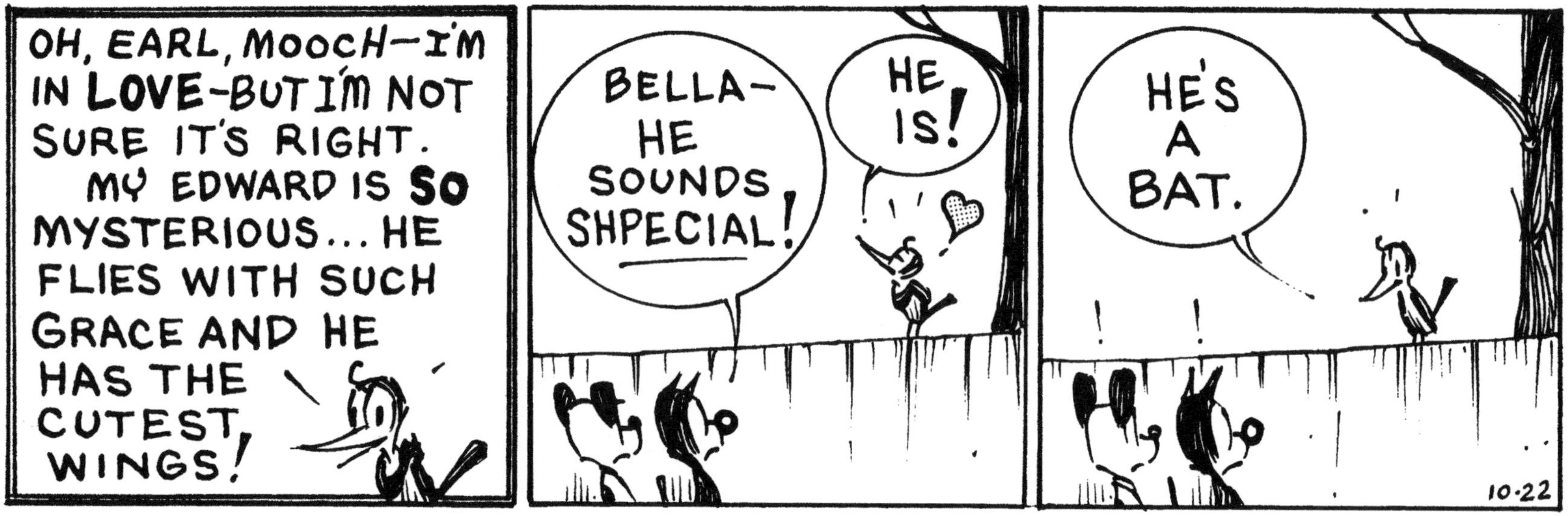
OH, EARL, MOOCH—I'M IN LOVE—BUT I'M NOT SURE IT'S RIGHT. MY EDWARD IS SO MYSTERIOUS... HE FLIES WITH SUCH GRACE AND HE HAS THE CUTEST WINGS!
BELLA—HE SOUNDS SHPECIAL!
HE IS!
HE'S A BAT.
10·22

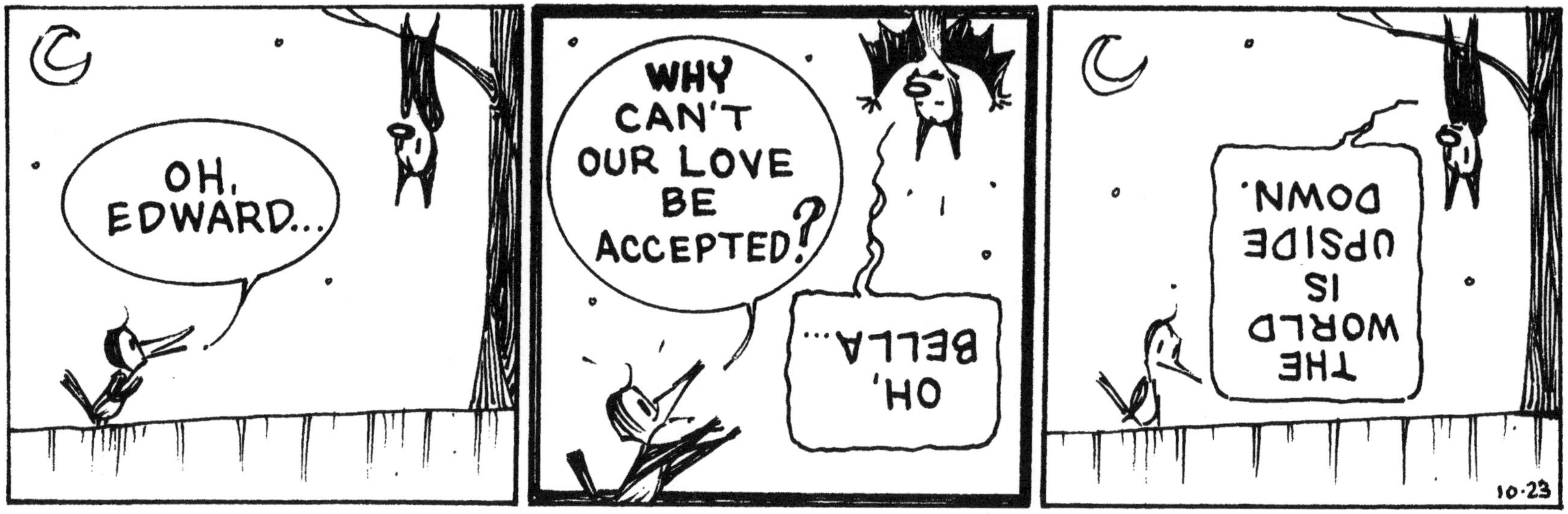
OH, EDWARD...
WHY CAN'T OUR LOVE BE ACCEPTED?
OH, BELLA...
THE WORLD IS UPSIDE DOWN.
10·23

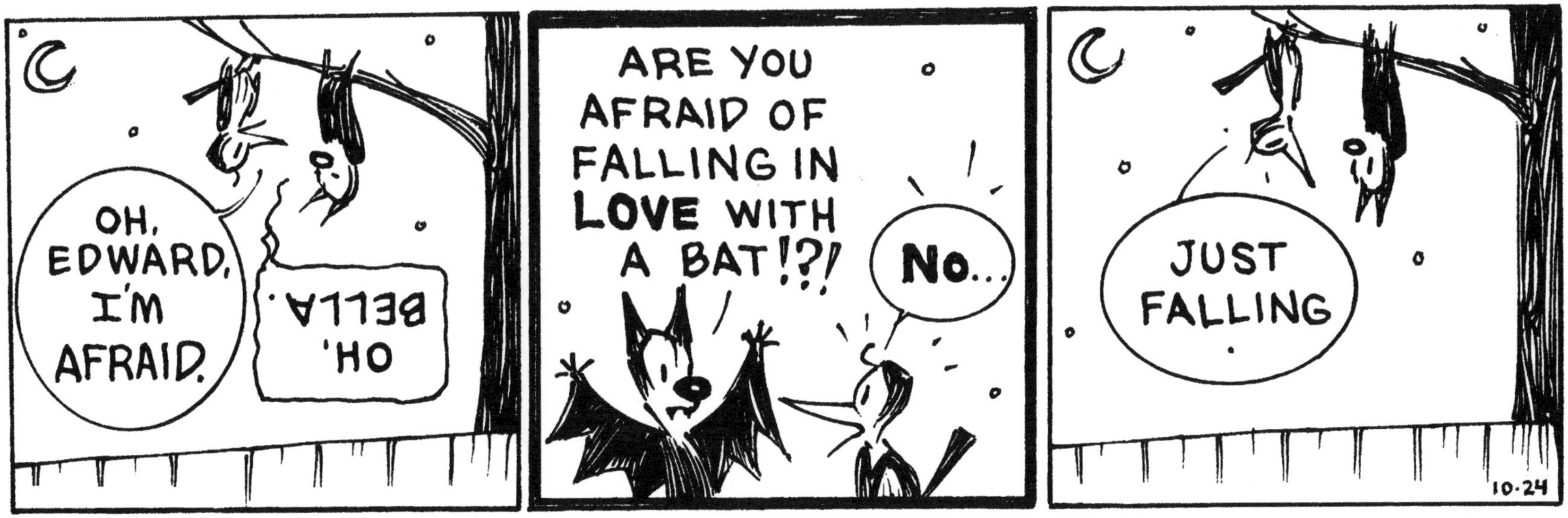
OH, EDWARD, I'M AFRAID.
OH, BELLA.
ARE YOU AFRAID OF FALLING IN **LOVE** WITH A BAT!?!
No...
JUST FALLING
10·24

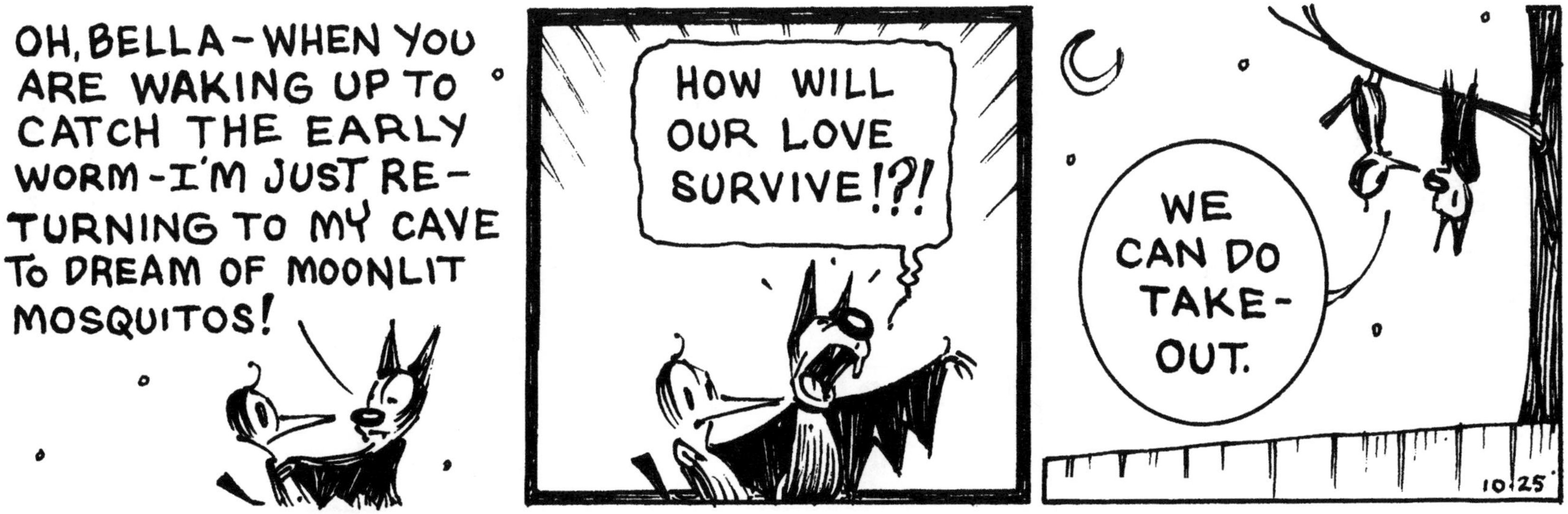
OH, BELLA - WHEN YOU ARE WAKING UP TO CATCH THE EARLY WORM - I'M JUST RE-TURNING TO MY CAVE TO DREAM OF MOONLIT MOSQUITOS!
HOW WILL OUR LOVE SURVIVE!?!
WE CAN DO TAKE-OUT.
10·25

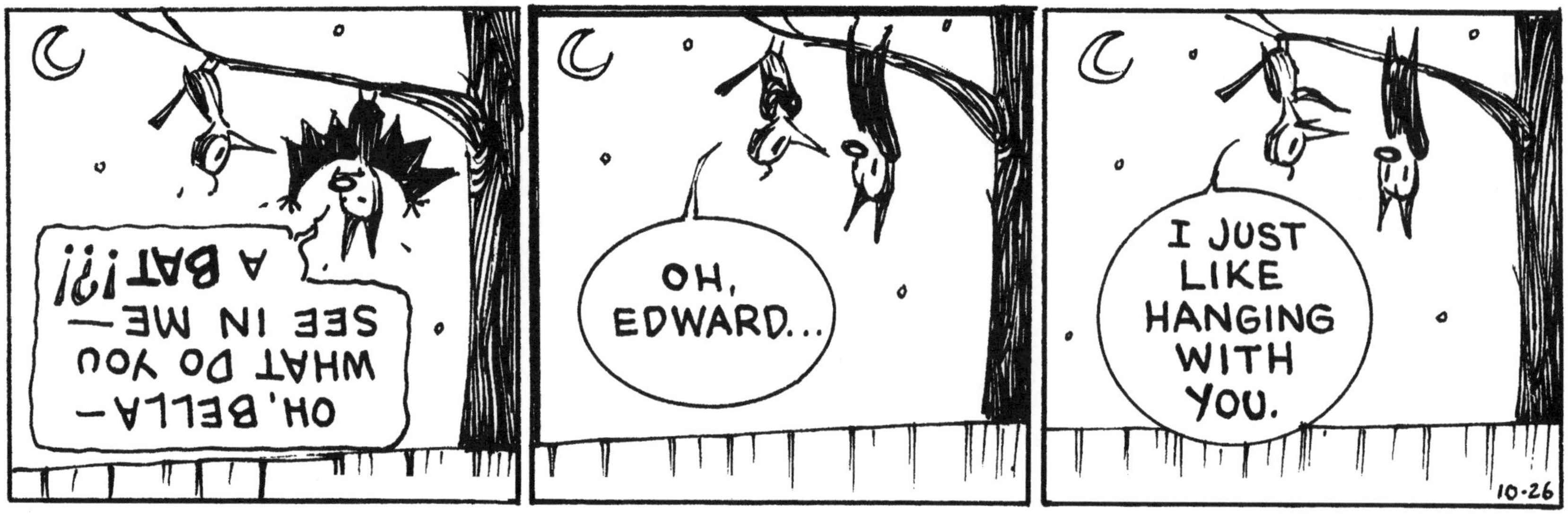
OH, BELLA— WHAT DO YOU SEE IN ME— A BAT!?!
OH, EDWARD...
I JUST LIKE HANGING WITH YOU.
10·26

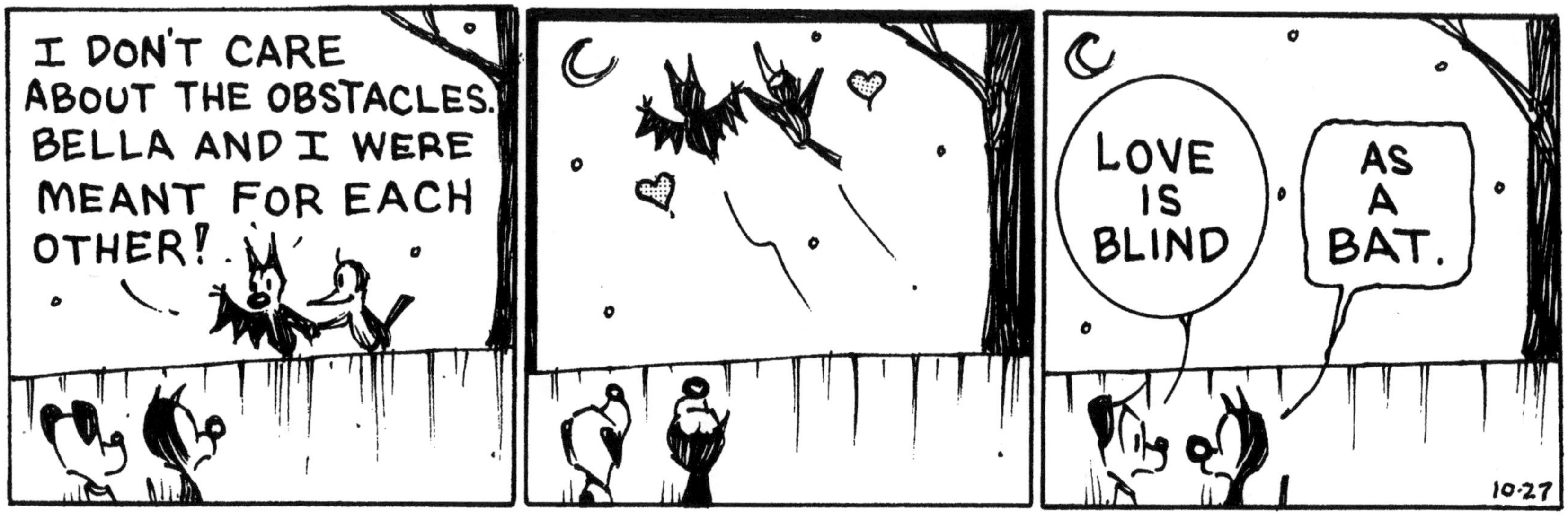
I DON'T CARE ABOUT THE OBSTACLES. BELLA AND I WERE MEANT FOR EACH OTHER!
LOVE IS BLIND
AS A BAT.
10·27

MUTTS

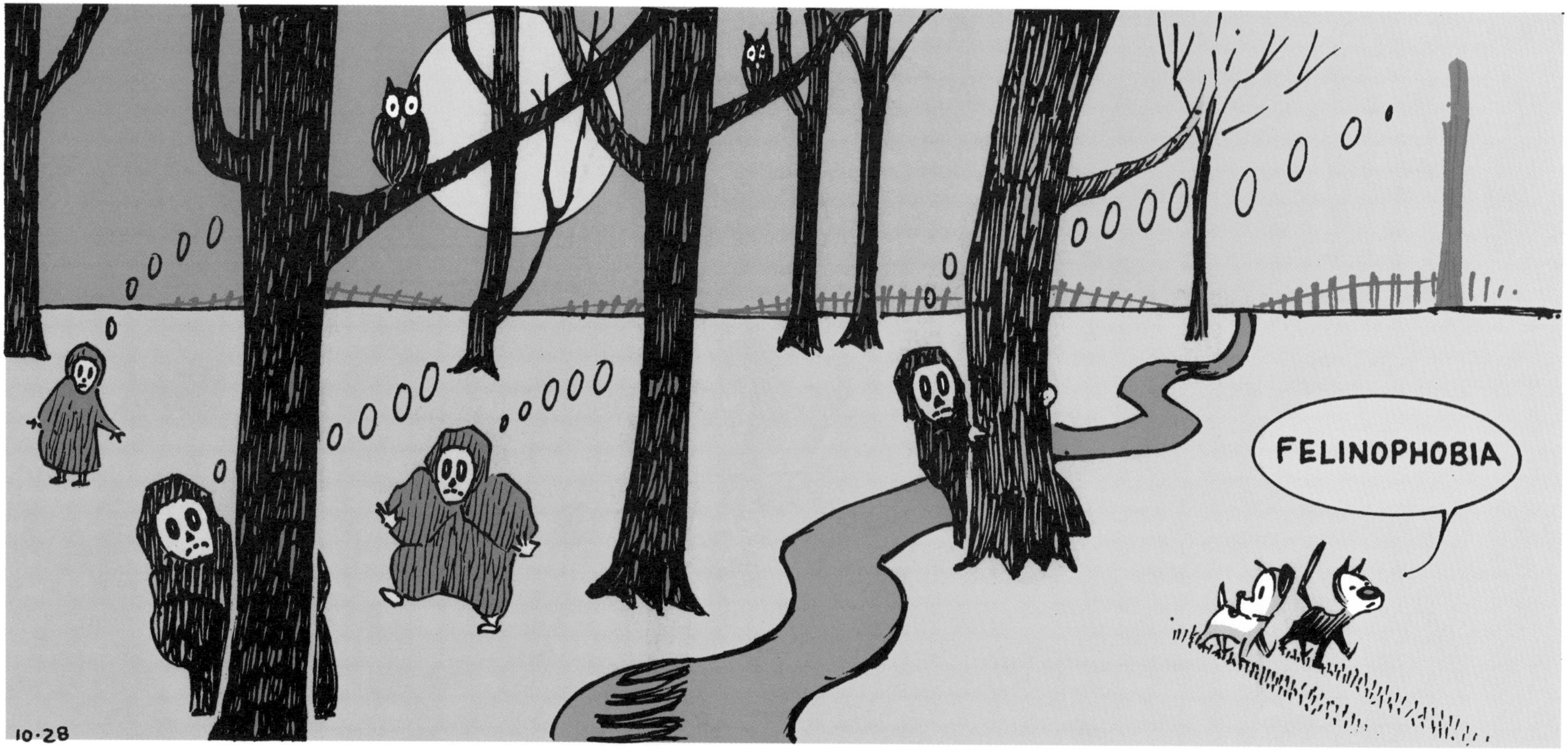
FELINOPHOBIA
10-28

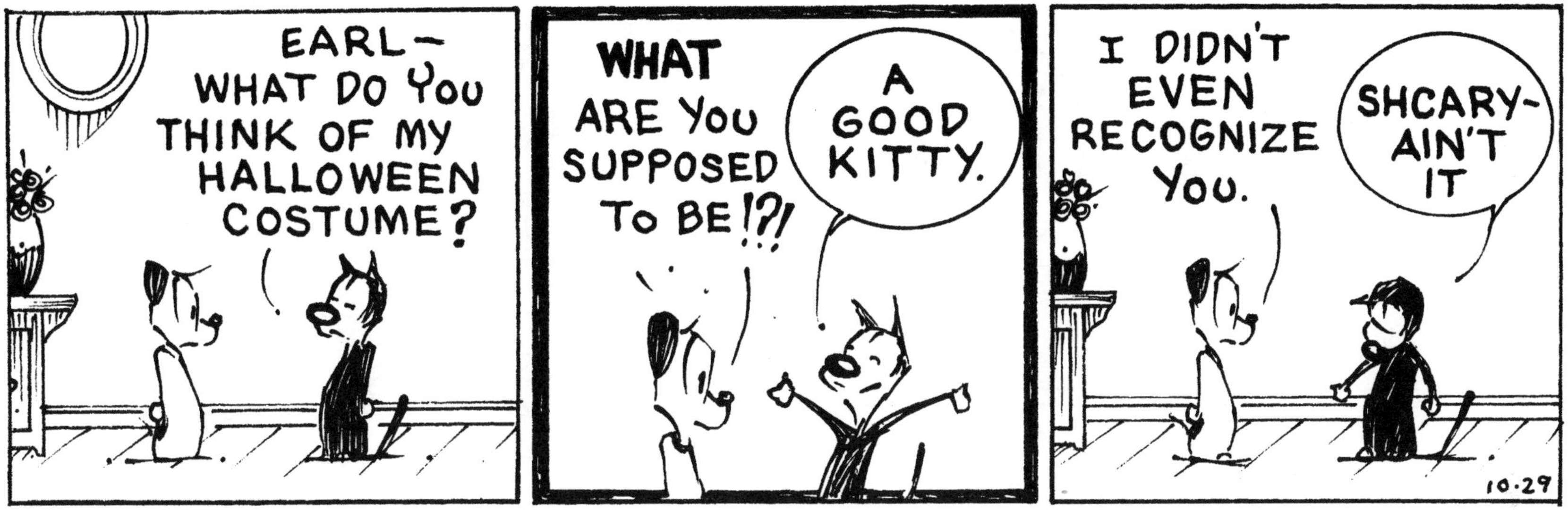
EARL–
WHAT DO YOU THINK OF MY HALLOWEEN COSTUME?
WHAT ARE YOU SUPPOSED TO BE!?!
A GOOD KITTY.
I DIDN'T EVEN RECOGNIZE YOU.
SHCARY–AIN'T IT
10·29

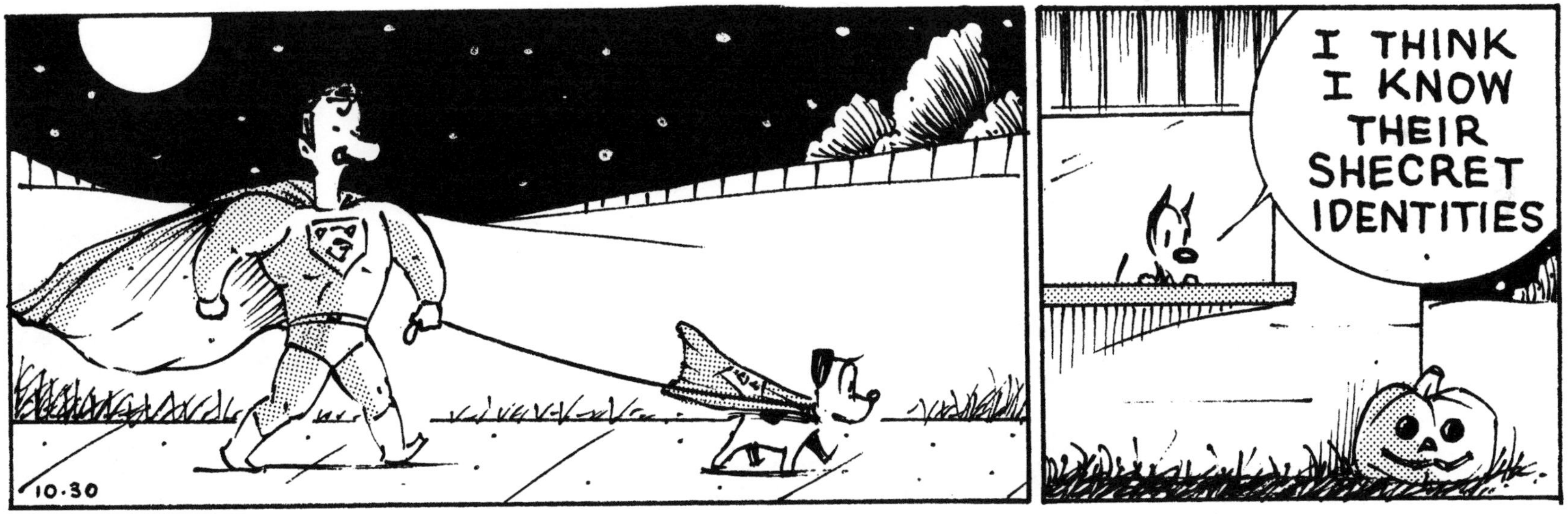
10·30
I THINK I KNOW THEIR SHECRET IDENTITIES.

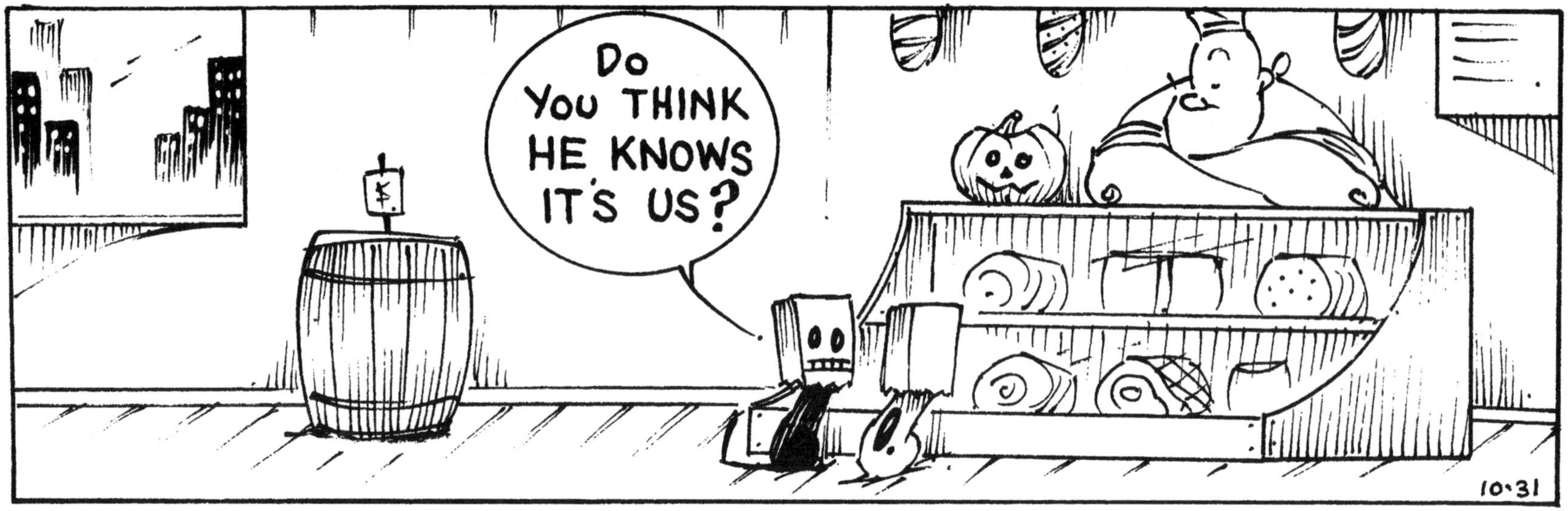
DO YOU THINK HE KNOWS IT'S US?
10-31

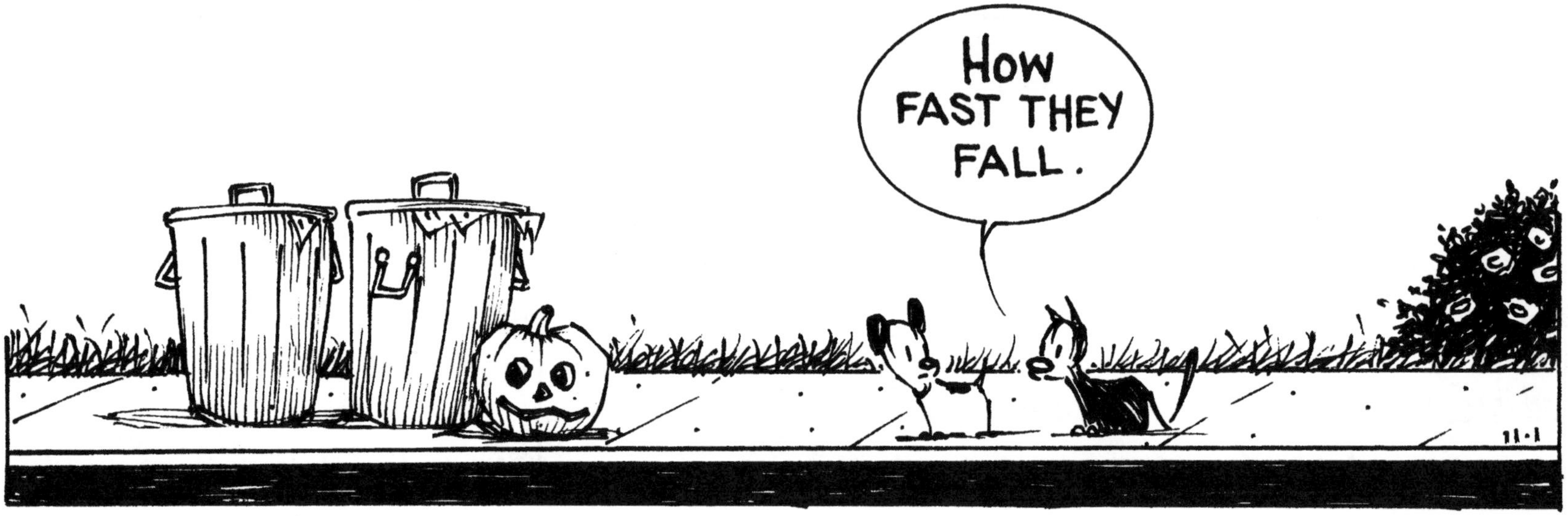
HOW FAST THEY FALL.
11-1

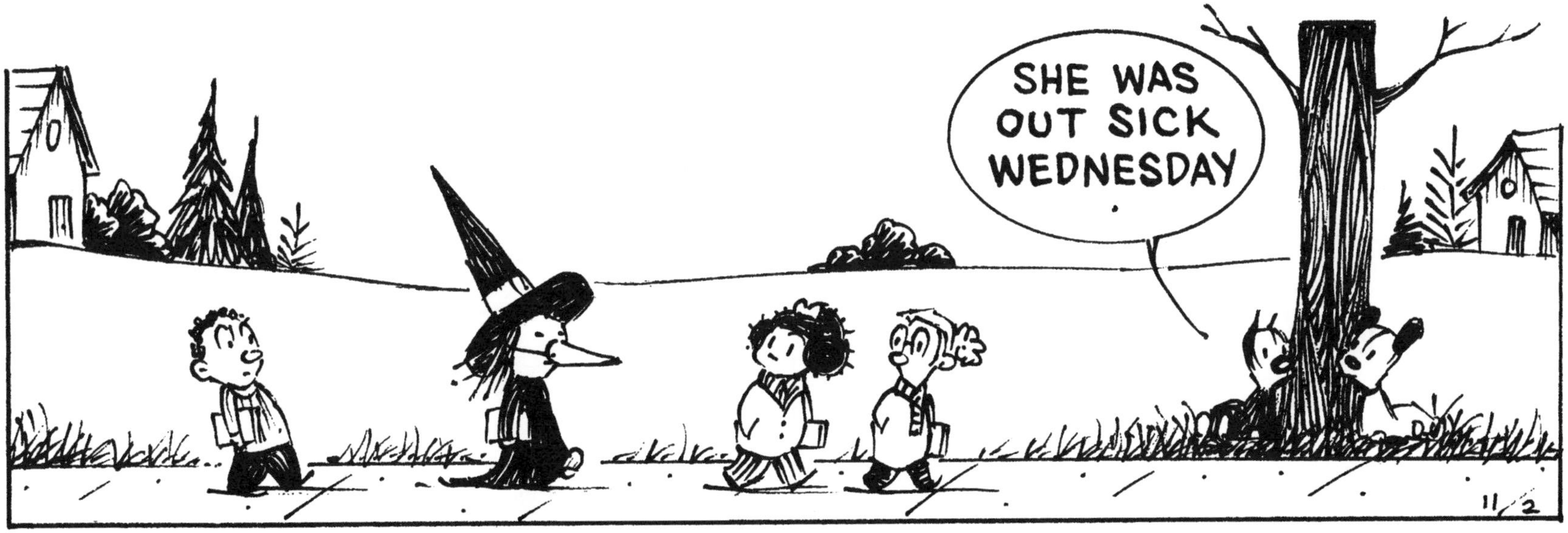
SHE WAS OUT SICK WEDNESDAY.
11/2

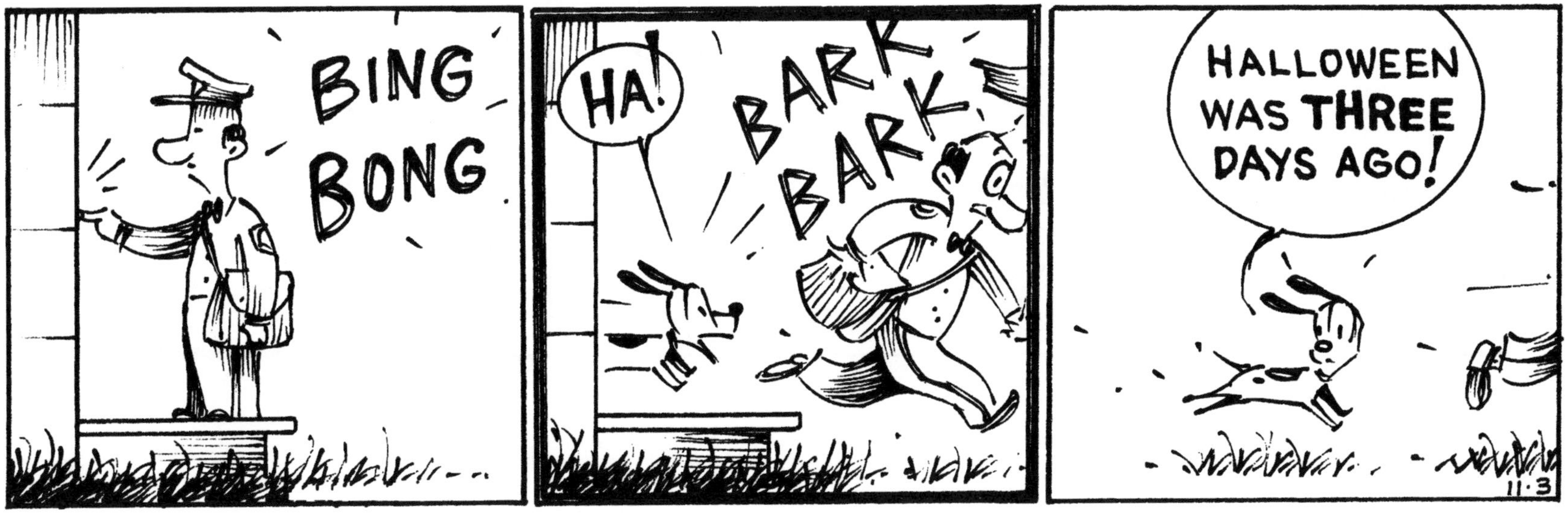
BING BONG
HA!
BARK BARK
HALLOWEEN WAS THREE DAYS AGO!
11·3

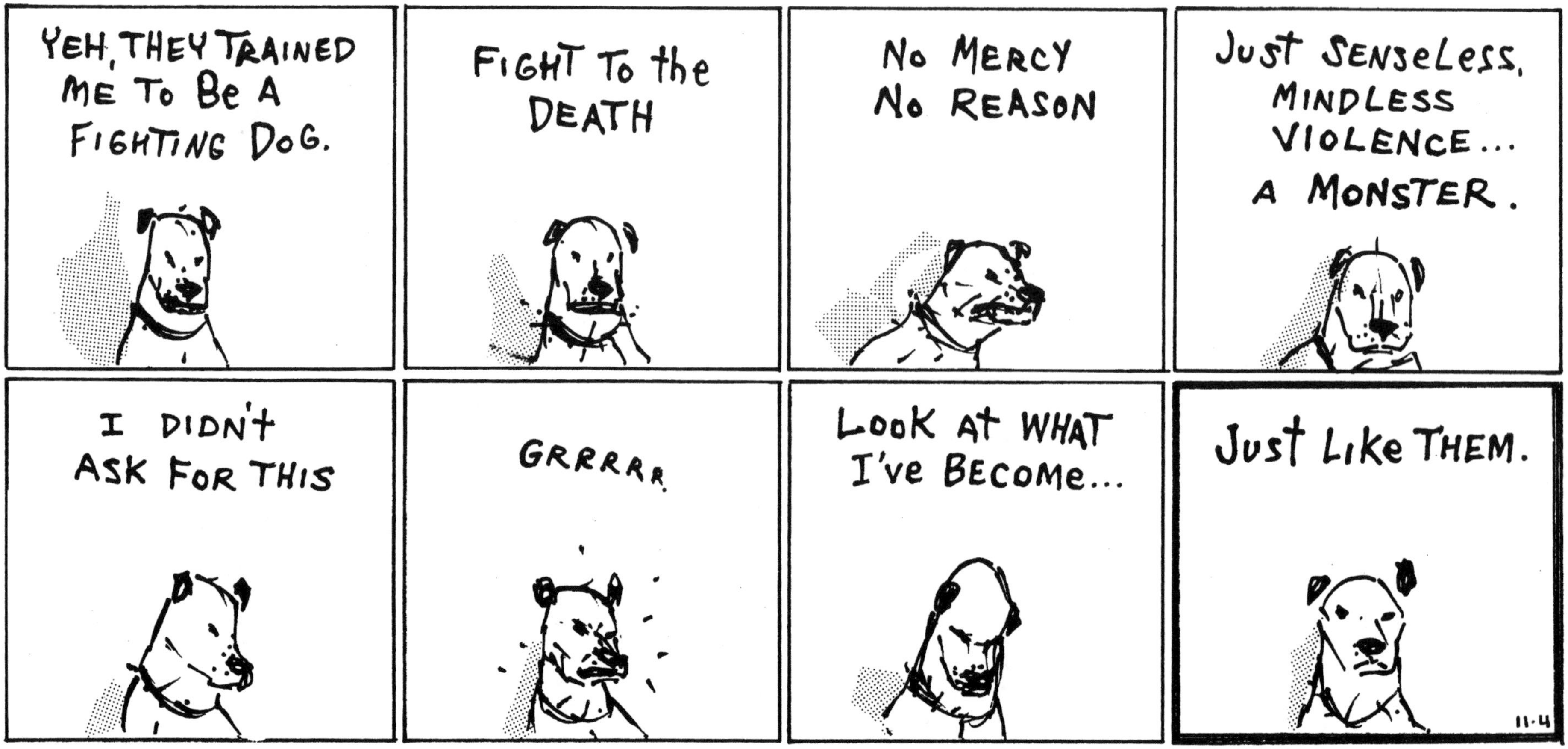
YEH, THEY TRAINED ME TO BE A FIGHTING DOG.
FIGHT TO the DEATH
NO MERCY NO REASON
JUST SENSELESS, MINDLESS VIOLENCE... A MONSTER.
I DIDN'T ASK FOR THIS
GRRRRRR
LOOK AT WHAT I'VE BECOME...
JUST LIKE THEM.
11·4

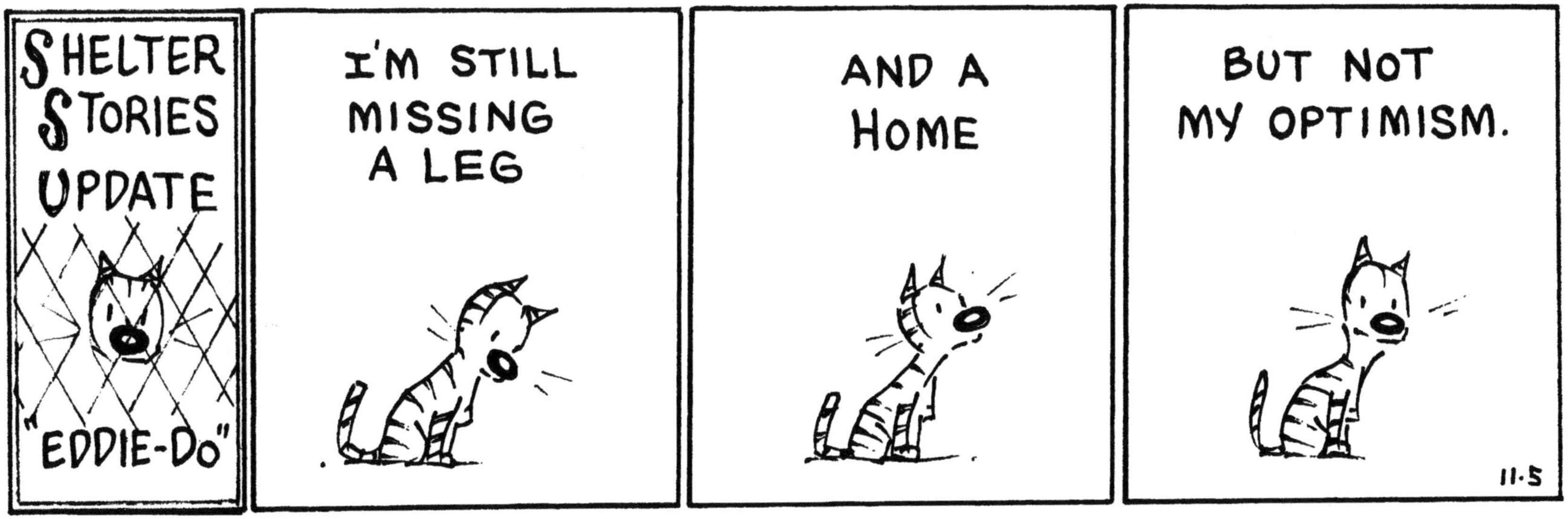
SHELTER STORIES UPDATE
"EDDIE-DO"
I'M STILL MISSING A LEG
AND A HOME
BUT NOT MY OPTIMISM.
11·5

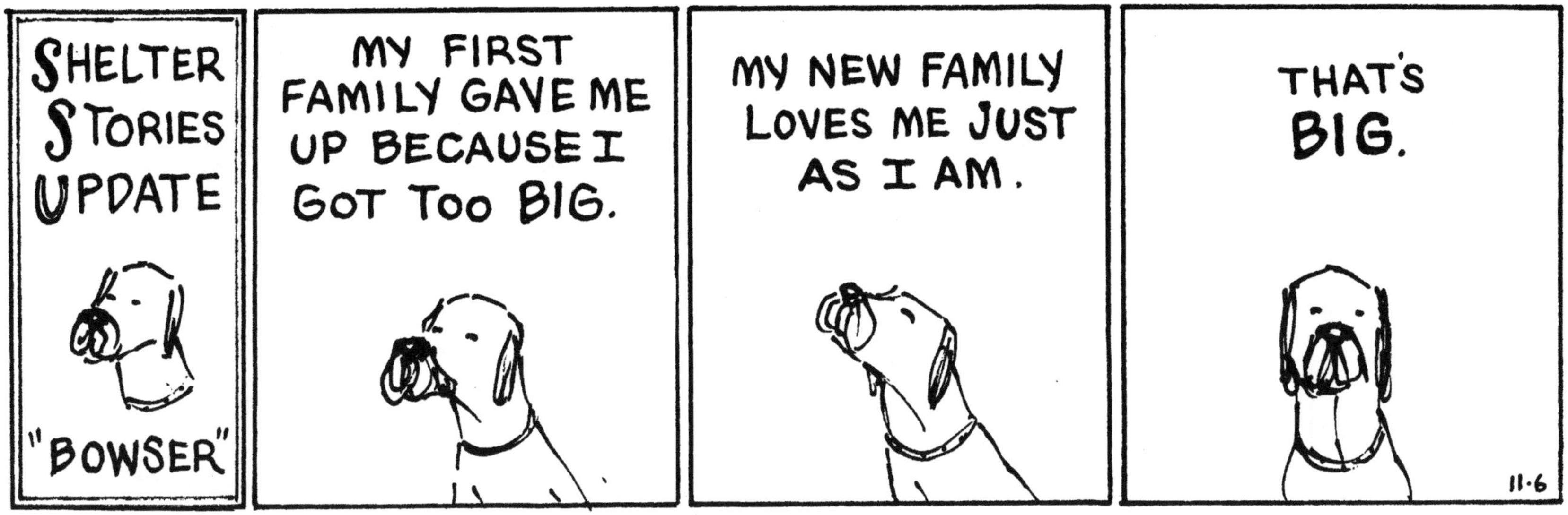
SHELTER STORIES UPDATE
"BOWSER"
MY FIRST FAMILY GAVE ME UP BECAUSE I GOT TOO BIG.
MY NEW FAMILY LOVES ME JUST AS I AM.
THAT'S BIG.
11·6

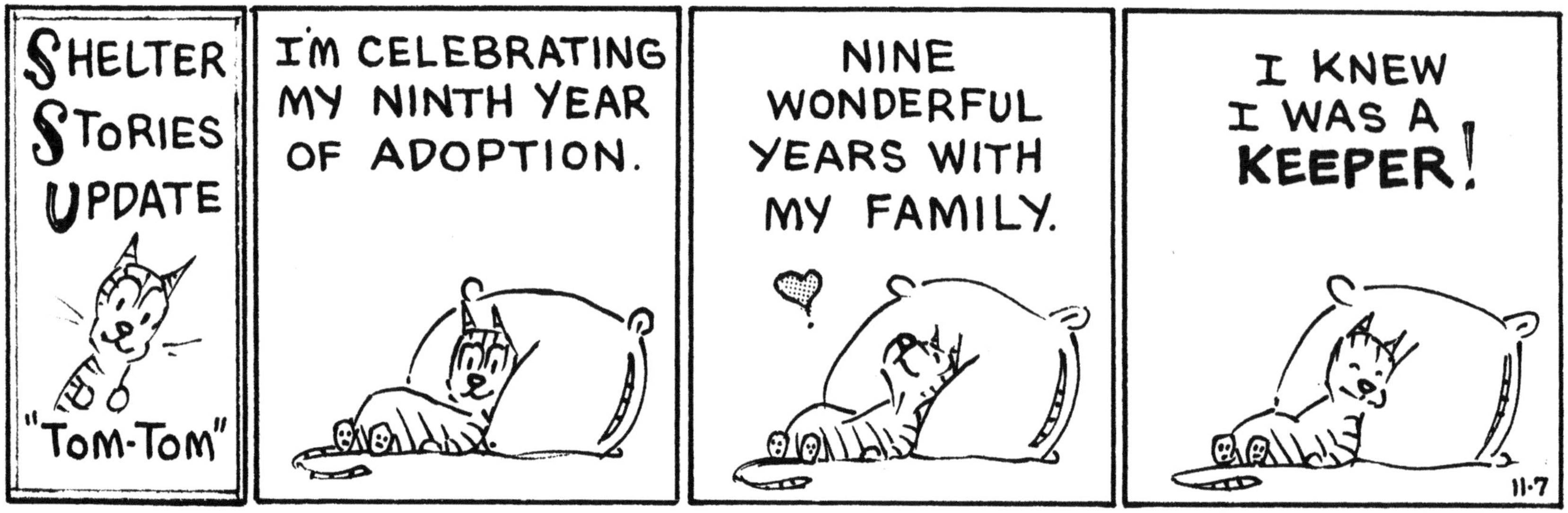
SHELTER STORIES UPDATE
"TOM-TOM"
I'M CELEBRATING MY NINTH YEAR OF ADOPTION.
NINE WONDERFUL YEARS WITH MY FAMILY.
I KNEW I WAS A **KEEPER**!
11·7

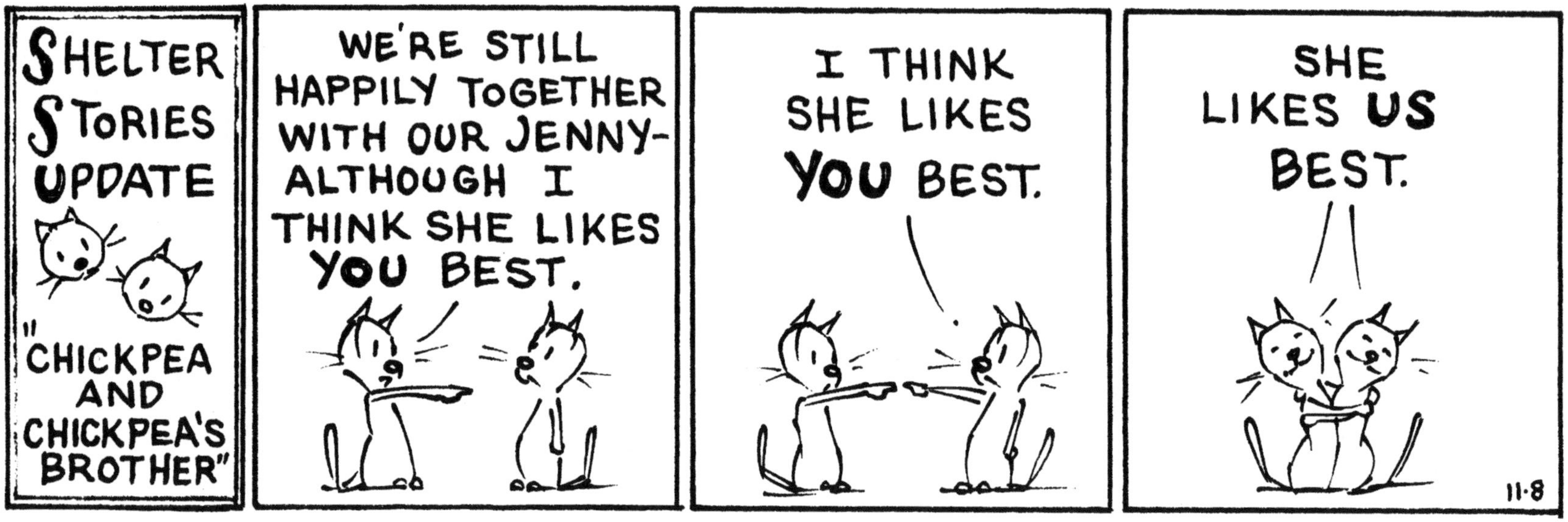
SHELTER STORIES UPDATE
"CHICKPEA AND CHICKPEA'S BROTHER"
WE'RE STILL HAPPILY TOGETHER WITH OUR JENNY- ALTHOUGH I THINK SHE LIKES **YOU** BEST.
I THINK SHE LIKES **YOU** BEST.
SHE LIKES **US** BEST.
11·8

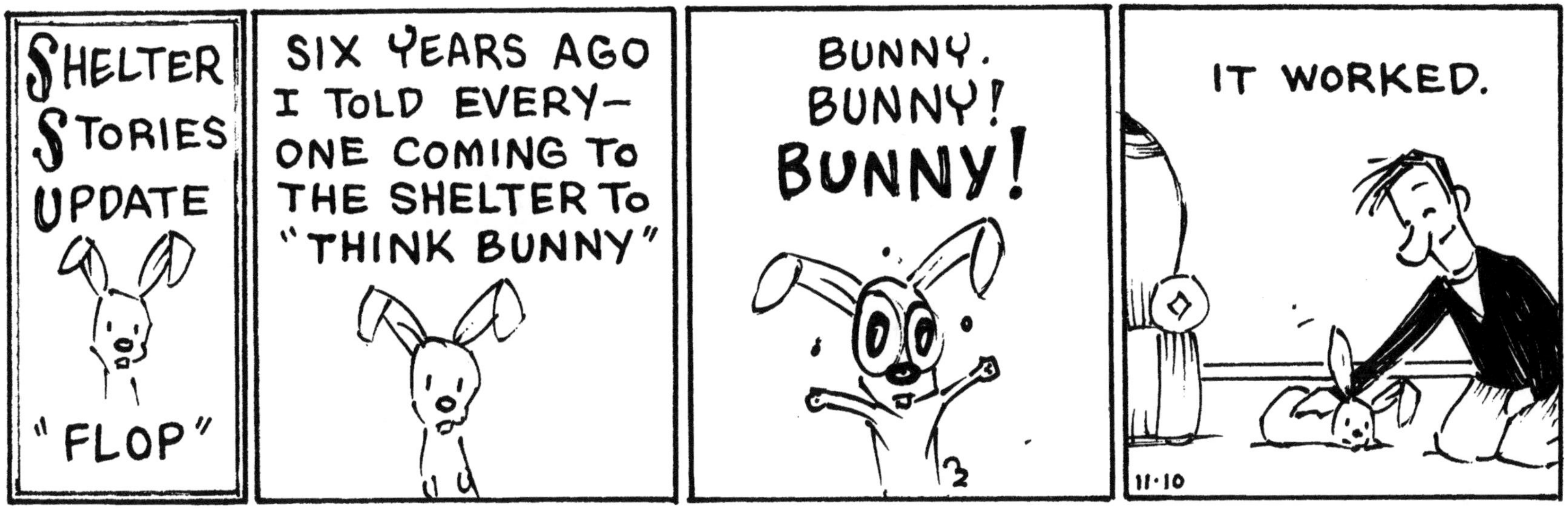
SHELTER STORIES UPDATE
"FLOP"
SIX YEARS AGO I TOLD EVERY-ONE COMING TO THE SHELTER TO "THINK BUNNY"
BUNNY. BUNNY! BUNNY!
IT WORKED.
11·10

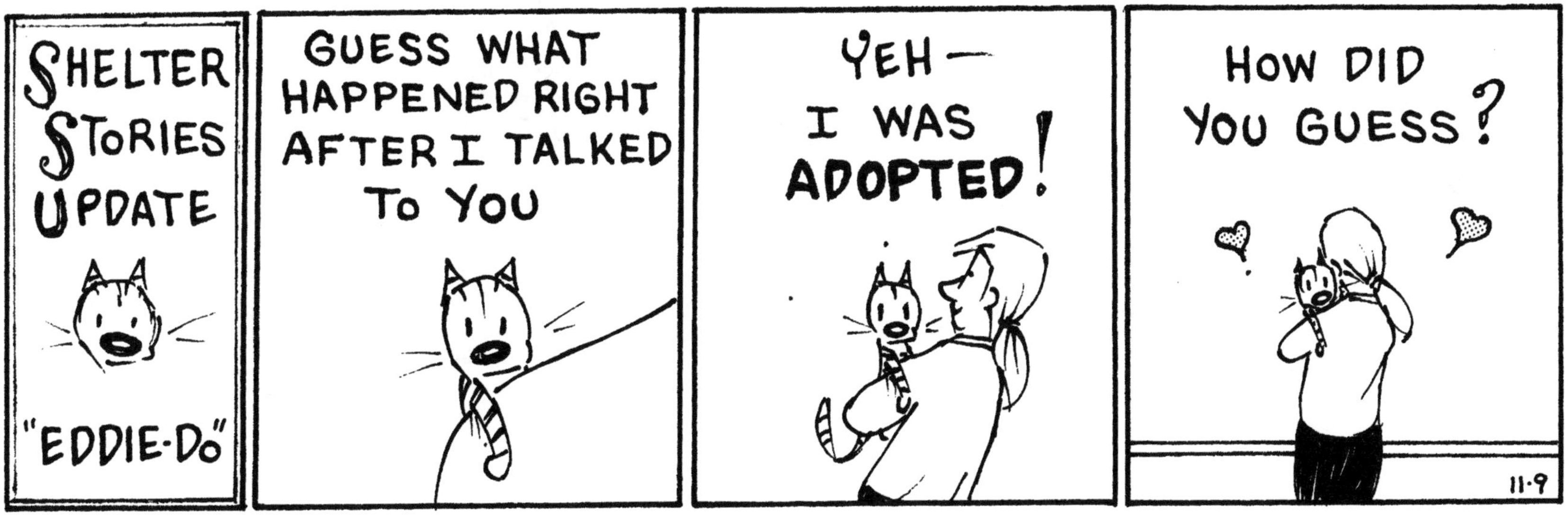
SHELTER STORIES UPDATE
"EDDIE-DO"
GUESS WHAT HAPPENED RIGHT AFTER I TALKED TO YOU
YEH — I WAS ADOPTED!
HOW DID YOU GUESS?
11·9

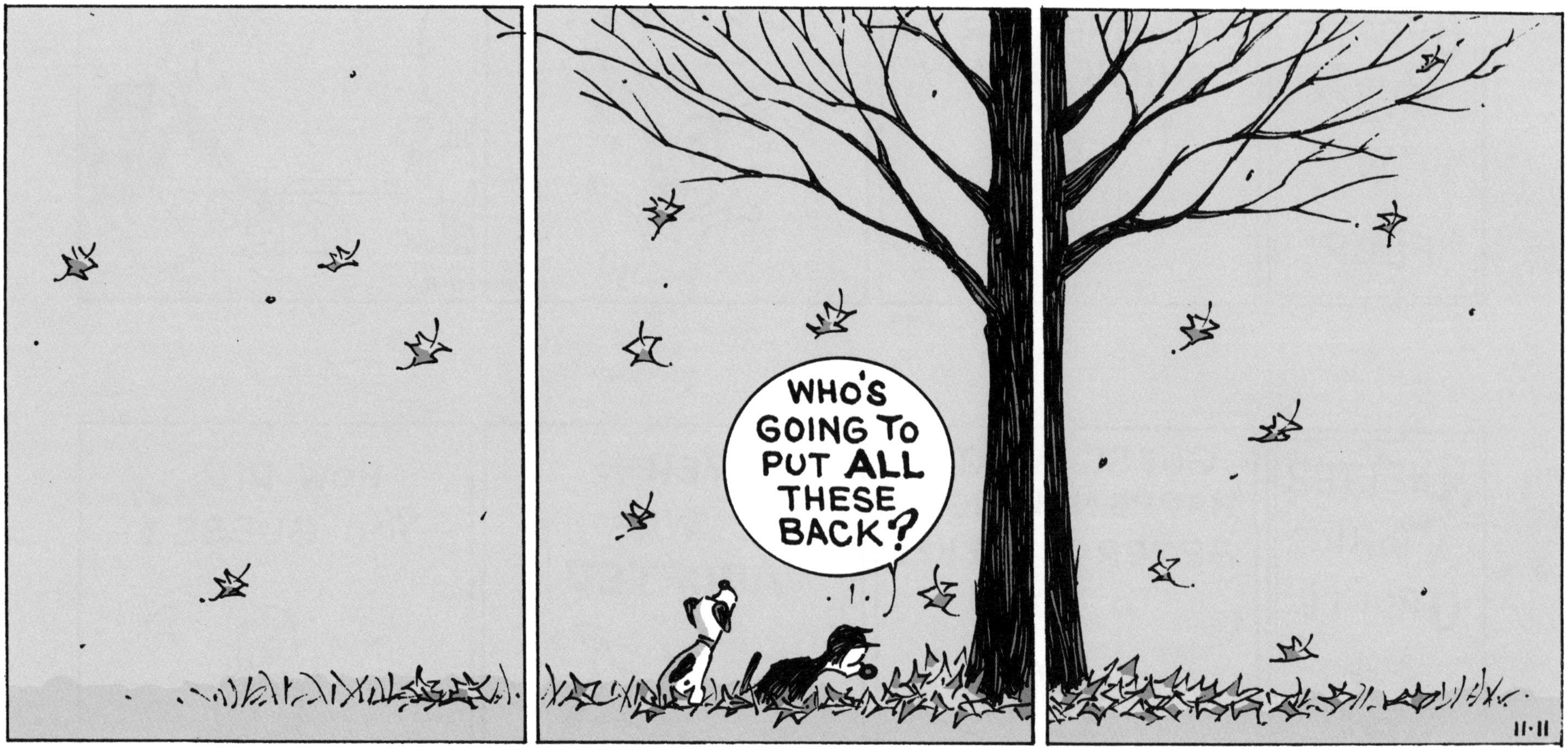
WHO'S GOING TO PUT ALL THESE BACK?
11·11

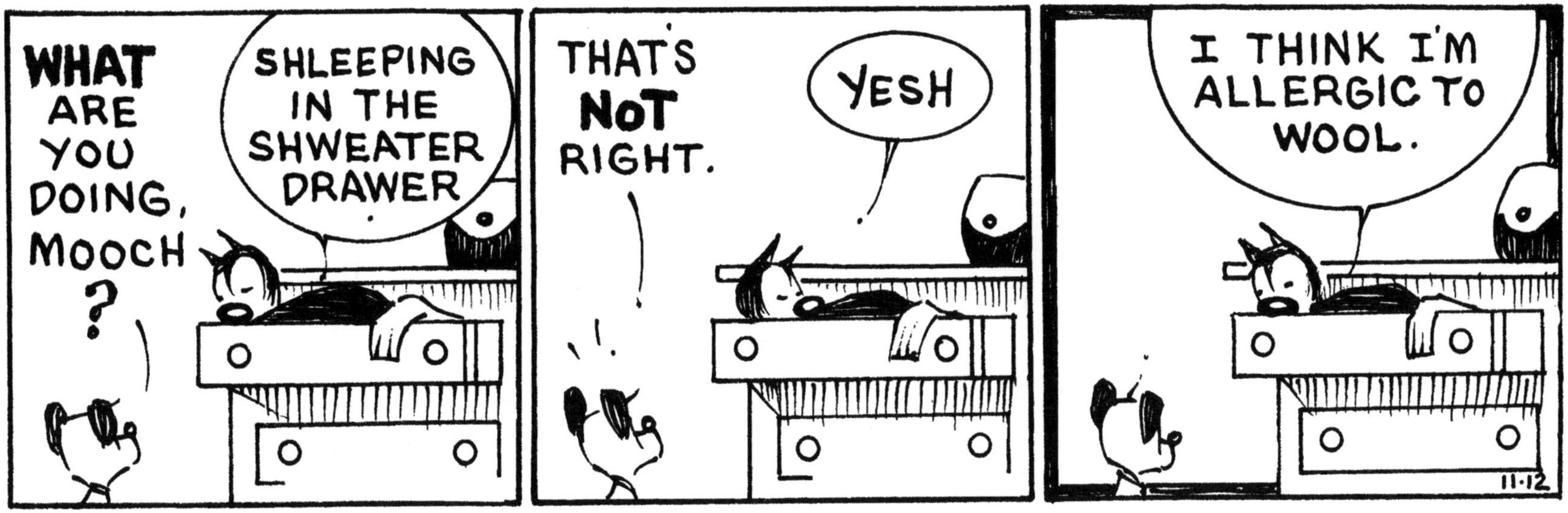
WHAT ARE YOU DOING, MOOCH ?
SHLEEPING IN THE SHWEATER DRAWER
THAT'S NOT RIGHT.
YESH
I THINK I'M ALLERGIC TO WOOL.
11·12

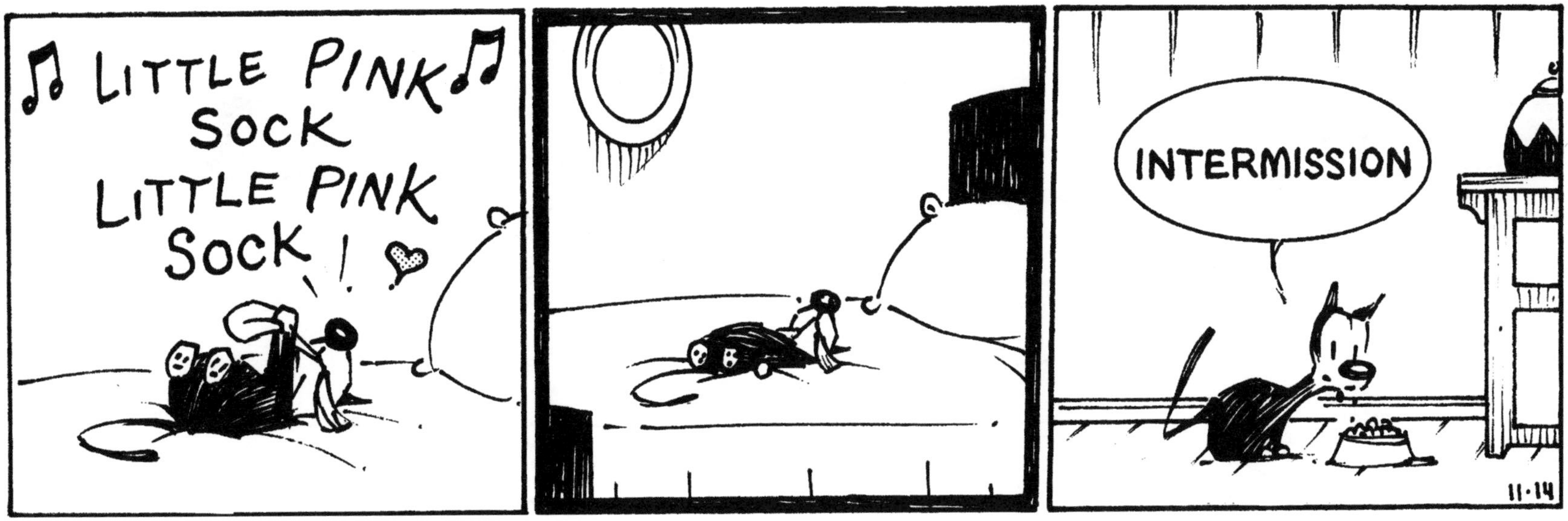
♫ LITTLE PINK ♫ SOCK LITTLE PINK SOCK !
INTERMISSION
11·14

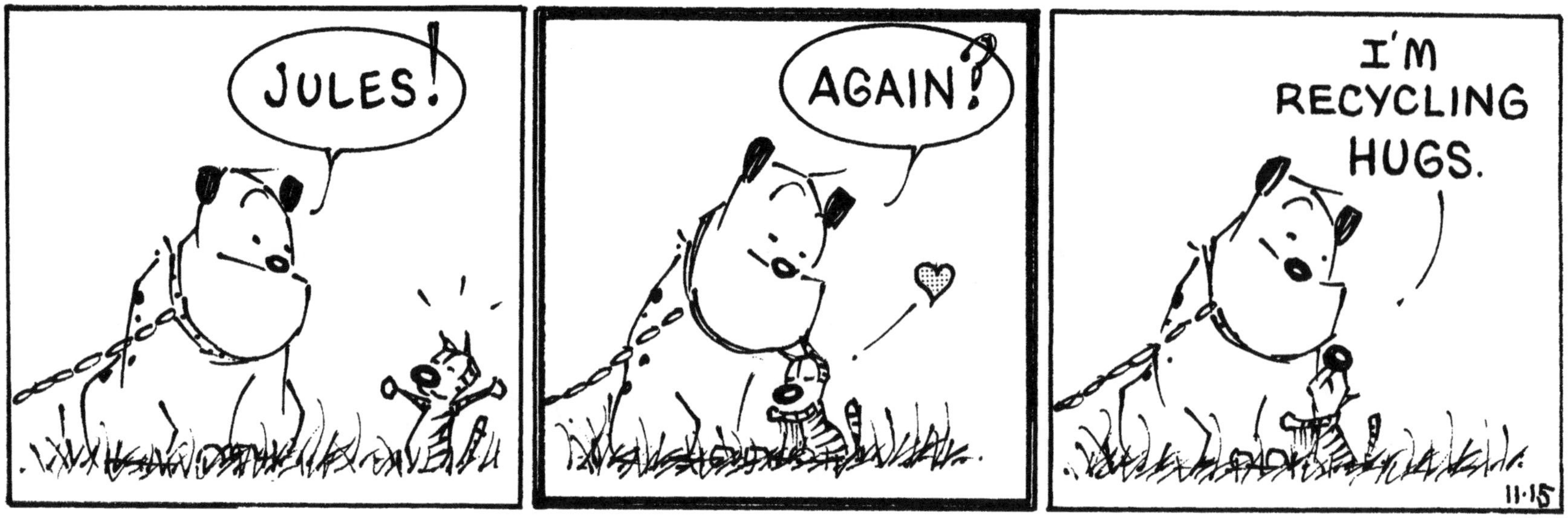
JULES!
AGAIN?
I'M RECYCLING HUGS.
11·15

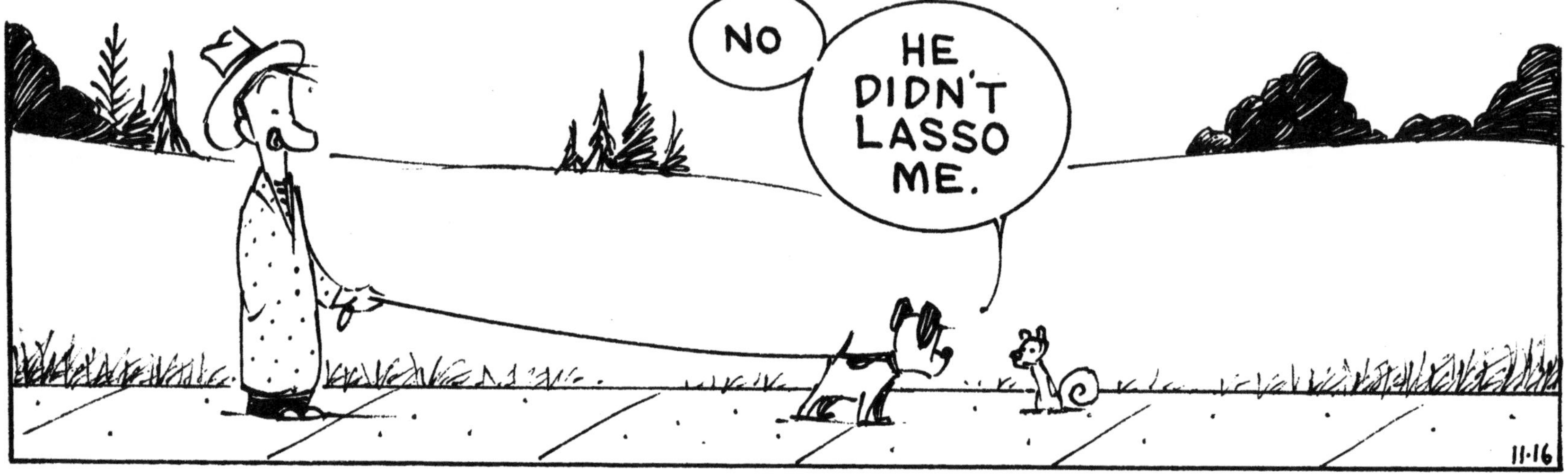
NO
HE DIDN'T LASSO ME.
11·16

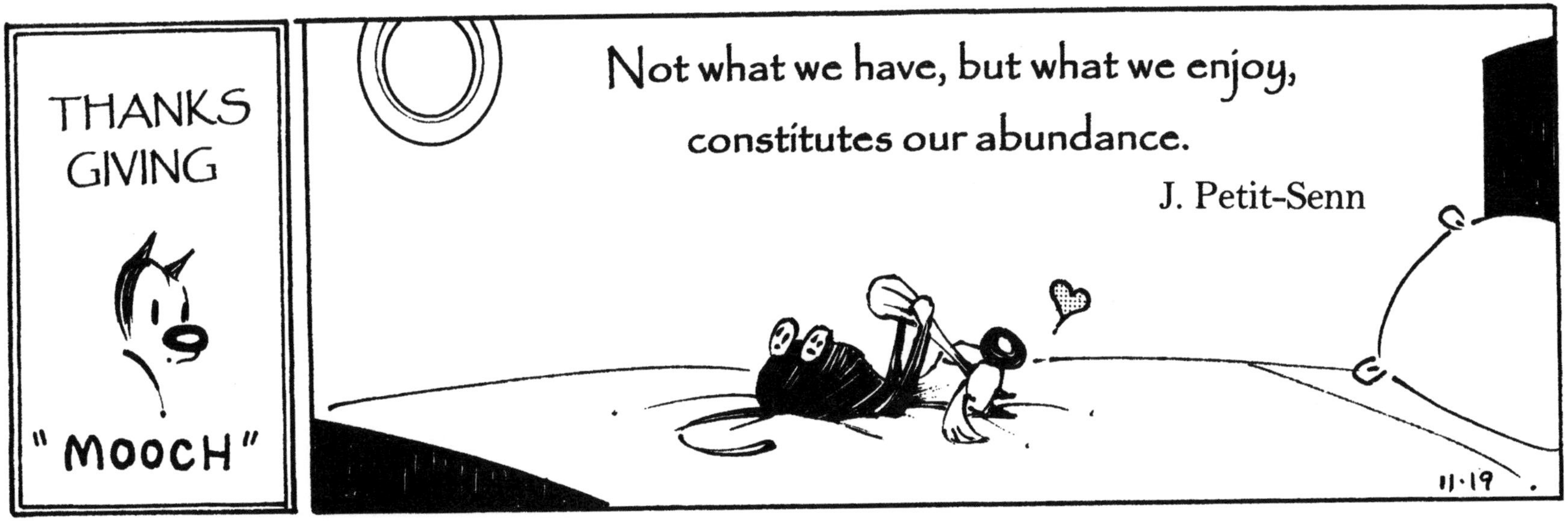
THANKS GIVING
"MOOCH"
Not what we have, but what we enjoy, constitutes our abundance.
J. Petit-Senn
11·19

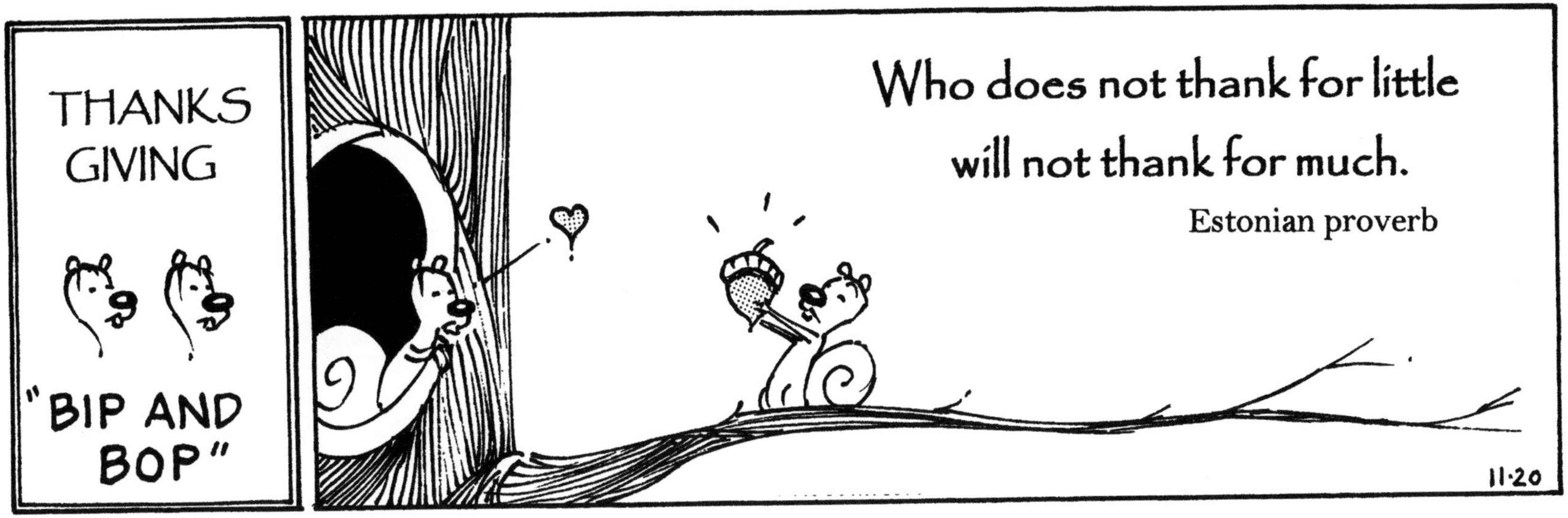
THANKS GIVING
"BIP AND BOP"
Who does not thank for little will not thank for much.
Estonian proverb
11·20

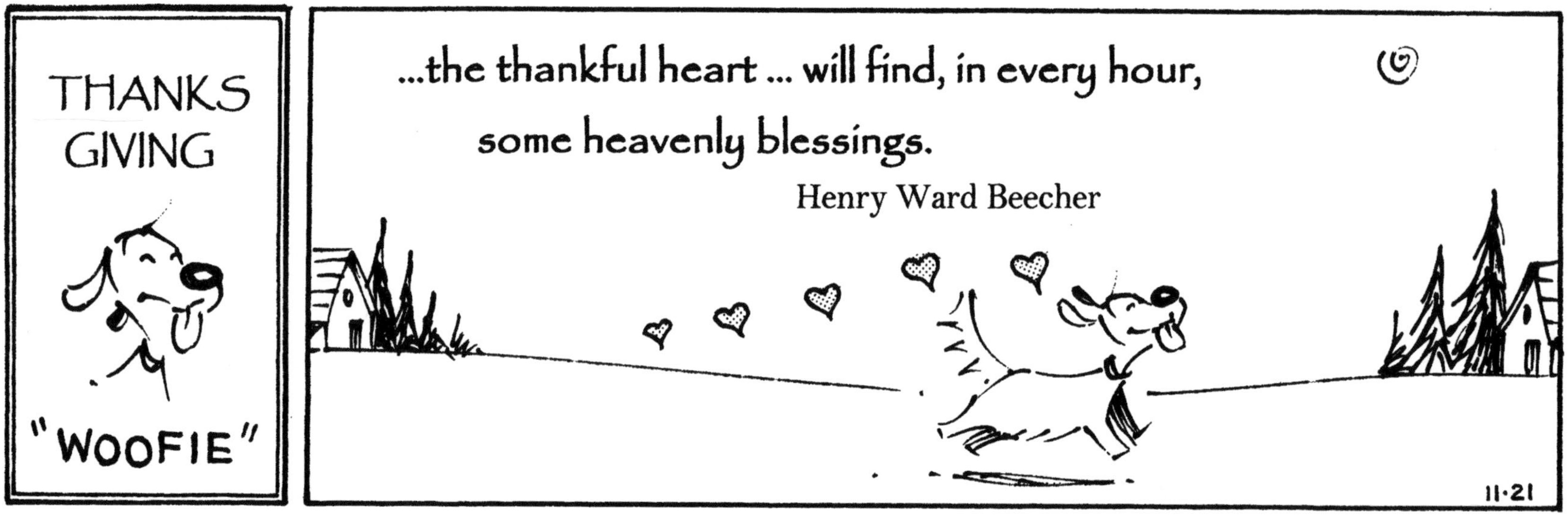
THANKS GIVING
"WOOFIE"
...the thankful heart ... will find, in every hour, some heavenly blessings.
Henry Ward Beecher
11·21

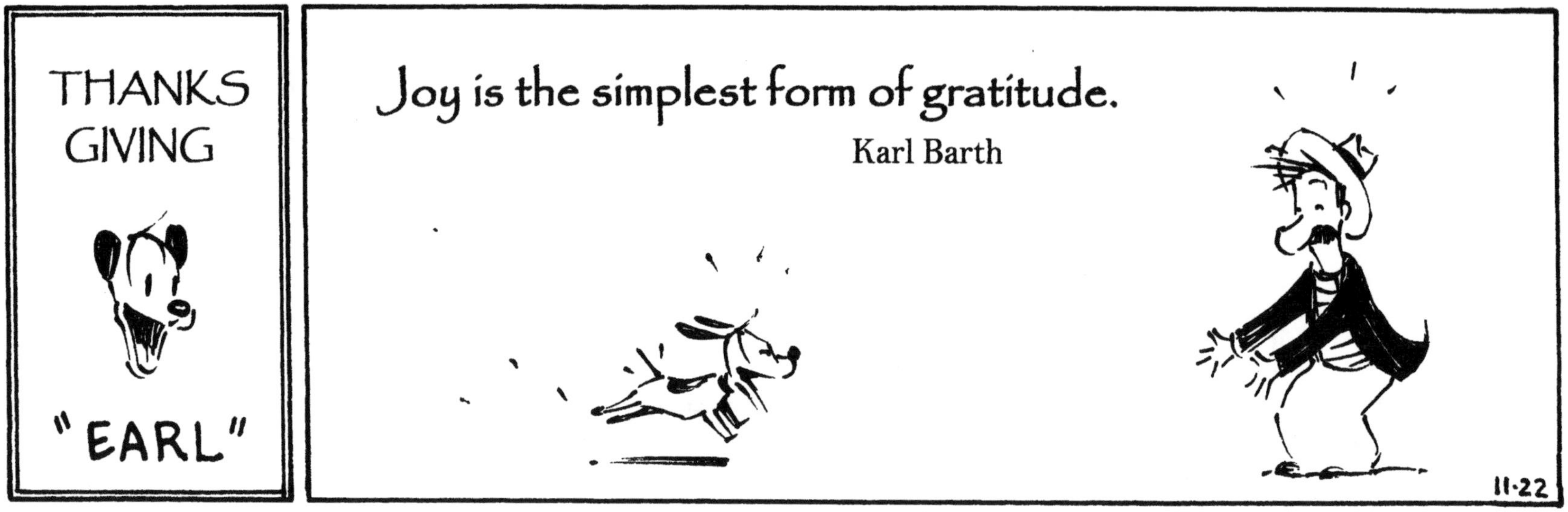
THANKS GIVING
"EARL"
Joy is the simplest form of gratitude.
Karl Barth
11·22

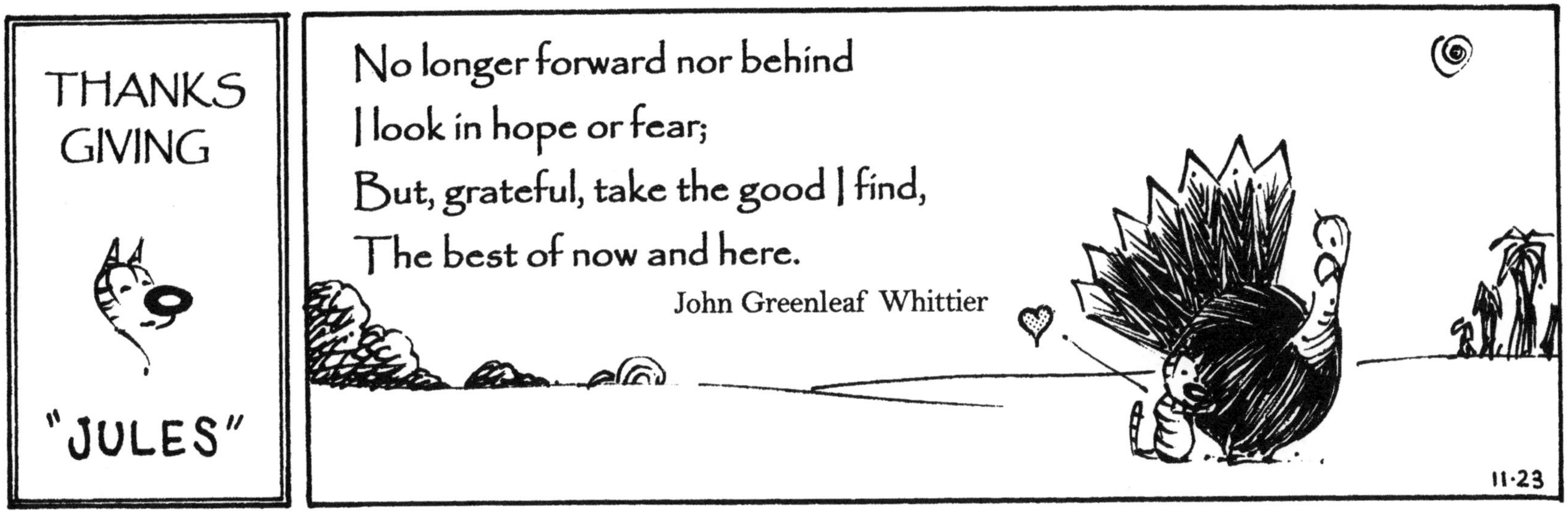
THANKS GIVING
"JULES"
No longer forward nor behind
I look in hope or fear;
But, grateful, take the good I find,
The best of now and here.
John Greenleaf Whittier
11·23

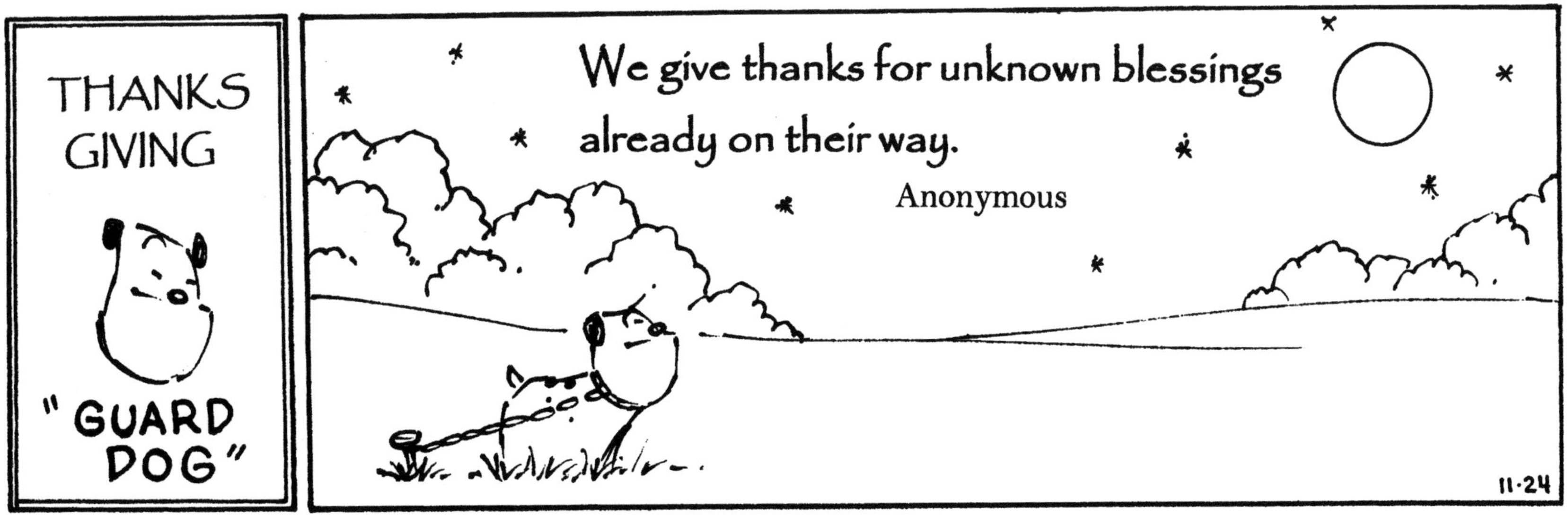
THANKS GIVING
"GUARD DOG"
We give thanks for unknown blessings
already on their way.
Anonymous
11·24

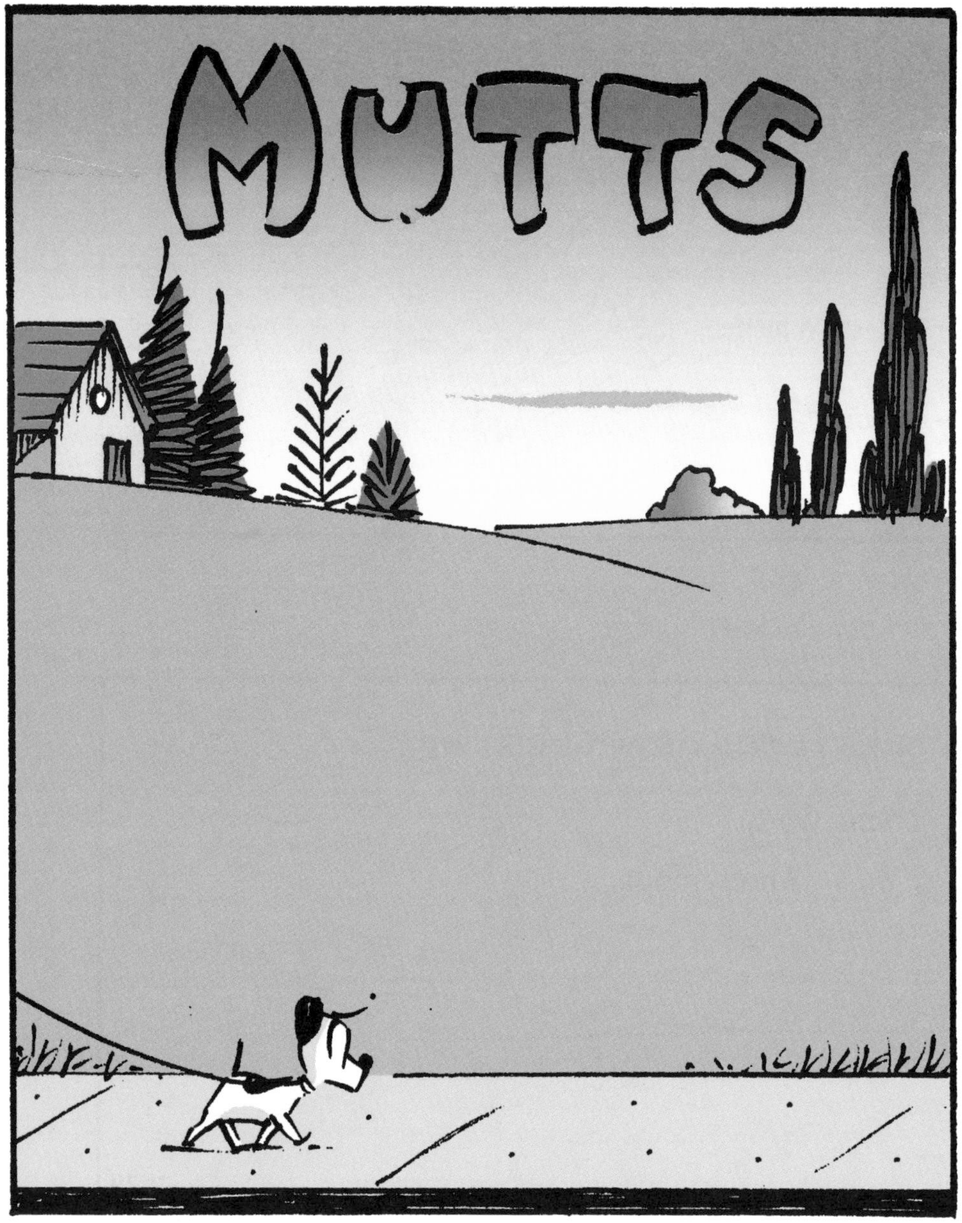
MUTTS

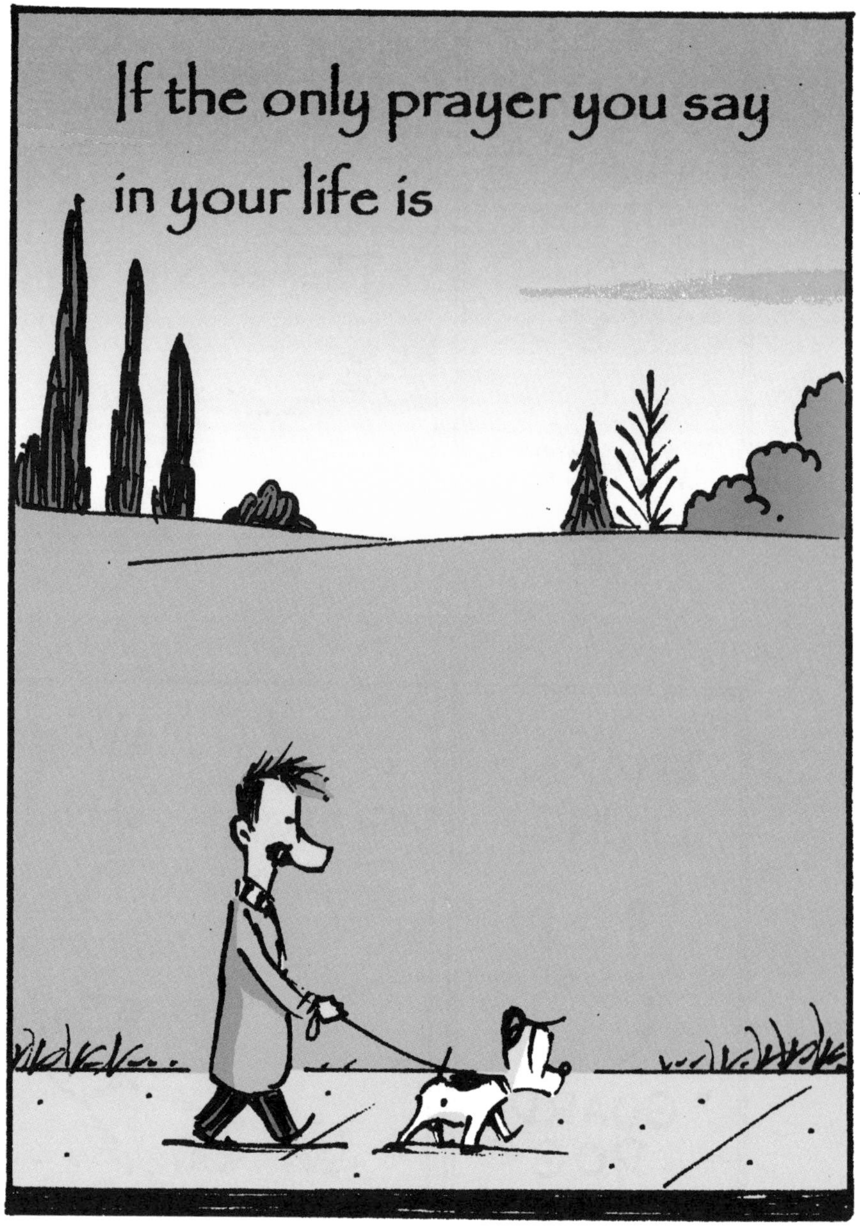
If the only prayer you say in your life is

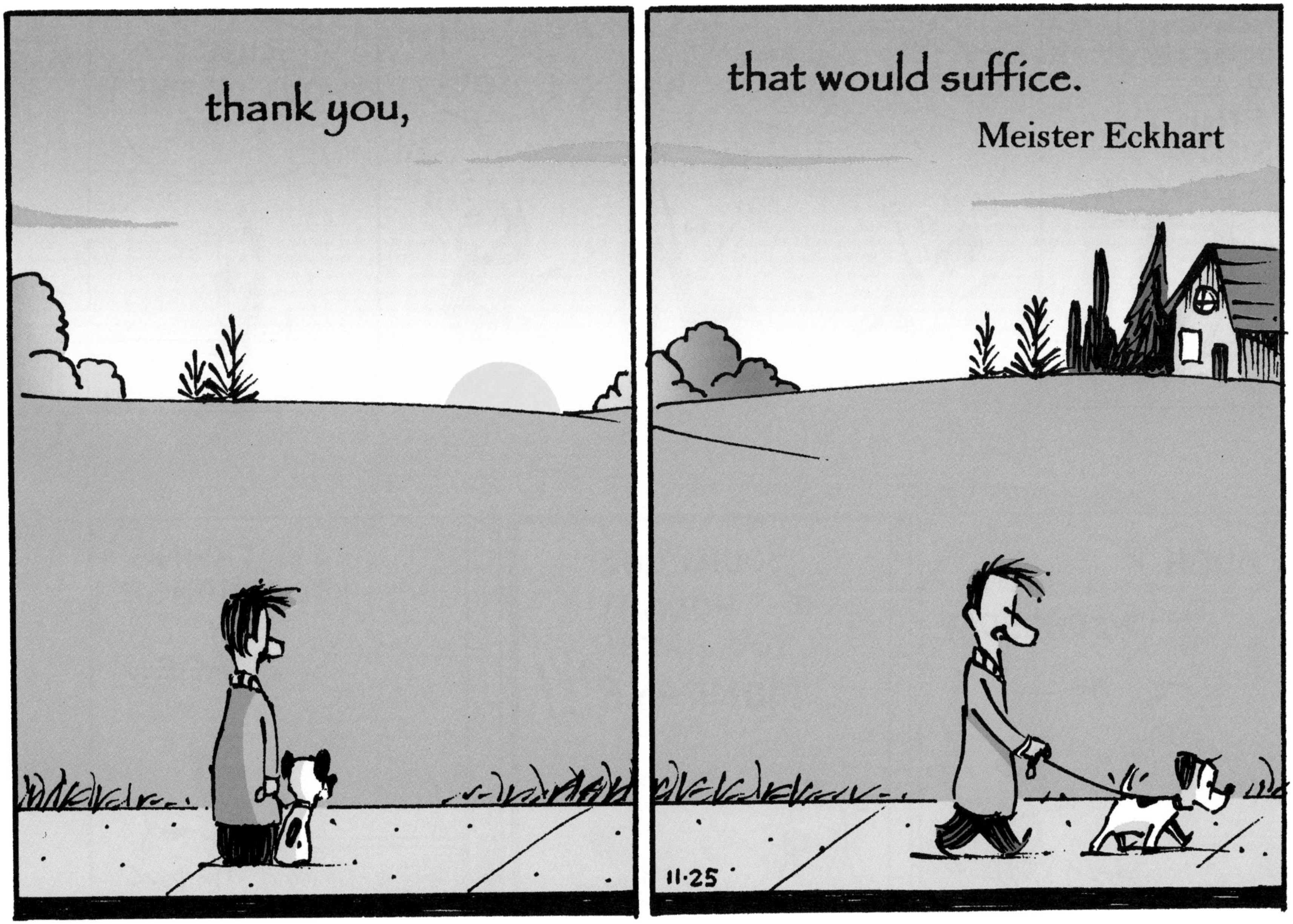
thank you,
that would suffice.
Meister Eckhart
11·25

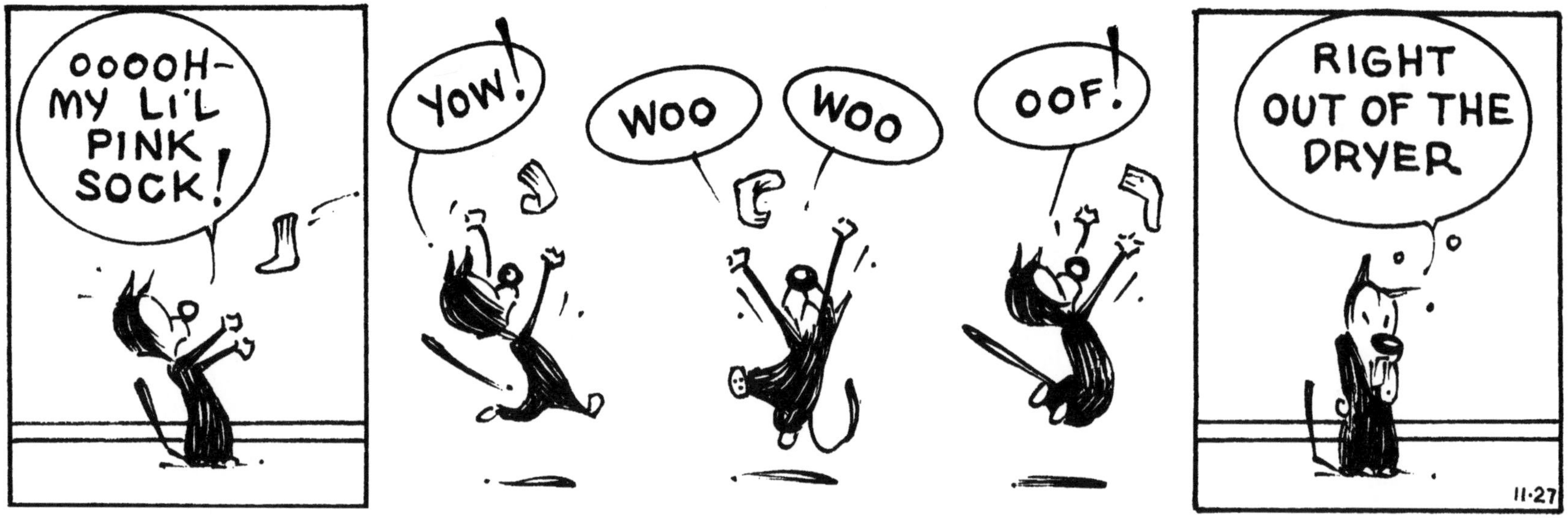
OOOOH-MY LI'L PINK SOCK!
YOW!
WOO
WOO
OOF!
RIGHT OUT OF THE DRYER
11·27

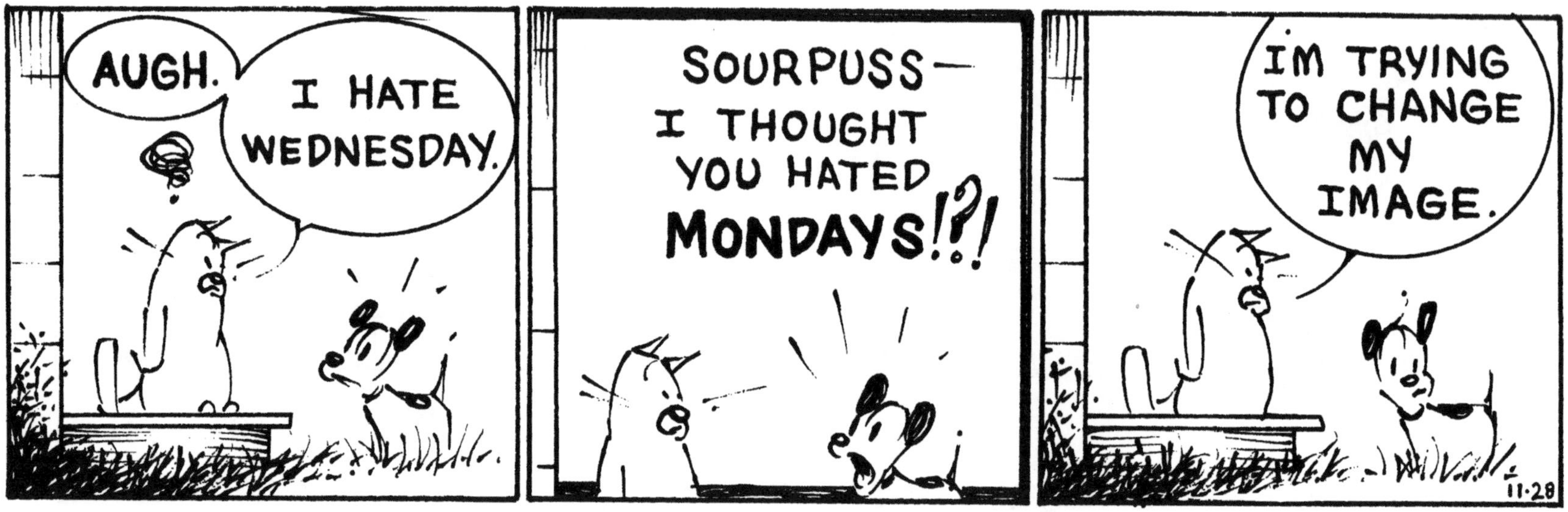
AUGH.
I HATE WEDNESDAY.
SOURPUSS— I THOUGHT YOU HATED MONDAYS!?!
I'M TRYING TO CHANGE MY IMAGE.
11·28

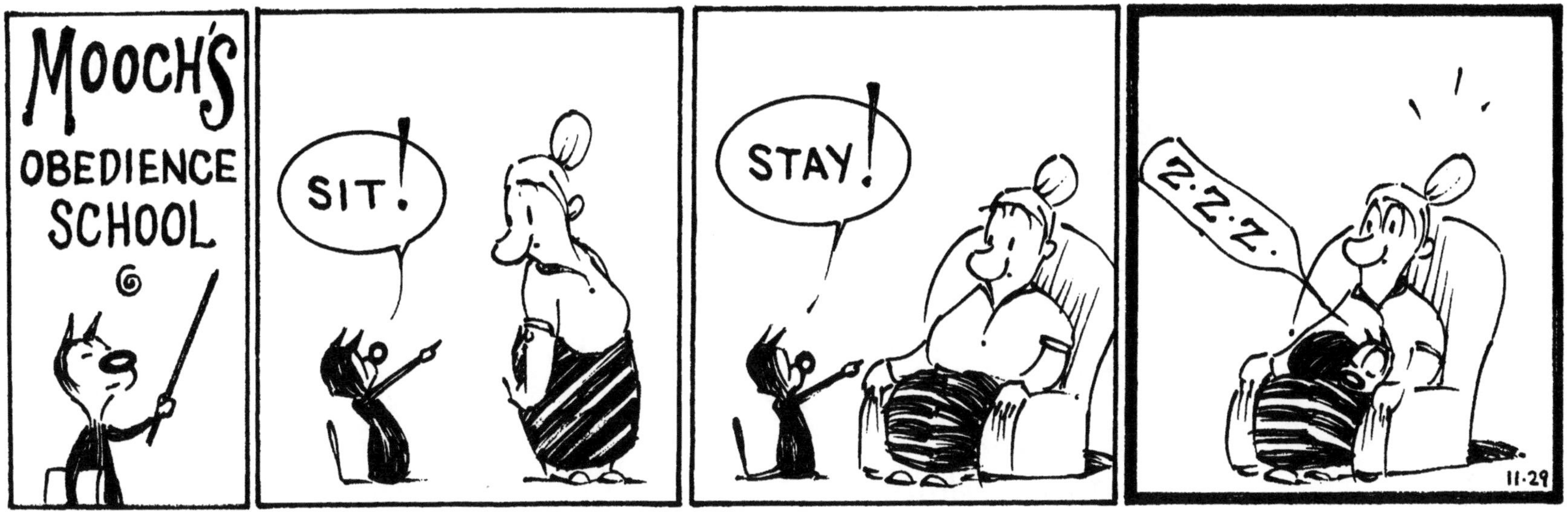
MOOCH'S OBEDIENCE SCHOOL
SIT!
STAY!
Z·Z·Z·
11·29

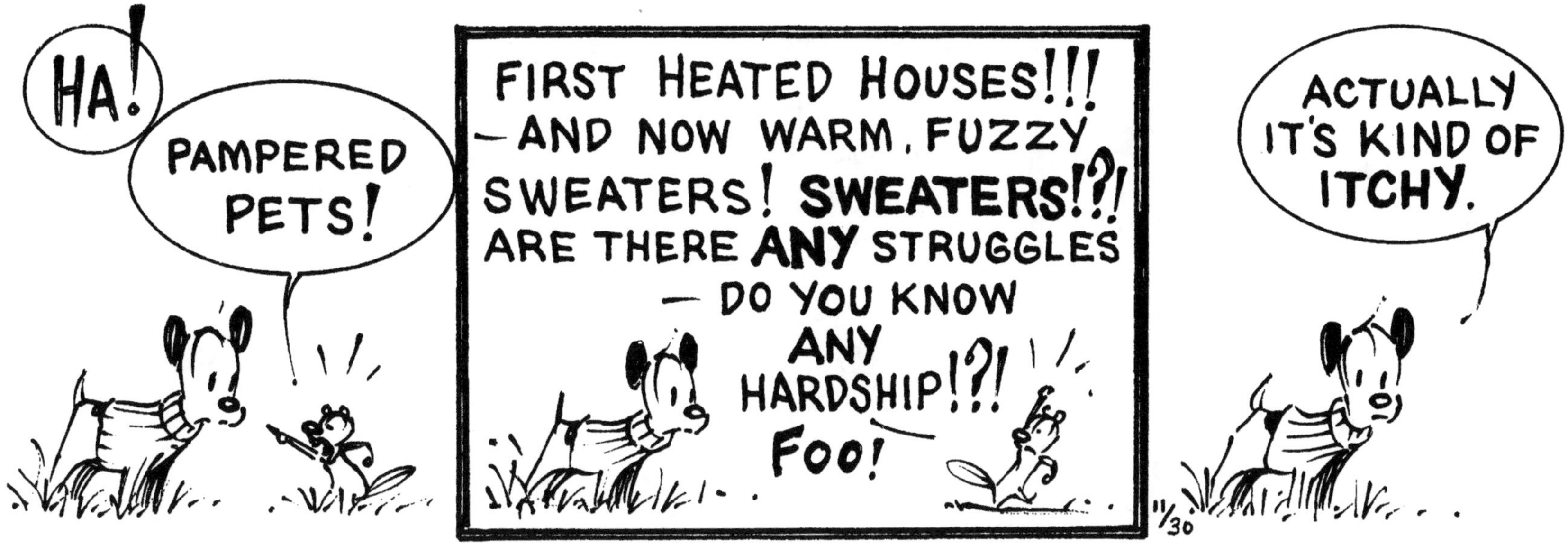
HA!
PAMPERED PETS!
FIRST HEATED HOUSES!!! —AND NOW WARM, FUZZY SWEATERS! SWEATERS!?! ARE THERE ANY STRUGGLES — DO YOU KNOW ANY HARDSHIP!?!
FOO!
ACTUALLY IT'S KIND OF ITCHY.
11/30

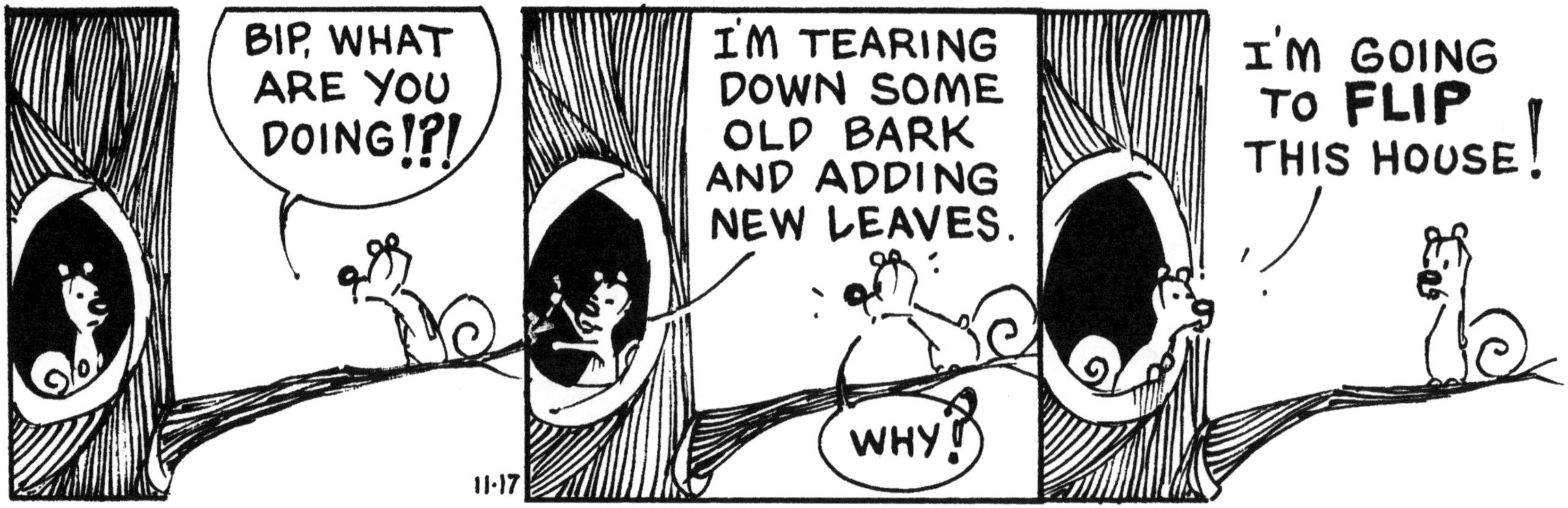
BIP, WHAT ARE YOU DOING!?!
I'M TEARING DOWN SOME OLD BARK AND ADDING NEW LEAVES.
WHY?
I'M GOING TO FLIP THIS HOUSE!
11·17

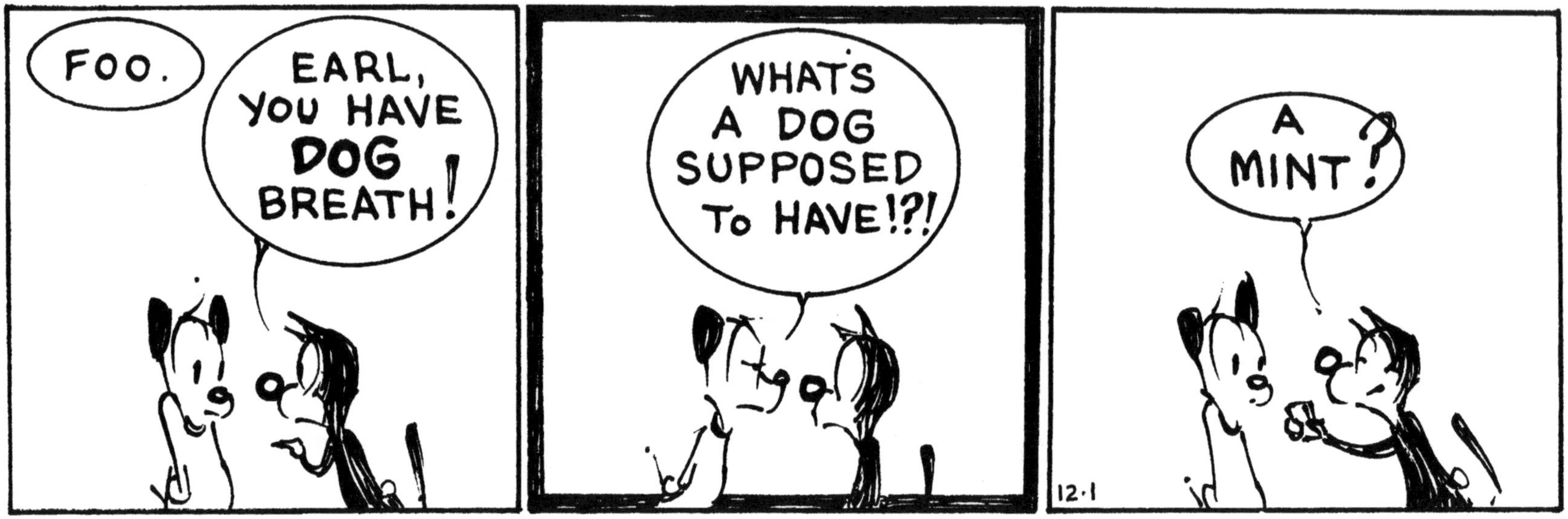
FOO.
EARL, YOU HAVE DOG BREATH!
WHAT'S A DOG SUPPOSED TO HAVE!?!
A MINT?
12·1

MUTTS

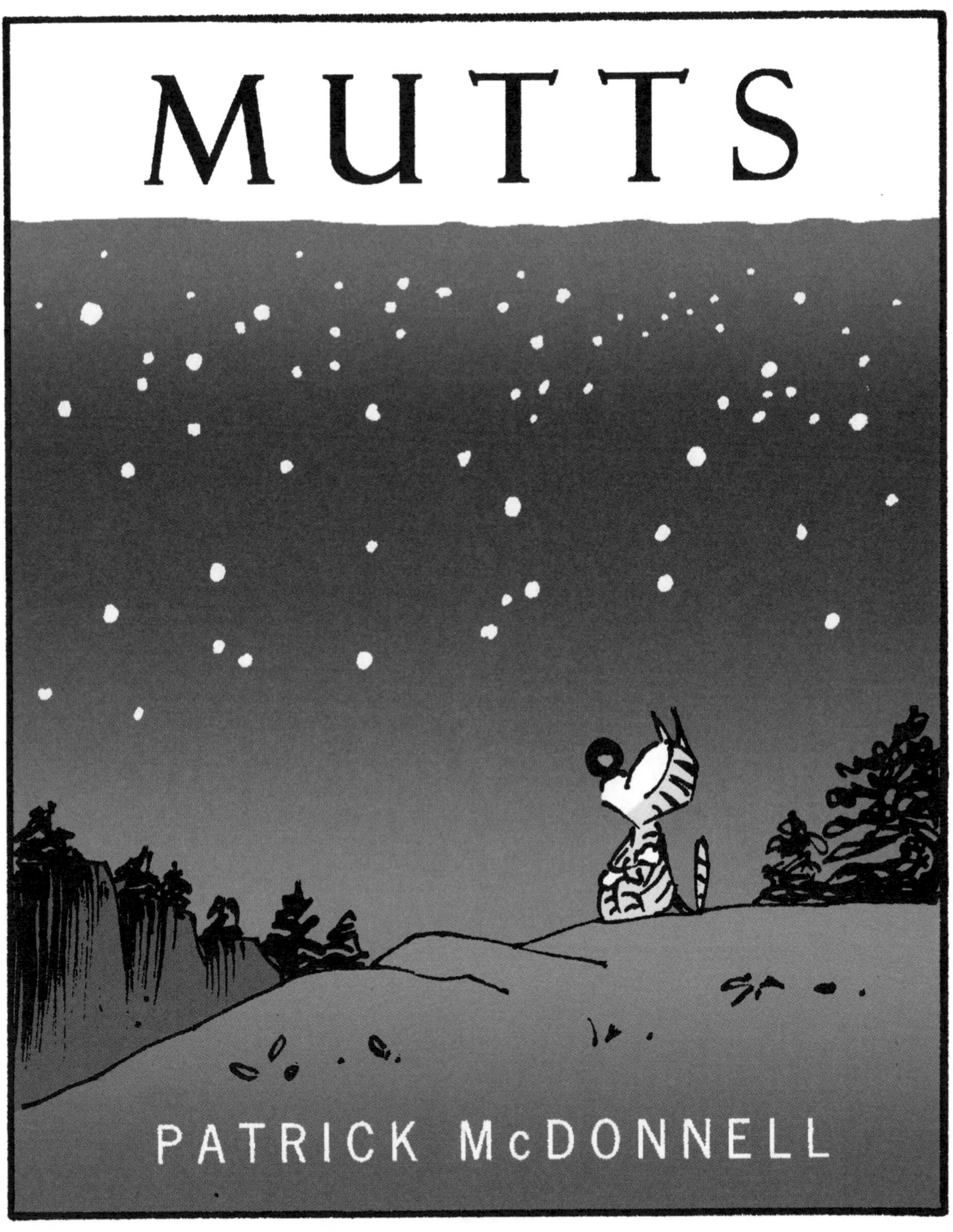

PATRICK McDONNELL

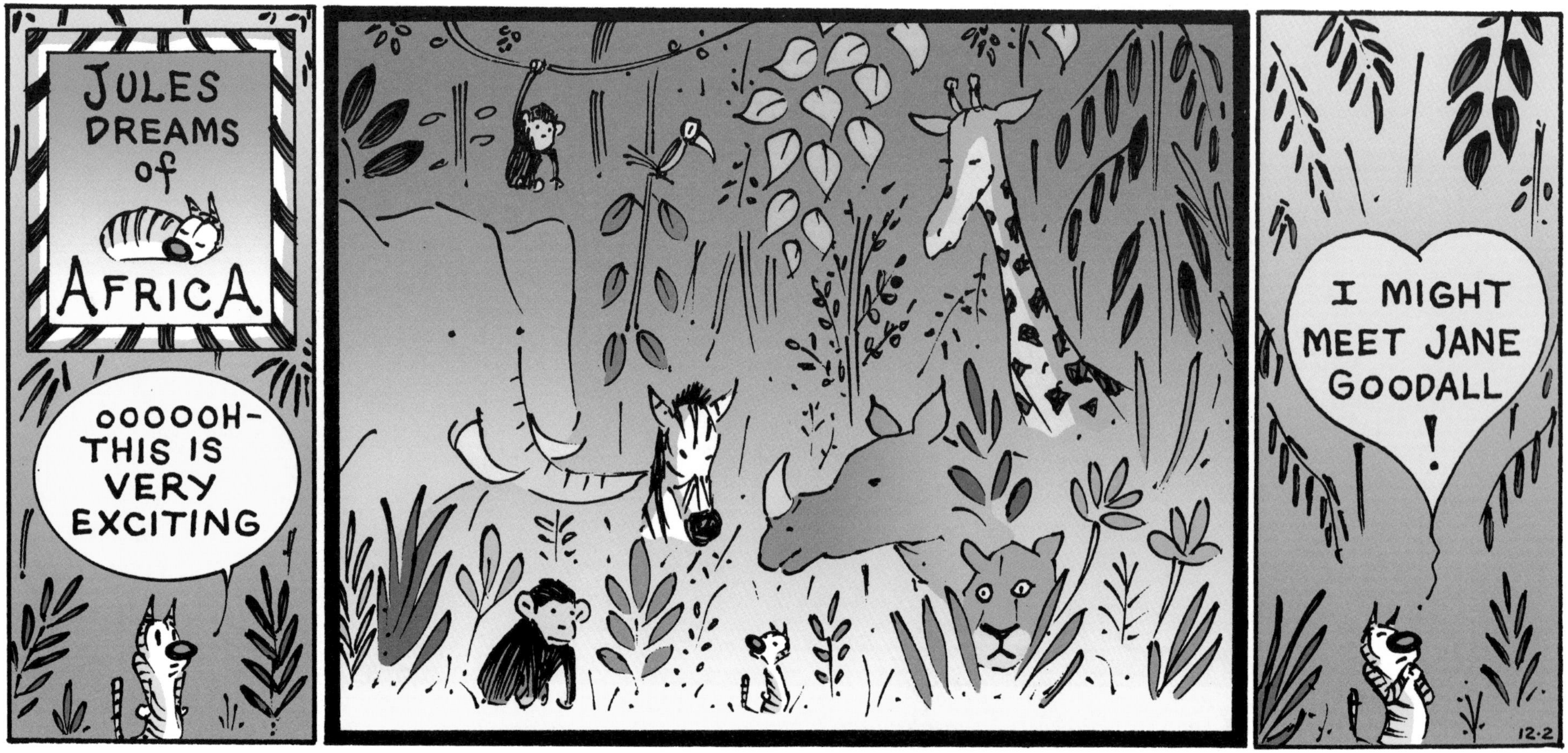
JULES DREAMS of AFRICA
OOOOOH- THIS IS VERY EXCITING
I MIGHT MEET JANE GOODALL !
12·2

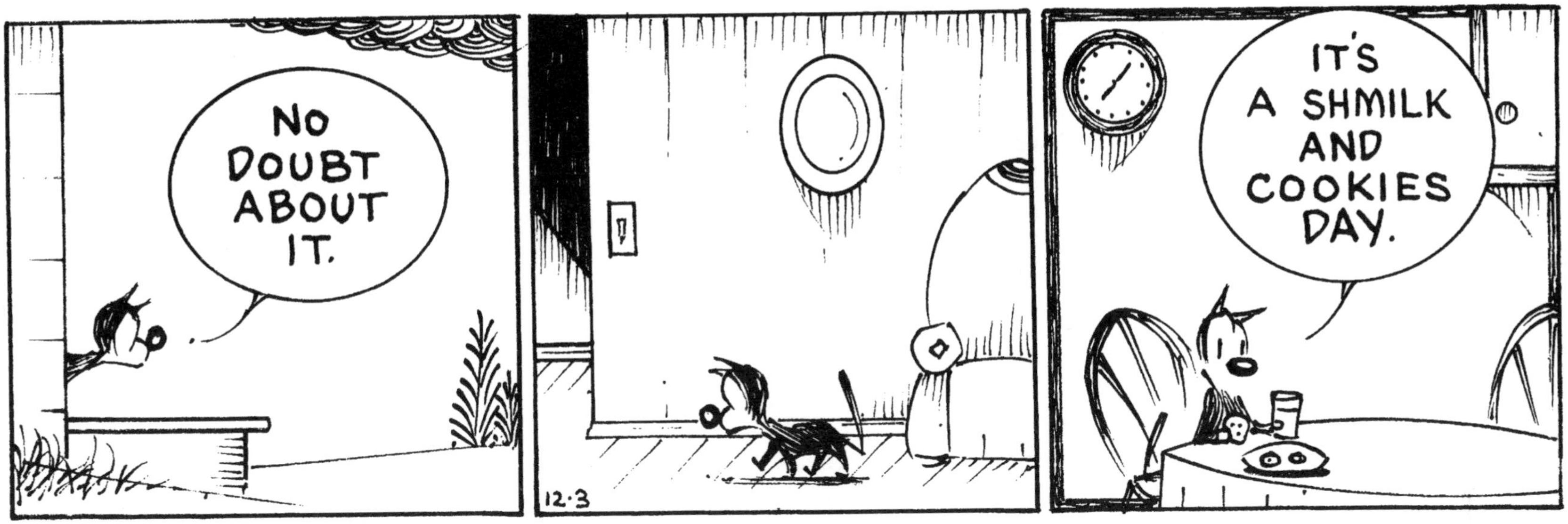
NO DOUBT ABOUT IT.
12·3
IT'S A SHMILK AND COOKIES DAY.

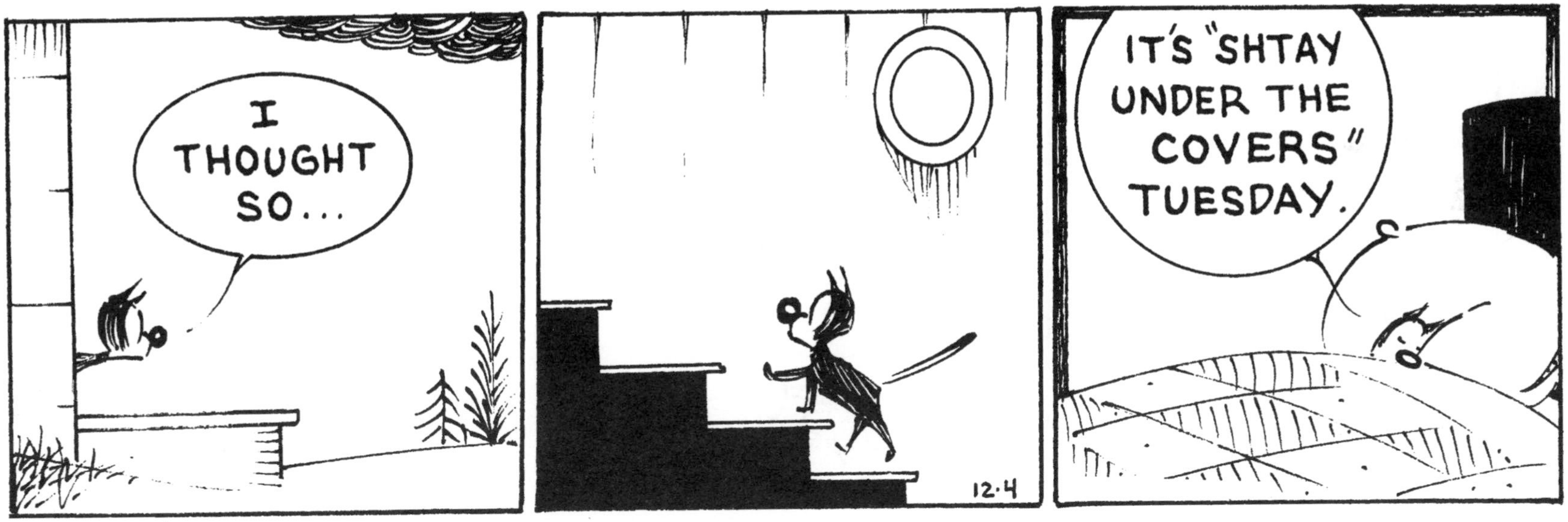
I THOUGHT SO...
12·4
IT'S "SHTAY UNDER THE COVERS" TUESDAY.

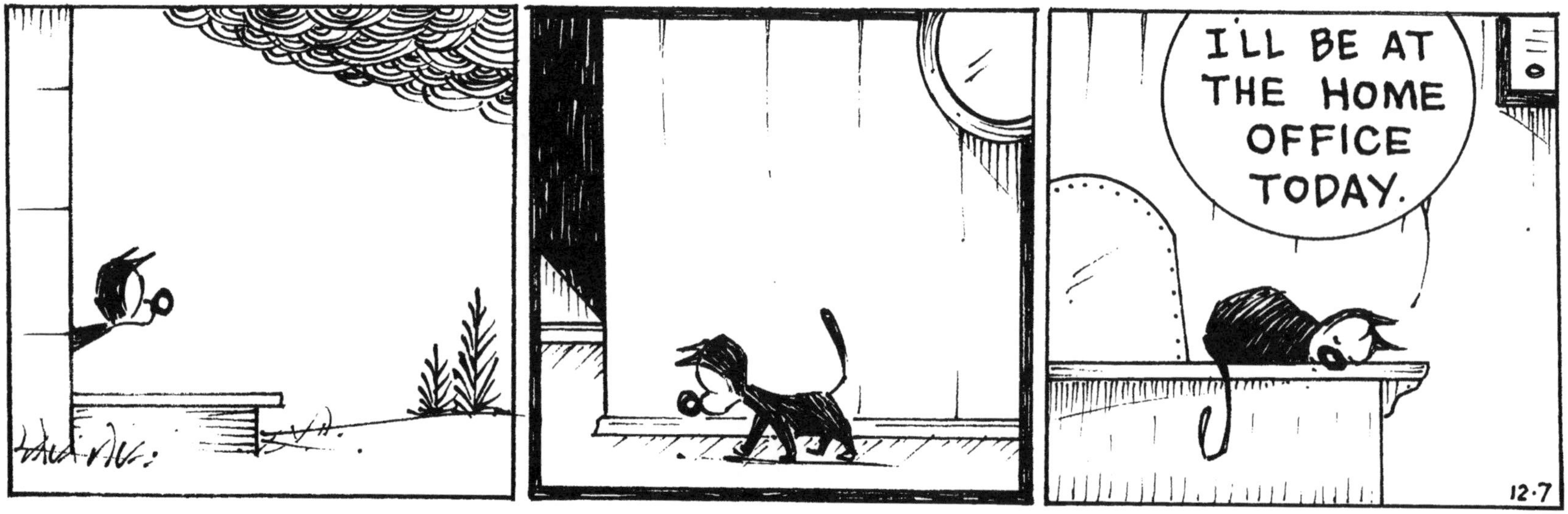
I'LL BE AT THE HOME OFFICE TODAY.
12·7

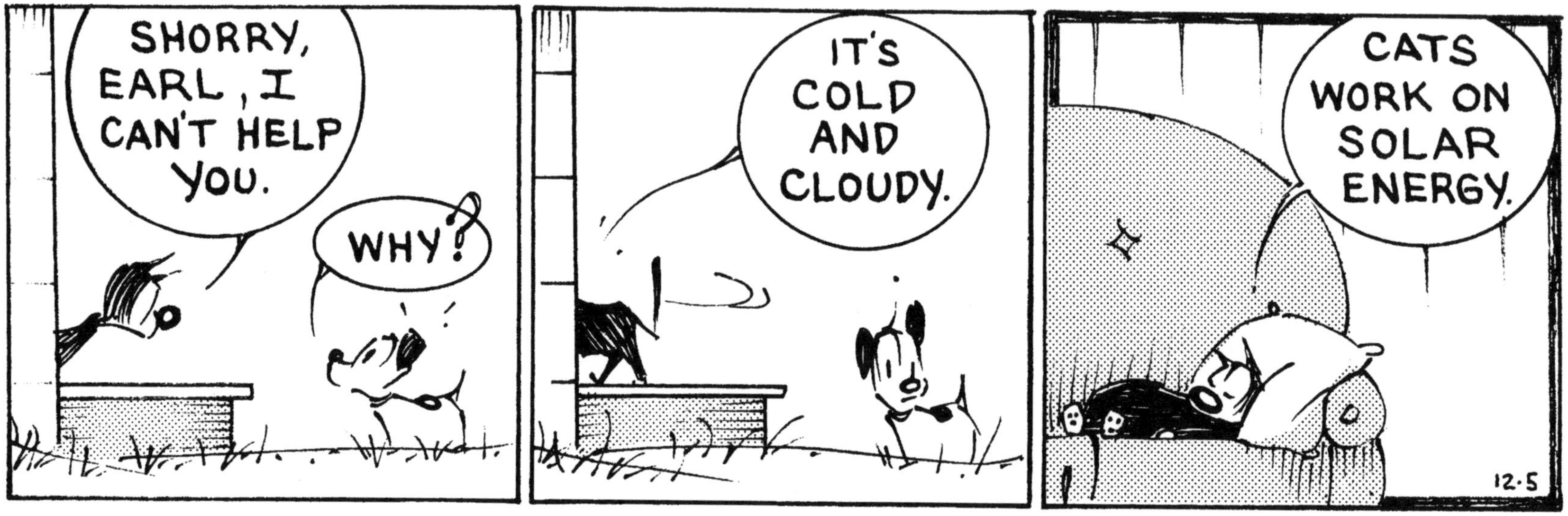
SHORRY, EARL, I CAN'T HELP YOU.
WHY?
IT'S COLD AND CLOUDY.
CATS WORK ON SOLAR ENERGY.
12·5

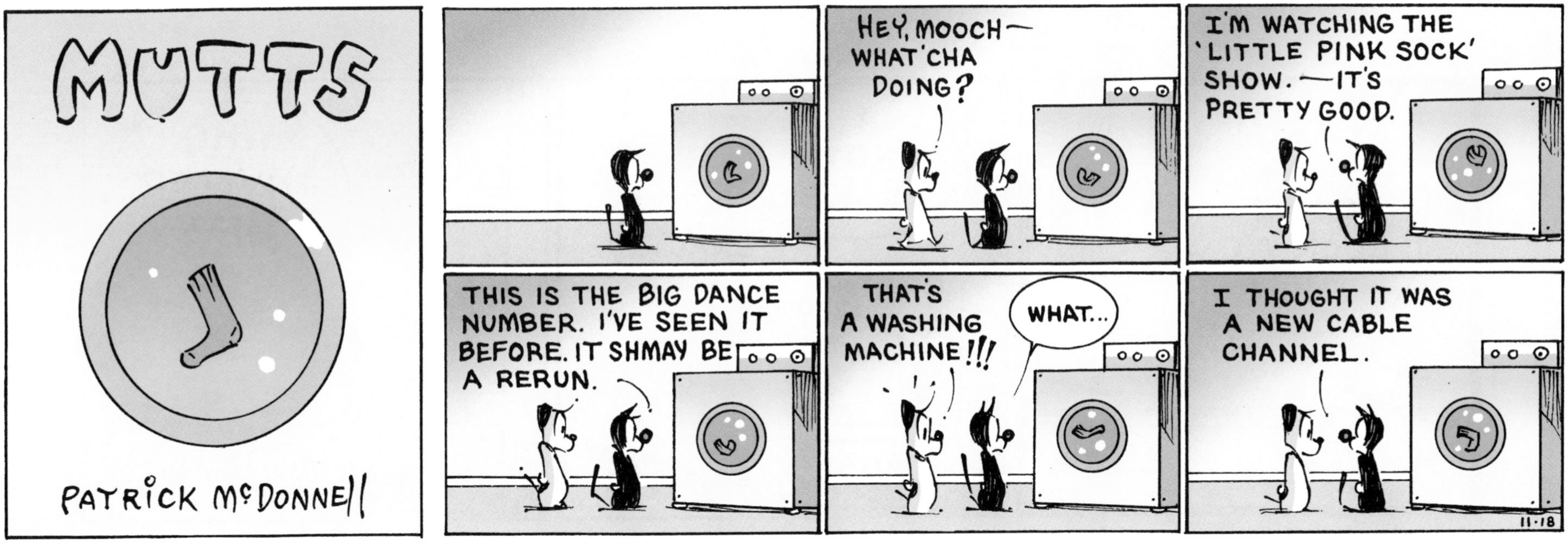
MUTTS
PATRICK McDONNELL
HEY, MOOCH— WHAT'CHA DOING?
I'M WATCHING THE 'LITTLE PINK SOCK' SHOW. —IT'S PRETTY GOOD.
THIS IS THE BIG DANCE NUMBER. I'VE SEEN IT BEFORE. IT SHMAY BE A RERUN.
THAT'S A WASHING MACHINE!!!
WHAT...
I THOUGHT IT WAS A NEW CABLE CHANNEL.
11·18

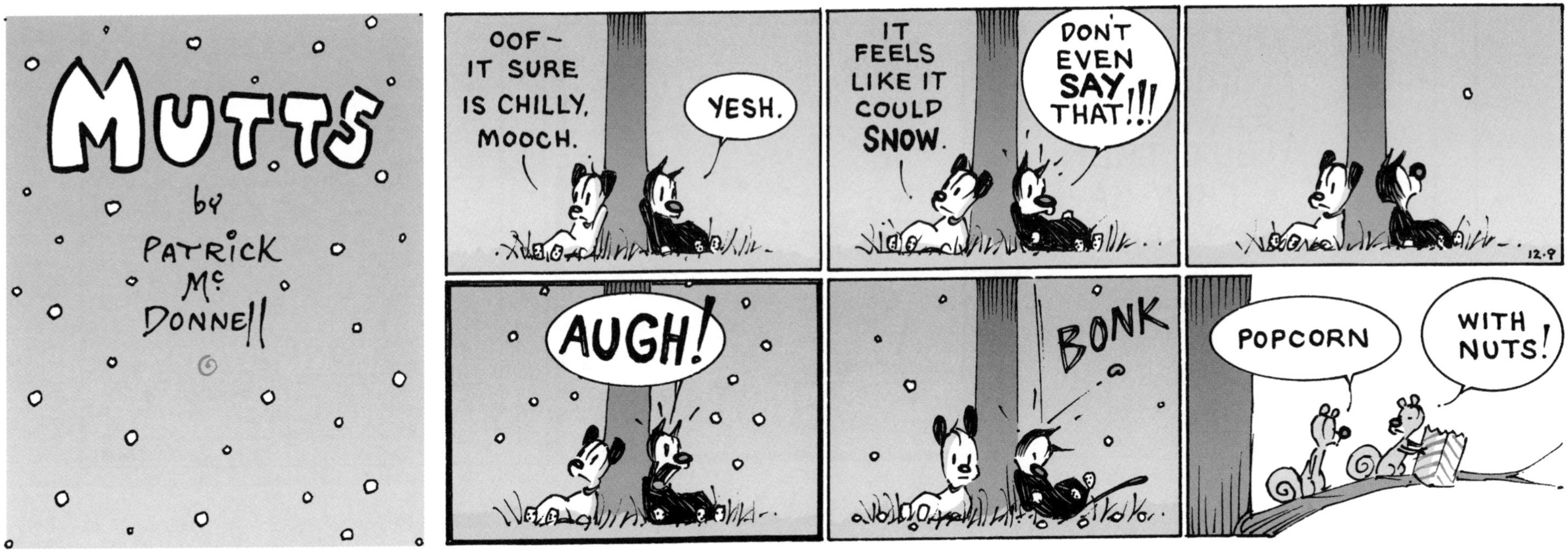
MUTTS
by PATRICK McDONNELL
OOF— IT SURE IS CHILLY, MOOCH.
YESH.
IT FEELS LIKE IT COULD SNOW.
DON'T EVEN SAY THAT!!!
12·9
AUGH!
BONK
POPCORN
WITH NUTS!

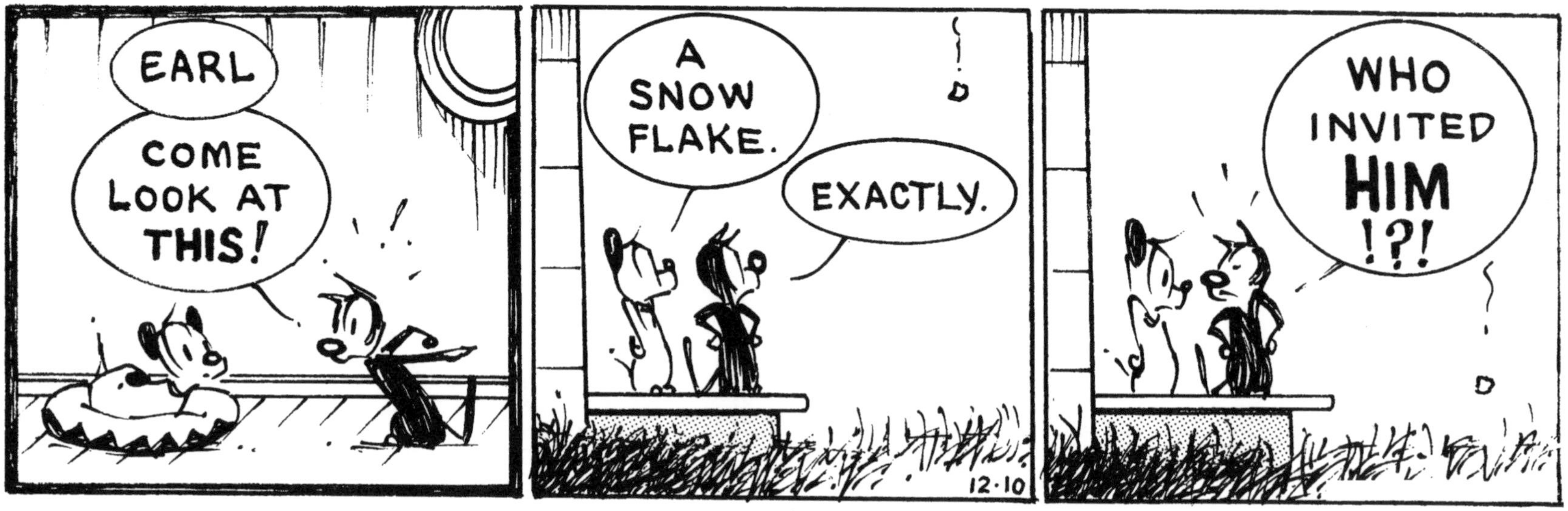
EARL
COME LOOK AT THIS!
A SNOW FLAKE.
EXACTLY.
WHO INVITED HIM !?!
12·10

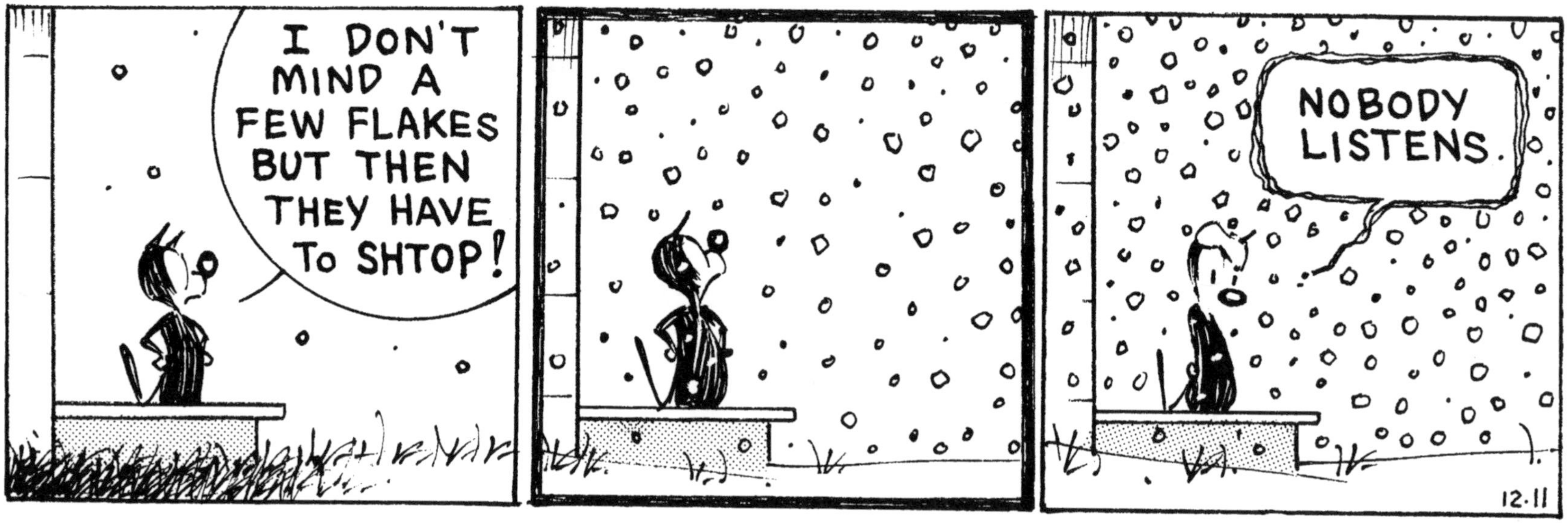
I DON'T MIND A FEW FLAKES BUT THEN THEY HAVE TO SHTOP!
NOBODY LISTENS.
12·11

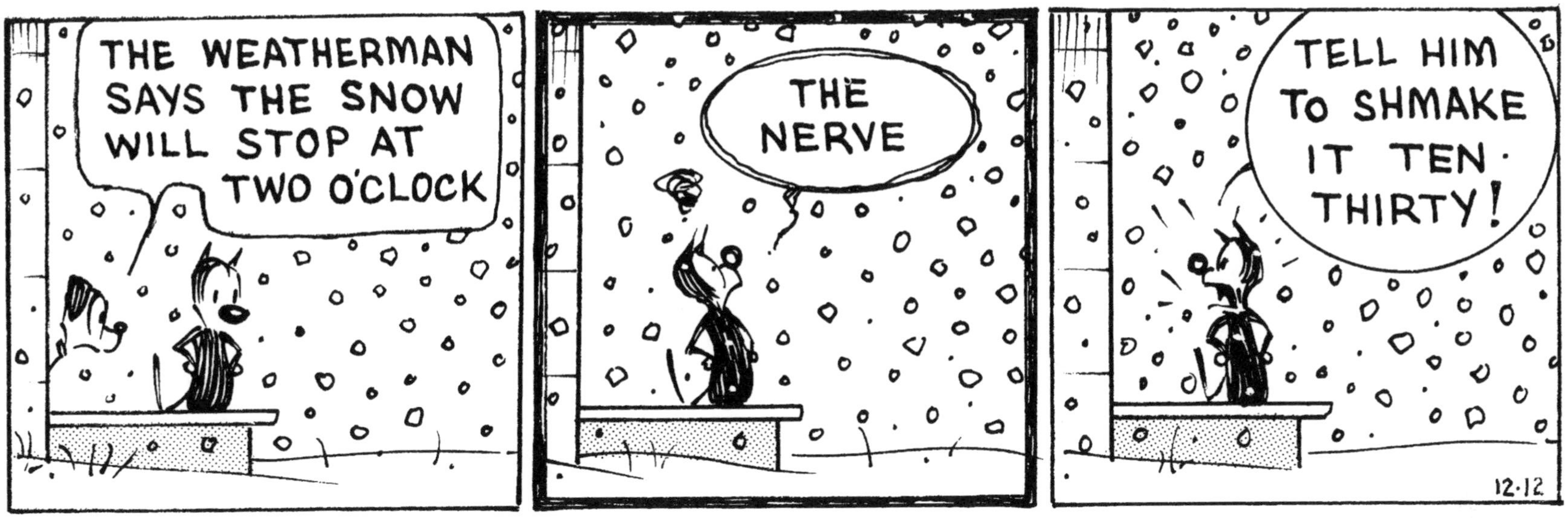
THE WEATHERMAN SAYS THE SNOW WILL STOP AT TWO O'CLOCK
THE NERVE
TELL HIM TO SHMAKE IT TEN THIRTY!
12·12

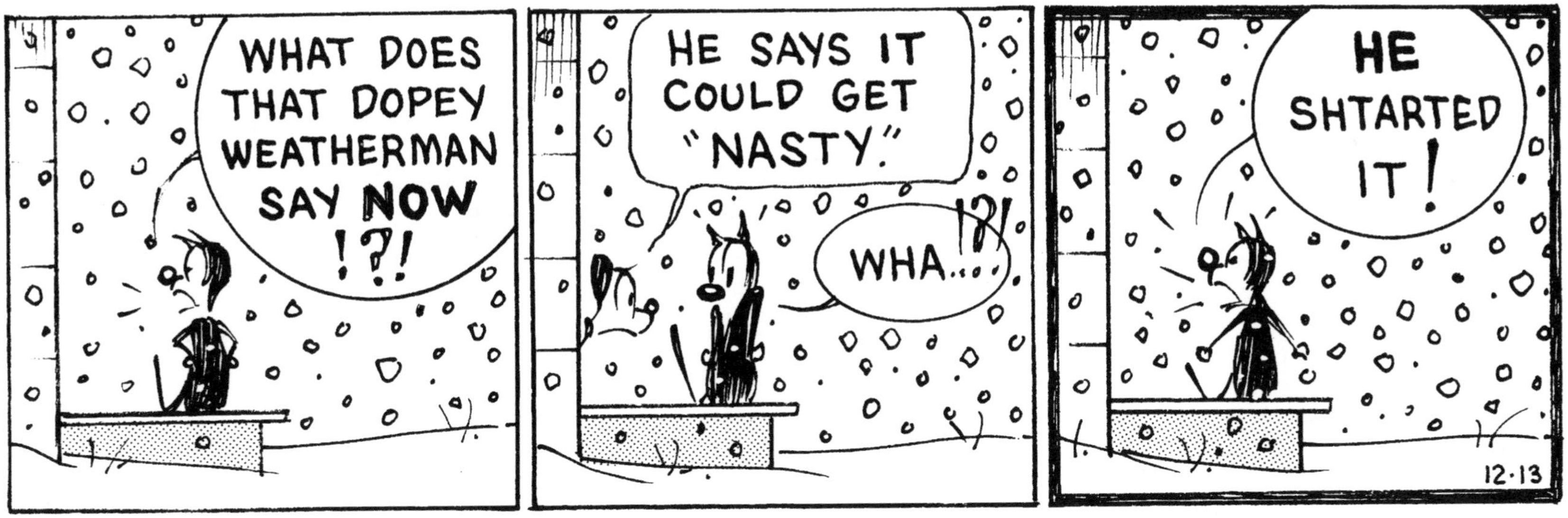
WHAT DOES THAT DOPEY WEATHERMAN SAY NOW !?!
HE SAYS IT COULD GET "NASTY."
WHA..!?!
HE SHTARTED IT!
12·13

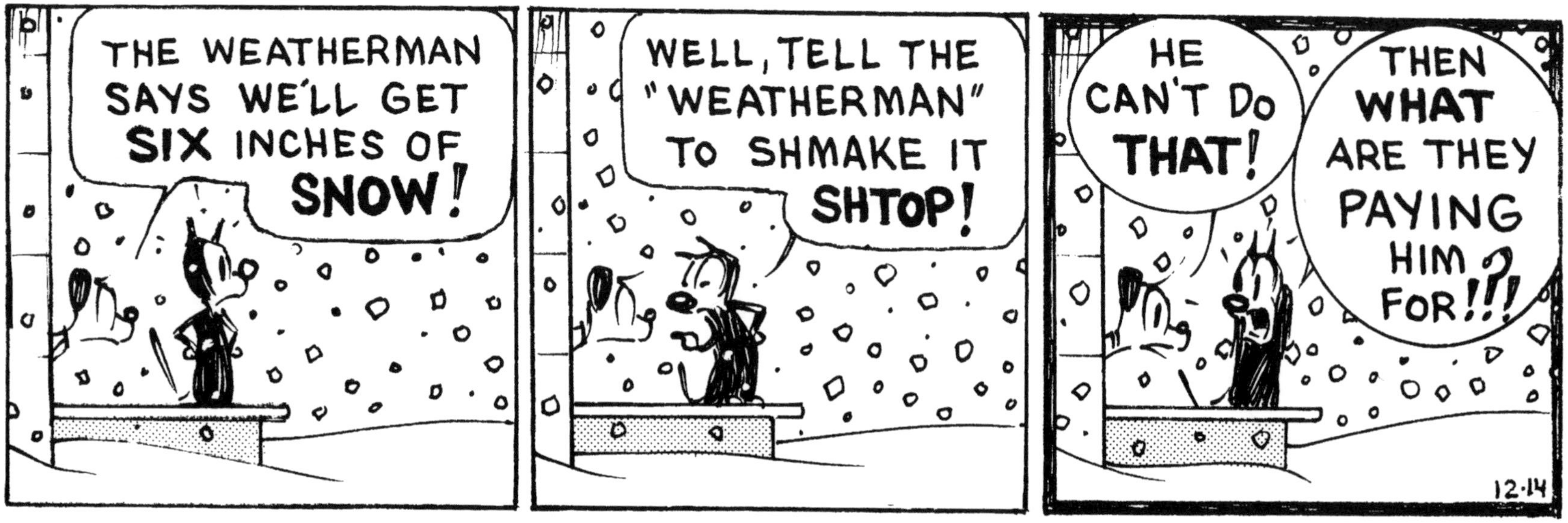
THE WEATHERMAN SAYS WE'LL GET SIX INCHES OF SNOW!
WELL, TELL THE "WEATHERMAN" TO SHMAKE IT SHTOP!
HE CAN'T DO THAT!
THEN WHAT ARE THEY PAYING HIM FOR?!?!
12·14

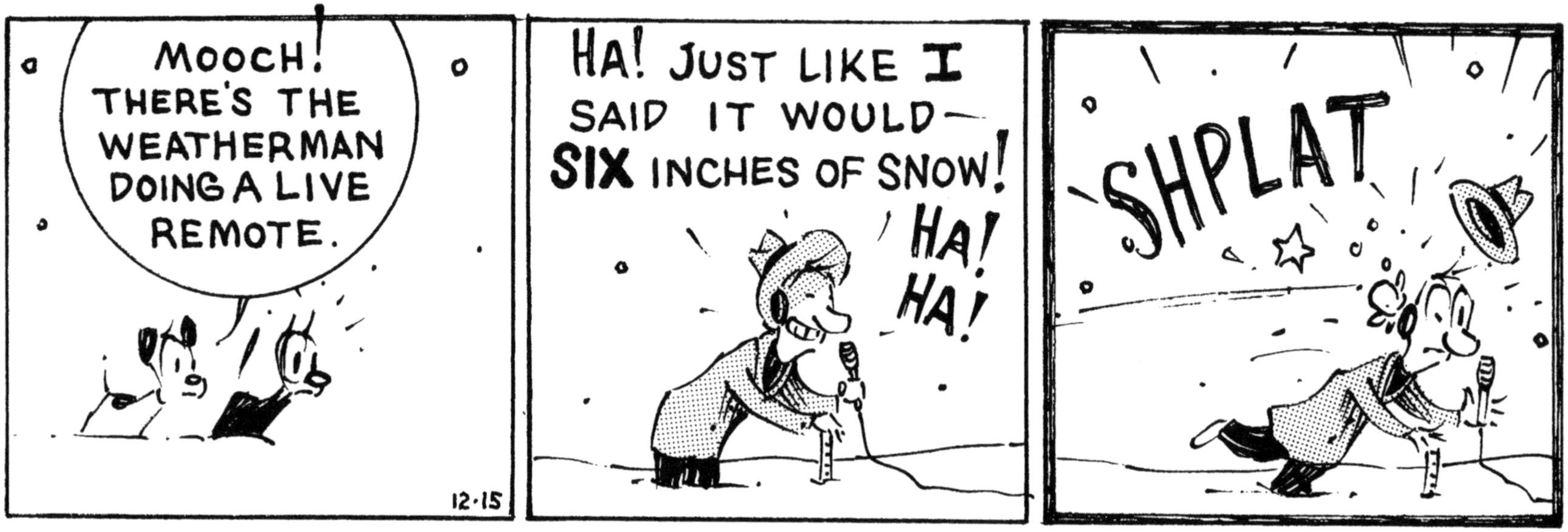
MOOCH! THERE'S THE WEATHERMAN DOING A LIVE REMOTE.
12·15
HA! JUST LIKE I SAID IT WOULD— SIX INCHES OF SNOW!
HA! HA!
SHPLAT

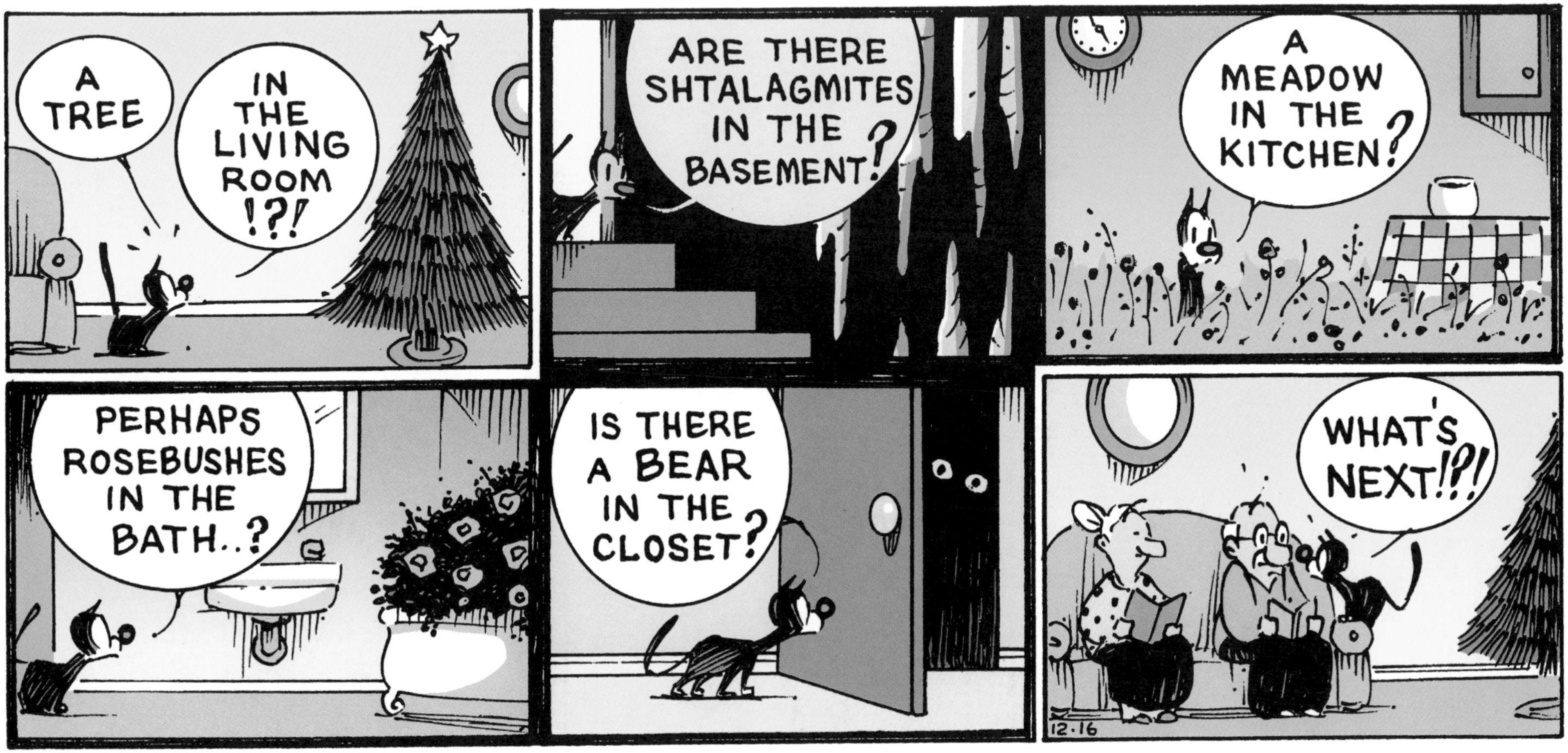
A TREE
IN THE LIVING ROOM !?!
ARE THERE SHTALAGMITES IN THE BASEMENT?
A MEADOW IN THE KITCHEN?
PERHAPS ROSEBUSHES IN THE BATH..?
IS THERE A BEAR IN THE CLOSET?
WHAT'S NEXT!?!
12.16

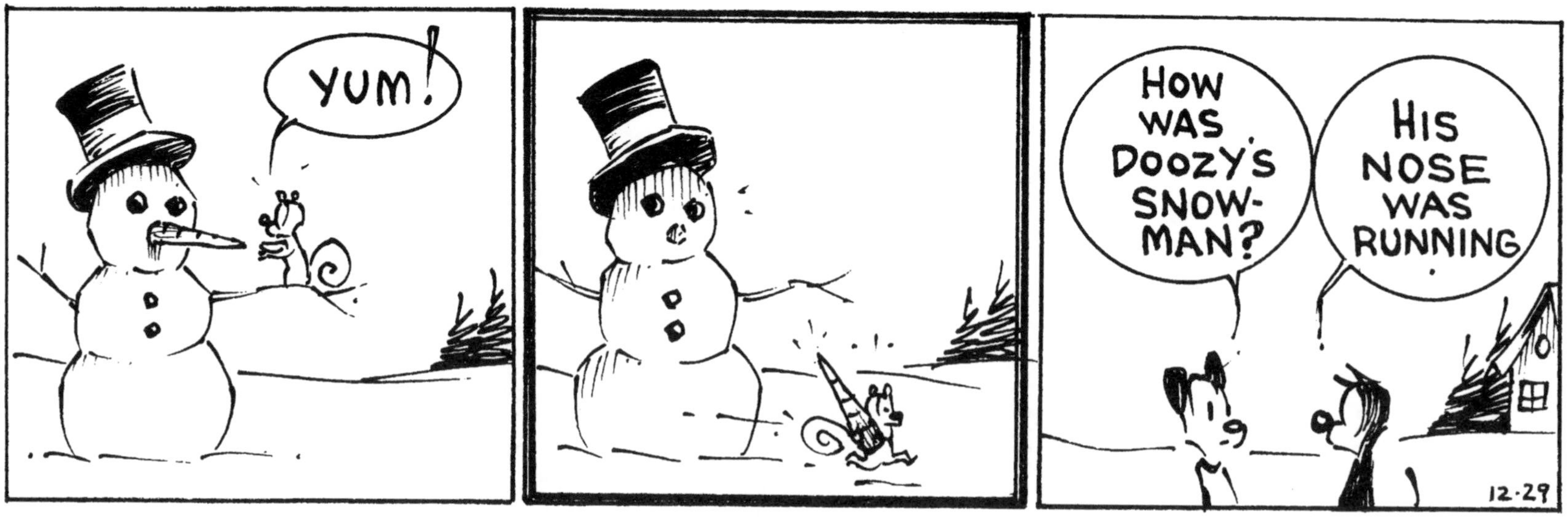
YUM!
HOW WAS DOOZY'S SNOW-MAN?
HIS NOSE WAS RUNNING.
12-29

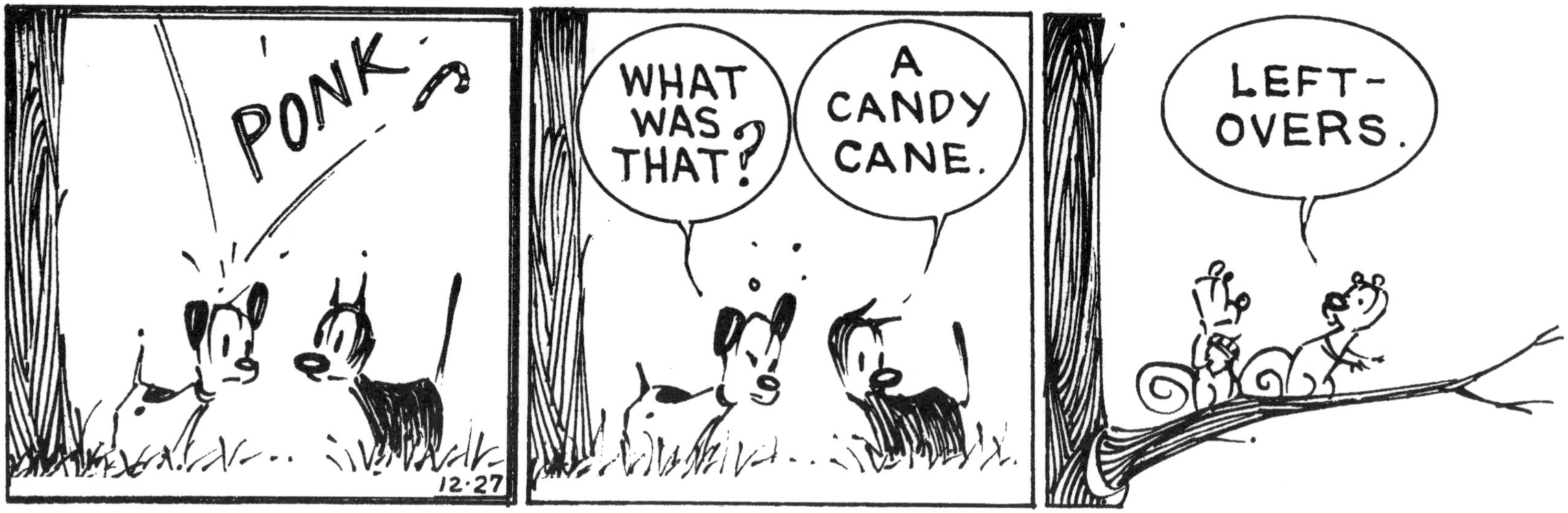
PONK
12-27
WHAT WAS THAT?
A CANDY CANE.
LEFT-OVERS.

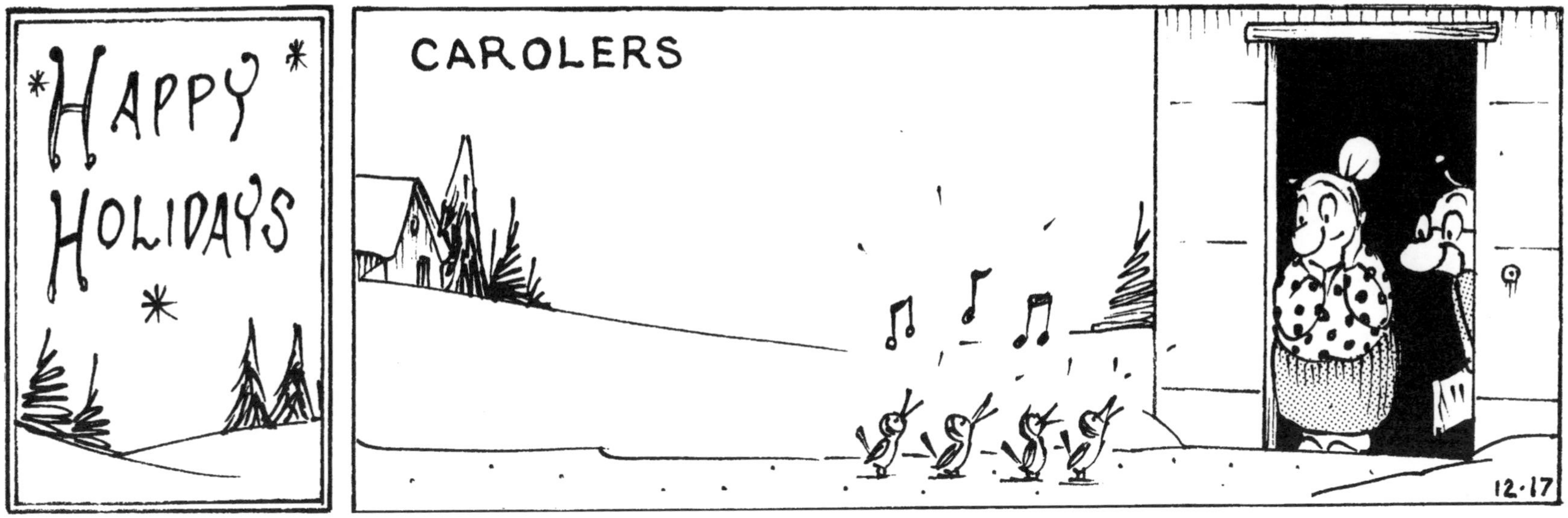

HAPPY HOLIDAYS
CAROLERS
12-17

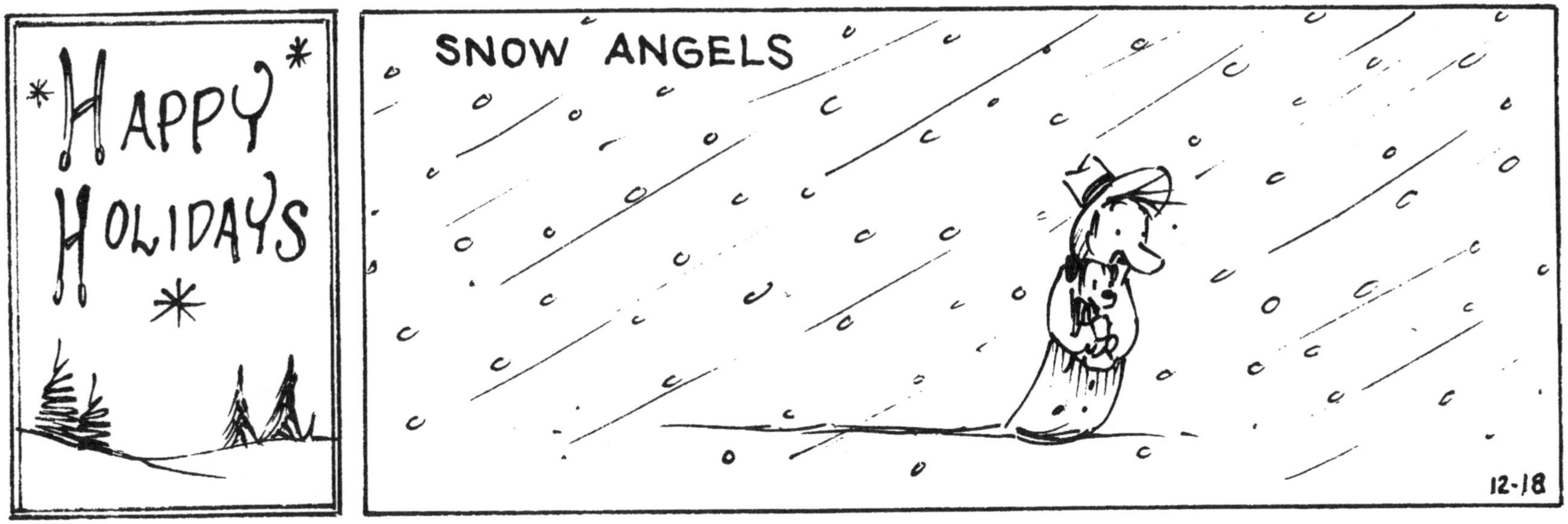

HAPPY HOLIDAYS
SNOW ANGELS
12-18

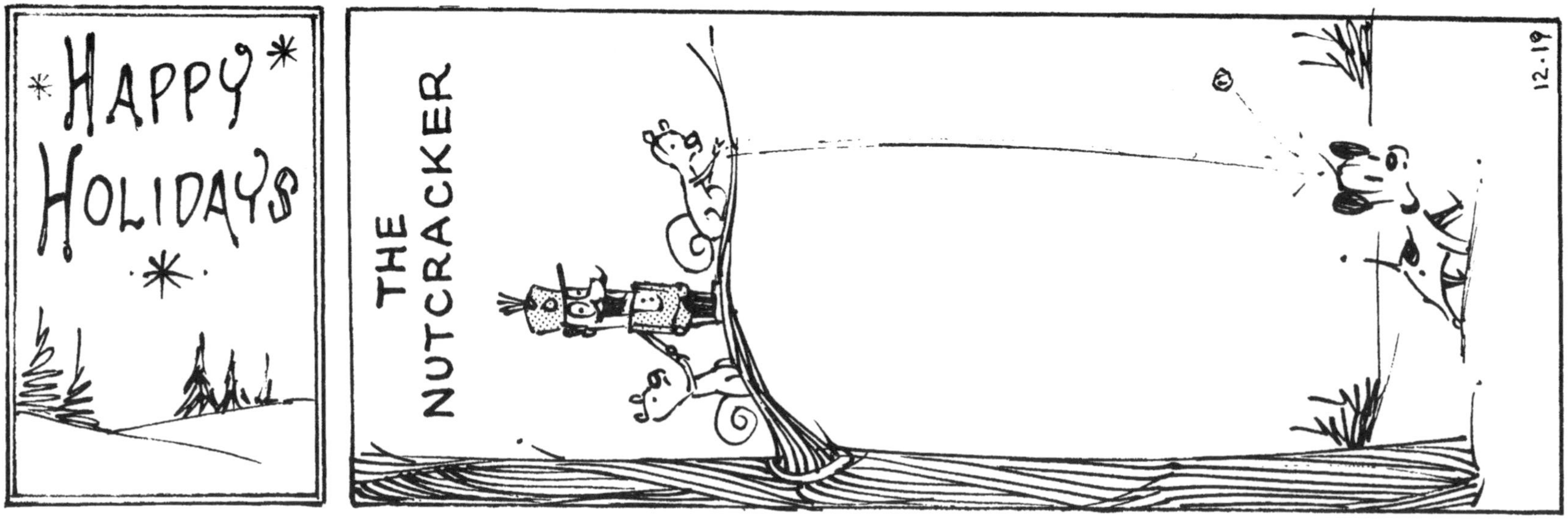
HAPPY HOLIDAYS
THE NUTCRACKER
12.19

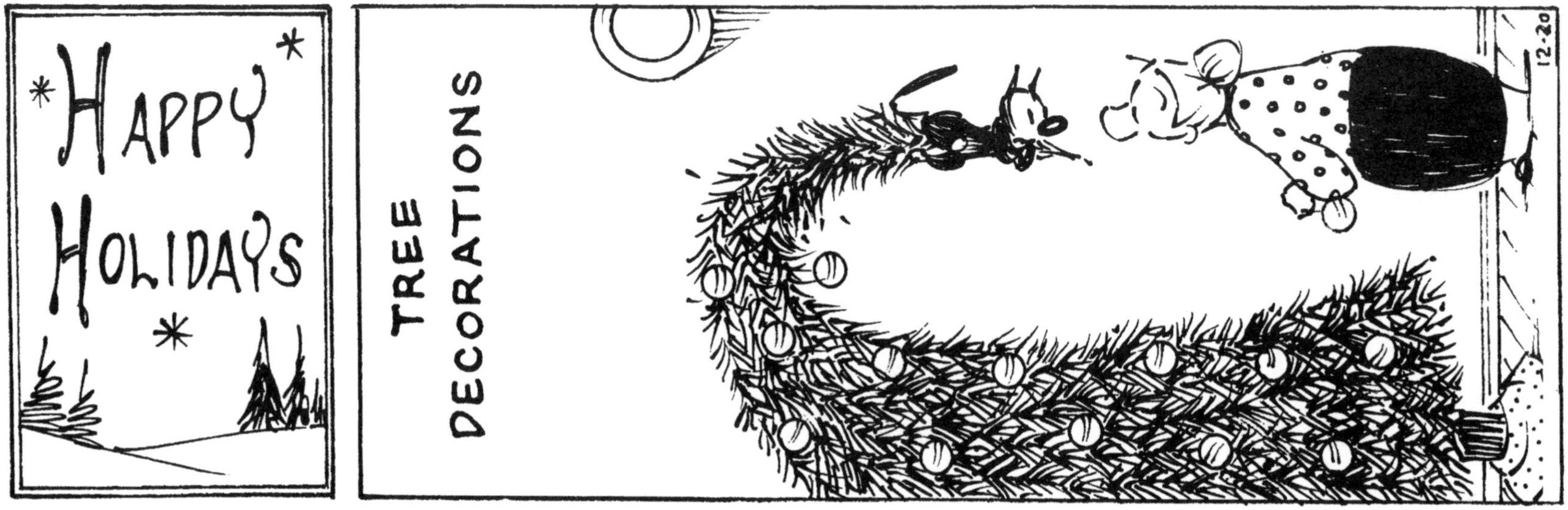
HAPPY HOLIDAYS
TREE DECORATIONS
12.20

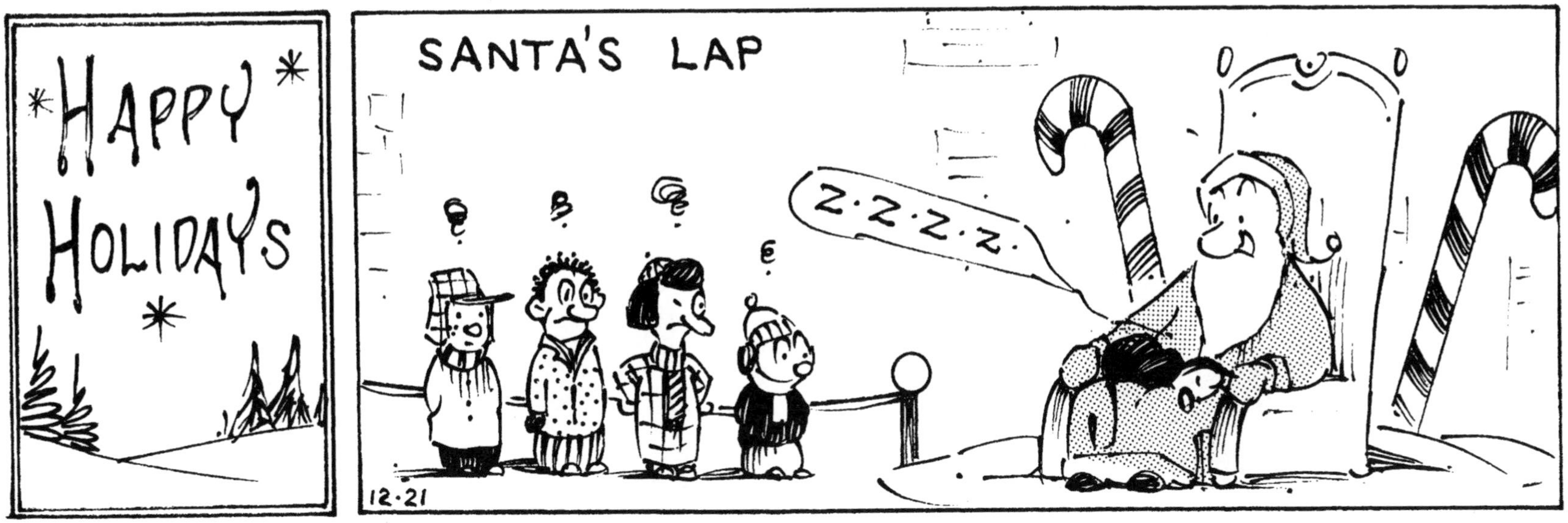
HAPPY HOLIDAYS
SANTA'S LAP
Z·Z·Z·Z·
12-21

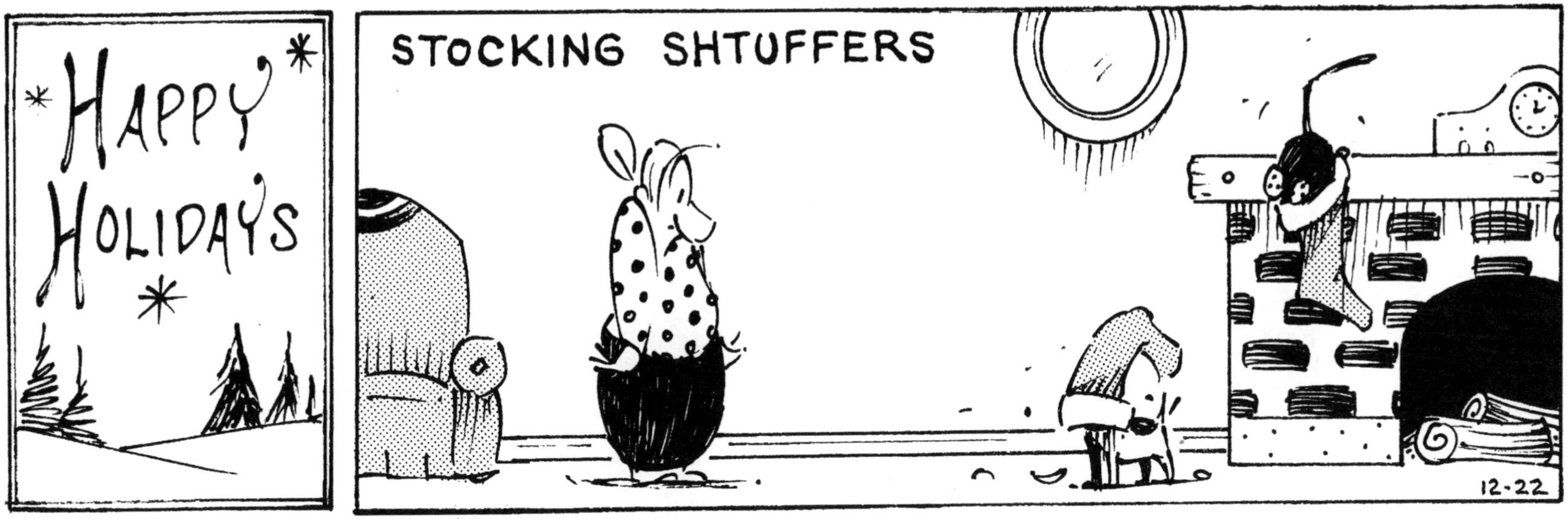
HAPPY HOLIDAYS
STOCKING SHTUFFERS
12-22

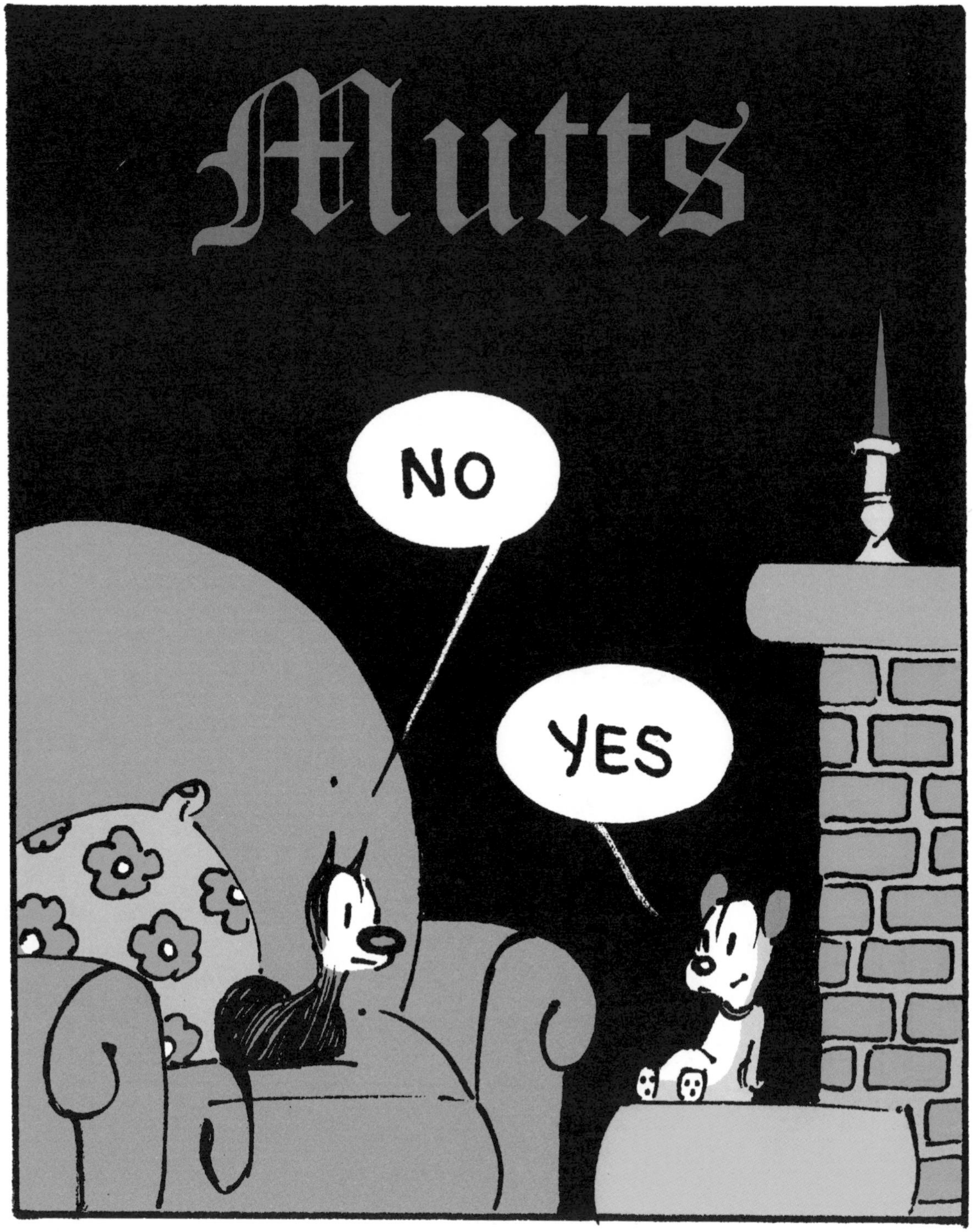
Mutts
NO
YES

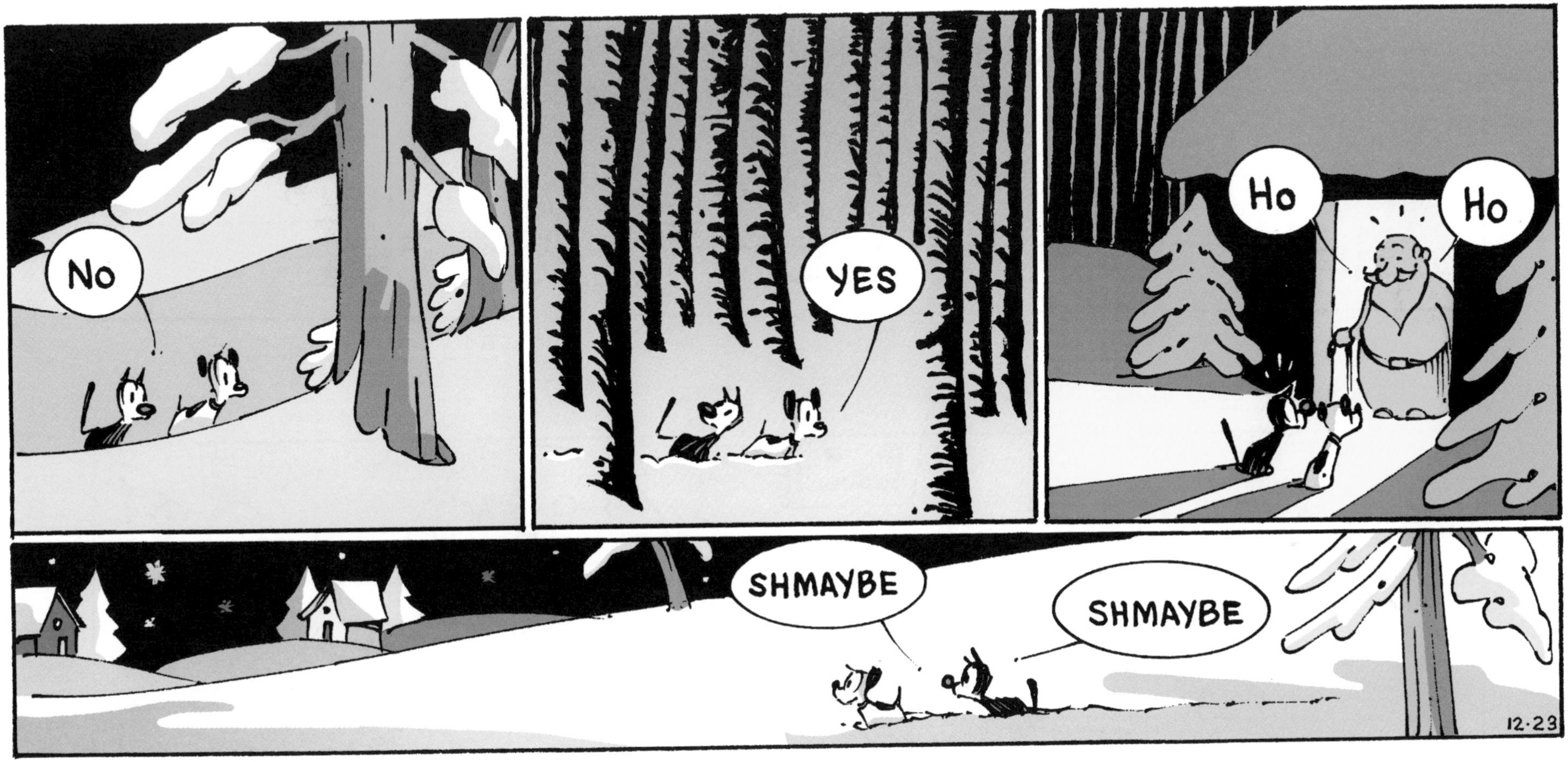
No
YES
Ho
Ho
SHMAYBE
SHMAYBE
12·23

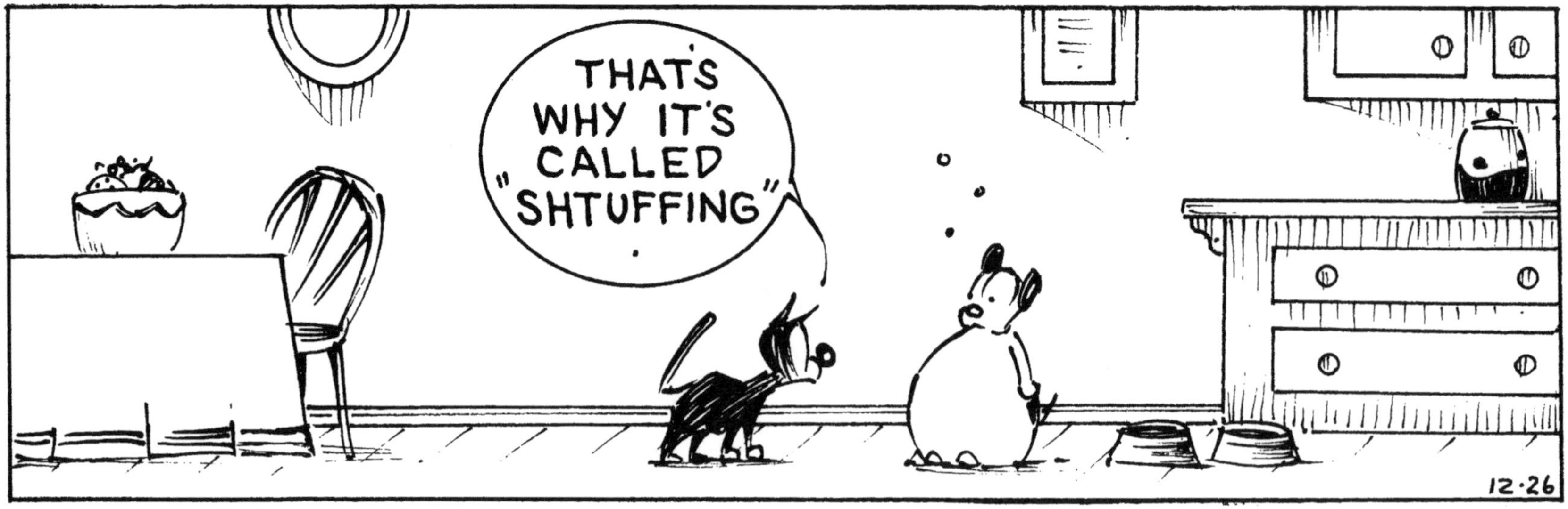
THAT'S WHY IT'S CALLED "SHTUFFING"
12·26

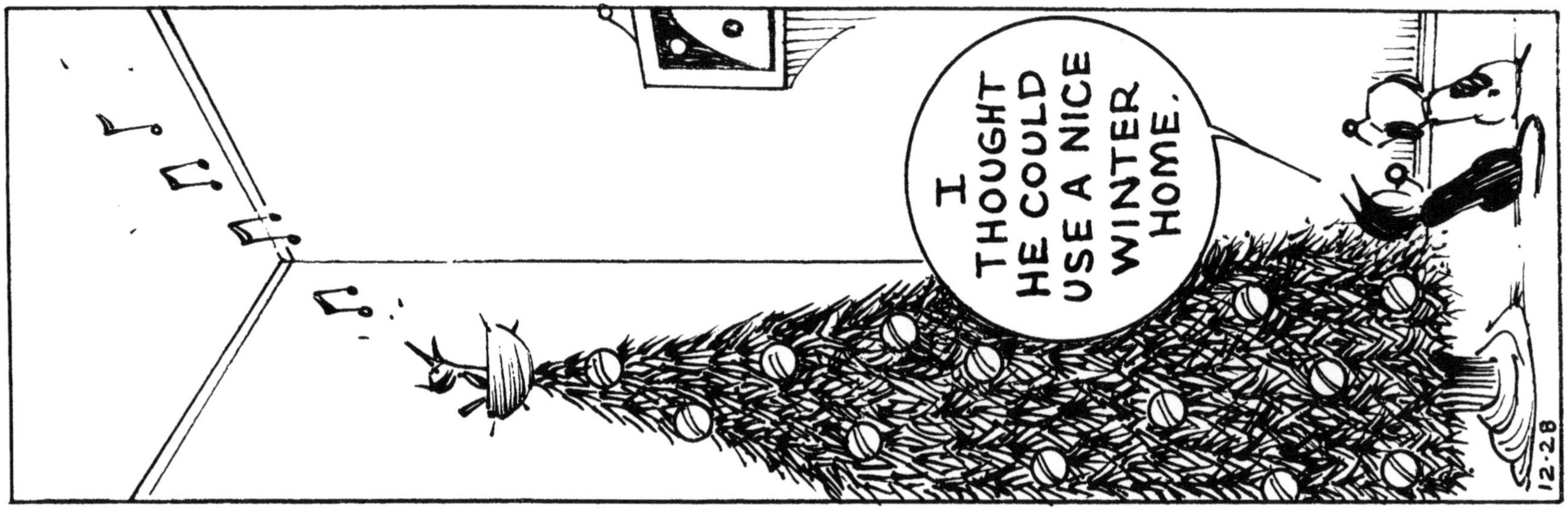
I THOUGHT HE COULD USE A NICE WINTER HOME.
12·28

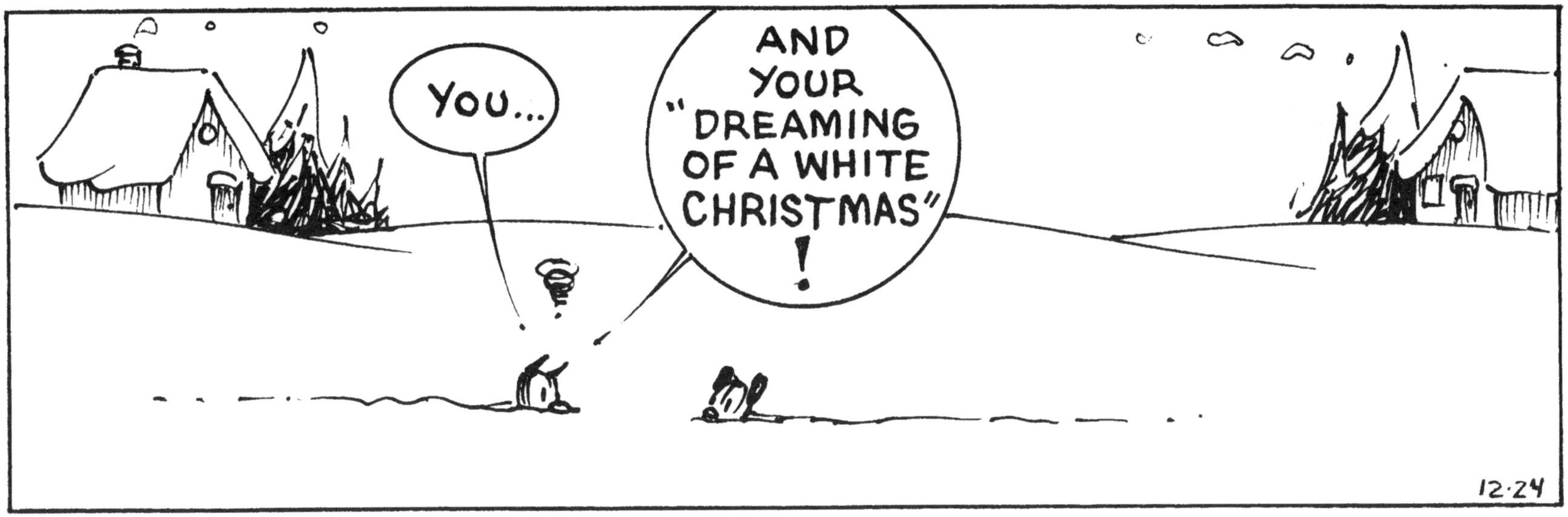
YOU...
AND YOUR "DREAMING OF A WHITE CHRISTMAS" !
12·24

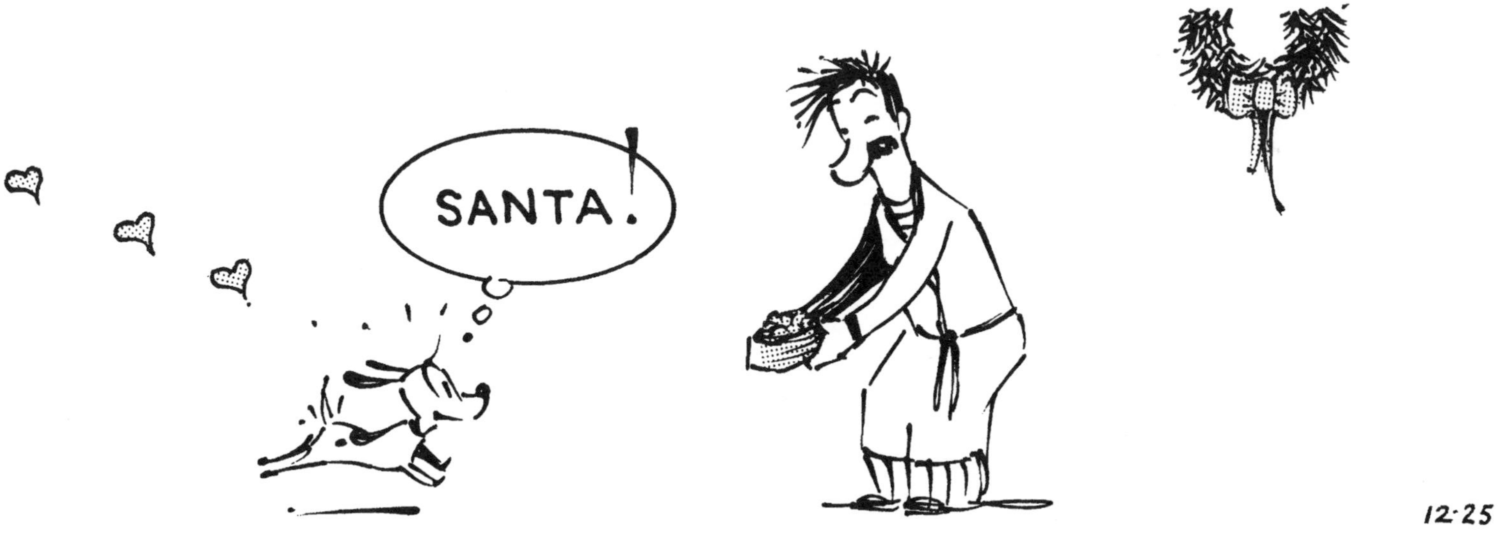
SANTA!
12·25

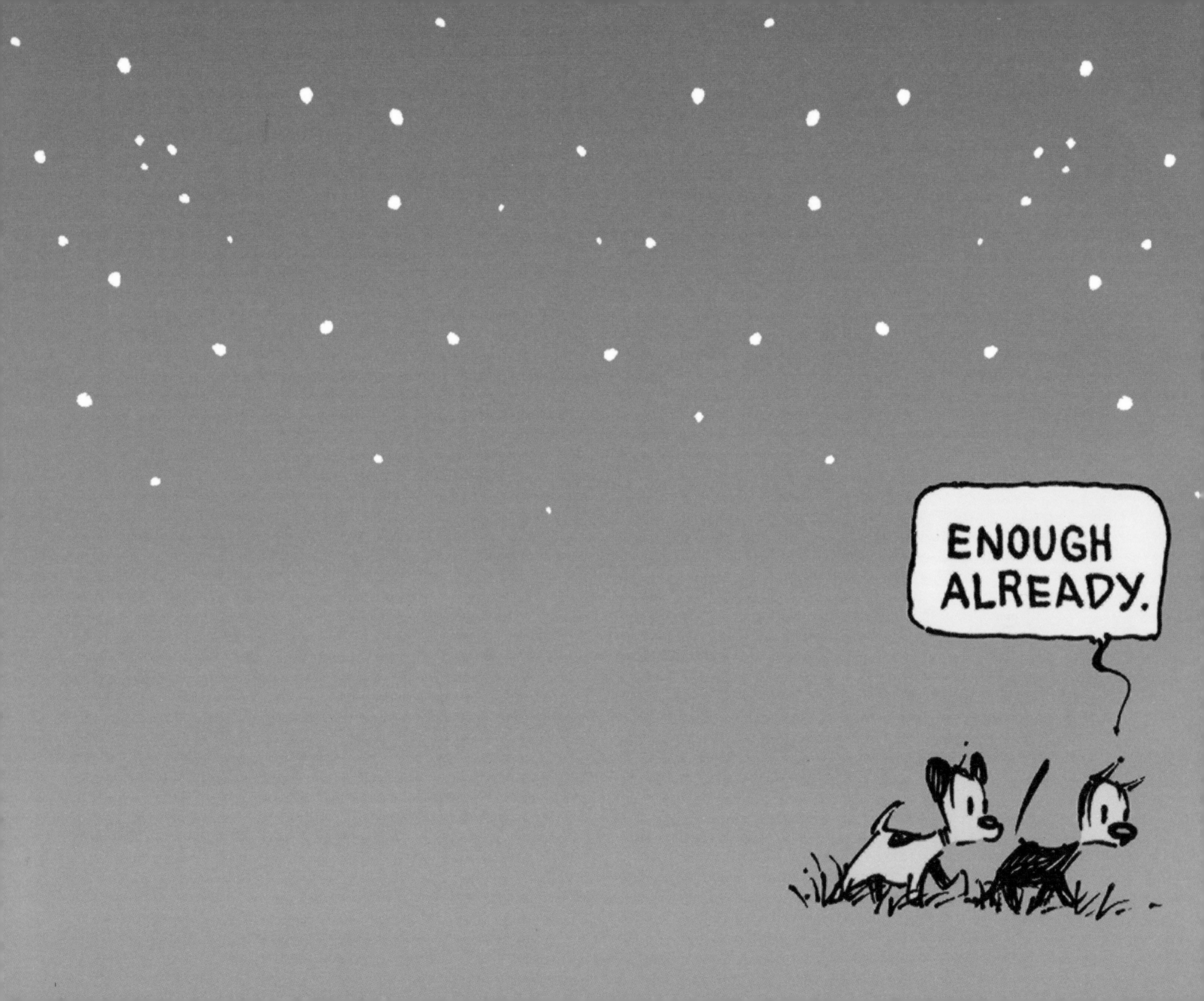
ENOUGH ALREADY.